D0937299

Michael Dillon is currently Visiting Professor at Tsinghua University in Beijing. He was formerly Senior Lecturer in Modern Chinese History and Director of the Centre for Contemporary Chinese Studies at Durham University. He is the author of *Contemporary China: An Introduction* (2008).

CHINA
A Modern History
Michael Dillon

I.B. TAURIS
LONDON · NEW YORK

Reprinted and first published in 2010 by I.B.Tauris & Co Ltd
6 Salem Road, London W2 4BU
175 Fifth Avenue, New York NY 10010
www.ibtauris.com

Distributed in the United States and Canada Exclusively by Palgrave Macmillan
175 Fifth Avenue, New York NY 10010

ISBN: 978 1 85043 582 2

A full CIP record for this book is available from the British Library
A full CIP record is available from the Library of Congress

Library of Congress Catalog Card Number: available

Printed and bound in the UK by CPI Antony Rowe, Chippenham and Eastbourne
from camera-ready copy edited and supplied by the author

CONTENTS

ACKNOWLEDGEMENTS

I am very grateful to Erik Zürcher, Professor of the Modern History of the Ottoman Empire and Turkey at the University of Amsterdam for the suggestion that I might write this book. His *Turkey: A Modern History* is a hard act to follow. I hope that he will not be too disappointed with my own effort. Lester Crook of I.B.Tauris has been a patient and tactful editor, and I am indebted to him for nursing the manuscript through the lengthy production process.

I would like to acknowledge the inspiration of all of the staff of the Department of Chinese Studies at Leeds University where I began to study China in the late 1960s and early 1970s. Although it is invidious to single out individuals, I would like to mention two people for particular encouragement and guidance in Chinese history. Owen Lattimore taught the history of China to first-year students and laced the lectures with anecdotes of his experiences in Chiang Kai-shek's wartime capital of Chongqing and on the camel caravans from Beijing to Mongolia. Bill (W.J.F.) Jenner guided me through the intricacies of Chinese historiography and supervised my PhD thesis on the industrial history of the pottery town of Jingdezhen. I appreciate their inspiration and insights.

At Durham University I am grateful to undergraduates who followed my Chinese history courses in the Department of East Asian Studies for keeping me on my toes with lively, challenging and occasionally irreverent questions. Postgraduate students brought experience of Asia, intelligent questions, and the necessary scepticism and humour to historical seminars and to discussions about their research. Keith Pratt, historian and Professor of Chinese, encouraged me in my research and many other members of the academic staff were supportive when the Department was forced to close down in 2007.

In China I have been fortunate over a period of twenty-five years in having had the opportunity of working with historians and other scholars at the Institutes of Modern History, Economics, World Religions and

Minorities of the Academy of Social Sciences in Beijing, and the regional academies in Shanghai and Guangzhou and in the provinces or autonomous regions of Anhui, Jiangxi, Gansu, Ningxia and Xinjiang. I have also found great benefit and pleasure in cooperation with colleagues in many universities, including Renmin University of China and Tsinghua University in Beijing, Fudan University in Shanghai, the Universities of Xinjiang in Urumqi and Ningxia in Yinchuan and the Hong Kong University of Science and Technology. In Taiwan I have carried out research at the Academia Sinica and enjoyed cooperation with colleagues at National Chengchi University.

These academic partnerships have been absolutely vital in assisting me to shape my understanding of the history of China and none of these visits would have been possible without financial and organisational support from the British Academy and the Universities' China Committee in London. This book, and the other publications which have resulted from these exchanges, would have been poorer without these academic exchanges, and it is a great pleasure to be able to acknowledge the generous support of these organisations over many years. The sole responsibility for any inaccuracies and omissions in the text rests, of course, with the author.

NOTE ON ROMANISATION

As far as possible the Hanyu Pinyin system of romanisation that was developed in the People's Republic of China in the 1950s has been used throughout the text. Some proper names, notably Sun Yat-sen and Chiang Kai-shek, have been left in an earlier spelling because the Pinyin forms have not been widely accepted. The Chinese name for the Nationalist Party has been written as GMD throughout, although the form Kuomintang is preferred in Taiwan.

INTRODUCTION

> It is a very common thing nowadays to meet people who are going to 'China', which can be reached by the Siberian railway in fourteen or fifteen days. This brings us at once to the question – What is meant by the term China?

This question was posed in 1911, just a few months before the revolution that brought about the collapse of the final dynasty of imperial China, by Herbert Giles, Professor of Chinese at the University of Cambridge and one of the leading sinologists of his generation. In the twenty-first century, when China can be reached from most of the developed world by a long-haul flight in less than 24 hours, it still requires an answer. The answer given by Giles was that, 'taken in its widest sense, the term included Mongolia, Manchuria, Eastern Turkestan, Tibet and the Eighteen Provinces': in his book on the civilisation of China, he proposed to confine himself to that portion of the whole 'which is known to the Chinese as the Eighteen Provinces and to us as China Proper'.[1]

'China Proper' is the primary, and the proper, focus of any study of China's modern history, but this book is concerned with the whole of the mainland which has been under the control of the Chinese Communist Party since 1949 as the People's Republic of China (PRC), and also with Taiwan, which retains its historic identity as the Republic of China (independent *de facto* but not *de jure* since the same year) and the former British colony of Hong Kong. Any history of the mainland must also take account of the contested histories of China's northern and western frontiers, notably those of Tibet, Xinjiang (Eastern Turkestan) and Inner (or Southern) Mongolia. Although the history of China's southwest is not contested in the same way, many of the indigenous peoples of that region are closely related to the majority communities of Vietnam, Thailand and Burma (Myanmar): social and commercial relations across the porous border have played a major role in shaping Yunnan province and the Guangxi Zhuang Autonomous Region.

Modern China: Conflict and Change

Conflict is a major source of, and stimulus for, historical change, and modern China has certainly had more than its fair share of conflict and change. There have been major struggles for power, both ethnic and political, within its borders, and there have also been military conflicts with external forces that have changed the balance of power in the whole East Asian region. Internal social, political and economic changes have altered the face of the world's most populous nation beyond recognition over the past 200 years.

However what and when was, or is, modern China? A brief reflection on the period in general and the meaning of the term modern China seem appropriate at the outset. Official Chinese historiography since the foundation of the People's Republic of China in 1949 has maintained a clear and rather inflexible distinction between modern and contemporary history. Modern history [*jindai shi*] is the period of humiliation that lasted from the Opium Wars of the mid-nineteenth century to the May Fourth Movement of 1919, the beginning of the nationalist upsurge that followed the Versailles settlement in Europe, which unexpectedly had profound implications for China's political development. Contemporary history [*xiandai shi*] is more positive and attractive to most Chinese historians as it traces the growth of nationalism, the rise of the Chinese Communist Party (CCP) and the eventual liberation of China from colonialism and the Japanese occupation. The maturation of scholarship, both in China and in the West, and particularly during the last 30 years when some of the many historical archives in the PRC have been opened to foreign researchers and academic exchanges have become routine, has led to a sharing of views that was hardly possible for the 30 years before that. This process has led to a timely and appropriate modification of the hard and fast periodisation that was insisted on by historians in China and a strong realisation that, in spite of the dramatic and revolutionary changes that China has undergone, there is a significant continuity of traditions, structures and attitudes: this continuity extends beyond the accession to power of the CCP in 1949, through the radical Maoist period and up to and including the dramatic reforms that began in the late twentieth century.

A broader understanding of the sense of modern China is therefore essential. China has exhibited signs of 'modernity' for centuries, beginning perhaps with the widespread commercialisation of the economy in the sixteenth century (in Chinese dynastic terms this is the middle period of the rule of the Ming house, which occupied the dragon throne from 1368 to 1644). Some historians look back even further to the Song dynasty (960–1127) for examples of this departure from autarkic rural communities. The Qing dynasty (1644–1911) which followed the Ming and was the last ruling house of imperial China is conventionally blamed by Chinese historians with a nationalist cast of mind for having delayed China's modernity. It was viewed as a foreign conquest dynasty because it was formed by the rulers of the Manchu tribal confederation who came down into China Proper from their homelands in the northeast in 1644 and were permitted by the remnants of the Ming military leadership to bring their armies through the passes into the capital to take the throne rather than permit it to fall into the hands of a rebel.

Although the Qing dynasty displayed many of the external trappings of a traditional Chinese dynasty, the Manchus also retained their own language and culture and were regarded as aliens by many Chinese, particularly by radicals and reformers, right up to the time of their political demise in the Revolution of 1911. From that time onwards, China has struggled to find 'modern' and national forms of political, economic and social organisation, beginning with the short-lived Republican governments of Sun Yat-sen, Yuan Shikai and Chiang Kai-shek.

After it had established the People's Republic of China in 1949, the government of the Chinese Communist Party initially followed the model of a planned, centralised economy offered by the Soviet Union in the 1950s before turning to Mao Zedong's revolutionary, romantic and ultimately disastrous experiments in mass mobilisation, the Great Leap Forward of 1958 and the Cultural Revolution of the late 1960s. Following the death of Mao in 1976, China embarked on a period that is identified as the era of 'reform and opening' [*gaige kaifang*]. It was inspired by Deng Xiaoping who died in February 1997 and, although this is less well known, by the legacy of the greatest political enigma of China's Communist establishment, Zhou Enlai, who died in 1975. The polity and the society that this reform programme has created appear stable, but many of the conflicts that fashioned it remain unresolved.

It is this broad definition of modern China that concerns the present work, which concentrates on the second half of the nineteenth century, the whole of the twentieth and the beginning of the twenty-first century. Modern China has been an epoch of momentous and diverse conflict, but no attempt has been made in this introduction to cover the whole range of social and political struggles that are detailed in the main body of the book: certain significant categories of conflict have been selected to illustrate the complexity and interconnectedness of the historical changes which were taking place.

The majority of the inhabitants of China are classified as ethnic Han, but there are significant non-Han populations, particularly in what are now the border areas of the PRC. Two major non-Han dynasties have ruled China since mediaeval times: the Mongol Yuan dynasty from 1271 until 1368 and the Manchus, ruling as the Qing dynasty from 1644 to 1911. The Manchus governed China with the assistance of those Han scholar-officials who were prepared to cooperate with them, numbers of whom increased as the dynasty progressed, in addition to Mongols and members of other ethnic groups, but they continued to maintain garrisons of Manchu troops in strategic locations around the country as a token, if increasingly ineffectual, reminder of their dominance. Nevertheless, there was conflict between Manchus and Han Chinese from the founding of the dynasty. A form of proto-nationalism, directed by non-elite Han Chinese against the Manchus, can be traced back to the conquest of 1644, which was deeply resented by the Han majority. Clandestine organisations including the White Lotus and other secret societies sustained their hopes for the extinction of the Qing and for a Ming revival through to the bitter end of the dynasty.

Other ethnic conflicts included clashes between the Han Chinese and different Muslim communities in Yunnan and in the northwestern provinces of Shaanxi and Gansu, and the invasion and hostilities that led to the independent regime of Yakub Beg in Xinjiang (Eastern Turkestan). These conflicts have a long and turbulent history and reached a peak in the mid-nineteenth century. However, even radicals who challenged the Confucian or imperial orthodoxy that China was a homogeneous society of *tianxia* (all under Heaven) have tended to downplay, if not completely ignore, the ethnic complexity of the empire and the potential for inter-ethnic conflicts. That tendency continued under the PRC, particularly during the Cultural Revolution when even trivial manifestations of ethnic difference were frowned upon.

Ethnic conflicts in China persist to the present day, especially in Xinjiang, Gansu, Ningxia, Tibet and Mongolia. The north–south divide is also a major issue in terms of economic development since the wealthier southeastern provinces exert far greater power and influence than those in the west and the interior. Although, as has been observed, the majority of the people living in China Proper are classified as Han Chinese, the linguistic and cultural differences are in some cases as great as would be found in separate European countries, and conflicts arise between communities which could be categorised as ethnic or sub-ethnic.

After the conquest of China by the Manchus in 1644 there was competition in government over the use of the Chinese and Manchu languages, which are not related either in speech or in script. By the eighteenth century, when the Qing dynasty had reached the height of its powers, Chinese, to all intents and purposes, had triumphed, as had been the case with previous conquest dynasties, and was in use on a day-to-day basis as the language of administration, both spoken and written, throughout the country. The Qing government sponsored a programme of translation from Chinese into Manchu to assist in the preservation of its own language, and it also retained separate collections of documents in Manchu language, which were a closed book to many of the Chinese officials. However Manchu entered a period of decline and has virtually died out as a living language of China, even in the old Manchu lands of the northeast. A form of Manchu survives as the Xibo (Sibe) language of an ethnic minority group of the same name who inhabit parts of present-day Xinjiang. Current research is re-evaluating the relative roles of the Manchu and Chinese languages in Qing China. More and more Manchu language documents have been discovered in the Qing official archives, and an increasing number of scholars in China have the ability, and the freedom, to translate and interpret them.

In the nineteenth century, a new and more destabilising conflict emerged: the clash of Chinese and Western values. This has been summed up as the *tiyong* debate, from the phrase *zhongxue wei ti, xixue wei yong*, 'Chinese learning for the essentials, Western learning for practical applications', first used in this sense in the nineteenth century but drawing on philosophical concepts that date back to the Warring States period (the fifth and fourth centuries BC). Chinese intellectuals were attempting to grapple with the implications of the powerful scientific and technical knowledge and related social and political ideas that were arriving from the West: they attempted to incorporate ideas and concepts that they considered necessary to strengthen China's defences and economy while tenaciously preserving values they perceived as essentially and unchangeably 'Chinese'. This conflict appears simplistic to the outside observer, but it resonates with many Chinese thinkers and has never been resolved: in present-day China, the social and economic system that emerged under the influence of Deng Xiaoping was known initially as 'socialism with Chinese characteristics' [*you Zhongguo tese de shehuizhuyi*]. This concept of 'Chinese characteristics', which was intended to demonstrate the persistence of essential Chineseness even in a time of radical modernisation, was applied enthusiastically to literature and to many social and physical phenomena.

Conflicts which are primarily religious in nature, such as those that can be found during the Reformation and Counter-Reformation in Europe and the spread of Islam throughout the Middle East, central and southern Asia and northern Africa, have played little part in modern Chinese history. Although the traditional religions of China, Buddhism and Daoism, have never been as pacific as some naïve and enthusiastic Western adherents might wish them to be, they have at least had the virtue of tolerance: exclusivity of belief has never been the problem in modern China that it is in Christendom or Islam. Certain conflicts have, however, contained significant religious elements. The Hui risings [*huimin qiyi*] of Shaanxi and Gansu in the mid-nineteenth century were inspired in part by the assertion of Islamic identity against a Confucian state but predominantly by conflicts that involved the plethora of Sufi and other orders that had emerged in north-western China since the seventeenth century. These religious orders persist to this day in the Muslim regions of China, and conflict between them and with the local authorities over issues such as tomb-building, land rights and Islamic education is still a regular occurrence.

The Taiping Rebellion, or Heavenly Kingdom of Great Peace [*Taiping tianguo*], which shook south-central China in the mid-nineteenth century and precipitated a substantial population decline, was the only uprising of the era that seriously threatened the authority of the Qing government. It offered an alternative society that appeared, at least for a time, to be viable and was unusual in that it was precipitated partly by a version of Christianity. In the Boxer Rising [*yihequan yundong*] of 1898–1901, it was, conversely, anti-Christian and xenophobic feelings among the peasants of northern China that turned what had been originally an anti-Manchu, and thus primarily an ethnic conflict into a xenophobic clash that was aimed at propping up the Manchus on the grounds that they were less foreign than the westerners.

Nineteenth century Chinese xenophobia, or 'anti-foreignism' as it is frequently translated, is a reminder that the major conflict with the West, and later with Japan, was primarily a conflict about trade and diplomacy although, as has been observed, it had cultural implications. The conflict with Britain that led to the Opium Wars of 1839–42 and 1856–8 and the creation of the Treaty Ports was the most significant, although naval battles with France off the coasts of Yunnan and Vietnam also served to open China to foreign influence: during the course of the century, most of the main European powers and the USA sought commercial and diplomatic influence in China. Russia pressed its own territorial and commercial claims on China's northern frontiers.

The Chinese and Manchu inter-ethnic conflict referred to above was also a factor in elite politics. The Imperial Court sought to maintain a balance between Manchu, Mongol and Chinese bureaucrats at the highest levels of the administration but this did not always lead to the greatest stability or to the appointment of the most able administrators. Towards the end of the nineteenth century, an ideological divide also opened between reformers and conservatives: this conflict overlapped to some extent with ethnic tensions, because Manchus were perceived as irredeemably conservative, and came to the surface during the abortive Hundred Days Reform of 1898.

Another significant aspect of elite conflict was friction between the centre and the provinces. Regional armies had been created to facilitate the suppression of the rebellions of the late nineteenth century, but the political power that resulted from the control of these colossal military forces led to the collapse of the structural protection against regionalism that had operated for centuries. In the early twentieth century, members of an emerging elite, modern and educated, and known as the New Gentry, exercised their power in the regional provincial assemblies. These assemblies came into their own in 1911 when the provinces seceded from the empire one by one in what became known as the Revolution of 1911. This decentralisation in turn laid the foundations for the emergence of regional warlords in the 1920s and 1930s and frustrated successive attempts to create a single Republican government.

Although China's first experience of conflict and disputes with foreign powers in the modern period was with the West, it was the challenge of Japan that proved to be more significant in the longer term. At the end of the Tokugawa period (1603–1868) Japan had emerged from a long period of isolation. During the Meiji restoration which followed, it embarked on an impressive programme of industrialisation and an aggressive policy of imperial expansion brought Taiwan, Korea and finally much of China within its colonial orbit.

Modern Chinese nationalism, although it has its distant origins in the resistance to Western pressure in the nineteenth century, developed essentially as a reaction to the increasing Japanese pressure on China in the twentieth century. The May Fourth Movement of 1919 was the most powerful manifestation of this nationalism and the two dominant political parties of modern China were created in its wake – the Chinese Communist Party (CCP), founded in 1921 and the Guomindang (GMD), which took its modern form in 1923. These parties were the expressions of two competing forms of Chinese (that is mainly Han Chinese) nationalism which came into conflict in the civil wars of the twentieth century.

Ethnic conflict within the traditional borders of China has also pitted Chinese nationalism against the nationalist independence movements of the Tibetans, the Uyghurs of Xinjiang and the Mongols, all of which include a powerful religious element that reinforces the political character of their separatist endeavours.

For orthodox Marxists, as members of the Chinese Communist Party perceived themselves to be in the party's formative period, the struggle of the working class in the cities should have been the focus of their political work. Nineteenth- and twentieth-century industrialisation and the migration of peasant labour to eastern coastal cities such as Shanghai and Tianjin had created a new urban working class as well as business and entrepreneurial groups. Trade unions played an important role in the early rise of the CCP and continued to be important in the period from the beginning of the century to the end of the Northern Expedition that was launched to reunify China. In 1927, in the Shanghai Coup, the GMD seized control of the cities, forced the CCP out into the countryside away from their working class base and removed them from what should have been their natural milieu of social conflict in the cities.

Before the Second World War, 80 per cent of China's population were farmers. A complex system of land tenure and agricultural practices that brought together extended family and lineage networks had evolved to manage conflict between landowners and tenants: there were, however, frequent and often violent confrontations over land ownership, rent and the payment of interest on loans to landlords. Members of the CCP had been involved in the peasant movement, which sought to advance the cause of the poorer peasants, from its earliest days, as exemplified by the work of Peng Pai in Guangdong during 1921–2, and Mao Zedong in Hunan in 1927, but this was considered to be a secondary focus in comparison with social and political initiatives in the urban areas. After 1927 when it had been excluded from the cities, the CCP was obliged to work in the country-side or it would have had no popular base at all. Ironically this was to stand it in good stead in the long run: the CCP was able to use the peasant nationalism that developed in the wake of the resistance to the Japanese invasion as its political base for taking power in China in 1949.

As a developing country, China in the modern period has witnessed conflict between the cities and the countryside: peasants have resisted urbanisation but have also contributed to it by migrating to the cities in search of work. The need to tax the peasantry in order to produce an agricultural surplus to fund the development of the industrial economy, land reform and collectivisation also exacerbated conflict between the state and the peasantry after 1949.

Although the CCP has by and large attempted to present a united front, there have been deep internal divisions over alternative strategies of economic and political developments and these divisions became dramatically public in the Great Leap Forward and the Cultural Revolution. The official designation for this intra-Party conflict was the 'struggle between the two lines', which is represented in most Western analyses as a battle between the moderate, conservative or pragmatic elements and the radical or Maoist factions. The death of Mao Zedong in 1976 and the advent of a reform-minded generation of CCP officials is presumed to have put an end to the 'struggle between the two lines' once and for all, although differences of

opinion on vital policies such as the state ownership of economic enterprises persisted.

Narrating the Political History of Modern China

This is a narrative history of China in the modern period. Most attention
has been paid to the twentieth century, divided as it is by the coming to
power of the CCP in 1949, but the nineteenth century is also examined in
some detail, and more recent developments are set in the context of
China's long history as an empire. Narrative history fell out of fashion to
some extent during the 1970s and 1980s, and many historians looked to
what was claimed to be the greater analytical power of the approach
favoured by social scientists. It has since had a welcome renaissance as it
became clear that social science methods could support the historian but
could not by any means supply all the answers or supplant a broad historical approach.

This account of modern China has at its heart a chronological narrative
of the political history of the country. Important social and economic
developments are also considered, and there is some treatment of cultural
history and the ideas that have stimulated change or encouraged resistance
to change but it is not primarily a cultural history. Greater coverage is given
to treaties and to constitutions than has been fashionable: these documents,
usually created during times of change and conflict and, in the case of
treaties, often forced upon vanquished nations or subjugated peoples, provide valuable evidence of the thinking of opposing parties and the political
processes that were involved.

Chinese history is often treated as if it were somehow separate from the
history of the rest of the world, a phenomenon that operates under rules
that are completely different from those that apply to history elsewhere.
This is not an appropriate or judicious approach. China has never been an
isolated or hermetically sealed society, in spite of periods during which it
has been politically isolated. This study therefore takes into account China's
relations with its neighbours, including Russia and the Soviet Union, the
central Asian societies that are now part of Kazakhstan, Uzbekistan and the
other successor states to the Union of Soviet Socialist Republics, Mongolia,
Korea and Japan, all of which have greatly influenced the course of Chinese
history – Russia and Japan most of all. Relations with more distant powers
were instrumental in shaping China's response to the modern world in both
the nineteenth and twentieth centuries – Britain, France and the USA being
among the most important.

Diversity and Contested Histories

China's history is complex because of its size and ethnic diversity. It is much the same size as Europe, and the histories of its different regions have followed different trajectories in the same way that European nations and peoples have had their own histories. To a greater or lesser extent, the size and diversity of China has been a determining factor in all periods of modern Chinese history. In the modern period, this was perhaps most obvious between 1916 and 1928 when political authority was fragmented. During these years, there was no effective central state authority, and power throughout the whole of China was in the hands of provincial military governors – 'warlords' – who for all practical purposes can be said to have run independent regimes.

Although the Han people are conventionally viewed as the homogeneous majority population of China, they are, as has been suggested, as diverse as the population of Europe in their spoken languages and local cultures and traditions. In some areas, the non-Han peoples, the ethnic minorities or the 'national minorities' as they are labelled in contemporary China, are not in reality minorities at all but constitute the majority population. Conflict between these communities and the Han has been one of the motive forces in modern Chinese history, most notably during the great rebellions of the nineteenth century that have already been referred to. In the border regions of China, the political authority and military might of the Chinese state have repeatedly come into conflict with the national and political aspirations of the Tibetans, the Uyghurs of Xinjiang and the Mongols. The histories of these regions are contested histories and the accuracy and legitimacy of historical accounts is disputed as much as are the territories from which the histories emerge.

Sources for Modern Chinese History

The main sources for this history include scholarly Chinese language accounts from both China and Taiwan, research monographs published in the twentieth century and academic journals in Chinese and European languages which focus on the history of China and the rest of East Asia. Particular attention has been paid to contemporary and eyewitness accounts of the events of modern Chinese history in English and occasionally in other European languages, many of them long out of print.

Students and scholars from the PRC are sometimes surprised, or even disappointed, to learn that the history of China as taught in the West is not so completely different from the version that they have learned in China. As China opened to the exchange of international academic opinion from the 1980s, there was an expectation, particularly among the younger generation of scholars, that the Western approach to history might undermine or revise the orthodox narrative that had been presented to them in China and could possibly provide answers to enduring intellectual problems.

In parallel with this, some Western scholars have become deeply suspicious of any historical studies emanating from the PRC, even to the extent of refusing to use editions of the traditional dynastic histories and other standard works that have been published on the mainland since 1949 without troubling to ascertain whether these editions are textually identical to the older versions. Although the government of the PRC has undoubtedly used history as a propaganda tool and has severely restricted the topics that could be studied, the manner in which they could be studied and the materials available to study them, this does not automatically invalidate all of the academic work that has been produced by the best professional historians in China, which can and should be subjected to the same critical appraisal as any history, wherever it is written.

Pre-1949 editions of source materials and scholarly studies that were completed well before the CCP came to power have been used in this study where appropriate, usually because they supply information and perspectives that have been ignored or forgotten. It is instructive to note that these sources do not suggest a completely new approach to the periodisation of Chinese history or to the major historical events and trends of China in its modern period, although they do offer new information and allow for the possibility of new interpretations.

There is as yet no close parallel between the way that historians can approach the modern history of China and newly developed methods for studying the history of the former Soviet Union and its successor states at the beginning of the twenty-first century. There has been no collapse of Communism in China, and there has been no consequent opening up of the most secret archive material that can be used to launch a complete reassessment of the history of the Communist Party and its policies. The economic opening and reform policies that have been pursued by Deng Xiaoping and his successors have persuaded some observers into thinking that China has been transformed overnight into a capitalist country or at least into a nation with a capitalist economy. This may happen at sometime in the future but, at the time of writing, the CCP seems secure in its authority and in its control over a rapidly developing mixed economy. Some national and local historical archives have been opened but the most interesting and important, notably the Party History archives, remain closed because they are also the most sensitive. It is possible to discuss most historical topics with colleagues in China, both formally and informally but there are still many taboo areas.

One of the problems faced in composing a general history of this nature has been the need to maintain a balance between the body of work that has gone before and has stood the test of time and newer interpretations of that history, which may turn out to be ephemeral. Some topics simply have to be included: a history of modern China that failed to cover, for example, the Opium War, the Taiping Rebellion, the Boxer Rising and the Long March, would be unacceptable. Twenty-first century interpretations of the significance of these conflicts may differ from those that prevailed in the mid-twentieth century, but they continue to influence thinkers and political actors in China and cannot be ignored.

Since the opening of China in the 1980s there has been an avalanche of publishing in all fields and history is no exception. Much of what has been published in Chinese is interesting and entertaining and some of it is also useful, but it is an impossible task to keep up with the quantity of books and articles in anything but a narrow specialist field. What complicates the situation even further is that history in China, especially the history of the CCP, is constantly being revised in light of changing political orthodoxies. This revision is carried out not only by professional historians but also by political actors, some of whom are using this medium to settle scores and vindicate their families or their political allies and to vilify old enemies. Some of the fascinating and dramatic material that is emerging about the Cultural Revolution and the factional disputes within the CCP is still too raw and untested to rely on as it takes time to sift fact from fantasy. It may, however, change our perception of these events radically in due course.

West Rainton, Durham
Tsinghua University, Beijing

1

RISE AND FALL
OF THE CHINESE EMPIRE

From 1644 to 1911, China was ruled by emperors of the Qing dynasty, a Manchu rather than a Chinese imperial family: it was to be the last in a succession of ruling houses that, by convention, stretches back in an unbroken line to the unification of the Warring States by the First Emperor Qin Shi Huangdi in 221 BC. A list of the dynasties of imperial China provides a comforting illusion of continuity and stability from the Qin to the Qing, but the collapse of one dynasty and its replacement by another was rarely a peaceful transition. Typically the ruling elite lost the confidence of the populace and its authority waned in a period perhaps of scandal at court or peasant rebellion, and a new house came to power claiming that it now possessed the Mandate of Heaven [*tianming*], the right to reign, which the deposed court were deemed to have lost by virtue of their defeat. By no means all the dynasties that ruled China were Chinese, in the sense that they were not all of Han origin. Long before the conquests of the Emperor Qin Shi Huangdi, the Chinese state and Chinese society had evolved through perennial conflict between the steppe and the sown; between the nomad stock breeders of the northern and western high pastures and the settled rice and millet farmers of the fertile basins created by the Yangzi and the Yellow River; between the Turkic, Mongol, Tungusic and Tibetan cultures of the frontier pastoralists and warriors and the Han Chinese culture of the central plains and eastern lowlands – the culture of the ideograph and the scholar bureaucrat.

The Chinese, as is the way with imperial powers, regarded their own culture as superior to all others, and the lands that they controlled were known as *Zhongguo* – the 'central kingdoms' – a concept that was later transmitted to the west as the Middle Kingdom. Chinese speakers, especially literate and educated Chinese speakers, often considered the frontier folk to be barbarians, but that did not prevent them from being overrun by these barbarians from time to time. Strict and loyal Confucian scholars might lament the loss of China to these uncouth herders and warriors, but the impact of the frontier peoples on the culture of China has been profound, and it is problematic to be precise about what in Chinese culture is of genuine Chinese origin and what came to the Middle Kingdom from the steppes of Mongolia, the Tibetan plateau or the mountains and forests of Manchuria, or indeed vice versa. From earliest times to the thirteenth century, the blending of nomad and farmer, of the steppe peoples with the men and women of Han ethnic origin, was a complex process although Chinese historians of an orthodox Confucian persuasion prefer to highlight dynasties such as the Han (206 BC–AD 221) and Tang (618–906) where 'Chinese' culture was thought to be at its most highly developed and have a tendency to play down the 'barbarian' dynasties which were disdained as temporary aberrations.[1] Some of these aberrations were to persist for centuries. The defeat of the Song dynasty by the Mongol armies of Khubilai Khan which captured the city of Hangzhou in 1279 led to the creation of a Mongol dynasty, the Yuan, to rule China but more significantly to the incorporation of the Chinese world into a wider, pan-Asian, Mongol empire that included Turks and Persians. The Yuan dynasty was overthrown in 1368 by what was ostensibly a 'native Chinese' dynasty, the Ming, but which in fact contained many non-Chinese elements including an influential community of Muslims. The Ming dynasty reigned until the late seventeenth century when its authority disintegrated amid the classic combination of palace corruption and peasant rebellion. The final years of the Ming were sorrowful and distressing for Chinese scholars and a painful ordeal for the population as a whole: the agony was brought to an end only when in 1644 the armies of yet another 'barbarian' people, the Manchus, marched down through the passes which lie to the north east of the present capital Beijing to take control of the Ming capital, which was about to be captured by the armies of a Chinese peasant rebel, Li Zicheng.

The Manchus were a confederation of tribal peoples who had created a powerful state to the northeast of China, in the area that was later named after them – Manchuria.[2] The name Manchu dates back only to 1635 and before that they had used a variety of tribal names including the ancient Nurchen. They were nomadic and organised into military units or banners but sought to emulate the imperial system that they saw across the border in China. In 1636, the Manchu ruler Hong Taiji (often referred to erroneously as Abahai in Western sources) who lived from 1592 to 1643 had given his state a Chinese name, Qing, which means pure or clear, although at the same time he enjoined his subjects to retain their Manchu language, dress and culture and the warrior virtues, particularly mounted archery, which he believed to be an essential part of their heritage. This attempt to marry a Chinese-style state system with values from their tribal homeland was to create tensions and conflicts throughout much of their rule in China. In his final years Hong Taiji embarked on his Great Enterprise, the conquest of China, a military triumph for the Manchus that he never lived to see. The posthumous title of Chongde was bestowed on him, and he can be considered to have been the founder and first emperor of the Qing dynasty – his reign being dated from 1636 to 1643 – although in conventional Chinese historiography the Qing dynasty begins with the Shunzhi emperor in 1644. His clan, the Aisin Gioro was to provide rulers for the Qing dynasty all the way through to the last emperor, Aisin Gioro Pu Yi in 1908.[3]

Manchu Conquest and Qing State

The history of modern China was dominated by the Han aspiration of throwing off the Manchu yoke, but how did China come to bear that yoke? When the Ming capital of Beijing was under threat by the rebel armies of Li Zicheng in 1644, generals of the Ming army made the decision that, rather than allow the peasant Li to take the imperial capital, they would invite in the armies of the Manchus to help them put down the rebellion. The Manchus did this with great success, but, having been invited into China, they stayed – for more than 250 years. Their conquest of China was prolonged and bloody. The fall of Ming cities to the Manchus was accompanied by massacres, notably the ten-day sack of the great commercial centre of Yangzhou in May 1645. These brutalities were long remembered by the Han Chinese and were evoked in the rallying cries of the revolutionaries who fought the Manchus in the late nineteenth and early twentieth centuries.

It was not until the suppression in 1681 of the Three Feudatories rebellion that the whole of China Proper was securely under Manchu rule. The Manchus had granted fiefdoms in the southern regions of Yunnan, Guangdong and Fujian to Ming officials who had collaborated with them during the conquest. The Kangxi emperor came to perceive these semi-independent kingdoms as a threat to his authority and to the unity of the Qing state and he decided to abolish the fiefdoms in 1673. The Three Feudatories rebellion was the resistance by the feudal princes to their abolition. The Manchu armies continued to counter all resistance to their conquest with campaigns of terror and mass slaughter and, to consolidate their control, they established garrisons of banner troops in the main towns of the conquered territories.[4] Western China would not be firmly under the control of the Qing until the late eighteenth century, and the island of Taiwan became a province only in 1885.

Kangxi and the Dzunghar Mongols

The expansion of the Qing dynasty westwards coincided with the eastward march of the Russian empire and also with the extension of Britain's empire in India. The first target of the Manchus was neither of these but a much smaller state which had been established by the Mongols, the former rulers of China who had been forced back to the steppes by the Ming dynasty and were in the process of creating their own Dzungar power base in Central Asia. The Manchus resisted the power of the Mongols but at the same time traded with them to acquire horses and forged military alliances with them. They invoked blood ties, a shared steppe heritage and a shared written language, for their script was derived from Mongol characters, but perhaps most of all they appealed to a powerful sense of the cultural difference between the two peoples of nomad heritage and the Chinese.

The Kangxi emperor, who reigned from 1662 to 1722, was the third son of the Shunzhi emperor, the first emperor of the Qing. His Chinese name was Xuanye and he was of the ruling Aisin Gioro clan of the Manchus, but he was also descended from Mongol aristocrats on his father's side. After satisfying himself that the defeat of the Three Feudatories in the south had secured China Proper for the Qing dynasty, he turned his attention to his northern borders and to the Mongols. Tribute missions from the powerful Galdan Tseren, who had become the Khan of the Dzungars in 1670 after a fratricidal civil war, were growing in size and in number and frequently behaved more like raiding parties than diplomatic and trade missions. Galdan had also built an alliance with Tibet on the basis of the Buddhism that the Mongols shared with the Tibetans. This form of Buddhism differs markedly in belief and organisation from the Buddhism of China and is sometimes called Lama Buddhism, although its adherents prefer the name Tibetan Buddhism.

In 1687 when Galdan's forces invaded the territory of the Khalkha Mongols, which was much closer to the Qing capital, Kangxi counter-attacked. The Qing supported the Khalkhas against Galdan and in 1690 Kangxi led his first military expedition against the Dzungars. Galdan's forces were not annihilated, which is what the emperor had intended, but they were forced to withdraw well beyond the borders of the territory that the Qing state controlled. This was a major victory for the Kangxi emperor but the campaign had been costly.

Diplomacy and Russia

This was the age of expanding empires by land as well as by sea, and the expansion of the Qing empire to the north and west could only proceed so far before it came into contact with the eastward expansion of Tsarist

Russia in search of furs to trade and the all-year-round warm-water port that its icebound navy needed so desperately for winter campaigns. In the seventeenth century, embassies from St Petersburg began their attempt to open China to trade and diplomatic representation, a policy that other western Europeans did not pursue until the eighteenth century. Negotiations were fruitless until a meeting at Nerchinsk in eastern Russia which followed conflicts between Russian and Chinese military units along the Amur River. Both sides accepted that it was necessary to clarify the position of the border between their empires. Manchu and Russian officials negotiated, not in Mongolian which would have been the most obvious medium as it was a *lingua franca* of the border regions but in Latin, which had been suggested by two Jesuits who had been attached to the Qing court. The Mongols were effectively excluded from the negotiations and in the Treaty of Nerchinsk which was signed in 1689, Russia gained territory along the Amur River, and its traders were given the right to enter China: China thus ensured that the Russians would not side with Galdan's Mongol forces. The Treaty of Kiakhta in 1727 took this agreement a stage further by confirming the boundaries between Outer Mongolia, situating it firmly within the Chinese empire, and the Russian region of Siberia. Russia established the town of Kiakhta as a frontier trading post.[5]

Qianlong's Frontier Campaigns

The Qianlong emperor's most notable achievement was the incorporation of the frontier regions of Tibet, Chinese Turkestan (Xinjiang) and Mongolia into his Manchu empire, thus determining most of what are commonly accepted as the boundaries of China right up to the present day. The Kangxi emperor had died in 1722 and was succeeded by the Yongzheng emperor (reigned 1723–36). Qianlong was the fourth son of Yongzheng and came to the throne in 1736, by which time the Qing had already begun to intervene militarily in Tibet and Turkestan, although the Manchus also used tried and tested methods of trade and tribute to keep the frontiers under their control.

When Galdan Tseren died in 1745, the Dzungar state, which under his rule had posed a serious challenge to Qing power in the west, began to unravel in a series of succession crises and by 1757 it had for all practical purposes ceased to exist. The Qing government had intervened on several occasions to protect what they regarded as their interests in Tibet, sending troops in 1717 to counter a Dzungar siege and dispatching a further contingent in 1728 to resolve a political crisis in its favour. After this intervention, the Qing established the office of the *ambans*, a permanent residency of representatives of the Manchu emperors in Lhasa, an institution that was to remain in place until 1912.[6] This time onwards, the Qing court attempted to control, or at least to influence, Tibetan politics through the *amban* system, and Tibet can be considered to have been a protectorate of the Qing empire at that time although it was not under Chinese sovereignty or direct control. The influence of the Qing in Tibet was at its greatest after another military intervention, on this occasion in the war between the Tibetans and the Nepalese Gurkhas in 1792 but it gradually weakened. The Tibetan authorities, both secular and clerical, wanted to remain as independent of China as they could and Tibet's remoteness from Beijing assisted them in this aim.[7]

With the Dzungars no longer a serious threat, Qing forces began to penetrate the deserts and oases of Eastern Turkestan. The only settled area of Eastern Turkestan was in the oases to the south of the Taklamakan desert, which were controlled by the Makhumzada Khojas, hereditary leaders of a powerful Sufi clan who had been clients of the Dzungars. The Qing established garrisons in Ghulja (Yining) in the northwest and Kashghar in the southwest but their control over the region was established only in the face of severe resistance, and it was not until 1765, when the city of Ush (now Ush-Turfan) was captured after a terrible and bloody siege, that the Qing could rest contented in their domination of Eastern Turkestan.[8]

The Qing government had also brought the Mongol regions under its control or had at least neutralised any threat by the Mongols to its power.

> When they came under Manchu rule, the Mongols neither adhered to the Manchus as a united people nor resisted the imposition of Manchu authority in the manner of a nation defending itself against foreigners. It is the piecemeal exclusion of the Mongols in the Manchu empire that accounts for the 'Outer', 'Inner' and other divisions of Mongolia and the Mongols.[9]

The Mongols were fragmented; they were a group of tribes rather than a unified nation, and they fought each other at least as frequently as they fought the Manchus. When, in the seventeenth century, the northern Khalkha Mongols were in danger of being overwhelmed by the western Oirat Mongols they sought help from the Manchus and the Oirats were repulsed. Outer Mongolia 'came within the Manchu empire as a special kind of protectorate, somewhat different in status from the administrative subdivisions of Inner Mongolia, and more loosely and indirectly ruled'.[10]

Qing Society and Economy

In spite of its inauspicious beginnings in conquest and carnage, the Qing dynasty was to prove to be a period of economic success and political and social stability for China – at least for the first 150 years of its rule. The population of China had fallen dramatically during the Ming-Qing transition, nt only as a result of the peasant rebellion and the conquest, but also because of epidemics which were rife during the 1630s and 1640s. As Manchu control stabilised the empire, the population began to rise and in the course of the eighteenth century it doubled, rising from some 50 million in 1700 to approximately 300 million by the end of the century. The reason for this dramatic increase is unclear but it is generally agreed that it was due to a decline in mortality rates rather than an increase in the number of births. That in turn has been attributed primarily to the reduction in social conflict and an increase in food production.[11]

Agriculture during the Qing period had changed little from the previous dynasties. Farming remained labour intensive with some use of oxen, water buffalo and donkeys as draught animals or in ploughing but very little use of machinery. The northern wheat growing area tended to have larger farms than the rice growing wet lands of the south and there were more tenanted farms in the south. Several innovations in agriculture had helped to feed the increasing population: the area of land under cultivation had been increased by the spread of terracing particularly in the poorer lands of the north; multiple cropping increased the yield of both rice and wheat. Fertilising the soil, however, depended heavily on animal and, especially, human manure. The agricultural economy of the early Qing had become more susceptible to the vagaries of the market as commercial investment in farms increased and both the management of farms and rural society became more complex.[12]

There was no industrialisation in the modern sense in the early part of the Qing reign, but handicraft industries had developed to a high degree and most villages had access to basic farm tools and everyday pottery, either from local producers or through the networks of pedlars and merchants who attended local markets. Higher quality goods were produced in specialist areas: pottery and porcelain from kilns including those of the imperial porcelain town Jingdezhen and the teapot specialists of Yixing; silk from Suzhou and iron ware from the town of Foshan in Guangdong province, which also produced pottery.[13]

Although commerce was officially disdained by the Confucian thinkers who considered it to be the lowest form of economic activity after the scholar-officials, the peasantry and the honest artisan, trade flourished during the early Qing period. Markets were held wherever it was possible to attract sufficient buyers: some villages and small towns only warranted periodic fairs, but in larger settlements a network of regular markets was established. In addition to local traders, these markets attracted travelling merchants from the great commercial syndicates that had flourished in the expansionary sixteenth century during the Ming dynasty and had been resurrected under the Qing once the wars of conquest were over. The greatest syndicates were the Shanxi traders from northern China who had originally made their money by supplying the frontier garrisons in exchange for licences to trade in salt, which previously had been a monopoly of the state, and the Xin'an or Huizhou merchants from the south of Anhui province who specialised in high value goods such as porcelain from Jingdezhen.[14]

Society

The social organisation of Qing dynasty China 'was highly stratified, with status distinctions that were carefully preserved in the vocabularies of both ritual and law'.[15] At the apex of the pyramidal structure of Chinese society were the hereditary nobles. These were either members of the imperial Manchu clan of Aisin Gioro and its allies or civil and military officials who had been honoured for their achievements or for their loyalty to the court with aristocratic titles. This status also brought them property, financial stipends and allowances of food – calculated according to their precise grade. Noble families outside the ruling clan had smaller allowances, Manchus had higher stipends than Mongols and the Han Chinese members of the elite received the lowest payments.

Ranking second only to the nobility were the members of the imperial civil service, the officials. Members of this group were assigned to one of nine ranks, and the entire imperial bureaucracy was subdivided into three levels, the top layer (ranks one to three), the middle level (ranks four to seven) and the lowest level (ranks eight and nine). Every rank was further divided into upper and lower levels, and each of these ranks and sub-ranks entitled the official to specific badges, buttons and belt clasps.

Below the office holders, although overlapping with them to a great extent were the scholar-gentry or 'literati', so called on account of the rigorous system of education and examination in the language, literature and philosophy of the Confucian tradition that they had undergone in their endeavour to secure high office, whether or not they attained that office. Entry to this group was by a series of graduated examinations, from the *shengyuan* degree, the holders of which had been examined in their own prefectures, to the *juren* degree awarded after an examination in the provincial capital and finally the highest degree, the *jinshi*, which was awarded to successful candidates in the metropolitan examinations that were held in the capital and was the prerequisite for entrance to the highest offices of state.

The scholar-gentry overlapped with the official class because all degree holders were potential officials although by no means all attained official positions. Nevertheless, the upper gentry (those who held the two highest degrees) had prestige and privileges that ranked with those enjoyed by lower officials, including immunity from corporal punishment and exemption from conscription into the corvee, the government labour service battalions. Many of the scholar-gentry who did not hold official positions were landowners who relied on income from their farms to maintain themselves and their families economically and socially.[16]

The remainder, and that meant the vast majority, of the population were commoners. Traditionally they were ranked in descending order as peasant, artisan or merchant, although this represented an ideal type of hierarchy according to the value placed on their occupations in Confucian morality rather than a representation of their actual power and influence in society.

The peasants, although considered as second only to the scholar-gentry in their value to a Confucian society, were the most disadvantaged group in Chinese society with the exception of some of the marginal or outlaw groups. They were the poorest and the least powerful although by no means all were living at the levels of extreme poverty that is associated with third world peasant farmers in the twenty-first century. Conditions for peasant farmers varied greatly from region to region and depended on the type of agriculture practised and the system of land ownership that prevailed in their locality. Southern rice farmers who rented the land that they worked for a reasonable sum might be comfortably off. Hill farmers in the northwest at the limits of crop growing typically found it extremely difficult to eke out a living even with the addition of sheep rearing and the associated trade in meat and fleeces. There was no tradition of primogeniture so landholdings divided on the death of the landowner and tended to be small: it was extremely difficult for peasants to amass capital and status. The pressure on land was often intense, and it is probably true to say that the majority of peasants were tenants and that many were landless and obliged to work as agricultural labourers. Working hours in the fields or rice paddies were long, and there was little in the way of mechanical aids to lighten the burden. If life was hard in normal times, it became impossible when natural disasters struck. Farmers were subject to periodic famines, floods and droughts, all of which wrought havoc on the carefully planned routines of ploughing, sowing, tending and harvesting that had been devised to keep the supply of food to the countryside flowing and provide the surplus needed for tax grain to feed the towns and cities. The worst natural disasters were accompanied by famine and death on a dreadful scale and by social dislocation that was often the precursor of peasant uprisings.

Farming families often manufactured some goods, whether this was oil for cooking, alcohol or clothes, household furniture and the other necessities of everyday life. This had led to the development of specialist handicraft-producing families and these craftsmen or artisans were considered to be a separate social group. Although some produced the simplest goods and operated at a village level, others were manufacturing high-quality commodities of great value, including silks and porcelains, and certain cities had developed reputations as producers of specific goods as was noted above.

Consigned by Confucian condescension to the lowest point in the social hierarchy were the merchants or rather the whole class of traders. This was a ridiculous fiction of snobbery as the most successful business families were often vastly wealthier than their social superiors, the officials, who frequently borrowed money from them. The merchant class ranged from the door-to-door pedlar through the traders at village and other local markets and brokers to members of the powerful and prosperous commercial networks, such as those based in the northern province of Shaanxi or the Xin'an (Huizhou) region of the southern province of Anhui. The financial reach of these merchant syndicates was astounding: they provided capital for the trade in high-value goods such as spices and jewellery and even invested in the production of luxury commodities such as porcelain and silks. Merchants from the Qing dynasty have left a record of their commercial travelling in the 'route books' in which they set down for their successors the most effective ways of travelling to the farthest-flung commercial outposts and the items that could be traded most profitably there. Often self-deprecating and reviled or at least patronised in print by the Confucian literati, these travelling traders knew China better than many of the officials sent out by the emperor to govern the provinces. However, such was the powerful draw of the official career structure that when they had amassed their fortunes, they settled down and saw to it that their sons were in a strong position to succeed in the imperial examination systems. Merchants have made little visible impact on the historical landscape of China with the remarkable exception of the crescent of ornamental archways in the village of Tangyue in the south of Anhui province which are dedicated to the memory of the men of the Huizhou merchant syndicate who went out to seek their fortune and returned to buy land and status in their home village. As the Qing dynasty drew to a close, the relationship between officials and merchants had become closer and more complex. Not only did officials borrow from merchants but some official families began to develop commercial sidelines such as managing warehouses, money-lending and pawnbroking to supplement the income from their official positions. By the nineteenth century it was often difficult to differentiate between the official and the commercial classes.

Some social mobility was possible in Qing China, which did not suffer the restrictions that existed in Japan under the Tokugawa Shogunate (1603–1858) where hereditary family occupations were enforced inflexibly. The examination system provided for a degree of opportunity but this was very limited, and only those whose families could support them for at least ten years' full-time study could ever hope to become graduates. In practice this meant that there was virtually no opportunity for boys from peasant or artisan families to move up the ranks of degree holders. There were rare and dramatic examples of exceptionally able boys from poor backgrounds who succeeded in the examination system with financial support from members of their extended family or lineage, and this gave rise to the image of the peasant boy preparing for his exams by studying the works of Confucius while sitting on the back of the water buffalo that he was guarding. This is an attractive myth but it became reality only occasionally. Needless to say, in a traditional society like Qing China, there was no question of girls preparing for examinations or for an official career.

Religion

Although religion played an important role in everyday life and seasonal rituals in Qing China, religious institutions were generally weak and relatively poor and did not challenge the political power structures of the dynasty.

The Manchus had traditionally practiced a form of shamanism, in common with their neighbours in northeastern Asia, the other Tungusic peoples, the Koreans and the Mongols, among whom it had not been entirely superseded by Tibetan Buddhism. Some Manchus, however, also followed Tibetan or Chinese Buddhism or even Daoism in homage to the culture of their powerful Chinese neighbour. Qing emperors patronised Buddhist temples while also retaining the shamanism of their ancestors. Shamanism in the Manchu lands was a form of animism which venerated the spirits that were believed to be present in the earth, water and all living beings whether they be plant or animal, a religious system not dissimilar to Shinto in Japan. Shamanism in northeastern Asia required the intervention and mediation of a shaman who would go into a ritual trance to communicate with the spirits and the shaman became a powerful figure in Manchu society. This belief in shamanism was an important factor distinguishing the Manchus from the Han but the Manchu elite did not accord it such prominence as the lower orders.[17]

For the Han population in Qing China, the cult of veneration of the ancestors that is associated with Confucian social thought, and is rather loosely referred to as ancestor worship, was almost universal. Much of this took place at the domestic level and included mourning rituals at family tombs and sacrifices in the presence of the kitchen god and other household gods. However this was also a state-sanctioned religion, and the ceremonies performed by the emperors were at the apex of a hierarchy of ceremonies performed in veneration of Heaven – a hierarchy of which the domestic remembrance of ancestors was a part. The clan (the common descent group of the extended family) also played an important role in collective ancestor worship, which centred on the ancestral temple, itself a physical representation of the power and authority of the past and present members of the clan. The ancestral altar might be home to hundreds of spirit tablets representing many generations of clan members and the whole atmosphere was designed to impress on individual family members that they belonged to and owed an obligation to the traditions of the clan.

Apart from Confucianism, which many prefer to regard as an ethical system rather than a genuine religion, there were Buddhist and Daoist monasteries, temples and other foundations. Buddhism and Daoism had been powerful social forces during earlier periods of Chinese history but by the Qing dynasty they had been marginalised and impoverished and many monasteries and temples barely survived on the donations of believers. They provided spiritual services including some that supported ancestor worship.

Secret Societies

If visible and mainstream Buddhism and Daoism had lost the authority that they had once wielded, their influence remained in a plethora of unofficial, underground and often illegal organisations that provided a counterweight to the institutions of imperial power. Many of them dated back to (or claimed that they dated back to) the Ming dynasty; some were avowedly political and aimed to restore the Ming as a Chinese dynasty after overthrowing the alien Manchu Tartars who they believed had usurped the dragon throne in 1644.

Secret society is a Western term for what were known in Qing China as *hui* [associations] or *tang* [lodges]. They were more common in the countryside than in the towns and were a focus for political and religious dissents and provided a social outlet for people denied entry to the official elites. They tended to be local organisations for local people and were not inevitably radical, revolutionary or opposed to the Qing state. However in times of social disruption they provided a degree of protection for local people against famine or attack by outsiders, and under certain circumstances they could coalesce into broader social movements which were capable of organising against the state.

The most significant societies were those that were associated with the White Lotus sect, which drew its inspiration from the Maitreya School of Buddhism; the messianic school focused on the Buddha of the future, although it also incorporated ideas and concepts from popular Daoism. Groups with links to the White Lotus were involved in all the major anti-Qing movements in the nineteenth and twentieth centuries, including the Boxer Rebellion and the Revolution of 1911. While their members came from all classes of society, they appealed particularly to marginalised and excluded groups such as peasants who had been forced off their land, failed scholars, boatmen, hired labourers and outlaws. Their legacy can still be detected in the modern Triad and other criminal organisations which have completely lost the religious and political values, which originally inspired the White Lotus groups but may retain some of their rituals or trappings.[18]

Women

Women in Mao's China were said to 'hold up half the sky' but that was certainly not the case under the empire of the Manchus. In the years before the establishment of the Qing dynasty, the Manchus had, like other traditional societies, used women as a diplomatic asset and the daughters and nieces of the Manchu khans were presented to their retainers to ensure loyalty and to draw potential challengers for power into the extended family.[19] The extended family had always been central to the society of China and this continued to be the case during the Qing dynasty. Marriage patterns had evolved to strengthen the role of the extended family, but they varied greatly depending on the social standing of the family concerned. For elite families, it was necessary to bring in a bride from a family of similar standing, if necessary from outside the area in which the groom's family lived. The bride brought with her a dowry and by convention was permitted to use at least a portion as she desired. The new wife would gradually acquire status in her husband's family and became the matriarch on the demise of other senior women, but her sphere of activity and influence would have been the home, and there were few opportunities to act outside this limited area. She might also have to accept that her husband would take a secondary wife or concubines. If her husband predeceased her, she would be expected to remain a 'chaste widow' rather than remarry. This form of marriage, which was the only form legitimised in Confucian rituals, meant that the bride moved completely from her parents' household into that of her husband and his parents, transferring her loyalty to the new household and accepting the authority of her husband's parents, in particular that of her new mother-in-law.

This high-status form of marriage was also found among the less privileged classes where it could be afforded, but there were other practical arrangements where money and rank were lacking. Poorer men often did not marry at all as they were unable to afford a bride, but the phenomenon of child-brides, girls who were taken into the households of their prospective husbands as infants, was relatively common. It was also possible for a man to marry into the family of a woman although this was less socially acceptable.[20]

Qing Culture: Manchus and Confucians

One of the paradoxes of the Qing dynasty is that Chinese language, literature and many forms of culture flourished in spite of the fact that the country was ruled by an alien elite with a distinct and different language and cultural heritage.

Members of the Manchu elite struggled to find a balance between retaining their commitment to the language and culture of their Manchu homeland – an essential part of their identity – and the literati culture of the Chinese elite with whom they found themselves in day-to-day contact and which they had come to respect even before the conquest. Some emperors took the lead by immersing themselves in the study of *wenyan*, classical or literary Chinese, and often became proficient not only in the language but also in the composition of poetry in classical forms and even traditional painting. This was controversial especially in the early years of the dynasty and the Shunzhi emperor's interest in elite Chinese poetry and literature was regarded by members of his entourage as decadent and unbecoming of a Manchu warrior. It was felt that this attitude conceded far too much authority and influence to the Chinese.[21]

Because they had adopted many aspects of Chinese culture while creating their own powerful state on China's border it was common to describe the Manchus as having become Sinicised, possibly even before, but certainly after the conquest of China. However archival research into documents written in the Manchu language – a language that is completely unrelated to Chinese in structure or script and is much closer to Mongolian – has compelled scholars to develop a far more sophisticated understanding of the relationship between the Manchus and the Chinese. Many members of the Manchu elite which took control of China, including the emperors, did indeed become highly adept at the Chinese literary language and immersed themselves in Chinese culture, but they also proudly maintained their distinct Manchu identity. Manchu remained a working language at court and documents in Manchu were produced well into the nineteenth century: in many cases documents were written only in Manchu with no Chinese equivalents and where versions in both languages have been consulted, the Manchu and Chinese language versions of documents have often been found to be significantly different.

The use of the written Manchu language in the garrison towns through-out China declined to a large extent after 1800, and Manchu families pressed their sons to learn Chinese to ensure their success in the imperial examinations. Nevertheless, spoken Manchu remained and was used to considerable effect as a secret or a security language, notably by Manchu officers during the Taiping rebellion.[22]

The Qing dynasty, whether because or in spite of the Manchu hegemony, is celebrated as a period of great flowering in Chinese culture. The poetry of the Qing, although published in great quantity may not have been a match for the striking and imaginative verses of Li Bai and Du Fu of the Tang dynasty or even the songs of Su Dongpo of the Song dynasty, but the achievements of Qing fiction are indisputable. *The Dream of the Red Chamber* (*Hong lou meng*) by Cao Xueqin is a masterly account, to a large extent auto-biographical, of the decline of a once great upper-class household. Eschewing simple narrative, the author reveals the psychology of the main characters from this highly cultured family, their powerlessness in the face of the authority of the court and their own psychological frailties. It is held to be the greatest of all the traditional novels and has been the source of inspiration for popular fiction, drama and television programmes. Another great novel, *Rulin waishi* by Wu Jingzi, which is known in English as either *The Scholars* or *An Unofficial History of the Literati* was written in Nanjing sometime between 1739 and 1750. It is a satire on Confucian society, its foibles and its decadence and is constructed in a picaresque form with perhaps 200 characters. It mirrored accurately the social conditions of the time, including the increasing irrelevance of the examination system, the sterile scholarship that it encouraged and the growing incompetence and corruption of the official class.

Qing painting likewise continued the old traditions but it had strayed from the simple and direct lines of the acme of Chinese brush work in the Song dynasty. It nevertheless remained, along with poetry, an important part of literati culture. Qing dynasty porcelain may not please Western, Japanese and traditionally minded Chinese connoisseurs as much as the delicate blue-and-white of the Ming or the subtle green celadons of the Song dynasty, but the ornate *famille rose* and *famille verte* designs and the armorial wares designed for export were a new and important phase in the development of Chinese ceramics and tested the technical expertise of the potters at the old imperial kilns of Jingdezhen. Culture in the Qing may have been dynamic and flourishing in the late eighteenth century, at the epoch of the expansion of the empire and imperial confidence. However, by the late nineteenth century, that culture seemed tired, listless and on the wane.

2

CHINA AND THE WEST:
THE ROAD TO THE OPIUM WAR

China's modern history was not completely determined by its relationship with the Western powers. Internal developments and complex interactions with its frontier neighbours and with the great Asian land empire of Russia were more significant until the nineteenth century. Even in the late nineteenth century it could be argued that it was China's contact with Japan, hardly Western except in the common but untenable view that Western and modern are somehow equivalent, that shaped the growth of Chinese nationalism which has been the main motive force of China's modern history. Nevertheless, had it not been for China's encounter with the West in the nineteenth century, the violent nature of that encounter and the commercial, political and cultural relationships that emerged from it, China's history would not have taken the direction that it did.

China has had many periods of political and diplomatic seclusion, but it has never been completely isolated from the outside world. Contact with the West has been continual, although with repeated interruptions as a result of political turmoil or military conflict, since the time of the Han dynasty (206 BC–220 AD) and the Roman Empire. This contact was frequently indirect. Trade and diplomacy followed the overland routes through the deserts and steppes of Central Asia that were later to become renowned as the Silk Route or more familiarly and fancifully as the Silk Road. There was never, of course, one road or one route: the romantic idea of the Silk Road was based on an authentic tradition of trade across the steppes, a system of linked commercial organisations and a series of preferred routes and trading posts that linked east and west. The capital of the Tang dynasty (681–907), which was known then as Chang'an but is today called Xi'an, is conventionally thought of as the eastern terminus of the Silk Route and was renowned for its multi-ethnic community and culture, a consequence of centuries of diplomatic and commercial intercourse with its neighbours to the west.[1]

Commerce also followed the sea lanes from the Gulf (the Persian Gulf or the Gulf of Arabia) to the Indian Ocean, eastwards to the spice islands of the Indonesian archipelago and thence north by way of the port of Malacca on the Malay peninsula to the southern coast of China. 'Indonesia's contribution [to the Indian Ocean trade] consisted chiefly of the supply of fragrant woods and aromatic resins, especially camphor, benzoin and pine resin, and also pepper, nutmeg and mace.'[2] Because spices were by far the best known and the most valuable commodities traded by sea, this trading network has sometimes been called the Spice Route by analogy with the Silk Route.

Arab, Portuguese and Dutch Commerce

The first traders from the Middle East to reach the China coast are usually referred to in Chinese texts as having come from *Dashi*, and this has been interpreted to suggest that they were all Arabs. It was in fact an imprecise description for all travellers and merchants from the Middle East, whom the Chinese authors did not distinguish clearly, and the merchants who ventured into the South China Sea probably included Persians and Jews as well as Arabs. These 'Arab' traders first established commercial bases in the ports of Changzhou and Quanzhou on the coast of Fujian province on the southeastern littoral of China and they later settled in these cities. Gravestones inscribed Islamic carvings in Arabic and Persian, on the stones of the Ashab mosque in Quanzhou which was built around 1009, and inscriptions on stone tomb-covers have survived in Quanzhou and are the clearest indication that Muslims from the Middle East had settled there by the eleventh century.[3] The descendants of these early migrants form part of the diverse Hui ethnic group of Chinese-speaking Muslims in China today.

The Arabs enjoyed a monopoly of trade for many centuries but this commercial supremacy was challenged by merchant venturers from Western Europe during the fifteenth and sixteenth centuries during the first period of European overseas expansion. At this time, Spain was preoccupied with its conquests in South America and, apart from its colonisation of the Philippines and some smaller neighbouring territories between 1565 and 1898, it played little part in trade and politics in East Asia. Portugal was the first leading European power to venture into the Indian Ocean in the quest for commerce, and its capture of Malacca in 1511 ensured that it occupied a commanding position on the East–West trade route, a position that it maintained until it was in turn ousted by the Dutch.[4] The Dutch, who were concerned to exclude their English rivals from the spice trade in addition to taking over from the Portuguese, had attacked Malacca in 1606 and again in 1615, and it finally came under their control in 1641. Malacca lost its position as the key port on the spice route, and the Dutch base of Batavia (the present day Indonesian capital of Jakarta) became the main trade link between Europe and the East.[5]

Although Portuguese and Dutch merchants had established a powerful presence in the East Indies, they traded only indirectly with China, and this business was mainly carried out through contacts with merchants from Chinese communities in the East Indies who acted as intermediaries. China still kept the Europeans at arm's length and there were no resident Portuguese or Dutch communities in China, with the exception of the Portuguese colony of Macao, which had been established in 1557 and retained by Portugal until it was returned to China in 1999, two years after the return of Hong Kong. Dutch attempts to open up direct trade with China began with the dispatch of a ship to Guangzhou (Canton) in 1604, but the Portuguese authorities in Macao objected and the Chinese authorities denied them permission to trade. When a second ship was sent in 1607 and suffered the same treatment, the Dutch abandoned the attempt to trade directly and settled temporarily for dealing with Chinese junk captains at ports in Japan, Java and India.[6] However, as European maritime power expanded, the allure of trade with the Qing Empire was too great, and the great powers once again directed their attention to the Chinese mainland. In the event, it was the British who first managed to breach the psychological and cultural barriers and began to negotiate, albeit at first unsuccessfully, for the right to trade directly with China.

East India Company

The China trade, which was such a magnet for Western merchants, is inextricably linked with the name of the East India Company. There were in fact several East India Companies, notably the Dutch *Verenigde Oost Indische Compagnie*, which was awarded its royal charter in 1602, and the French *Compagnie de Chine*, founded in 1604. However it was Britain's East India Company, the Honourable East India Company, or 'John Company' as it was known familiarly, that played the most important role in the opening of China to Western trade, and it is the British company that is usually referred to when the name East India Company is mentioned.[7]

In the late sixteenth century British merchants had attempted to break into the East India trade, which at the time was monopolised by the Portuguese, and they found themselves in direct competition with the Dutch. Like the Dutch, they began to establish trading posts or manufactories that became known as 'factories', after the factors (managers) who were stationed there and the 'manufactures' that they dealt in. Competition between the two maritime powers led to friction, and the conflict culminated in a failure of attempts to secure Anglo-Dutch cooperation and a 'massacre of the English by the Dutch' at Amboina in the Moluccas in 1623.[8] It was in this febrile atmosphere of intense competition for trade and political influence that the East India Company was born:

> On the last day of the century, 31 December 1600, letters patent were issued by [Queen] Elizabeth incorporating a company under the title of 'The Governor and Merchants of London Trading into the East Indies' and granting to it a monopoly for 15 years of trading between the Cape of Good Hope and the Straits of Magellan. The monopoly was made perpetual by a charter of James I issued in 1609, was strengthened by another of the Lord Protector Cromwell in 1657, again by another of Charles II in 1661.[9]

The first venture of this company involved the creation of a fleet of five ships, which sailed to the spice islands of Indonesia in 1601. Four ships made up the second expedition in 1604, three vessels ventured east in 1607 and that year onwards trading expeditions were dispatched on an annual basis.[10] As the Dutch had failed to gain access to trade with Guangzhou (Canton) and the Portuguese continued to block all other foreign commerce from their stronghold at Macao (Aomen), the East India Company decided to follow the Dutch example and to trade indirectly with China by way of ports in the Malay Archipelago or on the coast of India. British attempts to expand trade were constantly frustrated by their relationship with the Dutch, a relationship which at best resembled an armed truce. In 1635 the East India Company secured an agreement with the Viceroy of Portugal in Goa for a truce and free trade with China, but the Portuguese governor of Macao conspired with the Chinese authorities to prevent any British ships from reaching China.[11]

These conflicts between the European merchants established a pattern that was to persist for 200 years. Direct and unrestricted trade with China was the great prize that all European traders sought: it remained so near and yet so far away. European traders were determined to prevent their foreign counterparts from succeeding if they could not; they were not prepared to cooperate with their rivals and all remained frustrated. The East India Company dominated trade with China until the late eighteenth century when the British government decided to restrict its powers. In 1813 a decision was made to remove the monopoly, which expired in 1834, after which the Company functioned as an arm of the government. In 1857, the year of the Indian Rebellion (or Mutiny as it was known at the time) the

Colonial Office assumed control over the East India Company, which ceased operations in 1873.

Breakthrough in Guangzhou

The European merchants achieved a major breakthrough when they established the right to trade in the port city of Guangzhou (Canton), which is on the eastern bank of the Pearl River Delta and much farther inland than the Portuguese trading station of Macao. The first British ships to reach Guangzhou were in a flotilla of four under the command of Captain John Weddell, who sailed them on behalf of the Courbeen Association, a consortium that was acting independently of the East India Company but under the instructions of King Charles I. The flotilla called in at the Portuguese territory of Goa on the west coast of India on 7 October 1636 and sailed into the Pearl River Delta in January 1637. It passed through the Bogue, the mouth of the Pearl River, on 23 July as soon as the Portuguese fleet that was on its way to trade with Japan had departed. The Chinese authorities resisted this intrusion, but Weddell's ships opened fire and captured a fort near Guangzhou. The Portuguese authorities who were based in the city negotiated with Weddell while conniving with the Chinese in an attempt to exclude his ships. The Weddell mission was ultimately a failure, but his attempt on Guangzhou foreshadowed later and more successful enterprises.[12]

The East India Company sent its ship the *Carolina* from London in October 1682 with the specific mission of setting up a factory in Guangzhou. The agents of the company on board the ship, who were known as supercargoes, were promised that they would be well paid for their venture, but they failed in their attempt to establish themselves in Guangzhou and were obliged to make do with a base at Amoy (Xiamen).[13] The supercargo was the senior commercial officer on a merchant ship and the term is probably a version of the Spanish *sobrecargo*, that is, the officer placed over, or supervising, the cargo. In a subsequent mission the *Macclesfield*, commanded by Captain John Hurle and with Mr Robert Douglas as Chief Supercargo, dropped anchor off Macao on 2 March 1699, and Douglas entered into negotiations with the Hoppo, the representative of the imperial Board of Revenue (Hubu), who was the superintendent of trade in Guangzhou. The *Macclesfield* agreed to sell its cargo but there was a misunderstanding over the terms and the ship was delayed. It had, however, been able to sail into the port of Guangzhou, and the Supercargo rented a house in the city for the period of the monsoon during which the *Macclesfield* was obliged to remain in port. It eventually set sail for Portsmouth, arriving there on 1 July 1701 'with a rich and full cargo'.[14]

There was as yet no 'factory' or permanent settlement in Guangzhou, but 'the English had now, at the opening of the eighteenth century, thrust their feet over the threshold of the China trade, but had not yet obtained a seat at the table'.[15] Trade at Guangzhou, and the system devised by the Chinese government to regulate it, evolved gradually during the first half of the eighteenth century: it is impossible to pinpoint one event that established Guangzhou as the port in which all Europeans desired to trade. France had 'established a resident factor on Canton [Guangzhou] as early as 1698', but this post was abandoned in 1724. It was not until 1770 that the Court of Directors of the East India Company took the decision that its Supercargoes should be based permanently in China, but in practice Guangzhou was the favoured destination long before that decision was taken.[16]

Further trade missions were dispatched by the East India Company to Guangzhou, but even at this early stage in the endeavour to penetrate the Chinese market it had become clear that there were few, if any, products that the British could persuade the Chinese to buy from them. The result of this was that Britain was exporting copious quantities of silver to China in return for the tea and spices that were being shipped home. This imbalance of payments was a serious concern for both the East India Company and the British government and, in the longer term, can be seen as the major underlying cause of the trade friction that led to the Opium War.[17]

Cohong and Canton System

By 1716, Guangzhou had become the main destination of the East India Company's trading vessels and the Supercargo of the *Susanna*, one of three ships sent that year, came to a formal agreement with the Hoppo, an agreement that provided for regular access to his office, the right to employ interpreters and other staff and the right to provision his ship and leave Guangzhou without hindrance.[18] This agreement was the first made by the Company with the Hoppo and to some extent regularised British trade with Guangzhou. In 1720 the Chinese merchants of Guangzhou constituted themselves as a guild for the purposes of regulating their trade with the foreigners.[19] This guild was the origin of the Canton System, which was to exercise tight control over China's foreign trade for the following century. The guild became known as the Cohong from the Cantonese pronunciation of the standard Chinese (Mandarin) word that would be written in modern Pinyin romanisation as *gonghang*. *Gonghang* can be translated on one level to mean 'public (or joint) company', but it also has the connotation of fair dealing.

The rationale behind the Cohong system was that it would manage direct contact between foreign traders and the Chinese market. The firms that constituted the Cohong were conventionally known as the Thirteen Hongs (Firms), although the number varied from year to year with a minimum of 4 and a maximum of 26. The Cohong was obliged to disband in 1771 because it had fallen into arrears with payments of silver tax that were due to the Imperial Court and a number of its constituent firms had become bankrupt, but it was allowed to resume its operations in 1782 because foreign merchants were making direct loans to Chinese traders and the state wished to exercise some control over these transactions. Although the main function of the Cohong was to supervise trade and (in theory at least) to guarantee the payment of taxes due to the Court, it also had a quasi-diplomatic role and managed foreign relations on the south China coast on behalf of the Qing Imperial Court. A series of regulations for the control of foreign trade were issued, first in 1760 and subsequently in 1809, 1831 and 1835, and these rules included strict prohibitions on the activities of foreign merchants: they were not permitted to overwinter in Guangzhou, sell firearms, indulge in private trade, enter the inner harbour or live outside officially designated residential areas. The restriction of foreign trade to Guangzhou in this period was the basis for the long-term and highly successful development of the local and regional economy which has persisted into the twenty-first century, but it also severely limited commercial, cultural and technical exchanges between the West and other regions of China.[20]

How should China's attempt to restrict foreign trade and intercourse with foreigners in the eighteenth and nineteenth centuries be assessed? The historian of the Qing dynasty, Xiao Yishan, writing in the 1930s, acknowledged that before the nineteenth century China was at fault in that it did not accept that any other country was of the same status as the Qing Empire:

> Although Westerners have been coming to China for two hundred years, have traded, spread Christianity and imported scientific knowledge, we have simply treated them as if they were Koreans, Vietnamese or Ryukyu islanders, completely indifferent to whether they came or not, treating them as if they were from vassal states presenting tribute gifts to the celestial dynasty.[21]

Li Jiannong in his history, which was published in 1947 only two years before the Communist Party's establishment of the People's Republic of China and covered the previous century, pointed out that before the outbreak of conflict between the Chinese and British in 1839, trade between

China and the West had been inequitable in three areas: taxation, limitations on the ports that could be used and the restrictive practices of the Cohong. Regulations for tax collection were, he argued, unreliable and in any case China had never been as rigorous in collecting communal taxes in cash as it had in its land tax system. Because of this tax officials commonly exacted exorbitant extra payments, especially from foreign merchants who were new to China and did not properly understand the language or local customs. Restrictions on commercial ports were unfair: since foreign merchants were concentrated in the Guangzhou area, local officials in Guangdong had an excellent opportunity to enrich themselves. When foreigners tried to trade in the ports of Xiamen and Ningbo to avoid the exorbitant demands of the Guangdong provincial officials, they found that they were treated in the same way there if not even more harshly. The Qing government was determined to restrict traders to these southern ports because it did not want foreigners intruding further into China. The Cohong monopoly replaced the system of 'official merchants' which had been established during the reign of the Kangxi emperor (1662–1722) to resolve disputes about trade. Although it had not been established on the orders of the government, it did have informal but powerful support from the imperial bureaucracy, especially local officials, some of whom used it secretly to line their own pockets.[22] The approach of both of these Chinese historians demonstrates much more sympathy and understanding for the problems faced by Western merchants than is normally found in Chinese accounts of the Guangzhou trade, particularly in books and articles that were written after 1949.[23]

Macartney's Embassy and Its Successors

During the eighteenth century the strength of British naval power ensured that it became the pre-eminent maritime trading nation in the world. Britain eclipsed Portugal, Spain and the Netherlands in the China trade; in large measure this was because of her control of India and naval supremacy in the Indian Ocean. Consequently it was Britain, rather than any other western nation, that brought to a head the issue of foreign access to the China market, and the expedition led by Lord Macartney to China in 1792–3 is generally accepted as having been the turning point in China's diplomatic and commercial relations with the West. It was by no means the first such diplomatic mission. Dutch embassies had been sent to the Imperial Court at Beijing from their base in Batavia (Jakarta) in 1656 and 1667; Russian embassies had been dispatched in 1692 and 1720; the Vatican had sent an ambassador in 1720, and a Portuguese mission had reached the Chinese imperial capital in 1753.[24]

All of these diplomatic initiatives had essentially the same aims: to persuade the government of China to allow Europeans to trade on terms that the Europeans considered to be reasonable and to establish relations at an ambassadorial level, on an equal footing, in place of the antiquated Tribute System in which China had seen itself as the supreme power, receiving offerings from minor powers in acknowledgement of their inferior status. Where the Macartney Embassy differed from all those that had preceded it was that it pressed the issue all the way to the Imperial Court: the question of whether Macartney performed the ritual *koutou* (kowtow) of submission to the emperor became not only a practical issue of diplomatic relations but a symbol of the changing relationship between China and the West.

Lord Macartney was a former member of the British Parliament who had also been governor of Grenada and of the Indian state of Madras. He set sail for China from the Spithead, a sheltered naval harbour in Hampshire on the south coast of England, on Friday 26 September 1792 aboard the 64-gun man-of-war *Lion* which was accompanied by the *Hindoostan*, which was an Indiaman, and the brig *Jackall*. His route took him to Tenerife in the Canaries, the Cape Verde Islands, Rio de Janeiro and Tristan da Cunha after which the ships rounded Cape Horn and set course westwards across the Pacific Ocean for the Dutch port of Batavia 'at which place we were most hospitably entertained and most magnificently feasted by the Dutch government.' He sailed on through the islands of the Malay Archipelago to the coast of mainland Southeast Asia which was then known as Cochin China.[25] The three original ships were joined by the brig *Clarence* and the flotilla left Tourane Bay in Cochin China on Saturday 15 June and first sighted the coast of China on Wednesday 19 June, anchoring some seven leagues southeast of Macau on the following day.[26] If the Dutch authorities in Batavia had treated them royally, the Dutch and Portuguese traders in Macau were less enthusiastic about the British competition, but Spanish representatives provided them with maps and charts of the Pearl River Delta in which lay the city of Guangzhou (Canton), their first objective in China.[27] Macartney's squadron sailed northwards along the Chinese coast in the direction of Tianjin, from where he intended to proceed to Beijing and the Imperial Court to set out his diplomatic and commercial demands. The mission encountered constant and diverse bureaucratic obstructions and Macartney had great difficulty obtaining pilots to navigate his flotilla through the Gulf of Beizhili (Bohai) and into Tianjin. However by 31 July there had been contact with various local officials and Macartney's ships were presented with provisions in such quantity that they were forced to turn some down, and it was felt that they were now being received with considerable hospitality and attention.[28]

On Monday 5 August, Macartney and his entourage travelled to the coast in the smaller ships of their fleet, leaving the *Lion* at the Dagu batteries, the forts that guarded the entrance to the Bai River and the approach to Tianjin. They arrived at the mouth of the Bai River, which is now known as the Hai River, and continued their journey on board a Chinese sailing ship, specially provided for the purpose. The Viceroy (*Zongdu*) of the administrative region of Beizhili, Liang Kangtang, had been sent by the court to receive the embassy at Tongxian and on 6 August he informed Macartney that the embassy was to be permitted to travel to Rehe (Jehol) for an audience with the emperor. Macartney observed that at this juncture, he and his mission were treated with great cordiality and courtesy:

> It is impossible to describe the ease, politeness and dignity of the Viceroy during the whole conference, the attention with which he listened to our requests, and the unaffected manner in which he expressed his compliance with them.[29]

At noon on Friday 9 August, the flotilla set sail to the sound of drums and gongs from the shore and moved up the river at a stately pace. On the morning of Sunday 11 August, the ships finally arrived at Tianjin where they were met by the Viceroy who had taken the shorter land route so that he would be there when they arrived. The Salt Commissioner of Tianjin, the Manchu official Zhengrui, also attended as a personal representative of the emperor. It was agreed that the embassy would continue up the Bai River as far as Tongxian, which lies to the east of Beijing, and then proceed overland to Beijing and the Imperial Court. Tongxian was reached at six thirty on the evening of Tuesday 16 August and Macartney and his crew prepared to spend several days unloading the presents that they had brought for the emperor and their own personal luggage, and putting everything in order for the twenty-mile journey overland to the Yuanmingyuan, the Summer Palace, in the north of the capital. They were quartered in a temple in the suburbs of Tongxian and set out from there early in the morning of Wednesday 21 August. The embassy must have been an impressive sight: 85 wagons, 39 handcarts, 209 horses and 2,495 men made up Macartney's party, and they were accompanied by even greater numbers of men and horses and carts belonging to the Chinese officials. By three o'clock in the afternoon the procession had passed through Beijing and arrived at the Yuanmingyuan, which, Macartney noted, was in a state of considerable disrepair.[30]

It was during the journey to Tongxian and while they were lodged in the temple there that the staff of the embassy became aware of some of the difficulties that lay ahead of them in their dealings with Chinese officialdom: the traditional rivalry between officials of Chinese and Manchu origin was becoming apparent; the quality of presents for the emperor and the manner of their dispatch was clearly of great concern to the officials; above all it was made absolutely clear to Macartney that he and his entourage would be expected to conform to the rituals and customs of tribute missions to China including the *koutou* or nine prostrations of the head to the ground from a kneeling position.[31] Macartney's view was that his mission was as an ambassador from one monarch, King George III, to another, on at least equal terms. The system of tribute missions, by which relations between China and her less powerful neighbours had been regulated for centuries, was not understood or at least not accepted by Western governments. The aims of the embassy were presented to the Chinese in what were considered to be the most diplomatic of terms. The British Secretary of State for Foreign Affairs, Henry Dundas, had agreed with Macartney that Britain's approach should be

> not to press for the redress of past grievances, but to convey the King's congratulations to the Emperor on the occasion of entering the eightieth year of his age, and incidentally to discuss arrangements for conducting trade in future to the mutual advantage of the two countries.

This presumption of equality was not appreciated by the Chinese.[32]

Macartney and his entourage took their leave of Beijing on Monday 2 September and travelled to the city of Rehe (Jehol), which is now known as Chengde, arriving on Sunday 8 September. Two audiences took place with the Emperor Qianlong at his palace in the old Manchu summer retreat, the first on 14 September and the second on 17 September, the emperor's birthday. Macartney continued to insist that he should not to be obliged to execute the *koutou*, but he did agree to perform in front of Qianlong the same ceremony of obeisance that he would have performed before his own monarch, King George III. Court officials maintained that he had in fact performed the *koutou*. In all probability he did not, but the eventual failure of the mission must be attributed partly at least to the wrangling over ritual, precedence and rank that took place at this juncture.[33]

Macartney attempted to fulfil the aims of his embassy by setting out the demands of the British government that had prompted his mission in a letter to the Grand Council, the main policy-making body of the Qing government, which exercised many of the functions of a Cabinet. The demands that he presented included the right of British merchants to trade in the ports of Zhushan, Ningbo and Tianjin; that the British be allowed to avail themselves of the right to a warehouse in Beijing, a privilege which the Russians already exercised; the establishment of a warehouse and the lease of a 'concession' for accommodation in an unwalled island settlement near Zhushan and the same rights in the vicinity of Guangzhou. Britain also insisted on the abolition, or at least the reduction, of transit taxes between Macao and Guangzhou and demanded that British merchants should receive permission from the emperor for the right of residence without taxation. The British also stipulated that they should be permitted to propagate their religion freely in China.[34] In light of the completely different perceptions that the Chinese and British had of the relationship between the two nations, it is hardly surprising that none of these requests was accepted by Qianlong's officials. Macartney and his delegation, having failed in their mission, made their way back southwards to Guangzhou, finally setting sail from Macao for the return voyage to England on Wednesday 15 January 1794.

The response of the Qianlong emperor to this mission, his letter to King George III, is by far the best known document from the Qing dynasty in the West as it has been reproduced frequently in English, usually in the translation by Sir Edmund Backhouse. It is a long document which rebuts in detail the demands made by Macartney and explains why it would have been impossible from the Chinese point of view for foreigners to be stationed in China. Two telling sections read as follows:

> You, O King, live beyond the confines of many seas, nevertheless, impelled by your humble desire to partake of the benefits of our civilisation, you have dispatched a mission respectfully bearing your memorial. Your envoy has crossed the seas and paid his respects to my Court on the anniversary of my birthday. To show your devotion you have also sent offerings of your country's produce....
>
> Swaying the wide world, I have but one aim in view, namely to maintain a perfect governance and to fulfil the duties of the State: strange and costly objects do not interest me. If I have commanded that the tribute offerings sent by you, O King, are to be accepted, this was solely in consideration for the spirit which prompted you to dispatch them from afar. Our country's majestic virtue has penetrated unto every country under Heaven, and Kings of all nations have offered their costly tribute by land and sea. As your Ambassador can see for himself, we possess all things. I set no value on objects strange or ingenious and have no use for your country's manufactures.[35]

How significant was Lord Macartney's venture in the development of China's relations with the West? In Europe it has been seen as a turning point and the inability of the British and Chinese to agree on the appropriate ritual and therefore the relative status of the two nations is considered to be a mark of the depth of misunderstanding between the two civilisations. In 1993, the two hundredth anniversary of the commencement of Macartney's mission, several books and television programmes presented this view.[36]

The overall attitudes of the Qing court to the British mission can be seen clearly in the gloriously dismissive missive of the Qianlong emperor, but it is instructive to examine how this view was arrived at. Initially, the Qing court saw Macartney's visit as just another tribute mission but one that should be accorded special consideration as the first such mission from Britain and also because it was congratulating the emperor on his birthday. However Qianlong was angered by what he perceived as the 'arrogant' way in which the scientific instruments and other presents were explained to him, the implication being that Macartney's staff were suggesting that Britain might be the possessor of a superior civilisation. After the contretemps over the embassy's gifts, Qianlong became even more insistent on the correct ceremonial to indicate to Macartney, and to his own officials, the inferior status of the mission. The reality was that there was a vast scientific and technological gap between China and Britain at the time, but the Imperial Court either refused to recognise this or simply failed to understand what they were being offered. Many Chinese accounts play down the significance of the Macartney Embassy, and it is listed as just one of the many unsuccessful attempts by Great Britain, the superpower of the late eighteenth and early nineteenth centuries, to gain an economic and diplomatic foothold in China. Two subsequent diplomatic missions sent by Great Britain, and led by William Pitt Amherst in 1816–17 and Lord Napier in 1834, the year in which the monopoly of the East India Company was due to come to an end, also ended in failure because of similar misunderstandings and conflict with Chinese officials.[37]

Opium

After the failure of the three diplomatic missions to China, Britain and the Qing Empire found themselves drawn inexorably towards military conflict: Britain desperately strove to extend its trading rights in East Asia, and China resisted obdurately. The two wars that ensued are known as the Opium War (1839–42) and the Arrow War (1856–8) or, alternatively, as the First and Second Opium Wars.

Although conflict over opium clearly played a major part in these wars, they were precipitated primarily by Britain's pressure for the expansion of its commercial empire and China's resistance. Opium was not the true cause, but it was the emotive and opportune issue over which the wars were fought. Reading some of the oversimplified accounts of the opium trade that have been produced in twentieth-century China, one might be forgiven for believing that in the nineteenth century the perfidious British suddenly introduced a hard drug to the native Chinese who had until that time taken nothing stronger than a cup of green tea. The reality was more complicated: opium had probably been introduced to China as early as the eighth century by maritime traders on the well-established shipping route from the Gulf of Arabia (Persian Gulf) to the coast of Fujian and was cultivated in southern China. The Portuguese were probably the first Europeans to import the poppy, but the East India Company certainly followed them enthusiastically although it fastidiously kept any dealings in opium separate from its mainstream trade in tea, silks and porcelain.

Opium, the narcotic drug derived from the unripe seed capsules of the opium poppy, *Papaver somniferum*, was first mentioned in a Chinese publication during the Tang dynasty (618–907), in a herbal entitled the *Bencao shiyi* which was written in the first half of the eighth century by Chen Cangqi. The opium poppy is also mentioned in the writing of the Tang poet Tao Yong and his more famous Song dynasty successor Su Dongpo. Herbals and pharmacopœias published in the Jin, Yuan and Ming dynasties, all of which pre-dated Western trade with China, commonly included descriptions of opium and advice on its medicinal uses. The Chinese word for opium, *yapian*, may derive from the Arabic or the Persian *afyun*.

As a medicine, opium was taken raw for its analgesic properties and its capacity for reducing stress and inducing relaxation. In the early seventeenth century, the practice of combining opium with tobacco and smoking the mixture was reported among the islanders of Taiwan and this habit spread, first across the Taiwan straits to the mainland's coastal provinces of Fujian and Guangdong and subsequently inland and throughout China. By the late eighteenth or early nineteenth century, the custom of smoking opium was, if not universal, without doubt extremely common and had become a recognised leisure activity of the wealthier and more educated sections of society. Opium, in the form of a tincture that is dissolved in alcohol, was familiar in Europe by this time as laudanum. Leisure use could lead to addiction and although the Chinese state had collected customs duty on the sale of opium in the sixteenth and seventeenth centuries, in 1729 the Qing government issued an edict prohibiting the sale and consumption of opium within China because of the deleterious effect it was having on the wider population and because the government was aware that trade in the drug was on the increase. In 1796 the import and cultivation of the drug was also made illegal.[38]

The first Westerners to import opium to China may have been Portuguese traders, but the East India Company began a trial trade in the drug in 1773 and when it became clear that this was likely to become a successful venture, the British established their own opium depot at Lark's Bay to the south of the Portuguese base in Macau in 1780. When the trade in opium was declared illegal by the Qing government in 1796 the East India Company was no longer officially trafficking in the drug, but it did nothing to prevent the private enterprise of its staff. The quantity of opium imported during the Ming dynasty and the early part of the Qing was relatively small, and it was the dramatic increase that followed the East India Company's venture into the trade that alarmed the Chinese authorities, branded the British as the major drug smugglers of eastern Asia and precipitated a trade war.[39] Hsin-pao Chang divides the opium trade before the outbreak of hostilities into three distinct periods. In the first period, 1800–1820, imports of opium by the British amounted to an average of 4,500 chests annually.[40] In part this reflected a slump in trade in the early 1800s that resulted from disputes between the British and the Portuguese and also from piracy. During this period the Chinese government took an increasingly firm line on the import of opium. Local officials received support from the emperor for their proposal to search Portuguese ships for the drug and in 1821 the governor-general of Guangdong and Guangxi, Ruan Yuan who was to acquire a reputation for both strictness and an ability to compromise with foreigners, ordered the arrest of 16 opium dealers in Macau. Foreign opium traders were forced out of the Pearl River and were obliged to establish a base on an island at the mouth of the river where they remained until the outbreak of the Opium War in 1839.[41]

The second period, 1821–30 saw the trade increase to 18,760 chests annually, 'the most remarkable event in the trade during this phase [being] the upheaval caused by the introduction of Malwa', a cheaper variety of opium produced in the princely state of Malwa, in what is now the state of Madhya Pradesh in western India, which was outside the jurisdiction of the East India Company. Before 1815, Malwa had been imported only in negligible amounts and was difficult to sell. An increase in the price that regular Bengal opium attracted pushed traders into dealing in Malwa, which rapidly came to dominate the market. To compete with this the East India Company expanded its production of Bengal opium and also attempted to buy up as much of the Malwa as it could.[42]

The third period, 1830–9, was one of an even more extraordinary increase in trade; this was partly because of the expansion of production in India that has already been alluded to, and partly because of the availability of new and faster ships – clippers – to transport the drug. However it was the impending end of the East India Company's monopoly on China trade (due to expire in 1834) that sparked off a growth spurt in opium trading.

Commerce in the drug spread along the whole of the south China coast and by 1840 total imports were of the order of 40,000 chests a year.[43]

From the British point of view, the economic rationale of increasing the sale of opium to China was clear enough. The China trade had been largely one-way traffic; the Europeans bought high-value goods such as tea, silks and porcelain from the Chinese and paid for them in cash. Cash in the early nineteenth century normally meant the Mexican silver dollars that were the main currency in the Pacific at the time, following the Mexican silver mining boom in the second half of the eighteenth century that had flooded the market with silver.[44] Western traders had been constantly on the look-out for commodities to sell to China to reverse the flow of silver from their coffers, and the growing demand for opium in China provided them with a perfect opportunity which they seized ruthlessly. This created the same problem in reverse for China as her balance of trade switched from export to import. As the clandestine imports increased, they were paid for in cash and as imports actually came to exceed exports, the outflow of silver created an inflation in the price of silver in relation to the copper coinage that was in everyday circulation.[45] It was this economic crisis rather than righteous indignation at the depredations visited by opium on the health of the Chinese population that created the vigorous official pressure to suppress the sale and use of opium.

Chinese Debate on Opium

The response of the Chinese government was neither unambiguous nor consistent. In 1835–6, immediately after the end of the East India Company's monopoly on trade with China, and in a year when more than 30,000 chests of opium were being imported, there were two distinct views on how the crisis should be handled.

One approach was exemplified in a memorial sent by Xu Naiji to the Daoguang emperor on 10 June 1836. Xu Naiji was a censor in the office of the Court of Sacrificial Worship and had previously served as a provincial judge in the province of Guangdong, where he had learned a great deal about the hidden workings of the opium trade. In his memorial he took great pains to demonstrate his understanding of the opium question by pointing out not only its medicinal uses in raising the spirits, preventing diarrhoea and warding off malaria, and citing Li Shizhen's great pharmacopœia of the Ming dynasty, the *Bencao gangmu*, but also indicating to the emperor the harmful effect of prolonged use. He described in detail the three main types of opium on the market at that time, all from British controlled Bengal or from Madras in western India. He pointed out that before the reign of the Emperor Qianlong (1736–95) opium had been taxed as a medicine but that it had later been banned and the penalties for taking it, which had been limited to the cangue (a large wooden collar or yoke that was placed around the neck of a convicted person) and the cane in the first year of the Jiaqing reign (1796) were made increasingly severe. In spite of the penalties the number of opium eaters continued to increase throughout the empire. Xu proposed reverting to the system of taxing opium as the lesser of two evils while prohibiting civil and military officials from using it or trading in it.[46]

On the other hand, many officials were in favour of a complete prohibition on the import and sale of opium and petitioned the emperor to reject the views of the legalisation lobby. One of the best known was Huang Juezi, the director of the Court of State Ceremonial, who sent a memorial to the emperor on 2 June 1838 but he was following Zhuzun, the Manchu President of the Board of Rites, who memorialised in favour of abolition in October 1836 and the censor Xu Qiu who strongly urged that foreign opium traders be arrested. These last two memorials were translated for the benefit of the British Foreign Office who would therefore have been aware of the debate that was taking place in the higher echelons of the Chinese government.[47] The Daoguang emperor was won over by the prohibitionist argument, perhaps not surprisingly in view of the powerful combination of economic rationality and xenophobia and its appeal to traditional Confucian morality and the physical and spiritual health of the Chinese nation. Two of Daoguang's sons had died at a young age, one of them possibly from the effects of opium addiction, and it is likely that this coloured his attitude to national policy.[48]

Commissioner Lin

Lin Zexu (1785–1850), Commissioner Lin, who was to become the hero of the opium conflict in the eyes of many Chinese for several generations, was born near Fuzhou in Fujian province and gained the *jinshi* degree (the third and highest level in the imperial examination system and sometimes equated to a Western doctorate) in 1811. He was admitted to the elite Hanlin Academy which provided the intellectual support for the compilation of court documents, served in various official capacities throughout China including the post of judicial commissioner in Jiangsu and also had responsibility for water conservancy and flood prevention. He was then acting governor general of Jiangsu and Jiangxi (Liang Jiang or the Two Jiangs) in 1835 and became governor general of Hubei and Hunan (Liang Hu, the two Hus) in 1837.

Huang Juezi's memorial proposing the complete prohibition on the sale and use of opium had been circulated to all senior provincial officials in the summer of 1838 and Lin Zexu memorialised the throne on the subject on 10 July. He supported Huang's proposal but, more importantly proposed a series of practical measures to implement the prohibition, including the destruction of the equipment used to make opium, a time limit for opium users to give up the habit and punishment for opium sellers. Furthermore he actually implemented these measures in the region under his jurisdiction, the provinces of Hubei and Hunan, insisting on addicts being given pre-scriptions to help cure them and confiscating 12,000 Chinese ounces of opium.[49]

The governor general of Liang Guang (the two Guangs, Guangxi and Guangdong) from February 1835 was Deng Tingzhen (1776–1846), who was the front line government official in the conflict with the British over the import of opium. Deng was sympathetic to Xu Naiji's conciliatory approach to the opium issue, seeing it as a politic, if controversial, solution to an intractable problem. When the Daoguang emperor made it clear that prohibition was to be the official policy, Deng lent his support to the growing anti-opium campaign in Guangdong, although there were com-plaints from the Imperial Court that he was too lenient with opium dealers and users. William Jardine, the pioneer trader reported in December 1838 that Governor General Deng 'has been seizing, trying, strangling the poor devils without mercy – the prisons are full, and three or four are carried off daily by confinement and bad treatment'.[50]

William Jardine (1784–1843), originally from the lowlands of Scotland, had qualified as a surgeon in Edinburgh and decided to join the East India Company to seek his fortune. He took advantage of the company's policy of allowing employees to engage in private dealing and eventually became one of the most able and successful foreign businessmen in the south of China. He worked in various companies in Guangzhou and in 1820 met James Matheson with whom he was to form a lasting business partnership. In 1832 the two men founded the limited company Jardine Matheson, which in time was to become one of the greatest of the overseas firms in south China: the economic development of Hong Kong was inextricably linked to the success of Jardine Matheson. Jardine had enthusiastically sup-ported the idea of expanding the opium trade, and Matheson had gone to London to petition parliament on the matter. Once the East India Com-pany's monopoly expired in 1834, Jardine was the first trader to send a private cargo of tea to England, but it was the opium trade that helped them to prosper.[51]

The editor of the *Chinese Repository*, a scholarly missionary journal, which had been established to publish knowledgeable articles by members of the Protestant missionary community, published a graphic account of the execution in April 1838 of an opium dealer from Macao. He had been employed 'as an opium broker, and also in seething and selling the prepared opium'. He had grown wealthy through his dealings and often lent money to local people but was denounced to the yamen runners by someone to whom he would not lend enough. He was found guilty and sentenced to immediate strangulation:

> He was dragged to the place of execution and placed standing upon a piece of brick, touching the cross with his back. The executioners commenced by lashing a rope round his legs, under the arms, then through the hole in the upper part of the cross, after which it was passed through the loops of the cord and twisted round several times for the purpose of tightening the loop to effect strangulation. No apparent signal, other than the removal of the piece of brick, from under the feet, was given for the fatal turning of the stick.[52]

In all probability, the unfortunate Guo Siping, who was the victim of this judicial strangulation, was not a particularly corrupt dealer. He had simply been reported to the local justices who felt the need to carry out an exemplary punishment in the prevailing political climate.

Even before the arrival of Lin Zexu in Guangdong, the tide of opinion had turned, and opium dealers and users were already the target of a severe campaign by local officials. However the campaign against opium, and in particular against foreign opium traders, has always been associated with Lin as a national hero resisting this aspect of what later became known as China's national humiliation [*guochi*]. Lin Zexu was summoned to the court of the Daoguang emperor in late October 1838. On the last day of the same year, he was appointed Imperial Commissioner [*qinchai dachen*] with extraordinary authority to attend to the opium problem in Guangdong. He was given overall command of all the naval forces in the province and the governor general of the two Guangs and the governor and Guangdong were ordered to give him their full support and cooperation. Commissioner Lin left the imperial capital on 8 January 1839 in a sedan chair with 12 bearers, an indication of his great rank and authority. After passing through the provinces of Hebei, Shandong and Anhui, his party travelled on the Gan River through Jiangxi as far as the mountainous border and then overland by the Meiling Pass that had been used by generations of traders bound for Guangdong. The complete journey of 1,200 miles took Lin two months, and he and his entourage arrived in the provincial capital, Guang-zhou (Canton), on 10 March to an official reception by Governor General Deng Tingzhen and the provincial Governor Yiliang (1791–1867), a Manchu of the Plain Red Banner, on the banks of the Pearl River. Lin established himself and his staff in the buildings of the Yuehua Academy and began to meet local officials and merchants.[53] The intervention of the new imperial commissioner was to prove decisive for two main reasons: first, there had been substantial connivance by local officials in the opium trade and many had profited from it; second, the foreign traders, particularly the British, simply did not believe that the Chinese government had the courage or the capability to stem the import of opium.[54]

Suppressing Opium in Guangzhou

Lin Zexu made his position clear on 18 March, a week after his arrival in Guangzhou, when he summoned the local Cohong merchants to a meeting and publicly informed them of two decrees, one aimed at Chinese traders and the other informing foreign merchants of the 'illegality and immorality of the sale of opium' and requiring them to surrender any opium on their ships within the territory of China and to sign undertakings that they would not smuggle opium into the country in the future on pain of execution.[55] The style of the decree was formal and polite, but the message was uncompromising. Lin emphasised the authority that he had been given by the emperor and his own home background in coastal Fujian, which he said gave him an insight into trade and the ways of foreigners. Not only did he threaten recalcitrant foreigners with the full force of Chinese law, but he also warned them of the indignation of the common people and indicated that he was perfectly prepared to call on the population en masse to assist him in bringing the opium trade to an end. Lin Zexu's stern warning was followed by swift and resolute action. Foreign merchants were required to surrender all opium on their ships within three days of the edict. The traders prevaricated, some claiming that they were unable to hand over the opium as it belonged not to them but to their suppliers in Bengal and Bombay. Lin had threatened to behead some of the *hong* merchants who ran the Chinese side of the trade if his orders were not complied with, but the Western merchants thought that this was an empty threat. On 22 March 1839 Commissioner Lin ordered the arrest of Lancelot Dent, a British trader who had been one of the prime movers in resisting his demands. Dent refused to answer this summons unless his safety was guaranteed and the foreign community supported him. The senior British official, Captain Charles Elliot, who had been appointed Chief Superintendent of Trade by the British Foreign Secretary, Lord Palmerston, in June 1836 after a successful naval career and appointments in the Colonial and Foreign Office, was not in Guangzhou during these events. He had left Macao on the day that Lin Zexu had arrived in Guangzhou, apparently in the belief that British interests were not under threat. He returned to the British factories on 23 March, personally escorted Lancelot Dent from his factory to try to prevent his arrest and reasserted his position that China had no jurisdiction over British subjects.

Lin's response was to issue an order demanding the immediate cessation of trade and the withdrawal of all Chinese cooks, servants, coolies and compradors from the factories. This left the foreigners isolated in their residences and effectively under siege as Chinese guards were posted to prevent them from leaving, although some supplies were allowed to be delivered the detained foreign community.[56] W.C. Hunter, an American businessman, and author of *The 'Fan Kwae' at Canton* and *Bits of Old China,* made light of the hardship suffered by the foreigners during their confinement and wrote instead of the humorous opportunities created by Westerners attempting unsuccessfully to carry out the menial tasks that Chinese servants had previously performed. Cooking rice, toasting bread and boiling eggs competently was apparently completely beyond them.[57]

Captain Elliot continued to negotiate with the Chinese authorities, who were delighted to find in him someone whom they could hold responsible for the actions of all the foreigners. On 25 March he asked Commissioner Lin for safe passage for all the British subjects in Guangzhou but was informed that the opium would have to be released to Lin in advance. On 27 March, Elliot wrote to Lin with his agreement that the opium would be surrendered, although in the notification that he sent to the besieged British on the same day he made it clear that he had been writing under duress. Between 27 March and 21 May the majority of opium in British hands was surrendered to the staff of Commissioner Lin. There were hitches and disputes over the total amount delivered and some opium trading continued along the coast, but Lin could justifiably claim that he had discharged his duties.[58] The method by which the opium was to be destroyed and disposed of was decided upon after the idea of transporting the entire stockpile by ship and bearer to Beijing, for inspection by officials of the Imperial Court had been seriously considered and rejected on the grounds of cost and security. Lin decided that it should be destroyed in the sea off Guangzhou and composed a prayer to the god of the ocean in deference to the impact that this desecration would have on the living creatures of the sea. Trenches, lined with flagstones at the bottom and timber at the sides, were dug at the village of Zhenkou. Opium was thrown into the trenches, water, salt and limestone were added and labourers mixed the contents with hoes and shovels until the opium had been completely dissolved, when the resulting liquid was allowed to flow into a nearby stream which took it into the sea. On 13 June Lin sent a memorial to the emperor detailing the disposal of the opium and the emperor signalled his approval in a reply.[59]

Captain Elliot, accompanied by the British subjects who had remained in the factories, had left Guangzhou for Macao on 24 May. This was to be

his provisional headquarters from where he planned to continue his negotiations with Commissioner Lin. The death, in a brawl with British sailors, of
Lin Weixi who was a farmer from the village of Jiangsha (which is now part
of Hong Kong's Kowloon district and better known today by its Cantonese
name of Tsim Sha Tsui) exacerbated an already impossibly tense situation,
especially as Elliot dealt with the case by means of a British naval court
martial rather than handing the sailors involved over to the Chinese
authorities:[60]

> By the summer of 1839 it was fairly clear to both Chinese and English
> that the difficulties between the two peoples were not to be removed
> without force. Race psychology, pride, and ignorance were the back-
> ground factors. On the part of the Chinese there was never a declar-
> ation of war, the nearest to this was the publication of [a] document
> 'calling on the people to arm themselves, to resist parties of English
> landing on their coasts'.[61]

Thus, Harley MacNair, writing in the early 1920s and using the language of
his time, which was close to that used during the Opium War period. A
translation of the call to arms, composed by Commissioner Lin Zexu, was
published in the *Chinese Repository* at the time for Westerners to read:

> We make proclamation to all the gentry and elders, the shopkeepers
> and inhabitants of the outer villages and hamlets along the coast, for
> their full information. Pay you all obedience hereto; assemble your-
> selves together for consultation, purchase arms and weapons; join
> together the stoutest of your villagers, and thus be prepared to de-
> fend yourselves. If any of the said foreigners be found going on
> shore to cause trouble, all and every of the people are permitted to
> fire upon them, to withstand and drive them back, or to make pris-
> oners of them. [62]

Lin was declaring open season on foreigners who tried to land but he
ordered the local population not to attack them while they remained on
board their own ships. He later authorised the magistrate of Xiangshan to
advertise bounties on the heads of Captain Elliot, John Robert Morrison
his translator and interpreter and other British naval and commercial figures. This deliberate involvement of the general public has been seized
on by nationalist historians writing under both the Guomindang and Communist governments as evidence of widespread popular resistance to the
opium trade and to the British presence on the south China coast.

Outbreak of War

The British did not drift aimlessly or inadvertently into a war with China. It is quite clear, from letters written by Captain Charles Elliot to the British Foreign Secretary Lord Palmerston that intervention and retaliation were in his thoughts as he remained incarcerated in the factory area of Guangzhou; this view was echoed by all of the British opium traders. There had been minor clashes between British and Chinese ships in the Pearl River Delta, but it was an engagement off Shajiao Fort (also known as Chuanbi, or Chuenpi in Cantonese) on 3 November 1839 that was generally considered at the time to have marked the beginning of hostilities although other dates can be chosen and some authorities prefer to date the outbreak of war to 1840. HMS *Volage* under Captain Henry Smith fired on a flotilla of 29 Chinese vessels under the command of Admiral Guan Tianpei who was enforcing a blockade of Guangzhou. Three Chinese gunboats were sunk during this engagement and several others sustained serious damage. Lin Zexu responded by announcing that trade with Britain would cease forthwith, and the emperor was later to approve this action in a decree promulgated in January 1840. Captain Elliot responded by ordering Smith of the *Volage* to blockade the port of Guangzhou. The two nations were now effectively at war although neither side had issued a formal declaration.[63]

Hostilities did not continue immediately and the months between the clash at Chuanbi and June 1840 were essentially a period of preparation for war by the British and by the Chinese civil and military authorities. A century later it would have been called a 'phoney war'. Lin Zexu busied himself and his staff with defensive preparations, strongly supported by the Daoguang emperor who enjoined him not to be timid but to demonstrate China's military might now that the British had made clear their intention of war. Lin's preparations were confined largely to attempts to prevent British warships from penetrating China's coastal waters but, in view of the huge disparity in military capability between the two sides, these preparations were doomed to failure. Lord Palmerston appointed Admiral the Honourable George Elliot (cousin of Charles Elliot) to the command of the British Expeditionary Force to China. The British force arrived in the Pearl River Delta in June 1840 with a complement of 16 ships of the line (warships), 540 guns, 4 armed steamships and substantial military support, fully prepared to blockade the Pearl River and the docks of Guangzhou. The first British ship to arrive off Guangzhou was the *Alligator* on 9 June and it was soon joined by the *Wellesley*, a troop carrier the *Conway* and transport ships.

The Elliot cousins led their naval force northwards on 30 June after having effectively placed Guangzhou under a blockade. The fleet passed Xiamen (Amoy), where a boat sent to deliver a letter to local officials was fired on by the local garrison. The British proceeded along the coast of

Zhejiang province in the direction of the great banking and commercial centre of Ningbo where a second attempt to deliver a letter from the British government was more successful. To achieve their objective, the British fleet moved to occupy the island of Zhoushan, which is the largest of a chain of islands just off the northern coast of Zhejiang and lies about 100 miles to the southeast of Shanghai. They decided to take the main town of Zhoushan, Dinghai, which is on the southwest of the island facing Ningbo. When the fleet had assembled off Dinghai, a senior British naval officer, Sir James Bremer, invited his Chinese opposite number to surrender. Although the Chinese commander had rapidly become aware of the impossible position that he was in, on account of the superiority of the British armaments, he made a token show of resistance and the British bombarded the town. Marines were deployed to take control of Dinghai on 6 July but found it to be almost completely deserted. The *Times* reported from London as follows:

> The British flag waves over a portion of the Chinese empire for the first time! Chusan [Zhoushan] fell into the hands of the English on Sunday, [5 July], and one more settlement in the Far East was added to the British Crown.'[64]

Continuing its mission towards the capital of the empire, the British fleet moved on to the estuary of the Bai River near Tianjin on 28 July. The Bai River (Bai He and often written Pei Ho in an earlier romanisation of Chinese) is better known today by its alternative name of Hai River (Hai He). The remaining letter to senior Chinese officials that had been prepared by the government in London was delivered to Qishan, the Manchu Governor General of Zhili, which was the provincial administration under the direct control of the capital. Qishan (often spelled Kishen by Westerners at the time), who was also Grand Secretary, had been transferred to Tianjin to take overall charge of defences against the threat of a British invasion. He accepted the letter and agreed to meet Captain Charles Elliot, hoping to persuade him to return to Guangzhou with his fleet. Qishan's responsibilities as governor general included the defence of the capital and the protection of the Imperial Court, and he was anxious to deflect any real or apparent threat as rapidly as possible.

Qishan was wealthy and well-connected and had the reputation of being an astute diplomat and a skilled negotiator. He was born into the Borjigid clan of the Manchu Yellow Banner, a clan which traces its ancestry in part back to the Mongol Chinggis Khan, and held the hereditary rank of *hou* (which is conventionally translated as the English order of nobility, Marquis) after the death of his father in 1823. Sir John Frances Davis of the

East India Company, a scholar and a diplomat himself with many years experience of Anglo-Chinese relations, praised the diplomacy of Qishan highly:

> If conciliation was required, the choice could not have fallen on a fitter person. His great tact, his imperturbable suavity, and perfect command of temper, were extraordinary. He could exchange fair phrases, protract discussions, and make promises innumerable, without keeping one; and though the catastrophe of war became inevitable, he certainly postponed it much longer than could have been expected.[65]

Qishan's aristocratic connections and natural tact enabled him to achieve some initial success in the diplomatic obstruction of the British mission to the capital, for on 17 September Captain Elliott agreed to return with his flotilla to Guangzhou, where, he was led to believe, negotiations would continue. As a reward for his success in preventing a direct confrontation between the British and the Imperial Court, Qishan was instructed to move from Tianjin to Guangzhou where he replaced Lin Zexu as High Commissioner and he was later appointed governor general of Guangdong and Guangxi, once again replacing Lin who had held that office since early 1840. Lin was dismissed from all of his official posts because he had failed to defeat the British completely, but he was also a casualty of the Manchu-Han rivalry in the Chinese bureaucracy as he was replaced by a Manchu. He was initially required to stay in Guangzhou but in May 1841 was sentenced to exile in Yining (also known as Ghulja) in the far northwest of the territory of Xinjiang, which at the time was not formally a part of China as it was not designated a province until 1884. He remained in Yining for three years and was then rehabilitated and permitted to take further official positions.[66]

Captain Elliot moved his ships down the coast to Macao and Qishan followed, arriving in Guangzhou on 16 December 1840. He negotiated with the British and attempted to conciliate them, an approach that contrasted with Lin Zexu's more belligerent manner. While amenable to British requests for the restoration and extension of trade relations, he refused Captain Elliot's demand that Hong Kong be handed over as a British base, on the grounds that the emperor would never agree to any Chinese territory being ceded to foreigners. Once Elliot realised that Qishan was not willing or able to give way on Hong Kong, he made preparations for an attack and on 7 January 1841 stormed the Chinese shore batteries at Sand Cape (*Shajiao*, which was also known as Chuanbi) and Great Cape (*Dajiao*) just outside the Bogue (*Humen*), placing his forces in an excellent position to take control of that strategically important waterway and consequently putting himself in control of all river traffic to and from the port of Guangzhou.

Convention of Chuanbi

Under pressure from the British naval blockade of Guangzhou, Qishan agreed peace terms, which were then enshrined in the protocol known as the Convention of Chuanbi and signed by both parties on 20 January 1841. Under the terms of the convention it was agreed that China would ensure on the following:

1. Surrender the whole of the island of Hong Kong to the British, although customs duties on transactions that were carried out on the island would continue to be paid to the government of China as if the trade were still being carried out in Huangpu (Whampoa) in Guangzhou.

2. Pay the British government compensation of six million Chinese silver dollars, of which one million was to be paid immediately with the remainder in annual instalments, the final payment due in 1846. This compensation is often referred to as an indemnity, a term which is now more frequently used for a guarantee against possible future loss or damage.

3. Conduct official business with Britain on the basis of equality and reciprocity.

4. Restore trade through the province of Guangdong by the beginning of February 1841.

There were two versions of the text of this convention, one submitted by Qishan to the court in Chinese and the other signed by the British: they differed significantly, particularly in the first clause where Qishan suggested to the emperor that what was being offered was an agreement to allow foreigners to reside in Hong Kong that might be extended, even indefinitely, rather than a permanent surrender of Chinese territory to foreigners.

The Convention of Chuanbi was important because it was the model for the later treaties that were concluded at the end of, and following, the Opium War, even as far the problems that arose because of variant versions in Chinese and English. The Convention was essentially the first truce of the Opium War, a practical agreement negotiated by the military commanders on the spot, Elliot and Qishan, to resolve the conflict between their forces. However it proved to be completely unacceptable to either the Chinese or the British government. Elliot was censured by the British government for not having secured a larger sum in compensation and for agreeing to the payment of customs duties for trade through Hong Kong. He was recalled and replaced by Sir Henry Pottinger. Qishan was also severely criticised by his own government for having exceeded his authority and, when the implications of the agreement became clear, for ceding Hong Kong to Britain without informing the court. The Daoguang emperor appointed his own son Yishan as imperial commissioner and 'General responsible for suppressing the barbarians' and dispatched him, together with Lungwen and Yang Fang as his deputy commanders, to Guangzhou with a substantial contingent of troops to remove the threat of the British once and for all. The diplomat Qishan was mortified at this undermining of his efforts and submitted a memorial to the emperor urging the continuation of peaceful negotiations, but his entreaties were rejected and he was dismissed and sent back to Beijing in chains and all his property was confiscated.[67] Hong Kong itself was now firmly under the control of the British but in a vain attempt to lessen the insult to the Imperial Court, Charles Elliot had handed back the Bogue [Humen] forts and Dinghai to China.

The newly appointed General Yishan assembled troops to repulse the British in the south. Captain Charles Elliot, in disgrace (but in fact still in command as Pottinger had not yet arrived to replace him) moved to reoccupy the Bogue forts, and Chinese and British troops fought until 25 May, by which time the British were in control of all strategic points around Guangzhou, and Yishan was obliged to negotiate a second truce through the merchants and local officials of Guangzhou.

Ransom of Guangzhou

The second truce, which became known as the Ransom of Guangzhou, was signed on 27 May 1841. The key points of this agreement were as follows:

1. Within one week, the sum of six million silver dollars was to be paid to the British military, one million of which would be handed over on the day of the truce.

2. Chinese troops would retire to a position 60 miles outside Guangzhou.

3. British forces would withdraw to the Bogue.

4. The issue of the cession of Hong Kong to the British would be deferred.

5. There would be an exchange of prisoners of war.[68]

With the signing of this truce, Guangzhou was spared, and this proved to be yet another opportunity for criticism of Charles Elliot who was accused of having conceded too much. The deputy commander of the Chinese forces, Yang Fang, was also reprimanded by the emperor for agreeing to the truce rather than resisting. The fact that Hong Kong, in spite of the smokescreen provided by the fourth clause of the truce agreement, had fallen to the British was concealed from the emperor: local officials were only too aware of their likely fate had he known the truth.

Yishan justified the payment of this ransom in a memorial to the emperor in which he described the desperate conditions being endured by the civilian population of Guangzhou. Given the size of the British force ranged against him, he had decided that it was his 'duty to retain the whole force within the walls [of the city] for its defence, rather than attack the enemy'. Local people had petitioned him to relieve what was effectively a siege, and the Hong Kong merchants were desperate to be allowed to resume their trade. Nevertheless, the need to pay the British to stay out of Guangzhou was deemed to be a disgrace to the Chinese empire. An unnamed Chinese official described it as 'a calamity at which I was stricken with shame and scarcely dare to express my sentiment in writing'. He complained of troops abandoning the defences, of Chinese traitors spying for the British and of the failure of the authorities to capture Charles Elliot. Fighting even broke out between the Chinese forces and local militias in Guangzhou:

> When, finally, our soldiers were driven into the city there arose a furious combat with the native militia, and innumerable bodies strewed the streets. All discipline was lost; a confused clamour filled the ways, and everywhere I observed plunder and murder.[69]

Charles Elliot's replacement, Sir Henry Pottinger, finally arrived in Macao on 10 August 1841. Pottinger, a 52-year-old Ulsterman, had previously been Resident Administrator in the Indian northwest frontier state of Sind. He was born on 1789 at Mount Pottinger in what was then a rural community to the east of Belfast. After his career with the East India Company in India he became the first titular governor of Hong Kong before returning to India to govern Madras. He died in retirement in Malta in 1856. In light of what were seen as Elliot's failures, Pottinger's instructions from the British Prime Minister, Lord Palmerston, were quite specific, including the precise amount of compensation to be extracted from the Chinese and the trading concessions to be obtained from them. He was also instructed that he should negotiate primarily with officials of the Imperial Court in Beijing rather than with local officials in Guangdong province. With Pottinger's arrival, the focus of military and diplomatic activities moved away from Guangzhou. Pottinger had at his disposal an expeditionary force that would eventually amount to over 50 ships and 10,000 troops. Most of his force he deployed in an assault on Xiamen (Amoy), a city opposite the island of Taiwan, on 26 August. Dinghai, which Captain Elliot had handed back, was recaptured on 1 October, Zhenhai was occupied on 10 October and the old banking centre of Ningbo on 13 October, by which time the entire coast of Zhejiang province was effectively under the control of the British Navy.

The Daoguang emperor appointed the Manchu General Yijing to lead a counter attack in Zhejiang but this failed completely under the onslaught of a reinforced British assault. By 18 May 1842, Zhapu, a port city just south of Shanghai, had fallen. Wusong fell on 16 June and Shanghai itself on 19 June. On 21 June the British advanced inland along the Yangzi River to the strategic town of Zhenjiang, which lies at the junction of the Yangzi and the Grand Canal and played a vital role in the supply of foodstuff and other goods from southern China to the capital in the north. By 10 August, Nanjing, the second city of the empire and a former capital was within reach of British artillery. At this point, the Qing officials bowed to the inevitable and once again sued for peace.[70] The fighting had been severe and the loss of life considerable. Before the war, each side had believed the other incapable of sustained campaigns. Afterwards each side had become more respectful of the capabilities of the other but this respect had been earned at great cost. When Zhapu was captured on 18 May it had been defended by its Manchu garrison of 300 to 400 troops, many of whom died under the British artillery bombardment that set ablaze the temple where the Manchus made their last stand. Most of the Manchu women and children lay dead, having killed themselves or each other for fear of how they might be treated by the alien invaders. 'An old woman had been prevailed upon by [British] soldiers…not to drown her daughter, but she watched her time and effected the girl's destruction, and afterwards her own, as soon as left to herself.' Similar scenes of carnage took place in Zhenjiang. In both Zhapu and Zhenjiang, the poor of the cities, who were overwhelmingly Han Chinese, looted the quarters of their defeated Manchu overlords.[71]

Treaty of Nanjing

The Treaty of Nanjing, or to give it its full title, the 'Treaty of Peace, Friendship, Commerce, Indemnity etc, between Great Britain and China' was signed by the representatives of the two imperial powers on 29 August 1842 and has been excoriated by historians and political leaders in modern China as the first of the 'unequal treaties'. Over two decades this series of treaties reduced China to the status of a semi-colony, subservient initially to the British and subsequently to the other European and world powers that took advantage of the end of the first war between China and a European power to advance their commercial and political interests in East Asia. Unequal it may have been, but strictly speaking it was not the first, since the text of the treaty drew in detail on the two truce negotiations that the Qing government had already conceded under fire; although the Treaty of Nanjing made far greater concessions to Britain. Sir Henry Pottinger was the signatory for the British side. For the Qing court, the key officials were Pitying, Yilibu, Liu Yunke and Niu Jian. Qiying and Yilibu were both Manchu aristocrats and imperial commissioners, although Yilibu had technically lost that commission after the capture of Dinghai. They had direct authority from the Imperial Court, which enabled them to overrule the regular local officials. Liu Yunke was governor of Zhejiang, which was the province closest to the location of most of the battles, and Niu Jian was governor general of Liang Jiang which is roughly equivalent to the present day provinces of Jiangxi, Jiangsu and Anhui.

The Daoguang emperor was reluctant to agree to a treaty that put China at such a clear a disadvantage. In part this was because even his most senior officials had shielded him from the dire situation that Chinese forces had found themselves in when confronted with the naval and military might of the British. After the capture of Wusong and Shanghai, Niu Jian sent a memorial to the emperor suggesting that a historical precedent might indicate a way forward. In the reign of the Qianlong emperor (the Daoguang emperor's grandfather) an imperial expedition had been sent to subjugate Burma, but troops were withdrawn in return for an agreement that the Burmese king send tribute to the Qing court, and Niu Jian suggested that the British might be persuaded to do the same. The Daogong emperor responded that the present situation was entirely different and made it clear that he was both angry at the proposals for a peace settlement and anxious about the threat, which he had great difficulty comprehending. This exchange, citing historical precedent in the traditional Confucian manner and turning to the archaic but still current tributary system for a solution, illustrates the mode of discourse in the court at the time and the limits of perception from which the imperial regime suffered. It was only after the additional loss of Zhenjiang that the emperor appears to have realised that he had little choice but to heed the advice of his front line officials and agree to a treaty.[72] At court the acceptance of the need to agree to a treaty was due, above all, to the acumen of Muchanga, Manchu Grand Secretary and chief Grand Councillor who was 'the chief supporter at the capital of the unpopular but unavoidable policy of compromise and surrender'. Muchanga had been the main supporter of Qishan and had advised the emperor to dismiss Lin Zexu in 1840.[73]

The British side took some persuading that the Qing officials with whom they were negotiating genuinely possessed the authority to agree to peace terms in the name of the emperor. Initial discussions took place on 1 August 1842 between Sir Henry Pottinger, accompanied by his secretary Major Malcolm and the Chinese 'peace commissioners', to establish each other's credentials. At a second meeting on 26 August the British agreed that their blockade of the Yangzi would be lifted immediately after the treaty was signed and that all areas under their control would be returned to the Chinese when the first instalment of the reparations had been paid.[74]

The formal ceremony for the signing of the treaty took place a little before noon on 29 August 1842 on board the British warship, HMS *Cornwallis*, anchored on the Yangzi river close by Nanjing. Harry Parkes, 14 years old at the time and already a student of Chinese under John Robert Morrison the official translator and interpreter to the British mission, gave a vivid account of the ceremony:

> Firstly the Treaty was signed by Mr Morrison as secretary to Sir Henry on the one side and by Wang, as secretary to [Qiying] on the other. There was the seal of the Imperial High Commissioners and Sir Henry's seal. This being finished and done, the table was drawn up to the sofa, and then [Qiying] [Yilibu] and [Niu Jian] signed their names.... Then Sir Henry did his. There were four copies of the Treaty signed and sealed. They were bound in worked yellow silk, one Treaty in English and the same in Chinese stitched and bound together formed a copy. This being finished they all came out of the after-cabin and sat down to tiffin, and the different officers seated themselves all round the table making plenty of guests. Almost directly after the treaty was signed a yellow flag for China at the main and a Union Jack for England at the mizen were hoisted, and at the same time a royal salute of twenty-one guns was fired.[75]

The treaty includes a preamble avowing that its purpose was to put 'an end to the misunderstandings and consequent hostilities which have arisen between the two countries' and 13 articles, the main terms of which were as follows:

1. There should be peace and friendship between China and Britain and security for the nationals of both states in each other's country.

2. British subjects should be allowed to reside in Guangzhou, Xiamen (Amoy), Fuzhou, Ningbo and Shanghai for the purpose of trade. British

consular officials would be appointed in those ports to oversee relations between merchants and Chinese officials.

3. The island of Hong Kong was 'to be possessed in perpetuity by her Britannic majesty, her Heirs and successors and to be governed by such Laws and Regulations as her Majesty the Queen of Great Britain etc shall see fit to direct'.

4. China would pay 'Six Millions of Dollars'. This was compensation for the opium surrendered in March 1839 'as a Ransom for the lives of her Britannic Majesty's Superintendent and subjects, who had been imprisoned and threatened with death by the Chinese High Officers'.

5. The Hong or Cohong merchant system was to be abolished and China would pay three million dollars to compensate for debts owed by the Cohong to British merchants.

6. China would pay the expenses of the British Expeditionary Force up to 12 million dollars, less sums paid as ransom by Chinese cities and towns after 1 August 1841.

7. This total of 21 million dollars was to be paid in instalments: 6 million immediately, 6 million in 1843, 5 million in 1844, 4 million in 1845 [the total payment was in fact made by the beginning of 1846 and this was estimated to be the equivalent of £4 to 5 million sterling at the rate of exchange current at the time.

8. British prisoners in China (whether of European or Indian origin) were to be released.

9. Chinese subjects who had worked for or dealt with the British were to be released if in prison and indemnified against any further proceedings.

10. A 'fair and regular' public customs tariff would be established in the 'treaty ports' listed in Article 2 and further internal duties would be proportionate.

11. This clause indicated the formal terms to be used by British representatives in communication with Chinese officials [These terms were crucial in identifying the relative status of officials within the structure of the extremely formal wording of Qing period documents].

12. British forces would withdraw from Nanjing and the Grand Canal, and also Zhenhai, on signature of the treaty and receipt of the initial payment, but Zhoushan and other islands would be retained until payments and the opening of ports had been satisfactorily completed.

13. Ratification of the treaty would be completed by the Queen and the Emperor as soon as time and distance permitted.

The treaty was signed and dated 29 August 1842, the 24th day of the seventh month of the twenty-second year of the Daoguang reign on board HMS *Cornwallis*. The Daoguang emperor ratified the treaty on September 8th and Queen Victoria added her written assent on 28 December 1842.[76]

The content and the tenor of this document were to set the tone of Anglo-Chinese relations, and indeed China's international relations in general, for at least the following century. In concrete terms the most significant articles were those that designated the five 'Treaty Ports' (Article 2) and formally ceded Hong Kong to the British crown (Article 3). However the payment of indemnity or compensation, and the use of terms such as ransom, contributed to the indignity felt by the Chinese side and the beginning of what many Chinese citizens still consider to be a long period of national humiliation.

Treaty of the Bogue

A supplementary agreement, the Treaty of the Bogue [*Humen tiaoyue*], was signed by Qiying and Sir Henry Pottinger on 8 October 1843. Although it was intended merely to clarify and qualify details of the way in which the Treaty of Nanjing would be operated, in the long term it proved to be of much greater significance than had been anticipated, as it extended the provisions of the Nanjing agreement to all nations and not solely to Great Britain. Clause 8 of the Treaty of the Bogue has become known as the 'most favoured nation clause'. It allowed citizens of all countries to trade 'on the same terms as the English'. Britain had never tried to reserve for itself exclusive privileges in China, and similar clauses were regularly inserted in treaties subsequently signed by foreign missions to China, notably in the Treaty of Wangxia agreed by Qiying and the United States envoy Caleb Cushing on 3 July 1844 and in the Treaty of Huangpu (Whampoa) concluded between France and China on 24 October 1844.[77]

In this way, the gains made by the United Kingdom in access to trade and consular representation in China were extended to all Western nations: all took advantage as China grew weaker in the course of the nineteenth century. The Treaty Ports were opened not just to British but also to

European and American traders, and they gradually acquired a distinctive and vibrant hybrid culture with the development of prosperous westernised cantonments that excluded virtually all Chinese, apart from servants and labourers who were permitted to be there during their hours of work.

Sanyuanli and Popular Resistance

Sir John Francis Davis (1795–1890), who served as Chief Superintendent of Trade in Guangzhou after the death of Lord Napier and as governor of Hong Kong from 1844, was a student of Chinese, had acted as interpreter for the East India Company for many years and was regarded by his contemporaries as a good judge of the condition of China. Writing ten years after the conclusion of the Treaty of Nanjing, he suggested that, in addition to international trade and diplomacy, Chinese domestic concerns had been an important factor in the decision of the Imperial Court to agree terms with the British:

> The peace was hastened, not more by the really formidable character of the British expedition, than by the universal anarchy and confusion that reigned internally; by the entire failure of every scheme grounded in ignorance, and defeated by its own folly; and, in fine, by the apprehension of a general revolution against the government, which was losing its hold on the minds of the people.[78]

The British invasion of China did meet with some resistance from the local population, but in the 'anarchy and confusion' that prevailed in southern China in the 1840s it is often difficult to disentangle genuine popular resistance from the activities of the long-established gangs of pirates and bandits who operated in the region of the Pearl River Delta and along the entire extent of the south China coast. One incident, however, stands out. On 29 May 1841, British and Indian troops entered the village of Sanyuanli, an important rural market about one mile to the north of the city of Guangzhou. They damaged a temple, disturbed graves, either out of curiosity or in search of grave-goods to loot and raped a number of local women. This provoked an angry response from the local community, which raised an impromptu militia to take reprisal on the British. The resistance spread to other areas and representatives from each village met in the hill village of Niulangang to agree on a common strategy of resistance. Each village agreed to establish its own self-defence force to fight under its own banner and the decision to attack was to be communicated from village to village by the sound of large gongs.

Lin Fuxiang's eyewitness account of this popular resistance was published in 1854. Lin (1814–62), who was originally from a gentry family in Zhongshan County in Guangdong, had studied both the Confucian classics and military subjects:

> The opposition to the foreigners in the Sanyuanli area was provoked by their plunder and licentious behaviour. Yang Ruzheng and I had been instructing the villagers of several villages for days and out of loyalty and fear they were fired up and ready to fight. On 29 May I agreed with village leaders that each village would set up a great standard with the name of the village written on it and assemble several large gongs. If danger threatened, a village would beat its gong and all the other villages would respond and I would lead the coastal militia. On 30 May early in the morning the stubborn foreigners went over to Niulangang to plunder the village. When I heard the ceaseless sound of the gongs I responded with my militia and over 80 villagers arrived with their banners; tens of thousands of people were there in the twinkling of an eye.[79]

Lin describes the massed ranks of villagers, armed with axes, hoes and anything else that could be used as weapons, attacking the British forces and surrounding them, and this reminded him of a famous siege from the *Romance of the Three Kingdoms*, a classic Ming dynasty novel of political intrigue and military strategy. He records that there were casualties on both sides and that one of his kinsmen, the 18-year-old Tan Sheng, was killed. The day had begun brightly but clouded over and thunder, rain and high wind had set in by the early afternoon. The British fowling pieces were soaked and could not fire, and the troops were wearing leather shoes, which were useless for trying to walk through sodden paddy fields. The Chinese coastal militia and villagers attacked the invaders and killed 12 of them. This gentry-led militia action successfully channelled the patriotic indignation of the peasantry. The British had been using the Sifang Fort which overlooked Guangzhou as their base, and after the battle at Niulangang they retreated to the fort, pursued by the villagers who surrounded their encampment. Qing government forces were in the vicinity, but they failed to come to the aid of the popular resistance and, when the British threatened to attack the city of Guangzhou, the local authorities persuaded the villagers to withdraw, leaving behind a feeling of bitterness and resentment against the Qing government as well as hostility to the British.[80]

Popular resistance to the British invasion continued as the naval forces moved north up the coast of the provinces of Fujian and Zhejiang. In the countryside around Ningbo, the Blackwater Party [*Heishuidang*] launched guerrilla attacks on the British at night. The salt panners on the north bank of the Yangzi River also attacked the British, and there was sporadic resistance throughout the remainder of the British naval and military campaign. The degree of resistance among the Chinese populace made clear their displeasure at the presence of foreign military forces in their towns and villages, but local people could only harry the invaders rather than halt the invasion or even delay its progress to any extent.

3

TAIPING, NIAN AND MUSLIM UPRISINGS (1850–1884)

As if its defeat in the Opium War and the pressing demands of the West for trading rights and diplomatic representation were not problems enough, in the mid-nineteenth century the Qing government faced a challenge that would have been familiar to a Chinese imperial regime from any era, namely an outbreak of widespread communal violence in the rural areas which, at its height, threatened the very existence of the Manchu state. Whereas the immediate and direct effects of the Opium War, including the popular unrest, were mainly confined to the coastal areas and had the greatest effect on the official elite in those areas, the social dislocation, conflict and rebellions of the second half of the nineteenth century affected most of the interior of China. The fighting laid waste to vast swathes of the Chinese countryside, which suffered catastrophic depopulation from which China took decades to recover.

Peasant Rebellions and Secret Societies

Rural disorder had been a regular feature of the history of the Chinese empire since earliest times: discontent over misrule or exorbitant taxation frequently led to riots or armed insurrection directed against the local representatives of the state and less frequently to full-scale rebellions, usually described as peasant rebellions, some of which consciously attempted to bring down the government. Rebellions on the larger scale typically occurred during a period of weakness in a dynasty and often did contribute to its downfall. In the traditional Confucian view of history, these rebellions could be interpreted as an indication that the ruling family had lost the confidence, or the mandate, of Heaven, the supreme spiritual authority in Chinese tradition. Once lost by the dynasty that had been overthrown, the mandate of Heaven [*tianming*] was transferred to the new regime, which by virtue of its success was assumed to have gained the confidence of Heaven.

The Qing ruling house had itself come to power during a period of serious social disorder, including a rebellion led by Li Zicheng at the end of the Ming dynasty (1368–1644). The leadership of the Manchu tribal confederation, which controlled extensive territories to the northeast of China, had seized the opportunity and marched its armies into Beijing to establish a new administration. The Manchus were not ethnically or culturally Chinese, even though their culture and state structure had been strongly influenced by close contact with the elite of the Ming dynasty, and they were perceived by many Han Chinese as an alien regime. For this reason alone there was resistance to their occupation of China, and defiance of the Manchus continued in some form or other throughout the dynasty. Among the most serious instances of opposition were the risings of insurgents associated with the secret society that is known as the White Lotus, which was an underground organisation that not only belonged to the millenarian tradition of Buddhism, but also borrowed heavily from popular Daoism.

A White Lotus insurrection affected much of north and central China between 1793 and 1796, at the very height of Qing imperial expansion and at the same time that the Qing court was preoccupied with the Macartney mission. The Eight Trigrams Society, a branch of the White Lotus, rose and attacked the Imperial Palace in Beijing in 1813, striking at the heart of Qing power. One of the leaders of the Eight Trigrams declared himself to be the reincarnation of Maitreya, the compassionate Buddha of the Future, a messianic figure who was central to the belief and ritual of the White Lotus. Followers of the White Lotus tradition looked forward to the return of Maitreya and the establishment of a new social order, and the society was instrumental in many other outbreaks of opposition to the government throughout the nineteenth century.

Secret societies, whether Buddhist or Daoist (or frequently a combination of the two with an admixture of local beliefs that cannot readily be classified as either), played an important role in traditional Chinese society. They enabled the deprived and the disenfranchised to obtain a degree of protection and a position in society. They tended to attract marginalised social groups and members of the poorer rural classes, including dispossessed peasants, itinerant traders, boatmen and porters. Some also had women members who, although poor, were able to play more of a role in these societies than many wealthy women played in the established political and social structures. Secret societies were anathema to the imperial government and to its local officials who attempted to suppress them whenever they emerged from the shadows. In spite of constant repression by successive governments, they have never been completely eliminated and continue to exist in the Chinese countryside well into the twenty-first century.

Although the historical anti-dynastic risings have usually been represented as peasant rebellions, from the membership of the secret societies which provided the recruits for these uprisings, it is clear that this is not entirely accurate. Peasants and the rural poor may well have constituted the majority of the insurgents, but the leadership often came from the educated, or partly educated, minor gentry, many of whom were never able to secure a paid official post in spite of their examination successes. Whether these risings were simply outbreaks of communal violence in response to immediate and desperate economic and social pressures or whether they were ideologically driven rebellions against the Chinese state has been a matter of much debate. The most significant uprisings of the nineteenth century, the Taiping Heavenly Kingdom in the south, the Nian in the north and the series of insurrections by Muslims in different regions of western China, exhibit a combination of these characteristics.[1]

Origins of the Taiping Rebellion

Of all the anti-government insurgencies of the nineteenth century, it was the rise of the Heavenly Kingdom of the Taiping that came closest to toppling the Qing dynasty. The Taiping Heavenly Kingdom was a movement that was riddled with paradoxes: it had an ideology that combined a simplistic interpretation of evangelical Christian texts with social radicalism; it was avowedly anti-Confucian yet constructed an administrative structure modelled closely on the Confucian system that it sought to replace; it was the product of a regional conflict but developed into a movement that transcended regional concerns; it owed its initial support largely to a minority ethnic group, the Hakka (*Kejia* in the pinyin romanisation of modern Mandarin), but it aspired to be a pan-Chinese anti-Manchu movement.

The movement had its origins in the province of Guangxi, famed for its dramatic karst mountain scenery. Guangxi lies in southwestern China between Guangdong and Yunnan and today shares a border with the northern part of Vietnam. It was one of the poorest provinces of the empire and had a reputation for being one of the most corrupt and mismanaged. It was part of the governor generalship of the Liang-Guang, together with Guangdong, but was badly neglected in comparison with its more prosperous eastern neighbour. Intercommunal feuds were common, and many of those displaced by the feuding found their way into rebel bands, the ranks of which were swollen by unemployed craftsmen, porters, boatmen and miners. Banditry and piracy were rife in Guangxi in the 1840s, and many of the coastal pirates were driven upriver from the Guangzhou Delta by the

British navy during the Opium War. Firearms, which in normal times had been strictly controlled, were widely distributed in southern China and irregular forces were encouraged to arm themselves against the British invaders. When the war came to an end, weapons remained in the hands of these unofficial resistance bands, and many of their members reverted to banditry. The Qing government, which had permitted the arming of the populace to resist the British, was unable to re-establish control after the cessation of hostilities. Throughout the 1840s there had been serious disturbances involving members of local secret societies, primarily the pantheistic Ming loyalist organisations known as the Heaven and Earth Society [*Tiandi hui*] which were part of the wider cluster of underworld groups that operated – and still operate today – across the whole of the south of China, including Hong Kong, and are also known as the Triads.

Between 1848 and 1850 the province was ravaged by drought, famine and pestilence which drove thousands of people into the arms of the secret societies. These groups provided a degree of protection in times of trouble and in an emergency they could also be a source of food, in some cases the only source, for hungry villagers through the inns and shops that were run by their members. The Heaven and Earth Society was supported by peasants, handicraft workers, hired labourers and the itinerant poor and the society rose in rebellion against the local representatives of the Qing state in the border lands between Guangxi and Hunan in 1847 and 1848. Thousands of fighters attacked county towns, and there were other smaller-scale insurrections throughout Guangxi. By the time that the Taiping movement was beginning to emerge, the province of Guangxi was already in turmoil.[2]

Guangxi is a multiethnic province which is home to Cantonese and Hakka (*Kejia*) communities and also has a substantial population of the Zhuang, Miao and Yao people who are classified as ethnic minority groups in China. Hakka people, who originated in northern China but live in the south, are not usually considered to be an ethnic minority, but are treated as a component of the Han majority population, as are the Cantonese. However, the spoken language of the Hakka communities is not Cantonese but is closely related to Mandarin with differences that can be accounted for by the date of the migration of the Hakka from north to south China and believed to have taken place mainly in the twelfth century. There was a clear distinction in the minds of local people between the Hakka and the Cantonese speakers (who are commonly referred to as the *Bendi* or the *Punti*), not only on the grounds of their different languages but also by their dress and customs.[3] Most noticeably, Hakka women did not as a rule have bound feet. Hakka and Bendi communities lived in separate villages and had separate social organisations, both legal and illegal, and from time to time feuds that erupted between the villages led to larger-scale conflict.

Hakka communities, as relative latecomers, occupied the less desirable farming land in the mountainous areas because the more productive land in the valleys had already been taken by the Cantonese-speaking *Punti* or *Bendi*. The languages and way of life of the Zhuang, Miao and Yao groups in Guangxi, as in other parts of south China, mark them out quite clearly from those of the Han, and they are culturally closer to the peoples of southeast Asia and are regarded as separate ethnic minorities in present day China.

Heavenly King – the Early Career of Hong Xiuquan

What could have been just another local conflict, one of many that might have flared up in any of the provinces of China, was transformed into a major insurrection principally by the ideas and activities of one charismatic and messianic leader, Hong Xiuquan. Hong was born on 1 January 1814 in the village of Fuyuanshui in Hua County which is in Guangdong province, to the north of the city of Guangzhou. His family were ethnic Hakkas, and they had their roots in a Hakka village in eastern Guangdong. His father was a small-scale farmer who owned land, at first in Fuyuanshui and subsequently in the village of Guanlubu, to where the family moved when Hong was very young. Hong showed considerable academic promise from an early age. According to his cousin Hong Rengan who was to become his first disciple:

> He started his study during childhood and his intelligence was beyond compare; there was no book that he did not read. He began to take part in the examinations when he was fifteen or sixteen, and he often came out one of the ten best students. His grandfather and father had preserved the family tradition of farming and studying.[4]

In fact Hong probably entered for the imperial examinations as early as 1827 when he was 13 years old by the Western reckoning. Although he passed at the preliminary level in the round of examinations held in Hua County in 1837, he failed in the second round which was held in the provincial capital, Guangzhou. If had he passed at this level, he would have qualified for the *shengyuan* degree, the key to entry into the gentry class with all the privileges that gentry status entailed. He tried and failed to pass this examination on many occasions, attempting it for the last time in 1843, and supported himself in the meantime by teaching in the local village school. Of all his failures, his disappointment in the examination of 1837 was the most critical. He became seriously ill with what would probably have been diagnosed in modern times as a nervous breakdown or an even more serious psychological condition: friends and relatives reported that his personality changed dramatically as a result of what was for him a personal catastrophe.[5]

Hong Xiuquan and his supporters were to interpret this transformation in quite a different light after Hong had assumed the role of the True Sovereign of the Taiping:

> When the Sovereign was twenty-five years old in [1837], on the first day of the third moon, at midnight, he saw innumerable angels descending from heaven, saying that they had come to take him up into heaven.... Presently, supported by angels, the true Sovereign was seated in a sedan chair, and they set out on their circuitous way along the great road to the east and ascended. The Sovereign in the sedan chair was most ill at ease. When they arrived at the gateway to heaven, beautiful maidens beyond number approached to receive him, but the Sovereign cast no sidelong glances at them. When they arrived in heaven the radiant light was dazzling. It was most different from the dusty world. He saw innumerable persons wearing dragon gowns and cornered hats, all of whom greeted the Sovereign. Subsequently an imperial command was passed down to cut open the Sovereign's stomach, remove the old and replace it by a new one. They also brought certain writings and arranged them in such a way that they could be passed continuously before him.

The Heavenly Father, God, ordered three sets of books to be set before Hong, the Old and the New Testaments, which were 'pure and without error', and the writings of Confucius which contained 'numerous errors and faults'. Confucius, who conveniently also happened to be in Heaven, was admonished for confusing people, brought before the Heavenly Elder Brother, Jesus, and whipped many times while pleading for mercy. He was spared because 'his meritorious achievements compensated for his deficiencies' but was told that he would never be allowed down into the world again.[6]

Taiping documents also refer to Hong ascending to heaven on another occasion and battling against devils with the help of the Heavenly Elder Brother, Jesus. The title of *Tian Wang* [Heavenly King] was bestowed on Hong by the Heavenly Father and 'the devils who invaded the high heaven were one by one executed and dropped into hell'.[7]

Hong Rengan, in his essay on Hong Xiuquan's childhood and youth, recounted a follows:

> In the *pingyuan* year [1836], he was in the prefectural city of [Guangzhou] for an examination; there he met a mysterious man wearing a

dress with large sleeves and with his hair dressed in a knot, who gave him a book entitled *Good Words to Admonish the Age* [*Quanshi liangyan*]. The contents of the book taught people to believe faithfully in God and Jesus Christ, to obey the Ten Commandments, and never to worship demons. When Hong later fell ill, his soul saw precisely what the book had said. Hence he followed the teachings of the book and acted accordingly.[8]

Although Hong Xiuquan appears to have been given this tract in 1836 by a Chinese Christian convert named Liang Afa, he does not seem to have acted on the message that it contained until after his final examination failure in 1843: another cousin, Li Jingfang, found it on his bookcase at about this time. Hong found an explanation for his illness in the text and interpreted it as a religious experience. In March 1847, he took instruction briefly from a protestant American missionary of the evangelical Southern Baptist Church, the Reverend Issachar J. Roberts, who was based in Guangzhou. Moved by his discovery of these new ideas, Hong started to preach to his family and friends and then to other people in his village and he began to write down his thoughts.[9]

God Worshippers and the Rising at Jintian

The organisation that Hong Xiuquan used to disseminate his new ideas was the God Worshippers Society [*Bai shangdi hui*]. In appearance there was little to distinguish it from the numerous other anti-Qing secret societies of the mid-nineteenth century, but it used some of the rituals outlined in *Good Words to Admonish the Age*, including baptism, and it can legitimately be considered as a Christian, or at least a quasi-Christian, organisation, whereas all the other societies were influenced by Buddhism, Daoism or a combination of the two with the addition of local religious practices.

The Daoguang emperor died on 25 February 1850 after a reign that had lasted for almost 30 years: he was succeeded by his fourth son Yizhu who took the reign title of Xianfeng (and reigned 1850–61). The Xianfeng emperor was 22 years old on his formal accession to the throne on 9 March 1850 and contemporary Western observers considered that, although he was strong and vigorous in contrast to many of his palace officials, he appeared to be callow, tactless and lacking in judgement.[10] The morale and credibility of the Qing administration had already suffered a crushing blow from the humiliating defeat at the hands of the British in the Opium War, and many felt that he did not possess the great wisdom and strength of purpose in directing the empire that was necessary to repair the damage.

The activity of the Taipings escalated during the period of transition between the two reigns. In July 1850 members of the God Worshippers Society congregated in the village of Jintian in Guangxi province. Supporters of the sect travelled to Jintian from villages throughout Guangxi and from further afield to answer a call to protect their fellow God Worshippers who had been attacked by the militia maintained by local officials. The gathering began in a small way with a group of 130 people at the house of Wei Changhui, a landlord and the owner of a pawnshop, whose entire clan had thrown in its lot with the God Worshippers. During this initial period of the Taiping rising, Hong Xiuquan and Feng Yunshan were not in Jintian but remained in Huazhou in Guangdong province: in June 1850, Hong asked his family to travel from Guangdong to join him in Guangxi in preparation for a major uprising.

A group of over 3,000 Hakkas, who had been driven from their land after a conflict with the *Bendi*, arrived to swell the ranks of the God Worshippers and, as other groups arrived from far flung villages, the numbers grew to between 10,000 and 30,000. Although the majority were probably Hakkas, there were some followers from the *Bendi* group, and that inevitably led to a degree of internal conflict within the movement. In terms of regional and social origin, the gathering was decidedly heterogeneous, and it included Triad groups and bandit gangs with their own chiefs who were not necessarily willing to accept the overall authority of the leadership of the God Worshippers.

Such a concentration of potential rebels naturally attracted the attention of the local authorities: troops were sent to deal with the massed gathering of God Worshippers at Jintian and the smaller group at Huazhou, where the two leaders Hong and Feng were still based. One of their followers, Yang Xiuqing, who appears to have been suffering from psychological problems very similar to those that had attended Hong's original visions, recovered and led his forces against the government troops, relieving the pressure on Hong and Feng. In January 1851, the two groups of God Worshippers joined forces and managed to defeat the government armies that had been sent to wipe them out. They returned to Jintian where Yang was appointed Chief of Staff and subsequently became the most powerful military leader of the rebel movement. On 1 January 1851, his thirty-eighth birthday, Hong Xiuquan issued a proclamation announcing the birth of a new dynasty – the Heavenly Kingdom of Great Peace [*Taiping tianguo*]. He declared himself to be the Heavenly King [*Tian Wang*] and, from that day, issued edicts under that title.[11]

It was not uncommon for Chinese rebel leaders to declare themselves to be the founders of new dynasties, whether or not the new regime ever came to fruition, but this declaration does give a clear indication of the long-term intentions of the Taipings. During 1851 the Taipings remained in south-eastern Guangxi and were involved in a series of clashes with the forces of the local government and also with groups of bandits and brigands, some of whom had allied themselves with the government against the rebels. It was during this early period of conflict that the military organisation of the Taipings began to emerge.

The first recorded edict of the Heavenly King, given at Jintian and dated 15 August 1851, set out the basic precepts of the Taiping:

> First, obey the Heavenly Commandments.
> Second, distinguish men's quarters from women's quarters.
> Third, avoid causing the slightest damage.
> Fourth, be public-minded and harmonious, and each of you obey your leaders' restraining hands.
> Fifth, unite your minds and combine your efforts, and do not, when going into battle, flee from the field.[12]

The commandments, the separation of men and women, the unquestioning obedience to the leadership and the importance of preparing for battle were all central to the thinking of the Taiping leadership. The religious element was not simply grafted on: the commandments were an integral part of the discourse within the movement. Moral, military and social policies and the edicts of the Heavenly King were all expressed in religious terms:

> The Taiping movement was forged into an indoctrinated army, the tool with which the Taiping leaders hoped to conquer the country and establish their rule. As the model for their army, the Taiping leaders used the classical *Zhouli* system, a utopian organisation as-cribed to the Duke of Zhou, the founder of the Zhou dynasty. In this system, the civilian and military organisations were combined. The people were farmer-soldiers who did their productive work for society and took up arms when the need arose. Their military of-ficers were also their magistrates, and the military and civilian aspects of government were not separated.[13]

The core of the Taiping military organisation was fashioned at Jintian and consisted of about 7,000 troops. Hong Xiuquan is credited with the organ-isation of the military units, but the assistance of his trusted second-in-command Feng Yunshan was also critical in the success of this process and there is considerable evidence to suggest that Yang Xiuqing, whose miraculous recovery in the summer of 1850 had saved the two most senior leaders, was the military genius behind the organisation.

Two of the key tenets of the Taiping movement, their policies on women and on the ownership of land, were also established during the Jintian period. The position of women in the movement was highly unusual. Women served in separate military units, and men and women were separated and lived in separate encampments. Sexual relations were prohibited, even between married couples, on pain of death. This prohibition was enforced on the basis of a religious ruling that God had ordained chastity for his followers. Relationship between men and women were to be only as between brother and sister. The regulations on chastity appear to have been implemented during the period of the revolution as a necessary disciplinary measure for a tightly organised and highly mobile military force. There was a tacit assumption that there would be a return to sanctioned marital relations on the basis of the Ten Commandments at some unspecified time in the future, but this was to come to pass only after the final victory of the Heavenly Kingdom. Taiping practice in these matters was far from consistent and although the enforced separation of men and women was maintained in some of the cities that they eventually captured, they were not able to apply it universally, especially in the villages. The Taiping leadership were exempt from these restrictions and had their own harems.[14]

Property was important to the Taiping movement, probably because many of their original supporters came from families that had owned little land or none at all. Some had been driven off their land before joining the movement, others had sold their property so that they could be more mobile but all contributed their wealth to the 'common treasury' of the Taiping. This could be interpreted as an example of primitive communism or as an extension of the common wealth of the traditional extended Chinese family to the family of the children of God. The principle of the 'common treasury' was to be used later as the basis for the agrarian law of the Taiping.

From Jintian to Yong'an

The massed ranks of the Taiping rebels left Jintian with the intention of taking their Heavenly Kingdom to the whole of China. They moved eastwards, then turned north and captured the town of Yong'an, just to the east of the Mengshan mountain range, where they remained from 25 September 1851 until 5 April 1852.

The Yong'an period was a formative one for the Taiping leadership and there are striking parallels with the Communist Party's sojourn in Yan'an during the 1940s, parallels not lost on the CCP which saw itself as the inheritor of some of the traditions of the Taipings. Although the rebel elite had emerged during the conflict in and around Jintian, it was at Yong'an that the hierarchical relationships between the leaders were formalised. Taiping documents of the Jintian period mention a group of seven 'brothers' who were elevated above the rest of the movement. The list of 'brothers' began with Jesus; Hong Xiuquan, as the younger brother of Jesus came second. They were followed by Yang Xiuqing, the military hero; Xiao Chaogui, who was close to Yang and claimed to be the channel for the spirit of Jesus; Feng Yunshan, the original organiser of the God Worshippers; Wei Changhui, the early convert and a pawnshop owner and Shi Dakai, a Hakka from Guixian who was also a failed examination candidate and who had led a large contingent to Jintian in the summer of 1850. This band of brothers was the core of the Taiping movement in its earliest phase but it was eventually to become the instrument of its destruction as heavenly cooperation turned into hellish strife and fratricide.

The Heavenly King had already appointed Xiao, Shi, Wei, Feng and Yang as commanders [*zhujiang*] of military units although the Taiping rebels were still in Jintian. Ensconced in Yong'an, he issued an edict on 17 December 1851, an edict in convincing imperial style and language, which was designed to guarantee his own status as Supreme Sovereign (but not as Holy because that epithet was to be reserved for the Heavenly Father and the Heavenly Elder Brother – Jesus), and to formalise the status of the other five Brothers, who became kings [*wang*] in their own right but were subordinate to the Heavenly King. Xiao was to be known as the Western King [*Xiwang*]; Yang the Eastern King [*Dongwang*]; Wei was to be the Northern King [*Beiwang*] and Feng the Southern King [*Nanwang*]. Shi became the Assistant King [*Yiwang*] and had direct responsibility for supporting the court of the Heavenly King. The Eastern King was to be in overall control of the Taiping administration, an appointment that reflected the real power that Yang Xiuqing had acquired even before the new designations had been announced. In 1851 or 1852 the *Taiping Ceremonial Regulations* [*Taiping lizhi*] were published. They prescribed in great detail the precise terms of address that were to be used to all the members of the family of the kings and to the civil officials and military officers of the Taiping. This is a further example of the way that the movement modelled itself on the Confucian practices of the Qing imperial court while trying to retain its revolutionary, quasi-Christian and anti-Manchu stance.[15]

March on Nanjing

From Yong'an, the reinvigorated and reorganised Taipings marched forth to spread their Heavenly Kingdom throughout China, their primary objective being the populous valley of the Yangzi River. They struck out northwards across the Guangxi border and into Hunan, taking care to avoid the towns and cities where they were likely to encounter troops loyal to the Qing and those parts of the countryside where the landlord militias were strong. They moved through the mountainous areas which are the natural borders between counties and provinces and where the writ of the imperial bureaucracy did not run. Resistance in Hunan forced them to divert westwards, but in spite of such military setbacks, including opposition from armed units organised by the local gentry which they were unable to avoid, the Taiping rebels attracted converts or supporters along their route and grew into a movement that may have been over a million strong by the time the rebels reached Nanjing.

In the autumn of 1852, although they failed to take one of their main targets, the Hunan provincial capital of Changsha, they were able to capture sufficient ships on Dongting Lake in the north of Hunan to give them a naval capability which enabled them to move their forces more rapidly towards the city of Wuchang, which they took in January 1853.[16] They organised the population of Wuchang into military units, divided of course into male and female contingents, and these units accompanied the Taiping forces on the next stage of their campaign, the march on Nanjing. On 9 February, 1853 they captured the Yangzi River port of Jiujiang which played a key role in the economy of the north of Jiangxi province, including the distribution and export of porcelain from the renowned ceramic city of Jingdezhen. Anqing, which was at that time the capital of Anhui province, was taken on 24 February, and on 19 March the rebel armies entered Nanjing. Nanjing was the second city of the Chinese empire and had been the first capital of the Ming dynasty from 1368 to 1403, so it was a considerable prize for the rebel armies, both in strategic terms and as a symbol of the threat that they posed to the Qing dynasty.

Heavenly Capital

Hong Xiuquan decided that Nanjing would the capital of the Heavenly Kingdom of Great Peace and renamed it Heavenly Capital (*Tianjing*). Nanjing was of great symbolic significance as it was the capital of the Ming dynasty, a predominantly Chinese dynasty between the conquest regimes of the Mongols and the Manchus. En route to Nanjing, two of the original band of brothers had been killed in battle: Feng Yunshan, the Southern King, fell during a skirmish on the Guangxi-Guangdong border, and Xiao Chaogui, the Western King and the channel for the voice of Jesus, was slain at Changsha. The death of Feng, who had been a close ally of the Heavenly King, left the Eastern King, Yang Xiuqing, in a commanding position, although the loss of Xiao who had been a key supporter was also a considerable blow.[17]

The Taiping leadership set about establishing their kingdom from their new headquarters in Nanjing, although there is evidence of a debate as to whether Nanjing was the proper place for a capital or whether they should move further north. Some scholars have argued that, by settling for Nanjing rather than pushing northwards towards the Manchu capital of Beijing, the Taiping rebels lost the chance to capture the dragon throne.[18] Nevertheless, the Taipings did stop at Nanjing, and it was there that they began to create their new society. It has been estimated that of the one million followers of the Taipings who were involved in the assault on Nanjing, only about 20,000 were originally members and supporters of the God Worshippers from Guangxi: these early disciples became the elite of the movement and the new ruling class of Nanjing.

An energetic publishing programme was launched with the intention of replacing traditional Confucian literature with Taiping alternatives. There was a new edition of the children's reading primer, the *Three Character Classic* [*San zi jing*], in which Confucian concepts were replaced with those of the Taiping. Chinese editions of the Old and New Testaments of the Christian Bible were prepared with annotations by Hong Xiuquan, annotations that were often confused and incoherent as he used these notes to integrate the story of his own life into the biblical narratives. Some Western missionaries were impressed by this endeavour and were optimistic about the opportunities that this might create for mass conversions.[19]

Hong Xiuquan's psychological problems, which had manifested themselves in the original visions of the Heavenly Kingdom, were becoming increasingly severe and the Eastern King, Yang Xiuqing, seized the opportunity to reduce Hong's influence in the movement and to promote himself. This was achieved partly by political manoeuvring and also by the manipulation of the scriptural material that was being published. The *Book of the Principles of Heavenly Nature* [*Tianqing daoli shu*], which was compiled in 1854 on the orders of the Eastern King, was a revivalist document designed to breathe new life into the revolution after the Taipings had been in Nanjing for a year: it was also intended to establish the increased authority of the Eastern King in the minds of the faithful. It is a lengthy text which retells the history and the myths of the Taiping movement, but with the Eastern King rather than the Heavenly King as the central character. The Eastern King consolidated his power over the army and the administration, and, in an imitation of the traditional imperial examination system, introduced a system of competitive examinations for the recruitment of officials to govern the Heavenly Kingdom.

Aside from the conflicts within the leadership, the Taiping administration had to confront two main issues: relations between the sexes and the ownership of land. The segregation of the sexes, which may have been a rational and practical measure for a mobile fighting force, made far less sense in a settled society, and the prohibition of sexual relations between married couples was hard to justify, particularly in view of the fact that the leadership had large harems. Opposition to the policy had grown and, fearing the loss of thousands of their supporters, the leadership reversed their puritanical stance in March 1855 and agreed to allow marriages.

The *Agricultural Property System of the Heavenly Dynasty* [*Tianchao tianmu zhidu*] or the Taiping land law as it is more commonly known was an attempt to apply the principles of military organisation to the administration of agriculture for the most efficient possible production of grain. It was not intended to implement a policy to redistribute land, as the land remained the property of Heaven. Land was to be allocated to groups of families who were supposed to farm it and take sufficient produce for their own use but were then required to make substantial contributions to the common treasury. The regulations were never put into operation to any significant extent, but the ideas that they represented, the blueprint for the centralisation of control of the economy and the militarisation of society, were to have powerful echoes in the course of the century that followed as the Chinese Communist Party drew on the rhetoric and the spirit of the Taipings for its own land policies.[20]

Northern and Western Expeditions of the Taiping

Although the Taiping leaders had settled on Nanjing as the capital of their new dynasty and had established elaborate defences to protect it from the armies of the Qing, they were deeply committed to the destruction of the Manchu empire, and to this end they deployed two expeditionary forces to the north and to the west of their stronghold during the spring of 1853. The soldiers of the Taiping Northern Expedition took the ancient commercial centre of Yangzhou on 1 April and moved rapidly through the provinces of Anhui and Henan, adding to their numbers as they marched and often gaining recruits from the scattered bands of Nian rebels in the northern provinces (see below). They failed to capture a strategic town on the Henan-Shanxi border after a siege that lasted for two months but they did manage to penetrate Zhili (the district administered directly from the imperial capital, Beijing, and roughly equivalent to the modern province of Hebei), and their forces reached the outskirts of the city of Tianjin, which was an important trading port by virtue of its access to the Grand Canal and a series of rivers that enter the sea at the Gulf of Bohai. By mounting this operation the Taipings had gravely overextended themselves, and in spite of the dispatch of reinforcements from the Heavenly Capital, the Northern Expedition was wiped out.[21]

The forces of the Western Expedition set out from Nanjing on 19 May and recaptured the Anhui provincial capital Anqing, which the Taipings had taken on their original march from Guangxi but had subsequently lost to Qing armies. The expeditionary forces then divided and the armies that took the southern route failed to take Nanchang but did capture Xiangtan in Hunan in April 1854. Although this was a significant military achievement, the Taiping rebel regime was now at the height of its influence and was unable to expand any further.

Taiping Leadership Crisis

The band of celestial brothers, now somewhat depleted by deaths in battle, had also become riven with factionalism; the factions of each of the kings were based on family, regional and personal allegiances. The Eastern King, Yang Xiuqing, controlled the most powerful faction and was a threat to the authority of the remaining kings, the Heavenly King (Hong Xiuquan), the Northern King (Wei Changhui) and the Assistant King (Shi Dakai). The political conflict within the leadership came to a head on 2 September 1856 when the Northern King's troops assassinated the Eastern King and had all his family and supporters killed, possibly as many as 20,000 men and women all told. To keep the myth of the divine leadership alive, the Taipings announced that the Eastern King had ascended into heaven. It is not clear whether the Northern King had decided on the massacre himself or whether he was acting on orders from the Heavenly King, whose authority the Eastern King had usurped, but in any event the Northern King was blamed for the killing and for attempting to annihilate the family of his rival the Assistant King. The Assistant King, who had been on manoeuvres with his troops in Hubei, returned to the Heavenly Capital to take revenge and the Heavenly King sent his own troops to assassinate the Northern King and to wipe out his family and supporters.

This left only two of the original kings, the Heavenly King and the Assistant King, but by this time, the Heavenly King's brothers, Hong Renda and Hong Renfa, were beginning to acquire considerable influence over their divine and unstable elder brother. Shi Dakai, the Assistant King, was persuaded by the Heavenly King to take on the dual role of head of the government and head of the military, but he remained in Nanjing only from the end of November 1856 until the end of May 1857. His position had been undermined by the two Hong brothers and he even felt that his life was in danger from their supporters. He eventually left the Heavenly Capital to strike out on his own, taking thousands of Taiping troops and some of the more able officers with him. In due course, he went on to become a thorn in the side of the Qing general Zeng Guofan, who was distracted by this disaffected band from his main preoccupation with wiping out the administrative centre and military and political power base of the Taiping.[22]

In the event it was not the two Hong brothers who came to the aid of the stricken regime, but a cousin, Hong Rengan, who had been a follower of the Heavenly King, Hong Xiuquan, since the early days of the Jintian rising. Hong Rengan had been prevented from taking part in the initial rising in Guangxi by his family, who had decided that he was too young, and instead he was dispatched to Hong Kong, where he studied with a Protestant Missionary, the Reverend Issachar Roberts, the same I.J. Roberts who had influenced the young Hong Xiuquan. Hong Rengan spent some time working with the China Inland Mission as a teacher to Chinese converts. After several unsuccessful attempts he finally succeeded in reaching the Taiping capital on 22 April 1859. He was warmly welcomed by his cousin and within a few weeks, and apparently to his great surprise, he was promoted into the depleted and increasingly desperate Taiping hierarchy with the title of Shield King [*Gan wang*].

Hong Rengang came to the Taiping capital with far more knowledge of Protestant Christianity, and indeed of the outside world, than any of the core of original leaders who had long been isolated, both on their march from Guangxi and in the Heavenly Capital. He had decided that the twin goals of his mission were to educate the Taipings in what he understood to be the true version of Christianity and to establish close relations between the Heavenly Capital and the western Christian community in China. He also advocated administrative reforms and established a new bureaucracy to replace the one that had collapsed after the assassination of the Eastern King. As the Heavenly King's health continued to decline, Hong Rengan's authority increased, but there were now two new rivals, Chen Yucheng and Li Xiucheng, who had been high-ranking Taiping generals before Hong's arrival, and had been installed respectively as the Heroic King [*Ying wang*] and the Loyal King [*Zhong wang*] shortly after Hong's own ennoblement. Hong did not have the ability or the authority to control the military, unlike Chen, and particularly Li, and he was rapidly moved to the sidelines.

Zeng Guofan and the Hunan Army

Although the members of the Taiping elite were preoccupied with factional conflict and the ensuing carnage and attempting, but failing, to salvage the Heavenly Kingdom, the Qing dynasty was devising new strategies for confronting this rebellion, which threatened, like no other in its history, to overthrow it. During the march of the Taiping forces on Nanjing, one of their failures had been an attack on the city of Xinning in Hunan province.

The regular troops of the Qing army who were stationed in Hunan were no match for the Taiping, but a new type of army, recruited and organised by the local gentry, had been successful in repelling the rebel attack.[23] The Manchus were eventually persuaded that this new-style army was the only way forward. This was a radical break with tradition as it had been axiomatic for centuries that locally raised armies were too great a risk: they could threaten the carefully balanced political structure of the imperial state and create the possibility of the establishment of new regional feudal kingdoms based on independent military power. Such was the threat from the Taiping that this tradition was put to one side and, while it was to succeed in its immediate objective of suppressing the rebellion, in the long term this solution proved to be fatal for the Qing. The military structures that evolved from these new regional armies were eventually to become the agents of destruction of not only the Manchu dynasty but also the entire imperial system in the Revolution of 1911.

The principal author of these military reforms was Zeng Guofan (1811–72), a career official in the imperial civil service and a native of Hunan province. He was designated as one of 43 superintendents of local gentry militia that the Qing had reluctantly commissioned in 1852 and 1853, specifically to counter the threat of the Taiping rebellion. Zeng realised that if he were to have any prospect of completing the task assigned to him in Hunan, he would need far more than a minor local militia, and he set about creating a substantial, tightly disciplined provincial army, the Hunan or Xiang Army [*Xiang jun*]. This new-style army recruited soldiers in the rural areas, and each unit consisted of men from the same village, speaking the same dialect and was led by a local officer to whom they owed loyalty. These officers in turn would be answerable directly to Zeng Guofan. Zeng attempted to pay his troops well and regularly, which was not always the case in the imperial Chinese military, and he had access to internal customs revenues (the *lijin* or likin tax) which made it possible for him to do this. To get this new and heterodox military development past the censorate in the Imperial Court, Zeng was careful to report only part of what he was actually creating.

Zeng's new army was organised in 1853 and first saw action against the Taipings in the early part of 1854. It suffered some reverses in its initial engagements but achieved significant victories in the battles of Xiangtan on 1 May 1854 and Yuezhou in July, both engagements taking place in Hunan, its home province. In October of the same year, Zeng's troops recaptured the Yangzi river towns of Wuchang and Hanyang. Government forces also blockaded the Taiping territory from bases to the north and south of Nanjing, and this blockade was broken only in June 1856 when Taiping units were redeployed from their battles with the Hunan Army.[24]

In 1860, Zeng Guofan was appointed governor general of the Liang Jiang, the central Yangzi region which corresponds roughly to the present-day provinces of Jiangsu and Jiangxi, and concurrently as Imperial Commissioner entrusted with the suppression of the Taiping rebellion. He had been out of action for a period of mourning following the death of his father but returned with greater powers and access to more funds to pursue his campaign. His appointment was in breach of the long-standing convention that no official could serve in his home province, a further indication of the severity of the threat to the Qing empire and the willingness of the court to compromise with tradition to preserve its rule. To supplement his Hunan army, Zeng supported the creation of the Huai Army under Li Hongzhang, which was based in the lower Yangzi valley, and a similar force, raised in Hunan and intended for deployment in Zhejiang and other areas south of the Yangzi under the command of Zuo Zongtang. Zeng had conceived a careful strategy for the destruction of the Taiping forces and their main positions were wiped out one by one, but these defeats were accomplished as much because of internal dissension within the Taiping movement as by the tactical brilliance of Zeng Guofan.

The final campaign against the Heavenly Capital began in the summer of 1862, but Nanjing did not finally fall to the Qing forces until 19 July 1864 when troops under the command of Zeng Guofan's brother Zeng Guoquan broke through a section of the city wall. The Taipings refused to surrender, and Zeng Guofan reported to the Imperial Court that over 100,000 people had been killed in the final assault. Much of the city was destroyed by fire. The Heavenly King died before the collapse of his kingdom, but not long before; he perished on 1 June 1864 after a long illness, possibly as a result of taking poison. His death was kept secret for several days and he was succeeded by his son, the Young Monarch, but the Taiping regime was finished, and it remained only for Zeng and his allies to mop up the remnants of the leaderless armies around Nanjing.[25]

Westerners and the Taiping Heavenly Kingdom

Many Westerners living in China in the mid-nineteenth century were impressed and encouraged by news of a revolutionary movement that appeared to be based on Christian teachings. Reports of the rise of the Taiping Heavenly Kingdom appeared in the journal *Chinese Repository* as early as August 1850, and an initial sense of alarm at news of an unfamiliar and powerful rebel movement not far from Guangdong province – where Western commercial interests were strongest – was tempered by the hope that the Taipings might prove to be sympathetic allies in the European and American missionary enterprise. Contacts were made with the rebels, first by the British navy and later by missionaries. After a closer examination of the nature of the Taiping regime and the spiritual claims made by Hong Xiuquan and his followers, especially Hong's claim to be the younger brother of Jesus, the initial enthusiasm of the missionaries began to wane, and the Taipings were denounced as imposters by most Western Christians in China. In the words of a missionary historian who was later to be the Bishop-designate of Eastern Sichuan, 'As the ideals of its leaders deteriorated and province after province was devastated ... opinion [among Westerners] rallied to the support of the Imperial Government'. Missionaries coming to terms with their disappointment regarded Hong Xiuquan as having been no more than a 'partly instructed enquirer' and conceded that the hopes based on his earlier proclamations, and his eagerness to circulate the Scriptures, were gradually disillusioned. Dr Griffith John, the pioneer Welsh missionary who was in China during the Taiping rebellion, tried to put a positive slant on the failure of the Taipings to live up to the optimism of Western missionaries and concluded 'that God [was] uprooting idolatry in this land through the insurgents, and that He will by means of them, in connection with the foreign missionary, plant Christianity in its stead'.[26]

The desire of Westerners to preserve their commercial and diplomatic interests prompted the creation of a Volunteer Corps (more unkindly, but probably more accurately, described as a mercenary army) that assisted Li Hongzhang's Huai army in its struggle against the Taipings. This army was organised and trained by an American swashbuckler, Frederick Townsend Ward and, after Ward's death on the battlefield in 1863, by the British officer, Charles G. Gordon. As a result of his exploits in the battle against the Taipings, Gordon became known as 'Chinese' Gordon to the contemporary chroniclers of the British Empire, but this soubriquet was replaced after his heroic death in the Sudan and he is more usually encountered in Western history books as Gordon of Khartoum. The Western-trained troops were rather optimistically named the Ever Victorious Army [*Changsheng jun*] by the emperor: they played a small role in the defeat of the Taiping rebellion but the real credit belongs to Zeng Guofan and Li Hongzhang, and their new model armies.[27]

Nian Insurgency

The rising of the Nian armies *Nianjun* which took place between 1851 and 1868 was almost exactly contemporary with the Taiping rebellion, but it affected the north rather than the south of China. The two rebellions were firmly both in the secret society tradition of the peasantry and the dispossessed, but there were striking differences between them: there was some overlap between the two and even a degree of cooperation but they were essentially separate uprisings. Unlike the Taipings, the Nian had no single charismatic leader, although there were individual commanders who enjoyed widespread support. Nor was there an ideological basis to the Nian rising other than a broad antagonism towards the rule of the Manchu Qing dynasty. Although there is evidence of a historical link to the White Lotus society or at least a loyalty to the White Lotus tradition, the Nian did not have a distinctive religious or ideological identity: its forces were essentially armed outlaw bands that had developed from village self-defence organisations. These bands had been organised for as far back as anyone could remember in times of famine, and in the nineteenth century they united in loose coalitions against Qing officialdom.[28]

The Nian heartland was in the region north of the Huai river (and therefore known as Huaibei, as *bei* means north), which straddles the borders of the present-day provinces of Henan, Shandong, Jiangsu and Anhui. It is on the southern limits of the North China Plain and is characterised by poor sandy soil, low annual rainfall and frequent drought. The main crops grown in the area were millet and *gaoliang*, which is a member of the sorghum family.[29] Although drought was an ever-present danger, the proximity of the Yellow River and poor drainage also exposed the Huaibei region to sporadic catastrophic flooding, and it was not unknown for floods and drought to occur in the same year. From 1851 to 1853, the flooding was unusually severe, and in July 1853 the Yellow River overflowed its banks, crashing through a major dike in Henan province and wiping out towns and villages as it gouged out a new course towards the ocean. Inevitably there was great loss of life and widespread famine, and it was in this time of despair and desperation that the Nian insurrection took shape.[30]

The origins and meaning of the term 'Nian' are obscure, and there is no complete agreement on what the name meant to the people of north China at the time: what is clear is that the name was used by the Nian themselves and was not a disparaging appellation used by the official and landowning classes. The most compelling explanation is that a *nian* was a torch made of strips of paper twisted around a wooden staff. This could be dipped into oil or tallow (animal fat) and set alight to serve as a lantern for night-time activities. 'Nian' also appears to have been used to refer to the groups of men who banded together to form the rebel bands, and the connection may be that they carried such torches or that they were bound together as tightly as the paper strips.[31]

Although the Nian did not have a conscious and developed ideology like that of the Heavenly Kingdom of the Taiping, they were strongly influenced by the traditions of the White Lotus society which had a long history of resistance to the Manchus in northern China: local officials reported during the rising that they considered the Nian to be remnants of the White

Lotus. The Nian dyed their beards red following the traditional practice of White Lotus members: red was the symbolic colour of the Ming dynasty, and this emotional attachment to the memory of the Ming can be seen in the title accorded to the only Nian bandit chieftain who came close to being the overall leader of the movement. He was known as the Great Han King with the Mandate of the Ming Dynasty [*Da Han Mingming wang*]. The inclusion of the name Han in his title implies an opposition by Han Chinese to the alien Manchus and the inclusion of the character for 'mandate' suggests that the mandate of Heaven was being passed to the rebels on the authority of the Ming dynastic line which had died out in the seventeenth century.

The favoured *modus operandi* of the Nian was the mounted raid. The Nian were skilled horsemen and the mobile raiding that they favoured was ideally suited to the North China Plain, a flat landscape with no large rivers to impede their progress. In addition to robbery, the Nian were experts in extortion and ransom, and they were also involved in contraband trade of all kinds, notably the smuggling of salt, which had been a state monopoly for centuries. Salt smugglers operated at night so they were known as 'salt owls' and this trade, which was dangerous but highly lucrative, provided the Nian with funds, and enabled the leadership to acquire organisational skills and authority.[32]

The Nian bands acquired greater authority because of their involvement with the inter-communal feuds that were a feature of Chinese rural life in the imperial period: they often provided local communal leadership when simmering peasant resentment against the authorities boiled over into insurgency. Until 1853, the Nian were still independent groups or bands of brigands, each under the authority of a *tangzhu* or 'lodge master', a name that had echoes of other secret society organisations such as the White Lotus or the Heaven and Earth Society. During the winter of 1852–3, there were determined attempts to combine and unify the diverse bands when the heads of 16 Nian groups agreed to put their resources under an overall leader, Zhang Lexing. The outlaw leaders made a sacrifice to a new flag, a sign that they were moving from banditry towards outright rebellion. The local prefect decided to counter this incipient insurgency in the time-honoured manner of incorporating Zhang and his followers into an officially sponsored militia and the idea of a Nian union was deferred for at least two years.

In late 1855 or early 1856 there was another attempt to consolidate the Nian, this time into five larger bands and once again Zhang Lexing emerged as the overall leader. Zhang was formally designated Lord of the Alliance [*mengzhu*] in January 1856, and the richly symbolic title of Great Han King with the Mandate of the Ming Dynasty was also conferred on him on this occasion. The five enlarged Nian units were organised as banners [*qi*] under a colour system that ironically mirrored the banner organisation of the hated Manchus. This represented a significant step forward for the centralisation of the Nian military organisation, but underlying this reorganisation there remained the powerful local clan system, which ensured a broad base of support for the Nian leaders.[33]

'Earth Wall' Communities and Nian Cavalry

Nian villages in the Huaibei region were defended by the construction of 'earth walls'. Although such defensive earthworks were not uncommon in rural China, the way they were utilised by the Nian was quite distinctive. Earthworks were reinforced with bricks and this construction was topped by parapets which could protect defenders while they were firing small arms if the village came under siege. It is not clear when they were first developed in the Huaibei region, but there are records of resistance by fortified villages to government forces in 1855, at about the same time that the Taiping rebellion was spreading northwards. Between 1856 and 1859 the Nian concentrated their forces in a series of these walled villages between the Sha and the Hui rivers in the northern part of Anhui province. Some of these villages were captured by the Nian and incorporated by force, but there is also evidence of popular support for the bandits who could provide protection for starving and desperate peasants against the depredations of unscrupulous local officials.[34]

Mounted warfare is not usually associated with peasant movements in China: it was rarely practicable in southern China where the terrain is mountainous, roads are poor and there are many rivers, large and small, that would impede the movement of cavalry units. However across the whole of the north of China, the horse has for centuries played an important role in rebellions and in the suppression of rebellions. The Mongols and Manchus were renowned for their skills as horsemen and cavalry units manned by Muslim Hui (Dungan) soldiers played a key role in the military organizations of northwestern China. The Nian cavalry were also part of this tradition and used mobile warfare tactics to outsmart government forces. They would mount raids for supplies, often far outside their home territory and then return with their plunder to the safety of their walled villages. It has been estimated that by 1869 the Nian had 20,000 horses at their disposal: some of these horses were bred in their own villages, others were seized as plunder on their expeditions or bought from traders in the north.

Suppressing the Nian

The main military units deployed by the Qing government against the Nian between 1858 and 1865 were detachments of the imperial army, notably the cavalry under the command of the renowned Mongol military hero, Prince Senggerinchin. The Banner forces of the Manchus and the ethnic Han Chinese Army of the Green Standard were neither sufficiently trained or motivated to respond to the severity of the threat to the Qing state that was posed by the rebels nor had sufficient numbers of troops or horses. The ambush and death in battle of Senggerinchin, and the defeat of his troops at Caozhou in the eastern province of Shandong in the spring of 1865 robbed the imperial forces of the only commander in their service whose forces stood a chance of defeating the Nian. Senggerinchin was honoured after his death by Manchus and local Chinese officials alike and in addition to being enshrined in the Ancestral Temple of the Manchus he is remembered in local shrines that still stand in Shandong province.[35] In 1862, after the beginning of the final campaign against the Taiping rebels, the government was able to deploy units of the newly created Hunan army to the north, but it was only after Zeng Guofan replaced Senggerinchin as Imperial Commissioner that the new armies were fully engaged against the rebels. He replaced the Hunan army with the fresher troops of the recently established Huai army and ordered them to deploy to the north to suppress the Nian.[36] By 1865 the Nian were at the height of their power. They had sent armed units to assist the Taiping's abortive northern expedition to Beijing and, as part of an attempt to coordinate the anti-Qing activities of the two rebel armies, the Nian leader Zhang Lexing had earlier been designated a king in the Taiping hierarchy even though he had been killed in an attack by the Qing armies in 1863.

Zeng Guofan moved his Huai army troops northwards in the late spring of 1865. Unlike previous Qing officials who had sought simply to eradicate the rebels, Zeng attempted to understand the social roots of the Nian movement. He surveyed the earth wall communities and helped the peasants to reinforce them as defences against bandit attacks while preventing the mounted Nian raiding bands from returning. Li Hongzhang, who succeeded Zeng as commander of the Huai forces, took the decision to extend his recruitment to the villagers of the Huaibei region, the core area of the Nian rebels: by 1868 as many as 70 per cent of the Huai army may have been from the Huaibei. This undermined the support that the Nian could expect from the villages. Li also actively adopted Western military technology, notably muzzle-loaded rifles which were the most advanced weapons available in China at the time, and developed cavalry units to counteract the mobile forces of the Nian, which had been so successful. He centralised the organisation of the Huai army, forging close bonds between himself and his officers.

Under pressure from the revitalised government forces, the Nian divided into Eastern and Western bands, the Eastern band concentrating on an attack on the strategically important Grand Canal while the Western band headed out to Shaanxi to join the Muslim insurrection that had broken out in the northwest of China. The Huai army mounted a successful blockade of the Nian villages. This deprived the mounted bands of much of their remaining popular support and reduced their ability to replenish their supplies. By the winter of 1867–8, the Eastern Nian had been wiped out. The Western Nian failed to link up with the Hui Muslim rebels and returned to the Huaibei where their military units were annihilated by the Huai army in 1868.[37] The Nian rising was over, but the mystique remained in the memory of the people of the Huaibei region, to be drawn on and rekindled by later generations of rebels and revolutionaries.

Muslim Rebellions – the Hui in Yunnan, Shaanxi and Gansu

Islam does not come immediately to mind as one of the principal religions of China, but there have been Muslims in the Middle Kingdom since the eighth or ninth century and the total Muslim population of China at the beginning of the twenty-first century is generally agreed to be of the order of 20 million although even this figure may be an underestimate. There are Muslim communities throughout China but the largest and most distinctive are found in the northwest, close to the borders with Central Asia and in the southwest especially in Yunnan province.[38]

The Muslim insurrections of the nineteenth century are often considered together a cluster of related rebellions, but in reality the three major outbreaks of violence involving Muslims in the mid-nineteenth century were quite separate geographically and did not have the same economic and social roots. The first insurrection was in Yunnan in southwestern China and was a conflict which lasted from 1855 until 1873 and is sometimes known as the Panthay Rebellion after a Burmese word for Muslim. The second was the Hui rising in the northwest provinces of Shaanxi and Gansu, which took place approximately 1862 and 1878. Hui is the usual name for Chinese-speaking Muslim communities rather than those who speak a Central Asian language. The third outbreak was the insurrection that lasted from 1865 to 1873 and was led by the Central Asian Muslim, Yakub Beg from the city of Kashghar, which he had taken as his capital city. The campaign against the Taiping Heavenly Kingdom, and to a lesser extent the Nian armies, preoccupied the Qing court during this period, and they were unable to deploy substantial numbers of troops to check the progress of any of the Muslim uprisings in their early stages. Once the Taiping and Nian insurrections had been brought under control, the Qing forces were able to turn their attention to suppressing, or as they put it 'pacifying', the Muslims which they did with a vengeance. The classification of these insurrections is important and care should be taken with the terminology: to refer to them as rebellions begs the question of the legitimacy of Qing rule over all the areas in which they took place, particularly in western China, and this legitimacy is disputed by many of the non-Chinese communities of the region.

Yunnan

During the winter of 1855, Han and Hui silver miners in Lin'an (today's Jianshui county, to the south of Kunming) came into conflict over mining rights. Previously productive mineral workings that belonged to Han miners were by this time virtually exhausted, and the Han wanted to work in Hui-owned mines. Hui miners had, however, been experiencing similar problems and turned down the request. The two sides took their cases to law, and the Han failed to secure an order that they be allowed to work in Hui mines. Economic conflict turned into communal violence and countless Hui people were slaughtered by their Han neighbours, their livestock were killed and their farms destroyed. This affected at least 700 families and, in retaliation, hundreds of Hui led by a man named Ma Linghan gathered at Xiaobanqiao, a few miles from Kunming, and took reprisals on anyone they could identify as having helped the killers. Government officials branded the Hui as plotters and the architects of disorder and on 19 May 1856, Qing Sheng, a local official, ordered the indiscriminate killing of Hui people. Han landowners assembled a militia at Lin'an and spent three days searching for and killing any Hui they found, male or female, old or young. Between 4,000 and 7,000 Muslims may have been slaughtered in this pogrom. The Hui community's outraged response to this massacre grew into an armed rebellion against the local officials who had backed their adversaries and, for many, a search for political independence.

In the summer of 1856, groups of Hui led by Ma Jinbao and Lan Pinggui rose in revolt at Yaozhou (known today as Yaoan). In August, Du Wenxiu, who was to become by far the best known Muslim leader of the insurrection, rose at Menghua and attacked and occupied Dali in the west of the province: Hui communities throughout Yunnan followed his lead. Because of the numbers involved, local officials offered an amnesty, but the rebels refused and laid siege to the provincial capital, Kunming, during which the governor, Heng Chun, committed suicide. The Qing authorities drafted in a new governor, Zhang Liangji, and a fresh military commander and instructed them to suppress the insurrection. However, when the siege still had not been lifted by February 1858, the officials had no option but to call in influential Muslim leaders from the provinces of Sichuan and Zhejiang to mediate. Agreements were signed, a compromise was reached and there was a temporary lull in the fighting. However conflict flared up again when Zhang Liangji reneged on the agreements and once again started killing members of the Hui community. The Hui massed in self-defence: Ma Rulong held a mass oath-taking rally in Kunming and Du Wenxiu retook Dali and by May, the entire province was in revolt. Attempts to divide the rebels were partially successful and Ma Rulong capitulated in 1862 and was persuaded to write to Du Wenxiu asking him to surrender. Du stood firm, declaring that the Manchus had occupied China for more than 2,000 years and that the time had come for Han and Hui to work together to overthrow them. He set up an independent government based in Dali and his offices flew a white banner on which were written the words, 'Deprive the Manchu Qing of their Mandate to rule' [*geming Manqing*]. The rebel administration styled its newly created state Pingnan (Pacified South) framed its own laws and established its own structures of government, using Islamic terms for any of its organisations and the titles of individual leaders and officials. At the height of the rebellion, Du Wenxiu's independent sultanate controlled almost half the territory of Yunnan. It was finally crushed by the forces of a new governor, Cen Yuying, who had access to foreign weapons and training methods. Du Wenxiu was captured and publicly beheaded. By the end of the 18-year insurrection in 1873, the death toll ran to hundreds of thousands.[39]

Shaanxi and Gansu

In 1862, the Qing military establishment was paying little attention to the Muslims of the northwest. It was concentrating on an attempt to recapture the old Ming capital of Nanjing from the Taiping rebels. Nanjing had been renamed Heavenly Capital [*Tianjing*] by the Taiping leadership and the Qing accurately identified this insurrection as the major threat to the dynasty. Troop movements to surround Nanjing had left something of a military vacuum in Shaanxi province and in March or April a peasant army from Sichuan and Yunnan, led by Lan Dashun, crossed the border from Sichuan into Hanzhong, the county in the southwest of Shaanxi. Lan Dashun was a Hui Muslim, originally from Shaanxi, who had moved to Yunnan in search of work at a time when the opening of new mines had been creating relative prosperity in southwestern China. Joining forces with other roving bands that had been associated with the Taiping and Nian insurgents, the peasant forces crossed the Wuguan pass and headed for Xi'an, which they reached on 17 May. They failed to capture Xi'an and set out to take other towns. Anti-Hui leaflets began to appear in Huazhou and Weinan. The prefect of Huazhou, while dealing with court cases involving disputes between Han and Hui litigants, had stated openly that the Hui were 'colluding with the Long Hairs (the Taipings) in plotting rebellion' and that 'killing a Hui means one less traitor'.[40]

Government troops in Shaanxi were under strength because of the priority that had been accorded to putting down the Taiping uprising and the provincial authorities encouraged local landlords and officials to establish their own private militias to fight off the rebels. 'Quite naturally, the Chinese gentry organised the Chinese while the [Muslim] religious leaders organised the [Muslims] independently of each other.' This led to tensions between the communities, which was exacerbated by Han accusations that the Hui had supported the Taiping rebels rather than assist the local Han people.[41]

An incident in Huazhou, one of the county-level administrative centres, to the northwest of Xi'an precipitated an episode of serious intercommunal violence and may have been the spark that kindled the conflagration. According to a memorial sent by the Manchu provincial governor, Yingqi, to the emperor, the incident began when a group of Hui soldiers, drafted by the Qing government to help suppress the Taiping rebellion but defeated and returning home, went to a Han trader to buy some bamboo poles. The Han seller suddenly increased the price and the Hui refused to pay. In a brawl that followed several of the Hui were injured and some died, and although the confrontation was brought to an end by local people, a Han crowd later went into the Hui village in the evening and set it alight. The Hui and the Han had already been mobilised into their separate local militias and the ensuing battles were violent and widespread. Fighting soon spread to Weinan which is to the west of Huazhou and Dali which is to the northeast and the rebellion was well under way.[42] The Huazhou militia, a Han armed force, burned down Hui villages and made off with Hui women and property. Provoked by this humiliation, the Huazhou Hui revolted, followed by other Hui people on both banks of the Wei River. The Hui of the Weinan region took up arms in their thousands and sent representatives to liaise with another group of insurgents which was led by a man named Chen Decai. Guided by the Huis, Chen Decai's forces moved into the Weinan region and in late April they arrived in the county town. The two armies stormed Weinan, killed the magistrate Cao Shihe and went on to take Huazhou. Jonathan Lipman has pointed out that the disorder that spread through the Wei valley 'did not follow any pre-arranged plan of rebellion, but rather ran along the lines of communication between Muslim communities, all of which feared and reacted against the threat of Han violence'.[43]

The area around the provincial capital, Xi'an, which had also been one of the ancient national capitals, had remained peaceful until a member of the Han rural elite, Mei Jintang, led a militia unit of more than 2,000 men to attack Hui villages in Chang'an County just outside Xi'an. Hui houses were burned to the ground and their occupants were killed. The militia then proceeded to attack a Hui village, Huichu in the county of Huxian. The entire village was razed to the ground and thousands were killed and their bodies 'left lying in the ashes'. These attacks were repeated in many Hui villages and while the old, the ailing and the helpless were slaughtered, those who could flee regrouped on the banks of the Wei river and organised themselves into armed bands, with which they could defend their remaining villages and then counterattack the Han militia to take their revenge.[44] The towns of Gaoling and Huayi were attacked and in May, the city of Xi'an was surrounded. Xi'an was put under siege on 29 June after the Hui forces had already besieged Tongzhou. Xi'an was almost cut off: it was overcrowded with refugees and its supplies of fuel, salt and other essentials were rapidly running out. Ma Dezhao, the military officer responsible for the defence of the city brought in salt and charcoal from the riverside village of Caodian in spite of an attempted ambush but the siege continued. In July, Hui forces launched an offensive on Jingyan, Sanyuan, Fengxiang and other towns and villages. The whole of Shaanxi exploded into violence. The Qing government's response came in August when the imperial commissioner, Sheng Bao, an officer of the White Bordered Manchu Banner and none too successful veteran of the campaign against the Taiping and Nian rebels, was dispatched to Shaanxi. His entourage was attacked as they crossed the Tong pass and he ensconced himself in Xi'an as soon as he reached the safety of the walled city: at first he resisted instructions to leave the town and suppress the rebels who were still active in Tongzhou and Chaoyi in the east of the province. His forces did eventually lift the siege of Xi'an, and he finally agreed to move to Tongzhou to carry out the policy of the court. In November, imperial forces under the experienced Manchu commander Duolonga entered Shaanxi and the fighting grew more intense. In January 1863, Duolonga was appointed commander of the imperial forces in Shaanxi in place of the disgraced Sheng Bao who was relieved of his command, taken into custody and had all his property confiscated. Duolonga's troops broke through the Hui lines at Wangge and Qiangbai, capturing them on 19 March. By the end of May, eastern Shaanxi was once again effectively under the control of the imperial forces. In October, Lintong, Sanyuan, Jingguan and Fengxiang were retaken and Hui commanders in Shaanxi began to liaise more systematically with their counterparts in Gansu province to the west. Two important cities in Gansu, Guyuan and Pingliang, had been occupied by Hui insurgents and some of the defeated Hui forces in Shaanxi were retreating in that direction.[45]

The Hui rebels of Gansu worked closely with roving bands from outside Shaanxi, including the bands led by Lan Dashun who came back in November 1863 and occupied the walled city of Zhouzhi. In 1862, Hui units in Weihe had responded to the movement of these other armies into Shaanxi by stepping up their anti-Qing activities but in the first month of 1864, some of the outsiders left Shaanxi to return to Nanjing in an attempt to defend the Heavenly Capital against the Qing forces surrounding it. Lan Dashun's forces were routed at Zhouzhi and dispersed in the third month of 1864. Duolonga was injured in the campaign to retake Zhouzhi and died of his wounds but the situation in Shaanxi had been reversed. Within a year, the Heavenly Capital of the Taipings had fallen to Qing forces and this was a major setback for the Hui in Shaanxi as the Qing government was finally able to divert forces to Shaanxi. In the autumn of 1866, Zhang Zongyu led a 60,000-strong Nian army into Shaanxi. Prompted by this move, Hui rebels, sometimes in conjunction with the Nian and sometimes alone, took up arms again and kept the Qing armies on the run. In 1867, Zuo Zongtang, governor [zongdu] of Shaanxi and Gansu and the protégé of Zeng Guofan, moved the units that had suppressed the Taipings to Shaanxi and by the sixth month of 1868 had eradicated the rebel bands within Shanxi and Shaanxi. Hui forces moved out and by the fourth month of 1869 had arrived in Gansu, bringing the conflict in Shaanxi to an end.[46]

At the height of the rising, the Hui forces consisted of approximately 200,000 men in 18 battalions, most of them drawn from the farms, but including also artisans, small traders and pedlars. Many of the main leaders including Ma Shengyan, Ma Zhenhe, Yang Wenzhi and Bai Yanhu were farmers or traders. Others including He Mingtang, Zou Yulong, Ahong Guan, Second Ahong Guo, Second Hezhou Ahong and Feng Junfu were religious leaders. He Mingtang was one of the first to take the lead in the insurrection, but he and Second Hezhou Ahong secretly took part in peace negotiations and the defeats at Wangge and Qiangbai have been blamed on their wavering. Before the end of the fighting in Shaanxi, He Mingtang and two other leaders had capitulated and others had withdrawn to Gansu with their troops, taking more than 100,000 men in total.[47]

After the defeat of the insurrection in Shaanxi, the focus of the conflict shifted westwards to Gansu, an area which then included not only the present Ningxia Hui Autonomous Region but also part of Qinghai province in the vicinity of Xining, and part of eastern Xinjiang stretching from Hami towards Urumqi (Dihua). The whole Gansu region and Shaanxi province was controlled by Zuo Zongtang, the governor general of Shaanxi and Gansu who was based in Lanzhou.[48] There were four main centres of the Hui rising in Gansu. The first was Jinjibao (near present-day Wuzhong) under Ma Hualong and the insurrections in the town of Ningxia (now Yinchuan) and the eastern part of Gansu province were linked to the Hui leadership in Jinjibao. The second was Hezhou (Linxia), which was Ma Zhan'ao's base. The third insurrection, the revolt in the area around Xining was led first by Ma Wenyi and later by Ma Guiyuan and Ma Benyuan: in these two areas, people of the Dongxiang and Salar ethnic groups, who were also Muslims, took part in the rising alongside the Chinese-speaking Hui. In Suzhou (now Jiuquan County) at the northern end of the Gansu corridor, Ma Wenlü was the main leader.[49] Gansu province covered an immense area and the political and military situation in the 1860s was complicated. In addition to the large Hui population, there were also many Han people who resented Manchu domination. On the borders of Gansu and Shaanxi there were also scattered bands of demobilised soldiers, refugees and others who had joined them. In 1869, Hui forces in Jinjibao launched a major campaign to defend their base against government forces. The Qing government unit commanded by a former Hunan army officer, Liu Songshan, suffered a series of defeats: casualties were heavy and many killed, including senior officers. In January 1870, Liu Songshan was shot dead; having lost their commander, the Qing forces beat a hurried retreat. The Hui insurgents launched a counter-attack and rapidly, but temporarily, gained the advantage.

For the Qing government, the turning point was the year 1869 when Zuo Zongtang was finally able to turn his attention away from the Taiping and Nian rebellions and concentrate on suppressing the Hui rising in Gansu. Jinjibao was besieged by government forces in July 1869. Fortified Hui settlements in the surrounding area were taken by the imperial forces and food within the city ran out, the inhabitants having only 'straw, the roots of wheat plants, cattle skins and corpses to eat'. In view of the desperate situation, Ma Hualong decided to surrender himself to the forces of the Qing in the hope that the lives of the besieged troops and people of Jinjibao would be spared. When the imperial troops entered the city in January 1871, they butchered the population. More than 1,000 people were slaughtered, including Ma Hualong, and the loss of their base of Jinjibao was a serious blow to the rebels. Ma Hualong is still revered as one of the heroes of the rising and is venerated by Muslims as a shaykh of his Sufi order. The name and the town of Jinjibao were erased after the defeat of the Hui insurrection, but not far from the site, near the thriving town of Wuzhong, is the Honglefu Sufi complex [daotang], which has a tomb said to contain the remains of Ma Hualong. It belongs to the Jahriyya [*Zheherenye*] order, the largest of the Sufi orders in China.[50]

Although the Jinjibao campaign was at a critical stage, Hui troops from Hezhou launched an attack eastward in an attempt to provide support. Their attack was launched via Anding (present-day Dingxi), Tongwei, Taian, Qingshui, Taizhou, Xihe and Lixian, posing a serious threat to the Qing government's Southern Route Army. In August 1871, Zuo Zongtang's forces took Anding, and Hui forces countered to defend Hezhou. They constructed robust defence works on the west banks of the Tao River placing their finest Hui, Salar and Dongxiang marksmen inside.[51] In early 1872, the decisive battle of Taizi Mosque broke out during which Qing forces attacking the Hui strongholds were badly beaten and dispersed. This was probably Zuo Zongtang's worst defeat in the northwest with losses of officers and men and serious problems with supplies of food. In 1873, Ma Zhan'ao, the senior Muslim commander in Hezhou, and probably a follower of the Khufiyya Sufi order, the main rival of the Jahriyya order, sent his subordinate, Ma Jun to negotiate a truce with Zuo Zongtang, effectively bringing to an end the ten-year campaign of the Hui in that part of Gansu. Rivalry between the Sufi orders and the many sub-orders had constantly frustrated any attempts at a united front by Hui Muslims against the Qing government. Zuo Zongtang was prepared to negotiate on terms other than an unconditional surrender for a number of reasons. The losses sustained by the Qing forces in the battle of Taizi Mosque had convinced him that a prolonged siege of Hezhou would be even more costly. He was also persuaded that Ma Zhan'ao, a follower of the more moderate Khufiyya order would be prepared to serve the emperor and that this would be a successful example of 'using the Hui to control the Hui' [*yi Hui zhi Hui*]. This can be seen as an instance of Hui and Han elites forming an alliance to control ethnic tension and the pressure from the Hui peasantry. Whatever the reason, Ma Zhan'ao and his extended family were able to preserve their control over the Hezhou region.[52] According to information given by local people to the members of a French expedition led by Comte Henri-Marie Gustave d'Ollone (1868–1945), which travelled through many of the Muslim areas of China at the dawn of the twentieth century some years after the capture of Jinjibao and Ningxia and the execution of Ma Hualong, Zuo Zongtang offered an amnesty to the Hui inhabitants of Hezhou. The only condition was that they were prohibited from living in the town itself. The mosques were converted to Buddhist temples and the Hui population was confined to the southern suburbs outside the wall.[53]

In September 1872, the fighting spread to Xining, the main town in the Qinghai region. Bai Yanhu, and other Hui from Shaanxi, together with Hui and Salar bands from Qinghai, joined forces to resist the Qing troops which had been sent to subdue their rebel bands. In the canyons and gorges to the east of Xining, the Hui insurgents constructed sturdy fortifications and fought more than 50 skirmishes with the Qing forces causing them heavy losses and driving them back. However, the offensive by the Qing army and what they perceived as their betrayal by the Hui gentry finally proved too much for the Hui rebels and they were forced to retreat. Bai Yanhu went north to Datong and turned again towards Hexi. Ma Guiyuan and his younger brother retreated to Xunhua. Xunhua fell to the imperial troops and the Ma brothers were executed. By January 1873 the insurrection in Qinghai had come to an end.

With the collapse of the Hui forces in Jinjibao, Hezhou and Xining, Suzhou (now Jiuquan) in the remote desert region of northwestern Gansu became the only remaining stronghold of the combined Shaanxi and Gansu Hui rebel forces which had harried the Qing armies since Spring 1865. This Suzhou is not to be confused with the city of gardens, canals and bridges in southern China but lies near the westernmost outpost of the Chinese empire, Jiayuguan. In March 1873, when Bai Yanhu retreated to Hexi, he joined forces with the Suzhou insurgents but they buckled under pressure from the government forces. Bai retreated to Xinjiang and the insurrectionary forces in Suzhou were able to hold out only until September: the besieged citizens of Suzhou were reduced to eating their horses but would not capitulate. When Zuo Zongtang's troops finally entered the town there was a massacre.[54]

Although the insurrections in Shaanxi, Gansu and Qinghai, like those of Yunnan and Xinjiang, are usually described as Muslim rebellions, the role of religion and religious affiliation was often confusing. Islam provided the most significant indicator of the distinction between the Hui and the Han. However, the diversity of sects and Sufi orders and their mutual antagonism militated against Muslim unity against the Han and contributed to the defeat of the risings. In addition, the likelihood of individuals or families supporting or opposing the risings could depend as much on their social position as on their creed or ethnic origins. Landowners, whether Hui or Han, often found that they had far more in common with each other than with Hui peasants and in particular with the roaming bands of dispossessed Hui insurgents who moved through their region.

After the suppression of the rebellions in the northwest, Zuo Zongtang, as governor general, issued a number of injunctions in a carefully thought out and methodically implemented plan designed to shatter Hui solidarity and undermine the authority of the religious structures that had underpinned the risings. In Gansu and Qinghai, for example, all those classified as Shaanxi Hui were required to leave their homes and return to Shaanxi, although in many cases they had been settled in Gansu for generations.

Thousands of Hui families were resettled in new colonies. Zuo ordered that they be allocated land to farm, tools and seed at the discretion of the government and that provision should be made for the poor and needy, especially orphans, widows and the disabled. Zuo ordered that on resettlement the Hui were not to be treated as rebels but as good and loyal subjects. However, permits were needed for any Muslim wishing to travel out of the reserved areas. Sufi and other sectarian organisations were outlawed and Muslims were forbidden to conceal horses, weapons or ammunition. Resettled families had to have a plaque on their doors indicating the names, age, native place and sex of the family members. The families would by this means be integrated into the neighbourhood watch system [*baojia*] that was used throughout China. Zuo Zongtang's policies are seen by the Han Chinese as determined but scrupulous, directed at integrating the Hui rather than exterminating them. Hui commentators tend to be less positive, viewing it as discrimination and confinement to reservations.[55] This demographic engineering predated Stalin's policies of forced internal migration by 60 years and it transformed the population map of northwestern China.

It is difficult to exaggerate the scale of the devastation caused to northwest China, and to its Muslim population in particular, by this insurrection and its suppression by the armed forces of the Qing dynasty and by a similar campaign waged after a subsequent uprising in 1895. Contemporary accounts of this later rising and its repression all focus on the carnage left in its wake:

> It is stated by those who visited the province soon after the rebellion, that the soldiers and not the insurgents destroyed and looted the villages and devastated the country. Rebel bands scoured the country and great distress and even cannibalism are said to have prevailed. Colonel Bell affirms that the population of [G]ansu was reduced from 15,000,000 to 1,000,000, and that nine out of ten Chinese were supposed to have been killed, and two out of every three Mohammedans. These figures may be somewhat overstated, but in an extended journey through the province he states that 'all the villages and farmsteads for miles and miles in all directions were in ruins, and the huge cultivable hills were for the most part deserted'.[56]

Zuo Zongtang, the official responsible for the suppression of the insurrection reported in a memorial to the emperor that 'with the exception of the 2,000 or more Muslims who fled together with Bai Yanhu, there are no more than 60,000 of the original 700,000 Shaanxi Muslims who have survived to be rehabilitated in Gansu'.[57] The number of refugees resettled was probably nearer to 70,000 to 80,000, but the scale of the slaughter is not in dispute.[58]

Yakub Beg and the Creation of Xinjiang

Modern Chinese politicians, whether affiliated to the Communist Party or the Nationalist Guomindang, contend that Xinjiang has always been an integral part of China: in reality it has been a contested territory for centuries. Indisputable political control by the Chinese empire over its northwestern Muslim frontiers, rather than simply a degree of political influence or a formal tributary relationship, dates only from the eighteenth century. The name Xinjiang (New Frontier) was probably not used for the first time until 1768 it was not designated a province of China until 1884 and until modern times the region was more commonly known as Chinese Turkestan, Eastern Turkestan, or, by most Chinese, as the Western Regions [*Xiyu*].

The Qing dynasty was expansionist and its armies conquered vast tracts of land on its inner Asian borders, almost doubling the amount of territory under the control of the emperor in Beijing. The Manchu homeland, Mongolia, Eastern Turkestan and Tibet were gradually incorporated into the vast empire of the Qing. As the armies moved westwards so did the influence of the Han Chinese, their language and their culture, although this was never the intention of the Qing administration, and there were strenuous attempts to restrict the migration of Chinese to the newly acquired frontier territories, particularly during the eighteenth century. Nevertheless, Han Chinese immigration into these regions was substantial. This was largely due to the problems faced by the Qing government in financing its garrisons in these distant outposts. The court became heavily dependent on merchants from China Proper for assistance in supplying these garrisons, and a complex relationship grew up between the Han Chinese, Hui Muslims (then more usually known as Dongan or Tungan) and local Uyghur traders, although the traders from China seem to have become the most prosperous.[59]

The administrative centre of the Qing conquerors of Eastern Turkestan was the city in northwestern Xinjiang, variously known as Ili in Russian, Yining in Chinese and Ghulja to the Kazakhs and Uyghurs: Ili had also been the capital of the Zunghar steppe empire. The Qing built a new settlement to the west of the old city of Ghulja, a practice that had been followed in the conquest of many of the other cities of northwestern China, and the old city was renamed Ningyuan. Although the region was heavily garrisoned, as far as possible the Qing officials ruled at arm's length. They relied on existing political and religious structures and did not have close contact with the indigenous population. There was little interference in the traditional religious beliefs and customs of the region, which were predominantly Muslim, and the Islamic calendar and traditional forms of dress were tolerated by the Qing authorities. In southern Xinjiang in particular, a complex and hierarchical native civil and religious bureaucracy evolved: these were based on the *begs* (heads of powerful families) and the *akhonds* (Imams) who controlled their villages or towns ostensibly in the name of the Qing emperor but in practice independently and by the application of Islamic law.

The city of Dihua, (also spelled Ti-hua or Tihwa but better known today by its modern name of Urumqi) became the military and administrative centre of northeastern Xinjiang, controlling communications to the north of the Tianshan mountains and the settlements of Hami and Turpan. Manchu or Mongol bannermen controlled the southwest of Xinjiang from their base at Kashghar. The rank and file of the garrison troops were drawn from a motley collection of people from northern and eastern China, perhaps some 20,000 in all, including bannermen from the area around Beijing, Mongolian nomads from the northern steppes, minority tribes from Manchuria including Xibo, Solon and Daghur Mongols and Chinese members of the Army of the Green Standard who were transferred westwards from their bases in Shaanxi and Gansu. These occupation forces were the basis for the non-Uyghur, non-indigenous layer of Xinjiang's social structure in the nineteenth and twentieth centuries.

The Qing dynasty's military administration encountered constant political and religious resistance to its control of Xinjiang, often allied to Islamic forces in the neighbouring khanate of Khokand which lay to the west. The city of Khokand is in the modern state of Uzbekistan between the capital Tashkent and Ferghana. Jahangir and Baha'ad-Din, sons of Samsuq, one of the Makhdumzada khojas who controlled Khokand, declared a *jihad* in 1820 and invaded southern Xinjiang after the Khan of Khokand's demands for commercial privileges in Kashghar were refused by the Qing authorities. This invasion was resisted but the massacre of the Khan's supporters in Xinjiang by the Qing army prompted a further incursion in 1826 and an attack on the Qing garrison of Kashghar, which the Khokandis held under siege for ten weeks. When food and water ran out, the Qing officers committed suicide, and their troops tried to escape but they in turn were massacred by the Khokandis. Jahangir's army took the fort of Kashghar and burned down the Manchu settlements. They held the town until a Qing army was sent to retake it in 1827, and Jahangir and his followers fled into the mountains. Jahangir was betrayed by fellow Muslims and was captured and executed by the Qing government. All trade and communication across the mountains to Khokand was banned and newly arrived residents were sent back in an attempt to isolate the citizens of southern Xinjiang from the Muslim communities outside the frontiers of China. There was a further attempt at an invasion in 1830, this time under the direct and explicit orders of the Khan of Khokand, but the attack was beaten off by Qing forces partly because the Khokandi troops were obliged to withdraw to deal with an escalating conflict between Khokand and the rival Central Asian khanate of Bukhara. The Qing authorities increased the number of troops stationed in the Altishahr, the south of present day Xinjiang, and fortified the city of Yarkand to act as their administrative centre. In 1831, in a complete break with previous Qing policy in Inner Asia, the first Han immigrants from China were allowed to move into southern Xinjiang to cultivate reclaimable land or to take over land that had been abandoned during the conflict. A treaty with the Khanate of Khokand was signed in 1835, and Khokand was given permission to station commercial agents in the Altishahr and to appoint an ambassador in Kashghar.[60] However, unrest among the Muslims of Khokand and their supporters in Kashghar was to continue for decades, culminating in an incursion into Kashghar in 1865 by Buzurg Khan who was eventually replaced by his deputy, the far better known Yakub Beg. Yakub Beg declared himself to be the ruler of an independent khanate based on Kashghar and expanded his influence into northern Xinjiang, prompting the invasion and occupation of the Ili region by Russian forces. Within the Qing court there was a prolonged debate on whether forces should be deployed to recover Xinjiang from Yakub Beg's 'rebel' regime. It was by no means a foregone conclusion that western Xinjiang would be recaptured, and this is one of the strongest arguments to suggest that the Qing court was at best equivocal about its legal title to the region and that there were also serious doubts about the viability, and even the necessity, of retaining it within the boundaries of the Chinese empire.

Among those who favoured allowing the territory to remain in the hands of the *khojas* and their supporters, the best known is Li Hongzhang, one of the greatest statesmen of the Qing and a proponent of the modernisation of China's defences and its economy. On the other hand, Zuo Zongtang, another major moderniser of the Qing period, argued persuasively that Xinjiang should be retained within the territory of the Chinese Empire. After the suppression of the Hui Muslim rebellion in Gansu in 1873, the government finally approved the proposal for the re-conquest of Xinjiang. Yakub Beg's forces were defeated by the armies of the Qing in 1878, and the region was formally incorporated into the Chinese empire as the province of Xinjiang in 1884 during the period of the intense British and Russian imperial rivalry in Central Asia that became known, somewhat romantically, as the Great Game.[61]

4

RESTORATION AND WESTERN COLONISATION (1856–1898)

In the final 40 years of the nineteenth century the Qing dynasty struggled to preserve its rule over China. This period is often considered to have been the 'restoration' of the Qing dynasty, a term that invites comparison with the Meiji Restoration of 1868 which marked the beginning of Japan's rapid modernisation, although that was an imperial restoration only on a superficial level. The restoration of Qing dynastic rule began during the reign of the Tongzhi emperor (1862–75) and has therefore been styled the Tongzhi Restoration, although the term is often used for developments that continued after the end of the Tongzhi reign period. There were heroic attempts to strengthen the defences of the empire and to develop a new economic sector of mining and heavy industry to support these defences, but these had limited success in the long term. Although there was also pressure for political reform, this was resolutely resisted by the conservative Manchu court. Only in the conduct of foreign affairs was there any significant political modernisation with the creation of the Zongli Yamen, which was established to enable the court to come to terms with the new reality of foreign powers that were confronting China on an equal or a superior basis, and not as inferiors which had been the assumption of the old tribute system. Towards the end of this period of restoration in China, the empire of Japan, which had been subject to similar pressures but had responded in a more positive manner, began to adopt an assertive foreign policy and embarked on its own colonial enterprise, beginning with incursions into the eastern frontiers of China.

Arrow War and *Zongli Yamen*

Even after the catastrophe of the Opium War, it took another 20 years, a second war with Britain and two humiliating treaties before the Qing ruling elite came to terms with the need to reform the way that it conducted its relations with the West. It has been argued that the failure to do so previously was mainly the result of factionalism within the bureaucracy, between Chinese and Manchu officials and also between different factions among the Chinese scholar official class, but the malaise had deeper roots in the cultural complacency that permeated the Chinese ruling elite.[1] The reform of China's diplomatic administration took place before the beginning of the Tongzhi reign but it did set the tone for the way the court of the Tongzhi emperor dealt with the foreign threat.

This reform was prompted by the *Arrow* incident. The *Arrow* was a ship, a hybrid vessel known technically as a *lorcha*, which had a Western hull but Chinese rigging. It was owned by a Chinese subject but was registered in Hong Kong and sailed under a British flag of convenience. On 8 October 1856, the *Arrow* was boarded off the port of Guangzhou (Canton) by Chinese troops who suspected the crew of engaging in piracy. The British Consul in Guangzhou, Harry Parkes, demanded an apology for the raid, which he considered to be an insult to the British flag. Although the crew were released no apology was forthcoming and in reprisal, the British navy shelled the city of Guangzhou causing widespread destruction. French and American forces supported the attack by the British, and the port of Guangzhou was besieged throughout the whole of 1857. It finally fell to a combined attack by the British and French on 29 December. This conflict, although it had no direct connection with the opium issue, is often known as the Second Opium War or alternatively as the *Arrow* War.[2]

The Treaty of Tianjin which concluded this brief conflict was signed the following year: it would be more accurate to describe it as a series of treaties becuase separate agreements were concluded with each of the major powers. Representatives of Britain, France, the United States and Russia travelled to Beijing on 17 May 1858 and demanded the right of audience with the emperor to negotiate their demands for the opening of additional treaty ports, the right to station diplomats in the capital and to send missionaries into the interior of China. These demands were firmly rejected by the Qing court as was their practice, so Britain and France occupied the Dagu forts that guarded the approaches to Tianjin on the estuary of the Hai River to bring pressure to bear on the Imperial Court. The Qing government capitulated and sent a delegation of negotiators to Tianjin: the most senior of these, the elderly and infirm Manchu imperial clansman, Qiying, who had negotiated the Treaty of Nanjing in 1842, arrived in Tianjin on 2 June. The demands that had been rejected in May were now accepted by the court under protest although they subsequently reneged on these agreements.

On 13 October 1860, a joint British and French expeditionary force under the command of James Bruce, the eighth Earl of Elgin, occupied Beijing and on Lord Elgin's orders, most of the old Imperial Summer Palace, the Yuanmingyuan, which lies to the northwest of Beijing was burnt to the ground between 18 October and 20 October to demonstrate that the Westerners meant business and to put renewed pressure on the Chinese court to agree to abide by the terms of the Treaty of Tianjin.[3] Supporters of Elgin's action have interpreted this assault as a reprisal for the torture and execution of British officials and have even suggested that it was a relatively lenient punishment as he had originally intended to destroy the Forbidden City in Beijing: it is more generally perceived to have been a callous and brutal act of vandalism. The remains of the palace are preserved to this day as a reminder of the ravages of colonialism in China and are set among a network of lakes in tranquil parkland.

Following the sacking of the Yuanmingyuan, the Convention of Beijing, under which the court guaranteed to respect the provisions of the Treaty of Tianjin, was dictated to Prince Gong, the younger brother of the emperor, and was signed on 24 October by the prince and Lord Elgin: a similar agreement was signed by the prince and the French envoy Baron Gros the following day. This embarrassing debacle created a crisis within the Manchu-Chinese elite and prompted a re-evaluation by the Chinese government of the system that the court had been employing to manage its diplomatic relations with the West. In the past these transactions had been conducted through the offices of the *Lifanyuan*, a body that had originally been set up by the Qing court to oversee its relations with the border peoples in Mongolia, Tibet and Turkestan. When it also assumed the role of inter-mediary between the court and the West it still operated on the assumption that China was innately superior to all foreigners and that the only relation-ship possible between the two was that of tribute bearing missions from inferior states to the Son of Heaven. The West could not accept or even comprehend this type of relationship and the *Lifanyuan* rapidly became ineffectual and obsolete.

Smarting from the humiliation of being compelled to sign the Conven-tion of Beijing under duress, Prince Gong and other reformers of the court's inner circle memorialised the emperor on 13 January 1861, propos-ing that a new body be established to oversee China's relations with foreign powers and that the sons of the bannermen elite should henceforth receive instruction in foreign languages so that they would be able to deal with foreign diplomatic missions more effectively. On 20 January an imperial edict was issued authorising the creation of an Office for the General Man-agement of Trade and Relations with All Countries [*Zongli geguo tongshang shiwu yamen*], which is usually abbreviated, both in Chinese and in English, to Zongli Yamen.[4] This was to become the first modern department of foreign affairs in China.

Under the auspices of the Zongli Yamen, a new-style institution of higher education, the College of Foreign Languages [*Tongwen guan*] was established in Beijing and the first ten students were enrolled in July 1862.[5] The new college divided opinion in the Imperial Court from the outset: the progressives, influenced by the ideas of Zeng Guofan and Li Hongzhang, advocated directing the brightest and best of the nation's students into the study of foreign languages and sciences, but the conservatives were petrified that this would contaminate the Confucian elite by weakening the influence of traditional culture and the literary language. As a result many of the scions of the traditional elite were deterred, and the student body of the College of Foreign Languages was drawn largely from the less privileged classes of Chinese society who saw the study of 'foreign matters' as a way of earning a living as much as a high moral and patriotic principle.[6] Similar colleges were set up in Shanghai, Guangzhou and Fuzhou. The teaching of foreign languages was grudgingly accepted by the ruling elite, but attempts to expand the curriculum to cover modern approaches to mathematics and astronomy were firmly resisted as these were deemed to be part of the traditional remit of the Confucian educational system.

Dynastic Succession and the Empress Dowager

On 22 August 1861, the seventh ruler of the Qing dynasty, the Xianfeng emperor Yizhu, died at the old Manchu palace in Rehe (now Chengde) in Manchuria at the age of 30. He had reigned since 1851 and died, it was said, disconsolate and humiliated at the concessions that the West had imposed on China. He was succeeded by his surviving son Zaiqun (a younger son having died in infancy) who would take the reign title of Tongzhi and reign until 1875. The Tongzhi emperor was only five years old when he acceded to the Dragon Throne and the Manchu court appointed eight regents to rule during his minority. His mother, a concubine of the Xianfeng emperor, whose Chinese name was Xiaoqin and who was known in Manchu as Yehonala, disapproved of the choice of regents and took the infant emperor to Beijing, accompanied by Xiaochen (the wife of the Xianfeng emperor) and aided by two of the late emperor's brothers. Xiaoqin and Xiaochen, both Empresses Dowager but better known by their respective titles of Cixi and Ci'an, deposed the regents in a palace coup and took power, ruling as regents jointly with Prince Gong. The most senior of the original regents, Sushun, was beheaded at the public execution ground, a humiliating death for an official of such an exalted status. The boy Zaiqun studied with private tutors until 1873 when he reached the age of majority but even then he was not permitted to exercise the power of an emperor. He died on 12 January 1875 at the age of only 18, officially of smallpox and without leaving an heir.

China was once again ruled by the two Empresses Dowager acting as regents: their choice as successor to the Tongzhi emperor was the four-year-old Zaitian, although according to the laws of dynastic succession he should have been ineligible as he was of the same generation as the deceased Xianfeng emperor. It is a measure of the influence that the Empress Dowager Cixi exercised over the court that she was able to prevail, for she was effectively exercising power on her own, and Zaitian was enthroned as the Guangxu emperor on 25 February 1875. Cixi and Ci'an ruled nominally as joint regents but Cixi was by far the dominant partner and Ci'an died suddenly on 7 April 1881: the rumour was that she had succumbed to poison. Cixi was left as the sole regent and was the effective ruler of China until her death in 1908, although the Guangxu emperor was the nominal head of state to avoid any breach of the Confucian ethical code and historical convention which prohibited and abhorred female rulers.

Tongzhi Restoration and Self-Strengthening

In spite of its inauspicious beginnings and end, the reign of the Tongzhi emperor was an indisputable turning point for the Qing dynasty. The rebellions that had threatened to bring down the dynasty were crushed, central control was re-established and the ideology and social values of Confucianism seemed to have been given a new lease of life. For those of a traditional Confucian way of thinking, the enthronement of the new emperor marked a restoration [zhongxing] in the fortunes of the dynasty and an upturn in the dynastic cycle, a pattern that was familiar to them as it followed precedents that could be discerned throughout Chinese history and with clear parallels in the classical periods of the Zhou, Han and Tang dynasties. It can be seen, in the words of Mary Clabaugh Wright, as an 'Indian summer in which the historically inevitable process of decline is arrested for a time'; it was also a breathing space for the rulers of the dynasty. However, nineteenth-century Chinese students of the history of their country would have been only too well aware of the temporary nature of such a restoration.[7]

In the late nineteenth century, the highest priority for the Manchu state was defence: there was general agreement among members of the ruling elite that the plight of the nation was due entirely to its inability to resist the incursion of Westerners with their insatiable demands for trade and improper diplomatic relations. The Opium War had cruelly revealed the inadequacy of Chinese naval power in the face of modern Western technology. The failure of the standing armies, both Manchu and Chinese, to halt the rebellions of the Taiping, Nian and Muslims had demonstrated the urgent need for a fundamental reform of the military. Under the new terms of the Tongzhi Restoration, this reform was to be achieved through what became known as the self-strengthening movement [*ziqiang yundong*]. As part of this movement, China was confronted with the need to adopt western methods of technology, the foreign matters movement [*yangwu yundong*] as it was known, and this provoked a crisis of national identity as the conservative elite once again resisted changes that might have appeared on the surface to be purely technical but that, in their view, undermined the essential Chinese nature of the Qing state and the society that it ruled.

One of the earliest published documents to acknowledge the need to learn from the West was the *Illustrated Records of the Maritime Countries* [*Haiguo tuzhi*] written by Wei Yuan. This detailed geography of the outside world, which drew on earlier material compiled by his close associate, the opium commissioner Lin Zexu, including translations of Western material in Western languages, was first published in an edition of 50 *juan* (sewn volumes) in 1844, and such was the interest that it aroused that it appeared in expanded versions of 60 *juan* in 1847 and 100 *juan* in 1852. In the preface to the book, Wei Yuan was quite candid about his intentions in writing it. 'Why was this book written? It was written to use barbarians to attack barbarians [*yi yi gong yi er zuo*]…and to learn the superior techniques of the barbarians in order to control them.'[8] It was not just an academic tome or a study born out of intellectual curiosity but a political tool intended to play a role in the service of a state in crisis. Wei called for the establishment of a modern shipyard and an arsenal to equip China's military to deal with the foreign threat, but he also clearly understood the need for China to understand the 'barbarians', their geographical situation and their strengths and weaknesses, in order that the Qing court might deal with them successfully.

The experience of fighting against the Westerners in the Opium War, of later conflicts against domestic rebels using some Western weapons and with armies organised on a Western footing such as the Ever Victorious Army persuaded the rising class of Han Chinese political leaders that modernising the defence forces was vital. Zeng Guofan and his protégé Li Hongzhang corresponded regularly on this question and these two military and political officials were largely responsible for creating the climate of opinion that made self-strengthening possible as well as for the creation of specific self-strengthening enterprises. In 1865, Zeng and Li sent a joint memorial to the Imperial Court requesting permission to build what was later to be known as the Jiangnan Arsenal. Their wish was granted and the Jiangnan Arsenal in Shanghai became the first major builder of modern ships, guns and cannon in China. It also created its own translation bureau to assist in the adoption of Western technology and established a branch arsenal in Nanjing. The Fuzhou shipyard was created on the estuary of the Min River at Mawei in Fujian province in1866 and a machine-building factory opened in the northern port city of Tianjin at about the same time. Chinese students were chosen to be sent to the USA to study the latest foreign thinking on defence and international affairs. Although they could not have been enacted without the new open-minded spirit of the time, these reforms were essentially the result of joint actions by Zeng, Li and Zuo Zongtang.

Li Hongzhang was also responsible for the establishment of the China Merchants Steam Navigation Company in 1872; for the manufacture of steel warships and for the dispatch of a group of students from Fuzhou to Europe in 1876. He also sponsored the sinking of the Kaiping mine in 1878; the founding of the Tianjin Naval Academy in 1880 and a military academy, also in Tianjin, in 1885; the Port Arthur shipyard and harbour facilities in 1882 and the Beiyang (Northern Oceans) Fleet in 1888.[9] These reforms were single-mindedly directed at defence and defence-related industries. Li had his critics, including Guo Songtao, the Chinese ambassador to the United Kingdom, who argued that China's long-term development would be better served by promoting the study of non-military technologies including railway construction and electricity. Guo argued that Japan was taking this broader view of how to respond to the West and that Japan was without doubt more successful in its moves towards modernisation than China.[10]

Treaty Ports

Clauses in the Treaty of Nanjing of 1842 and subsequent treaties between China and the Western powers that provided for the opening of specific ports for trade were to change the face of China for generations to come. When the Treaty of Nanjing specified that 'British subjects … be allowed to reside in Guangzhou, Xiamen (Amoy), Fuzhou, Ningbo and Shanghai for the purpose of trade [and] British consular officials be appointed in those ports to oversee relations between merchants and Chinese officials', it was setting in motion the creation of a network of open ports that were in time to become renowned as the Treaty Ports. The five ports that were opened in 1842 were all situated on the southeastern coast of China, but under the terms of the Treaty of Tianjin, which was signed in 1858, a further ten posts were opened, and some of these, including Jiujiang in Jiangxi province and Hankou, which is now part of the metropolis of Wuhan, were not coastal ports at all but were located a considerable distance inland along the navigable section of the Yangzi river. The Treaty Ports were the birthplace of a new form of social organisation for China, a Sino-Western amalgam that was dominated economically by the commercial muscle of the Westerners. Western investment flowed into the Treaty Ports, and this in turn attracted the investment of Chinese entrepreneurs and wealthy officials who became the middlemen in negotiating trade between the foreigners and the vast interior of China. These middlemen were known as *compradores*, a term which means 'buyer' in Portuguese and reflects the pioneering role of the Portuguese in the commerce of the South China Sea, although by this time they had long ceased to play any leading role in the trade of the region.[11]

The Treaty Ports began simply as the headquarters for the economic activities of foreign merchants. Around the warehouses and offices of the primarily European firms, foreign settlements evolved and in these communities life was lived as far as possible in the approved manner of the middle classes of the home country. It was possible to get a passable baguette in the French quarter in Shanghai, and the German tradition of *kaffee und kuchen* was stoutly maintained at Kiesslings in the German concession of the northern port of Tianjin. As the expatriate communities became more established they created their own schools, newspapers and postal services and even their own independent systems of policing and law courts. The commercial class was reinforced by the arrival of missionaries, who often had a vocation for medical or educational work in addition to their religious calling, and then by colonial civil servants who were recruited to run the postal or the customs services. What had begun as a system for regulating foreigners had a profound impact on the economic life of the local Chinese population as more and more people were drawn into the expanding Treaty Port economy as labourers, domestic assistants, interpreters or employees.

Two important concepts were developed to cope with the special position occupied by the foreign community during the latter half of the nineteenth century: concessions and extraterritoriality. Concessions were those areas reserved in the Treaty Ports by agreement for the exclusive occupancy of foreign residents. In some of the ports, including Tianjin, Hankou and Guangzhou, the concessions were leased from the Chinese government, whereas in Shanghai Westerners were able to purchase the land that they needed. The foreign communities took responsibility for local administration, including policing, the maintenance of roads and sanitation: these were paid for out of taxes that were levied by the foreigners on their own residents. The system of extraterritoriality ensured that foreign residents were governed by their own laws rather than by the laws of China. In the French concession of Shanghai the *Code Napoléon* reigned supreme, but in the British concession, infractions of the law were dealt with just as if they had been in Birmingham or Manchester. Overseeing the whole system were

Western diplomats accredited to the Qing court in Beijing and their consular officials in each of the Treaty Ports.

Although these arrangements were innovations in nineteenth-century Qing China, they were not entirely without precedent. During the Tang (618–906) and Song (960–1279) dynasties, similar arrangements had been put in place to regulate the residence and the commercial activities of Muslim traders from the Arabic and Persian-speaking world who had established communities on the southeastern coast of China. There were of course similar treaty ports in Japan and Korea and coastal cities in India, other Asian countries, Africa and Latin America which performed similar functions and in which similar hybrid societies had developed, but they were not known by the same name.

It is difficult to generalise about the nature of the Treaty Ports of nineteenth and twentieth century China. They ranged in size from small settlements such as Yichang and Beihai to sections of major cities, notably the International Settlement in Shanghai. Relations between the foreign residents and the host Chinese community in different ports also varied considerably. In most cases the foreigners were intent on living their own very separate European lives, in spite of being in China, and with as little contact with the native population as possible. Racial prejudice and antagonism were rife and the very notions of concession and extraterritoriality created a separation of cultures that is in many ways reminiscent of the *apartheid* system of South Africa. In time, the effect of wealth to some extent mitigated that of race, and some prosperous and educated Chinese families found their way into the foreign concessions, especially in Shanghai. There were, naturally, honourable exceptions to the all too common denigration of Chinese culture, and it was in the Treaty Ports that the serious modern study of the Chinese language and Chinese culture among Westerners began, taking up where the Jesuits had left off. Missionaries took an active interest in the religious life and thought of the people they hoped to convert. This was, to be sure, part of their evangelical endeavour, but it nevertheless contributed to the wider understanding of the key thinkers of the Chinese tradition. James Legge, who worked in Hong Kong as Principal of the Anglo-Chinese College from 1843 to 1870, studied and translated the canonical classics of Confucianism in collaboration with Chinese scholars and published the first volume of his translations in 1861. Although they are considered to be somewhat archaic, his translations were the foundation on which modern research on the history and philosophy of China was built in the English-speaking world, and they are regularly consulted by sinologists. Legge returned to Britain in 1870 to take up the first Chair of Chinese at the University of Oxford and was one of the great British sinologists of the nineteenth century.[12]

In Shanghai the foreign presence was more concentrated than in any of the other Treaty Ports, largely as a result of its strategic position at the mouth of the Yangzi estuary. It had been an unassuming fishing and trading settlement before the Opium War but it developed more rapidly than most of the other port communities that were created by the treaties. Even in the twenty-first century, when the image of Shanghai that is usually presented to the world is the ultra-modern development of the Pudong district, the nineteenth and twentieth century architecture of the Bund, the *Waitan*, on the opposite bank of the Huangpu River to Pudong still bears witness to the financial power and influence of nineteenth-century Europeans. Glimpsed out of the corner of the eye it could be the banks of the Thames in London or the area dominated by the Liver Building in Liverpool. The International Settlement of Shanghai attracted earnest commercial and spiritual entrepreneurs, but it was also a magnet for shifty adventurers and criminals on the run, and it rapidly gained a reputation for a fast and louche lifestyle.

Hong Kong was a special case. Under the terms of the Treaty of Nanjing, the island of Hong Kong was 'to be possessed in perpetuity by her Britannic Majesty, her Heirs and successors and to be governed by such Laws and Regulations as her Majesty the Queen of Great Britain etc. shall see fit to direct'. It was therefore a colony and as such was governed directly by Britain through a series of governors. Nevertheless the commercial attitudes and the lifestyle of the foreign community in Hong Kong were the Treaty Port attitudes and lifestyle writ large.

Sino-French War

The conflicts between China and Britain and China and Japan (see below) were the most significant in determining the course of China's history but there were other military confrontations which also contributed to the weakening of the power of the Qing Empire and the Sino-French War can represent these. China and France had been involved in a long-running dispute over access to the state of Annam which is in the northern part of what is now Vietnam. France had been attempting to trade with Annam since the seventeenth century and in 1874 had managed to impose a treaty, the Franco-Vietnamese Treaty of Peace and Alliance which was signed in Saigon on 15 March and which allowed France to trade, promote Christianity and exercise overall sovereignty over the part of southern Vietnam that was then known as Cochin China.

The Qing court regarded Vietnam as a tributary state of the Chinese empire and attempted to reassert what it regarded as its own traditional rights over the region but France annexed the territory in 1884 and declared it to be a French protectorate. An agreement between Li Hongzhang and the French representative, Captain François Ernest Fournier was signed on 11 May 1884. Under the terms of this accord, the Li-Fournier agreement, China agreed to open Yunnan and Guangxi to trade with France and to withdraw its troops from Tongkin, the name the French used to describe the densely populated and rich agricultural region centred on the delta of the Red River in northern Vietnam close to the modern city of Hanoi. Neither side complied fully with the agreement; fighting broke out and spread northwards along the coast into China. French forces attacked and destroyed the naval dockyard at Fuzhou and blockaded the Yangzi ports. China conceded defeat and a treaty was signed in Tianjin on 9 June 1885: it confirmed France's protectorate over Annam.

Korea and the Sino-Japanese War

Relations between China and Japan were in the long run the most momentous of all. They were close neighbours but they had responded in quite different ways to the challenge posed by the West. The turning point was the Meiji Restoration of 1868: in spite of its grand title suggesting a conservative revival, it was essentially a coup by modern-minded samurai from the western regions of the country who had seen the power of the West at first hand and overthrew the moribund Tokugawa Shogunate. Japan embarked on an assertive foreign policy to underpin its drive for modernisation and to defend itself against commercial and diplomatic pressure from the United States and other Western powers. It began to look for possibilities to expand its territory beyond its four main islands. Hokkaido in the north, already part of Japan proper but backward and home to the non-Japanese Ainu nation, was ripe for development and in the south the archipelago known to Japan as the Ryukyu Islands and to China as Liuqiu was a natural outlet. The Liuqiu islanders spoke languages related to Japanese but had their own independent cultures and kingdom.

However it was Korea that was to be the initial source of conflict between Japan and China. Korea, like Annam, had been a tributary state of China for centuries, although the degree of control and influence had varied greatly depending on the policies of different Chinese and Korean governments. Japan, for its part, had been trying to open Korea to trade since 1876, in the same way that Western commerce had been trying to open Japan. Korea has its own distinctive language and culture although, like China, it considers itself to be a Confucian society. The Korean language is not related to Chinese but for centuries it was tied to Chinese written culture by the use of the Chinese script. The invention of the Hangŭl writing system in the fifteenth century allowed written Korean to develop independently: Chinese characters continued in use and are still used in conjunction with Hangŭl in the Korean language as written in South Korea, although not in the North. During the early part of the Yi dynasty (1392– 1910), which is also known as the Chosŏn period, the Confucian elite in Korea was strongly influenced by the court of the Chinese Ming dynasty, but when the non-Chinese Manchus took power in 1644, official contacts decreased, and the Korean royal court adopted a more independent posture. China tried to reassert its traditional dominance in the final years of the nineteenth century in response to Western, and then Japanese, attempts to seek influence in Korea. The Qing court dispatched a Resident Director-General to the Korean capital of Seoul in an effort to manipulate the policy of the court of the powerful Queen Min. A military revolt in 1882 present-ed China with the excuse to send troops to Seoul to restore order and from 1882 to 1894 China maintained a strong and visible presence in Korea. A Chinese garrison was stationed in the country, and it was Chinese officials who carried out negotiations with foreign powers on behalf of the Koreans.

In the spring of 1894, another insurrection, the *Tonghak* rebellion, rocked Korea. *Tonghak* means 'eastern scholarship', as distinct from the Western scholarship of foreign missionaries, in particular Catholic missionaries. The *Tonghak* was also the name of a radical nationalist sect, supported by both peasants and unemployed members of the *yangban* ruling class. The move-ment had begun in 1864 in the province of Kyŏngsang and was vehemently opposed to Christianity and to the Confucian elite who were judged to be too accommodating to foreigners. Although the *Tonghak* was suppressed by the government, its influence grew as European and American penetration of the Korean peninsula escalated 1866 onwards. Japan moved to counter Western influence by attempting to establish diplomatic relations with the court in Seoul and Tokyo had come to an agreement with China that neither country would intervene militarily in the politics of Korea without informing the other. When the *Tonghak* rising broke out in the Chŏlla region in February 1894, China ignored this agreement and sent 1,500 troops to suppress the insurrection. Japan countered by deploying its own forces and the two countries found themselves at war on Korean soil.[13]

The Chinese mobilisation was triggered by a telegram sent on 8 May 1894 by Yuan Shikai, who was the Chinese ambassador in Korea (and was to become President of China in 1912), to Li Hongzhang, then governor general of the northern Chinese province of Zhili which is close to Korea, asking him to assist the Korean court in suppressing the rising. The Korean monarch, King Kojong did not formally request this assistance until 31 May, but China was determined to intervene to preserve its position in Korea. The Chinese intervention was perceived as a threat by the Japanese cabinet of Itō Hirobumi and Japan decided to send its own troops to Seoul on

2 June. Both sides built up their forces in the Korean peninsula during June and July despite requests from the diplomatic representatives of the USA, France, Russia and the United Kingdom that they both withdraw. Japan attempted to compel King Kojong to state publicly that Korea was independent and was not a tributary state of China. On 23 July Japanese forces occupied the Imperial Palace in Seoul, arrested Queen Min and her family and incarcerated them in the Japanese legation. The *Daewŏn'gun,* (often written *Taewŏn'gun* – the title means Prince of the Great Court and is a traditional one for the father of a reigning monarch) who was the father of King Kojong and had served as regent during his son's minority, was brought out of retirement to act as the figurehead for a Japanese puppet government in spite of the fact that he personally had a history of opposing Japanese influence in Korea.

Hostilities broke out on 25 July 1894 when Japanese troops sank a British registered vessel, the *Kowshing,* which was transporting Chinese reinforcements to the Korean front. The two sides formally declared themselves to be at war on 1 August. The major engagements of the war were a Japanese bombardment of the port of Weihaiwei on 10 August; the battle of P'yŏngyang which raged on 15 and 16 September after which the Chinese army was forced to retreat to Manchuria; and the defeat and almost total destruction of the only modern Chinese naval force, the Beiyang Fleet, just outside the mouth of the Yalu River. The Japanese army was able to occupy the whole of Korea between October and December and even seized territory across the border into China. On 22 December the Qing court sued for peace but suffered a further defeat at the hands of the Japanese navy in the Battle of Weihaiwei on 12 February 1895. After mediation by Western diplomats, peace negotiations began in the Japanese port city of Shimonoseki which is located on the southwestern tip of the island of Honshū and a ceasefire was agreed. Li Hongzhang was sent by the Guangxu emperor to negotiate on behalf of the Qing court and arrived in Shimonoseki on 19 March with an entourage of 135 staff. The negotiations were conducted in an atmosphere of great tension as Japanese forces continued their aggression, taking the Pescadores islands between Taiwan and the Chinese mainland on 23 March. There was an assassination attempt on Li Hongzhang on 24 March: a Japanese man shot at him and he was slightly wounded when the bullet grazed his left cheek.

Treaty of Shimonoseki

The Treaty of Shimonoseki which marked the end of the war was concluded on 17 April 1895. The text of the treaty was in Chinese, Japanese and English, the last having been added as a safeguard in the event that differences of interpretation might arise. The treaty was signed by Itō Hirobumi, Japan's first Prime Minister under its new modern constitution, and his Foreign Minister Mutsu Munemitsu and for China by Li Hong-zhang and his son Li Jingfang, the Chinese Ambassador to Japan. Under the terms of Article 1, China agreed to recognise the 'full and complete independence and autonomy' of Korea. The payment of tribute and the acknowledgement of any formal subservience to the Chinese court would cease. Article 2 ceded to Japan the southern part of the province of Fengtian that is usually known as the Liaodong Peninsula; the island of Formosa (Taiwan) and all islands belonging to it; and the Pescadores (Penghu) Islands. Article 4 provided for the payment by China to Japan of a war indemnity in the sum of 200 million *taels*. Under Article 6, Japan was to be accorded Most Favoured Nation Status, the right to trade in an additional four specified ports and the entitlement to navigate with steam vessels on the Upper Yangzi as far inland as Chongqing and on the Wusong River and the Grand Canal from Shanghai to Suzhou and Hangzhou. Japan was also given the right to manufacture goods on Chinese territory.[14] This right to establish an industrial base was to prove of great consequence for the capacity of Japan to colonise parts of China in the years to come.

Chinese officials on Taiwan tried to prevent the takeover by the Japanese of what had only recently become a full province of China by declaring an independent republic, but Japanese troops landed on the island, close to the town of Jilong (Keelung) on 29 May. Taiwan was formally handed over to Japan on 2 June; Japanese troops took Jilong the following day and entered Taibei (Taipei) on 7 June. Taiwan was to remain a colony of Japan until the end of the Second World War in August 1945 and since then has remained outside the control of the mainland Chinese government.[15]

The outcome of the Sino-Japanese War transformed relations between the two key states of East Asia, the venerable imperial power, China and the vigorous young upstart, Japan. Japan's victory over China was an indication that Japan's strategy of modernisation was succeeding whereas China's was not. The balance of power had changed and Japan was now in control of two regions that China considered to be part of its own historical territory or sphere of influence – Taiwan and Korea – although the status of Japan's rule in Korea would not finally be resolved until 1910. Japan was beginning its transformation from Asian backwater to world power. It was actively seeking colonial possession and the mainland of China was firmly in its sights.

Hundred Days Reform

Defeat at the hands of the Japanese was traumatic for the Qing court and for Chinese thinkers, particularly the conservatives. Japan was still seen as the 'younger brother', the junior partner in the Confucian world, in spite of its greater level of economic development, and for this inferior culture to defeat the nation at the heart of Confucian civilisation was profoundly disturbing. At the time of the peace negotiations in Shimonoseki, the emperor received 130 separate memorials signed by a total of more than 2,500 individuals demanding that the war be continued so that China would avoid the shame and humiliation of defeat by a subordinate.

One of the most remarkable responses was a petition by successful graduates of the provincial level examinations who were gathered together in Beijing to sit the papers for the prestigious *jinshi* degree, the qualification that was required for the most senior official appointments in the empire. Led by Kang Youwei and Liang Qichao, they submitted a petition to the emperor on 22 April 1895 demanding that the Treaty of Shimonoseki be rejected. On 2 May this was followed by the Ten Thousand Character Petition, signed by 603 of the graduates, also protesting against the acceptance of the treaty by the Qing court but in addition demanding that the government move the capital inland where it could be defended and, significantly, that it implement a programme of social reform.

On 29 May 1895, the day that Japanese forces landed on Taiwan, Kang Youwei composed a personal memorial to the emperor. He called for the court to reject the Treaty of Shimonoseki and demanded that the court implement a comprehensive programme of modernisation and reform. The young Guangxu emperor read the memorial and indicated his approval on 3 June. By doing so he was putting himself at some considerable political and personal risk as he was aligning himself with the reformers against the conservative establishment in the Qing court including its most powerful member, his aunt the Empress Dowager Cixi.[16]

Many members of the scholar-gentry class who had not been able to secure official positions became involved in political associations *xuehui* in the wake of the protests against the Treaty of Shimonoseki: one of the most influential of these alliances was the Self-Strengthening Society which was created by Kang Youwei, Liang Qichao, Yuan Shikai and others in September 1895. Liang became editor of the society's newspaper, *The Globe* (*Wanguo gongbao*), and he used its pages to urge the court to implement a radical reform programme and to move away from ruling by decree towards a constitutional monarchy. The Qing state reacted by proscribing the Self-Strengthening Society and the impetus for reform was temporarily halted, although popular support for radical change did not diminish. The Guangxu emperor, who at 27 years was close in age and sympathies to the petitioners and had in theory been ruling in his own right since the formal retirement of Cixi as regent on 4 March 1889, was anxious to find a solution to the worsening condition of the empire, and he signed a decree on 11 June 1898 indicating his support for the idea of reform and self-strengthening. This marked the beginning of the heady Hundred Days of reform which lasted until 21 September. On 16 June 1898, after months of applying unsuccessfully, Kang Youwei was granted an audience with the emperor. He presented a proposal for a raft of reforms including the restructuring of the government and the creation of a cabinet, a national assembly, a constitution and a Bureau of People's Affairs which would involve the restless scholar-gentry in the reform programme. He was appointed secretary to the Zongli Yamen, the prestigious foreign affairs bureau.

For the duration of the Hundred Days, Kang, Liang and their supporters worked feverishly drafting edicts on reform and attacking what they saw as the evils that pervaded Chinese society. The reformers were proposing a modern education and examination system; the abolition of the system of extraterritoriality; the promotion of agriculture, medicine, mining and trade and the modernisation of the military, the police and the postal service. These were by no means unrealistic aims. All of their proposed reforms had already been carried out in Japan, which functioned somewhat curiously as both a threat to China and as the chief inspiration for Chinese radicals:

> During this time, under the inspiration of Kang Youwei, reform decrees were issued by the dozen. Foreigners and Chinese were left breathless with amazement at the sweeping orders for change: institutions, great and small; officials, powerful and insignificant; century-old customs – all were affected.[17]

The reform programme was too much for the conservatives in the court to countenance: the attack on the primacy given to classical studies and the condemnation of official corruption threatened their position and they rallied around the Empress Dowager, relying on her to stifle the tide of reform. The Guangxu emperor had intended to imprison the Empress Dowager to prevent her from blocking his reforms, but his aunt's sources of intelligence were better than his own and she acted more swiftly. Cixi left her seclusion in the Summer Palace, came out of retirement and, with the Manchu commander of her household guard, Ronglu, promptly placed the Guangxu emperor under house arrest in the Lake Palace just outside the wall of the Forbidden City. She resumed the regency and, with what was effectively a coup d'etat, brought to an end the Hundred Days of reform. Kang Youwei and Liang Qichao escaped to Japan but other reformers including Tan Sitong were executed. The emperor remained in seclusion and was not allowed to play any further part in the affairs of state. The Empress Dowager died on 15 November 1908. It was announced that the Guangxu emperor had died just one day earlier but it was widely assumed that he had been murdered on the order of the conservative faction after her death, although this has never been conclusively proven.[18]

From 1898 to 1908, Cixi had been once again the de facto ruler of China, in complete contravention of all Confucian ethics and in spite of the professed intention of the conservatives to preserve the imperial status quo.[19] Although the Hundred Days had ended in defeat, this was by no means the end of the vision of the reformers of the Qing period, merely an interruption. The impetus for reform was too powerful to be stifled completely and reform edicts, strikingly similar to those prepared by Kang and Liang, would be introduced in the early years of the twentieth century as the power of the Empress Dowager waned. After her death in 1908 major constitutional reforms were proposed, but they came far too late and in most cases their implementation was overtaken by the Revolution of 1911.

Scramble for Concessions

The urgent need for reform was underlined by the response of the West to China's defeat in 1895. China's weakness was only too obvious and the great powers responded by seizing even more parcels of its territory as new concessions. These events are often referred to as the 'scramble for concessions' by analogy with the 'scramble for Africa', the partitioning of almost the entire continent of Africa by Belgium, Britain, France, Germany, Spain and Portugal that was carried out between the French occupation of Tunis in 1881 and the end of the second Boer War in 1902. Although China was never colonised as thoroughly as Africa, the intention was the same: the most powerful nations moved to establish their own spheres of influence before their imperial rivals could establish themselves.

Germany had a long-standing interest in Shandong province and particularly in the Bay of Jiaozhou (Kiaochow) and the port of Qingdao which guarded the entrance to its sheltered harbour. Its main rivals in this part of China were Japan and Russia. On 1 November 1897, two German Catholic missionaries were killed in Caozhou which is in the west of Shandong province and their churches were badly damaged in what was probably a manifestation of local xenophobia of the kind that was later to develop into the Boxer movement. On 14 November a German naval force attacked and routed the Chinese garrison at Qingdao and took control of the city and thus effectively of the whole of Jiaozhou Bay. From this position of strength, and using the death of the missionaries as a lever, Germany's ambassador to the Qing court, Baron von Heyking, demanded the right to sink mines and build railways in Shandong and claimed the right to lease the Bay of Jiaozhou. The Zongli Yamen rejected these demands on 22 November and on 4 December German forces entered the town of Jiaozhou which lies at the head of the bay and thereby gained a foothold in China, a policy that Kaiser Wilhelm II endorsed without delay in a speech.

On 18 December 1897, Russian naval vessels sailed into Lüshun (Port Arthur) in response to the German presence in Shandong and on 27 March 1898, China and Russia signed a treaty which granted the lease of the twin ports of Lüshun and Dalian, often known jointly as Lüda, to Russia for 25 years and allowed Russia to construct what was to be the first phase of the South Manchurian Railway. This agreement clearly defined the German and Russian spheres of influence in northeastern China.

Further south, the French fleet sailed into the harbour of Guangzhou in April 1898, seeking to secure a lease of the whole of Guangzhou Bay for France. The aim of this operation was to extend existing French influence in Yunnan and Vietnam into lands further east. An agreement to do this was not concluded until 16 November 1899 but it was to remain in force until August 1945. Meanwhile, on 9 June 1898, Britain had signed a lease that would allow it to make use of Kowloon peninsula, the territory on the Chinese mainland that is directly opposite Hong Kong Island, for 99 years. The terms of this agreement were to prove momentous as it was the imminent expiry of this lease that finally compelled Britain to negotiate with China on the handover of Hong Kong in 1997. Britain also took control of the port of Weihaiwei in Shandong on 1 July 1898.

Sun Yat-sen and the Revolutionary Movement

The path of reform and the struggle for a constitutional monarchy, as exemplified by the activities of Kang Youwei and Liang Qichao during the Hundred Days reform period, was not the only reaction by Chinese political thinkers to the crisis faced by the Qing state. Other political activists, weary of the repeated failure of reformist politics, turned to ideas of revolution and dreamed of replacing the empire with a republic. The most celebrated of the early revolutionaries was Sun Yat-sen, the father of the Chinese Republic, as he was to be dubbed later. Whereas Kang and his followers had pinned their hopes on influencing the ruling elite of Qing China, and especially the emperor, Sun recognised the futility of this approach and concluded that meaningful change would be possible only on the basis of radical action by the lower orders.[20]

Sun Yat-sen (Sun Yixian) was a native of Guangdong province who had spent his early life in Hawai'i and had been educated in Christian schools and in the medical faculty of the University of Hong Kong. He practiced medicine briefly in Macau but then moved to Guangzhou in 1893 and devoted the remainder of his life to seeking radical change for China. In 1894 he formed the Revive China Society [*Xing Zhong hui*] and set about creating an insurrectionary army that would be strong enough to challenge the Qing regime. A rising by this army was planned for the Double Ninth, the ninth day of the ninth lunar month (26 October 1895) and Sun's modest initial aim was to take control of the city of Guangzhou. Plans were made in Hong Kong and the insurrection took place as planned but it was a failure. Many of the revolutionaries were arrested and a number of the leaders of the Revive China Society were executed. Sun escaped to Hong Kong under threat of arrest by the Guangdong authorities. His first attempt at revolution had been a failure, but he had learned valuable lessons from this and withdrew to fight again another day.

5

BOXER RISING AND IMPERIAL DECLINE (1899–1911)

The Boxer Rising, or Boxer Rebellion, acquired its name in English from militia units that practiced ritual boxing as a form of self-defence and group discipline. In Chinese it is known as the movement of the *Yihequan*, the Righteous and Harmonious Fists, or the *Yihetuan*, the Volunteers of Righteousness and Harmony. The rising broke out at the very end of the nineteenth century, and its origins and the motivations of its leaders and supporters are complex and often confusing. The Boxers are usually considered to have been the descendants of a millenarian anti-Manchu movement, based on groups associated with the secret society known as the White Lotus, a name which first appeared in the resistance to the Mongols in the fourteenth century and was associated with a number of insurrections during the early part of the Qing dynasty. During the three years of the insurrection (1899–1901) its focus appeared to shift dramatically away from its anti-Manchu traditions and many of the Boxer units were persuaded to transfer their allegiance to the Qing court in the struggle against the growing, and what many Chinese considered to be the greater, menace of Western influence in China.[1] Research in the Qing archives in both Beijing and Taiwan that became available in the 1980s suggested to some historians that the anti-dynastic stance of the early Boxers had been exaggerated and that, from their inception, they were essentially village defence militias that enjoyed a degree of official support.[2] However, it should be remembered that most of the written records of these events were created by officials of the Qing dynasty or other members of the literati class, and it was not necessarily in their interest to draw attention to the anti-dynastic nature of the movement. There is strong evidence of the opposition of the often illiterate Boxers to the Manchu Qing in the folklore and oral history of the movement.[3]

In popular Western accounts of the Boxers, the emphasis has been on the xenophobia of the rebels and the siege of the Western legations in Beijing, which was relieved by a multinational force of which the Japanese were by far the most numerous.[4] The resilience of the Westerners blockaded in their diplomatic quarters was an Asian parallel to the relief of the siege of Mafeking in the Boer War which was fought at approximately the same time between the British and the Afrikaners in southern Africa. There was much more to the Boxer rising than this and, in spite of the ambivalence of the movement's attitude to the Manchus, in its actions and its thinking, it can be considered to be a forerunner of the nationalism that was to bring down the Qing dynasty a decade later.

North China at the Turn of the Century

By the late nineteenth century there was widespread resentment among all social classes in China at the expanding foreign presence, at least in those areas close to the Treaty Ports. The gentry and local officials were concerned that the power and authority that they exercised in the name of the Imperial Court was being undermined by Christianity, and newly established church missions were often seen as rival centres of power. China was experiencing a severe economic downturn, and this slump was popularly blamed on the availability of foreign goods, the establishment of Western businesses and railways and the circulation of foreign currency. The economic crisis was severe: the decline in village handicrafts, which were unable in many cases to compete successfully with foreign imports, and the deterioration of domestic trade led to serious unemployment and grinding poverty. Cautious analysts of the Chinese economy of the late nineteenth century, such as Albert Feuerwerker, have been sceptical about the nationalist argument that places the blame for China's poverty entirely on the Western dominance of certain sectors of the economy, but he nevertheless conceded that 'significant structural changes in the handicraft industrial sector took place'…and that 'the strain and dislocation occasioned by these developments adversely affected substantial parts of the population'.[5] In addition to the pressures of unemployment that were directly attributable to foreign penetration of the Chinese economy, there was the financial and social impact of the Qing government's military campaigns against both foreigners and domestic rebels. Heavy taxes were levied to pay for these wars and for the financial penalties (indemnities) which had been imposed by the foreign powers. At the close of hostilities, troops were demobilised, often without pay, and many turned to banditry and other forms of criminal activity.

In 1852, the silt-laden Yellow River, known for good reason as China's Sorrow, had flooded to such an extent that within three years it had completely changed its course and had found a new route towards the sea, emerging into the Gulf of Bohai on the north coast of Shandong Province. In August 1898, it burst its banks again and flooded more than 400 villages in Shandong, causing widespread suffering and the complete failure of that year's harvest. There were also floods in the southern provinces of Sichuan, Jiangsu, Jiangxi and Anhui and, at the same time, severe drought in northern China. These were far from unique occurrences and indeed between 1875 and 1895 there was a serious natural disaster of one kind or another every year. Popular superstition blamed these calamities on the presence of foreigners who had been building factories and churches and constructing railway lines without taking into account traditional ritual practices such as *fengshui* [geomancy] which prescribed rules for where and how buildings could be constructed: the floods were clearly the revenge of heaven for the foreigners' interference with nature.[6]

Origins of the Boxers

The Righteous and Harmonious Fists [*Yihequan*] were part of a popular religio-political tradition that combined aspects of Buddhist and Daoist beliefs and practices and can be dated back to the Chinese resistance to the Mongol conquests in the thirteenth century. Its immediate predecessor was the Eight Trigrams [B*agua*] Secret Society, the organisation that had launched an attack on the Imperial Palace in 1813.[7] One of the leaders of the Eight Trigrams claimed to be the reincarnation of the Maitreya, the Buddha of Compassion who is also known as the Buddha of the Future, a messiah figure, and their revolt is best understood as part of the continuing resistance by adherents of the White Lotus tradition to the Qing dynasty. The attack on the palace was repulsed and the rebels were wiped out in an assault by government troops in January 1814, but the millenarian tradition persisted in northern China and it was on this rich heritage that the Boxers drew. It is impossible to establish clearly the existence of any continuity between the different strands of the White Lotus and to attempt to do so would be misleading, but the creative reinvention of the millenarian tradition had sufficient popular resonance to serve as a focus for a mobilisation against the Manchus. The term *Yihequan* may have been used as early as 1808 when it referred to a number of individual and uncoordinated self-defence groups that were found throughout the provinces of Shandong, Henan, Jiangsu, Anhui and Zhili (the province directly administered by Beijing and roughly equivalent to present-day Hebei).

The Boxer groups were small, perhaps 20 to 25 strong, and each owed allegiance to a single leader who had complete authority over his group. The groups acted against any manifestation of the foreign presence in their own territory. They identified three categories of adversary: foreigners themselves were known as the Great Hairy Ones [*da maozi*]; Chinese Christian converts and individuals involved in the construction and operation of foreign economic enterprises were identified as Secondary Hairy Ones [*er maozi*], whereas those who merely used foreign products were the Tertiary Hairy Ones [*san maozi*].

An uncompromising Boxer proclamation of 28 May 1900 made their intentions crystal clear:

> Hear ye, townsmen and villagers of the Central Plains [an archaic term for China]. The Catholics and the Protestants have been maligning what we hold sacred; they have bullied the officials and oppressed the black haired people of China. Gods and men are angry with them but the people keep their counsel so we have trained ourselves in the sacred boxing of righteousness and harmony to protect China, drive out the foreign invaders and check and kill the members of the churches so as to avoid the subjugation of the masses. After the publication of this proclamation we instruct all villagers, wheresoever they may be, to drive away any converts with haste and burn their churches and other buildings so there is no trace left of them.[8]

Although membership of the Boxer groups was drawn from a wide social spectrum, they included a high proportion of socially marginal individuals who had no land or regular employment and were excluded, or had excluded themselves, from mainstream society. The two most prominent overall leaders of the Boxer movement were Zhang Decheng, who had been a boatman and Cao Futian a former soldier: both occupations are representative of the marginalized population from which the Boxers drew their support. The Boxers were frequently in conflict with officialdom and their beliefs and practices appear irrational and theatrical, relying heavily on ritual and magic. The core of their practices was the sacred boxing from which they came by their name, and this was intended to promote both physical fitness and spiritual enlightenment but there were also sessions of hypnotic trances, a type of shamanism or spirit-possession and a panoply of 'charms, prophecies and magic formulae assuring the invulnerability of the faithful and of the leaders [and which] destroyed or claimed to destroy the military potential of the enemy'.[9] These magic powers also offered control over the weather, particularly the rain, and this was particularly appealing to people living on the poverty line in a drought-stricken region.

Boxer activities were focused on altars or shrines [*tan*], which were their sacred areas.[10] A long-established *tan* could sponsor a new unit and appoint its master and the movement developed in this way. The Boxers recruited young men, mainly teenagers although some were as young as ten years of age, and subjected them to strict military discipline. They were organised into companies of ten, with ten companies combining to form a brigade [*dadui*]. They pledged total obedience to their leader or master and swore not to accept presents, steal or molest the common people; they also pledged to have no relations with women, eat no meat and drink no tea. Even more intriguing, given how few opportunities there were for women in traditional Chinese society, were the female brigades of the Boxers. The Red Lanterns were girls between the ages of 12 and 18 who trained and fought alongside their brothers and the Blue Lanterns were a force of mainly middle-aged women.[11]

The Rising

The impetus for a coordinated rising of all the Boxer militia was the campaign that had been waged against Christian churches by another popular underground organisation, the Big Sword Society [*Dadao hui*] in Shandong province. The Big Sword, which was also an offshoot of the White Lotus, was active in the southwest of Shandong and can be regarded as an early manifestation of the Boxers: the Boxer societies proper had their origins in the northwest of the province. The Big Sword had attacked churches in two counties of Shandong in 1896 and in another five counties the following year, but it was their attack on two German Catholic missionaries that brought matters to a head. The two were killed on 1 November 1897 and their churches in the town of Caozhou were badly damaged. The German government responded by demanding the dismissal of the Governor of Shandong, Li Bingzheng, and the payment of compensation: it also insisted that Germany be given mining and railway rights in the province. When it became clear that the Chinese were not prepared to accede to these demands, the Germans occupied Jiaozhou in the bay near Qingdao on the south coast of Shandong province. Li was then dismissed (from the Vicerealty of Sichuan to which he had been transferred) on 11 December and was replaced in Shandong by Yuxian, his former deputy.[12] German forces consolidated their position in Shandong and the undercurrent of resistance and revolt continued to grow. Li Bingheng had been a covert supporter of the Big Sword society and had encouraged them in their campaign against Chinese Christians, arguing that members of the churches were bullying and intimidating non-Christians with the protection and backing of foreign diplomats. His successor, Yuxian, also patronised the Boxers, encouraged them to adopt the slogan 'support the Qing and exterminate the foreigners' [*fu Qing mie yang*] and gave them financial support in return for helping to train his own troops. He officially sanctioned a change of name by which they were transformed into a semi-official militia and they were henceforth known as the Volunteers (or Militia) of Righteousness and Harmony [*Yihetuan*].

On 9 October 1899, Boxer units under Zhu Hongdeng (Red Lantern Zhu), who already had a reputation for attacking Christian converts, fought and defeated government troops in the vicinity of Pingyuan in Shandong Province. The harvest in Pingyuan had failed that autumn and there were allegations that the missionaries were conspiring with local landlords and merchants to hoard grain and were benefiting from the price rises that were a consequence of the shortage. Zhu was one of the first of the Boxer leaders to argue that their main priority was to support the Qing against the foreigners. The Minister (Ambassador) of the United States, Edwin H. Conger, protested that the authorities in Shandong were doing nothing to protect American citizens, particularly missionaries and Yuxian became the second official to be removed by the Qing government under pressure from foreign diplomats when he was dismissed from the governorship of Shandong. He was recalled to Beijing on 6 December and Yuan Shikai, future president and would-be emperor, was appointed in his stead with a clear brief to wipe out the *Yihetuan*. The forces of the Boxer leader, Zhu Hongdeng, were defeated by Qing troops and Zhu was killed on 24 December. On 26 December Yuan Shikai arrived in Shandong with units of his New Army. He issued a proclamation declaring the *Yihetuan* to be illegal and threatened to crush any opposition with whatever force was necessary. He recruited 20 battalions of troops in Shandong to supplement the units that he had brought with him and by the spring of 1900 he had more than 20,000 men under arms at his disposal. The Boxers moved many of their supporters into Zhili (present-day Hebei), which is much closer to the capital, Beijing, and they joined forces with anti-foreign peasant groups that were already operating there, moving closer to the capital. In a confidential despatch to St Petersburg on 4 May 1900 according to the Russian calendar, the Russian Ambassador to China reported that the influence of the Boxers had recently increased and that, after moving into Zhili in the direction of Beijing, they had dispersed into the villages where they had achieved considerable success in recruiting followers. He reasoned that it was impossible to estimate how many of them there were all told, but hundreds had appeared in the outskirts of the capital and their leaflets were already being distributed in the outer city, the Chinese, rather than the Manchu, part of Beijing. Their intentions were quite clear from the slogan 'Support the Qing and Exterminate the Foreigners' that appeared on their banners.[13]

The main Boxer force, which numbered more than 10,000 fighters, captured the town of Zhuozhou in Zhili on 27 May; on 31 May the foreign legations in Beijing were reinforced by European, American and Japanese troops. By 6 June the Boxers were fighting with foreign units outside Tianjin and on 13 June, after destroying the railway line from Tianjin at the approach to Beijing and cutting the telegraph wires that linked Beijing and Tianjin, large numbers of Boxers made their way into the capital. Foreign troops under the command of Admiral Sir Edward Seymour had been sent to counter the Boxers but they were prevented from reaching their objective by Qing forces. The Imperial Court held a series of crisis meetings of senior officials and Manchu princes beginning on 16 June to discuss how the government should react to the emergency and on 19 June decided to issue an ultimatum to the foreigners and to demand that the legations in Beijing be evacuated within twenty-four hours, effectively taking the side of the Boxers.

On 17 June1900, Yuan Shikai had received a decree from the Chinese emperor ordering him to move his forces to Beijing but he only complied with this instruction to a certain extent, transferring just some of the units under his command to the border of Shandong and Zhili provinces. The reasons for his reluctance to comply are not entirely clear but it is likely that he preferred to retain the bulk of his troops in territory that he controlled himself rather than risk having them attacked by both the Boxers and the troops of the foreign legations.[14]

Legations under Siege

As information about the approach of the Boxers filtered through to the foreign community in Beijing, they gathered together in three main areas of the city: the Legation Quarter itself, which was in the south of the capital and to the east of the gate of Qianmen in the neighbourhood between Dashalan and Zhukou roads; the compound of one of the Roman Catholic Cathedrals, the Northern Cathedral [*Beitang*], which was just inside the imperial city to the west of the Zhonghai lake and the compound of the American Methodist Mission which was situated north of another gate, Hatamen. Throughout the month of May, the expatriate community had talked of nothing but the Boxers and the attitude of the Empress Dowager and her court to the Boxers, that is nothing, apart from the oppressive heat and the dust from the Gobi. One eyewitness and participant in the siege was not deeply impressed by the way that the foreign community had conducted itself as the crisis developed:

> The Old Peking society has…vanished, and in its place are highly suspicious and hostile Legations – Legations petty in their conceptions of men and things – Legations bitterly disliking one another – in fact, Legations richly deserving all they get, some of the cynics say. The Peking air … is highly electrical and unpleasant in these hot spring days with the dust rising in heavy clouds. Squabbling and

cantankerous, rather absurd and petty, the Legations are spinning their own little threads, each one hedged in by high walls in its own compound and by the debatable question of the *situation politique*.[15]

This legacy of petty quarrels extended to the garrisoning of the Legations and, together with conflicting orders from the sundry governments, made it extremely difficult for the officers commanding the national detachments to agree on a joint strategy for defence against the Boxers.

The period between 8 June and 20 June has been described as a state of 'semi-siege'. Small numbers of Boxers had been sighted close to the Legation Quarter. Putnam Weale's diary entry for 9 June was prescient.

It is, therefore, becoming patent to the most blind that there is going to be something startling, something eclipsing any other anti-foreign movement ever heard of, because never before have the users of foreign imports and the mere friends of foreigners been labelled in a class just below the foreigners themselves.[16]

The terms Great Hairy Ones [*da maozi*], Secondary Hairy Ones [*er maozi*] and Tertiary Hairy Ones [*san maozi*] had finally reached the ears of the expatriate community in Beijing.

On 14 June a force of Boxers broke through into the Tartar City via the Hatamen Gate. They attacked and burned houses and offices belonging to the foreign-controlled Imperial Maritime Customs, missionaries and others with foreign connections, set fire to the Roman Catholic Eastern Cathedral [*Dongtang*] and put to death with great brutality many whom they assumed to be Catholic converts.[17] Great confusion reigned as the Legations staff erected barricades and attempted to consolidate their resources. Technically, relations with the Chinese government had not changed at all: the Qing authorities were temporising in such communications as there were and the foreigners simply had to wait to see what line they would take. On the nights of 16 and 17 June a great fire started in the Chinese City around the main thoroughfare of Qianmen Avenue.[18]

A cursory but unambiguous ultimatum from the Zongli Yamen that all Legations must be evacuated from Beijing within 24 hours was received in the Legation Quarter on 19 June. Twelve copies were delivered in red envelopes to the 11 Legations and to the Inspectorate-General of Customs. It was now abundantly clear to the foreign community that the Chinese government had finally taken the side of the Boxers and that this meant war. There was fear and panic throughout the Legation Quarter. The diplomatic body met and, after heated discussions and much mutual recrimination, a message was sent to the Zongli Yamen, accepting that there was no alternative to evacuating the Legations and agreeing to move all staff to Tianjin, but asking the government for more time.[19] By nine o'clock on the morning of 20 June the hoped-for response from the Zongli Yamen had not arrived and a proposal that all of the Ambassadors should visit the Yamen en masse was discussed but rejected. The German ambassador Baron Freiherr Lemens Von Ketteler announced that he had a previously arranged appointment at the Zongli Yamen, which he intended to keep. He returned to the German Legation and emerged in his official green and red sedan chair, accompanied only by his interpreter and two Chinese outriders. Shortly after leaving the Legation Quarter he was ambushed and shot dead and his interpreter was gravely injured. The rest of the diplomatic community realised that a safe evacuation to Tianjin was no longer possible and preparations were made to bring food and other supplies into the Legations, 'payment being made in some cases and in others postponed until a more propitious moment'. Shops near the Legations ceased trading, and many Chinese servants and workers slipped quietly out of the Legation Quarter.[20]

Cavalry units of General Dong Fuxiang's feared Gansu Army [*Ganjun*], mainly Hui Muslims who were conspicuous by their black turbans and were equipped with Mannlicher rifles which had been standard issue in the Austrian army since 1886, appeared beyond the Austrian Legation, heading westwards to the Imperial City to reinforce the government garrison. Dong Fuxiang, although a Muslim himself, had been commissioned by the Qing government to suppress the Muslim rebellion in Gansu in 1894–5. His predominantly Muslim troops were also fiercely loyal to the Manchus and had a reputation for taking no prisoners. It was believed, but never established beyond doubt, that it was soldiers of the Gansu Army who had killed Von Ketteler. They were unable to break through the defences of the Legations and there was some confusion as to what authority they had to attack the foreign residents. In a letter to Ronglu, the Manchu governor general of Zhili, written after the insurrection and when he was under arrest, Dong Fuxiang maintained that he had repeatedly received instructions from his superior, Ronglu, to 'lay siege to and bombard the Legation Quarter' although Ronglu later claimed that he had merely been trying to protect the diplomats from the depredations of the Boxers.

The members of the foreign community, numbering some 500 in total, were obliged to defend themselves behind what was known as the Tartar Wall against attacks from the north by Chinese artillery and fires which had been started with the intention of driving them out, but they held on to their positions for almost two months.[21] A former mission school student, Ma Luotian, who had lived in Beijing for a year, managed to leave the city on 26 June when a Manchu soldier friend lent him a military uniform that he wore to slip away in disguise. He described how in the days following the assassination of the German ambassador, there was fighting everyday between the Legation guards on the one hand and the combined forces of the Gansu army of Dong Fuxiang and the Zhili troops under the command of Ronglu on the other:

> Some days it was said from 200 to 300 native troops were killed at other times 30 or 40, and the onlookers were compelled to carry the dead bodies out of the city. The remarkable thing was that the Foreign troops were seldom seen, as they kept behind walls. Their firing was so deadly that the native troops did not dare to travel on Legation Street, nor even on the wall within reach of Foreign guns. The native houses between Legation Street and the city wall, also near the British Legation, were soon all burned and the inhabitants killed by native troops.[22]

The international force that finally relieved the beleaguered foreign community on 14 August 1900 was made up of troops of the Japanese, Russian, British, American, French, Austrian and Italian armies. According to Harley MacNair, who was, it should be noted, American, 'The American flag was first on the walls of the city; the British were the first to enter the legations at three o'clock in the afternoon. Two days later the Pehtang [*Beitang*] cathedral's siege was raised.'[23] The relief forces had advanced on Beijing after first taking the Dagu forts in Bohai Bay and occupying the port city of Tianjin. The first to reach the Legations were Sikh troops of the British army from India 'who were cheered lustily by men and women of every nationality'.[24]

The allied forces had arrived at Tongzhou on 12 August and sent out a reconnaissance patrol to within six miles of the capital the following day. The general attack on Beijing had been planned for 15 August but this was brought forward when heavy fire was heard from the direction of Beijing at 2 a.m. on 14 August and the British contingent was ordered to advance. On arriving at their initial objective some six miles from Beijing, it became clear to their officers that the noise of gunfire had been caused by the Russian and Japanese units of the relief force, which had already started their attack. The British troops found the East Gate of the Chinese City virtually undefended and, although coming under fire from Chinese sentries at Hatamen, were able to pass though a sluice gate in the Tartar Wall and enter the British Legation at 2.30 p.m., two hours before any of the other units arrived. The Americans, Japanese and Russians followed.

On 17 August the allied troops took part in a triumphal march through the Forbidden City, a march 'which seemed a rather ridiculous procedure. Detachments of every regiment and branch of service in Peking formed part of the procession, headed by their bands (in the cases of those who had them), but somehow the Russians managed to get about 1,500 to 2,000 men into their part of the procession.'[25]

The international nature of the relief forces has often been stressed but this should not be taken to imply either an equal contribution or a common purpose beyond the immediate concern for the rescue of foreign diplomats. Anglo-Russian rivalry, spurred on during the Great Game, was clearly undiminished. The Japanese component of the force was by far the largest (8,000 men out of a total of 18,000 – the Russians contributed 4,800 and the British 3,000), perhaps not surprisingly given the closeness of Japan to Beijing and the involvement of Japan in continental East Asia since the Sino-Japanese War of 1894–5. This important contribution to the international relief effort raised the profile of Japan in China and, from the time of the Boxer Rising, its importance in the diplomacy of East Asia was at least equal to, and often exceeded, that of the Western powers.

Shops, houses and offices in Beijing were systematically looted by troops of all the national contingents and also by some of the formerly besieged foreign residents. Some of the more knowledgeable – and ruthless – of the foreigners seized the opportunity to acquire valuable antiquities including seventeenth century instruments from the Beijing observatory and many rare books.[26]

Boxer Protocol

It was more than a year after the arrival of the relief forces before negotiations between China and the foreign powers had reached a point where a treaty could be signed. The delay was as much the result of the inability of the foreign powers to agree among themselves on the terms and conditions of the treaty, as any unwillingness on the part of the Chinese to negotiate. Eleven ambassadors signed the treaty, including three whose countries had taken no part in the conflict. This treaty, the Final Protocol between the Foreign Powers and China for the Resumption of Friendly Relations was signed in Beijing on 7 September 1901, and there were two versions, one in French, the diplomatic language of the period, and the other in Chinese. There were 12 articles in the Boxer Protocol as the treaty became known:

1. China agreed to an apology and a memorial for the murdered German ambassador Baron Von Ketteler.

2. There would be death sentences or banishment for senior officials of the court and the government and the suspension of official examinations for five years in towns in which foreigners had been murdered or ill-treated.

3. An apology would be made for the murder of a Japanese diplomat, Mr Sugiyama.

4. Monuments of expiation would be erected in foreign or international cemeteries that had been desecrated and funds would be set aside by the Chinese government for that purpose.

5. China would forbid the import of arms and ammunition and also the means to manufacture them.

6. By an Imperial edict of 29 May 1901, China agreed to pay foreign powers an indemnity (compensation) of 450 million *Haiguan* or Customs *taels*, annual payments to be made until the end of 1940. This was the renowned Boxer Indemnity.

7. The Legation Quarter was to be recognised as a foreign quarter in which no Chinese had the right of residence. The Chinese side acknowledged the right of foreign legations to defend the Quarter and to organise their own troops and police. A map delineating the boundaries of the Legation Quarter was attached as Annexe 14.

8. The Dagu forts and any other fortifications that impeded communications between Beijing and the sea were to be demolished.

9. The foreign powers were given the right to occupy 12 towns to give them access to the sea.

10. Edicts forbidding membership of anti-foreign organisations, advising on the suspension of examinations and reporting on the punishments inflicted by the Imperial Court were to be published in all county towns throughout the Chinese empire.

11. Treaties could be renegotiated in the interests of the foreigners.

12. The Zongli Yamen would be reorganised as a Ministry of Foreign Affairs at the request of the foreigners and would take precedence over the other six ministries of the government. The foreign governments agreed to withdraw all troops, apart from the Legation guards, from Beijing by 7 September 1901 and from the region of Zhili by 22 September.[27]

The tone and content of the Boxer Protocol, the one sided nature of the treaty and the severe punishments that were inflicted on Chinese officials were a bitter humiliation for the Manchu government from which it never recovered.

Russo-Japanese War

By the terms that it was able to dictate in the Treaty of Shimonoseki in 1895, Japan had amply demonstrated its supremacy over China, and this was strengthened by the role it played in the suppression of the Boxer Rising. Japan's main rival in Asia was Russia, whose imperial ambitions over the centuries had led to the expansion of its territory eastwards across the vast expanses of Siberia to establish a naval base in Vladivostok, a port within striking distance of Japan. Many Japanese politicians were concerned that an alliance between France and Russia, which seemed to be imminent, would pose a danger to Japan's aspirations to be the major power in Asia. Some members of the Japanese ruling elite, notably the former Prime Minister, Marquis Itō Hirobumi, favoured negotiating an alliance between Japan and Russia and Itō was planning to visit St Petersburg to discuss a treaty with the Tsar, but on 30 January 1902, and to the considerable surprise of most of the international community, the Anglo-Japanese Alliance was created. The prime mover on the Japanese side was Hayashi Tadasu, who had studied in Britain and was Tokyo's ambassador in London from 1900 to 1906. With the conclusion of this agreement, Britain had stolen a march on Russia. Russia was also Britain's chief rival in Asia after decades of the Great Game which had been played out in Central Asia as Britain strove to protect its interests in India.[28]

As the first day of the new year of 1902 dawned, Russian troops found themselves in control of the strategic region of Manchuria that they had occupied after the Boxer crisis. This was a cause of great concern for Japan and Britain as well as for China. A diplomatic agreement, the Russo-Chinese Convention, which provided inter alia for the withdrawal of Russian troops and the re-establishment of the authority of the Chinese Imperial Court in Manchuria, was signed on 8 April 1902. By 8 April 1903, in spite of the three-stage timetable set for the withdrawal of troops under the Convention, Russian troops remained in the Chinese towns of Shenyang, Niuzhuang and Jilin. The Russian government prevaricated and throughout the whole of 1903 continued to propose a series of new conditions for the withdrawal of its forces. On 28 October the Russian military took control of the local government offices in Shenyang and imprisoned the Military Governor Zengqi: on 11 December Russia made it clear to Japan that it was no longer prepared to negotiate over its position in Manchuria. Japan lost patience with Russia, broke off diplomatic relations on 8 February 1904 and launched a naval attack on Port Arthur on the same day. Russia formally declared war on 9 February 1904 and Japan reciprocated a day later.

The odds were stacked heavily against Russia from the outset. It had at its disposal in its Far Eastern region no more than 83,530 troops of whom 70,000 were infantrymen and 4,200 cavalrymen. In theory the Russian forces in total could have matched those of Japan but most were stationed in the west of the country in European Russia and, as the Trans-Siberian Railway had not yet been completed, reinforcements could not be transported to the theatre of war in time. Japan, on the other hand, was able to mobilise 850,000 fully trained soldiers and had reserves of over four million. Japan's navy was even more impressive than its land forces and could deploy far more fire power than the Russians. Russia had two naval bases in the Far East, Port Arthur which was not large enough to accommodate battleships and Vladivostok which was ice-bound for many months each year, whereas Japan had four fully operational naval bases in addition to many other harbours that its warships could use. Although Japan was at the peak of its drive for economic modernisation, a policy which attracted the support and enthusiasm of much of the population, Russia was embarking on the process of internal disintegration that would lead to the Revolution of 1905 and finally the October Revolution of 1917.

Japan's military strategy was to contain the Russian fleet in the two bases of Port Arthur and Vladivostok and to annihilate it ship by ship as they ventured out to sea, giving Japan control of the sea lanes at a very early stage in the war. The Russian land forces were swiftly overrun by superior Japanese formations in Korea, the first land battle of any significance being the battle of the Yalu River on the border with China where the Russian army was forced back on 11 April 1904. Amphibious landings near the tip of the Liaodong Peninsula cut off the Russian Army from Port Arthur which was the main source of its supplies and Japanese armies marched northwards into Manchuria. The second major land engagement of the war, the battle for Shenyang (Mukden) began on 23 February 1905 and continued until 16 March, by which time the Russian forces had once again been forced to retreat in spite of the fact that they had initially outnumbered the Japanese. Japan won a decisive victory at Shenyang and occupied the city: by the end of the battle Russian losses amounted to 90,000 killed or wounded and the comparable figure for the Japanese army was 70,000.

Port Arthur had fallen on 2 January and the Russian Pacific fleet was wiped out in the Straits of Tsushima, together with the Baltic fleet (renamed the Second Pacific Squadron) that had been sent out to reinforce it. By the end of May, the Russian army had also been vanquished and pushed back westwards although it had not been annihilated. On 8 June the president of the United States, Theodore Roosevelt (in office 1901–9), proposed a peace conference. Both sides agreed and the conference was held in Portsmouth, New Hampshire where the Treaty of Portsmouth was signed on 5 September 1905.[29]

Russia had no choice but to accept Japan's dominance in Korea and Manchuria:

> The Imperial Russian Government, acknowledging that Japan possesses in [K]orea paramount political, military and economic interests, to obstruct nor interfere with the measures of guidance, protection and control engages neither which the Imperial Government of Japan find it necessary to take in [K]orea.

Both sides agreed to remove their forces from Manchuria with the exception of the strategically important Liaodong Peninsula and Russia transferred 'to the Imperial Government of Japan, with the consent of the Government of China, the lease of Port Arthur, [Dalian] and adjacent territory and territorial waters and all rights, privileges and concessions' associated with the territory. Japan had therefore secured exclusive rights over the most important naval base in Manchuria. Japan also acquired

> the railway between Changchun and Port Arthur and all its branches, together with all rights, privileges and properties appertaining thereto in that region as well as all coal mines in the said region belonging to or worked for the benefit of the railway.

This railway line, the South Manchurian Railway, was to become one of the key instruments of Japan's military and political control over Manchuria and the base for its invasion of China Proper in 1937. The administration of the remainder of Manchuria was to be returned to China.[30]

China had officially been neutral in the conflict between Russia and Japan. 'The position of a neutral [was] a difficult one at all times and doubly so for a country not well grounded in the theory and practice of international law and in close proximity to the belligerents'.[31] Most of the combat took place in Manchuria, which was still technically Chinese territory even if it was not under Chinese control: it was impossible for the Qing government to remain uninvolved, particularly since both sides sought to supply their forces from China. China was criticised, mainly by Japan, for not having observed the conventions of a neutral state and this was addressed in a report prepared by Captain W.F. Tyler, formerly of the Royal Navy but subsequently an official of the Maritime Customs Service, for the International Congress at The Hague, the conference that resulted in the Hague Convention of 1907. Tyler concluded that, broadly speaking,

China had fulfilled its international obligations as a neutral state, in spite of allegations by the Japanese government that it had favoured the Russian army and navy.[32]

After the conclusion of the treaty negotiations in Portsmouth in 1905, Japan decided to consolidate its position in Korea and appointed a Resident General in Seoul to 'control and direct' Korean foreign affairs. Subordinate officials, designated as Residents, were appointed to represent Japanese interests in the Korean treaty ports and other strategic regions of the country. For the time being domestic matters were left to the Korean court but, after the Russo-Japanese War, Korea came firmly under the control of Tokyo: in 1910 Korea was formally annexed and the country was run as a constituent part of the Japanese state until 1945. Not only had China completely lost control over its former tributary state, it now faced the growing threat of the expanding and increasingly belligerent Japanese empire on its northeastern frontier.

Social and Political Reform

Although the 1898 Hundred Days' reform movement had ended in failure and in exile or death for many of its leaders, the ideas of the movement and the momentum for reform had endured. In the wake of China's comprehensive defeat in the war with Japan and the Boxer debacle, and during the Empress Dowager Cixi's temporary absence in her refuge from the Boxer troubles in Xi'an, the less conservative court officials decided that the time was right to put forward proposals for a series of reforms, many of them modelled on the plans made by Kang Youwei and Liang Qichao in 1898 but rejected by the conservatives at that time. These reforms have been variously criticised for being too little and too late, or for showing weakness and hastening the downfall of the Qing. In retrospect, they paved the way for major constitutional changes that helped to create the necessary conditions for the Revolution of 1911. In April 1901 a new government department, the Bureau for the Promotion of Political Affairs [*Tuban zhengwu ju*] was given the responsibility for overseeing the implementation of reforms, and although this was almost certainly just a concession by the Grand Council of which the new Bureau was a subsidiary section, it was important symbolically as an acknowledgment from the most senior institutions of government that reform was acceptable or even necessary. Proposals were also put forward for educational, military and administrative reform.

The aim of the imperial edicts on education that were published in January 1901 was to create the academic basis for a modern educational system, partly on the model of Japan which, having shown its military capability in the war with China, was viewed as the state most worthy of emulation in all essential matters. Under the new proposals, a network of new schools was to be established, covering the whole of China and inspired by schools that had been set up in Shandong under Yuan Shikai. Part of the curriculum was to include scientific and technical education to encourage industrialisation. Traditional methods of teaching and assessment were to be abandoned, notably the tightly structured and cumbersome 'eight-legged essay' [*baguwen*], a commentary on classical Chinese texts that had for centuries been deemed to be essential for the Confucian understanding of politics and philosophy, and was named after the eight prescribed sections that students had to write. It was replaced with essays on current affairs and finally became obsolete when the entire imperial examination system came to an end in 1905. Students were sent abroad for the first time, mainly to Japan, and the first institutions of higher education independent of the state were established. Yanjing University, the precursor of Beijing University, was founded in 1902. In 1906 a Ministry of Education was created to supervise the reforms and many provinces developed their own educational societies to investigate and promote modern education.

The Qing military system had demonstrably failed in its response to external threats, although it had been successful in suppressing internal rebellion. In comparison with the armies and navies of the Western powers and especially Japan, it was desperately weak and under-equipped. Under the new reforms, part of the Army of the Green Standard (the Chinese auxiliary to the Manchu banner forces) was disbanded. Modern weapons and military training methods were to be introduced under new provincial military academies which were to come into being on 1 September 1901, three days after the abolition of the traditional military examinations that had existed for centuries alongside the civil service examination system. The Northern [*Beiyang*] Army, which had been created by Yuan Shikai, would remain and the regionally based new armies that had been created to suppress rebellions would also be retained.

In addition, new-style government ministries were established beginning with a Foreign Ministry, the successor to the Zongli Yamen, in 1901; a Ministry of Trade in 1902 and Ministries of Police, Education and War in 1906. A governmental mission was sent abroad in 1905 to study the workings of constitutional monarchies. The traditional policy of balancing Manchu and Chinese representation in government was discontinued but the abolition in 1907 of the restrictive quota of Chinese officials caused considerable resentment among the Manchu elite who were now in danger of losing their privileged position. An edict promulgated on 1 September 1906 endorsed the principle of moving towards a system of constitutional government.

Death of the Empress Dowager

The position of the Empress Dowager Cixi and the most conservative elements in the court had been much weakened since the Boxer rising. During August 1908 the principles on the basis of which a constitutional government could be created were finally published. Cixi died on 15 November at the age of 73, one day after the death of the Guangxu emperor who was only 37. Ever since the demise of the Empress Dowager, there has been speculation that the Emperor was poisoned by courtiers, or even that he was murdered by Cixi herself.

Yun Yuding, who had been one of the court officials in closest contact with the emperor, argued in his book *Records of Despatches from the Lofty Mound* [*Chongling quanxin lu*] that the emperor had enjoyed excellent health and had never missed his official duties for one day because of illness. It appears that after the Guangxu emperor's return to the court from Xi'an with Cixi following the end of the Boxer Rising, the eunuchs who had previously attended him were replaced by staff loyal to the Empress Dowager. He took no further part in the affairs of state and was isolated and possibly depressed when doctors were brought to the palace to examine him in the autumn of 1908. Prince Qing, one of the most influential court officials, was sent away by Cixi on 11 November, almost certainly on a pretext, and did not return until 14 November, the day on which the Guangxu emperor was found dead and one day after Prince Chun (Zaifeng) had been proclaimed regent. The Guangxu emperor was succeeded by Puyi, the son of Prince Chun and Cixi's great-nephew. The Regent, Prince Chun, was the nominal but ineffectual ruler of China during the reign of his infant son and court policy remained in the hands of members of the old clique of conservative Manchus until the Revolution of 1911.[33]

In 1909, the idea of constitutional government became a reality, if only in a restricted sense, when the first Provincial Assemblies were convened. There was only very limited suffrage since voting rights were restricted to scholars and landowners. In Shandong, for example, the electorate was 119,000 out of a total population of 38 million and Hubei, which had a population of 34 million, had only 113,000 voters. In spite of their narrow mandate, these assemblies fulfilled a vital role as they became a focus for opposition to the central government from the provinces.

The following year, in February 1910, delegates from the assemblies demanded that a national parliament be convened and in October a National Consultative Assembly was summoned: this was not in any sense a democratically elected body since half of the representatives were appointed by the Qing government. However, an undertaking was given that a parliament would be in place by 1913. In April 1911, a 'cabinet of princes and nobles' was created (taking as its model, the reformed Japanese political system) as a first step on the road to a cabinet-led parliamentary system.[34]

Railway Nationalisation and Popular Protest

In the early years of the twentieth century, new railway networks had been constructed as part of the modernisation of the Chinese infrastructure, mostly by foreign firms, and the control of these railways had aroused a great deal of public concern. In the northeast, the Chinese Eastern Railway and the South Manchurian Railway from Harbin to Dairen were Russian-owned operations and the Shandong Railway was German. In China Proper, the main routes ran from Beijing to Hankou (now part of Wuhan), which was completed in 1906 and from Tianjin to Pukou (Pukou is a district of the city of Nanjing and the line was an important part of the rail link between Beijing and Shanghai). The total length of railways built before 1912 was only 9,244 kilometres, which was far too little to have any significant impact on the national economy.[35] In the early twentieth century, the railways were notable not so much for their economic value as for the degree of opposition that they attracted. Nevertheless they were seen as the transport of the future and investors were keenly interested in becoming involved in their development.

Although some of the opposition to the building of railways was based on the popular superstition and xenophobia that had arisen during the Boxer Rising, there were also more sophisticated arguments and disquiet at the control of these major economic and strategic assets by foreigners. Both the Manchu-dominated national government and the newly created Chinese provincial authorities attempted to assert their rights over the railway network. Between 1909 and 1911 there were heated and long drawn-out discussions over who should own and manage the railways. Financial negotiations between the Qing government and the foreign powers had produced an agreement that was signed on 15 April 1911 for a loan to underwrite the reform of the monetary system and the economic development of Manchuria. Following this, at a meeting in Paris in the early part of May 1911, the bankers, who were to become known as the Four-Power Consortium, came to an agreement on the division of the financing of the railways in central China including the Hankou–Sichuan line and the northern portion of the Hankou–Guangzhou line. The banks involved were the Hong Kong and Shanghai Bank (Britain); Deutsch-Asiatische Bank (Germany); Banque de l'Indo-Chine (France); J.P. Morgan, Kuhn Loeb and Co, First National Bank and National City Bank, all of New York (USA). On 9 May, in response to a memorial from the Minister of Posts and Communications, Sheng Xuanhuai, the Imperial Court issued an edict ordering the nationalisation of all the main railway lines. This brought them under the control of the Qing state which used its new powers to mortgage the network to the foreign bankers. Sheng signed a contract with the Four Power Consortium on 20 May for a loan of £10 million which was to be disbursed in two tranches to pay for the construction of the Sichuan–Hankou and Hankou–Guangzhou railways and was repayable over a period of 40 years from customs duties and salt taxes which were to be collected in the provinces of Hubei and Hunan. Under the agreement, 'construction and control' of the railway lines was to be 'entirely and exclusively vested in the Chinese government' although foreign engineers would supervise the project and local materials were to be used wherever possible.[36]

The Railway Protection League was established in Sichuan province on 17 June 1911 to protest against this policy of nationalising the railways. The main objection of the founders of the League was not to the idea of public control of major economic assets but that nationalisation involved the handing over of Han Chinese-owned railways to the Manchus and then to their paymasters, the foreign powers. A mass meeting of 10,000 of its supporters held in the city of Chengdu on 13 August supported a proposal for a series of strikes by students and traders and a tax boycott. Support for the Railway Protection League was particularly strong in the commercial world of Sichuan, Hunan and Hubei because local businessmen, supported by the banking muscle of the wealthier merchant community of Guangzhou, had an existing and extensive financial interest in the construction of the railways, sections of which had already been completed. Opposition to the nationalisation programme went far beyond the narrow commercial interests of the business class. The impetus was as much nationalistic and anti-Manchu as economic.[37]

Xenophobia was already rife in China. A boycott of American goods, the first in China's history, had been decided on by the Chinese Chamber of Commerce and a number of other business organisations in Shanghai on 10 May 1905, largely in protest at discrimination against Chinese immigrant labour in the USA. The boycott spread to all the main commercial cities of southern China and on 27 August the Chinese Foreign Ministry felt obliged to dissociate itself from the campaign in the face of American protests. It was not only the United States that found itself the target of Chinese nationalist sentiment. The *Tatsu maru* incident of 1908 was the first national movement directed against Japan. A Japanese ship, the *Tatsu maru*, was seized by the authorities off the Chinese coast and held on suspicion of smuggling weapons into China on behalf of the revolutionary organisation, the *Tongmenghui*. The Japanese government demanded its release and these demands precipitated mass boycotts of Japanese goods in Guangzhou and then nationwide.

Revolutionary Organisations

Although Sun Yat-sen (Sun Yixian) is revered as the father and ideological guide of the nationalist revolution in early twentieth century China, the revolutionary movement at the time was influenced far more by a short popular book, *The Revolutionary Army* [*Geming jun*] which had been written by Zou Rong (1885–1905). Zou Rong came from a prosperous merchant family background in Sichuan, and therefore belonged to that part of society that was most deeply affected by the railway agitation. He was politically active at school and refused to enrol in classes to prepare for the imperial examinations but went instead to Japan to study. While in Japan he came into contact with other exiled revolutionaries including members of the Revive China Society [*Xing Zhong hui*] and he wrote *The Revolutionary Army*, which was published in 1903, on his return to China. He was arrested by the police of the International Settlement in Shanghai and died in prison in April 1905. He is considered by the Chinese Communist Party to have been a martyr of the 'old democratic' or bourgeois revolution and to a much broader spectrum of Chinese opinion he was a pioneer of militant nationalism. *The Revolutionary Army* is a deeply patriotic and anti-Manchu work, written with all the ardour of a young revolutionary. Zou argued passionately that there should be a political revolution in China as there had been in England, America and France, recognising that it would at first be destructive. He excoriated the Manchus for their bloody repression of the Chinese population during the conquest in the seventeenth century, quoting from two violently anti-Manchu books that were circulating widely underground, *Diary of Ten Days in Yangzhou* [*Yangzhou shiri ji*] and *Massacre in the City of Jiading* [*Jiading tucheng ji*], both of which recounted in graphic detail the brutality of the Manchu conquest and were required reading among the revolutionaries. He also made no secret of his contempt for Chinese 'traitors', including major political figures like Zeng Guofan, Zuo Zongtang and Li Hongzhang, who had accepted ministerial appointments under the alien Qing dynasty.[38]

There were thousands of Chinese students attending universities and colleges in Japan at the time of Zou and many of them were involved in political clubs of one kind or another. Revolutionary books and journals sprang up like the 'first shoots of bamboo after the rain' [*hao bi yu hou de sun*]. A number of radical and revolutionary organisations emerged during this period. The most significant was the Revive China Society [*Xing Zhong hui*], which had been established by Sun Yat-sen in Manila, the capital of the Philippines, in 1894 with a handful of members. Sun had attempted to expand the influence of this group in the expatriate Chinese community in Honolulu the following year but had very little success and complained bitterly of the reactionary political atmosphere and of the conservatism of the Chinese community in Hawai'i. He then moved to Hong Kong where he established his headquarters in February 1895 and he also set up a branch of his party in Guangzhou. An uprising against the Qing dynasty was planned for the Double 9th (26 October in the modern calendar) 1895 but the organisation was betrayed; more than 70 rebels were arrested and the leaders of the attempted coup were executed. Sun fled to Japan.

On 30 January 1905 at a conference in Tokyo, the Revive China Society and other radical émigré groups merged to form the United League [*Tongmenghui*] under the chairmanship of Sun Yat-sen. In his autobiography, Sun recalled that the organisation was originally going to be called the Revolutionary United League [*Geming Tongmenghui*] but that too many people were afraid to use the term *geming* (revolution) at that time, so it was agreed that it should simply be known as the Tongmenghui, and it is commonly referred to by this Chinese name even in English-language works. The Tongmenghui had about 400 members at the time of the merger although this number would increase to almost 10,000 by 1911. It did not have a coherent programme and it was organisationally weak but it was the first nationalist party in China and in 1912 it was to become an important constituent part of the first incarnation of the Nationalist party, the Guomindang.[39]

In the three years that followed the death of the Empress Dowager, there were four serious but ultimately unsuccessful attempts at insurrection against the Manchu state by members of the revolutionary organisations. On 19 November 1908, Xiong Chengji led a revolt in Anqing, which was the provincial capital of Anhui province at that time. In February 1910, there was an insurrection by the New Army in Guangzhou. Wang Jingwei, Huang Fusheng and others attempted to assassinate the Manchu regent Zaifeng in March 1910. On 27 April 1911, the Guangzhou Rising, an attempt at a coup d'etat, was staged in Huanghuagang at the foot of Baiyun Mountain in the eastern outskirts of Guangzhou (Canton): it costs the lives of 72 activists, the elite of the Tongmenghui, who were later to be honoured as revolutionary martyrs. These uprisings were either organised by or inspired by the Tongmenghui but there were many other riots and disturbances that contributed to the general malaise and to the feeling that a revolutionary upheaval was imminent. However the failure of the Guangzhou Rising was a devastating setback to the revolutionary cause and the surviving leadership of the Tongmenghui dispersed and planned to regroup in Wuhan, which seemed to offer the greatest opportunities for revolutionary activity.[40]

Mutiny at Wuchang

Wuchang is one of the three towns (the others being Hankou and Hanyang) that make up the modern industrial city of Wuhan in Hubei province. It lies on the east or right bank of the Yangzi River and is the oldest and most important of the three settlements. Urban Wuhan had developed economically during the latter half of the nineteenth century, partly as a result of the positive attitude that Zhang Zhidong, the governor general of Hubei and Hunan, had adopted towards reform and westernisation during the 'self-strengthening movement', but the province of Hubei had been badly affected by flood and famine and Wuhan became the magnet for the destitute and dispossessed of the surrounding countryside. Significantly, Wuchang was also the base for the New Army units responsible for the security of Hubei province.

As early as 1904, revolutionary groups in Wuhan had begun to disseminate nationalist and anti-Manchu propaganda among the military. The two main radical organisations operating in the city were the Literary Association (*Wenxueshe*) and the Society for Mutual Progress (*Gongjinhui*), which was an offshoot of the Tongmenghui. Wu Yuzhang, who was active in the 1911 revolution in Sichuan and later became a member of the Chinese Communist Party and president of People's (Renmin) University in Beijing, described the work of the two groups. 'The Literary Association used literature as a front behind which they carried out intensive activities among the soldiers of the new army for the purpose of expanding revolutionary organisations.'[41] It published its own newspaper, the *Great River News* (*Dajiang bao*), the Great River being the Yangzi on which Wuhan stands, and by July 1911 claimed a total membership of 5,000. The New Army was 16,000 strong and as many as one-third of its soldiers belonged to the Literary Association. The Society for Mutual Progress had been established in Japan in 1907 when the members of various underground groups joined forces. Its leading members returned to China and attracted a great deal of support in Hubei and Hunan. They merged with the Literary Association in the summer of 1911 and set up a joint headquarters in Wuchang.

In September 1911, the government ordered the New Army garrison in Wuchang to deploy troops to Sichuan where they were to be utilised to defuse the tension created by the railway agitation. The revolutionaries feared that dividing the New Army in this way would reduce the effectiveness of their own agitation among the troops and organised a meeting on 2 September to prepare for an uprising which they decided would be on 6 October, the day of the traditional Mid-Autumn Festival. Rumours spread through Wuhan that there was going to be a rising against the Manchus that would be as memorable as the legendary Chinese revolt against the Mongols in the fourteenth century. However, the planned uprising was postponed until 16 October because the rebels did not feel that they were adequately prepared: they were overtaken by events and on the morning of 9 October, a group of revolutionaries were making bombs in a house down a lane in the Russian concession of Hankou when there was an explosion which seriously injured one of the bombers. The police raided the house and took away documents, seals, banners and other paraphernalia belonging to their organisation, blowing their cover. The revolutionaries tried to organise an immediate uprising, but their headquarters was raided and many of the leadership were arrested. On 10 October 1911 (the tenth day of the tenth month and thus the Double Tenth) revolutionaries belonging to the 8th Engineering Battalion of the 8th Regiment of the New Army in Wuchang attacked their officers when the plans for an insurrection were discovered. The British Minister (Ambassador) in Beijing at the time described the unit as being 'in a very unsatisfactory state of discipline' and reported that 'considerable disaffection existed in its ranks'. The mutineers took control of an armoury and were joined by other units. An initial attack on the *yamen* [office] of the Governor-General was bungled in the confusion but the revolutionaries regrouped and attacked again, obliging the Manchu Governor-General Ruicheng to flee by climbing over a wall and leaving the town in a gunboat. By the following morning the whole of Wuchang was under the control of the revolutionaries and had an independent government.[42]

The surprising and accidental (according to Sun Yat-sen) success of the revolutionaries at Wuchang left them with no obvious leader. A military government was established and Li Yuanhong, a popular senior officer in the New Army, was apparently compelled to assume the leadership of the revolutionary forces at gunpoint after having initially been arrested by his own troops. He rapidly became an enthusiastic convert to the cause of China's liberation from the Manchu yoke. The revolutionaries were happy to see order restored to Wuhan after the representatives of the hated Manchus had been driven out and they did not attack the foreign legations in the city. Li Yuanhong notified the foreign consuls that he would respect existing treaties and agreements with the foreign powers as long as they did not give any assistance to the Manchu government.[43]

The revolt in Wuhan and its effective secession from the Qing Empire triggered a chain reaction: city after city and then province after province declared their independence from the Manchus. The provinces of Zhili, Henan and Shandong which were closest to the capital and the northeastern provinces of the Manchu homeland took the longest to respond and the Qing authorities in Nanjing did not finally relinquish their control until 12 December. The imperial navy declared its allegiance to the Revolution on 11 November and by the end of 1911, most of the provincial authorities considered that they were part of a Chinese Republic that had not yet been formally constituted.[44] The speed with which the empire collapsed was remarkable and reveals how fragile Qing control had become. The Revolution took the Qing government by surprise and few Western observers were prepared for the cataclysmic changes that were about to engulf China.

6

STRUGGLE FOR THE REPUBLIC
OF CHINA (1911–1916)

Of the three revolutionary periods of China's twentieth-century history, 1911, 1926–7 and 1946–9, only the first is known simply as a revolution in China today and is acknowledged to have been a revolution by both the Chinese Communist Party and the Nationalist Guomindang. The usual Chinese name for the revolution of 1911 is the *Xinhai geming*, the revolution of the *xinhai* year, which is 1911 in one of the traditional Chinese systems of indicating the date. In this system, the years are designated by pairs of characters known respectively as the 10 heavenly stems, *tiangan*, and the 12 earthly branches, *dizhi*. The combination of these yields a series of 60 pairs and thus a cycle of 60 years. This system was adequate for denoting years within most reign periods but not for any longer stretch of time, and the alternative system of counting the years since the accession of the emperor is often preferred. Once the Republic of China was established the latter system was also used, so 1912 was Minguo (Republic) 1. The use of the term *xinhai* was particularly appropriate for naming a revolutionary year: the revolutionary forces overthrowing the Qing could not use a Qing reign date and there was as yet no tradition of using a Western or a universal calendar.[1]

The Qing government was overthrown, not by a single rebellion but by a decentralised movement that devolved power to the provinces. However it proved extremely difficult to replace it with a government that was acceptable to all the provinces and all the regional economic and political interests that had been involved in the struggle to bring down the Manchus. Support for a constitutional monarchy had ebbed away and there was broad agreement among political activists that China needed a republican government, but there was no common understanding of what that would involve in practice, how it should be implemented and, of more immediate importance, who should be in power.

The struggle to create a functioning republic was bedevilled by intractable internal conflicts and contradictions. There was the long-standing division between the north and the south of China, reflected in the acrimonious debate on whether Mandarin or Shanghainese should be the national language. Democratic institutions were weak at the provincial level and creating a national parliament on this basis was never going to be easy. Revolutionaries who wanted to change everything and former supporters of the Qing dynasty who wanted to preserve their own positions and as much of the structure and culture of the *ancien régime* as possible were never going to see eye to eye: the struggle for power between Sun Yat-sen and Yuan Shikai was only the most obvious example and can be seen as the symbol for all of these conflicts. Underlying all of the political battles were the twin problems of China's desperate underdevelopment and the control of the country's key economic resources by foreign interests, both Western and Japanese.

Sun Becomes President

In his autobiography, Sun Yat-sen recalled his journey from Paris to Shanghai while, in China, the revolution was taking place. He arrived in Shanghai in late December 1911, a month after leaving France: the negotiations between the northern and southern power brokers were already under way. Rumours had spread that he was bringing back to China a huge sum of money to aid the revolution, but he had to disappoint his supporters. Provincial delegates of a republican cast of mind met in Nanjing to decide on the presidency of the infant republic and Sun was elected Provisional President on 29 December:

> On January first, A.D, one thousand nine hundred and twelve, I went through the inauguration ceremony. On that day, I proclaimed the Republic of China, and adopted the solar calendar for the first year of the Chinese Republic. On that day I saw the successful accomplishment of the great ambition for which I had struggled during thirty years, the restoration of China and the establishment of a Republic.[2]

In his inaugural proclamation as president, he declared that his highest priority was to organise a provisional government that would be able to negotiate with the foreign powers, reunite the provinces that had seceded from the empire and bring Mongolia and Tibet back into the fold. He recognised that his government might be a temporary one, an administration forged during a revolution, the duties of which would be at an end once the Chinese Republic had been firmly established.[3]

In the event, Sun Yat-sen's presidency was even more short-lived than he had anticipated. Yuan Shikai had already been appointed prime minister, in place of Prince Qing, by the National Assembly that had been set up under the auspices of the doomed Qing government on 7 November 1911. The entourage of the five-year-old Xuantong emperor, Pu Yi, was coming under increasing pressure to make him abdicate but as late as 28 December the Empress Dowager Longyu, widow of the Guangxu emperor, niece of Cixi and the adoptive mother of Pu Yi, was able to postpone the decision by issuing an edict that proposed the establishment of a National Convention which would decide on the future form of the government of China. However, on 27 January 1912, officers of the Beiyang Army, Yuan Shikai's own troops, demanded the abdication of the emperor and a provisional parliament was convened on 28 January with representatives from 17 provinces.

Abdication of Last Qing Emperor and Presidency of Yuan Shikai

On 12 February the boy emperor finally abdicated by means of a document signed by Empress Dowager Longyu; Yuan Shikai declared his support for the Republic on 13 February and on the same day, Sun Yat-sen expressed his willingness to step down as president in favour of Yuan. The edict of abdication was prepared in the third year of the Xuantong emperor, the last year that China was ruled by an imperial dynasty: it carried the seal of the Imperial Court and the signatures of Yuan Shikai as prime minister and ten cabinet ministers (some of them *in absentia*). It recognised that the empire had been like 'a boiling cauldron' because of the popular unrest and the support this had received from the provincial authorities and that there was 'wide divergence of opinion between the North and the South' to the extent that there had been 'an entire stoppage of trade and suspension of ordinary civil life'. Accepting that the majority of the population of China were in favour of a Republic it conceded that this clearly expressed 'the will of Heaven'. Under the terms of the abdication, sovereignty was handed over to the people, and Yuan Shikai, who 'having been elected some time ago as president of the National Assembly at Peking, is therefore able at this time of change to unite the North and the South' was authorised to form a provisional government.[4]

The terms of the abdication agreement which had been agreed with Yuan Shikai allowed for the preservation of the imperial tombs and the completion of the mausoleum of the recently deceased Guangxu emperor. The Xuantong emperor, Pu Yi, would be allowed to retain his title and his existing properties; he would be awarded an annuity of 4 million *taels*; he would be allowed to remain in the Imperial Palace until a move to the

Summer Palace could be arranged and he would be permitted to continue performing religious rituals at the ancestral tombs. Members of the Manchu aristocracy would also be allowed to retain their hereditary titles.

Yuan Shikai notified the Nanjing government of the abdication and took power. Sun Yat-sen sent a telegram to Yuan on 14 February agreeing to resign as president in Yuan's favour but insisting that a Republic could only be created by the will of the people and not 'by any authority conferred by the Qing emperor. The exercise of such pretentious power will surely lead to serious trouble. As you clearly understand the needs of the situation, certainly you will not accept such authority'.[5] Yuan Shikai was declared President on 15 February 1912 and formally inducted into office on 10 March. Sun clearly had the moral authority to remain as president but he had committed himself to put the unity of China before his own position and, had he not done so, the consequence would almost certainly have been immediate civil war between the northern and southern armies. He resigned himself to forming an opposition party and devoting himself to the educational and economic betterment of China. The civil war that he had feared eventually broke out in spite of his patriotic gesture.

Provisional Constitution, Parliament and Political Parties

The National Assembly [*Canyiyuan*] formally approved the Provisional Constitution of the Republic of China [*Zhonghua minguo linshi yuefa*] on 10 March 1912. The constitution defined the territory of the Republic as the twenty-two provinces of China Proper, which included Xinjiang, and also Inner and Outer Mongolia, Tibet and Qinghai. The rights of the people, including freedom from racial, social or religious discrimination were also outlined. The composition and function of the National Assembly was also explained as was the process by which it would, within ten months, be dissolved when a parliament (*guohui*) would be convened by the provisional president to take its place. It also set down the roles of president, vice-president and ministers of state and the justice system.[6]

At the same time, Yuan Shikai was inaugurated as provisional president. On 9 April the National Assembly was transferred to Beijing, which became once again the capital of China. This was a considerable triumph for Yuan as it brought the seat of government back into the area controlled by his military forces and denied a power base to the opposition in the south.

Political parties were a novelty in China. Under the empire, to be a member of a party, or a faction [*pai*] which was the term more commonly used meant effectively to be disloyal and possibly a conspirator against the legitimate government of the emperor. That amounted to treason and could be punished by exile or with the death penalty. There had been court factions, either with known names such as the *Donglin* faction of the Ming dynasty, or unnamed factions, including eunuch groupings, which acquired considerable power within court circles from time to time during the Qing dynasty. There were secret societies, some of which had close links with the ruling elite. There were also the outlawed revolutionary bodies such as the Revive China Society [*Xing Zhong hui*] and the Tongmenghui but these could function effectively only outside China.

With the establishment of a parliament came a profusion of political groupings, which were broadly speaking either constitutional or radical and revolutionary. They defined themselves in terms of their relationship to the Beiyang warlords or militarists, which was the name given to the supporters of Yuan Shikai, and there was much debate about the degree of cooperation that was possible with Yuan's government. The constitutionalists vacillated but tended to support Yuan, so the major conflict was between the revolutionaries and the Beiyang military elite.

The Tongmenghui was transformed from an underground secret society into an open political party. Political negotiations and the amalgamation of the Tongmenghui and other parties created a new coalition, the Guo mindang or National People's Party. This was primarily the initiative of one of the prominent leaders of the Tongmenghui, Song Jiaoren, who engineered an agreement between his party, the United Republican Party and other smaller groupings in August 1912. The Guomindang that emerged from this process was by far the largest political alliance in the first parliamentary election. Its platform included the political unification of China; the development of local self-government; the abolition of racial discrimination; improvement of the standard of living and the maintenance of international peace. However there were conflicting ideas within the Guomin dang on the balance to be achieved between centralisation and decentralisation. This early version of the Guomindang was not precisely the same as the party that emerged from a further reorganisation in 1923 and continues to exist today in Taiwan, although they were broadly within the same tradition. None of the political parties could be said to have a genuine popular base because they relied almost entirely on the educated gentry elite. 'They were all like duckweed, floating on the water with no roots' [*dou chengle shuishang wugen de fuping*].[7] It is difficult to be precise about the policies of the parties at this time as they changed regularly but throughout this formative period for the new Republic there was really only one problem for them to confront: how to deal with Yuan Shikai. As the parties lacked popular support or substantial armed forces of their own, they were ineffective in the face of his military strength.

Assassination of Song Jiaoren

The opposition to Yuan was fragmented and had no coherent policy. Although Sun Yat-sen, determined on creating an effective movement that would modernise China, was willing to cooperate with Yuan, this approach was regarded by many of his colleagues as high-minded and sincerely meant but totally impractical. Song Jiaoren accepted the need for a degree of formal cooperation with the cabinet and with Yuan but continued to work independently in an attempt to bring the Guomindang to power through the legal and constitutional mechanisms that had been established under the Provisional Constitution. In Spring 1913, the attention of the political elite turned to the provincial elections and in the first election the Guomindang gained 360 seats, making it by far the largest party in the lower house of the National Assembly, but there was considerable confusion as a number of representatives appear to have stood for more than one party. Nevertheless, it was accepted that the Guomindang commanded a majority.

Song Jiaoren campaigned for the cabinet to be brought under the control of the majority party: this was not implicit in the constitution or indeed the Japanese model that had strongly influenced it. Although he continued to advocate that Yuan should remain as president, his criticisms were anathema to the Beiyang military clique. On 20 March 1913, while waiting at the railway station in Shanghai to catch a train north to Beijing, Song was shot and he died two days later. His assassin was Wu Shiying who had been aided and abetted by Ying Guixing. Neither was a known political activist but when the police raided their homes, they found documents which implicated the Cabinet Secretary Hong Shuzu, the Prime Minister Zhao Bingjun and even Yuan Shikai himself in a conspiracy to murder Song. Wu and Ying were arrested: Ying escaped from prison in Shanghai and asked for his case to be re-examined but he was murdered on the train between Beijing and Tianjin on 19 January 1914. Wu was found dead in his cell. Shortly afterwards, Zhao Bingjun 'died violently with the blood gushing from his seven orifices' [*yi qi kong liuxue baowang*], apparently after complaining to Yuan about the murder of Ying. In 1916, after the death of Yuan Shikai, the cabinet secretary Hong Shuzu was arrested by Song's son, was tried and sentenced to death. The reasons behind the assassination of Song Jiaoren can only be speculated upon but Yuan Shikai almost certainly feared that a powerful Guomindang would be able to wrest control of the cabinet from him. He had decided that the party could only be destroyed if he eliminated its leadership.[8]

Second Revolution and Yuan Shikai Dictatorship

The murder of Song Jiaoren galvanised his colleagues in the Guomindang. On 25 March, Sun Yat-sen, Huang Xing and others met in Shanghai to devise an appropriate response. The party was in a state of confusion, with some members advocating a military assault on Yuan, and others preferring the legal route who favoured attacking him in the courts for illegitimately negotiating a foreign loan, the 'Great Loan', to support his military ambitions which were to pre-empt the civil war that he was anticipating. In June 1913, Yuan dismissed a number of provincial governors who had supported the Guomindang and formally severed relations with the opposition party. Military action by forces loyal to the Guomindang began on 12 July when the deposed military governor of Jiangxi, Li Liejun, declared war on Yuan. The provinces of Anhui, Jiangsu, Guangdong and Hunan declared their independence from Yuan Shikai's government, but by 1 September when troops loyal to Yuan reoccupied Nanjing, this attempt to overthrow Yuan by force, which was to become known as the Second Revolution, had come to an end and the smaller military forces supporting the Guomindang had been comprehensively defeated.[9]

Sun Yat-sen had fled to Japan in August 1913 in fear of his life, and he was joined there by his old comrade Huang Xing and by hundreds of Guomindang supporters. Once again the revolutionary movement had been driven into exile. In July 1914, the Chinese Revolutionary Party (*Zhonghua geming dang*) was formed by exiles loyal to Sun but, in defeat, Sun had reverted to an organisational form that was more akin to a traditional secret society with its members pledging loyalty to an individual leader, himself, than to a modern political party with an open political programme, and some of his erstwhile supporters deserted him. The remnants of the Guomindang found themselves in the political wilderness, divided over policies and tactics and without any influence in the political process in China.

In spite of the defeat of the Second Revolution, a radical nationalist movement continued to develop inside China, primarily in response to the growing political and economic encroachment of Japan. Sun Yat-sen's pan-Asian philosophy and his admiration for Japan began to seem out of place in the face of this mounting threat. On 13 October 1913 Yuan Shikai issued instructions for the arrest of members of the provincial assembly in Jiangxi who had supported the military action against him,, and on 4 November he ordered the formal dissolution of the Guomindang and declared that its members could no longer serve in the National Assembly, which, consequently could not deliver a quorum and was not able to meet. On 12 November, Yuan ordered that all representatives in the provincial assemblies who were also members of the Guomindang should be dismissed. On 26 November he issued an order that the National Assembly should be replaced by a Political Conference, a completely new organisation that he had invented and that was completely under his control: it met for the first time on 15 December 1913.

On 1 May 1914, Yuan annulled the 1912 Provisional Constitution and replaced it with a constitution devised by his Political Conference which had now been renamed the Constitutional Conference. His new constitution allowed for a legislative chamber and a council of state; it effectively abolished the cabinet as a body with any authority and consolidated Yuan's own personal control over the machinery of government. On 29 December 1914 a new Presidential Election Law was promulgated, also devised by Yuan's Constitutional Conference. The term of office of the president was to be ten years, with no restriction on the number of terms that the president could serve, and he could be re-elected on a vote of two-thirds of the Administrative Council. Under certain conditions the president could be permitted to serve for an additional term without the necessity for an election.

More significantly, in light of his long-term monarchical ambitions which were an open secret, Yuan Shikai had made a sacrifice at the Temple of Heaven on 12 December: this was one of the religious rituals that had been reserved for the emperor. This act was not performed casually. President Yuan was driven to the temple in an armoured car and the 'entire route was covered with yellow sand, as was customary for an imperial drive, and was lined three-deep with soldiers who had been stationed there in the biting cold since the evening before'. He was transported from the southern gate in a vermillion coach and carried in a sedan chair into the temple where he changed into ceremonial robes. The entire ritual had been modified slightly to suit the Republican sentiment of the times but the continuity with centuries of imperial sacrifice was unmistakeable.[10]

Yuan had effectively established himself as a military dictator for life, using the constitutional processes when they suited him and abandoning them when they proved to be an obstacle to his authority. He was viewed as a 'strong man' by many foreign observers who felt that, even as a republic, China needed a figure with the authority of an emperor. His period in office was dominated by two major issues: the growing Japanese insistence on political and economic control of China and the restoration of the monarchy.

Japan and Shandong

Japan, like China, had been an underdeveloped, predominantly rural, society until the mid-nineteenth century when the West, in this case the USA, began to insist that it open its ports for trade. Unlike China, Japan had responded by changing its political structure radically after the Meiji

Restoration of 1868 and embarking on a period of rapid industrialisation and modernisation. This was accompanied by expansion into Taiwan, which became a Japanese colony in 1895 after the Sino-Japanese War, and then into Korea which came under Japanese control at the end of the Russo-Japanese War in 1905 and was annexed to Japan in 1910, from which date it was considered to be a part of the mother country. China's natural resources made it the next obvious target, and Japan had been building up its commercial and industrial influence on the Chinese mainland for some years.

Between 1914 and 1918 the major European powers were preoccupied with the Great War, the First World War, which was fought mainly on the battlefields of northern France and Belgium and in the eastern Mediterranean and the Middle East on the fringes of the collapsing Ottoman Empire. The USA entered the war in 1917. Japan, although technically an ally of the United Kingdom since the signing of the Anglo-Japanese Alliance in 1902, was not involved in any military action; however it did send a token squadron of ships to the Mediterranean in 1917. It was the only significant military power in East Asia and took the opportunity that the war offered to extend its influence in China. China had declared itself to be neutral by means of a presidential decree issued by Yuan Shikai on 6 August 1914.[11]

On 15 August 1914, Japan issued an ultimatum, requiring Germany to withdraw all her naval vessels immediately from Japanese and Chinese waters, to disarm any which could not be removed and 'to deliver on a date not later than 15 September to the Imperial Japanese authorities, without condition or compensation, the entire leased territory of Jiaozhou with a view to the eventual restoration of the same to China'. Japan was clearly intent on securing control over Qingdao which was the main port in the Jiaozhou region of Shandong province, but at this stage was claiming that it would in due course be returned to China. Britain acquiesced, under the terms of the Anglo-Japanese Alliance, on the understanding that Japan would only involve itself with German-controlled territories.[12]

Not only was Qingdao Germany's most important possession in China, it was also the largest German overseas naval base and home to the East Asiatic Squadron. The East Asiatic Squadron was under the command of Admiral Graf von Spee and comprised two battle cruisers, the *Scharnhorst* and the *Gneisenau* as well as three smaller light cruisers. Japan declared war on Germany on 23 August: the Imperial Rescript announcing the declaration of war complained of Germany, 'busy with warlike preparations' at Jiaozhou, 'its leased territory in China, while her armed vessels, cruising the seas of Eastern Asia, are threatening our Commerce and that of Our Ally [Great Britain]'.[13] On 2 September, Japan deployed troops in Shandong. They occupied Qingdao on 7 November and it was formally surrendered on 10

November. The East Asiatic Squadron sailed out into the Pacific in search of a new base. It eventually reached South America and but was destroyed off the Falkland Islands in a celebrated naval battle on 8 December 1914.

The Chinese Foreign Ministry protested at the occupation of Qingdao, a warlike act by a supposedly friendly power, but to no avail. A British contingent had taken part in this operation but withdrew after the capture of Qingdao, leaving it entirely in the hands of the Japanese military. On 9 November 1914, the Japanese occupation forces issued the Regulations of the Japanese Military Administration of Jiaozhou. Japan established military administration offices in the towns of Qingdao and Licun (now known as Laoshan and famous for its mineral water) which were to be subordinate to the Qingdao garrison Divisional Commander who was authorised to levy taxes on the local population.[14]

Twenty-One Demands

On the evening of 18 January 1915, during a private audience, the Japanese ambassador to Beijing, Hioki Eki, presented Yuan Shikai with a document that has become infamous as the Twenty-One Demands (*Ershiyi tiao yaoqiu*). It outlined the relationship that Japan expected to have with the new government of China and, if it had been accepted entirely, would effectively have conceded to Japan control over all key areas of the Chinese economy and government. China would have become a partial colony or protectorate of Japan:

> Not only were the Demands unprecedented in their nature, being, as the Chinese government pointed out, such as might be presented by a military conqueror to its victim, but the method of presentation itself was in disregard of diplomatic usage. By diplomatic convention the demands should have been presented to the Ministry of Foreign Affairs, not to the chief executive. The fact that the paper on which the Demands were written was watermarked with dreadnoughts [battleships] and machine guns was felt by the Chinese to be of peculiar significance.[15]

Ambassador Hioki had requested that the Twenty-One Demands remain confidential but within a week they had been leaked and widely discussed in the diplomatic community in Beijing: their import had also been reported in the Chinese press. Japan initially denied that the Demands existed, but on 14 February Tokyo finally made available a document that contained a version of them.[16]

The Twenty-One Demands are usually summarised only in the five groups in which they were organised, but the implications for Japan's intentions towards China at the time and in the future were so profound that they deserve more detailed consideration.

Group 1 *Shandong*

1. China to agree automatically on any arrangement that the Japanese and German governments came to on rights and concessions in Shandong.
2. China to agree not to lease any territory in Shandong or off its coast to a third party.
3. A Japanese railway from either Yantai (Chefoo) or Longkou to link up with the existing Jiaozhou–Jinan line.
4. Additional ports in Shandong to be opened for foreign trade and residence, the details to be agreed later.

Group 2 *South Manchuria and Eastern Mongolia*

5. Leases of Port Arthur (Lüshun) and Dalny (Dalian), the South Manchuria Railway and the Andong to Shenyang (Mukden) Railway (the An–Feng railway) to be extended to 99 years.
6. Japanese subjects to have right to lease or own land for trade, manufacture or farming in this region.
7. Japanese subjects to be free to reside and travel in the region and engage in any business or manufacture.
8. Japanese subjects to have the right to open up mines in the region.
9. Japanese government to be asked for permission before a third power was allowed to build a railway, or raise loans for building a railway, in South Manchuria and Eastern Inner Mongolia or before any loan raised with a third power using local taxes as security.
10. Political, financial or military advisors or instructors in China could be employed only after consultation with the Japanese government.
11. The control and management of the Jilin–Changchun (Ji–Chang) railway was to be handed over to the Japanese government for 99 years.

Group 3 *Hanyeping Company*

12. Hanyeping Company, in which Japanese financiers had a close interest, to become a joint Chinese–Japanese concern at an appropriate time.
13. No mines in the neighbourhood of the Hanyeping mine to be worked by outsiders.

Group 4 *Coastal territory*

14. China not to cede or lease to a third power any harbour, bay or island along the Chinese coast.

Group 5 *Miscellaneous*

15. The Chinese Central Government [*Zhongguo zhongyang zhengfu*] to employ influential Japanese advisors in political, financial and military matters.
16. Japanese hospitals, temples or monasteries [*siyuan*] and schools in the interior of China to have the right to own land.
17. Police forces in key areas to be jointly run by China and Japan or employ large numbers of Japanese.
18. China to buy at least 50 per cent of its munitions requirements from Japan or establish a joint arsenal with Japanese technical experts and using Japanese material.
19. Japan to be granted the right to construct railways from Wuchang to Jiujiang and Nanchang; and from Nanchang to Hangzhou and Nanchang to Chaozhou
20. Japan to be consulted if foreign labour were needed for sinking mines or the construction of harbours and railways in Fujian.
21. Japanese subjects to be permitted to propagate the teachings of Japanese Buddhist sects in China.[17]

Yuan Shikai accepted the majority of these humiliating conditions on 9 May, although he did reject the demands in Group 5. It was suggested at the time that this last group of conditions had been deliberately included by the Japanese drafters to provide room for manoeuvre, and to give the impression that there had been some genuine negotiation. In reality Japan was not overly concerned that these demands had been rejected.

Apart from the fact that Japan already controlled the key areas of Shandong, the main reason for Yuan's willingness to accept this document was that the Japanese government was promising support for his campaign to be recognised as emperor. These negotiations were carried out in secret but the prime minister of Japan, Okuma Shigenobu (1838–1922), who had formed his second cabinet in April 1914, was reported in a newspaper interview as having said that, since Japan was a monarchy the political systems of the two countries would work together more smoothly if China also had an emperor.[18]

Restoring the Monarchy

In Beijing during the period immediately after the Second Revolution of 1913, a small but influential body of opinion was emerging to argue that the republican experiment was not working because it did not suit the conditions of China: the monarchy should therefore be restored. This current of thought was associated with Yuan Shikai's family, especially his eldest son Yuan Keding, and also with the remaining members of the Manchu imperial family, although not surprisingly they were more interested in restoring to power the Xuantong emperor who had abdicated in 1912, Aisin Gioro Pu Yi, rather than the upstart Yuan Shikai.

Yuan Shikai had already started behaving like an emperor, by ordering the worship of Confucius and making the traditional offerings to Heaven. Liang Qichao, the great reformer who was serving as Minister of Justice, was fundamentally opposed to the restoration, and there is no evidence that there was any serious popular support for Yuan to be declared emperor. Yuan asked his constitutional adviser, Dr Frank J. Goodnow, an American who later became president of Johns Hopkins University, to advise him. Goodnow temporised but effectively came down on the side of monarchy, arguing that a Republic required a society with a high general standard of intelligence.[19] Yuan proceeded with his plan to have himself enthroned as emperor. An office to oversee the ceremonial details was established in September 1915 and the name Hongxian (Glorious Constitution) was chosen for the new dynasty, apparently with no sense of irony. Yuan sent one of his officials Guo Baochang, to Jingdezhen in Jiangxi, the city that had supplied porcelain to the Imperial Court since the Tang dynasty. Guo's remit was to supervise an order for 40,000 pieces of porcelain for the palace of the new emperor, at a total cost of 1.4 million yuan.[20]

The question of the restoration was discussed at great length in all the institutions of the government but there was mounting opposition in the provinces and on 21 May 1916, five days after the declaration of independence by the southwestern province of Guangxi, Yuan Shikai decided to abandon his monarchical pretensions in the hope that this would avert a civil war. He died on 6 June and was succeeded by his vice-president, Li Yuanhong, a veteran of the 1911 Revolution. Li was the New Army officer, who had been forced at gunpoint by his own troops to become the leader of the revolutionary forces in Wuchang.

The foreign community, by now well established in China, recorded the transition of power after Yuan's death in its English language newspaper, the *North-China Daily News* and its weekly edition, the *North-China Herald*. These were both published in Shanghai, which was 'North-China' to the business community whose natural stamping grounds were the southern port cities of Guangzhou and Hong Kong. On Friday 9 June 1916, the *North-China Daily News* carried a report from Reuters' correspondent in Beijing that, 'after lying in state surrounded by his sons, daughters and wives, the men on the left and the women on the right,' Yuan's remains had been brought by train to the capital, 'dressed in the sacrificial dress which the late president wore at the annual sacrifice to Heaven with the diadem on the head'. The reporter commented that China had adopted the 'foreign mode of mourning', that the *Government Gazette* had been published with black borders and that soldiers and police were all wearing black armbands.

Li Yuanhong's formal installation as president was carried out on 7 June in the presence of a number of senior cabinet ministers and military officials but no foreigners witnessed the ceremony. There was relief but some surprise among the expatriates that there were no disturbances associated with the handover of power. The editorial in the *North-China Daily News* of Friday 16 June, commenting on the constitutional difficulties inherited by President Li, argued that 'for the moment, the country is in danger of being controlled by the dead hand of Yuan Shikai'. Yuan had indicated in his will that Li Yuanhong should succeed him, in accordance with the provisions of the Constitution, but there was considerable disagreement as to which of the two existing constitutions should be applied in this case.

Yuan Shikai's funeral took place in Beijing on 28 June. It was, said the *North-China Daily News*, 'a mixture of the Occidental and the Oriental, gorgeous in places, commonplace elsewhere'. Since there was no precedent for a ceremony to accompany the death of a republican head of state in China, advice had been sought from the United States of America. The coffin of the Chinese President travelled from the Imperial Palace to the railway station by way of two of the gates to the Forbidden City, Tian'an men and Qianmen, at the head of a mile-long procession and thence by train to his ancestral province of Henan.[21] The death of Yuan and the ignominious failure of his ambitions to be emperor appeared to be the end of the monarchy, but there was an abortive attempt to restore Pu Yi to the throne and to bring back the Qing dynasty on 1 July 1917 during one of the first clashes between warlord armies in Beijing. Pu Yi, the 'Last Emperor', was later to be 'restored' again in 1932, but then it was by the Japanese, as emperor of Manzhouguo (Manchukuo). China was about to enter what is known as its warlord era, a period with no effective central government, during which power was in the hands of provincial or regional governors, whose only claim to legitimacy was the level of military force that they had at their disposal.

Warlords

After the death of Yuan Shikai in 1916, there was no administration that could indisputably be described as a national government of China until the Guomindang took power in Nanjing in 1928. In the intervening years, there were nominal governments and titular presidents based in Beijing, but their authority was almost entirely limited to the capital and to relations with foreign powers: the political structure of China was completely fragmented.

Provincial governors ruled as autocrats in their own regions, relying for their authority on the actual or potential exercise of military power. These warlords, as they became known, formed political relationships with each other: these were sometimes long-term coalitions but more frequently they were shifting alliances, resembling the traditional politics of the pre-imperial Warring States period in the fourth and fifth centuries BC. Although the warlords as a class are often characterised as ruthless despots, their conduct towards their subjects and their social and economic policies varied greatly.

The establishment of political and military regional factions during the conflict that accompanied Yuan Shikai's monarchical machinations was the basis for the rule of the warlords. The relationship between them was complicated and depended to a certain extent on personal and family connections, but probably the most important influence on the membership of these factions was the attendance of senior officers at the military academies that had been created during the Self-Strengthening Movement. Although there were also provincial academies, it was the elite national military colleges that provided most of the senior officers of these factions. The most influential of the national academies was the Beiyang Military Academy that had been founded by Li Hongzhang in 1885. Many leading political figures, including Duan Qirui and Feng Guozhang, who were both to serve as Prime Minister, and a long list of provincial military governors who were associated with the Beiyang Army had attended this academy.[22]

Fengtian Warlord Clique in Manchuria

In the northeast (Manchuria) Zhao Ersun who was the governor general at the end of the Qing dynasty, had invited Zhang Zuolin, at the time a junior officer, to bring his troops to assist in the running of the province. When units of this section of the New Army in Fengtian (Liaoning) mutinied in 1912, Zhang was appointed commander of the twenty-seventh battalion and in the factional squabbles that followed was chosen as military governor (*dudu*) of Fengtian and also served as acting governor of the province. Xu Lanzhou took power in neighbouring Heilongjiang and, with Zhang's support, became the local military governor. This was the basis of the alliance that became known as the northeastern or Fengtian military clique.

Shaanxi and Guangzhou Warlords

In Shaanxi, Chen Shufan replaced the previous military governor who had been a supporter of Yuan Shikai. Guangzhou province fell under the control of Lu Rongting, the old warlord of its neighbouring province, Guangxi. Sun Yat-sen, with the support of the Chinese navy, established a military government in Guangzhou. He had arrived in the city on 20 July 1917 on board the warship *Haichen* (Sea Treasure) and was supported by the governor of Guangdong Province and the assembly members of the province. On 5 August he assembled a fleet and sailed to Huangpu, which is some ten miles from Guangzhou. He organised an extraordinary meeting of parliamentarians in Huangpu and the establishment of a military government in the city was approved on 30 August, with Sun nominated as Grand Marshal [*Da yuanshuai*] which effectively made him the warlord of Guangzhou, although that is a designation that is usually avoided by those who prefer to remember him solely as a symbol of China's national unification. Negotiations with Beijing were attempted but failed. The military government was reorganised in April 1918 and Sun was replaced by a military committee. Similar conflicts and rivalries occurred throughout the provinces, most of them having only local or regional implications.[23]

Beiyang Warlord Clique

The dissent within the Beiyang clique, in contrast, had longer lasting results, not surprisingly, as that clique controlled the capital, Beijing. Yuan Shikai had himself been the leader of the Beiyang military clique and his death provoked tension within that group as a replacement was sought. The dispute was ostensibly about the validity of two versions of the constitution but it was above all about military and political power. The outcome was the division of the Beiyang warlords into two: the Zhili clique and the Anhui clique and by the autumn of 1920, the armies of these two factions were fighting each other.

The Beiyang clique had control over the process of selecting a new President. After Yuan Shikai's death, the succession of the Vice-President, Li Yuanhong was announced in a message to the nation on 6 June by the Prime Minister Duan Qirui. Duan, who wished to install Li as his puppet, claimed that the succession was in accordance with the constitution of the Republic. In fact, it reflected the terms of the revised election law of October 1913, which had been drawn up by Yuan and had not been acceptable to many members of the Guomindang, rather than the original constitution of 1912. Consequently the legitimacy of the succession remained in dispute and confusion reigned.

Li Yuanhong was eventually confirmed as president, a cabinet with Duan Qirui at its head was agreed upon, and the National Assembly or Parliament, which had been dissolved in 1914, reconvened on 1 August 1916. This cabinet and the convening of Parliament was intended to reunite the North and South of China, but many of the Guomindang leaders felt that their party had not been represented adequately in the cabinet. The North and the South were once again at loggerheads, and the final break came after the abortive attempt to restore the monarchy on 1 July 1917 and the assumption of Presidential powers by Feng Guochang. The cabinet in Beijing was hopelessly split and the southern provinces refused to acknowledge its authority.

War between the Military Cliques

War broke out between military factions in Hunan and Sichuan. Members of the Anfu clique, the warlords of Anhui and Fujian, attempted to create a national parliament, the New Parliament, and to operate it under their control. This assembly met in early August 1918 and was able to shore up the dwindling power of Duan Qirui, who was in constant conflict with the Acting President Feng Guochang.

None of these regimes had sufficient support or authority to form a national government and when the First World War came to an end in Europe, foreign interests in China turned their attention to the search for a negotiated peace between the warlord factions. A peace conference was organised in Shanghai during February and March 1919, but it rapidly became a vehicle for the foreign powers to increase their influence over China. Japan, for one, was more interested in new acquisitions in Shandong province than in patching up differences between regional warlords. The peace conference concluded on 15 May without any agreement but the meeting was completely overshadowed by a demonstration on 4 May in which students in Beijing protested against the terms of the Paris Peace Conference, the much weightier European peace negotiations, which had been convened to conclude a treaty between the combatants of the First World War and was about to hand over substantial territorial concessions to Japan. This was the beginning of the May Fourth Movement, which was to radicalise a significant part of the Chinese population and heralded a new phase in Chinese nationalism.

Negotiations between the warring factions continued but the situation deteriorated rapidly. Duan Qirui's clique, which many people held responsible for the failure of the negotiations, lost power in Beijing. The Military Government in Guangdong, which had already rejected Sun Yat-sen, was dissolved. In July 1920 war broke out between the armies of the Zhili and Anhui factions and in August, Guangxi and Guangdong went to war with each other. Yunnan and Sichuan were in conflict from May to November. In northern China, the Fengtian and Zhili armies under their respective warlords Wu Peifu and Zhang Zuolin fought in the spring and summer of 1922. Zhang Zuolin's forces were routed and forced to withdraw beyond the Shanhaiguan pass to a position nearer the Zhili faction's original power base in Manchuria. China was in the grip of a confused and bitter civil war. The idea of a reunited China under one Republican government seemed hopelessly optimistic. Federalism, a voluntary association of independent provincial governments was perceived by some progressive thinkers as the new solution to China's crisis. A conference of teachers and businessmen was convened in Shanghai in March 1922. It proposed that individual provinces draft their own constitutions and that a federal constitution be drawn up on the basis of those provincial documents. None of the established political or military figures supported this proposal, which, although it appeared immensely practical, was therefore doomed to failure.

New Republic, New Language

One of the key issues faced by the government of the new republic was a decision on what was to be used as the official national language. China is a nation of continental proportions and has the linguistic variations that might be expected across such a continent. Leaving aside the non-Chinese languages of its inner Asian frontiers, of which Tibetan, Uyghur, Mongolian and the almost defunct Manchu were the most important, the new republican government was faced with a multiplicity of Chinese languages, the pronunciation of which differed, and still differs, at least as much as Portuguese and Romanian in Europe: Portuguese and Romanian are distantly related as members of the Romance family of Indo-European languages but are not mutually comprehensible. Men and women from the coastal province of Fujian, which faces the island of Taiwan, could not readily understand their fellow Han Chinese living in the north-western inland provinces of Shaanxi and Gansu, although their Min or Hokkien language was readily understood on Taiwan. The Cantonese of Guangzhou and Hong Kong was not understood in the shops and *hutongs* of Beijing.

Because officials of the empire had for centuries been required to serve in provinces other than their own, as a protection against nepotism and corruption, a *lingua franca* had developed in the Imperial Court and among its provincial officials. This language was known as *guanhua* the 'speech of officials' and was based somewhat broadly on the form of Chinese spoken in the Beijing region but omitting many of its local idiosyncrasies of pronunciation and vocabulary. In the West it became known as Mandarin. It is commonly assumed that this name was derived from the Portuguese verb *mandar*, which translates as to 'send, despatch or order' and refers to the officials delegated by the court to govern on its behalf. However, *Hobson-Jobson*, in its day the ultimate authority on the Anglo-Indian vernacular that was used widely in the Malay states and in the China coast trade, assures us that it derives ultimately from the Hindustani (Hindi–

Urdu) word *mantri*, an adviser or minister of state and was transmitted to the West as *mandrim* by the Portuguese.[24] Mandarin, as the existing language of administration, had a head start and was the firm favourite for the national language of the Chinese Republic but there were other runners, mainly the dialect of Shanghai, part of the Wu language of China's southeast.

An additional complication was the Chinese script, the mastery of which had dominated the education of scholars and officials alike. The script is complex, has its origins partly in pictographs and symbols and is only partly phonetic. Historically this had the advantage that it could be used throughout the Chinese-speaking world (and indeed beyond in Korea, Japan and Vietnam) irrespective of the spoken language of the readers or writers and this was one of its great strengths. Its complexity was its weakness as it denied literacy to anyone who was unable to set aside the many years required for study. A modern republic needed to address the issue of illiteracy, and it would therefore have to attend to the issue of how modern Chinese should be written.

The first Minister of Education in the new administration was Cai Yuanpei (1868–1940) who had achieved the highest qualifications under the imperial examination system but had become disillusioned with the rule of the Qing dynasty and had devoted himself to educational reform. Under his guidance, the Ministry of Education embarked on radical measures to reform the Chinese language. An educational conference was convened in Beijing, followed by a conference on the unification of pronunciation. The aim of this second conference was to agree on a national standard pronunciation for Chinese written characters and to devise phonetic symbols to represent this pronunciation. Although this idea was regarded as revolutionary for China, it was not unprecedented. Vietnam had abandoned Chinese characters in the seventeenth century in favour of an alphabetic script, *quoc ngu*, which is based on the Latin script and was devised with the assistance of French Roman Catholic missionaries intent on converting the Vietnamese to Christianity.[25] The Korean Hangŭl script, which is phonetic but retains much of the aesthetic appeal of the Chinese characters that it replaced, dates back to the fifteenth century.

The conference on language reform met in Beijing on 15 February 1913. By this time the divisions in the new Republic of China, between north and south and between the reactionary Yuan Shikai and the radical Sun Yat-sen, were already apparent and were beginning to affect every aspect of the administration. Academic and personal wrangles complicated political differences and the conference dragged on for weeks. There was great opposition to the adoption of a roman alphabet, and in May 1913 it was agreed that a phonetic script based on Chinese characters (the *Zhuyin zimu* or phonetic alphabet) would be used. In spite of heroic efforts like James

Yen's Mass Education Movement of the 1920s, the *Zhuyin zimu* phonetic script was never accepted and it survives only in sinological dictionaries and teaching manuals that were published before and during the Second World War. There had been, moreover, deep division as to what form of speech this alphabet would represent, and this again reflected the political divisions of the Republic: the two main competing blocs of delegates supported respectively the Mandarin group of dialects and the Wu group of Jiangsu and Zhejiang, of which the urban dialect of Shanghai was the most important. Weeks of stalemate were followed by political chicanery: in the end, Mandarin, which was to be known as *Guoyu* (National Language), defeated its southeastern rivals. *Guoyu* was promoted as the national standard in schools throughout the whole of China, irrespective of the local spoken language.[26] It survives today as the national language in Taiwan and in the People's Republic of China under the name *Putonghua* 'common speech' or *lingua franca*. It is far from being the universal language of the nation and a survey published in *China Daily* in September 2006 revealed that only 53 per centof the population of the People's Republic of China regarded themselves as fully competent in *Putonghua*.

Mongolia, Tibet and Xinjiang at the End of the Empire

The end of Qing rule had a profound and lasting impact on China's border regions. Although it was stated explicitly in the Provisional Constitution of March 1912 that they were all to be included in the territory of the Republic of China, this was never achieved in practice. As the Republic was never able to control even all of the provinces of China Proper before the establishment of the Nanjing government of Chiang Kai-shek in 1928 and even then only partially and with considerable difficulty, it is hardly surprising that the frontier regions with their mainly non-Han Chinese populations eluded its grasp during that period. The border regions had enjoyed independence to different extents at different times before the Qing dynasty brought them into the Chinese empire in the eighteenth century, and the collapse of the Qing dynasty was an ideal opportunity for local political forces to make a bid for independence from China. This aspect of China's history is keenly contested as are the border regions themselves. Chinese of a rigid nationalist turn of mind find it unthinkable even to acknowledge that these territories were ever beyond the control of the Chinese empire, whereas many Mongols, Tibetans and Uyghurs maintain that the degree of independence that they enjoyed in the years following the Revolution of 1911 is their natural birthright and a legitimate political goal.

Mongolia

For the Mongols of Inner Mongolia [*Nei Mengu* in Chinese], that part of Mongolia that lies closest to the centre of Chinese political authority in Beijing, the main impact of the Revolution of 1911 was that it delivered them

> into the hands of Chinese warlords with limited local interests. From 1911 to the establishment of Chiang Kai-shek's regime in 1926–7 there was no central government strong enough to impose a continuous national policy on the warlords who had at their mercy the various sectors of Inner Mongolia.'[27]

Inner Mongolia was no different in this respect from the other areas of China that had fallen under the control of warlords.

In complete contrast the region that had traditionally been known as Outer Mongolia [*Wai Mengu*] 'immediately slipped out of China's control'.[28] Chinese, or more accurately Manchu, control over this part of Mongolia (which is Outer because it is further from Beijing) was always less direct than in Inner Mongolia and the impact of trade with China on the traditional economy was also less significant. The 'old order' of feudal nobles, and religious power, based in the Buddhist monasteries which followed the Tibetan rites and presided over by the Jebtsundamba Khutukhtu the Living Buddha of Urga, was also much stronger in Outer Mongolia. Urga, the Mongolian capital, became Ulaanbaatar after the revolution of 1924. The Mongol elite in this part of Mongolia had sought help from the government of Tsarist Russia in their bid to create an independent state, believing that Mongolia could only be independent of China by linking itself closely with Russia, which also had a population of Mongolian subjects living in what is now called Buryatia. A delegation of Mongol Princes was despatched to Russia in 1911. Russia was expanding its influence eastwards at this time and saw Mongolia as a useful buffer against China. Some elements in the Tsarist government in St Petersburg favoured bringing Mongolia under direct Russian control but a more conservative view prevailed, namely that Russia should simply prevent Mongolia from reverting to China or falling into the hands of Japan, which had defeated Russia in the 1904–5 war and was aggressively prosecuting its own imperial interests in northeastern Asia.[29]

A sovereign Mongolia was effectively created in 1911 by a declaration of independence and coup d'état: this took place on 1 December when the Mongols took control of Urga, and the last Manchu *amban*, the title of the Qing dynasty's colonial administrators in Mongolia and Tibet, was escorted out of the city followed immediately by the Manchu garrison troops. On

28 December the Jebtsundamba Khutukhtu, the Living Buddha of Urga, was proclaimed Great Khan in the capital city and the new Mongolian state was inaugurated. Russian sources often claim that the independence of Mongolia was a result of the political manoeuvring of Tsarist diplomatic agents. Although Russian political agents clearly played an important part in the independence movement, it was 'essentially a nationalistic movement' and the Mongolians were by no means simply pawns in this game.[30]

Mongolia's autonomy was formally guaranteed by an agreement with Tsarist Russia on 3 November 1912, although in a subsequent treaty, Russia was to agree to China's continuing right to suzerainty over the country, thus leaving room for an element of confusion.[31] Contact with St Petersburg led to continuing Russian involvement in Mongolia, including military intervention and assistance, and the army of the new Mongol state was created in Urga in March 1912 when Captain Vasiliev of the Russian Army and a team of twelve instructors arrived to begin to train new recruits.

There were also links between the emerging nationalist leaders of Outer Mongolia and Russian revolutionaries: Russia had gone through its first revolution in 1905 at the end of the war with Japan and the success of the October Revolution in 1917 attracted radicals in Mongolia as well as in China.[32] However, between the collapse of the Tsarist regime and the establishment of Soviet power in Siberia, Mongolia's neighbour to the north, Chinese politicians reasserted their interest in Mongolia and by February 1920 were on the point of bringing the Jebtsundamba Khutukhtu's government under their control and reasserting the traditional feudal relationship between China and Mongolia.

Two Mongolian revolutionaries, Sukhebatur and Choibalsan, formed separate political clubs in Urga during the winter of 1919 and later amalgamated them to create the Mongolian People's Party. The members of these clubs were from a mixture of backgrounds and included poor labourers, lamas (Buddhist monks) and even some minor aristocrats, but their ideological motivation at that stage was more nationalist than Bolshevik. Comintern advice and training followed and the party established a provisional government in 1921 after Chinese forces had been expelled from Urga. From 1921 to 1924 Mongolia was a constitutional monarchy, albeit one under the tutelage of its new Soviet military advisers. Sukhebatur, the senior of the two revolutionaries, whose statue still stands today in the square named after him in Ulaanbaatar, died in 1923, and Mongolia became a People's Republic in 1924, nominally independent but closely allied to and economically and militarily dependent on the USSR.[33] The other senior revolutionary, Choibalsan, became Commander-in-Chief of the Mongolian army, and was Premier of the Mongolian People's Republic from 1939 until his death in 1953. Of all the frontier regions, Outer Mongolia was the only one to remain free of Chinese control and this was possible only because of its relationship with the USSR.

Tibet

The influence of the Qing dynasty in Tibet declined as the Manchus became preoccupied both with the challenge of Western incursions on the coast and with domestic rebellion further inland which was closer to their capital, Beijing than the Tibetan plateau in the far west. Any problems that they might face in Tibet were at least temporarily ignored. By the mid-nineteenth century, Manchu and Chinese influence in Tibet was 'minuscule' and 'Chinese overlordship had become more symbolic than real'. The spiritual ruler of Tibet during this period, the thirteenth Dalai Lama, Thupten Gyatso (1876–1933) who was the immediate predecessor of the contemporary fourteenth Dalai Lama, Tenzin Gyatso, became known as the Great thirteenth partly because of the extraordinary personal authority that he exercised, even for a Dalai Lama, and partly because it was during his rule that Tibet emerged from under Chinese control.

Following an expedition in 1903–4 that was commanded by Sir Francis Younghusband and developed into a full-scale invasion of Tibet by the forces of British India, the thirteenth Dalai Lama left Lhasa, the Tibetan capital, and took refuge in Urga, the capital of Mongolia which was also (and remains today as Ulaanbaatar) a bastion of Tibetan Buddhism. He arrived in Urga in October 1904 and, in his absence the Chinese government declared that he had been deposed. Tensions arose between the Dalai Lama and the Jebtsundamba Khutukhtu, the Living Buddha of Urga who had established a rival spiritual power base in Mongolia, and the Dalai Lama returned to Tibet where he attempted to arrive at an agreement with the Chinese government.

The Anglo-Chinese Convention of 1906 effectively repudiated the gains made by Younghusband's adventure and reaffirmed China's suzerainty over Tibet. In 1908, Zhao Erfeng was charged with bringing the eastern province of Kham and eventually the whole of Tibet more firmly under Chinese control and assimilating its institutions into the Chinese empire. Troops under Zhao's command began to arrive in Lhasa in February 1910 and the Dalai Lama, believing that the Chinese government had reneged on the pact that he had agreed with them, fled once again, but on this occasion to Darjeeling in India.

When the news of the Chinese Revolution of 1911 reached Lhasa, a group of Tibetans rose against their Chinese masters, directed by a 'secret War Department' that the thirteenth Dalai Lama had established in India:

By April 1912, the Tibetans had prevailed: about three thousand Chinese troops and officers surrendered and were permitted to leave Tibet via India. In the fifth Tibetan month of the Water-Mouse year (1912), the Dalai Lama returned to Tibet, staying first in Chumbi and then, in January 1913, finally entering a Lhasa free of Chinese troops and officials for the first time since the eighteenth century.

Although the new president of the Republic of China, Yuan Shikai, attempted to build bridges with the Dalai Lama by restoring his former secular titles, the Dalai Lama insisted that he would from then on exercise both spiritual and temporal authority in Tibet and 'cut even the symbolic tie with China'.[34]

The position of Tibet in the years following the collapse of Qing rule has been described as 'static and non-changing, living in splendid isolation and illusionary independence'.[35] Its independence may have been an illusion but, in practical terms, it was a period of genuine separation from China that lasted until 1951 and that period has ever since fired the aspirations of Tibetans who seek to create an independent state.

Xinjiang

After the suppression of the Hui Muslim rebellion in Gansu in 1873, the Chinese government finally agreed on plans for the military reconquest of Xinjiang. Yakub Beg's forces were defeated by the armies of the Qing dynasty in 1878, and Xinjiang was formally incorporated into the Chinese empire as a province in 1884. Yang Zengxin became governor of Xinjiang in 1911 and ruled until he was assassinated in 1928. In many ways he maintained the status quo in the region, retaining for all practical purposes the framework of civil administration that had been used by the Qing Imperial Court to govern its most distant subjects. He kept the region tightly under control, partly by isolating it from the political factionalism of the warlords and politicians in China Proper, but he also kept open a weather eye for Russian, and later Soviet, interference and influence. In Owen Lattimore's words, he was 'an experienced official of the civil service, who flew the flag of the Republic but ruled the province for himself until his assassination in 1928'.[36] It is both significant and ironic that even the administration of a Chinese governor sought to isolate Xinjiang from the rest of China to keep it under control.

Yang Zengxin's successor, Jin Shuren, had none of the power or authority that Yang had wielded and under his direction there was a marked increase in tensions between the Chinese administration and the native Uyghur leaders with whom Chinese officials had to negotiate. In 1930, Shah Makhsud the native leader of the Uyghurs of the eastern Xinjiang city known as Hami or Qumul, who was known to the Chinese as Wang or Prince and to the Uyghurs as Khan, died of natural causes at the age of 66, having been Khan since the death of his father in 1908. Although his son Nasir succeeded him, Jin Shuren used the old Khan's death to assert his authority over the Hami region and the resentment that this provoked was the immediate cause of the insurrection of the Uyghurs against the Chinese authorities in 1931, a rising that was supported by the warlord Ma Zhongying, an ethnic Hui, one of the community of Chinese-speaking Muslims who are also known as Dungans in Xinjiang. Ma brought his Gansu Hui armies into Xinjiang, ostensibly to support the local Muslims but in fact to enable him to establish his own power base in Kashghar.[37] Xinjiang was to remain separate and politically unstable throughout the period of Republican government in China.

7

MAY FOURTH MOVEMENT: COMMUNISTS AND NATIONALISTS (1917–1924)

During the six years that followed the death of Yuan Shikai, a sequence of momentous events which took place both within China and overseas coalesced to create a radical climate of opinion during which the main political currents that would dominate the entire twentieth century history of China emerged. The most important external factors were the Russian Revolution and Japan's designs on Shandong province, but domestic political and cultural issues, including the part that Confucianism and classical Chinese language and culture should play in a modern society also played a crucial role in driving forward political change.

Russian Revolutions

The revolutions in Russia in 1905 and 1917 that overthrew the Tsarist regime had a lasting impact in China, as they did in many other countries, particularly in the colonies of Western powers and other developing societies. It is often forgotten how close China and Russia are to each other geographically. Although Beijing and St Petersburg are at the opposite ends of the Eurasian land mass, the expansion of the Russian empire in the eighteenth and nineteenth centuries had taken it across the far north of Asia and had given it extensive borders with the Chinese empire. The city of Irkutsk to the north of Mongolia was a Russian outpost which had diplomatic and commercial contacts with China: Vladivostok, the strategic port on the Sea of Japan, which was established in 1861 as the base for Russia's Pacific Fleet, is just over the border from Manchuria and only 830 miles to the east of Beijing. These far-flung settlements and the railways that linked them to Mother Russia were built by gangs of workers from the west of Russia, European Russia, and the radical ideas of anarchism and social democracy that were spreading among the industrial workers of St Petersburg and Moscow travelled east with them.

When Russia went through its period of revolutionary turmoil, these were not events in a distant country but the contemporary politics of a near neighbour, and what is more, an Asian neighbour that had many social and geographical similarities to China in spite of the obvious linguistic and cultural differences. European Russia, dominated by the court of the Tsar, the nobility, the bureaucracy and the Orthodox Church, was only part of Russia. Most of the territory of the Russian empire was in Asia, including Siberia, and was populated by non-Russians and indeed non-Europeans, including speakers of a wide range of Turkic and Mongolian languages and followers of Islam or Lama Buddhism of the Tibetan school. Radical ideas had also spread to China by way of Japan and in the early decades of the twentieth century, anarchism, Marxism and other forms of socialism were all known in the major cities. In the early twentieth century, it was anarchism that was most popular at first as can be seen from the contents of the radical journal *The People* [*Minbao*], which had begun life as Marxist but had followed the current fashion in Japan and by 1906 was changing its stance in favour of anarchism.[1] Classical Marxism, with its emphasis on the role of the industrial proletariat and class struggle in the towns and cities, did not appear to many local activists or observers to be relevant to the condition of China, although it did have its adherents such as Chen Duxiu and Li Dazhao, who were to play important roles in the political and ideological conflicts of the 1920s.

The Russian Revolution completely changed the way that Marxism was perceived in China. It was successful; it had taken place in a nation that had comparable social conditions and it had a new leader, Lenin, who was admired by many Chinese radicals. There were two revolutions in Russia in 1917: the first in February was 'the spontaneous outbreak of a multitude exasperated by the privations of war and by manifest inequality in the distribution of burdens.' Support came from elements of the middle class and officials of the Tsarist bureaucracy who had lost confidence in the system that they served. The Provisional Government that was established after the February revolution depended on these people for its support and the revolutionaries were not involved directly. In fact most of the Bolsheviks were not even in St Petersburg and some, including Lenin, were out of the country.[2] In St Petersburg (Petrograd), groups of workers created a Soviet of Workers' Deputies. This idea proved popular and similar soviets (*sov'ets* or councils) were set up, initially in Moscow, later in smaller cities and finally in the rural areas. By the end of March 1917, an all-Russian conference of soviets had been convened to bring together delegates from all the regional councils.[3] On 7 November after a summer of political conferences and intense discussions and disputes between the Bolsheviks and their opponents, Lenin proclaimed in St Petersburg that all power had been transferred to the Soviets of Workers', Soldiers' and Peasants' Deputies, having first taken the precaution of establishing control over all the key installations of the city in advance. Real power was invested in the Military Revolutionary Committee which had masterminded the transfer of power and in which the Bolsheviks had greatest influence.[4] This was a coup d'etat, but it was an almost bloodless coup and the manner in which it was carried out deeply impressed the Chinese revolutionaries. The word 'soviet' eventually found its way into Chinese as *suweiai* and was used by the Chinese Communist Party to describe its early experiments in government in the 1930s.

The most direct and immediate impact of the Russian Revolution on China was in the city of Harbin in the Manchurian province of Heilongjiang, which shares a border with Russia. On 7 December, *Sovnarkom*, the Council of People's Commissars, had issued an appeal to 'All Muslim Toilers of Russia and the East' to overthrow the colonialists, but East Asia was not included in this manifesto. Nevertheless, on 12 December 1917, a Workers' Soviet inspired by the Bolsheviks took control of the Chinese Eastern Railway, which was owned and administered by Russians, and expelled its Russian manager, General Horvath. Troops from the provincial garrisons of Jilin and Heilongjiang were despatched to put down this rising, which had caused great disruption to the operation of the railway. On 26 December, Chinese troops disarmed the workers and soldiers who had supported the Soviet and sent them back to Russia. The military governor of Heilongjiang, Meng Enyuan, was behind this move to support the administration of General Horvath against the Bolsheviks, but his successor Bao Guiqing subsequently had to defend Chinese interests in the railway against the White anti-Bolshevik forces that had rallied in Siberia, which was the 'main theatre of war against the Soviet Government' from the summer of 1918 to the spring of 1920.[5] The Russian Revolution was making its presence felt on the very doorstep of China.

Confucianism and the Chinese Renaissance

The direct impact of the Russian Revolution brought home to many educated Chinese the changes that were taking place in the outside world, but the indirect influence, the spread of ideas, was to have more enduring consequences. China was ripe for change. For many of the Chinese intelligentsia, what was needed was not simply a change of government and the ejection of the Manchu elite, or a change of name from the Qing Empire to the Chinese Republic, but a thorough social and intellectual revolution that questioned the philosophy that had underpinned the empire for centuries – Confucianism.

Confucianism (or *Rujiao*, the 'teachings of the scholars', to give it its more accurate Chinese name) is notoriously difficult to pin down or to define adequately. It was, and remains on one level, a quasi-religious system with a canon of classical texts that are regarded as almost sacred; it has temples and rituals, but there is no liturgy and no priesthood. It has never been fully accepted as a religion because it does not place the same emphasis on the numinous, the concept of a present spirit or deity that is found in Buddhism, Daoism and in the many local popular cults and religions of China. In spite of, or possibly because of this, the importance of Confucianism in Chinese culture is at least as important as are religions in other cultures. It is a rational and coherent, although not entirely consistent, philosophical system with a discourse that proceeds from the *Lunyu* (*Analects*) of Confucius (550–479 BC) and the *Mengzi* of Mencius (371–289 BC) in the days before China became a unified empire; through the neo-Confucian texts of Zhu Xi (1130–1200) and other influential writers and thinkers of the Song dynasty right through to the twentieth century. Confucian texts had become the core curriculum of the state education and examination system during the Han dynasty (206 BC–AD 221) and subsequently generations of candidates in the imperial examinations were required to prove themselves worthy of appointment as government officials by demonstrating in the austere examination cells their ability to memorise large sections of the classical texts which dealt with questions of leadership, good government and ethics and were written in technical and sometimes deliberately abstruse Classical Chinese [*wenyan*]. They were also required to comment on these texts according to the prevailing political orthodoxies. Classical Chinese, in which all historical, philosophical, literary texts and official documents were written, remained relatively unchanged for centuries, whereas the spoken language of the people had been transformed radically, and this made it a difficult subject of study that, with very few exceptions, was accessible only to members of the landowning elite who had the financial ability to devote many years to full-time study.

Confucianism also represented the deeply entrenched conservatism of Chinese society and political structure. The emperors began to make ritual sacrifices to Confucius during the Han dynasty, guaranteeing its position as a state cult if not an official religion. The influence of Confucianism went far beyond the ruling elite because the basic tenets of Confucius were incorporated into popular concepts of correct behaviour. The key social relationships, the five relationships [*wulun*] of Confucianism, were known to all: ruler–ruled; father–son; elder brother–younger brother; husband–wife; friend–friend. All apart from the last of these were relationships that implied superiority and inferiority, and this way of viewing the world through a framework of interacting hierarchies was applied to all aspects of society and even to relations between China and the smaller and weaker states that surrounded it. This was the Confucianism that the reformers of the late nineteenth and early twentieth centuries fought against, believing it to be responsible for holding China back and preventing it from achieving modernisation.

The attack on Confucianism had already begun with the Hundred Days reform movement of 1898, although it was not unambiguously articulated as such at the time. The reform of the educational system that eventually took place in the last years of the Qing dynasty, above all the abolition of the imperial examination system in 1905, was a practical move towards reducing the influence of Confucianism, but scholars during the period of the New Culture and May Fourth movements after the end of the First World War were determined to go even further. The New Culture [*Xin wenhua*] movement was one of the names given to the radical intellectual current that began in China in 1917. It was also known as the New Thought or the New Tide Movement. In 1918, students at Beijing University began publishing a monthly journal called *The Renaissance*. It aimed to 'promote a new literature in the living language of the people to take the place of the classical literature of old'; it was part of a movement protesting 'against many of the ideas and institutions in the traditional culture', and it was also a humanist movement which sought to reinterpret that culture in light of modern critical techniques. Hu Shi, one of the leading Chinese intellectuals of the time and a liberal academic and writer who was later to become a staunch anti-Communist, borrowed the title of the students' magazine to represent the movement as a whole in a series of lectures that he delivered in the Department of Comparative Religion in the University of Chicago in the USA in 1933: the lectures were eventually published under the title *The Chinese Renaissance*.[6]

Language Reform

In 1913, the nation had debated the question of what should be the appropriate spoken language for the new republic. In 1917, attention turned to the written language. Hu Shi was already a proponent of the reform of the Chinese written language, which he regarded as the *sine qua non* of cultural and social developments. The influential radical journal *New Youth* [*Xin qingnian*] which was the icon of the young intellectuals and boasted the chic French subtitle *La Jeunesse*, had published his article 'Tentative proposals for the reform of literature' [*Wenxue gailiang chuyi*] in its edition of January 1917. This essay became one of the key texts of literary reform. Hu Shi's modest title concealed a revolutionary proposition. He and his supporters, including the editor of *New Youth*, Chen Duxiu, intended that in future

Chinese should be written in the vernacular [*baihua*] a written form that was to be as close as was practicable to the spoken language of the time, rather than in the ossified classical language [*wenyan*] that could only be mastered with a colossal investment of time and considerable intellectual resources.

Although classical Chinese was the key to the culture and wisdom of 2,000 years of Chinese history and at its best can be elegant, sophisticated and refined, it was a closed book to the population as a whole and a barrier to literacy and education. The move from *wenyan* to *baihua* can be understood as having an impact similar to the shift from Latin to the Romance vernaculars of French, Spanish, Portuguese and Italian in early modern Europe. It would empower the poorer sections of society and remove the monopoly over knowledge and scholarship that was controlled by the *literati*, the educated sons (never officially the daughters) of the landowning elite.[7] Modern-minded writers began to use the vernacular language, not only in articles in reformist magazines but also in their essays and short stories, often struggling to escape from the stranglehold in which their literary education had restrained them. A whole new vernacular literature was born and writers such as Lu Xun, Yu Dafu and Mao Dun began to make a name for themselves in the modern written style.

Treaty of Versailles

The Paris Peace Conference, which had been convened to settle the terms of the post-war settlement between Germany and the Allies, ended on 28 June 1919 with the signing of the Treaty of Versailles. China had finally declared war on Germany and its principal ally, Austria, on 14 August 1917 and was therefore included among the Allies at the treaty negotiations, although Chinese forces had made no appreciable contribution to the war effort, apart from the Chinese labour battalions that supported the British and French troops on the battlefields of northern France and whose final resting place can still be seen in carefully tended Chinese cemeteries in rural Normandy and Picardy.

Although most of the text of the treaty dealt with the European settlement, certain key clauses that concerned Germany's possessions in China were to reverberate in East Asian politics for decades. Under Articles 128–34 of the Treaty, Germany agreed to renounce 'in favour of China all benefits and privileges resulting from the provisions of the final Protocol signed at Peking on [7 September] 1901' [in other words the Boxer Protocol]. All German-owned properties in Tianjin, Hankou 'or elsewhere in Chinese territory' were to be returned to China with the exception of diplomatic premises. However clauses 156–8 which dealt with Shandong were more problematic for the Chinese delegation. These Shandong clauses included the statement that:

> Germany, renounces in favour of Japan, all her rights, title and privileges – particularly those concerning the territory of [Jiaozhou], railways, mines and submarine cables – which she acquired in virtue of the Treaty concluded by her with China on [6 March] 1898 and of all other arrangements relative to the Province of Shandong.

The Chinese delegation to the conference, led by Lu Zengjiang and Thomas Zhengting Wang refused to sign the treaty because of the Shandong clauses, although the Chinese government, under its then President Xu Shizhang, acknowledged that it had no quarrel with the remainder of the treaty and that it was no longer at war with Germany. These controversial Shandong clauses of the Treaty of Versailles were to become the *cause célèbre* for patriotic Chinese and led to the radicalisation and politicisation of members of the intelligentsia who had hitherto been focusing on cultural, linguistic and literary reform.[8]

May Fourth Movement

Even before the formal signing of the Versailles treaty, news of China's failure to achieve any of its aims at the Peace Conference in Paris and rumours of a secret agreement between the Chinese government and Japan had spread like wildfire throughout China, and it was assumed that China had simply acquiesced to Japan's acquisition of the German concessions. Although the immediate cause of the nationalist ferment was China's humiliation in the Versailles negotiations, the humiliation felt by many thinking Chinese after Japan's Twenty-One Demands of 1915 still rankled. A number of student organisations including the New Tide Society, the Citizens Magazine Society, the Work-Study Society, the Common Voice Society, and the Cooperative Society met at the end of April 1919 and agreed to organise a mass peaceful demonstration for 7 May, which was National Humiliation Day, the fourth anniversary of Japan's presentation to China of the Twenty-One Demands. The student bodies of the main universities in Beijing, including Beijing University, the Higher Teachers' College, the Higher Industrial College and the College of Law and Political Science all supported this planned protest. A declaration on behalf of all students in Beijing was telegraphed to the press and government bodies:

> Our demand for the restoration of Qingdao is going to fail; and 7 May is near at hand. All of our people must awake to this situation. We hope

that you will one and all hold protest meetings on that day to oppose unanimously foreign aggression. Only in this way can our nation survive the crises.

The protests were not confined to student organisations. The Chambers of Commerce in Beijing and Shanghai demanded support for China's position at the Paris Peace Conference and the Citizens' Diplomatic Association called for a citizens' meeting [*guomin dahui*] to be held on 7 May. When it became clear that the Beijing municipal government was planning to crack down on the protests, a group of student activists convened an emergency meeting on the evening of 3 May. This meeting took place in an orderly but emotional atmosphere and it was decided to bring forward the demonstration to the following day, 4 May. At 10 o'clock on the morning of Sunday 4 May, student representatives met to agree on the publicity for their demonstration and on the route which they planned to take. The march was to begin at the Gate of Heavenly Peace, [*Tian'anmen*], on the southern wall of the Forbidden City, proceed southwards through the Legation Quarter [*Dong jiaomin hang*] and onwards from there to the commercial district on Hatamen Boulevard [*Chongwenmen*].

By half-past one in the afternoon of 4 May, more than 3,000 students from 13 universities and colleges had assembled in front of the Gate of Heavenly Peace to protest against China's acceptance of the Japanese demands and also the presence in Beijing of three protégés of former Prime Minister Duan Qirui who had supported the cession of Shandong to Japan and who were regarded as traitors. A representative of the Ministry of Education, the commandant of the Beijing garrison troops and the chief of police tried to persuade the students not to demonstrate: this delayed the start of the march but it did not deter the students. The demands of the students were made public in the Manifesto of all the Students of Beijing, a brief document written, in the spirit of the literary and cultural revolution, in clear *baihua* vernacular Chinese: it was circulated at the meeting and on the march. A more formal declaration, written in literary Chinese [*wenyan*], was also distributed nationally after the demonstration.

The demonstrators left Tiananmen at two o'clock after the meeting and set off southwards. National flags were carried at the front of the procession and some protesters carried mock funeral scrolls with the names of Cao Rulin, Lu Zongyu and Zhang Zongxian, the 'traitors' of the Shandong issue. Slogans of the demonstrators included 'Return our Qingdao', 'Abolish the Twenty-One Demands', 'Refuse to sign the peace treaty', 'Boycott Japanese goods', 'China belongs to the Chinese' and 'Death to the traitors Cao, Lu and Zhang'.[9] The demonstration moved slowly towards the foreign residential area, the Legation Quarter, which had been formally established after the signing of the Boxer Protocol, and was surrounded by high walls and heavily fortified. The students tried to enter the Legation Quarter to see the American ambassador but were turned back by foreign guards and also by Chinese police and troops. They marched north along East Chang'an Street to the Dongdan arch and soon found the residence of Cao Rulin, the minister of communications, at 2 Zhaojialou Street near the Foreign Ministry. Cao, who had been a member and financial backer of the pro-Japanese Anfu (Anhui-Fujian) warlord group, was regarded as one of the worst of the traitors and was therefore the number one target of the students.

What had until this point been a peaceful demonstration suddenly became violent, because of a combination of the students' frustration at not being able to convey their message directly to a foreign diplomat and heavy-handed police and military tactics. Cao's house was stormed and it was set on fire. Cao claimed that the students had caused the fire, but some of the demonstrators alleged that it had been started by Cao's family, who were trying to destroy confidential documents. The students found Zhang Zong-xiang, the Chinese ambassador to Japan who was staying with Cao Rulin, in the sitting room with the Army Minister Ding Shiyuan and a Japanese journalist Nakae Ushikichi (1889–1942) who had been a long-term resident of Beijing and was a renowned scholar of classical Chinese and Western philosophy. Zhang was severely beaten and carried unconscious by the police to the Tongren Hospital, which was run by Japanese nationals. Nakae and Cao also escaped (Cao in disguise) to seek sanctuary in the Legation Quarter.[10] Thirty-two students were arrested but they were released three days later. Martial law was declared in the area around the walled Legation Quarter. Demonstrations also took place in Shanghai and Chinese students attending universities in Tokyo organised their own protests.[11]

The series of demonstrations, strikes and boycotts that followed the demonstrations of 4 May became known as the May Fourth Movement. Chow Tse-tsung suggests that the term New Culture Movement, which had already been used before 1919, 'gained currency' in the six months following the demonstrations and was taken up by the editors of literary journals and political newspapers. Sun Yat-sen gave the movement and its name his imprimatur in 'A letter to the overseas comrades of the Guomindang, which he wrote on 29 January 1920, endorsing the spirit of patriotism of the May Fourth demonstrators.[12] To all intents and purposes, the May Fourth and New Culture Movements were one and the same, a continuum of political and cultural thought and deed. This was the electrifying and radical milieu in which the Chinese Communist Party and the revived Nationalist Guomindang were able to develop.

Birth of the Chinese Communist Party

The Chinese Communist Party (CCP) was founded in July 1921 and its intellectual and ideological origins have been the subject of controversy ever since. During the Cold War, some Western scholars, following the position taken by the defeated Guomindang in Taiwan, strove to demonstrate that the idea of a Communist Party was a wholly foreign concept, imposed on China by the Communist Third International (Comintern) from Moscow. When the CCP later asserted its independence from Moscow, great emphasis was placed on the indigenous nature of Chinese, as opposed to Russian Marxism, and its origins in the political clubs of the May Fourth Movement and earlier. Analysts attempted to account for the development of 'Maoism' by arguing that the CCP had characteristics that were particular and peculiar to Chinese culture and attitudes.

The CCP could not have been formed without the example of the Communist Party of the Soviet Union (Bolshevik), the CPSU (B) which is more commonly known as either the CPSU, or just the Bolsheviks. Equally, in spite of the similarities between Asiatic Russia and China, the history and culture of radicalism in China was very different from the corresponding trends in Russia and it is not surprising that the CCP eventually took a different political direction. The origins of the CCP lie in the creative tension between the experience of the Russian revolution and the CPSU, as explained to Chinese Communists by emissaries of the Comintern, and the Chinese response to their own internal political factors. These include the low level of urbanisation that China had achieved by the early years of the twentieth century and the relationship between the CCP and other domestic political parties, notably the Guomindang.

In April 1920, a delegation sent by the Vladivostok branch of the Bolsheviks' Far Eastern Bureau and led by Gregory Voitinsky, head of the Far Eastern Bureau in Irkutsk, visited Beijing and Shanghai. Voitinsky brought with him political literature on the Bolshevik Revolution including key texts by Lenin and a copy of John Reed's classic and stirring account of the October Revolution, *Ten Days that Shook the World*. In Beijing Voitinsky met Li Dazhao and other radical academics and students and in Shanghai he held meetings with Chen Duxiu, who was at the time the single most prominent radical of the May Fourth generation. It was during these meetings that the idea of creating a Chinese Communist Party emerged, but that idea was only possible because there already existed in China a number of study groups such as the New Peoples' (or Citizens') Study Society [*Xinmin xuehui*] in Hunan province, the Awakening Society [*Juewu she*] in Tianjin and the Social Welfare Society. In Beijing, the Society for the Study of Marxist Theory [*Makesi xueshuo yanjiuhui*], which had been formed in March 1920 by radical intellectuals associated with Li Dazhao and had in fact existed informally for some time before that, predated the Voitinsky visit.[13] The first Communist group in China was probably one set up in Shanghai in August 1920. It operated as the provisional central body of the CCP until the First Congress, which took place the following year and it had even issued its own rudimentary manifesto in November 1920.[14]

The First Congress of the CCP began in secret in Shanghai on 23 July 1921. It was held on the premises of a girls' school, which was closed at the time as it was the holiday period, in the French Concession of Shanghai. The location was chosen to avoid the prying eyes of police, who were working for the local warlord, but undercover agents were eventually alerted to the meeting and for the final session the delegates moved to a boat on the South Lake near Jiaxing in Zhejiang province where they continued their deliberations while pretending to be holidaymakers.[15] Thirteen delegates attended this First Congress, and they represented the 53 members of the local Chinese Communist groups in existence at that time (and one in Japan represented by Zhou Fohai) at the time. Shanghai was represented by Li Da and Li Hanjun; Beijing by Zhang Guotao and Liu Renjing; the Hunan delegates were Mao Zedong and He Shuheng; Hubei sent Dong Biwu and Chen Tanqiu; Wang Jinmei and Deng Enming came from Shandong and Chen Gongbo represented Guangdong. Neither of the two most prominent left-leaning radicals of the time, Chen Duxiu and Li Dazhao, attended. Although some of these delegates, notably Mao and Zhang Guotao, were to become well-known in the Chinese Communist movement, many of the others fell by the wayside in the ideological and military conflicts that were to follow.[16] It was from this seemingly insignificant and inauspicious beginning that the Chinese Communist Party grew to become the government of China in 1949.

The conference issued a programme and a document on the objectives of the CCP. The programme called for the revolutionary overthrow of capitalism; the establishment of the dictatorship of the proletariat and an alliance with the Third International, the Comintern. It detailed criteria for membership, organisation and finances and made it clear that, for the time being, 'the doctrines of the party and even membership in it must be kept secret'. The list of objectives, which were essentially the CCP's initial plan of action, covered the formation of trades unions, propaganda and publication of magazines, pamphlets and newspapers under the control of the party's Central Executive Committee and the organisation of schools to educate the working class. The CCP was to be exclusive and completely independent of any other party but would subordinate itself to the Third International and maintain contact with the Comintern's Far Eastern Bureau in Irkutsk.[17] Many of the Chinese Communist Party's contacts with

Russia, and subsequently the Soviet Union, during this period were with the Russian Far East rather than directly with Moscow.

By the time the CCP held its Second Congress, once again in Shanghai, in July 1922, the emphasis on exclusivity and independence had been significantly watered down. In part, this reflected the desperate situation that China faced after the Washington Conference (see below). The CCP perceived the Washington Conference as simply a mechanism for the foreign powers to formalise the division of China in to increase their economic dominance and indeed the Soviet Union organised its own conference, the Congress of the Toilers of the East, in response. The influence of the Dutch Comintern agent, Maring (also known by his real name of Hendricus Sneevliet) in persuading the nascent party to work with other groups was decisive. The view from the CPSU, transmitted by Maring and reflected in the Manifesto issued by the Second Congress, was that the CCP, in common with the Communist parties of other underdeveloped countries, could not hope to seize power unaided and should seek a political alliance with representatives of the 'enlightened bourgeois democratic movement'. It was agreed that the most appropriate group for them to negotiate an alliance with in China was the Guomindang, which had been organising an administration in Guangdong province under the respected Sun Yat-sen. The Manifesto also identified the peasantry as the 'most important factor in the revolutionary movement', rather than identifying the urban working class as the sole progressive force. The tone of the document was more confident than the Programme of the First Congress, and it formally identified the CCP as a branch of the Comintern.[18]

Sun Yat-sen and the Rebirth of the Guomindang

The military government that Sun had established in Guangzhou had been reorganised in April 1918 in such a way that Sun Yat-sen himself had been effectively excluded from power. Relocated to Shanghai, he then concentrated on attempting to reorganise his revolutionary political movement on a national basis. With no opportunity to exercise any genuine authority, he was able to devote all of his energies to creating an organisation that would one day take power. He also wrote two of his key works, his *Political Autobiography* [*Sun Wen xueshuo* – Sun Wen was one of Sun Yat-sen's formal names] and *Revolutionary Strategy* [*Geming fanglüe*] in which he outlined his plan for a revolution in three stages, beginning with military conquest which was to be followed by political tutelage (a benign dictatorship designed to prepare China for democracy) and concluding with constitutional government.[19] In 1921 Sun launched a military expedition, which was the forerunner of the 1926 Northern Expedition against the warlords. Although the expedition captured some key towns it failed, largely because of a dispute between Sun and the warlord of Guangxi and Guangdong, Chen Xiongming, which nearly cost Sun his life. Sun returned to Shanghai, determined to rebuild his power base in Guangzhou. He deployed the armies of his warlord supporters and was able to oust Chen Xiongming in January 1923 and return in triumph to Guangzhou on 21 February. The military government was re-established, with Sun as Grand Marshal *Da yuanshi*. This was the original Chinese term for Generalissimo, the title by which his successor Chiang Kai-shek was commonly known. It has been almost forgotten that it was originally used to describe Sun Yat-sen.[20]

A committee for the reorganisation of the nationalist parties had been established in the autumn of 1922 and Hu Hanmin and Wang Jingwei drafted a manifesto, which was approved by Sun on 16 December. The manifesto announced that the Chinese Revolutionary Party, the name that supporters of Sun Yat-sen in exile in Japan had used after the failure of the Second Revolution in 1913, had changed its name to the Chinese Guomindang. It was also announced that it would base its political platform on a modified version of what were now being referred to as Sun's Three People's Principles [*San min zhuyi*]: national self-determination, people's rights and people's livelihood.

Sun sought the support of the Soviet Union, the Union of Soviet Socialist Republics (USSR), which had been formally established on 30 December 1922, and was making overtures to non-Communist nationalist parties in other countries that were considered to be progressive. While still in Shanghai, Sun had entered into negotiations with the Comintern representative Adolph Joffe. An agreement between the two was announced on 26 January 1923 in which the USSR agreed to assist in the unification of China and both sides placed on record their common view that China was not yet ready for a Communist government. The USSR also renounced the privileges that Tsarist Russia had enjoyed in China and agreed not to encourage Mongolian independence, although this was already more or less a *fait accompli*. Sun sent his protégé, Chiang Kai-shek [Jiang Jieshi], to Moscow in the summer of 1923. Chiang was not able to meet Lenin who was gravely ill, but he did make the acquaintance of Leon Trotsky. He was deeply impressed by the organisation of the Soviet military system, Trotsky's particular achievement, and by the discipline of the Soviet Communist Party. Admiring the methods, if not the ideology of the CPSU, Sun and Chiang resolved to revitalise the Guomindang using the organisational structure of the CPSU as a model. The Comintern agent, Mikhail Borodin, was sent to Guangzhou to advise the Guomindang's new Central Executive Committee.[21]

The founding congress of the reconstructed Guomindang took place in Guangdong 20 to 30 January 1924. Each province was represented by six delegates but only three of them were elected by the province: the other three had been appointed by Sun Yat-sen. Sun, in his inaugural speech, went out of his way to stress that the task of the GMD was national reconstruction rather than merely the party political undertaking of establishing an administration. Members of the CCP were allowed to join the GMD although some delegates at the conference were opposed to this. Li Dazhao explained that members of the CCP who wished to enrol in the GMD were joining as individuals rather than as a group that would function as a faction and attempt to take over the whole party. The support of the USSR for the new party was demonstrated by a telegram from the Soviet ambassador, Karakhan, but the celebration of Sino-Soviet cooperation was marred by the news of the death of Lenin. Lenin had suffered a series of strokes and the fourth and fatal one had occurred while he was at his *dacha* (country home) outside Moscow. His death triggered a power struggle in the USSR, in which the main contenders were Stalin and Trotsky. Stalin's ultimate victory had serious repercussions, not only for the course of the history of the Soviet Union but also for the future of the Chinese revolution. The agreement between the CCP and the GMD is known in the historiography of the two parties as the beginning of the First United Front, which is deemed to have lasted from 1923 to 1927.

The political position of the Guomindang was made public in the Manifesto that was issued by the National Congress of the party on 30 January 1924. This document was essentially an expanded version of the 1923 Manifesto and was primarily the work of Sun Yat-sen. It was in three parts:

Part 1, *The Present Situation in China* began with a historical survey of recent politics in China, beginning in 1894 but concentrating on the 1911 Revolution and the role of Yuan Shikai. It then analysed the solutions to China's problems proposed by the constitutionalists, the federalists, the pacifists who favoured an international peace conference and those who wanted to hand over the running of the government to businessmen.

Part 2, *The Principles of the Guomindang* summarised Sun's three principles of National Self-determination, People's Rights (often translated as democracy but only democratic in a very limited sense) and People's Livelihood (sometimes translated as socialism, which it was not). By this time the three principles had been enshrined as the basic ideological tenets of Chinese nationalism.

Part 3, *The Guomindang Platform* expanded on the foreign and domestic policies of the GMD and the methods that would be used to implement them. The last section envisioned progress towards a democratic system evolving through the three stages that Sun had been developing for several years (i) military dictatorship, (ii) political tutelage (or guidance) and (iii) constitutional government. Sun made it clear that he did not consider the people of China to be ready for immediate democracy: that could only come with training and education. The policies outlined in the Declaration of the Guomindang were almost entirely those of one man – Sun Yat-sen.[22]

Washington Conference

These domestic political developments took place against the backdrop of two major international conferences, as the 'great powers' attempted to hammer out their policies towards Asia in the aftermath of the First World War.

The Washington Conference took place in Washington D.C. in the USA between November 1921 and February 1922. According to J.O.P. Bland, the pessimistic if not downright reactionary chronicler of the dying years of the Manchu court who was in China during that period:

> The significance of the Washington Conference was twofold. It was, in the first place, an outward and visible sign of the American nation's consciousness of its new rôle of predominance in world affairs; in the second place, it inaugurated a new alignment of the Powers, in substitution for that of the Anglo-Japanese alliance, pledged under American initiative, to a policy of non-interference and patient conciliation in China.[23]

The idea for the conference emerged from concerns that American foreign policy analysts had expressed about the possible future ramifications of the Shandong controversy and the renewal of the Anglo-Japanese Alliance, which were the two burning questions for Westerners in East Asia. On 8 July 1921, President Warren G. Harding asked the Department of State to sound out the governments of Great Britain, France, Italy and Japan as to their willingness to take part in a conference on arms limitation and the problems of the Far East. The responses were favourable and formal invitations were issued on 11 August 'to participate in a conference on the subjects of Limitation of Armament, in connection with which Pacific and Far Eastern questions will also be discussed, to be held in Washington on the 11th day of November 1921'. Belgium, China, the Netherlands and Portugal were also invited 'because of their interest in the Pacific and Far Eastern questions'. It speaks volumes for the attitude of the non-Communist great powers towards East Asia at this time that Japan was included in the early consultations whereas China was part of the afterthought.

The opening ceremony of the conference took place on 12 November in the Memorial Continental Hall in Washington. This was one day later than had originally been planned and the delay was to allow time for the delegates to attend the ceremony of the interment of the Unknown Soldier at the Arlington National Cemetery in Virginia on Armistice Day, a reminder if any were necessary, that the conference had been convened to deal with the aftermath of the First World War and with problems that had been left unresolved or exacerbated by the Treaty of Versailles in 1919. The conference continued, in plenary session and in specialist committee meetings, until 6 February 1922. China was represented by Dr Sao-Ke Alfred Sze, its ambassador to the USA and by Dr V.K. Wellington Koo the ambassador to the UK, Wang Zhonghui the chief justice of the supreme court, and Mr Wu Zhaozhu, supported by over 130 advisors, interpreters and translators and other technical experts.[24]

The priority for the American negotiators was the Anglo-Japanese Alliance of 1902, which they viewed 'with deep concern' and as 'seriously prejudicial to our interests'. By this they meant that it undermined the US policy of the 'open door', which can be defined simply as the right of all nations to have equal access to commercial and diplomatic relations, in particular with China:

> It was, therefore, a matter of the greatest gratification that the American Delegation found that they were able to obtain an agreement by which the Anglo-Japanese Alliance should be immediately terminated. No greater step could be taken to secure the unimpeded influence of liberal opinion in promoting peace in the Pacific region.[25]

The Alliance was replaced by the Four-Power Treaty which was approved by the USA, the British Empire, France and Japan and signed on 13 December 1921. Senator Henry Cabot Lodge, one of the American delegates, summed up the treaty as an understanding that the four powers would resolve any conflict over their 'insular possessions and dominions' in the Pacific by mutual agreement and that no provision had been made for the use of force. A supplementary treaty signed on 6 February 1922 was found necessary to clarify the position of the main islands of Japan which were not to be included, although Karafuto (southern Sakhalin), Taiwan and the Pescadores islands were covered by the treaty.[26] Shandong, however, was the problem that most concerned China, and the Chinese and Japanese delegations took the opportunity presented by the Washington Conference to agree on a treaty, which the two parties signed on 4 February 1922. Japan agreed to restore Jiaozhou and its region to China within six months, to withdraw troops and to transfer the Qingdao–Jinan railway to Chinese ownership at a cost of 53,000,000 gold marks to China. Great Britain announced at the same time that the British concession of Weihai would also be handed back to China. Weihai (also known as Weihaiwei) is on the northern coast of Shandong and had been a useful summer anchorage for British warships that were based in the southern part of China.[27]

The Washington Conference ended with the signing of a Nine-Power Pact that guaranteed the territorial integrity of China and included an agreement on the restoration of Chinese sovereignty over the parts of Shandong occupied by the Japanese. An open-door policy for foreign relations with China was also proposed. At the same time, the powers agreed on the Washington Naval Limitation Treaty, which limited the number and size of warships and fixed the ratio of naval ships between the great powers. This policy was unenforceable largely because of opposition to it in Japan, and its provisions were ignored in practice by the Japanese and were finally repudiated by a right-wing government in Tokyo in 1934.

Congress of the Toilers of the Far East

The Congress of the Toilers of the Far East was held in Moscow 21 January–2 February 1922 as the Soviet Union's response to the Washington Conference, from which it had been excluded. The West had pursued a policy of isolating or ignoring the USSR since the abortive allied intervention in the Civil War that had followed the October Revolution. The proposal to convene the Washington Conference was made at the same time as a meeting of the Third Comintern Congress, and the Comintern immediately decided to organise its own conference of revolutionaries from the Far East in opposition. There was a brief initial meeting in Irkutsk but the main conference was held in Moscow from 21 January to 1 February and held its final session in the Uritzky Palace in Petrograd (St Petersburg) on 2 February in a joint session with the Petrograd Soviet. Grigoriy Zinoviev, who chaired the first session of the conference and gave the closing speech, outlined the Comintern's view of the Washington Conference in his report and concluded that 10 December 1921, the date of the Four-Power Agreement, was 'one of the blackest days in the history of mankind', arguing that the powers had 'concluded between themselves an armistice for the purpose of more successfully oppressing the nations at the expense of whose blood these imperialist robbers have been living for many a year'.[28]

Speakers from China, Korea, Japan and Mongolia reported on the situation in their respective countries and the congress concluded with a resolution supporting Zinoviev's report; condemned the 'imperialist plot of the four robbers of Washington' and, not surprisingly, called for 'an indissoluble union of the workers of the Far East under the flag of the Communist

International', as the only possible solution to the problems of the region. The Chinese Communist Party sent a delegation and a representative of the Guomindang, Zhang Qiubai, is also reported to have attended, although a careful reading of the 39 delegates from China, by age, social position, education and party membership, does not record any member of the Guomindang attending.[29] The Congress of the Toilers of the Far East may have had the edge in rhetoric but in terms of economic or military muscle it was no match for the Washington Conference and the great powers.

8

NORTHERN EXPEDITION
AND UNITED FRONT (1923–1927)

The period from 1923 to 1927 is the second of the three epochs of up-heaval and transformation in twentieth-century China that are commonly described as revolutionary by historians, although it is not normally called a revolution in China today. The other two periods are the overthrow of the Qing dynasty in the Revolution of 1911 and the coming to power of the Chinese Communist Party in 1949 after its victory in the civil war. The years between 1923 and 1927 were also known as the period of the First United Front, the name for the first period of cooperation between the CCP and the Guomindang. This included the series of military actions that culminated in the Northern Expedition, during which the CCP and the GMD appeared to have forged a common bond in trying to create a united republican China out of the chaos of the fragmented warlord system.

The actions of both the CCP and the GMD were influenced, and argu-ably distorted, by the power struggle between the supporters of Stalin and Trotsky that was taking place in the Soviet Union following the death of Lenin on 21 January 1924. The policies of the Soviet Union under Stalin were a significant factor in the failure of the Chinese revolution in 1927: this was to have a long-lasting effect on the relations between the Com-munist Parties of the two countries and was one of the underlying causes of the breakdown of fraternal relations between the two Communist powers in the 1960s. The history of this period remains fiercely contested by parti-sans of the factions involved.

Huangpu (Whampoa) Military Academy

Although the establishment of the two political parties, rivals but cooperat-ing uneasily under the paternalist guidance of the Comintern, was of endur-ing importance, another institution that was created in 1924 was of far more practical significance in the short term for the revolutionary forces. The Huangpu Military Academy [*Huangpu junguan xuexiao* or *Huangpu junxiao*] was designed to train the leadership of a united revolutionary army, a task that had for years been one of Sun Yat-sen's highest priorities. It was finally established on 3 May 1924 at the site of the former Imperial Naval Academy, on an island in the Pearl River Delta to the east of the city of Guangzhou. Chiang Kai-shek was appointed commandant of the new academy on his return from Moscow, where he had been studying the organisational and training methods of the Red Army that had been inspired primarily by Leon Trotsky, the Bolshevik Commissar for War. Chiang had also been negotiating with the Moscow authorities for the supply of weapons to support the nationalist revolution in China.[1] Chiang Kai-shek wrote about his early experiences in the Soviet Union in 1956, during his seventy-first year and after his final defeat in the Civil War with the CCP. While his memoirs are coloured by bitterness at what he perceived as the betrayal of the Guomindang by the Comintern, they do shed light on his activities in Russia. He left Shanghai on 16 August 1923 after a meeting with the Comintern agent, Maring, and on 25 August crossed the border at Manzhouli, a busy transit point between Russia and China that lies close to the borders with Outer Mongolia, reaching Moscow on 16 September. Chiang and three other Guomindang members spent three months in Russia and concentrated on studying political and military organisations, including a tour of the Central Party Headquarters, attending meetings of the Comintern, and visiting the Military Academy in Moscow, the Naval Academy in Petrograd (St Petersburg) and the fleet at Kronstadt. As Lenin, the leader of the Bolsheviks, was seriously ill and near to death Chiang was not able to meet him and he had more discussions with Trotsky than with any other Soviet leader, finding him to be 'the most forthright of them all, both in speech and in conduct'.[2]

Sun Yat-sen had made clear his reasons for the establishment of the military academy in a speech at the opening ceremony:

> Because we have lacked a revolutionary army, the warlords have dominated the Republic and impeded the progress of the revolution. Our aim in opening this academy is to create the revolutionary task anew from this day and students of this academy ... will be the bones and the trunk of the forthcoming Revolutionary Army.[3]

Students were selected as much on the basis of the level of their political understanding of Guomindang ideology as their physical capacity and suitability for army life. Within the Academy there was a Guomindang representative whose status and authority was at the same level as that of the principal of the academy, and a party organisation permeated the academy parallel with the traditional military hierarchy. This commissariat system, which was based on the system that had been developed in the Red Army

of the Soviet Union, was later extended to the whole of the National
Revolutionary Army of the Guomindang, and in due course to the Workers
and Peasants' Red Army and the Peoples' Liberation Army of the Chinese
Communist Party. The original intention was to enrol 300 students in the
academy but 3,000 applications were received, and it was decided to limit
the number admitted to 500 of those who had passed an entrance examination. The first cohort graduated after a short course and 400 more were
admitted. When Chiang Kai-shek reported on the state of the academy in
May 1924, he was concerned about a lack of funds and an inadequate
supply of weapons for training purposes. Nevertheless, the Huangpu Academy did become operational and it was the nucleus of the National Revolutionary Army that Chiang created to mount the Guomindang's Northern
Expedition against the warlords.[4] Support from the Soviet Union was vital,
and the academy was

> supplied and operated with Russian funds, staffed with Russian mili-
> tary advisers. Before long, shiploads of Russian arms were coming
> into Canton [Guangzhou] harbour to supply the armies which rallied
> to the new banner as soon as the Guomindang began to display the
> new strength with which all these activities endowed it.[5]

The first shipment of munitions from Russia arrived at Huangpu on 7 October 1924 and consisted of 8,000 rifles and 4 million rounds of ammunition.[6]
Russian instructors at the Huangpu Academy were led by General Vassili
Konstantinovich Bluecher, operating at the time under the name of Galen,
who was later to become commander-in-chief of the Soviet Red Army in
the Far East, the force that defeated the Japanese in Manchuria in the Second World War. The curriculum of the Academy was modelled explicitly
on the Command Colleges that Trotsky had created for the Red Army and
the greatest emphasis was on subjects that can broadly be described as
political education, including the study of patriotism, socialism, imperialism
and the role of the National Revolutionary Army.[7]

As the terms of the agreement between Sun and Joffe allowed for individual members of the CCP to join the GMD, it is not surprising that many
of the more able Communist activists found their way into the Huangpu
Academy. Indeed, as many as 80 of the first cohort were members of the
CCP, and the director of the Political Department, the head of the political
commissariat, for much of the time was none other than Zhou Enlai, who
was to become the Premier of the People's Republic of China. The Academy was an ideal base for the recruitment and education of a future
Communist Party elite.[8] Although there was cooperation between CCP and
 members at Huangpu, there was also considerable ideological tension and

some of the GMD cadets joined the Sun Yat-sen society, which had been established in the academy specifically to counter Marxist teachings.

Northern Expedition

The Northern Expedition [*Beifa*] or Northern Expedition of Unification [*Beifa tongyi*] that had long been planned by Sun Yat-sen to bring China under one republican government, was formally launched on 5 September 1924 at a conference in Shaoguan, which is in the north of Guangdong province and close to the border with Jiangxi. The National Revolutionary Army was far from being in a state of operational readiness and Sun was under no illusion about this, but his hand was forced by two major considerations. First, hostilities had broken out between the warlord armies of Jiangsu and Zhejiang on 1 September, and it was patently obvious that the Fengtian and Zhili armies were also on the verge of war with each other. Second, Sun's own position in Guangzhou had become untenable because the people of Guangdong had grown resentful of the burdens that the presence of his military units had imposed on the province. Prices had been driven up, corruption was rife and there had been many instances of indiscipline among the troops. Sun came to the conclusion that his only possible course of action was to march northwards and engage the northern warlords in battle. On the one hand this would be part of the fulfilment of his dream for a united China; on the other he was able to promise the people of Guangzhou an independent municipal government and the abolition of some of the more onerous taxes that had been levied to support his military establishment.[9]

The relationship between the warlords was complex and the extent of the territory that was under their control varied over the years and indeed at times from month to month, but a snapshot of the situation on the eve of the Northern Expedition gives an indication of the task faced by the nationalist troops. Feng Yuxiang of the Zhili faction ruled most of the northern and northwestern regions and after seizing Beijing on 23 October 1924, he renamed his own army the 1st Army of the National Army of the Chinese Republic [*Zhonghua minguo guominjun*] and his subordinates Hu Jingyi and Sun Yue became commanders of the 2nd and 3rd Armies. Feng ordered his troops to expel Puyi, the last Manchu emperor, from the Imperial Palace where he had lived under the agreement made in 1912 and Puyi fled to Tianjin. Feng also ousted Wu Peifu, the old Zhili warlord and Cao Kun, the titular but powerless president of China. The renaming of his army and the capture of the old Qing capital are an indication of Feng's aspirations to national rather than merely regional power. He issued proclamations to the people of Beijing, to the north of China and to the nation as a whole, calling for a peace conference and an end to the rule by militarists and he appeared to be moving towards an alliance with the Guomindang.

Feng Yuxiang's main rivals in the north and northeast were the forces of the Fengtian clique under the Manchurian warlord Zhang Zuolin. The Fengtian armies controlled the whole of Manchuria, Shandong and much of Zhejiang, Anhui and Jiangsu, including the old Ming capital of Nanjing. They recaptured Beijing from Feng Yuxiang in early 1925. Yan Xishan ruled the province of Shanxi independently and played the larger warlord factions off against each other. The Zhili forces under Wu Peifu had control of most of Hubei from Wu's base in Hankou. In October 1925, another Zhili warlord, Sun Chuanfang, claimed jurisdiction over Zhejiang, Fujian, Anhui, Jiangxi and Jiangsu. Sichuan was not under the overall control of any single warlord; Yunnan in the far southwest was the fief of Tang Jiyao; Zhao Hengti ran Hunan. Guangdong and Guangxi were under the control of the forces of the Guomindang, which at the time could easily have been taken for just another warlord army. Only with hindsight is it apparent that their ideology, national perspective and determination set them apart from the other regional forces of that period.[10]

Sun Yat-sen died in Beijing on 12 March 1925 at the age of just 58 and on 20 August, Liao Zhongkai, the administrator of the Huangpu Academy, minister of finance in the fledgling National Government, and one of the chief architects of Soviet-Guomindang cooperation, was assassinated. The way was clear for Chiang Kai-shek and other non-communist officers to make a move to boost their influence. On 20 March, Chiang ordered the seizure of the gunboat *Zhongshan* that had sailed into Guangzhou and the arrest of its captain, a member of the CCP who may have been ordered into the city by Soviet advisers. Chiang also had a number of CCP political commissars and Russian advisers arrested and he disarmed the Workers' Guard, a militia that was controlled by the CCP. In what has often been called the 'Zhongshan incident' or the Guangzhou Coup, Chiang Kai-shek seized control of the Huangpu Academy and, by doing so, consolidated his own power in the Guomindang. Soviet advisers accepted this coup and supported Chiang at this time.

The National Revolutionary Army (NRA) [*Guomin geming jun*], that had been formed around the nucleus of the Huangpu-trained officers, grew rapidly between 1924 and 1926 and other regional forces joined to swell its ranks, notably the Guangxi army in February 1926. In April and May, the NRA moved northwards in support of the Hunanese warlord Tang Shenzhi who had been attacked by the forces loyal to his Shandong rival Wu Peifu. On 9 June, Chiang Kai-shek formally became commander-in-chief of the expanded NRA forces and on 1 July he made public the Mobilisation Order for the Northern Expedition at a meeting to celebrate the first anniversary of the establishment of the National Government in Guangzhou by Sun Yat-sen in 1925. The Guomindang leadership took an oath of loyalty to the principles laid down by Sun, and Chiang, as chairman of the party's Military Council, read out the order:

> Our army keeps alive the will of the late generalissimo and hopes to carry out his revolutionary proposals. To protect the welfare of the people, we must overthrow all warlords and wipe out reactionary power so that we may implement the Three People's Principles and complete the National Revolution. Now, gather we our armies, first to occupy Hunan, then Wuhan, and pressing further to join up with our ally the [National Army, *Guominjun*] to unite China and restore our nation.[11]

The strategy was clear and explicit: the Northern Expedition was being legitimised as a continuation of the vision of Sun Yat-sen.

The NRA marched into Hunan, taking the provincial capital, Changsha on 1 July and then moved into Hubei, capturing the Yangzi River towns of Hanyang and Hankou on 6 and 7 September. The walled city of Wuchang, the third part of the Wuhan conurbation, in which there was a sizeable community of foreign missionaries, remained under siege until 10 October. Other units took control of the treaty port of Jiujiang in Jiangxi province on 5 November and the provincial capital, Nanchang, on 8 November.[12] By the end of 1926, the NRA had taken all the major towns and cities of the provinces of Hunan, Hubei, Jiangxi and Fujian and was in control of almost the whole of central China south of the Yangzi River. If the provinces of Guangxi and Guizhou which were already allies of the NRA and the original base of Guangdong are added to this, the National Government in Guangzhou could be said to have had authority over a population of approximately 170 million. The territory under NRA control expanded during the campaigns of spring 1927 as the army moved in a northeasterly direction and the cities of Hangzhou in Zhejiang, Hefei in Anhui and, most importantly, Shanghai and Nanjing were occupied in February and March. The lack of resistance to the advance of the NRA was remarkable. This was without doubt due in part to the conflict between the feuding northern warlords and their inability to coordinate what should have been superior military forces, but popular support for the Northern Expedition, both among the peasants and in the burgeoning workers' movement in the cities, also played an important role.[13]

Chinese Labour Movement

One of the consequences of Western and Japanese colonial expansion in China during the nineteenth century was a rapid increase in urbanisation and industrialisation, but only in certain regions. A modern industrial sector grew very rapidly in areas where previously there had only been handicraft industries. To a large extent this industrial sector was confined to the northeast and the Treaty Ports where foreign capital had found a ready supply of cheap labour, either *in situ* or willing to migrate from the impoverished countryside. New-style factories, long familiar in the West and already established in Japan, were created in the ports, which were situated either on the eastern seaboard or inland in the towns and cities along the Yangzi River. Working conditions were often atrocious, conflicts between employees and management were frequent and by the 1920s there was already a strong tradition of trade (labour) unions and a history of strikes and workers' protests.[14]

As early as November 1916, there had been a wave of strikes in the French concession of Tianjin, in the Jiangnan shipyards of Shanghai and among the basketmakers and papermakers of the Hunanese capital, Changsha. The industrial action spread across the country and increased year by year, developing in parallel with the student and intellectual activism of the May Fourth Movement.[15] From these strikes grew a movement of organised labour, a network of craft and trade unions. Although the GMD did have some political involvement with the labour movement, it was dominated by the CCP, which in its early years focused on creating and supporting the organisations of the urban working class, almost to the complete exclusion of the peasantry.

The CCP was involved in three major strikes in the two years after its first congress. The Hong Kong Seamen's Union took strike action on 13 January 1922 in support of demands for a wage increase, demands that the employers had refused. The industrial unrest spread to Shanghai and Shantou and the British colonial government in Hong Kong ordered that the Seamen's Union should be disbanded and arrested the leaders of the strike. Other unions joined the dispute in sympathy and on 26 February a general strike was called for all Hong Kong, involving as many as 120,000 workers at its height. Troops of the British garrison in the colony fired on a demonstration of strikers on 3 March, injuring hundreds of workers, of whom four died, and the strike was settled on 5 March when the employers agreed to the wage increases and released the detained leaders of the trade unions.

On 17 September 1922, miners at the Anyuan colliery in Jiangxi province downed tools in support of demands for improved wages, better working conditions and the official recognition of their trade union. The strike was led by, among others, Liu Shaoqi (later to be China's first Communist head of state) but was celebrated in the 1970s in a painting that depicted the spruce and youthful Chairman Mao Zedong walking to organise the strike dressed in the traditional robes of a Chinese scholar. The miners' demands were accepted. On 24–25 August, there was a strike by more than 3,000 employees on the Beijing–Hankou railway and some concessions were secured by the workforce. When the railwaymen met in what is now the great Henan railway hub city of Zhengzhou on 2 February 1923 to create the Beijing–Hankou Railway General Trade Union, they were hounded by troops and police of Wu Peifu's warlord government and their leaders were imprisoned. A major industrial action began and Wu Peifu's troops shot and killed many of the strikers. In spite of support from students and workers in Beijing, the strike was put down by the police and the army.[16]

The most dramatic increase in labour agitation followed the May Thirtieth Incident. On 30 May 1925, students and workers were attending a memorial service in the International Settlement of Shanghai to commemorate strikers who had been killed and injured at a Japanese-owned factory earlier that month. A British inspector of police ordered his men to open fire on the demonstrators and at least 9, possibly 12, were killed and many others were seriously injured: a large number of arrests were also made. This incident was followed by a wave of strikes, boycotts and demonstrations and a call for a general strike. In the agitation that followed, more demonstrators were shot and killed by British police on the island of Shamian in the city of Guangzhou. The strikes spread to Beijing and Hankou and especially to Hong Kong and Guangzhou where British goods were boycotted. In Beijing on 10 June, a crowd of over 100,000 people, standing outside the Gate of Heavenly Peace [*Tian'anmen*] in the pouring rain, heard demands for the National Government to take action against the British Legation. The demonstration was carefully choreographed and led by students but there were also

> contingents of merchants, teachers and workers, students and journalists encircling the politicians occupying the central platform. A total of 157 groups were represented, ranging from professional associations… like the chamber of commerce and the journalists association, to provincial clubs, merchant and craft guilds, religious organisations, Marxist study groups and labour unions.[17]

Local grievances merged with nationalist outrage and textile workers in Tianjin and Qingdao, cotton mill workers in Shanghai, miners in Anyuan, and many others left their jobs and took to the streets. At the beginning of May the All-China Labour Federation met in Guangzhou and the Shanghai General Trades Union was organised on 31 May. These were attempts at establishing national bodies to reflect the views of the hundreds of thousands of workers who had been involved in local strikes. The CCP was in the forefront of these organisations. In Tianjin, the level of trade union activity increased rapidly after the May Thirtieth Incident and the workforce, much of it newly arrived from the countryside, proved amenable to the organisations that the CCP were helping to establish, often using their knowledge of family and native-place networks to draw in recruits. 'Many millhands became active in unions while a small but important core of activists was recruited into the CCP.' [18]

As the National Revolutionary Army moved into Jiangxi province in the autumn of 1926, demonstrations and strikes by workers and students helped to facilitate the capture of the provincial capital, Nanchang, which fell in September, and the treaty port of Jiujiang which was taken in November. After the arrival of the forces from the south, a General Union of 73 trade associations was formed in Nanchang. It was some 40,000 strong and was led by the printers and telephone workers: railwaymen on the Nanchang–Jiujiang line also went on strike.[19] The experience of Jiangxi was typical of the impact that the NRA had in the provinces that it passed through. On the one hand the labour movement supported the Northern Expedition and eased its passage; on the other, the arrival of the NRA stimulated the formation of new trade union activities and radicalised substantial numbers of urban residents. Industrial protests were not limited to the modern sector: there are records of more than 540 separate strikes involving handicraft workers of all trades between 1921 and 1929 in places as far apart as Beijing, Shanghai, Guangzhou, Hangzhou, Chahar, and Chongqing.[20] The porcelain town of Jingdezhen in Jiangxi province was deeply affected by the labour movement that flourished in the wake of the Northern Expedition. Nanchang came under the control of the NRA in September 1926 and, when Jiujiang was taken two months later, the first trade union in the area, the General Union, was formed: in the following year plans were made to organise a federation of trade unions based on workers' organisations that were already taking shape in Nanchang, Anyuan, Jiujiang and Jingdezhen.[21] Embryo Communist groups were also being formed, and one of these, led by Fang Zhimin, was involved in a strike for better food supplies that took place in Jingdezhen in 1929.[22]

Putsch in Shanghai

The relationship between Communist and non-Communist members of the Guomindang during the Northern Expedition was complex and often tense. Communists were extremely useful to the commanders of the NRA: their exceptional network of contacts with local underground party cells and trades unions meant that they could travel ahead of the main force and provide intelligence to the military. They could also organise factory work-ers and townspeople to strike and demonstrate so that the authority of the warlord administrations was undermined and the towns and cities that they controlled would fall more easily to the nationalist forces. As the NRA moved northwards, these strikes and protests erupted in the towns and cities through which it passed.

However it was clear to both sides that each group had its own agenda. Chiang Kai-shek was much less sympathetic to the Communists than Sun Yat-sen had been, but he was prepared to make use of their energy, organ-isational skills and local knowledge. Many members of the CCP were un-happy about being forced into an alliance with the GMD by the policy of the Comintern but the Northern Expedition provided them with an un-paralleled opportunity to organise and recruit members for the party or for its affiliated trades unions. Although in the short term the interests of the GMD and the CCP were complementary, in the long term a struggle for power seemed inevitable. It was only a matter of time before this uneasy alliance came to an end.

The NRA entered Shanghai on 22 March 1927. There had been no opposition to their advance and they were able to march into the city with-out firing a shot. This was largely because the All-China General Trades Union in Shanghai had called for a general strike and demonstrations in support of the NRA and the workers' government that they hoped would be established on the arrival of the Northern Expedition. The general strike, which was the result of months of organisation by the CCP, had begun on 21 March and Shanghai welcomed the NRA troops. Although Chiang Kai-shek benefited from the CCP's influence and organisational skill, he had become increasingly alarmed by their authority and by the level of support that they had in the cities and was determined to purge the Communists once and for all and abandon the United Front.

The signal for the purge was a bugle call from Chiang Kai-shek's head-quarters at four o'clock in the morning of 12 April, followed by a blast on the siren of a gunboat that was anchored off Nantao, a Chinese quarter close to the French Concession on the banks of the Huangpu River that was later to be devastated by Japanese bombing in 1937. Armed members of the Shanghai underworld's Green Gang and Red Gang, wearing white armbands identifying them as *gong*, 'labour' pickets, moved through the working-class areas of the city, attacking the offices of trade union organ-isations that were affiliated with the Communist Party or any that might conceivably have pro-Communist sympathies. Officials and strike pickets were shot where they were found or tied together and marched off to be executed elsewhere. The last building to be attacked that morning was the Commercial Press where more than 400 pickets held out for hours until the gangland thugs were reinforced by regular troops of the NRA who stormed the building and wiped out the resistance. Contemporary reports put the death toll at between 400 and 700, but many more were injured or arrested and hundreds of people disappeared in the confusion. Although the General Union and the CCP organisations remained in existence, their links with the local community had been broken and their influence had been all but eliminated. Chiang Kai-shek's ruthless action against his erstwhile allies has been called the Shanghai Coup, the Shanghai Massacre or the White Terror.[23]

Chiang was still not entirely in control: since December 1926, Wuhan had been the base for a left-wing opposition to Chiang Kai-shek's Guomindang. This was in line with the strategy of the Comintern's representative in China, Mikhail Borodin, who wanted the CCP to continue to cooperate with the left-wing of the Guomindang, which meant essentially working with the leaders of factions opposed to Chiang. On 17 April 1927 after the Shanghai Coup, the Wuhan government, now headed by Wang Jingwei who had returned from Paris at the beginning of April, announced that it had expelled Chiang from the Guomindang and dismissed him from all his political and military positions. This was a futile gesture as the Wuhan government was in no position to influence events: it was bankrupt and powerless and at most could only claim to have authority over parts of three provinces – Hubei, Hunan and Jiangxi – whereas Chiang Kai-shek was in control of the wealthiest and most developed region of China and was able to gain the confidence of industrialists and financiers. Jiang established his own national government in Nanjing on the following day and this was to be the beginning of a decade of Guomindang rule. The CCP continued its activities in Wuhan as long as possible, even holding its Fifth Congress in the city 27 April–5 May. Chen Duxiu, the CCP secretary general, persuaded the delegates to the congress that they should continue to support the government of Wang Jingwei in a united front against Chiang Kai-shek. The CCP withdrew its members from the Wuhan government on 13 July but remained nominally in cooperation with the GMD. The final break in the united front came on 15 July when the CCP members of the GMD were ordered by the GMD to renounce their Communist Party membership on 15 July. Faced with that choice the Communist Party withdrew completely from the alliance.

Political Centres, Political Symbols

As the forces of the nationalist revolution moved through China in the first quarter of the twentieth century, distinct regimes were established in a number of key cities, some of them transient and others more enduring; some of these cities became symbols of particular types of political culture.

Beijing, as the centre of Manchu rule, was the symbol of the ancien régime. Its image was that of a conservative, corrupt and moribund city, and the presence of the last emperor, Pu Yi, in the Imperial Palace until 1924 only served to confirm this. Nevertheless, there was grudging respect for the city that had been the capital of China continuously from 1421 to 1911 and the capture of Beijing was one of the main objectives of warlords and nationalists alike.

Guangzhou, the power base of the Guomindang, was seen as radical, nationalist, and politically active. It was a Cantonese city, with a vital language and culture that were very different from the dour Mandarin of the north. It had experienced Western commercial and diplomatic pressure at an earlier stage than any other Chinese city and also had close connections with the Chinese diaspora in Southeast Asia, the USA and Europe. It was more cosmopolitan and open to outside influences than any other city apart from Shanghai.

Shanghai was 'different, and was seen and rejected as such by the Guomindang and then by the Communists, both of whom described the city as foreign.'[24] Indeed, in 1949 there were serious proposals to disperse as much as half of the population to the countryside and relocate schools and factories to the provinces of the interior, although these plans were vigorously opposed by local people and were never implemented. A writer in *Economic Weekly* [*Jingji zhoubao*] described Shanghai as 'a non-productive city. It is a parasitic city. It is a criminal city. It is a refugee city. It is the paradise of adventurers.'[25] Shanghai was of course the city in which the CCP had been founded in 1921 and defeated in 1927. It was later to play a radical role in the Cultural Revolution of the 1960s and was one of the leaders of the dramatic economic growth in the 'reform and opening' period of the 1980s.

Wuhan, the capital of Hubei province, lies on the middle reaches of the Yangzi River and was one of the inland treaty ports. It was the setting for the Wuchang rising that began the collapse of Qing power in 1911. As the base for the Left Guomindang and the last attempts of the Comintern to shore up the more progressive elements of the Chinese nationalists after Chiang Kaishek's takeover of the GMD, it became a symbol of compromise and failure.

Nanjing, the original capital of the first Ming emperor in 1368, had not played a significant role in Chinese political life since the Yongle emperor had moved his administration to Beijing in 1421: it retained the status of an imperial city, governed directly by Beijing but it was a political backwater. It was to become Chiang Kai-shek's base in 1928, the symbol of Guomindang rule of China and, after the Rape of Nanjing in 1937, the emblem of the brutalities of the Japanese occupation.

Rural China in the 1920s

Although the most dramatic political events of the 1920s took place in the cities, it was in the rural areas, apparently lethargic, unchanging and backward, that the movement that was eventually to shake the nation took root. For centuries, peasant movements and peasant risings had been the forces that had risen to overthrow Chinese dynasties, and in the twentieth century it was once again to be a peasant movement that resolved the question of who would rule China. In many ways, rural China was China: the total population of China in the 1920s and 1930s was something of the order of 450 million, of whom at least 345 million, 75 percent, lived and worked on the land.[26]

The quality of life and the standard of living of Chinese peasants in the 1920s varied greatly. By and large it was a life of grinding, repetitive manual work with few mechanical aids and desperate poverty, but the degree of poverty was much greater for farmers working the poor soil of the hilly areas of northern and western China than it was for their counterparts tending the wet paddy fields in the productive rice bowl of the southeast. There were also great contrasts in the system of land tenure and the class structure of the countryside in different parts of the country. In the wealthier regions, the system of land ownership had become quite sophisticated, with a hierarchy of landlords, wealthy peasants, poor peasants and labourers. In the less productive areas even the poorest peasants might own a small amount of land. Regional customs and the influence of religious foundations and clans or extended families, which frequently owned and rented out land, complicated the situation even further.

Village society was complex and in constant flux and was not at all the simple bucolic life that is sometimes imagined. In addition to the main economic activity, agriculture, which followed the seasonal needs of the seeds and the crops, there was often a thriving craft tradition and there were sometimes small industries such as breweries or factories making processed foods or tools. Although transport and communications may have been underdeveloped, most villages were not isolated units but were linked to other villages by networks of markets and to the county town where the local representative of the central government was based. Social and ritual life revolved around the local Buddhist or Daoist temples (or in some communities, the mosque or the church) and the ancestral hall where the tablets commemorating the departed ancestors were preserved in the Confucian tradition. There was an annual round of festivals from Spring Festival (Chi-

nese New Year) through Qingming, the festival of the sweeping of ancestral graves, to the Mid-Autumn festival and its mooncakes. There were also
many local festivals and religious cults.

Secret societies that were typically associated with one or other of these
religious organisations, played an important role in village life, especially for
the poor and for others excluded from the time-honoured Confucian
power structures, particularly women. The type of underground brother-
hoods that had produced the activists of the Boxer rebellion persisted long
after the collapse of the Qing dynasty. Societies such as the Red Spears
[*Hongqiang*] the Elder Brother Society [*Gelaohui*] and the Way of Unity
[*Yiguandao*] were an important force in the countryside in different parts
of China. In the 1920s, the Red Spears were active across the north China
plains, mainly in the rural areas of Shaanxi, Henan, western Shandong and
southern Hebei. They also had support among the railwaymen on the
Longhai line and many were simultaneously members of the Elder Brother
Society. They carried red-tasselled spears, after which they were named,
practised a style of ritual boxing and wore amulets, which they claimed
made them invulnerable: they were worthy successors to the Boxers who
had operated in much the same area. The Red Spears, together with the
White and Yellow Spears who were associated with them, functioned essentially as village self-defence organisations during a period of chaos and
confusion as the armies of rival warlords criss-crossed the plain. They
attempted to live independently of the villagers whom they sought to protect, had a simplistic ideology of village self-government and at one point
occupied a number of towns in Shaanxi province. In Hua County in the
northeast of Henan province, the Red Spears were at the forefront of peasant resistance to additional taxes imposed by the warlord General Feng
Yuxiang when he brought his National Army [*Guominjun*] forces into the
county in September 1926 during the Northern Expedition. Red Spear
members moved into Hua County and took up residence in the Liu'an
temple where they provided free meals for the poor peasants who joined
them. The Red Spears organised a highly successful tax boycott, which
lasted throughout the autumn of 1926 and the spring of 1927 and came to
an end only after the victory of Chiang Kai-shek's Guomindang forces later
that year. In September 1927, Feng Yuxiang's troops moved against the
Red Spears and killed their leaders, after which the tax collectors moved
back into Hua County.

The Red Spears' combination of rebellious independence, military
organisation and primitive concepts of democracy attracted the attention of
both the Comintern and members of the CCP who looked to them as possible allies. Li Dazhao wrote what was probably the first attempt at a Marxist analysis of a Chinese secret society in his article 'The Red Spears of

Shandong, Henan, Shaanxi and other provinces' [*Lu-Yu-Shen deng sheng de hongqianghui*] and appealed to the CCP to try to mould them into a revolutionary peasant movement. The Left Guomindang government in Wuhan also attempted to cultivate them. However, the Red Spears like many of the other secret societies tended to be loyal to their own local groups and were fiercely independent and not easily assimilated into any national movement. They were by no means purely a movement of poor peasants although it was from that class that they drew most of their manpower. They were led and often financed by local landowners, gentry and merchants and in some ways operated as a militia for the landowning classes of their own clans. This made it difficult for the CCP to assimilate them into their own peasant revolutionary force.[27]

In rural China, poverty was a constant companion and famine a recurrent fear. The crops were vulnerable to drought or to excessive rain that could fill the rivers and cause disastrous floods. The distinguished English economic historian, R.H. Tawney, who surveyed the rural economy of China in 1931, observed that 'A tolerable standard of well-being cannot be said to prevail as long as some considerable proportion of her rural population is under-fed and under-housed, decimated by preventable disease, and liable to be plunged in starvation by flood and drought.'[28]

In 1920 and 1921, a large part of northern China was hit by a severe drought which brought famine to the provinces of Zhili (the area around Beijing), Shandong, Shaanxi and Henan. It has been estimated that at least 500,000 people died of starvation in that famine. International relief workers confirmed that this was a genuine famine rather than a continuation of the chronic grinding poverty that northern China was used to. In addition to the deaths and individual suffering, the famine devastated the economy of the entire region. Villages were deserted, land values collapsed, people were reduced to selling their children and hundreds of thousands of people left their homes in search of some way of earning a living. The immediate cause of the famine was lack of rainfall in the months leading up to the harvest in the autumn of 1920, but there were also structural reasons which include overpopulation and overuse of the land; logging had removed the tree cover from the hillsides and allowed the free flow of dusty soil; roads and irrigation works had been neglected by central and local government and had not been properly maintained. In 1923 there was widespread drought and flooding which killed more than 100,000 people and over the following summer, the province of Hunan was badly affected by serious flooding which later spread south to Jiangxi, Guangdong and Guangxi and north to the area between Beijing and Tianjin. In 1925, Sichuan experienced a severe famine, which caused the deaths of more than 3 million people and left much of the rural population destitute. In the summer of

1926 the Yangzi River flooded in Hubei and Anhui provinces and the Gan River overflowed its banks in Jiangxi. Drought and famine devastated the whole of north China from Gansu to Shandong in 1928–1930, affecting more than 20 million people. Contemporary observers estimated that as many as 2 million people had already died in Gansu alone and another 2 million were on the verge of starving to death. The rural areas were in deep crisis and peasant farmers were desperate and open to new ideas to resolve their problems.[29]

Peng Pai and the Guangdong Peasant Movement

Although Mao Zedong eventually took the credit for identifying the peasantry as the most important revolutionary force that the CCP should nurture, he was a relative latecomer to this idea. In the early 1920s, Peng Pai, a member of the CCP whose name was virtually written out of the official history of the party and the revolution during Mao's lifetime, created a network of peasant associations in Guangdong province and demonstrated that an alliance of peasants and Communists was viable.

Peng had been born into a landowning family in Haifeng County in Guangdong province in 1896 and had studied economics at Waseda University in Tokyo, where he also encountered Marxist ideas for the first time. He returned to his home county to run the education department but was dismissed for organising a Labour Day demonstration on 1 May 1921. He began organising peasant associations in 1922 in Haifeng and in Lufeng, the neighbouring county: the two counties are often collectively known as Hailufeng. The associations campaigned against the landlords, making demands for the reduction of rents and also struggled against social injustices. In 1924 Peng Pai was appointed First Secretary of the Guomindang Peasant Department in Guangzhou and head of the Peasant Movement Training Institute. Members of the peasant associations that he had organised were among the supporters of Chiang Kai-shek's 1925 Eastern Expedition which was a precursor to the Northern Expedition. Peng Pai later left Guangzhou and returned to the countryside to continue his work with the peasant associations. After Mao Zedong was appointed head of the Peasant Institute in succession to Peng in February 1926, he took the entire student body to Haifeng for two weeks where they attended lectures by Peng Pai and experienced the radical peasant movement in action. After the split between the CCP and the GMD in April 1927, Peng Pai led an insurrection that created a Soviet government which lasted from 29 April to 9 May and then a longer lasting regime that finally collapsed in February 1928. Peng continued to involve himself in peasant associations until his arrest by the

GMD. He was held in the Longhua prison in Shanghai and executed on 31 August 1928.[30]

The success of the peasant movement, initially in Guangdong but then as it spread further north in the provinces of Jiangxi, Hubei and Hunan, had posed serious ideological and practical problems for the CCP. On the one hand the party wished to capitalise on the momentum of the agrarian revolution; on the other, until April 1927 it was still attempting to maintain its alliance with the Guomindang, and most GMD members had no interest in mobilising the peasants. When the CCP's Central Executive Committee met in Shanghai from 12 to 18 July 1926 to discuss the way forward during the Northern Expedition, it considered a detailed report on the peasant movement in Guangdong. Although the party was generally positive about the progress made by the organisers, there was also criticism and concern that the movement had grown so large that it could not be controlled effectively by the CCP members in the province. Between 4 January and 5 February 1927, Mao Zedong travelled to the five counties of his native Hunan province in which the peasant movement had been most active: during this visit, he formed a much more definite impression of the role that peasants could play in the Chinese revolution than most of his fellow Communist leaders. He expounded these ideas in an article entitled 'Report on an investigation of the Peasant Movement in Hunan', which was published on 28 March 1927. This document marked a complete break with official CCP policy towards the peasantry, which was still seen as secondary to the urban proletariat as the motive force of the revolution. Although Peng Pai had been the first Chinese Communist to organise the peasants, it can be argued that Mao was the first to attempt to persuade the Party centre that the entire focus of their strategy should be altered and that in future it should be based on the rural areas and in particular on the poorest section of the rural population.[31] Mao's report raised the peasant question in the Party but did not resolve it by any means, and this was to become one of the key issues that divided Party opinion in the struggle to reorganise after the defeat of April 1927.

Cultural Life in the 1920s

It would be quite erroneous to imagine that the 1920s in China were years in which there was nothing other than war, revolution and peasant poverty, however much this was the reality for large sections of the population. As is so often the case during times of conflict and radical social change, the 1920s saw a flowering of the arts, especially literature which benefited from the new opportunities afforded by the move away from the classical language of Literary Chinese [*wenyan*] to the vernacular written style. However the development of the old and the flowering of new forms of culture were predominantly urban phenomena and literacy, education, and the appreciation of the arts were immeasurably more highly developed in the major cities such as Beijing, Shanghai, Guangzhou and Hong Kong than in the poor rural areas.

The most striking development of the 1920s was the creation of a new style of vernacular [*baihua*] fiction. Vernacular fiction was far from a new idea as there are extant examples of 'prose romances' from as early as the Tang dynasty and there was a flourishing tradition of novels in the Ming and Qing dynasties that were written in a style of literary Chinese that was closer to the spoken language although it was still heavily influenced by classical styles and vocabulary.[32] The new twentieth century vernacular fiction was epitomised by the writing of Lu Xun (also written Lu Hsün), the pseudonym of Zhou Shuren (1881–1936). Lu Xun started to write for publication in 1918 with a short story, 'Diary of a Madman' [*Kuangren riji*], which is reminiscent of Gogol and was published in the leading journal of the May Fourth Movement, *New Youth* [*Xin Qingnian*]. He became best known for his novella 'The True Story of Ah Q' [*A Q zhengzhuan*], which was published together with 'Diary of a Madman' in the influential collection *Outcry* [*Nahan*] in Beijing in 1922. Ah Q – Lu Xun used the English letter Q in his Chinese title – became the symbol for what depressed and infuriated the author most about his Chinese fellow countrymen of the time. Ah Q was a self-deluding bully and coward who, being himself oppressed, responded by oppressing those who were weaker than he was and in the end failed and was executed. Lu Xun became the literary icon of the Chinese Communist Party and was the one writer who never went out of favour in Beijing under the PRC, perhaps because he died young and before he could become involved in the literary–political struggles of the 1940s. Although he professed his support for the use of the vernacular language [*baihua*] in literature, in common with many writers of the time, Lu Xun's writing retained many of the conventions and much of the vocabulary of older types of fiction. Another noted writer in the vernacular was Ba Jin (1904–2005), who began his literary career in 1927 while studying in France, where he wrote his first novel *Destruction* [*Miewang*] while reading and translating some of the classic works of anarchism which greatly influenced his thinking. He went on to write many successful novels including *Family* [*Jia*], *Spring* [*Chun*] and *Autumn* [*Qiu*] and in spite of his interest in anarchism, he managed to retain the favour of the CCP and occupied a number of senior cultural posts after 1949. He failed to gain re-election to the Chinese People's Political Consultative Conference in March 2003 as he was considered to be too old at the age of 99 and was bedridden when he died on 17 October 2005. Mao Dun (1896–1981), who became well known as a novelist in the 1930s with Midnight [*Ziye*] among many other books, had taken part in the Northern Expedition and learned his trade as a writer and journalist in Hankou in the late 1920s.

In addition to the writing of Lu Xun, Ba Jin and others that has been accepted into the modern Chinese literary canon, at least on the mainland, there was a considerable growth in popular fiction in the 1920s. This was widely read among the new urban classes and particularly by young women. Mass produced and not always of the highest literary quality, it reflected the widespread unease about the introduction of Western lifestyles and values. Often modelled on romantic stories from classical literature, this new genre was criticised for its sentimentality and escapism and its unwillingness to engage with the radical social concerns and national politics of the period after the May Fourth Movement. It was known, somewhat disparagingly, as 'mandarin duck and butterfly literature', taking its name from the popular symbols for devoted lovers in the classical tradition. It found a ready market in the new wave of newspaper, book and magazine publishing that emerged in the 1920s.[33]

A new generation of poets also relished the freedom that was afforded by the new vernacular. Classical forms of poetry were by no means abandoned and even the revolutionary Mao Zedong, who prided himself on the quality of his poetry, adhered closely to traditional metre and rhyme even if he did address modern themes. Xu Zhimo and Wen Yiduo are perhaps the most enduring of the poets of this period and they embraced the new forms enthusiastically. Xu Zhimo (1897–1931) was a romantic who had a particular affection for the English poets Keats and Shelley and also translated some of Baudelaire's verse. He visited the USA, but preferred England where he studied in London and at King's College, Cambridge. He also visited the Soviet Union in 1925 and came away with negative impressions: this contributed to his political outlook, which was anti-Communist and anti-left. He returned to China, and in 1927, he was one of the founders, with his friend Hu Shi, of the right-wing Crescent literary society in Shanghai.[34] Wen Yiduo [1899–1946, also written as Wen I-to] studied in the USA after a classical Chinese education in Hubei province and became a great enthusiast for poetry in the vernacular. He returned to China in 1925 and was torn between the life of a bohemian aesthete and involvement in politics. His best known poems are 'Dead Water' [*Sishui*] which on one level symbolised the state of China as he saw it and 'The Laundry Song' [*Xi yifu*, literally 'washing clothes'] which lamented the lowly position and demeaning occupations that were the fate of many of Chinese migrants to the USA. After the Japanese occupation of China in 1937, Wen Yiduo finally joined the Democratic League, which was created to offer a third way, a political alternative to both the Guomindang and the CCP; he was shot and killed in July 1946 by opponents of the League, who were almost certainly hired agents of the Guomindang.[35]

In spite of the great interest in the new wave of literature and other arts, traditional opera remained popular in Beijing but especially in the provinces. The tradition of renowned actors creating a troupe around their own artistic personalities continued and so did operatic training schools. Of all the actors of the Republican period, only Mei Lanfang (1894–1961) achieved a reputation outside China. He was particularly noted for his performance in stylised female roles, which are copied by singers in China today, and toured Japan, Europe and the USA. Traditional opera had many regional forms and these continued to be popular among all social groups throughout the 1920s and subsequently.[36]

The cinema had been known in China since the first Western film had been shown there in 1895, and short films were produced in a studio in Beijing soon afterwards. In the 1920s, feature films were produced after American producers had visited China and Shanghai became the centre of the new industry. Chinese films in the 1920s were usually tied to traditional styles of theatre and opera, for example, the film of *Tale of the Western Chamber* [*Xi xiang ji*] directed by Hou Yao that appeared in 1927. However, *A String of Pearls* [*Yichuan zhenzhu*] which was directed by Li Zeyuan and appeared in 1926 was an adaptation of the well-known short story *The Necklace* by the nineteenth-century French writer Guy de Maupassant. In the 1930s one film actress, Lan Ping began to make a slight impression on the large screen in Shanghai, but fled to the northwest of China in common with many other artists and intellectuals. She joined the Communist Party, married Mao Zedong and changed her name to Jiang Qing. She was to come to political prominence during the Cultural Revolution of the 1960s and 1970s.

9

NANJING DECADE AND THE LONG MARCH (1927–1937)

The period between 1927 and 1937 is often referred to as the Nanjing Decade. The Guomindang established itself in Nanjing, claiming to be the legitimate government of the whole of China, and it was indeed the first to be able to do so with any justification since the death of Yuan Shikai in 1916. The GMD was accepted by most of southern China and by much of northern China but its writ did not run in Manchuria and the loyalty of many of the former warlords was, to say the least, questionable. The international community accepted the administration as legitimate and Chiang Kai-shek was feted as a strong head of state. There was, however, growing international concern about the nature of the Guomindang government which began to adopt many of the trappings of the fascist regimes of Europe.

By the end of 1927, the CCP appeared to have been destroyed or at least reduced to a small group, politically impotent and divided on strategy. The factional dispute in the USSR in which Joseph Stalin defeated the supporters of Leon Trotsky not only left deep scars in the CCP but also left open the door for a new political approach based on the mobilisation of the poor peasantry, the approach favoured by Mao Zedong. The CCP were driven out of the cities which had been their natural milieu, among the workers and trades union organisations, and were forced to set up new bases in the countryside. Their most important rural bases were initially in the south of China, in Jinggangshan on the border between the provinces of Jiangxi and Hunan and then in the Jiangxi Soviet, which had its administrative headquarters in the town of Ruijin in the south of that province. For the CCP this period became known as the First Revolutionary Civil War and military conflict with the forces of the National Government finally drove the communists out of Jiangxi. The series of retreats and forced marches that led the CCP out of Jiangxi and to relative safety in Yan'an in the northern Chinese province of Shaanxi have become celebrated and mythologised as the Long March. In the background, and constantly in the minds of Nationalist and Communist political leaders alike, was the increasing pressure of Japan on northern China. This led to the occupation of Manchuria in 1931 and finally to the invasion of China Proper in 1937, an invasion which was to alter fundamentally the direction of China's history.

Nanjing Government

On 24 March 1927, two days after it had taken Shanghai, the National Revolutionary Army entered the old Ming capital of Nanjing, under fire from British and US warships which were attempting to protect foreign possessions from looting by pro-Communist militia. There were attacks on foreigners and their property during the NRA's capture of Nanjing and this came as a surprise to the members of the foreign community who had remained in the city because there had been no similar incidents previously during the Northern Expedition, but they illustrate plainly the xenophobia that was a component part of the broad and complex movement of Chinese nationalism.[1]

On 18 April, less than a week after the coup in Shanghai, Chiang Kai-shek established his National Government in Nanjing, in opposition to the left-wing Wuhan administration of Wang Jingwei. At this point there were therefore two rival national governments, both claiming to be the legitimate representatives of the nationalist movement. On 13 May the Nanjing government proclaimed its intention of attacking and annihilating the Wuhan government, but Wang Jingwei clung to power in the city. He eventually decided to throw in his lot with Chiang Kai-shek and expelled the CCP from his Wuhan administration so the two factions were notionally reconciled in August 1927.[2] Wang Jingwei ended his career running a puppet administration for the Japanese occupation forces and was condemned as a traitor by both Communists and Nationalists.

The Northern Expedition was almost at an end, and Chiang was close to achieving his objective. In August 1927 he announced his retirement and went into retreat in a Buddhist monastery in Zhejiang, but this was very much a diplomatic retirement and he received a constant stream of visitors. On 1 December 1927, Chiang married Song Meiling, the sister of Sun Yat-sen's widow Song Qingling, in Shanghai. This marriage brought him into an alliance with two extremely powerful men of the Christian Song (or Soong) family, T.V. Soong (Song Ziwen) who was the brother of Qingling and Meiling, and H.H. Kung (Kong Xiangxi) who was the husband of Song Ailing, the third of the Song sisters, and who was also a descendant of Confucius. Both men had been educated in the USA and were prominent in banking circles and both in turn were to serve the National Government as finance minister. The influence of the family on the National Government was such that people talked of a new Song (Soong) dynasty.[3]

Units of the National Revolutionary Army continued their march north-wards and finally took control of Beijing on 6 June 1928 and Tianjin six days later on 12 June. The military unit that took Beijing was in fact the Third Army Group which was the name assumed by the forces of the Shanxi warlord Yan Xishan, who, like Feng Yuxiang, had thrown in his lot with Chiang Kai-shek. The name of Beijing [northern capital] was altered, subtly but significantly, to Beiping [northern peace] as an unambiguous sig-nal that Nanjing [southern capital] was to be the only capital city of the new government.

The position of the National Government in Shandong and Manchuria took longer to resolve. Troops of the NRA had advanced into Shandong in late April and occupied Jinan on 30 April. Japan had despatched naval and military units to protect its interests in the province on 20 April, and there were serious clashes between Japanese troops and the NRA on 3 May with many deaths and casualties. Chiang was obliged to order the temporary withdrawal of NRA forces from Shandong and during May Japanese forces bombarded the city of Jinan. The Japanese government also sent a diplo-matic note to Zhang Zuolin, the warlord of Manchuria, on 18 May indica-ting that it was prepared to use force to protect its interests in his territory; on 4 June Zhang was assassinated when his train was blown up by explo-sives planted by an officer of the Japanese Guandong army.[4] The actions of the Japanese military had imposed a strict limit on the expansion of the power of Chiang and the GMD in northern China. On 6 August 1928, Zhang Xueliang, who had formally succeeded his murdered father Zhang Zuolin as warlord of Manchuria on 4 July, received a message from the Jap-anese Prime Minister Tanaka Giichi warning him of Japan's opposition to his intention to ally Manchuria with the government of the GMD. In spite of this intimidation, he pledged his support for the National Government on 29 December.

In August 1928, the Chinese Ambassador to the USA, Wu Chao-chu, delivered two lectures on the domestic and foreign policies of the Guomin-dang to the Institute of Politics at Williamstown, Massachusetts in the USA.[5] Ambassador Wu was also a member of the Central Executive Com-mittee of the Guomindang and a former foreign minister. He based his lectures on Sun Yat-sen's *Three People's Principles* and began with the prin-ciple of Democracy [*minquan*] claiming that traditional China had always been democratic, as attested by the meritocratic system of selecting govern-ment officials by competitive examination. He outlined the introduction of the government's proposed legislation, which was at the time still at the drafting stage. This included plans for a reinvigorated examination system and a modernised censorate, modelled on the official historians of the imperial period, whose records of the words and deeds of emperors, he argued, served as a check on possible excesses. He neatly sidestepped the question of whether the GMD was socialist but pointed to the vague and frequently debated principle of People's Livelihood [*minsheng*] and another influential book by Sun Yat-sen, *The International Development of China*, as the basis for a programme of investment by the state in Chinese industry and communications, especially the railways. Wu indicated that the support of foreign capital was welcome provided that it was interested in legitimate business propositions and had no ulterior motives. If this sounded naïve in light of the history of China's experience with foreign businesses, his understanding of the rural problems of China were even more so. He argued that China did not share the land problems of 'many of the old countries', including Russia and several European countries in which 'a great percentage of the land…is in the hands of a few who are able thereby to exploit the peasants'. The lack of primogeniture and the preponderance of the small land holding could be dealt with, he argued, by organising the peasantry and by the introduction of agricultural banks.[6] The Guomindang have been criticised frequently for their lack of understanding of the conditions in rural China and nothing in Ambassador Wu's lectures undermines that argument.

Wu's second lecture, on the foreign policy of the Guomindang, took as its starting point Sun Yat-sen's principle of Nationalism [*minzu*], and he went to great lengths to make a distinction between this and chauvinism or jingoism. Disavowing any anti-foreign sentiment, he nevertheless made clear the objections of the GMD to 'the *régime* under which foreigners live in China' and 'the position of special privilege which foreigners occupy in China'. The core of the GMD's foreign policy, he argued, was the ending of these privileges by the abrogation of the unequal treaties which had governed China's relations with the outside world since 1842. In fact this had long been the position of both the Communists and the Nationalists, and Wu Chao-chu had already made the point clearly in a statement of 11 May 1927 when he was minister of foreign affairs. Although he referred obliquely to the 'Manchurian difficulty' during his speech to the Institute of Politics and in remarks made at a separate conference on the problems of the Pacific, he acknowledged that the National Government did not have a satisfactory answer to Japan's insistence on its right to control Manchuria.[7]

To legitimise its control over China, the Guomindang enacted two major pieces of legislation on the structure of the new government. The Organic Law of the National Government of the Republic of China was ratified on 2 October 1928 and made provision for a chairman or president, a State Council and the Five Yuan, the Nationalist's name for the branches of government. Chiang Kai-shek was formally installed as chairman or president of the National Government, and concurrently as 'Commander-in-Chief of the land, naval and air forces' on 10 October 1928, the seventeenth anniversary of the Wuchang uprising of 1911. The Five Yuan were the Executive Yuan, which as the highest executive organ functioned as a cabinet; the Legislative Yuan, which had the power to decide on legislation, budgets and treaties and was to comprise between 49 and 99 members 'appointed by the National Government at the instance of the President of the said Yuan'; the Judicial Yuan, which had overall control of the courts and the legal system; the Examination Yuan to supervise public service examinations and the Control Yuan, which would serve as the modern day censorate. Their functions were detailed in the Organic Laws of the Five Yuan which were approved on 20 October 1928. The Five Yuan system of government was retained by the GMD in Taiwan after 1949 and is still in use by the government of the Republic of China in Taipei.[8]

Jinggangshan

In spite of appearances to the contrary, the CCP had not been completely destroyed by the August putsch of 1927, but it had lost the political support that it had constructed so assiduously in the cities and was in considerable disarray. The attacks on CCP supporters and trades unions in Shanghai had been repeated in other cities throughout China and it was in the rural areas that it began its recovery. On 1 August 1927, unrest in Nanchang, the sleepy capital city of Jiangxi province on the banks of the Gan River escalated into an insurrection that was to become celebrated in the history of the CCP. The uprising was led by Ye Ting, He Long and other CCP members, and it is commemorated in the history of the CCP as the Nanchang Rising. The insurgents took control of the city in the name of the newly created Workers' and Peasants' Red Army but they were surrounded by GMD forces and forced to leave on 5 August, withdrawing eastwards into the hills. A crisis meeting of the CCP, the August 7 Conference, was held in the Jiangxi city of Jiujiang, one of the Treaty Ports which lies on the banks of the Yangzi River. Chen Duxiu's leadership of the Party was denounced and a new strategy of agrarian revolution, in opposition to the 'white terror' of the Guomindang, was adopted. The Nanchang rising, although universally acknowledged to have been a failure, is celebrated as the birth of the CCP's military force and 1 August is still commemorated as Army Day in the PRC. Streets and buildings in Nanchang are to this day named 1 August [Bayi] in memory of the insurrection.

Peasant armies had also laid siege to Changsha, the capital of Hunan province, at the end of May 1927, but the CCP forces in Hunan were ordered to withdraw by Chen Duxiu in the interests of the United Front.

On 8 September, Mao Zedong, Qu Qiubai and other members of Communist units of the National Revolutionary Army, which had been redesignated as the Workers' and Peasants' Red Army, took part in what was to become renowned as the Autumn Harvest Uprising [*Qiushou qiyi*]. They were supported by local peasant militias and bands of miners from the Anyuan colliery, and they managed to take control of the town of Liling and destroyed sections of the Guangzhou–Hankou railway line before they were forced out of the area by troops loyal to the landlord militia. They retreated to the region of Jinggangshan, a picturesque but remote mountain fastness, on the borders of Hunan and Jiangxi in October and this was to become the first base area of the sections of the CCP associated with Mao's rise to power. Although the Autumn Harvest Uprising was a complete failure, Mao regarded it as a valuable lesson and it persuaded him that no revolution could succeed in China unless it had the support of the peasant masses.

In Guangzhou, a government modelled on the soviets (councils) of the Russian October Revolution, the Guangzhou Commune, was set up on 11 December by Ye Ting, Zhang Tailei and other members of the CCP, taking advantage of a dispute between officers of the GMD army. This was a continuation of the policy of armed attacks on towns in spite of the failure of earlier attempts including the Autumn Harvest Uprising. The Guangzhou Commune had the support of thousands of local workers, but it was brutally suppressed two days later and thousands of people are believed to have been killed. The failure of the Guangzhou Commune was part of the urban insurrectionary phase of the CCP's strategy, which is associated with Li Lisan, who dominated the Party in 1929 and 1930, and who was Mao Zedong's most significant political rival at the time. Li Lisan was a native of Hunan province, as was Mao, but he had studied in France and Moscow, which Mao had not. Li launched the urban insurrections after the National Government had been diverted from its attacks on the CCP bases by a conflict with the joint armies of the warlords Yan Xishan and Feng Yuxiang on 5 April 1930. The insurrections were a disaster, and Li Lisan lost all the authority and influence that he had enjoyed in the Party. At the time, Mao was ambivalent about Li's policies although later versions of the history of the Party depict him as having been a resolute opponent. Li Lisan was a strong advocate of guerrilla warfare, a strategy that Mao was later to make his own: in 1930, Mao's criticism of Zhou Enlai's caution on the possibility of successful urban insurrections certainly lent tacit support to Li Lisan's policies.[9]

Jinggangshan became the focus of the rural activities of the CCP. It was a collection of mountain villages, many of them settled by Hakka [*Kejia*] families, and secret society activities and banditry were rife. Zhu De and

Chen Yi who had been leading remnants of the Nanchang Uprising in southern Hunan finally joined forces with Mao in Jinggangshan in April 1928 and in December a CCP meeting in the town decided on a military strategy to respond to the encirclement campaigns of the GMD armies which had been launched to wipe out the Communist strongholds. Mao and Zhu De were to take command of the 4th Red Army which would attempt to link up with other Communist bases in southern Jiangxi and western Fujian while the 5th Red Army under Peng Dehuai would remain to guard the Jinggangshan base. The Communists held on to their base until 14 January 1929 when it was retaken by GMD forces under the command of He Jian.

Jiangxi Soviet

Forced out of Jinggangshan, the political and military leadership of the CCP, including Mao Zedong, Zhu De and Chen Yi, moved into the southern part of Jiangxi province, and eventually took control of a county seat, Ruijin, and from their headquarters in the town they established an administration in the region that surrounded it. This government was called the Jiangxi Soviet [*Jiangxi Suweiai*], its name once again drawing inspiration from the workers' and peasants' councils that had been set up after the October Revolution in Russia. It was created in November 1931 and remained in existence until October 1934 when most of the members of the CCP and its associated military units withdrew to take part in the Long March. The term Jiangxi Soviet is normally used to refer to the Central Soviet that was based on Ruijin, but smaller Soviets were also established in the surrounding areas and by the summer of 1930 there may have been as many as 15 CCP rural bases. Among the most important were the Xin River Soviet established in northeastern Jiangxi by Fang Zhimin, whose forces became the 10th Army of the Workers and Peasants' Red Army; and the 4th Army Group of the Hubei-Henan-Anhui (E-Yu-Wan) border region under Zhang Guotao and Xu Xiangqian, which was located in Xinxian county in the south of Henan province, a great distance from the main Jiangxi Soviet.[10] Communication with the outposts was extremely difficult as the Guomindang were constantly attempting to eliminate the Communists and for much of the time the individual bases effectively operated independently. Official historians of the history of the Chinese Communist Party have attempted to demonstrate a degree of continuity between these bases and the later leadership of Mao Zedong, but there was no such simple correlation. After the First All-China Soviet Congress which took place from 7 to 20 November 1931, the Ruijin Soviet was acknowledged as the centre of the revolutionary movement, and the outlying Soviets fell prey to attacks by the GMD, forcing many of their members to move to Ruijin, but there were persistent and often bitter factional disputes between Communists from the different bases.

This was a formative and significant period for the CCP. For the first time the revolutionary organisation had to take on the role of a government, albeit the government of a small area. It had to deal with problems of administration, finance and the administration of justice, and it created its own organisations to do this. The Party was also confronted with issues that were later to be vital to its success, both in gaining power and in retaining it. These included acquiring an understanding of the system of social classes in the rural areas and the related matter of land ownership. The measures that the CCP employed to deal with these issues in the Jiangxi Soviet, both successfully and unsuccessfully, were to influence its policies for at least the next 20 years and in some cases for much longer. It was in many ways a laboratory in which the CCP was able to experiment with policies that would later be implemented in the PRC.

In Jiangxi and the other areas in which it established its authority, the CCP created basic-level Soviets (in the sense of administrative committees) at the local village [*xiang*] level in the countryside; intermediate Soviets at district, county and provincial level; with the Soviet Central Government at the top of the pyramid. The members of the Soviets were elected but the electoral process was subject to a considerable degree of control and the vote was restricted to people who were at the very least not opponents of the CCP. The main deliberative organ was the National Soviet Congress and this elected (or selected) the Central Executive Committee, the Presidium or Political Bureau and the Council of People's Commissars which had a membership of 10 or 12. The functions of these bodies were set out in the Organic Law of the Central Soviet which was enacted in February 1934. These institutions did not last long and there was conflict between the political realities and the legal framework, but it was a first attempt by the CCP to construct a politico-legal structure. The names and functions of the bodies were modelled on the experience of the Soviet Union, and they were to a large extent the basis for the system of government that the CCP was to establish in all of the areas that it controlled in China until the end of the Civil War in 1949 and subsequently in the People's Republic of China. The government of the Central Soviet was faced with considerable opposition, which it regarded as counter-revolutionary, and it instituted its own judicial system to deal with this as well as with more mundane criminal activities. A People's Commissariat of Justice oversaw a Supreme Court and a series of local courts and policing functions were carried out by the State Political Security Bureau [*Guojia zhengzhi baowei ju*] and by various militias. Prisons and labour reform camps [*laodong ganhua yuan*] were also developed.[11]

At the founding conference of the Jiangxi Soviet, which took place from 1 to 5 November 1931, Mao Zedong's views on peasant revolution were still a minority position, and he had failed to gain control of the CCP's military units, which were the responsibility of Zhu De as the chairman of the Central Revolutionary Military Commission and his deputies Peng Dehuai and Wang Jiaxiang. Nevertheless, he was elected chairman of the Central Executive Council of the Soviet on 27 November. There had been serious differences between the political factions of the CCP during the creation of the Soviet and in December 1930 there had even been a massacre of Communist forces at Futian by troops loyal to Mao Zedong: this factionalism continued during the life of the Soviet, and Mao began his rise to supremacy by the ruthless exclusion of his political opponents from power. From January 1931, the CCP was formally under the control of a group of its members who had been trained in Moscow and were known as either the Returned Students faction or the Twenty-Eight Bolsheviks. They were led by Wang Ming (Chen Shaoyu), who was supported by the Comintern representative to China, Pavel Mif, and they had come to power in opposition to the 'Li Lisan line', which had promoted the disastrous strategy of urban insurrections. The Wang Ming group still believed that the future of the Chinese revolution lay in the cities and not in the countryside, and they were scornful of what they described as the 'mountain communism' of Mao Zedong. The Returned Students had been based in Shanghai, but were forced out by the Guomindang police and were then obliged to move to the Soviet areas, where they played a more direct role in the factional politics of the Soviet Government.[12]

Two of the major social issues that the CCP encountered in Jiangxi were the subservient position of women in Chinese society, especially rural society, and the inequalities in the ownership of land. In the Soviet area, greater freedom of marriage and divorce was encouraged, initially by CCP decrees and then by the Regulations on Marriage that were promulgated by the Soviet Government on 1 December 1931. The preamble to the Regulations on Marriage outlined the principles of the CCP's thinking on marriage and divorce: in the areas under the control of the Soviet government, men and women should be economically independent and free to marry or divorce as they wished, without the feudal social constraints of the past. What is more, given that women had suffered more in the feudal past, their interests and those of children should be given priority. The Regulations were not universally welcomed in what was still essentially a fiercely traditional rural society, but there was a significant increase in marriages and divorces that were in line with the new system and the Regulations were the starting point for the legislation on marriage reform that the CCP was to enact after 1949.[13]

Although the CCP's positive policies towards women were to prove vital in attracting support, it was the land question that was more significant in their eventual victory. The land policies of the Jiangxi Soviet were in the beginning a carbon copy of the anti-kulak policies of the Soviet Union at the time. The *kulaks* in Russia were the owner occupiers of farming land who resisted collectivisation. There was no precise equivalent to the *kulaks* in China but the Chinese Communists substituted the class of rich peasants, and these became their main target. During the Land Investigation Movement [*chatian yundong*] of 1932–3, teams of cadres went into the villages to mobilise the poor against the rich and, after a document by Mao Zedong on the differentiation of classes in the countryside had been accepted by the Central Committee in June 1933, the policies were modified to ensure that the middle peasants, who were seen as potential allies rather than enemies of the CCP, did not have their landholdings expropriated. The Land Investigation Movement was directed by Mao and was one of his most important power bases in the factional conflicts that raged in Jiangxi. The importance of this movement in the history of the CCP is not so much the actual changes in land ownership, although they did take place, but the adoption of models of rural class struggle and confiscation and redistribution of land that were to prove vital to the Party's rise to power in the 1940s.[14]

Japan in Manchuria 1931–2

Japan had been increasing its economic and political pressure on China since the Twenty-One Demands of 1915, but the rise of militarism in the 1920s and the growing involvement of the army in Japanese domestic politics posed an even greater threat to the security of China. Japan appeared to regard China as fair game for its expansionist policies, especially the north-eastern region, which is closest to Japan and to Korea, its colony since 1905. The Meiji Constitution, which came into effect in November 1890, placed the army directly under the control of the emperor rather than the cabinet, which gave the military scope for operating with considerable independence. Manchuria was regarded by many in the military, and in the popular imagination, as Japanese by right in recompense for the tens of thousands of Japanese troops who had died there during the Russo-Japanese War of 1904–5. During that war, the siege of Port Arthur alone may have cost as many as 60,000 Japanese lives by the time the Russians surrendered on the last day of December 1904. The battle for Shenyang [Mukden] lasted from 23 February to 16 March 1905 and involved 750,000 men. The Japanese armies defeated the Russians and took control of Shenyang but lost more than 40,000 men in the process. Manchuria was also viewed in Japan as a buffer zone which could be used to counteract the expansion of the Russian empire, and later Bolshevism. During the 1920s, the Manchurian warlord Zhang Zuolin had tried to maintain a conciliatory relationship with Japan while retaining his own independence, but with the rise of the Guomindang and the establishment of the National Government in Nanjing in 1928, Japan was concerned that Manchuria might once again be integrated into a strong unified China. Zhang Zuolin was assassinated that year and his son and successor, Zhang Xueliang, proved to be a nationalist strongly opposed to Japan's presence in Manchuria.

On 18 September 1931, a bomb exploded on the track of the South Manchurian Railway line to the north of Shenyang (Mukden), the city which is now the provincial capital of Liaoning province. There was very little damage and virtually no disruption to the timetable but the Japanese Guandong Army (*Kantōgun* in Japanese) based in Manchuria used this 'Mukden Incident' as an excuse to launch a full-scale assault on the Chinese garrison in Shenyang. The Guandong Army moved out of the South Manchuria Railway zone, which it was supposed to be defending, on 21 September and by early 1932 had taken control of virtually the whole of Manchuria. Manchuria was proclaimed an independent state as Manzhouguo (Manchukuo, and Manshūkoku in Japanese), and Puyi, the last emperor of the Manchu Qing dynasty was installed as its emperor. Manzhouguo was, of course, independent only from China and functioned as a puppet state completely dependent on Japan which now had a colonial empire that included Taiwan, Korea and the northeast of China. Although it has been argued that the Mukden Incident was primarily a local affair and that the attack on the garrison was an overreaction by relatively junior officers, there is overwhelming evidence that tacit approval at least was given by the command of the Guandong Army and that the action was condoned by the government in Tokyo. The annexation of Manchuria was condemned by the League of Nations, but this was completely ignored by Tokyo and the Guandong army continued its westward march and took control of the eastern part of Inner Mongolia.

The invasion of Manchuria was a direct attack on the National Government's claim to sovereignty over the whole of China. Unable to resist militarily because its forces would have been defeated easily by the Japanese military, the Guomindang administration adopted a twin track strategy. It used diplomatic channels in a vain attempt to persuade the international community to act against Japan and at the same time it utilised a wave of popular dissent and trade boycotts in an effort to use the combination of economic muscle and political nationalism to undermine the advance of Japan. Demonstrations and boycotts had preceded the Mukden Incident but afterwards they were given a semi-official status. The underlying disunity of China, and in particular the inability of the Guomindang to establish its control over the north of the country, combined with the GMD's lack of grassroots support, fatally undermined any resistance.[15]

Encirclement and Suppression Campaigns

Although the Japanese Guandong army was busy invading Manchuria, the GMD were preoccupied with annihilating what they regarded as the rump of the 'Communist Bandits' in Jiangxi. They mounted a series of five military expeditions, the Encirclement and Suppression [*weijiao*] Campaigns against the Jiangxi Soviet. These military campaigns, the first of which was launched in November 1930, were, as the name suggests, designed to surround and annihilate the Communist bases. For the CCP, defence became the highest priority, but the defence of the bases was compromised by the factional disputes within the Party hierarchy. Nevertheless, there were successes. During the First Encirclement and Suppression Campaign, the GMD's National Government troops under the command of Zhang Huizan attacked the CCP bases in Huangpi, Jiangxi but were repulsed by forces led by Mao Zedong and Zhou Enlai. CCP sources claimed that in the five days after the initial contact between their troops they had annihilated 15,000 enemy soldiers and that the remnants of the Nationalist units fled in panic. They also captured Zhang Huizan. At this point the Red Army established for the first time its own system of radio communications in an attempt to collect intelligence reports from outlying areas. Radios were so unfamiliar to the rural population that peasant soldiers of the Red Army who came across the remains of GMD equipment on the battlefield after their victory at Longgang gleefully destroyed transmitters, electric motors, battery chargers and batteries without the slightest idea of what they were. Mao ordered that in future anything that was found when a battlefield was being cleared should be brought to headquarters and as a result of this order, at the battle of Dongshao, a GMD radio station was captured intact. The Red Army were able to listen in to GMD news broadcasts and also military transmissions which gave them a much clearer idea of the whereabouts of Nanjing's troops. The GMD did not realise that the CCP were intercepting their transmissions so they did not bother to observe basic radio security and often broadcast details of their movements well in advance. By 1 January 1931, the Red Army had comprehensively defeated Zhang Huizan's troops at Longgang, the remnants withdrew, and the First Encirclement and Suppression Campaign came to an end.[16]

Mao Zedong, ever the romantic revolutionary with an eye to the historical significance of his mission, commemorated this victory in his poem 'Repulsing the First Great Encirclement and Suppression Campaign', which

was based on the rhyme schemes and tonal pattern of the classical poem
'Pride of the Fisherfolk' [*Yu jia ao*] by Yan Shu (991–1,040).

Ten thousand trees blaze bright beneath a frosty sky,
The anger of heaven's soldiers soars skywards;
A thousand crags are dimly visible in misty Longgang.
Call out with one voice,
Zhang Huizan has been captured at the Front!

Two hundred thousand soldiers return to Jiangxi,
Wind and dust roll in and fill the air,
Arousing workers and peasants in their millions,
All of one accord.
Red flags are the final act below Buzhou Mountain.[17]

The Second Encirclement and Suppression Campaign started at the end
of February 1931 when He Yingqin led a 200,000-strong army against the
Central Soviet. The major battles of this campaign took place between
16 May and 30 May on the Jiangxi-Fujian border. The GMD forces under
He Yingqin were defeated and the CCP extended the territory under its control, ending the second campaign in a stronger position than when it had
begun. Radio began to play a central role in the strategy of the Red Army:
the CCP established their own radio station that summer and developed an
expertise in code-breaking as the GMD had finally realised that their mes-
sages were being intercepted and had begun to encrypt their transmissions.[18] The Third Encirclement and Suppression Campaign was launched
personally by Chiang Kai-shek on 1 July 1931 at a military conference in Nanchang, the birthplace of the Red Army. GMD troops took the Jiangxi town
of Guangchang on 15 July and by 3 September had moved to Nankang
where they were in position to besiege the Central Soviet area. However the
invasion of Manchuria by the Japanese Guandong Army on 18 September
diverted the attention of the GMD leadership and the third campaign was
aborted. The beginning of the Fourth Encirclement Campaign is usually
considered to date from Chiang Kai-shek's arrival in Hankou on 28 June
1932. The government of the Central Soviet decided to embark on a policy
of expanding its military forces and the area under its control. The Central
Soviet was attacked by GMD military units in November 1932, but the Red
Army succeeded in wiping out most of them in a counter-attack in
February 1933 and the campaign had disintegrated by the end of March.

Chiang Kai-shek had concluded that he was not in a position to deal
with the military threat from Japan in the north and the CCP in the south
simultaneously. He announced that the Communist bandits in Jiangxi were

a far greater threat to the existence of the Guomindang state than were the Japanese and mobilised his forces for a fifth expedition to wipe out the Central Soviet. The Fifth Encirclement Campaign was launched in October 1933. It was under the personal command of the generalissimo, and he committed far greater forces to it than had been deployed in the previous campaigns. A new strategy, of creating blockhouses as each strategic point was taken and then building new roads which would be used to link the blockhouses to each other and to supply bases and reserve forces in the rear, proved highly successful. At this time the CCP was going through one of its periodic bouts of internal strife, in this case a campaign against the Fujian Party Secretary, Luo Ming, who was accused of 'pessimism', although his call for the adoption of flexible military tactics seems merely pragmatic given the situation in which the CCP found itself.[19]

On 10 November, GMD forces took the town of Yihuang in Jiangxi, and this assault proved to be the first of a series of hard-fought battles against the Red Army. By April 1934, the Central Soviet was completely surrounded, and the decisive battle for the strategically located town of Guangchang began. The CCP made conciliatory gestures towards the GMD, tentatively suggesting a united front against the Japanese but the Communist's position in Jiangxi was becoming untenable. Ren Bishi's 6th Army Corps broke through the GMD blockade in July and Mao Zedong and Zhu De led their 1st Front Army westwards out of Ruijin on 16 October. GMD forces captured Ruijin on 10 November and the Jiangxi Soviet was extinguished. This strategic withdrawal by the CCP, unplanned and unwanted, was the beginning of what was to become part of the founding myth of the People's Republic of China – the Long March.

Long March of 25,000 *Li*

According to Liu Bocheng, who commanded units of the Red Army on the Long March, and was writing in the late 1950s shortly after he had become a Marshal of the People's Liberation Army:

> In the two full years from October 1934 to October 1936, the Chinese Workers and Peasants' Red Army left its original bases and staged the Long March of 25,000 *li* which astounded the world. During the Long March, the Red Army seized pass after pass; forded treacherous rivers; killed or repulsed millions of troops who were pursuing them or blocking their way; crossed snow-capped mountain peaks that disappeared into the clouds and trekked across remote and uninhabited grasslands.

This introduction by Liu Bocheng to a collection of reminiscences of the Long March by men and women who had participated in it conveys the awe in which the event has been held in China. The translation of the term *changzheng* as Long March is unfortunate as it gives the impression of a single orderly military manoeuvre. The reality was much more confused and disorganised. *Zheng* has historically been used to mean a journey or, in the military sense, an expedition or a campaign and this would have been a better translation. However, the idea of the Long March is so entrenched that it will remain the authorised version for many years.[20] Liu Bocheng's dramatic depiction of the Long March is an excellent example of the way in which it has since been portrayed in fiction, drama, film and in museum exhibits in China since 1949: the combination of romance, courage in the face of unimaginable hardship and snatching victory out of the jaws of defeat has contributed to the important role played by the trek in the process of legitimising the Chinese Communist Party's rule.[21] For the first forty years of the People's Republic of China, a significant number of the leadership were veterans of the Long March: it was, therefore, beyond criticism and its importance in the rise to power of the Party could never be subjected to critical analysis.

The route, or rather routes, of the Long March have been well documented and Chinese and Western scholars and journalists have taken great pains to reconstruct it from documentary sources and from the memory of participants.[22] The march was not one single co-ordinated manoeuvre but rather the withdrawal from Jiangxi of a number of different groups of the CCP which gradually made their way through the western regions of China. Many, but by no means all, of the participants finally converged on the town of Yan'an in the northern province of Shaanxi. The route of what has usually been regarded as the main column of the March, the First Front Army under Mao Zedong, can be divided into four phases. Phase one (October 1934–January 1935) was the withdrawal from the Soviet bases in Jiangxi of perhaps 86,000 troops and the trek westwards to the province of Guizhou, one of the poorest regions of China then, as it is now. Phase two (January 1935) was the period spent in the region of Sichuan province then known as Xikang (Sikang) on the borders of Tibet. Phase three (August–October 1935) was the trek of the main body of marchers from Sichuan into Shaanxi.

In phase four (October 1935–October 1936) there was a period of consolidation during which other military units of the CCP that had not formed part of the main column rejoined their comrades in Shaanxi.

The CCP was far from united at this time: it was divided into a number of political factions and there were serious differences about strategy, including the question of where a new revolutionary base should be established. Although Mao's First Front Army is considered to have been the main force, this is with the benefit of hindsight. Zhang Guotao had initially planned to establish a base in western China with the units under his control and when his detachments and those led by Mao met in June 1935, a celebratory rally masked a bitter power struggle between the two men. At this point Zhang had far more troops under his control than Mao. In the course of a series of meetings in a Buddhist monastery at Maoergai in Sichuan in July and August 1935, Zhang had insisted on retaining his forces independently in the west, whereas Mao pressed his view that a united march northwards was the correct strategy. The CCP forces continued to be divided and some units led by Zhang Guotao, He Long and Zhu De did not join the main column until much later in the march. On 22 October 1936, the First, Second and Fourth Front Armies of the Red Army once again joined forces in the Huining-Jingning region of Gansu and Zhang Guotao finally threw in his lot with the political group dominated by Mao Zedong.[23] In December 1936, the CCP established its headquarters in the province of Shaanxi, first at Bao'an and finally in the legendary redoubt of Yan'an. By this time Mao was firmly established as the leader of the Party although this did not mean that he was supported by all factions.

Irrespective of the hyperbole that it has attracted in the PRC, the Long March was genuinely important for two main reasons. In the first place it removed the CCP from a region of China in which it would have been vulnerable to the Japanese invasion of 1937 as well as to attack from the forces of the GMD. It was also the occasion for a number of crucial Party meetings which were to have a profound effect on the leadership and the policy of the CCP for the next 40 years.

Zunyi Conference

The most important of these meetings took place in the town of Zunyi in Guizhou province, probably from 6 to 8 January 1935, during a brief period when it was occupied by the CCP before its recapture by Guomindang troops on 19 January. It was a conference of the Politburo, or more accurately an enlarged meeting of that body, and it is generally regarded as the point at which Mao Zedong became the undisputed leader of the CCP. For many years, official Chinese sources maintained that Mao was elected chairman of the Politburo at the end of the conference on 8 January and this is taken to be the beginning of his legitimate authority over the CCP. Although Mao was indeed elected to the Standing Committee of the Politburo following the purge of the previous secretary general of the Party, Qin Bangxian (Bo Gu) and the Comintern's German military and political adviser, Otto Braun, known by his Chinese name Li De, he certainly did not become chairman at this point. Qin Bangxian was replaced as Secretary-General by Zhang Wentian, a man whose name was to disappear almost entirely from the history of the CCP during the years of Mao's leadership of the Party, and whose role during the Long March was only publicly acknowledged after Mao's death. President Yang Shangkun and others who came to power after the death of Mao made a point of asserting that Zhang Wentian was known as Chairman Zhang in 1935. Mao certainly did become more influential as a result of this meeting, particularly in matters relating to military strategy so the Zunyi conference was an important stage in his rise to power even if it was not the single decisive event.[24]

Xi'an Incident

Chiang Kai-shek and the National Government had indicated unambiguously that their number one priority was to annihilate the Communist Party and the Red Army and that the Japanese threat was a secondary problem that could be dealt with later. This policy caused considerable disquiet within the ranks of the Guomindang and its warlord allies, especially among politicians in the north of the country for whom the Japanese army was an ever present reality rather than a remote threat. There were repeated and urgent discussions between the major political figures of north China, notably Zhang Xueliang, the warlord of Manchuria (whose father Zhang Zuolin had been murdered by the Japanese), Yang Hucheng, the pacification commissioner for Shaanxi and the Shanxi warlord Yan Xishan.

On 4 December 1936, Chiang travelled to the Shaanxi provincial capital of Xi'an with Zhang Xueliang to attend a meeting that he had called to finalise preparations for a Sixth Encirclement Campaign to wipe out the Communists. Chiang stayed at the Huaqing Hot Springs, a beauty spot and resort at Lintong just outside the city.[25] On 7 December, Zhang drove to Huaqing in the hope that he could persuade Chiang to change his mind and to try to demonstrate to him that the creeping pressure of Japan was a desperate threat to the survival of the Chinese nation. In spite of hours of wrangling Chiang would not be diverted from his determination to resist the CCP above all else. Yang Hucheng also tried, but the more he argued the more determined Chiang became. He firmly believed that he had almost wiped out the CCP and that all that was required was a final push. Since persuasion and 'tearfully remonstrating' [*kujian*] with the ruler in the time-honoured feudal fashion had failed to move Chiang, Zhang and Yang felt compelled to 'become outlaws' [*shang liangshan*]. It was the events of 9 December that ultimately pushed Zhang and Yang into taking action. 9 December was the first anniversary of the patriotic student movement that had demonstrated in Beijing against Japanese imperialism and the attempt to impose an autonomous Hebei-Chahar Political Council that would have served Japanese interests.

On 9 December 1936, 10,000 students marched in Xi'an in the teeth of a biting north wind, carrying placards and banners calling for an end to the civil war and the creation of a unified resistance to Japan. They assembled in front of the gate of the Guomindang's Northwest Bandit Extermination Headquarters [*Xibei jiaofei zongsiling* – the 'bandits' were the CCP]. The building was heavily guarded by men of the GMD secret police who fired warning shots at the demonstrators, wounding a primary school student. This incensed the students and some of them wanted to go immediately to the Huaqing Hot Springs at Lintong to confront Chiang Kai-shek directly. When Chiang heard of this plan, he ordered Zhang Xueliang to put a stop to the demonstrations. If not, he threatened that he would order the demonstrators to be shot. Zhang went to the demonstration but was apparently so moved by their patriotic fervour that he guaranteed that he would respond to their demands within the week. Chiang Kai-shek upbraided him for taking an interest in the demands of the demonstrators and insisted that he choose between the students and the Guomindang state. Chiang had already called a meeting of his staff officers and had made known his determination to issue orders for the Sixth Encirclement Campaign against the Red Army on 12 December. He made it clear that if Zhang Xueliang and Yang Hucheng resisted these orders, their forces would be disbanded. On 10 December, Chiang telegraphed regional commanders with his plans for eliminating the Red Army and on the same day, he met Zhang at Lintong near the hot springs and firmly rebuffed his proposal for a united front with the Communists against the Japanese. The following day, Zhang and Hu finally resolved that Chiang should be taken into custody.

At 4:30 on the morning of 12 December, the day that the orders for mobilisation were due to be issued, shots rang out at the Huaqing Hot Springs resort while Chiang was asleep. When his guards woke him, he rose from his bed in haste, donned his dark blue satin night attire, climbed out of the window at the back of his five-room suite, scrambled over the wall that enclosed the villa and clambered up the hill as fast as he could, assisted by his guards. When Zhang Xueliang's Northeastern Army troops arrived at the villa, they found Chiang's briefcase and his false teeth on his desk and his coat and hat still hanging in the wardrobe. Following his trail up the hill, they discovered a pair of shoes where he had climbed the wall and finally found Chiang himself in a cave half way up the hill-side, white-faced, barefoot, covered in mud and wrapped in a quilt. Legend has it that when the officer commanding the detachment, Sun Mingjiu, found him, Chiang asked him to kill him there and then, but Sun said, 'No, we just want you to fight the Japanese'. Chiang was helped down the hill and driven to Xi'an in

Sun's staff car. Zhang Xueliang and Yang Hucheng held Chiang and a group of his senior advisors hostage for a week and presented him with a list of eight demands which essentially called for an end to the civil war between the National Government and the CCP and for a united armed resistance to the threatened incursion of the Japanese military.

The demands were publicised in a telegram issued by Zhang and Yang:

1. Reorganisation of the Nanjing government to accommodate all parties and factions with the common responsibility of saving the nation

2. Halt to all civil war

3. Immediate release of patriotic leaders detained in Shanghai

4. Release of all political prisoners in China

5. Lifting of restrictions on the mass patriotic movement

6. Guarantee of political freedom for the people to assemble and associate
7. GMD should genuinely follow the testament of the president (i.e. Sun Yat-sen)

8. Immediate convening of a National Salvation Convention.

The detention of Chiang and the demands for national salvation were welcomed by the populace of Xi'an who demonstrated in their thousands on 13 December, expressing their support for Zhang, Yang and the eight principles and demanding that Chiang be put on trial publicly or even that he be executed.

In Nanjing, it was the redoubtable Song Meiling (Madame Chiang) who took the lead in trying to secure her husband's release. She sent her own representative to Xi'an to negotiate and strenuously rejected the idea that the city should be bombed. Finally on 22 December, she and a trusted group of advisors, including the Guomindang's sinister secret police chief Dai Li, arrived in Xi'an. Dai Li played a crucial role in the negotiations and was probably the man who was able to persuade Zhang Xueliang that if he released Chiang Kai-shek, his safety and liberty would be guaranteed. It was not to be. The situation was resolved by a number of mediators including Zhou Enlai who flew to Xi'an from Bao'an where the CCP was based at that time before it moved to Yan'an. An agreement was negotiated and was to become the basis for the Second United Front. Zhou Enlai, who had served under Chiang at the Huangpu Military Academy and owed him a degree of loyalty, has been given the credit for the success of these negotiations. The agreement established Zhou as the main liaison officer between the two parties, a responsibility that he was to continue to exercise for some years. Chiang Kai-shek was set free and Zhang Xueliang went back with him to Nanjing: Zhang was arrested and sentenced to ten years imprisonment after a court martial. He spent the rest of his life effectively under house arrest and died in Taiwan on 14 October 2001 at the age of 103. Throughout the crisis, Zhang had been in an impossible position as he had been negotiating secretly with the CCP for some time in the hope that he would be able to secure an agreement for national resistance to the Japanese.[26]

The kidnapping of Chiang Kai-shek was not part of the CCP's formal strategy, but the Party was more than happy to take advantage of the situation: 'The Xi'an Incident is an internal matter of the GMD Nanjing government. Our party took absolutely no part in it. However, after the Incident occurred, our party immediately published a telegram proposing a peaceful solution.' [27] The peaceful solution that they proposed was to call a halt in the civil war and to capitalise on the patriotic fervour shown in Xi'an. The CCP proposed a ceasefire line between their forces and those of the Nanjing government and requested the immediate convening of a peace conference in Nanjing which would draw on the political parties and a broad range of participants from all walks of life with the sole aim of resisting Japan.[28] The Guomindang was about to be dragged, kicking and screaming, into an alliance with its bitterest enemy in the interest of national resistance.

10

JAPANESE INVASION, SECOND UNITED FRONT AND CIVIL WAR (1937–1949)

In the first week of July 1937, fighting broke out between Japanese troops stationed near Beijing and the local Chinese garrison. Japan was entitled to garrison troops in the region under the provisions of the 1901 Boxer Protocol. There had been sporadic clashes between the two sides since 1935 but this outbreak of hostilities was far more serious and the response of the Japanese government and the local military commanders ensured that on this occasion the fighting spread until it developed into a full-scale Japanese invasion and occupation of China which was to last until August 1945. There was no formal declaration of war.

The initial clash, no more than a skirmish, took place on 7 July at the Lugouqiao or Marco Polo Bridge, an elaborate stone bridge decorated with almost 500 carved lions, which dates back to the twelfth century. The bridge, just outside the southwestern boundary of Beijing, had been built to cross the Yongding River although that had dried up long ago. Japanese troops were engaged in night-time manoeuvres when they were challenged by the local Chinese garrison commander. The Japanese did not respond and the Chinese troops opened fire. A Japanese soldier was reported missing but was later found safe and well and there were no casualties on either side. The following day, the commanding officer of the Japanese forces in Beijing demanded the right to carry out a house-to-house search in Wanping, which was at that time a separate walled town on the southern side of the Marco Polo Bridge. When Chinese officers finally agreed to allow their Japanese counterparts into the town, there was an exchange of fire and both sides suffered casualties. Negotiations between the two sides were marred by further clashes including a Japanese attack on Wanping on 10 July in which they deployed more than 600 men, 4 tanks and heavy artillery. Japanese reinforcements including a motorised division were sent from Shanhaiguan and Tianjin. By 27 July the situation was virtually out of control from the point of view of the Chinese and their 29th Army had already lost 5,000 men in fighting around Beijing. On 29 July Japanese forces occupied Beijing and by 8 August they had it firmly under their control and had put in place a garrison of 3,000 troops. This was the beginning of the Japanese occupation of China and for the people of China it was the start of the Second World War.[1]

Although there is no evidence to suggest that the outbreak of fighting was carefully planned, it did provide an excellent opportunity which expansionist elements in the faction-ridden Japanese army were quick to exploit. The Japanese army during most of the 1930s was dominated by the Control [*Tōsei*] Faction, which was committed to the development of a military state and expansion into Manchuria and China. The minister of war from 4 June 1937 to 3 June 1938 was Sugiyama Gen, a supporter of the Control Faction, and his decision to deploy reinforcements from Manchuria and Korea to China, against the wishes of the Prime Minister Konoe Fumimaro, exacerbated the situation.[2] The occupation of China was swift and dramatic, an example of the *blitzkrieg* strategy that was later to be employed in Europe by the German military, almost before the term had been heard of in the West. The Japanese advance followed the railways southwards, and city after city fell to their motorised columns, infantry and armoured units.[3] Tianjin fell on 30 July; fighting broke out in Shanghai on 13 August and Japanese warships that were anchored off the coast near Shanghai were bombarded by aircraft of the National Government. Wusong, which is close to Shanghai, was taken on 1 September and the Japanese navy set up a blockade which cut off almost the entire coast of China. Nanjing was bombed regularly from 20 September until it finally fell in December and Shanghai was finally subdued on 12 November. On 20 November the National Government abandoned its capital of Nanjing and moved to relative safety in Chongqing in the southwestern province of Sichuan, where it was to remain until the end of the war.

The attack on Shanghai was much more difficult than senior Japanese officers had envisaged. Marie-Claire Bergère has described the siege of Shanghai as 'an unprecedented catastrophe for the town'. Civilian deaths were caused by misdirected Chinese bombing as well as by the Japanese attack and Shanghai effectively became a puppet city state under Japanese administration. As there was no possibility of trading with their usual markets in the interior of China, many Shanghai businessmen cooperated with the Japanese occupying forces.[4] The Japanese had expected a swift and easy victory, but Shanghai held out for four months and the siege of the city cost the lives of many thousands of Japanese soldiers. It has been suggested that one of the reasons for the brutality of the Japanese military after they had moved on from Shanghai to Nanjing was retribution for the loss of the lives of their comrades in Shanghai.

Nanjing Massacre

During the Japanese military occupation of China which lasted until 1945, there were countless civilian deaths and many examples of atrocities against the civilian population, but one episode stands out above all for the degree of brutality unleashed by the Japanese military against the people of China. This was the Nanjing Massacre or the Rape of Nanjing which took place in the days that followed the entry of the Imperial Japanese army into the former Nationalist capital on 13 December 1937. The Japanese troops embarked on a frenzied and unprecedented orgy of looting, burning, murder and rape that was not only unchecked by their officers but appears to have been encouraged by them:

> The Nanjing rampage seems all the more atrocious in that it involved not what has seemed so horrifying about the Holocaust – its bureaucratised planning and mechanical execution – but the often gleeful killing of perhaps hundreds of thousands of civilians by individual soldiers using sword and bayonet as well as bullet. The killings were all the more appalling in that they were unnecessary for the military objective, continued after the victory was secured, and apparently involved such joyful or at least indifferent murder.[5]

Two aspects of the atrocities in Nanjing made the events stand out. First, the scale of killings, rapes and mutilations was unparalleled in even the most brutal of modern warfare. Second, the testimonies of Chinese victims were supported by robust and consistent eye-witness reports from foreign residents of Nanjing who documented the massacre thoroughly and contemporaneously and published these accounts in the Western press.[6] Although there is no agreement on the precise number of victims of the massacre, it is safe to conclude that as many as 200,000 people were probably killed during the Japanese occupation of Nanjing and that at least 20,000 women and girls were raped. These figures were broadly accepted by the International Military Tribunal for the Far East, also known as the Tokyo War Crimes Trial, which took place between May 1946 and November 1948. Chinese sources put the figure even higher than this. When a memorial to the massacre was erected on 15 August 1985 in the outskirts of Nanjing close to one of the burial sites associated with the massacre, the wall opposite the entrance was inscribed with the words 'Victims 300,000' and the names of tens of thousands of victims are written on the walls around the displays of bones from the grave pits and the detritus of the massacre.

In spite of the weight of the evidence, the very fact of the massacres has been denied regularly in Japan, notably by right-wing nationalist historians who were not prepared to accept the verdict of the trials and offered their own revisionist version of the war in China. The nature of the Japanese attack on Nanjing and the scale of the atrocities did not come to the attention of the wider public outside China until the 1980s. The revelation was partly the result of the work of the Chinese-American journalist and historian Iris Chang, but much credit is also due to a group of progressive Japanese historians, many of them Marxist, who challenged the consensus that the Nanjing massacre was a fabrication and have sparked a debate that continues to rage in Japan.[7]

Japanese Push Southwards and Second United Front

Before the Japanese attack on Nanjing had taken place, the threat to the national capital had prompted the CCP to approach Chiang Kai-shek once again with proposals for a second united front against the Japanese. Zhu De and Peng Dehuai were sent by Mao Zedong to Nanjing to negotiate with the National Government. These negotiations were more successful than on previous attempts and on 22 August, the CCP's Red Army was redesignated the Eighth Route Army to mark its nominal incorporation into the united national armed forces under the generalship of Chiang Kai-shek. Zhu De was named as the commander-in-chief of the Eighth Route Army with Peng Dehuai serving as his deputy. On the previous day, the National Government had signed a non-aggression pact with the USSR in Nanjing, a necessary precondition for the new alliance. The CCP's Shaanxi-Gansu-Ningxia Soviet base area in the northwest of China was renamed a Border Region on 6 September and on 12 October, the units of the Red Army that had remained south of the Yangzi river after the Long March were redesignated the New Fourth Army. Thus began the Second United Front which was to last officially until the end of the Japanese occupation of China in August 1945 but which was so riven with contradictions and internal conflict that it was virtually ineffective from the outset.

Japanese army units of the 5th Division under General Itagaki Seishiro had marched on Shanxi province and attacked the forces of the provincial warlord Yan Xishan in September 1937. They easily outfought Yan's soldiers but were repulsed by the Eighth Route Army supported by the Nationalist Fourteenth Army under Wei Lihuang in what was one of the few genuine examples of effective cooperation between the two armies. As dawn broke on 25 September, the Communist 115th Division of the Eighth Route Army which was commanded by Lin Biao launched an attack on Japanese units that had become trapped below them in the pass of Pingxingguan. More than 3,000 Japanese soldiers were killed with the Chinese suffering only 400 losses. This victory in the battle of Pingxingguan is attributed by CCP historians to the successful application of guerrilla tactics. The Japanese regrouped and joined their own First Army and after initial successes, the Chinese forces found themselves outnumbered and were obliged to retreat to the shelter of the mountains near their Shaanxi base.[8]

From the end of 1937, the main Japanese thrust was southwards although there were also operations to consolidate their control of northern China. From December 1937 to May 1938 Japanese columns marched through the provinces of Shandong and Henan; Wuhan, the erstwhile capital of the left wing of the Guomindang, fell on 25 October 1938 after a campaign that had begun on 10 June and may have cost the lives of as many as one million Chinese soldiers. The Japanese march south was augmented by amphibious landings on the coast of Fujian province in May 1938 and this pincer campaign led to the capture of Guangzhou by 21 October. The following February, Japanese forces occupied the island of Hainan which lies off the southwestern coast of Guangdong province and is the most southerly part of Chinese territory.[9] Between April and October 1939 the Japanese army attempted to capture the strategic city of Changsha in Hunan province, but its troops were repulsed by the forces of the Nationalist general Chen Cheng in what was to become known as the First Battle of Changsha. In the Second (September 1941) and Third (December 1941–January 1942) Battles of Changsha this ferocious defence was repeated and the Japanese were unable to take the city.

The Japanese advance into central China was marked by punitive operations of great brutality against the civilian population, particularly in the rural areas. This policy which was known as the Three All – kill all, burn all, destroy all – had its origins in the strategy adopted by General Okamura Yasuji when he had assumed command of the North China Area Army in the summer of 1941. Peasants who were prepared to cooperate with the occupying forces were transferred to 'protected villages' where they were allocated food supplies, but those who remained outside were likely to be killed or starved to death. This 'Three All' policy is still remembered as an example of the inhumanity of the Japanese occupation of the Chinese countryside and is featured regularly in film and fiction that is set during the Sino-Japanese War. The policy was designed to undermine the guerrilla war strategy that had been adopted by the Chinese Communist Party and for which Mao Zedong is usually given the credit. It was intended to deprive the Communist guerrilla units, and what can be loosely described as the regular troops of the Eighth Route Army, of the practical and moral support of the peasant population in which they had their roots. It met with some success, but in the long term it did not manage to annihilate the guerrilla opposition.

The greatest political triumph for the Japanese occupation forces came in the winter of 1938–9. Japanese forces had moved into Hankou on 25 October and they completed their occupation of the triple city of Wuhan (Hankou, Hanyang and Wuchang) on 26 October. Wang Jingwei, the *eminence grise* of the Left Guomindang in Wuhan, left the Guomindang headquarters of Chongqing on 18 December and flew to Hanoi, convinced that cooperation with the Japanese was the only possible option for the Chinese Nationalists. On 22 December, the Prime Minister of Japan, Konoe Fumimaro, set out his terms for ending the war with China and proposed a 'new order in East Asia'. Prince Konoe had been one of the chief architects of Japan's new imperial ideology and his 'new order' claimed to offer 'Asia for the Asians', self-sufficiency for East and Southeast Asian nations, world peace and stability, and was explicitly anti-Communist. For China this would have meant that all military and political activity in the country would be under the control of Japan. The concept of pan-Asian self-sufficiency was developed further in the concept of the Greater East Asia Co-prosperity Sphere which was first referred to in a speech by the Japanese Foreign Minister Matsuoka Yōsuke in August 1940.

Chiang Kai-shek, speaking from his internal exile in Chongqing, de-nounced the 'new order' proposal as a thinly disguised plan for annexing China (as Japan had already annexed Taiwan, Manchuria and Korea) and extinguishing any independent Chinese political organisations. Wang Jing-wei, who was in still Hanoi, argued for the acceptance of Prince Konoe's proposals and endorsed the idea of a peaceful settlement of the conflict between China and Japan. Chiang formally expelled Wang from the GMD on 1 January 1939: from that time onwards he would be excoriated by one and all as a traitor to the Chinese cause.

Eighth Route Army Liaison Office in Xi'an

During the Japanese occupation of China and the ill-fated Second United Front, the main centres of national political power were in the city of Chongqing in Sichuan province, where the Guomindang National Govern-ment had established its temporary wartime headquarters, and in Yan'an, the small town in the hills of northern Shaanxi province where the main body of the CCP had settled at the end of the Long March. Commu-nications between the two establishments were difficult and were depend-ent on radio, the telegraph, slow motor convoys and occasional air travel. Most of the journeys by land passed through the ancient capital city of Xi'an, the scene of Chiang Kai-shek's ignominious abduction in 1936, which lay roughly half way between the two and played an important role in the attempts to create a united resistance to the Japanese occupation.

The CCP had established its own bureau, the Red Army Liaison Office, in Xi'an. At first this was a covert operation. Liu Ding, who had been working with Zhang Xueliang's forces was entrusted by Zhou Enlai with the task and managed to persuade a sympathetic German dentist, Herbert Wunsch, who had been practicing in Shanghai, to move to Xi'an and lease a building at No 1 Qixianzhuang (Village of the Seven Worthies) which would be run as the German Dental Hospital. Dr Wunsch was killed by a stray bullet shortly after the Xi'an Incident so he never saw the results of his contribution to the Chinese revolution. Until August 1937 the office was known as the Red Army Liaison Office [*Hongjun lianluo chu*] and was run by Ye Jianying and two assistants, Li Tao and Xuan Xiafu. As discussions on collaborative resistance against Japan developed, the office was gradually transformed into what was essentially the first public presence of the CCP in the GMD-controlled areas after ten years of bitter civil war. In September 1937, it changed its name to the Eighth Route Army Office in Shaanxi [*Balujun zhu Shaan banshichu*] to reflect its new role in the period of CCP–GMD cooperation. The office became associated particularly with Zhou Enlai who had a room in the building for his political work. It is now a museum and among the exhibits are many everyday items that belonged to or were used by Zhou when he worked there.[10]

Hundred Regiments' Campaign

The resistance against the Japanese occupation organised by the Chinese Communist Party is usually represented as having been conducted primarily by means of guerrilla warfare. However during the Second United Front the CCP had sizeable military formations at its disposal and on occasion used them in large-scale battles. One of these occasions was the confrontation with Japanese forces in north China that has been described as the Hundred Regiments Campaign. Some 400,000 soldiers of the Eighth Route Army, organised in 105 regiments, were pitted against the Japanese in a campaign that began on 20 August 1940. The initial target was the railway network which the Japanese had taken control of to ensure their ability to move troops quickly. Chinese sources estimate that there were 1,820 battles or skirmishes with the Japanese military and that more than 25,000 enemy troops were killed or injured. During the fighting a total of almost 300 miles of railway track was destroyed together with 260 stations and many bridges and tunnels. Almost 1,000 miles of road were rendered useless to the Japanese and fortifications and other military installations were also destroyed, especially in the second wave of the attacks that began on 20 September.

The final phase of this campaign took place over a period of two months between 6 October and 5 December, and the CCP troops concentrated on countering incursions that the Japanese had made to recapture the railway lines had been lost to them in the earlier stages of the campaign. Although the Communist forces enjoyed considerable success in confronting the Japanese they were obliged to concede that in terms of positional warfare they were no match for the Imperial Japanese Army. The Eighth Route Army suffered great losses in these operations with as many as 17,000 killed or wounded but the battles had inflicted severe damage on the Japanese ability to control the countryside. It was as a result of this highly successful resistance that the Japanese military decided to reassess their strategy and introduce the Three All policy, which has been considered above, to terrorise the rural population which had been providing support for the Eighth Route Army.[11]

Chinese Communism without Mao and the New Fourth Army

It is important to bear in mind that in the 1930s and 1940s there was not a single Chinese Communist movement dominated by Mao Zedong and his faction. The history of some Communist groups has been ignored and the influence of others has been marginalised in the official histories of the PRC if their role threatened to undermine the myth that Mao's political strategies alone had always been correct.

One important group of China's Communists did not participate in the Long March after the Party was forced out of Jiangxi in October 1934. This group of guerrillas took to the hills to maintain their opposition to the Guomindang and carried on their own independent three-year battle with the troops of the National Government. They were obliged to mount a patient campaign with no immediate prospect of success, and their strategy was a combination of classic guerrilla warfare with the creation of a powerful civilian support network. Once Japan had invaded in 1937 and the CCP were once again in an alliance for national salvation, these guerrillas descended from their mountain refuges and contributed to the resistance against the Japanese occupiers in the Yangzi Delta. These survivors of the three-year war of resistance became an important component of the New Fourth Army which was closely associated with Shanghai and its more enlightened attitudes. Gregor Benton has argued that this southern band of communist rebels had a much more modern and cosmopolitan outlook that contrasted with the introspective anti-modern attitude of Mao's northern communists.[12]

The wartime alliance between the Guomindang and the CCP was fragile at the best of times but the impossibility of long-term collaboration was demonstrated clearly in early October 1940 when the GMD 89th Army under the command of Han Deqin attacked units of the CCP's New Fourth Army, which was commanded by Chen Yi, at Huangqiao in the central region of Jiangsu province not far from the north bank of the Yangzi estuary. The New Fourth Army had been created in August 1937 from the Communist units left behind in southern China after the Long March and was under the overall command of Ye Ting. After two weeks of bitter fighting, the New Fourth Army emerged as victors in this battle of Huangqiao and claimed to have killed 11,000 GMD soldiers. On 10 October, Chen Yi's forces linked up with the Fifth Column of the Eighth Route Army which had been moving south and together they founded the Northern Jiangsu Anti-Japanese Base Area.

There was an ill-tempered exchange of telegrams between the commanders of the Communist forces and the Nationalist generals He Yingqin and Bai Chongxi, who were, respectively, chief and deputy chief of staff of the Military Council of the National Government. The GMD was attempting to regain control of the Eighth Route and New Fourth Armies, but the rift in the anti-Japanese coalition was by now beyond repair.

On 4 January 1941, 9,000 troops of the New Fourth Army moved northwards, apparently in line with instructions from the GMD higher command, although they followed an indirect route and initially marched west. When they reached Jingxian in southern Anhui, they were attacked by seven divisions of GMD troops numbering some 80,000 men. After a week of fighting, their supplies of food and ammunition were exhausted and the majority were killed or captured, although as many as 2,000 may have broken through the enemy lines and escaped. The New Fourth Army commander Ye Ting was taken prisoner and his deputy Xiang Ying and Chief of Staff Zhou Zikun were killed as was the political commissar Yuan Guoping. On 17 January, Chiang Kai-shek condemned what he described as a mutiny by the New Fourth Army. This 'Southern Anhui Incident' was the final nail in the coffin of the Second United Front. The GMD blockaded all the areas under CCP control, and this was in a sense the beginning of civil war between the two sides, although outright hostilities did not resume until some time after the surrender of Japan in 1945.[13] On 20 January, the CCP Central Committee ordered the New Fourth Army to establish a new headquarters, which it did on 28 January at Yancheng in Jiangsu, with Chen Yi as acting commander of the 90,000-strong force, and Liu Shaoqi as its political commissar. This brand new New Fourth Army was completely independent of the Guomindang. Ye Ting was eventually released and died in an aircraft accident on 8 April 1946 as he was on his way from Yan'an to Chongqing as part of the post-occupation negotiations between the GMD and the CCP.[14]

Pearl Harbor

The attack by aircraft of the Japanese Navy on the headquarters of the US Pacific Fleet at Pearl Harbor on the Hawai'ian island of Oahu on Sunday 7 December 1941 did not have any immediate impact on the war in China but in the long term it was to change the entire course of the Pacific War and thus the fate of China. The Japanese fleet prepared for its strike at the naval base of Kure, which was close to the great military city of Hiroshima, and then assembled on 26 November off the south coast of Etorofu, one of the Kurile Islands, which lie to the northeast of the Japanese island of Hokkaido, to sail to Hawai'i. The fleet consisted of six large aircraft carriers, two battleships and other support vessels. Within two hours of the beginning of this audacious and highly effective attack, 5 US battleships and 14 other ships had been sunk or put out of action, 120 aircraft had been destroyed and 2,400 people had been killed. The Japanese pilots targeted the hangars of the aircraft deployed to defend the fleet before turning to strike at the naval vessels themselves.[15] The US Congress declared war on Japan on 8 December and on 11 December Germany and Italy, Japan's axis allies, declared war on the USA.

The attack on Pearl Harbor remains controversial. Many contemporary accounts maintain that it was entirely unexpected, not least because the attack took place while diplomatic negotiations between Japan and the USA were taking place in Washington. Some Japanese sources claim that a note breaking off the negotiations was delayed by an incompetent typist. The US military and naval intelligence have been blamed for their failure to recognise that the attack was imminent, and there have been persistent suggestions that the US government failed to respond to the signals intelligence that was made available to them because they were looking for a convenient excuse to declare war on Japan. Whatever the truth, the attack on Pearl Harbor and the US declaration of war changed the outlook for China completely. Before December 1941, the Chinese were entirely alone in their resistance to the Japanese occupation and had been alone since 1931. After Pearl Harbor they could finally expect support from the outside world, although it was to take almost four years before their enemy was defeated and the occupation of their country lifted.

Mao Zedong and the Yenan Years

Mao Zedong had become one of the leading members of the CCP during and after the Long March but he was far from being the single unchallenged leader that his acolytes would later suggest. There were two serious rivals to his leadership: Zhang Guotao had led a far larger military force on the Long March, had not attended the Zunyi Conference at which Mao had emerged as a major figure and did not accept the decisions of that conference; Wang Ming, the head of the CCP's mission to the Comintern, who opposed Mao's view that the CCP should be more independent in the United Front, had returned from Moscow to Yan'an in November 1937. Mao consolidated his position by outmanoeuvring his opponents during a restructuring of the Party's organisation. During the Sixth Plenary Session of the Sixth Central Committee of the CCP, which took place in Yan'an between 29 September and 6 November 1938, a new Party organisation, the Central Secretariat, emerged as the body that was entrusted with the day-to-day running of Party affairs. Mao was nominated as head of the Secretariat and this greatly strengthened his position in the Party. His standing was also enhanced by indications from Moscow that his leading position in the CCP had been endorsed by the Comintern. The capitulation of Wang Jingwei and the Left Guomindang government in Wuhan to the Japanese in November 1938 seemed to give support to Mao's preference for complete independence from the Guomindang.

The Yan'an period was decisive in the creation of a new type of CCP organisation that was being groomed for power. Yan'an was the headquarters of the CCP from the end of the Long March in December 1936 until their withdrawal on 18 March 1947 during the civil war, the day before the forces of the GMD captured the town. It is also, together with the Long March, part of the foundation myth of the PRC and, after 1949, the leadership in Zhongnanhai would often evoke the spirit of Yan'an, a nostalgia for the poverty, frugality, comradeship and egalitarian spirit of the cave dwellings in this remote and mountainous northern rural township. The myth and the reality are often difficult to disentangle, partly because the leadership realised quite astutely that to retain control over the organisation they had to have control over its history. During the Yan'an period, when they were isolated and not directly threatened by the Japanese occupation, the core leadership of the CCP focused on defining their ideological standpoint, reorganising the party into a tight Leninist structure and rewriting the history of the 1930s to show that the leadership of Mao Zedong and his colleagues had been correct throughout all the political crises and controversies and was the only legitimate authority in the Party. This period of reorganisation and consolidation is known as the Rectification Movement [*zhengfeng yundong*] and was at its height between 1942 and 1944.

The Rectification Movement began formally on 1 February 1942 when Mao Zedong made the opening speech at a meeting of the Central Committee's Party School in Yan'an. His speech, which was later published as 'Rectify the Party's Style of Work', built on an earlier talk 'Reform Our Study', which he gave in May 1941 and in which he had called for a more systematic study of China's history and the situation in which the CCP found themselves, based on a Marxist–Leninist analysis. The ostensible aim of the Rectification Movement was the eradication of dogmatism in the CCP, and in particular the dogmatic imitation of Soviet models. This was in fact a thinly disguised attack on Wang Ming and his supporters who had been the main obstacles to Mao in his attempt to gain supremacy in the Party. Wang Ming was one of the Moscow-trained '28 Bolsheviks', also known as the Returned Students Faction, who had been sent back to China to lead the CCP in 1930 after the disastrous failure of the policy of mounting urban insurrections that is associated with the name of Li Lisan. Although the movement was not simply a method of purging Wang Ming, the attacks on Wang as the 'foreign formalist and dogmatist' made the target of the campaign quite obvious. There was no actual purge but the end result of the campaign was that Wang's group had lost any real influence.

The methods used in the Rectification Campaign are important, not only because of the results that they achieved at the time but also because they were the model for campaigns that were to be used in the People's Republic for many years after 1949. The operation was carried out in three phases. Phase 1 was an extended period of study and discussion (although the exchanges of views were more vigorous and less open than that bland description suggests), during which two months were spent in the Party School and three months in Party organisations. Phase 2 was an investigation of Party work by the organisations and schools, and Phase 3 was the conclusion and the final report by the CCP's Propaganda Bureau.[16]

The style of management that was developed in the Rectification Movement was one of consolidation and control. It could be argued that this proved useful in uniting a community that had diverse roots. Some method was needed to turn it into an effective resistance force and an organisation that was fit to take power as a national government. In Yan'an, in addition to the original Long Marchers, the population had expanded as refugees travelled there from the areas occupied by the Japanese. Many of these were students or young urban professionals and creative artists who had made the arduous trek to Yan'an out of a sense of frustration at the inability of any other group to resist Japan and out of a sense of patriotism and social justice rather than an educated theoretical commitment to Marxism. The aim of the Rectification Movement was to restrict the free-thinking and broad-minded approach that many of them had arrived with and persuade them that ideas and culture were there for one purpose and one purpose alone, to serve the revolution: that meant putting their talents at the disposal of the Chinese Communist Party without question. This atmosphere of control and constraint brought about the tightly disciplined force that Mao considered essential, but in the longer term the cost to

China's social and cultural development was colossal. The cadre of senior CCP members and officials that emerged from this programme dominated the Party and the government for decades after the foundation of the People's Republic. Although they could not be faulted for their sense of purpose and loyalty to the Party, the country was to suffer for decades from the narrow-minded and intolerant attitudes that they cultivated. This emphasis on a tightly disciplined force was similar to that of both Sun Yat-sen and Chiang Kai-shek and stemmed from the early involvement of both the CCP and the GMD with the organisation and methods of the Soviet Union.

Japan at War 1941–45

The Japanese occupation of China was part of a broader strategy in what is generally referred to in Japanese as the Great East Asian War [*Dai Tōa Sensō*]. On 10 December 1941, troops of the Japanese South Seas Detachment landed on the Pacific Island of Guam and at key bases in the Gilbert Islands (now renamed Kiribati, but at the time part of the British colony of the Gilbert and Ellice Islands) before taking control of the US military base on Wake Atoll in the north Pacific Ocean in preparation for the invasion of the Philippines. In China, the US Yangzi patrol vessel *Wake* (named after the Pacific naval base) was captured and the US garrison in Shanghai surrendered on 8 December: two days later the contingent of US Marines with responsibility for American interests in Beijing and Tianjin also surrendered.

The British crown colony of Hong Kong came under attack from the Japanese 38th Division on 8 December 1941 immediately after the attack on Pearl Harbor. Hong Kong's defences relied on a Royal Navy flotilla and four infantry battalions, which in July 1941 were the 2nd Battalion the Royal Scots, the 1st Battalion (Machine Gun Battalion) of the Middlesex Regiment, the 5th/7th Rajput Regiment and the 2nd/14th Punjab Regiment with support from local and volunteer units. There was no air defence cover and no anti-aircraft artillery, and it was widely recognised that the colony could not be held for any length of time in the face of a sustained assault, but infantry units from the Royal Rifles of Canada and the Winnipeg Grenadiers were sent to Hong Kong as reinforcements. The Japanese attack began with an aerial assault and three infantry regiments advanced from the mainland and were met by resistance from the defence forces in hand-to-hand combat. The defending forces withdrew to Hong Kong Island on the night of 9–10 December and the Japanese strategy was to try to force Hong Kong to surrender by means of a concentrated bombardment from the air and heavy artillery. By 19 December the Japanese had occupied most of the island and the colonial government formally surrendered on 25 December. The fighting had cost the lives of 4,500 on the British side and 2,750 on the Japanese. The Malay Peninsula was firmly under Japanese control by January 1942; Singapore surrendered on 15 February; and the Philippines were in Japanese hands by April as Tokyo took control of the western Pacific Ocean.[17]

For Chinese on the mainland, this was the War of Resistance to Japan [*Kangri zhanzheng*].[18] The Japanese military controlled the main towns and cities and the railways of eastern China, but they did not by any means occupy the whole of the country. The journalist Stuart Gelder was war and special correspondent for the British newspaper, the *News Chronicle*, reporting from the China–Burma–India theatre of the war between 1943 and 1945. He made no secret of his frustration with the Guomindang government in Chongqing, particularly its inaction in the resistance against Japan and its suffocating system of censorship: like many foreign correspondents at the time, he was impressed by the vigour of the resistance of the CCP in spite of the fact that it had far fewer resources:

> What was the position in China in the winter of 1943? The Japanese possessed all the ports and the major cities. They controlled the entire coastline. The Burma Road was closed. They had driven far inland into the provinces of Zhejiang, Fujian, Guangdong, Jiangxi, Anhui, Jiangsu, Henan, Shandong, Hebei and Shanxi. American military estimates put their total military strength in China at half a million men. These were well trained, clothed and fed and adequately equipped with rifles, automatic light arms and pieces of artillery, ranging from mortars and howitzers to seventy-five-millimetre guns. Tanks were not employed, but there was a small, efficient air force. Supply lines from Japan and Manchuria were secure. The Chinese Guomindang Government forces ... were officially reported to number between 2,000,000 and 3,000,000 men. Of these, half a million were employed in blockading the Communists in the north and preventing any intercourse between them and the rest of free China. They were never in action against the Japanese....The Guomindang constantly excused military inaction by quoting the closure of the Burma road as the reason why they could not receive sufficient armament to enable them to take the offensive. The truth was that the quantity of supplies flown over the Himalayas far exceeded the total taken over the road, and would have enabled an efficient and determined army to deliver effective blows against the enemy, and forced him on the defensive, or compelled him to reinforce his troops from other theatres.[19]

> The truth was that the Japanese could have overrun [Guomindang] China any time they wished, if they had wished. They did not do so because it would not have brought them worth-while gain. They had already achieved their aim – to seize the ports and principal lines of communication, at the minimum of military sacrifice. Occupation of the whole of China would merely have meant the liability of garrisoning it with troops which were required elsewhere. In other words, there was no object in further advance. Fighting was therefore restricted to periodic raids into rice-growing areas to steal crops and destroy those which could not be carried away. The same policy would have been pursued in the north if the Communists had allowed it.[20]

This is a powerful contemporary indictment of the failure of the Guomindang to mount any active resistance to the Japanese invasion of China and it is supported by first-hand evidence from many other Westerners who served in, or reported on, the Nationalist capital Chongqing during the war with Japan. The matter of the closure of the Burma Road is a controversial one and some historians have supported the contention that, following the Japanese capture of Burma and the closure of the overland link to what was still an outpost of British India, resistance from Chongqing was impossible. In any case there was a strategy, masterminded by Claire Lee Chennault, whose independent American Volunteer Group, more popularly known as the Flying Tigers, had devised a plan for supplying Chongqing over the Himalayas (known colloquially to the allied military as 'the Hump').[21] Equally controversial are the roles played by the CCP and the GMD in the resistance. Historians unsympathetic to the Communist Party, have claimed that the CCP, like the GMD, effectively sat out the war and waited for the United States to defeat Japan.[22] There is no serious support for claims that the Guomindang put up any effective resistance, but there is convincing evidence that peasant guerrilla units under the control of the CCP in northern China played a significant role in at least harrying the Japanese military so that they could not expand their area of control any further.

Chiang Kai-shek in Chongqing

Chongqing (or Chungking as it was spelled at the time) was not a popular choice for the location of a government in exile. It 'was known even in China as a uniquely unpleasant place. For six months of the year a pall of fog and rain overhangs it and coats its alleys with slime. ... It was a rural city and its sounds and smells were those of a great feudal village'. Before the war it had been a walled city with almost the entire population of 200,000 packed within the walls and because of its remoteness was remarkably backward compared with other cities of China. After the Japanese occupation, the bulk of the government and administration of China migrated to Chongqing as this remoteness was now also its great attraction. The winter fog did have its uses: to some extent it protected the city from air-raids. From the autumn of 1938 to the spring of 1939, officials of the Guomindang poured into Chongqing:

> Government offices were migrating en masse. They came by bus and sedan, by truck and ricksha, by boat and on foot. Peddlers, shop-keepers, politicians, all ended their march in the walled city. The population of 200,000 more than doubled in a few months; within six months after the fall of [Hankou) in 1939 it was nudging the million mark. The old town burst at the seams.[23]

Chongqing came under sustained attack by the Japanese air force from 3 May 1939. The bombings were in response to Chiang Kai-shek's rejection of the Japanese peace overtures of December 1938 and began as soon as the fog had lifted sufficiently to allow the bombers to see their targets. The bombing was relentless and thousands of civilians lost their lives in the waves of incendiaries that were dropped at first by night and later also by day. The attacks on Chonqqing continued until 1941 and the bombing created an atmosphere of solidarity among the ill-assorted population, similar to that experienced by Londoners in the Blitz that began with Luftwaffe air raids in August 1940.[24]

The political atmosphere in Chongqing can best be described as a siege mentality. The rail link to Hanoi was cut in June 1941 after pressure by the Japanese on the French colonial authorities in Vietnam and the British came under pressure to close the Burma Road in the same month, even though the Japanese did not invade Burma until January 1942. The influx of refugees from the occupied areas imposed a great strain on the re-sources, not only of Chongqing, but of Sichuan province more generally, notwithstanding the fact that in normal circumstances it was one of the most fertile regions in the whole of China. The bureaucracy of the government in exile attempted to juggle the supply of money and food but corruption became endemic. The Guomindang that Chiang Kai-shek led was far from being a united organisation. Chiang was not able to function as an absolute dictator because he had to balance the demands of powerful individuals and factions inside the Party, but the war-time regime that he ran was certainly not democratic. Although there were genuine nationalists within the GMD who desperately wanted to resist the Japanese invasion and were prepared to support the United Front, there were others who were more or less entirely preoccupied with suppressing the Communist Party which they saw as a far greater threat to the long-term future of China. Chiang himself was famous, or more accurately notorious, for his pronouncement that 'the Japanese are a disease of the skin; the Communists are a disease of the heart. They say they wish to support me, but secretly all they want is to overthrow me'.[25]

Owen Lattimore (1900–89), who had been recommended as special adviser to Chiang by the US Treasury, travelled to Chongqing in 1941. Initially he found the Generalissimo to be reserved but fully in control of himself. Chiang felt that the Japanese had reached the point of diminishing returns and that any further push southwards would overstretch their resources and lines of supply. Even before the attack on Harbor, he was convinced that the USA would enter the war against Japan and was content to bide his time. Lattimore later complained about the difficulty of communication with Chiang who preferred to surround himself with a coterie of sycophants and yes-men.[26] The distinguished American reporters, Theodore White and Annalee Jacoby were impressed by Chiang's frugality and his lack of concern for personal possessions and were prepared to believe that he was not personally corrupt even if he was dealing with an astonishing degree of corruption, duplicity and extortion among his staff and supporters. He inspired a considerable degree of loyalty in the early years of the Japanese occupation but this loyalty had begun to crumble by 1943. Regional warlords resented his rise to national prominence and there was growing criticism of his inaction and of the paralysis of the Guomindang regime. Rumours of discontent and even riots in the rural areas under Guomindang control began to spread in Chongqing as early as 1942, further undermining his position.[27]

The official American envoy to Chongqing was General Joseph W. Stilwell (1883–1946), an old China hand who spoke Chinese, knew the country well and had a great deal of respect for the people of China but much less for their leaders. He was sent to China in March 1942 by President Franklin D. Roosevelt to serve as commander-in-chief of Allied Forces in the China–Burma–India theatre of the war, the Cinderella of all the military theatres. His lack of tact and his remarkable ability to offend anyone and everyone earned him the soubriquet of Vinegar Joe. He never established a working relationship with Chiang Kai-shek, for whom he had little respect, and he was highly critical of Chiang's reluctance to commit Guomindang forces against the Japanese. From Chiang's point of view, however, Stilwell's worst crime was that he had been too impressed by the military organisation of the CCP and had argued strongly for genuine cooperation with them. Chiang regarded him as a dupe of American Communists and their sympathisers in the State Department who he considered were too inclined to regard the CCP as harmless agrarian reformers. Stilwell resigned at Chiang's request and was succeeded by Major-General Albert C. Wedemeyer in October 1944. Wedemeyer and the US ambassador Patrick Hurley were more sympathetic to Chiang's anti-Communism but by this time the war in China was becoming increasingly marginal to the grand strategy of the US and Washington's attention was focused almost entirely on defeating the Japanese in the islands of the Pacific and moving its naval and land forces steadily towards the Japanese homeland.[28]

Dixie Mission

A mission mounted by the US Army Observer Group to the CCP head-quarters in Yan'an was a missed opportunity in Sino-American relations, and the history of that mission and the subsequent fate of its members during the McCarthy period of 1950 to 1955 can serve as a microcosm of those relations. The Observer Group arrived in Yan'an on 22 July 1944 in a Lockheed C-47 transport of the US Air Force, the first US military aircraft ever to land at the CCP's base. The group of nine members of the 'Dixie' mission (as it became known) and the pilot had taken off from the China–Burma–India war headquarters at Chongqing and made a brief stopover in Xi'an as was the normal practice for flights between the two cities. The task of the mission had been set out, albeit in rather general terms, in a memorandum from the Allied Headquarters of the China–Burma–India theatre of operations to its leader, Colonel David D. Barrett. He was to obtain such information as he could in the Communist-controlled areas, including the order of battle of the CCP forces and their opponents; the strength of the CCP forces and their intelligence operations and a complete list of CCP officials, a 'Who's Who' of Chinese Communism.

The memorandum specifically asked for information on the 'most ef-fective means of assisting [the] Communists to increase the value of their war effort' and an 'evaluation of [the] potential contribution of [the] Com-munists to the war effort'. It is quite clear from the context as well as the document that the US forces in China were beginning to realise that the CCP were not simply a group of rebel backwoodsmen but were, potentially at least, valuable allies in the war against Japan. Patchy and irregular reports from Yan'an had suggested that the CCP were turning into a formidable fighting force, and it was the task of the mission to seek independent con-firmation of this. When they arrived in Yan'an, the members of the mission were briefed by senior members of the CCP and by officers of the Eighth Route Army (in many cases one and the same individual wearing two hats) and had the opportunity to meet all ranks informally and to observe and form an opinion of life in the Yan'an base area. Reports were sent back to

Chongqing, at first to General Stilwell and then to his successor General Wedermeyer. Colonel Barrett concluded that the CCP's armed forces were not in a position to mount large-scale operations after the losses that they had sustained in the Hundred Regiment offensive of 1940, but that they were excellent guerrilla fighters, and that 'after some training, and supply with adequate amounts of American arms and equipment, they could engage in regular operations against the Japanese'. These recommendations were rejected by Chiang Kai-shek and were never put into effect.

In the MacCarthy era witch hunt that followed the success of the CCP, Colonel Barrett was denied promotion as a result of his participation in the Dixie Mission. John S. Service, second secretary to the US Embassy in China and also attached to the mission to Yan'an was dismissed from the foreign service, although he was later exonerated and reinstated. Another foreign service officer, John Paton Davies, who had strongly recommended the dispatch of the Dixie Mission, was also dismissed and charges of disloyalty against him were not repudiated for many years. Owen Lattimore eventually left the USA to establish the Department of Chinese Studies at Leeds University in the United Kingdom. The USA lost the service of some of its best qualified China specialists in this dark and disturbing period of its history.[29]

Wartime Universities

China's universities had inevitably suffered as a result of the invasion. Nankai University in Tianjin was attacked on 28 July 1937 and the buildings were flattened by an aerial bombardment, which was followed by artillery fire at short range. In Beijing the National University, which had played such a prominent role in the May Fourth Movement, and Tsinghua (Qinghua) University were both occupied by the Japanese military which converted their buildings into barracks for the duration. Staff and students were active in the resistance to Japan and many lost their lives. Others were able to leave the occupied areas and joined guerrilla units, but some were determined to recreate a university in spite of the wartime privations. Administrators from Tsinghua and other universities responded to an invitation to move to the Hunan provincial capital of Changsha and on 1 November 1937, lectures began at the Changsha Temporary University [*Changsha linshi daxue* or *Linda*]. After the fall of Nanjing in December 1937, it became clear that Changsha was too vulnerable to an attack by the Japanese. Some students and staff moved to the northwest to join the courses offered by the Resistance University [*Kangda*] that was being run by the CCP in Yan'an. The leadership of *Linda* made preparations to move to the southwest and the university was reconstituted as the Southwest Associated University

[*Xinan lianhe daxue* or *Lianda*] at a new campus in the city of Kunming in Yunnan, the province in the far southwest of China. Although the primary objective of the move to Yunnan was to preserve as far as possible the pre-war university system, the exigencies of wartime prompted a debate on the nature of university education more generally and whether it was realistic or even appropriate to try to teach a liberal curriculum when the existence of the nation itself was under threat.[30]

Women in Revolutionary China

Although women were far from invisible in the historical record of China in the nineteenth and early twentieth centuries, there is significantly less information on their lives and their activities than that of men. It was assumed that the domestic realm was the only proper sphere for women, and they were explicitly excluded from the political system. Women did play an important informal role in local affairs, often through religious foundations associated with Buddhist and Taoist monasteries and temples and sometimes by membership of secret societies. There are examples of individual women who played a significant political role, including the Empress Dowager Cixi, the revolutionary Qiu Jin and the formidable Song Meiling, the wife of Chiang Kai-shek, who contributed enormously to his international credibility, but these are rare cases.

The Chinese Communist Party was the first national political organisa-tion in China to take seriously the non-elite women of the country and this at least partially accounts for their success in the 1940s. The reasons for their interest in what was to become known as 'woman-work' [*funü gongzuo*] are probably twofold. First, there was the influence of Marxist–Leninist culture which emphasised the equality of the sexes and this was reinforced by the example of the Soviet Union in its early revolutionary phase where there was a genuine attempt to introduce policies based on equality. Sec-ond, the CCP was concerned to develop the widest possible political base and many of its members, especially those who had been educated abroad, were aware of the political potential of women.

In the Jiangxi Soviet period of the early 1930s, there were genuine attempts to involve women in the work of the CCP and the Red Army, for practical reasons if nothing else, although it is fairly clear that defence and land reform took priority. Women's congresses were established and this provided an opportunity for women to become active in political discus-sions. The 1931 Land Law of the Chinese Soviet Republic acknowledged that the redistribution of land was vital for liberating poor rural women: the Marriage Regulations of 1931 and Marriage Law of 1934 were designed to break down the traditional system of arranged and unequal marriages and to give women the protection of a legal union. Because the Jiangxi Soviet lasted only until 1934 it is difficult to assess the impact of this legislation on the population: its importance was as a model for the future. Women were not especially active in the Red Army during the Jiangxi Soviet period although there were exceptions, including Kang Keqing who was married to the Red Army Commander Zhu De and Li Zhen who rose to the rank of major-general after 1949. There were, however, opportunities to serve in local self-defence units such as the Women's Guards and in the Women's Aid Corps which undertook nursing duties and ensured that supplies reached the front line troops.

After the Long March and the decision to establish the Yan'an base, survival and the creation of a self-sufficient local economy were the highest priority, but the CCP also created mass organisations to ensure the participation of women in the war effort and the revolution. The Women's Committee of the Central Committee [*Zhongyang fuwei*] was in overall charge of 'woman-work' and in 1945 a preparatory body for the development of a Women's Association was created for the liberated areas. In the countryside, women were organised in the Women's National Salvation Association, and this was absorbed into the Women's Association after the Japanese surrender in 1945. Reports constantly complained of the shortage of female cadres, but it is not always clear whether this was because women were reluctant to come forward or whether it was because of resistance from male party members.[31]

August 1945

Although Chinese politicians on both sides would like to have claimed credit for the final victory over the Japanese, there is no doubt that their salvation came from outside China. On 26 July 1945, the British Prime Minister Winston Churchill, President Harry S. Truman of the USA and Generalissimo Chiang Kai-shek (by radio contact) issued the Potsdam Declaration which called on Japan to surrender unconditionally or face complete destruction and set out stringent terms for its surrender, including the loss of the Japanese empire, the total demilitarisation of Japanese society, the punishment of war criminals and the military occupation of the country.[32] The demand came during the Potsdam Conference which was not primarily concerned with the war in the Far East, but had been called to settle the fate of post-War Germany and which Stalin also attended on behalf of the Soviet Union. The Soviet Union was not at war with Japan at the time and was in negotiations with China on a new peace treaty but it did subsequently give its support to the Declaration. The precise history of diplomatic contacts between Japan and the allies in the days that followed the Potsdam Declaration remains ambiguous, but it is safe to say that there was considerable resistance in the military and political leadership in Tokyo to the idea of surrender, especially as it threatened the quasi-religious position of the emperor. There is, however, also evidence that significant political figures in Japan were moving towards an agreement on surrender in the first few days of August.

On 6 August the *Enola Gay*, a Boeing B-29 Superfortress of the US Army Air Force, dropped an atomic bomb on the city of Hiroshima which lies in the west of Honshū, the main island of Japan. This was the first use of the new weapon in war and caused the death of up to 200,000 Japanese civilians who were caught below the airburst. On 8 August the Soviet Union declared war on Japan, invaded Manchuria and overran the Japanese Guandong army within a week. On 9 August, a second atomic bomb was dropped on the port city of Nagasaki which is on the southern island of Kyūshū and was the old gateway for the introduction of Western learning in Tokugawa period Japan. Amid fears that Tokyo would be bombed next, the cabinet debated for several days and the final decision to accept unconditional surrender was taken just before midnight on 14 August and broadcast to the Japanese nation at midday on 15 August. Japanese forces began to withdraw from the areas of south China that they had occupied and the question of the surrender of military units created a political conundrum. Chiang Kai-shek, who was formally the commander-in-chief of all Chinese armed forces, was unwilling to allow the Soviet Red Army (which was active in Manchuria) or the Chinese Communist Party to take the surrender of Japanese commanders so he asked for assistance from the United States Army in transporting Guomindang troops to the north by air and by sea. This effectively resurrected the civil war between the GMD and the CCP which had been largely in abeyance during the occupation: the willingness of the USA to assist indicated that Washington was firmly aligned with Chiang Kai-shek and the National Government.[33]

The Chinese Communist Party held its Seventh National Congress in Yan'an between 23 April and 11 June 1945. Mao Zedong's keynote speech to the delegates was entitled 'On Coalition Government' and reflected the assumption that, after the defeat of the Japanese, the United Front between the CCP and the Guomindang would be transformed into a government of national unity in which all political parties would be able to play a role. This assumption was also shared by international observers, including those from the USA and the Soviet Union. However, the level of criticism aimed at the GMD was an unambiguous signal that the CCP was also preparing to stand alone if necessary. The Congress also adopted a new constitution for the Communist Party, which was piloted through the conference by Liu Shaoqi. Liu's report gave new prominence to the role of Mao Zedong and praised Mao Zedong Thought as 'the development of Marxism with regard to the national democratic revolution…at once Chinese and thoroughly Marxist [and] the foundation of the present revised party Constitution'. The entire speech was marked by obeisance to Mao Zedong Thought, a sign of things to come.[34] The members of the Political Bureau of the Central Committee who were elected at this Seventh Congress were essentially the group of men who were to take control of China after 1949.

Coalition Negotiations 1945–46

In the immediate aftermath of the defeat of the Japanese, both of the major parties in China entered into negotiations to create a coalition government although both were simultaneously making preparations to govern on their own. On 28 August 1945, Mao Zedong and Zhou Enlai flew to Chongqing from Yan'an, together with the US ambassador, Patrick Hurley, to negotiate with Chiang Kai-shek. Mao and Chiang met in Chongqing the following day. The formal surrender of Japanese troops in China was accepted by the Nationalist General, He Yingqin, in the former capital of Nanjing on 9 September and American marines and warships moved in to assist in the disarming and evacuation of Japanese forces. The Chongqing negotiations continued and on 10 October, the anniversary of the 1911 uprising in Wuhan that had begun the overthrow of the Qing dynasty, representatives of the GMD and the CCP signed a memorandum of agreement in which both parties agreed to attempt to avert a civil war and to build a new China that would be independent, free and strong. However, it was obvious to participants and observers alike that there were many unresolved issues, and Mao returned to Yan'an on 11 October not at all convinced that a coalition would be possible.

Ambassador Hurley resigned, criticising US policy in China, and was replaced by General George C. Marshall who flew out to China in December. Marshall is better known as the author of the Marshall Plan for the reconstruction of post-War Europe. His aims in China were to facilitate a ceasefire, and the creation of a coalition government and a national army. It became clear during the course of 1946 that these negotiations were not going to succeed and the GMD and CCP each positioned its own party to take control of the country. The GMD attempted to reconstitute its prewar administration in Nanjing, at first on the basis of a coalition of political parties but as that proved increasingly unrealistic it prepared to go it alone. A National Assembly was convened on 15 November 1946 although it was boycotted by both the CCP and the Democratic League which had been formed in an attempt to offer an independent third-party political strategy. The National Assembly adopted a new constitution, retaining the Five

Yuan system of the early Republic and promising universal suffrage and a secret ballot but it closed on the same day that it had opened. On 12 July 1946, the leader of the Democratic League, Li Gongpu, was assassinated in Kunming. His fellow Democratic League activist, Wen Yiduo, who was also one of the country's finest modern poets, attended the funeral on 15 July and was himself assassinated. It is assumed that these were political murders carried out by agents of the Guomindang, and to many outside the Guomindang this was further confirmation of the futility of any further negotiation.

Civil War

On 1 May 1946 the CCP's forces which had been nominally integrated into the national army under Guomindang command during the Japanese occupation were formally redesignated as the Chinese People's Liberation Army [*Zhongguo renmin jiefangjun*] and would henceforth be known in English by the acronym PLA. This symbolic renaming was a powerful signal of the CCP's intention of taking control on its own. By June or July skirmishes between the two armies had escalated into a full-scale civil war. Negotiations continued in Nanjing but Marshall, having failed in his mission, left China on 8 January 1947 to return to the USA and take up his appointment as secretary of state (minister of foreign affairs).

During a three-day battle for the town of Laiwu in Shandong province that began on 20 February, the PLA defeated the GMD forces comprehensively, and this battle was one of the early turning points in the civil war. The GMD were forced onto the defensive although on 19 March they did manage to capture Yan'an, the former Communist headquarters, just after the CCP had evacuated it. A major nationwide PLA offensive began in June 1947 as they moved to a strategy of positional warfare and by the end of the month they were in almost complete control of Shandong and more than 40 counties in Manchuria. In December the PLA attacked GMD positions in central China along the Beijing–Hankou and Longhai railway lines and began a new campaign to consolidate their control over Manchuria. In September 1948 the first of three decisive campaigns in what would later be known as the 'War of Liberation' began. This was the Liaoxi-Shenyang campaign in which the forces of the PLA were under the overall command of Lin Biao. The second campaign, the battle of Huai-Hai, to the north of Nanjing, under Chen Yi began in November and the third, the Beijing-Tianjin campaign, also under the direction of Lin Biao started in December. These campaigns overlapped with each other and were fought over a period of many weeks but by January 1949, virtually the whole of Manchuria and northern China was under CCP control, including the key cities of Beijing and Tianjin.[35]

Peasant Nationalism and the Yan'an Way

After the victory of the People's Liberation Army and the establishment of the People's Republic of China, Western analysts, many of whom had discounted the possibility of a Communist victory, struggled to come to terms with what had happened. Many studies were produced but two stood out for their attempts to establish a theoretical framework for the dramatic political change that had taken place in China. Chalmers A. Johnson argued in the early 1960s that the success of the CCP was not due to widespread support for its economic and political programmes such as Land Reform or the influence of the international communist movement but the mass mobilisation of the peasantry in response to the Japanese invasion. This argument was made more persuasive by comparing the Chinese experience with the rise of Tito's administration in Yugoslavia, which had extricated the country from Nazi rule independently and, crucially, without the assistance of the Soviet Red Army. It found a ready audience at a time when there was little sympathy in the West for Stalinist states such as China, but the concept of 'peasant nationalism' has remained influential and is an important part of any complete explanation for the success of the CCP.[36]

Mark Selden argued against the 'peasant nationalism' thesis and suggested that the very real suffering and discontent among the peasantry in the regions in which the CCP were influential was not sufficient alone to create the revolutionary change. He contended that more weight should be placed on the active involvement of the CCP cadres in the rural areas, their understanding of local social conditions and their ability to generate a strategy for channelling the discontent of the peasants into a revolutionary movement. The issue that mobilised the peasants was the land revolution and the political method used was the 'mass line' in which the policy makers of the CCP went to the masses to try to understand their needs, hopes and fears and then distilled these into policies that would ensure popular support. Selden's analysis was also a product of its time and had a resonance in a period when the Third World was undergoing a profound revolutionary transformation and the Chinese way was being examined as a possible model by emerging revolutionary regimes in Africa and Latin America as well as in Asia.[37] With the benefit of hindsight and the availability of more evidence both from documentary studies and fieldwork in rural China, it is sensible to conclude that the Johnson and Selden theses were not polar opposites as has been claimed but complementary aspects of a complex revolutionary movement.[38]

Taiwan before 1950

Taiwan did not play a significant part in mainstream Chinese history until the middle of the twentieth century. It is a large island off the southeast coast of China, and it is a maritime frontier region in the same way that Manchuria, Mongolia, Xinjiang and Tibet are inland frontier regions. The indigenous population of the island is of Malay or Polynesian origin and small numbers of their descendents remain today and live mainly in the central highlands and in protected communities throughout the island but particularly in the south and east. During the sixteenth and seventeenth centuries, Han Chinese from the province of Fujian began to migrate to Taiwan, and from this migration emerged that part of the community that is referred to today as Taiwanese, that is the speakers of the *Minnan* or southern Fujian (southern Hokkien) language, part of the family of Chinese languages but quite distinct from Standard Chinese or Mandarin.

The island was an important commercial base for Portuguese and then Dutch merchants from the fifteenth to the seventeenth century, and between 1661 and 1683 it was the headquarters of an independent regime under Zheng Chenggong, often known as Koxinga which is an archaic spelling of his soubriquet, *Guo xing ye*, which means 'Lord of the Imperial Surname' and refers to the fact that he was permitted to use the name Zhu, the surname of the Ming emperors, in recognition of his loyalty to the Ming cause after the Manchu invasion of China in 1644 and the establishment of the Qing dynasty on the mainland. Zheng Chenggong was part of a prominent merchant family and had originally been based in Xiamen (Amoy) on the Fujian coast, but he moved to Taiwan when his home was attacked by the Qing forces which captured the Dutch stronghold there. Zheng died in 1662 and Taiwan officially became part of the Qing empire in 1683 as a prefecture of Fujian province. It came under pressure from the commercial and strategic interests of the expanding Japanese and French empires and was elevated to the status of a province in its own right in 1887. At the end of the Sino-Japanese war of 1894–5, Japan's imperial ambitions in the area were finally realised when it acquired both Taiwan and the Penghu archipelago (the Pescadores), which lies between Taiwan and the mainland, under the Treaty of Shimonoseki which was signed on 17 April 1895. Taiwan remained under Japanese control until 1945, but in spite of the difficulties created by the political divisions between Taiwan and the mainland, family, cultural and commercial contacts with Fujian have endured and continue to endure over the generations.

In the mid-twentieth century, Taiwan was a Fujianese-speaking Chinese society which had to a large extent become accommodated to Japanese colonial rule. Japanese was the second language of the island, especially among administrators and intellectuals, and many Taiwanese thinkers regarded Japan as the model of modernisation to which they should aspire, even though they also yearned for independence from their colonial masters. As part of the agreements signed by the wartime allies in Cairo on 22 November 1943 and in Potsdam in July and August 1945, it was established that Taiwan would be returned to China after the defeat of the Japanese, notwithstanding a significant body of opinion on the island that favoured outright independence.

As China moved inexorably towards civil war, it became increasingly clear to the Guomindang that Taiwan was going to be vital for them as an offshore base. The former governor of Fujian province, Chen Yi, was sent to Taiwan to take over as governor of the island in October 1945. He took with him a considerable entourage of military and civil servants and this group became the basis for the new mainlander elite on the island. These officials established themselves as the government in Taibei (Taipei) with scant regard for the feelings of the native Taiwanese population:

> As the armies of the [Guomindang] struggled in their death agonies, over a million refugees began to pour into the sanctuary of the island. The place was put on a war footing and thousands of Chinese soldiers, sailors and airmen followed in the wake of the refugees to prepare for what promised to be a last desperate and possibly unavailing stand, and Formosans in [Taibei] and other places began to evince uneasiness.[39]

The popular resentment at the imposition of a 'mainlander' government boiled over in the 1947 uprising that is known as the February Twenty-Eighth (2–28) Incident. On 27 February, officials of Chen Yi's administration had shot and injured a woman who was selling cigarettes on the streets of Taibei during a raid on suspected dealers in contraband tobacco. She had refused to hand over tobacco that the monopoly bureau were trying to confiscate and was shot in the course of an altercation. A bystander was also shot dead and there was a demonstration and a strike the following day. Shops were closed, factory workers went on strike and students left their lectures. The demonstrators attacked the warehouses belonging to the government's monopoly bureau and burned them down. Troops fired on unarmed demonstrators, killing three people and injuring a further three. The situation escalated and the demonstrators destroyed the Trade Bureau offices in Taibei and occupied the radio station. In Taizhong, a citizens' assembly proclaimed the formation of a People's Government. The National Government dispatched troops from the mainland and the uprising was suppressed with great brutality and considerable loss of life.[40] Chen Yi was dismissed as governor on 22 April 1947 and replaced by Wei

Daoming. The 2–28 Incident disappeared from view during the Guomin-dang imposition of martial law in Taiwan, but it had not been forgotten and when the DPP came to power in 2000, the park opposite the Presidential Palace was renamed the 2–28 Peace Park in memory of those killed and injured in the 1947 disturbances.

Chiang Kai-shek, still on the mainland at that time, appointed Chen Cheng as governor to replace Wei Daoming on 5 January 1949, primarily to strengthen his position, but then announced his retirement as president of the Republic of China on 21 January and stood down in favour of Li Zongren. He nevertheless retained overall control of the Guomindang, its finances and the military but retired to Ningbo, his home town to prepare for exile in Taiwan. Chiang ensured that the bulk of the financial resources of the Guomindang, gold and silver bullion and foreign currencies, esti-mated at over US$300 million were moved to Taiwan, together with nationalist troops and their equipment. In December 1948 he asked the US government to transport to Taiwan all the supplies that had been promised to the Nationalists when they were in control of most of the mainland.[41]

Li Zongren remained the titular head of state as Acting President, but when Chiang Kai-shek eventually arrived in Taiwan, Li was prepared to stand down and Chiang formally resumed his position as president of the Republic again on 1 March 1950 after Li had travelled to the USA for medical treatment.

INTERLUDE:
NEW CHINA, NEW HISTORY?

For the Chinese Communist Party, their supporters and sympathisers, 1949 was the beginning of a new era – New China. In the heady atmosphere of the time changes were made that had echoes of the period immediately after the French Revolution of 1789 (although there was no declaration of a completely new revolutionary calendar) or the Russian Revolution of 1917. It was not a Year Zero such as the Khmer Rouge were to announce in Cambodia in 1975, but even so the implication was that everything had changed and that the year 1949, the year of Liberation [*jiefang*], was a completely new start. From that time it was believed, the history of China, New China, would have to be written in an entirely different way.

One of the greatest challenges in attempting to understand New China is to establish how much did in reality change and how much remained the same but under a new name. The influence of politics on the everyday life of the majority of the population was unprecedented, and it is impossible to give a clear account of the period without dealing at some length with the political campaigns and the political meetings of the Chinese Communist Party and its associated organisations. These affected almost the entire population which would be aware of them not only from the media but also from personal involvement, usually whether they liked it or not, in their workplaces and residential areas.

Below the political level, life continued: in many ways, especially in the rural areas, there was a great deal of continuity with the way life had been lived under the Guomindang or even under the Qing dynasty. New political terms often concealed the recycling of older forms of social control or administrative organisation. Yet there were also profound changes, especially in the way that the country was governed through the combination of Party and State bodies, and it is the nature of this government that is most difficult to assess with any degree of accuracy. Government and Party business was, and still is, conducted in an atmosphere of great secrecy and often of suspicion, mistrust and fear. Documentation which might ordinarily be available to the historian or the general public in the West is likely to be restricted as *neibu* 'internal': documents with this classification are often regarded as state secrets and may not be obtainable by legitimate means. This applies to many mundane subjects in addition to documents relating to matters of defence and genuine national security, which are restricted in most societies. Documents or summaries of documents do leak out, either accidentally or as part of the political strategy of an individual or a faction within the Communist Party, and these are useful in shedding light on the most secret workings of the CCP and its government.

It is useful, and often necessary, to use meetings of the decision-making bodies of the CCP and the government to construct the basic chronology of the period although they were not the only decisive events. The Central Committee of the CCP and its Politburo had, and continue to have, regular scheduled meetings and the public pronouncements issued by these bodies meetings provide considerable insight into the policies of the Party and its internal difficulties. The rather less regular sessions of the CCP National Congress, although primarily a party rally rather than a serious body for political discussion, have also provided essential information about political developments in the absence of the kind of information that would be available in a more open society. The absence of scheduled meetings has also been suggestive of problems that the Party has faced. Likewise the public assemblies of government bodies, notably the National People's Congress which is the nearest approximation that China has to a parliament and the Chinese People's Political Consultative Conference, an advisory and consultative body that has a membership beyond the CCP, are a barometer of political changes. The proceedings of meetings of the bodies that actually make decisions, such as the Standing Committee of the Politburo and the State Council, are not made publicly available although there are from time to time leaks of discussions in these secretive bodies and they do report to the relevant public forum.

Since the death of Mao Zedong in 1976, the inauguration of the economic reforms of Deng Xiaoping and the greater openness that has accompanied them, there has been a vast increase in the publication in China of documents on government, society and history. The publication of books and articles has increased exponentially and this creates challenges for historians and other academics who struggle to keep up with the latest material. Topics that were previously taboo can now be discussed in China within limits, for example, the independence or separatist movement in Xinjiang, for which there is now a small number of partisan but useful accounts in Chinese: it is not yet possible to discuss Tibet in quite the same way. Archives of historical materials for the Qing and Republican periods are open to investigation, although this is no easy task, especially for the foreign historian. However there has been little change in the availability of the most sensitive and potentially the most informative documentation: the most secret archives on Government and Party history have not been opened to scholars and there is no sign of that happening in the foreseeable future. The CCP prefers to exercise complete control over its own past and of the history of the PRC.

11

LIBERATION AND THE BIRTH OF THE PEOPLE'S REPUBLIC OF CHINA (1949–1954)

The Civil War came to a symbolic end on 31 January 1949 with the capture by the People's Liberation Army of the city of Beiping. The name, Beiping (Peiping) which means 'northern peace' or 'the pacification of the north' was used at that time for the old imperial capital of Beijing (which means 'northern capital') because the capital city of the Guomindang state was Nanjing, the 'southern capital' and there could only be one capital. The PLA's advance into Beiping was in the event peaceful although fighting continued throughout much of the rest of China and it was many years before the country would be at peace. Once the military conquest was more or less secure the Chinese Communist Party turned its attention to consolidating its authority and creating a state structure. This was achieved in two ways which were complementary but dissimilar in their approach and in their impact on Chinese society.

On the one hand there was a serious attempt to create a constitutional basis for the rule of the CCP which would continue some of the spirit of the less than successful United Front and which would be inclusive, with a degree of representation for minority political, social and religious groups, although not for those who had been members of or associated with the Guomindang or its armies or who had collaborated with the Japanese. On the other hand the party launched a series of mass campaigns designed to root out hidden enemies and to attempt to impose the Party's values on those sections of society that were most likely to oppose them – the urban middle classes and educated professionals. Although these two approaches were complementary they were not compatible and the campaigns isolated and alarmed many of those to whom the constitutional inclusive approach was designed to appeal. This illustrates the contradictory nature of the CCP and reflects the conflict between the civilian and military approaches which were difficult to resolve. The advent of the Korean War in 1950 created a sense of great tension and isolation in China and this increased the tendency towards paranoia and the search for hidden traitors, which favoured the militaristic approach.

Liberation

Derk Bodde, an American academic who had gone to China as a Fulbright Fellow to study modern Chinese philosophy and to continue his work on the translation of Feng Youlan's *History of Chinese Philosophy*, had not expected to witness a revolution or to observe the liberation of Beiping. His first-hand account of the arrival of the Communist armies is an extraordinary contemporary source. The news of the surrender of Fu Zuoyi's Nationalist garrison reached him on 23 January 1949 and three days later posters from Communist units began to appear all over the city, stuck to walls and telegraph poles, 'exhorting the population to conduct itself peacefully and work for the building of a new China'. By Chinese New Year which fell on 29 January in 1949, the traditional spring festival celebrations, the display of red door couplets and the sound of firecrackers, were accompanied by the news that a temporary peace committee, consisting of four Communists and three non-Communists had been nominated to run the city. There were rumours that some Nationalist troops had been unwilling to accept the surrender and that riots and looting were imminent, but at around four o'clock in the afternoon on 31 January the first units of the Peoples' Liberation Army marched into Beijing with no opposition:

> At their head moved a sound truck (apparently supplied by the municipality), from which blared the continuous refrain 'Welcome to the Liberation Army on its arrival in Peiping! Welcome to the People's Army on its arrival in Peiping! Congratulations to the people of Peiping on their liberation!...' Beside and behind it, six abreast, marched some two or three hundred Communist soldiers in full battle equipment. They moved briskly and seemed hot, as if they had been marching a long distance. All had a red-cheeked, healthy look and seemed in high spirits. As they marched up the street, the crowds lining the side-walks, including our Chin [pedicab driver and houseboy to the Bodde family], burst into applause. Near their head walked a rather nondescript, shabbily dressed civilian – apparently some kind of official. Behind the soldiers marched students carrying two large portraits: one of Mao Tse-tung, the other presumably of Chu Teh, commander in chief of the People's Army. A military band came next, and finally a long line of trucks carrying more soldiers, students and civilian employees of the telephone company, railroad

administration, and other semi-official organisations. In about ten minutes the parade was over.[1]

The Peoples' Liberation Army continued its relentless progress across China during the spring and summer of 1949. Peace negotiations had opened in Beijing on 1 April but the Nationalists had rejected an ultimatum from the CCP, and Mao and Zhu De immediately ordered a nationwide advance. The Second Field Army, commanded by Liu Bocheng, and the Third Field Army which was under the command of Chen Yi crossed the Yangzi River on 21 April and pushed south. The Nationalist capital, Nanjing, was captured on 23 April and the remnants of Chiang Kai-shek's government evacuated all civilian and military personnel with the initial intention of establishing a temporary capital in Guangzhou. Cities fell to the PLA like ninepins: Taiyuan fell on 24 April, Hangzhou on 3 May, Wuhan on 17 May, Xi'an on 20 May, Nanchang on 22 May, Shanghai on 27 May and Qingdao on 2 June. One by one the provincial capitals were falling into the hands of the PLA, many of them with virtually no resistance from the demoralised Nationalist army. Fuzhou, the capital of the coastal province of Fujian, capitulated on 4 August, and, as the PLA advanced westwards, the Gansu capital, Lanzhou, was taken on 26 August and Xining in Qinghai province surrendered on 5 September.[2]

Chinese People's Political Consultative Conference

Although its military units were taking control of the key towns and cities, the senior leadership of the Chinese Communist Party was working to establish its political authority and attempting to make common cause with political, religious and intellectual leaders who were not committed to supporting the Guomindang Nationalists. This reflected the United Front policy which characterised the early years of the People's Republic but which began to disintegrate in 1956 when Mao became aware of the depths of distrust that many educated Chinese felt for his government. The first instrument of the United Front policy was the Chinese People's Political Consultative Conference [*Zhongguo renmin zhengzhi xieshang huiyi*], usually referred to by its initials, CPPCC. The conference opened on 21 September 1949 in one of the halls of the Forbidden City in Beijing and closed on 30 September. It had been due to meet earlier in the year but was delayed as a result of the breakdown of negotiations on a possible coalition government with the Guomindang. The United Front Bureau of the CCP had contacted potential sympathisers and had organised a Preparatory Committee for the CPPCC. This committee, which began its work in the Forbidden City on 15 June, was given the responsibility of setting the date and time for the meeting, drawing up an agenda and drafting a Common Programme [*Gong-tong gangling*], the first statement of national policy under the new Communist government.

The 662 delegates to the CPPCC included members of the non-communist minority parties, PLA troops, individuals from the ethnic and religious minorities and representatives of overseas Chinese communities. Direct representatives of the political parties, including the CCP were in a minority, although their supporters were present as representatives of trades union, students, women's and military organisations. The CPPCC functioned as a provisional parliament and approved two Organic Laws: the first outlined its own powers, authorising it to exercise supreme authority over the state and empowering its National and Standing Committees to act in its stead between meetings; the second, the Organic Law of the People's Government legitimised the Central People's Government, the new government of New China. The CPPCC elected the Central Government Council 'by secret ballot on nomination lists previously discussed by all delegates' and ministers in the new ministries of state were appointed after discussions at the conference. The guiding principle was the concept of New Democracy in which the Communist Party claimed to lead a four-class block of peasants, workers, petty bourgeois and national bourgeoisie. No secret was made of the fact that this was a transitional policy on the road to communism and that the CCP was to lead this block in a 'dictatorship of people's democracy' which would, if necessary, use force to ensure that its objectives were met.

Common Programme

The CCP had produced initial drafts of the Common Programme but these were then handed over to the Preparatory Committee of the CPPCC, which consulted the constitutions of the USSR, the newly emerging countries of Eastern Europe, the USA and Germany and circulated its own draft among delegates. There were detailed discussions in plenary sessions which took place in the afternoons and in small group discussions in the evenings. The debate continued until a consensus had been achieved.[3] Zhou Enlai, who had been made responsible for the Common Programme, went to great lengths in his report to the Conference to demonstrate the level of discussion and consultation that had gone into producing the document. The initial draft had come from a group of the Preparatory Committee, which had gone over it three times. It had been discussed a further three times by the 500–600 delegates in small groups, twice by the Standing Committee of the Preparatory Committee and finally submitted to the second plenary session of the Preparatory Committee before being presented to the CPPCC itself for ratification.[4]

The Common Programme contained 60 clauses and a preface and was effectively the first constitution of the Peoples' Republic of China. The preface proclaimed that victory in the Chinese people's war of liberation had brought to an end the era in which imperialism, feudalism and bureaucratic capitalism had controlled China. China had been transformed from an exploited country to a country in which the Chinese were the masters of a new society, in a new state in which the dictatorship of people's democracy replaced the reactionary rule of the feudal, compradore, fascist Guomindang. The new-style dictatorship was to be the political expression of the United Front of workers, peasants, petty bourgeoisie and national bourgeoisie, together with other patriotic elements, but based on the alliance between workers and peasants and with the working class taking the lead. In practice this meant that the Communist Party would effectively be in control as the representative of the working class in accordance with Marxist theory. The CPPCC was envisaged as the embodiment of the will of the nation in its support for the establishment of the People's Republic of China and the organisation of 'the people's own central government'.

Although the stilted, Stalinist language of the Common Programme had been commonplace within the CCP, it was new and probably mystifying to many of the non-Communist delegates. This style of analysis was to become the normal level of discourse in the Chinese media: they had no option but to accustom themselves to it and to learn to read between the lines. Section 1 of the Common Programme elaborated in more detail the general principles outlined in the preface. Clause 4 gave citizens of the PRC the legal right to vote and to be elected, and under the terms of clause 5, all citizens were entitled to freedom of thought, speech, publication, assembly, association, communication, freedom of the person, residence, migration or change of residence, religious belief and the right to demonstrate. Clause 6 affirmed the abolition of feudal restrictions on women, their right to equal treatment with men in political, economic, cultural, educational and social spheres and the freedom of marriage for both men and women. Ethnic minorities within the borders of the PRC were to be accorded equal rights and responsibilities. However, the right of the PRC to suppress all counter-revolutionary activities and the role of the army and the police in protecting the independence and territorial integrity of the new state were also stated explicitly. Clause 11 committed the PRC to unite with all countries and peoples that loved peace and freedom, principally the USSR, the People's Democracies that had been created by the USSR in Eastern Europe after the Second World War and all oppressed nations, and to stand on the side of international peace and democracy against imperialist aggression. Section

2 established the organs of state power, and these have remained in place in China to the present day although there have been changes in their functions and, in some cases, their names. A network of People's Congresses [*Renmin daibiao dahui*] at different levels would be created by general elections [*puxuan*] and these would elect the corresponding People's Governments at their level. The highest level of these congresses would be the National People's Congress or NPC [*Quanguo renmin daibiao dahui*]. The CPPCC would remain as a United Front organisation with representatives of the working class, peasants, revolutionary military personnel, the intelligentsia, the petty and national bourgeoisie, ethnic minorities, Chinese living overseas [*guowai huaqiao*] and other patriots and democrats. Provision was made for the military control of newly liberated areas before the election of Peoples' Congresses; the principle of democratic centralism was to be adopted by all congresses; all Guomindang laws and decrees and the judicial system that they had established were to be abolished; organs of the PRC had to be run in an honest, simple and frugal manner; supervisory bodies would be established in all People's Governments above county and town level to ensure that duties were being carried out correctly and individuals or organisations had the right to complain to these bodies.[5]

Naturally the newly victorious Communist Party wished to claim that it represented the interests of the majority of the population in China, but is it possible to assess with any certainty how much genuine support there was for the Common Programme in 1949? Peter Townsend first came to China in 1941 to work with the Friends Ambulance Unit, an organisation established by Quaker conscientious objectors that saw distinguished service in China during the Second World War. He later transferred to the Chinese Industrial Cooperatives movement, inspected cooperatives throughout China during the war, was present in Shanghai and later Beijing during the CCP's rise to power and was an experienced and well-informed observer of the revolutionary political changes taking place. After talking to non-Communist delegates to the CPPCC, he formed the opinion that they had accepted the CCP's programme willingly. Guomindang pressure on them not to take part in the consultations had been intense and 'ideals of unity, independence and industrialisation were held in common'; there was also a broad measure of agreement on the need for land reform which was promised as a central policy of the CCP.

Many of the non-Communist delegates had been surprised at the inclusive nature of the Common Programme and the willingness of the CCP to moderate its objectives, at least in the short term. The idea of state involvement in the economy was not a novelty and the Common Programme appeared to offer an improvement on the Guomindang's monopoly of finance, trade and mineral resources. There was more disquiet about the proposed international links as many of the delegates were temperamentally more inclined to look to the USA rather than the Soviet Union, partly because of their own background and education, but partly because they were not convinced that the USSR had the means to support the modernisation of China. Others felt that the USA's continued support for Chiang Kai-shek had effectively ruled it out as a future ally. Delegates from religious, educational and professional organisations told Peter Townsend that they had been pleasantly surprised at the thoroughness of the discussions at the conference and the amount of revision of the documentation that was permitted – as many as six drafts had been discussed and revised by the time the final documents were approved. Zhou Enlai made a point of drawing attention to the extraordinary degree of consultation, discussion and redrafting in his report to the plenum of the CPPCC on 22 September 1949.[6]

For the CCP, the theoretical Marxist basis for the construction of a new China had already been outlined in a key essay by Mao Zedong 'On the Dictatorship of People's Democracy' [*Lun renmin minzhu zhuanzheng*]. This was published on 30 June 1949 to coincide with the anniversary of the foundation of the CCP and, in the article, Mao reviewed the history of the Chinese revolution and summarised his view of the political system that would be developed in the new People's Republic. He envisaged China being governed by a coalition of four social classes: the working class, the peasants, the urban petty bourgeoisie and the national bourgeoisie, by which he meant the wealthier middle classes who had not thrown in their lot with the Japanese during the occupation. In accordance with classic Marxist theory he argued that the working class would lead the coalition and that, in practice, this meant that the CCP, as the representative of the most advanced elements of the working class, would take the leadership role, the classic Stalinist approach of substituting the party for the class. It was ironic that the CCP, after years in the rural backwaters of China, had almost completely lost touch with what was in any case a small urban working class and was in effect a party with a peasant culture and a peasant mentality. Mao also made it clear that any possibility that there might have been in the past of cooperation with, or assistance from, either the British or American government was now a fantasy, and that China must 'lean to one side' [*yibian dao*]: it could not remain neutral in the post-war conflict between the Communist and the non-Communist world.[7] The contrast between the democratic and inclusive atmosphere of the CPPCC and Mao's clear view that the leading role of the CCP was not negotiable was a foretaste of the conflicts that were to unfold in the 1950s and 1960s.

A further indication of the prevalence of confrontation over harmony was an order-in-command by Zhu De, the legendary Commander-in-Chief of the PLA, which was issued on 1 October and congratulated all who had contributed to victory and to the creation of the People's Republic. He warned, however, that the task was not yet concluded and that remnants of the enemy continued to conspire against the new government and were soliciting foreign intervention against it. He called for members of the PLA at all levels to comply with Mao Zedong's directives to rid China of the enemy and liberate all those parts of China's territory that had not yet been liberated while exterminating all bandits and counter-revolutionary gangsters and suppressing opposition and trouble makers.[8] It was this document and others like it, rather than the inclusive constitutional deliberations of the CPPCC, that set the stage for the mass political campaigns that were to dominate the lives of most of the population of China during the 1950s.

Mass Political Campaigns

After the military victories of 1948–9, the CCP initiated a series of mass campaigns to establish its political control. It could be argued that the most important of these campaigns was Land Reform, the continuation of policies that had begun in the 1930s, but this will be dealt with separately for the reason that, in addition to its political function, it had profound implications for planned changes in the economy and society of rural China, in which of course, the majority of the Chinese population lived and still live.

One of the most important priorities of the CCP was to take control of the towns and cities, which had been their base in the 1920s but from which they had been largely excluded since the break with the Guomindang in 1927. There were members of the Communist Party who had remained in towns and cities across China throughout the civil wars and the Japanese occupation, working underground in conditions of great secrecy and often in danger of their lives, but the cities were alien to many new members of the CCP who had been recruited in the countryside. The cities were also the natural habitat of their enemies, the members and supporters of the Guomindang and the middle classes, who were certainly not instinctive supporters of the Communist Party although they were to be included in the coalition of 'the people' and recognised as an important part of the governance of new China.

The three most important political campaigns that were launched to control and win over the urban population in the 1950s were the Movement for the Suppression of Counter-Revolutionaries, and the Three-Anti and Five-Anti Campaigns. They followed on from each other and to some extent overlapped: they also took place at a time of great international tension – the outbreak of the Korean War – during which the isolation of the People's Republic of China became almost complete.

Suppressing Counter-Revolutionaries

The first targets of the mass campaigns were individuals who were deemed to have been active counter-revolutionaries. This category included leading members of the Guomindang and senior officers of its army as well as the highest ranking police officers and secret agents who had worked for the former regime. There is no doubt that such people existed and that in many cases they had vigorously opposed the Chinese Communist Party, but as the campaign unfolded, it drew in thousands of minor officials who had worked for the Guomindang administration or who had simply been associated with it and their past conduct was investigated in detail. Many were exonerated but others were convicted and imprisoned or even executed.

Between January and October 1950, there were 13,812 arrests of people accused of being counter-revolutionary agents. Zhou Enlai signed an order on 23 July ordering the more active pursuit of counter-revolutionaries. The movement which later acquired the formal name of Eliminate Counter-Revolutionary Elements [*Suqing fangeming fenzi*] explicitly followed the example of Stalin's purges in the USSR during the 1930s with *People's Daily* quoting approvingly from the Soviet leader's 1937 speech in an editorial on 29 December 1950. On 19 December, Mao Zedong had sent a telegram to two activists congratulating them on the tactics that they had employed in suppressing counter-revolutionary elements: 'I received your comprehensive report on 7 December; it is excellent, your policies are correct. Counter-revolutionary elements must be attacked firmly, surely and ruthlessly so that no one at all has any doubt.' [9]

The movement now had the imprimatur of the highest leader of the CCP and it remained only to legitimise it by codifying the crimes of the counter-revolutionaries and the punishments considered to be appropriate. The document entitled Regulations on the Suppression of Counter-Revolutionaries was ratified by the Central People's Government on 20 February and published on 21 February 1951. It set out severe penalties, including sentences of death, even for those deemed to have opposed the Communist Party before it had come to power.

The Regulations claimed to derive their authority from the Common Programme and defined counter-revolutionary crimes as those aimed at the overthrowing or disruption of People's Democracy. Anyone found guilty of collaborating with imperialists to betray the motherland faced the death penalty or life imprisonment. The same fate would befall senior people who bribed public employees, the military or the militia or otherwise enticed them to turn traitor. Minor participants faced a term of up to ten years in prison. Spies risked execution or life imprisonment, and, depending on the severity of the crime, there was the threat of execution or a long prison term for a list of offences including the theft of state secrets, supplying intelligence to domestic or foreign enemies, identifying bombing targets for enemy aircraft or ships and supplying the enemy with munitions or other material for military use. These were wartime regulations and serve as a reminder that, although the PRC was a new government that was attempting to reconstruct its economy and society, China still considered itself to be in a state of war with Taiwan and with the USA.[10]

Although the movement was aimed primarily at spies and those who were actively resisting the new government, particularly former members of the Guomindang and organisations associated with it, it also targeted leaders of the traditional Buddhist and Daoist secret societies which had their main body of support in the countryside but also enjoyed a substantial following in the cities. The campaign was carried out in part through the courts, but it was also a mass movement which is said to have involved 80 per cent of the population. There were mass meetings at which alleged counter-revolutionaries were denounced before being executed and individuals were forced to betray people who they knew had been involved with the previous regime. Factories, schools, government offices and street organisations established their own committees for the elimination of counter-revolutionaries to supply names to the security forces and to the police.[11]

One of the mass meetings that took place in Beijing in March 1951 was described in some detail in *New China Monthly* [*Xinhua yuekan*], the authoritative journal of the CCP, and this was clearly intended as a model to be followed in other parts of China. The meeting was presided over by Peng Zhen, the mayor of Beijing and concurrently secretary of the Beijing City Party Committee who was also first deputy chairman of the government's Political Legal Commission. Peng called enthusiastically for the execution of those accused of counter-revolutionary crimes, and these included workers, peasants, secondary school students and members of Daoist secret societies; rather he persuaded the assembled crowd of 5,000 to call for the executions. A second mass meeting in May 1951 was organised by Peng Zhen and Luo Ruiqing, the Security Minister who was also responsible for security in the capital and a number of 'counter-revolutionaries' were sentenced to death or life imprisonment (technically a death sentence suspended for two years). Luo Ruiqing, in his address to the meeting, announced that 199 counter-revolutionaries had been executed in Beijing since the March meeting. He continued:

A great number of people have denounced counter-revolutionaries. Wives have denounced their counter-revolutionary husbands; children have denounced their fathers. Young students have caught counter-revolutionaries and brought them to the security offices. This shows that the great propaganda has moved the masses to struggle against the counter-revolutionaries and that the People's Government and the People struggle together. Accusation meetings have been held in many quarters of Beijing, and a total of 200,000 people have taken part in them. Many have written letters to the police. Many, however, have not dared to sign their letters in fear of revenge. The masses have nothing to fear. The government will eradicate the counter revolutionaries totally. In recent days we have examined the cases of 500 persons. Most of them were denounced by others; 221 will be executed.[12]

Members of Daoist secret societies, including the Way of Unity [*Yiguandao*], which was powerful in northern China, including villages in the rural outskirts of Beijing and other cities, were also among the 277 killed and 56 sentenced to life imprisonment on 10 July 1951 during the campaign in Tianjin, along with members of a Buddhist organisation, the New Buddhist World Association.[13] These attacks on religious or quasi-religious secret societies were deliberate and were a logical consequence of the distrust felt by educated and radical Chinese in the cities for what they regarded as fraudulent religious practices and archaic superstitions that held sway throughout much of rural China.

It is difficult to make an accurate assessment of the scale of the campaign and particularly of the number of people executed after the mass meetings or trials. These statistics became a subject for propaganda and counter-propaganda in the cold war between the PRC and Taiwan. A figure of 500,000 to 800,000 deaths, based on a statement made by Mao in 1957 is often quoted but it is impossible to say whether this referred to the campaign specifically or whether it also included deaths in the last stages of the civil war and the land reform campaign. In 1951, Zhou Enlai reported to the CPPCC that 800,000 Guomindang bandits had been 'mopped up' and Bo Yibo was quoted in the 16 October 1952 edition of *People's China* as saying that 'more than two million bandits' had been liquidated. These figures were often assumed to be admissions by the PRC of the number of executions but there is no reliable evidence that this is so. There were, to be sure, many executions, of counter-revolutionaries: this was after all the end of a violent civil war which had lasted more than 20 years and there were many scores to settle. However there were also many instances of people being charged with counter-revolutionary crimes and then released. Many others were imprisoned or sent to labour camps. The psychological pressures of forced confessions in small groups and mass meetings is also said to have led to hundreds of thousands of suicides but it is difficult to verify these numbers although there is sufficient anecdotal evidence to suggest that it was a widespread phenomenon.[14]

Three-Anti Campaign

The Three-Anti [*Sanfan*] Campaign was publicised as a mass movement to counter the three evils of corruption, waste and the culture of bureaucracy and it was essentially an urban campaign. It was intended primarily for urban cadres, particularly officials who were employed in government departments responsible for financial and economic affairs and who were suspected of being implicated in corruption through official contacts with the old commercial and banking elite. It was carried out on a trial basis in the Northeast region of China by Gao Gang, the most senior CCP figure in that region, before being launched nationally. A report published in 1957 stated quite explicitly that the 'Three-Anti Campaign was aiming at a quota of 25 per cent of Party members to be purged and this figure was almost certainly reached'.[15]

The movement was piloted in the Northeast in August 1951, as were so many of China's political experiments, but it was launched as a genuinely national campaign on 7 December 1951 when the Government Affairs Council[16] approved a proposal from Zhou Enlai to launch a nationwide campaign for frugality and economy and to counter corruption, waste and 'bureaucratism'. The CCP Central Committee had drawn attention to the importance of the new movement which it felt able to promote after the 'great victories' in the Resist America – Aid Korea Campaign which had been introduced to muster public support for China's participation in the Korean War. Detailed regulations laid out the levels of punishment for corruption depending on the amounts involved. By the end of December 1951, the Three-Anti had taken over from other campaigns including an internal party rectification campaign as the highest priority of the government, which was trying to come to terms with the problems of managing an advanced urban economy and what they perceived as the widespread corruption it fostered.[17]

It was a direct intervention by Mao Zedong on 1 January 1952 that galvanised many organisations and persuaded their management to take the campaign seriously. China had seen campaigns like this before, including the puritanical New Life movement of the Guomindang in the 1930s which was a Confucian attack on dirtiness, untidiness, laziness and dishonesty but conspicuously failed to have any effect. Because the Three-Anti Campaign also targeted government officials, it had a degree of credibility that the New Life movement had lacked. Meetings were held during which CCP cadres drew attention to the financial and other inducements that the commercial world was offering to government officials who were weak or corrupt. These were reinforced by articles and cartoons in the press and displays in shop windows. It was very difficult for anyone to avoid the campaign and once it was activated in shops, offices and factories through 'mass struggle meetings' [*douzheng dahui*], it drew in almost the entire urban population. The meetings were not merely general denunciations of evils. Individuals whose actions were deemed to exemplify the crimes targeted in the campaign were singled out, humiliated and denounced with verbal if not physical violence, often while being forced to kneel on a platform in front of their colleagues. They were not permitted to say anything in their defence: only confessions were allowed. Not all 'struggle meetings' were carried out with such intensity and venom, but the nebulous charges and the possibility of such retribution created a climate of fear. Western observers, teaching in the science department of Yanjing University at the time, noted the way that the Three-Anti Campaign 'drove through Government institutions with the thunder and tempest which [Mao Zedong] had conjured up'. All types of institution were affected, not merely those that were connected to the commercial world.[18]

Although the Three-Anti Campaign was important in its own right, it also served as a template for future mass campaigns in having a percentage target for the number of offenders which had to be achieved (whether or not there were genuinely that number of offenders); by the use of stage-managed meetings to accuse individuals and by running a trial campaign in one region before the policy was applied nationwide.

Five-Anti Campaign

At the same time as the Three-Anti Campaign was targeting government cadres, a parallel campaign was being mounted against another set of evils, this time five in number: bribery, tax evasion, fraud, the theft of government property and the leakage of state secrets. This was the Five-Anti [*Wufan*] Campaign, and it was directed against the 'national bourgeoisie', the industrialists and powerful merchants who had until then been treated more or less as allies, since only those who had not collaborated with the Japanese could be included in that category. The new drive was more specific than the Three-Anti and its toughness reflected the tensions that had developed during the Korean War. It was launched in January 1952 at a time when there was a stalemate in the war. Like the Three-Anti Campaign, it was primarily an urban movement and it affected all of the major cities

and towns. It was directed against industrialists and traders who were suspected of breaking the law, especially the wealthiest capitalists, who could
be accused of many different economic crimes including swindling the state
and the wider public. However the underlying aim of the movement was
the destruction of the power and authority of the national bourgeoisie
which was perceived to be a serious impediment to the CCP's ability to
achieve its objectives.

The Five-Anti Campaign strengthened the CCP's control over businesses because, for the first time, it gave activists in workers' organisations
the opportunity to examine the finances of their employers and to search
for evidence of tax evasion or other malpractices. In turn these activists
became members of a new type of middle management and were assigned
to replace cadres and others who were purged because they were considered to have been corrupt. Businesses also became more dependent on
the state because the anti-corruption drive had the effect of weakening
them financially, resulting in applications for new loans and government
contracts. On occasion the government lent money to businessmen so that
they were able to pay the fines that they had incurred as a result of the Five-
Anti investigations. This led to an intricate arrangement in which business
leaders were in debt to, and obliged to be deferential to, senior party
officials. During the campaign, CCP branches were established in many of
the larger businesses: one of the important outcomes of this was that the
Party gained a great deal of information and understanding about the
workings of the private sector in China's towns and cities.[19]

Treaty of Peace and Friendship with the Soviet Union

If there had ever been any doubts about the international allegiance of the
new government in Beijing after Mao's promise to 'lean to one side', these
should finally have been resolved by the extended visit that Mao Zedong
made to Moscow in the winter of 1949–50. The meeting was tense and
difficult for Mao as Stalin continued to make it clear that the Soviet Union
expected all Communist states, including China, to subordinate their own
interests to the interests of world communism as a whole, which in practice
meant whatever interests were dictated by Moscow.

Mao had tried to arrange a meeting with Stalin as early as September
1948, well before the end of the Civil War, but Stalin was not willing to
proceed with a face-to-face encounter at that stage. Instead, there were
exploratory meetings involving Mikoyan for the Soviet side and Liu Shaoqi,
acting for Mao. Anastas Mikoyan, an experienced Soviet statesman, had
been a member of the State Defence Committee since 1942 and was responsible for the procurement of supplies for the Russian military during

the Second World War. He became deputy prime minister in 1946 and was the USSR's specialist on international trade. Mikoyan arrived in China on 31 January 1949 and visited Mao at his wartime centre of operations which was in Xibaipo in the province of Hebei. The Soviet authorities insisted that the visit be kept secret as it might cause difficulties in their relations with Washington, their wartime ally. Mao reported on the progress of the CCP in the civil war and on his political intentions once victory had been achieved. Mikoyan indicated plainly that Mao could expect recognition from Moscow once a government had been established, but there were already distinct disagreements about the likely scope and level of bilateral relations. Moscow had serious reservations about the possibility of the CCP forming a successful administration on its own and there were also doubts about China's rural policies. Mao subsequently made adjustments to his public pronouncements on party policy to placate Stalin, announcing that the cities were now the main focus of the CCP and even suggesting that their emphasis on the peasantry would be more restrained.

Mao Zedong dispatched a delegation to Moscow, headed by Liu Shaoqi, who was the second in seniority in the Party, to prepare the ground for his discussions with Stalin. The group spent about five weeks in Moscow in July and August 1949. Some progress was made, although not on the most difficult issues such as Soviet influence in Xinjiang and its military presence in Manchuria. Stalin had not been ready to make any firm promises but it appeared that enough solid groundwork had been laid for a productive visit by Mao to be feasible. Mao arrived in Moscow – his first visit to the headquarters of world communism – on 16 December 1949 and had a meeting with the Soviet leader, Joseph Stalin. He remained in the capital of the USSR until March, a stay of some nine weeks and was deeply frustrated at not being able to obtain from Stalin the concessions he required on economic assistance and territorial and boundary problems. The USSR had been the first country to recognise the People's Republic of China but that did not mean that it was willing to treat it as an equal partner. Stalin was reluctant to return to China the territories in Manchuria that the Red Army had occupied in 1945 and the Manchurian railway; he was also concerned about the rise of yet another independent Communist leader after the political disagreements that had erupted between Moscow and Tito's Yugoslavia and the acrimonious split in 1948. The Soviet authorities were not at all sure how to evaluate Mao's status: the revolution in China had developed independently of the Comintern and there had been relatively little contact between Yan'an and Moscow. There was little mutual understanding or empathy between Stalin and Mao during Mao's visit, and although Mao declared that basic agreement had been reached on a treaty between the two states, there was only a deadlock.

The impasse was broken when Zhou Enlai joined Mao in Moscow, and this was an early example of Zhou's renowned charm and diplomatic facility being deployed effectively in the interests of the PRC, in sharp contrast to Mao's notorious earthy peasant directness. On 2 January, Mao had sent a telegram to the Central People's Government in Beijing and reported that

> There have been important developments in the work here in the last two days. Stalin has agreed that Zhou Enlai can come to Moscow and to a new Sino-Soviet Treaty of Friendship and Alliance as well as agreements on credit, commerce and civil aviation.

He went on to note that on 1 January an interview that he had given to a correspondent from the Soviet News agency, TASS, had been published and that Comrades Molotov and Mikoyan had visited him on the evening of 2 January to consult on the contents of the treaty and other matters. Zhou Enlai arrived in Moscow on 20 January and on 14 February he and his Soviet counterpart Andrei Vyshinsky signed the Treaty of Friendship, Alliance and Mutual Assistance which was intended to bind the two Communist states together for eternity. At the same time the two sides signed separate agreements on the withdrawal of Soviet troops from Manchuria and the return of the Manchurian railway and other property in Dalian and Lüshun (Port Arthur) to China. By these agreements the Soviet Union effectively abrogated all of its special privileges in China. The USSR also agreed to provide China with loans to a total value of US$300 million, to be repaid at an annual interest rate of 1 per cent. Stalin has been criticised for not having behaved more generously towards his new and poorer ally but the USSR also faced enormous challenges in reconstructing its economy after the depredations that had been inflicted by the armies of the Third Reich. Mao and Zhou returned to Beijing on 4 March 1950. Although the treaty was hailed as a great triumph for the new People's Government, the experience had soured Mao's view of Moscow and the eternal alliance was to last for barely ten years.[20]

Korean War

Although people in China's cities were undergoing the trials and tribulations of the three mass political campaigns, a major international drama was unfolding on the borders of the People's Republic. In 1950 Korea once again became the battleground for a war between great powers: in 1894–5 the powers had been China and Japan; now it was the USA and the Soviet Union. China was acting as proxy for the Soviet Union and the USA was fighting as part of a coalition sponsored by the United Nations. This was a major battle on the eastern front of what had until then been the Cold War. The Korean War had a lasting and, on balance, detrimental effect on China's standing in the world and also on the attitudes and policies of the government of the PRC.

For centuries, Korea had been an independent kingdom although it was closely allied to the Chinese empire and acknowledged its formal sub-servience by paying tribute to the Chinese imperial court. Because of its dis-tinctiveness and isolation it was often known as the Hermit Kingdom; it was also called, somewhat fancifully, the Land of the Morning Calm after a possible translation of the Chinese characters in its name, although history has not bestowed calmness on it in recent times. Over the centuries, Korea had adopted many of the characteristics of Chinese Confucianism but it retained its own distinctive language and culture. After the Sino-Japanese War of 1894–5 it came under the control of the expanding Japanese empire and was conquered in 1905 and fully incorporated into Greater Japan in 1910. Japan attempted to eradicate the Korean language and culture and the repressive nature of Japanese rule stimulated the development of nationalist sentiment, notably in the 1 March demonstrations of 1919. Many national-ists were forced into exile, among them Syngman Rhee [Yi Sung-man 1875–1965] who established a government in exile in the USA and Kim Il-sung, a shadowy figure who had probably fought against the Japanese along-side Soviet and Chinese guerrilla forces in Manchuria.

After Japan had conceded defeat in 1945, the Red Army moved from Manchuria into the northern part of Korea on 9 August, one day after the USSR's formal, but in military terms irrelevant, declaration of war on Japan. US forces advanced into the southern part of Korea in September and the two armies, theoretically allies at the time, it should be recalled, met in the centre. The 38° line of latitude, the 38th Parallel, was chosen as an arbitrary dividing line between the advancing armies. The Soviet forces would take the surrender of the Japanese military units to the north of it, the USA to the south. This temporary arrangement turned into a permanent border. In the south the ultra-nationalist and anti-Communist Syngman Rhee emerged as victor in the elections of May 1948, and he was proclaimed president of the Republic of Korea on 15 August 1948. Kim Il-sung became head of the Peoples' Committee in the north and mobilised the peasant masses in a land reform campaign which was very similar to the strategy that had been adopted by the Chinese Communist Party. A United Nations commission which had been appointed to assist in the reunification of Korea was expelled by Kim, the north held elections on its own and on 9 September 1948, Kim Il-sung became the leader of the Democratic People's Republic of Korea: he was to become known as the Great Leader.

At this stage the People's Republic of China was not involved in Korea at all. The Civil War between the CCP and the GMD was reaching its climax and Korea was the last thing on the minds of the CCP leadership. Even after the foundation of the PRC in October 1949, the new government was more concerned with Taiwan, land reform, domestic reconstruction and forging its new alliance with the USSR than with Korea. As late as the beginning of June 1950, Mao's speeches and reports to the meeting of the Third Plenary session of the Seventh Central Committee of the CCP concentrated on large-scale retrenchment in government expenditures and there was no suggestion of any military intervention in Korea.[21]

On 25 June 1950, North Korean forces invaded the south and on the following day Kim Il-sung claimed in a broadcast that the north had been obliged to launch a counter-offensive to push back an invasion of enemy troops. Although it was true that there had been many border incidents, including exchanges of fire, since the establishment of the two states in 1948, no credence is given to this claim although it was supported by the Soviet Union. On 27 June, China still maintained that it was not involved in Korea and the media in the PRC was far more concerned about the mobilisation of the US Seventh Fleet in the Taiwan Strait. China, it seemed, was reluctant to become involved in what appeared to be solely a North Korean military adventure. Documents that emerged from the archives which were opened after the collapse of the Soviet Union in 1991 told a rather different story. Kim Il-sung had visited Moscow on 27 February 1950 with a proposal entitled the 'Korean People's Army Pre-emptive Strike Plan'. Kim stayed in Moscow for three days with a seven-member strong military delegation and discussed his strategy with the Soviet General Staff. Kim visited Moscow again in April 1950 to discuss his plans: Beijing had still not been officially informed although there were reports that a senior member of the Korean Party of Labour, Pak Chong-ae, had visited Beijing in March to warn the CCP leadership that an attack on the south of Korea was imminent. Stalin approved the invasion plan and the Soviet Ambassador to Pyongyang, General Aleksey Shitikov, was involved at every stage. On 25 June he sent a telegram to Stalin informing him, 'Attacks have been going as planned. By evening, People's Army units advanced 20–40 km on all fronts. Enemy defences are being destroyed with ease.'[22] It later transpired that, although Kim Il-sung had not consulted the Chinese leadership about his plan formally or in detail, he did visit Beijing between 13 and 16 May 1950 to solicit Mao's approval in general for the invasion of South Korea. At this point, Stalin effectively distanced himself from the Korean problem and made it clear that the Koreans would have to take the responsibility themselves, with the support of the Chinese if necessary. Kim's visit to Beijing was probably at the insistence of Stalin. Mao is reported to have offered to contribute several Chinese units, but this was refused by Kim Il-sung. Shi Zhe, who acted as interpreter for many of these high level meetings, reported that Mao Zedong found Kim's tone arrogant and the North Korean leader insisted that his forces could complete the re-conquest of the South Korea with the assistance of Korean Communist guerrillas in the south and did not need Chinese help.[23]

It is important to appreciate that the relationship between the Chinese and Korean Communist Parties was close but not unproblematic. Korean Communists had worked with the CCP in Shanghai and in some of the guerrilla bases: during the Chinese Civil War some units of the Chinese People's Liberation Army consisted mainly of ethnic Korean troops. As China itself has a sizeable ethnic Korean population, particularly in the Northeast, this is not surprising but it does help in part to explain the sensitivities of relations between the two ostensibly fraternal parties.[24]

China publicly made known its formal interest in the conflict on the Korean peninsula on 20 August when Zhou Enlai sent a telegram to the United Nations demanding that China be represented at discussions on Korea. The United Nations counter-offensive, which was led by the USA, was launched on 15 September 1950 with amphibious landings at the port city of Inchon which is just to the west of the South Korean capital Seoul. On 1 October, the first anniversary of the foundation of the People's Republic of China, South Korean troops crossed the 38th Parallel into the North. Under pressure from Stalin, Mao Zedong issued a directive to contribute units of the Chinese People's Liberation Army to the North Korean war effort and these were mobilised under the title of Chinese People's Volunteers, CPV [*Zhongguo renmin zhiyuan jun*]. The date of the directive is usually given as 1 October, which was highly symbolic for China, but Mao did not give his agreement until 7 October and it took another week of discussions in the CCP Politburo before the decision was finally ratified. For China this was now the War to Resist America and Aid Korea [*Kang Mei yuan Chao zhanzheng*], and Chinese troops were urged to fight under the slogan 'protect your homes and defend the country' [*baojia weiguo*]. The troops of the CPV were placed under the command of the veteran General Peng Dehuai and sent to the front line on 25 October. They went into battle in their regular PLA uniforms, but with the addition of a small rectangular cloth badge with the insignia of the CPV sewn onto their jackets. Peng Dehuai was later to claim that a majority of the CCP leadership had been opposed to involvement in Korea but that Mao had overruled them and that he, Peng, had supported Mao or at the very least had not opposed him.[25] Mao was concerned that the very existence of the PRC would be endangered if North Korea were defeated, and he realised that his support for Kim was important in the power play within the Communist bloc.

Vanguard units of the CPV moved south across the Yalu River, which marks the border between China and Korea, on 18 October 1950 and were soon facing American soldiers of the First Corps. Peng had some 400,000 troops under his command and they were drawn from his most experienced and battle-hardened units which were fresh from their successes in the Civil War. The performance of the CPV impressed even their adversaries, many of whom had previously subscribed to the myth that Chinese people could not be trained as good soldiers. Although there were logistical and communications problems, the experience of many of the PLA commanders in guerrilla warfare gave them advantages in terms of mobility, deception and surprise. Between October 1950 and July 1951 there were five major campaigns. Tactics such as the attacks by 'human waves' of infantrymen with fixed bayonets, in the face of concerted enemy fire with virtually no air or artillery support, were extremely effective but they took a dreadful toll and cost the lives of thousands of Chinese troops. The UN forces were forced back to the 38th Parallel and the initial objective of securing North Korea for Kim Il-sung's Korean Workers' Party had been achieved but at a great cost.

Towards the end of January 1951, the Chinese People's Volunteers were beginning to feel under intolerable pressure and Peng Dehuai flew back to Beijing to consult with Mao. By the summer of 1951 Chinese troops were fatigued to the point that they could fight no more: the spring offensive in late April and early May alone may have cost the lives of as many as 200,000 CPV troops. Mao and Zhou Enlai met Kim Il-sung in June 1951 to try to find a way to extricate their armies from the situation and agreed that a ceasefire was the only viable option available to them. When the United Nations proposed negotiations for an armistice in July 1951, the Chinese and North Koreans were only too ready to accept this. The negotiations began on 10 July in the village of Kaesong on the front line but were then transferred to another village, Panmunjom, which was located in the demilitarised zone established after the cessation of hostilities, and which has ever since been synonymous with the ceasefire and with the stalemate that was the only outcome of the peace talks. The negotiations were long and drawn out and in the end failed to reach a satisfactory conclusion, with the result that no peace treaty was ever signed. An armistice agreement was signed on 27 July 1953 at Panmunjom by Peng Dehuai for the CPV, representatives of the Korean People's Army and the United Nations. This marked the formal end of the war although there had been no fighting since July 1951. Peng Dehuai was honoured as a war hero both in the North Korean capital, Pyongyang, and in Beijing.

It has been estimated that the total number of Chinese casualties in the Korean War was 900,000, greater than the losses of any of the other nations involved and probably greater even than the total number of Korean troops killed and injured. Mao Zedong's son, Mao Anying ('Volunteer Number 1'), who was working as a secretary and Russian interpreter, died in an American bombing raid on the CPV headquarters on 25 November 1950. He was 28 years old and, as he had been placed by Mao under the personal protection of Peng Dehuai; this was to sour relations between the two men for years to come with serious repercussions for Chinese domestic politics. Peng himself only narrowly escaped death in the raid.[26] On the home front in China, the Resist America – Aid Korea Campaign became a mass movement and this added to the CCP's credibility as a patriotic party, a status that it had already attained with its history of defiance in the War of Resistance against Japan. The political campaigns, particularly the Campaign for the Suppression of Counter-Revolutionaries, were intensified as a result of the tension and suspicion created by the fear of invasion and the numbers of people executed as counter-revolutionaries or traitors may have been greatly increased because of this.[27] For China, one of the most significant consequences of the Korean War was that Beijing was excluded from the United Nations and from the international community more generally for 20 years because it was considered to have been an aggressor. The UN had not accepted Beijing's claim to sovereignty of all of China after 1949 and the outcome of the Korean War made it unlikely that it could ever do so. The isolation of the People's Republic of China was an important factor in the atmosphere of distrust and fear that affected the country in the 1950s and 1960s. It fuelled tensions within the CCP that led to ideological and personal battles between party factions and ultimately to the Cultural Revolution.

Constitution of 1954

By 1954, the Korean War was over, the most violent phase of the political campaigns had been concluded and the PRC was ready to move towards the adoption of a written constitution. The first constitution was adopted by the first National People's Congress on 20 September 1954. It was drafted by a constitutional committee, and it drew heavily on the 1936 Soviet Constitution. It lacked the inclusiveness of the Common Programme and Article 1 enshrined the principle that the People's Republic of China would be led by the working class, which effectively guaranteed that the CCP would dominate China for the foreseeable future.

The Constitution outlined the structure of the Chinese government and its major organisations of state. The highest authority was to be the National People's Congress [*Quanguo renmin daibiao dahu*, the NPC], made up of deputies elected from the provinces, autonomous regions (created in acknowledgement of the large non-Chinese populations in some of the areas under the control of the CCP) and the largest cities. It was intended that it would serve for a term of four years and meet annually: it would have the ultimate power to amend the Constitution, enact legislation, elect the Premier and the head of both the Supreme People's Court and the Procurate, and rule on economic plans. When the NPC was not in session, its functions would be exercised by a Standing Committee, which had very wide powers, including the authority to conduct the election of the deputies, to convene its own sessions, to interpret the legislation that had been enacted and to supervise other state bodies including the State Council and the Courts. The NPC would also elect a chairman of the People's Republic of China, the equivalent of a president in most republics, who would have the power to nominate the premier and other senior ministers and officials, and who would exercise supreme authority in relations with foreign countries.

The State Council [*Guowuyuan*] was created as the executive body of the state, under the premier and with ministries and commissions subordinate to it. It was to be responsible to the NPC and to its Standing Committee when the full NPC was not in session. Local people's congresses were also established at provincial and local levels, creating a hierarchy of bodies in which, broadly speaking, the lower organs elected deputies to the higher. The Constitution also outlined the rights and duties of citizens and adopted the national flag which is a red flag with five stars (Article 104), and the national emblem, the gate of Tiananmen under the light of five stars in the centre, surrounded by ears of grain and a cogwheel at the base (Article 105).[28] The flag was chosen as a result of a competition and represented the political symbolism of the time. Mao Zedong is said to have chosen the final winner from a shortlist. The red background was intended to represent 'revolutionary enthusiasm' but it also had echoes of the Ming imperial colour, whether those responsible for choosing it were conscious of that or not; the large star represented the Communist Party and the four smaller ones the four classes of 'the people' that were in alliance with the CCP in the period of New Democracy, in other words the national bourgeoisie, the petty bourgeoisie, the working class and the peasantry.[29] It is also oddly resonant of the flag of the Guomindang's Republic of China and the nationalist concept of the five nations of China: Han, Manchu, Mongol, Tibetan and Muslim. There is some confusion in China today about the precise symbolism of the stars; many accounts simply say that the stars represent the relationship between the CCP and the people of China.

Although the Constitution was couched in democratic terms with many references to elections, it does not require very close reading to discern the considerable power that would be wielded by the Standing Committee of the NPC and the Chairman of the State. Control of the Standing Committee and the post of Chairman, which were permanently in the hands of the most senior members of the CCP, ensured that the Party had control of the government. Elections did take place, but the electoral procedures, which were elaborated in separate legislation, made it possible for the CCP to control the nomination of candidates to the elections at all levels and thus to control the entire process. The term Central People's Government gradually fell into disuse but the executive arm of the government of China is still known as the State Council.

Purge of Gao Gang and Rao Shushi

Official accounts of the early years of the PRC always stress the unity of purpose and solidarity of the leadership of the CCP. It is true that China never experienced the mass purges, show trials and the murder of party officials that was characteristic of the Soviet Union in the Stalin era but there had always been factional struggles within the Party. Trotskyists and anyone suspected of sympathising with them were expelled in the 1930s and Wang Shiwei's incarceration and subsequent death in Yan'an illustrated what could happen to a dissident or an oppositionist.[30]

However the only serious purge that took place in the PRC before the Great Leap Forward was the expulsion of Gao Gang and Rao Shushi from the government and from the Communist Party in 1954. Gao Gang was a member of the Politburo and Director of the State Planning Commission who also served as the most senior party, government and military official of the Northeast, Manchuria. Rao Shushi was similarly the leading CCP figure of the eastern China region around Shanghai and was the Director of the Organisation Department of the Central Committee and a member of the State Planning Commission. They came under sustained criticism at the Fourth Plenary Session of the Seventh Central Committee which took place in Beijing from 6 to 10 February 1954 and were accused by Liu Shaoqi in his formal report to the committee of having conspired against the CCP in attempting to set up 'independent kingdoms'. At specially convened and stage-managed meetings of party cadres from the Northeast and eastern China that were held from February through to August 1954, the allegations against the pair were revealed to the massed ranks of the Party. They were expelled from the Party and dismissed from all of their government posts at the National Conference of the CCP that ran from 21 to 31 March 1955 in Beijing.[31]

This episode is one of the most obscure and murky in the early history of the PRC, but what is indisputable is that it involved policy differences over the speed of China's economic development, Gao's closeness to the Soviet Communist Party, the implications that this relationship might have had for relations between the two states and for China's ability to forge an independent path and tensions between the centre and the regions.[32] However it was primarily a power struggle by Gao and Rao to wrest control of the CCP bureaucracy from Liu Shaoqi and Zhou Enlai who were known to be cautious about the pace of economic construction and agricultural cooperation. Whether Gao was acting on his own behalf or as an agent of the more impulsive Mao Zedong, who approved of his track record in the Northeast is not clear. Gao had drawn up an alternative list of Politburo members and had canvassed support for it, at which point Mao decided to distance himself from him, criticised him and gave his support, for the time being, to Liu Shaoqi. Gao, who was only 49 years old, apparently attempted to commit suicide in February 1954: he finally succeeded in ending his own life the following August. Although that particular crisis had ended, it did expose many of the factional and policy fault lines within the CCP which were to come to a head during the period of the Great Leap Forward of 1958 and later in the Cultural Revolution.

12

ECONOMIC AND
SOCIAL POLICIES
(1950–1957)

Military victory, the establishment of a new government and the elimination of enemies and political rivals were the highest priorities for the leaders of the CCP when they took power in 1949, but they were also determined to implement policies that would help to resolve some of the fundamental problems that had affected China for decades. At the top of the list were economic reconstruction for a land devastated by almost 40 years of conflict; the more equitable redistribution of agricultural land; marriage reform to alleviate the suffering of millions of women and the thorny problem of how to deal with the educated and professional classes, many of whom were temperamentally inclined to support New China from patriotic motives but were also, by profession and by disposition, extremely critical. The Party leadership had made commitments to their supporters that they would take action on these measures: they knew that the Guomindang had been weakened by these perennial problems and that unless they acted swiftly and decisively, their own authority could be undermined in the same way.

Building a Planned Economy

China's economy, when the CCP came to power in 1949, can be characterised as almost entirely pre-modern. The Middle Kingdom was predominantly an agricultural country that used traditional technology that had been in place with little change for hundreds of years.[1] Population growth and the scarcity of arable land made it extremely difficult to produce adequate amounts of food, and this accounted partly for the famines the country had experienced in the 1920s and 1930s. War and civil war had also played their part in this. In 1949, grain production was a mere 113 million tons, an amount that was totally inadequate to feed the population. Urban China amounted to perhaps 20per cent of the total in terms of population, and the cities had to be fed from the surpluses generated from the countryside, surpluses that were seldom sufficient if the villagers were also to be fed adequately.

Industrial development had been patchy. There had been advances in modern heavy industry in the provinces of the Northeast (Manchuria) largely as a result of the Japanese occupation. Manchuria had been vital to the development of the Japanese economy as it possessed immense resources of coal and iron, which Japan lacked. Coal mines and iron workings had been developed by Japanese enterprises since the 1920s, as had the railway infrastructure that was required to transport their products back to Japan. There had also been significant developments in manufacturing in and around the Treaty Ports, which were spread along the southeast coast and inland along the Yangzi River. Textile manufacture, food processing and other light industries were widespread but their growth was hampered by the low level of technical skills and by major problems in distribution and lack of investment. The 'foreign matters' movement that followed the Tongzhi restoration had also left a legacy of industrial development to underpin the naval and armament industries created by the modernising proto-warlords of the late Qing period, but this was also predominantly in the coastal areas.

The problems of underdevelopment and rural poverty had been exacerbated not only by decades of war and civil war but also by the hyperinflation of the 1940s, so the first significant economic action of the new People's Government in 1949 was a fiscal one, the centralisation of finance and taxation accompanied by restrictions on the circulation of foreign currency. These measures, outlined in a Government Administration Council (GAC) document entitled Decisions on the Unification of the Nation's Financial and Economic Work were published on 3 March 1950 and had the effect of breaking the inflationary spiral.[2]

China was on course to follow the Soviet model of economic development. After the failure of international attempts, led by the USA, to form a coalition government in 1946 and 1947 and Mao's decision to 'lean to one side' in 1949, there was no realistic alternative and the Soviet system was, in any case, the only modern economic and social approach of which most of the CCP leadership had any real experience or understanding.[3] Adhering to the Soviet model meant the construction of a centrally planned economy and specifically the setting of Five-Year Plans. The First Five-Year Plan (1953–7) was regarded by many contemporary analysts, Communist and non-Communist alike as having been broadly successful. It was the only Chinese plan that followed its natural economic course without political upheaval, and it is therefore a good measure of the efficacy of this type of economic management in the Chinese context. Long-term planning on a national scale could not begin until the outlying provinces had been conquered and mass campaigns in rural and urban areas had left the CCP leadership confident of their political control. Initial attempts at long-term economic strategy had been hampered by the lack of expertise in both planning and statistics, by the demands that the Korean War had placed on the Chinese economy and by difficulties that China had encountered in negotiating an aid package with the Soviet Union. At first, plans were drawn up on an annual basis only, but by 1953, when the Korean War had finished and aid negotiations with the USSR had been concluded, planning for five years became feasible. The principles of the First Five-Year Plan were published in 1953, but it was not until April 1955 that a full version was made publicly available.[4] In 1952 two government bodies were established to assist in the implementation of the Plan: these were the State Statistical Bureau and the State Planning Commission, which were to become highly influential in the management of the Chinese economy. The task of the State Statistical Bureau was to generate the data needed for planning; the State Planning Commission, which reported directly to the State Council under the 1954 Constitution, was responsible for both long-term and annual plans until 1956 when short-term planning was devolved to the State Economic Commission.[5]

In common with so many other policies of the CCP, the economic plans were given a dry run in one region, the Northeast, before being applied nationwide. The Northeast was not only one of the most developed areas of China but it had also come under CCP control early in the civil war, and a rough plan for revitalising the region had been drawn up as early as 1949. The Northeast Administrative Area was run by Gao Gang and, on the strength of his experiences in Manchuria, Gao was put in charge of the State Planning Commission: he introduced to the whole country accounting and planning practices that he had experimented with in the Northeast. Gao was ousted in 1954 in the only major purge of the CCP in the early 1950s and was replaced by Li Fuchun, his former deputy in the Northeast.[6]

The thinking behind the First Five-Year Plan was that China required a massive expansion in its heavy industry sector and that this could only be funded by extracting surpluses from the agricultural sector. It followed that industrial production was to a large extent dependent on the success of the harvest which could fluctuate considerably depending on the weather. Major institutional and social changes took place in the period of the First Five-Year Plan: the private sector was virtually eliminated and modern industry came under state control, although many handicraft workshops and small shops remained in private hands or were organised in cooperatives. The push towards nationalisation, the 'socialist transformation of industry' as it was termed, was at its height in 1955 and 1956. Even earlier, many businesses had been converted into joint state–private companies as a halfway house. These were usually created with the provision of substantial government investment and by nominating Party cadres to the boards of directors. During the nationalisation drive, businessmen were persuaded to sell their firms in return for compensation from the government which was often set at a generous level. In general the directors remained on the board as their expertise and inside knowledge were still required, and they were entitled to receive a dividend on the shares that they owned, an entitlement that lasted until 1962. Most of the resistance to this programme had been pre-empted by the Five-Anti Campaign.[7]

In line with the experience of the USSR, the strategy of the new government of the PRC was to place most of its emphasis on capital construction and the development of heavy industry. During the First Five-Year Plan, life expectancy increased, the number of children in primary schools went up dramatically, urban housing standards improved and consumption and real wages also grew. There was very little outside help: the USSR supplied capital goods but these were not donations and were paid for at the time or on short-term credit.[8]

A positive estimate of the plan by a leading scholar of the economy of the early People's Republic ran as follows:

> Measured in terms of economic growth, the First Five Year Plan was a stunning success. National income grew at an annual average rate of 8.9 per cent (measured in constant prices), with agriculture and industrial output expanding annually by about 3.8 and 18.1 per cent respectively. Since annual population growth was 2.4 per cent, output grew at 6.5 per cent per capita, a rate at which national income would double every eleven years. Compared to the pattern of growth in China during the first half of the twentieth century, in which output grew barely as fast as population, the First Five Year Plan marked a decisive acceleration. China's experience also compares favourably with most newly independent developing countries in which per capita growth averaged about 2.5 per cent per annum during the 1950s. For example, India, another continent-sized agrarian economy with initial economic conditions similar to those in China, achieved a per capita growth rate well under 2 per cent during the 1950s.[9]

Critics of the plan have pointed to problems in the coordination of targets – for example, the plans for electrical power generation and manufacturing industry were not entirely compatible – and have argued that there was inadequate emphasis on agriculture, water conservancy and forestry which restricted the availability of food and agricultural raw materials.[10]

The Second Five-Year Plan was due to follow on immediately from the first and was scheduled to run from 1958 to 1962, but by 1955 Mao was already concerned that, under the First Five-Year Plan, agriculture had been growing too slowly and desperately wanted to increase the pace of economic development. He was also beginning to look for ways to distance himself from the Soviet Union and to create a specifically Chinese way of changing the economy and society. An old slogan, 'more, quicker, better, more economically', which sounds much snappier in the Chinese original of *duo, kuai, hao, sheng*, was revived in November 1956 and Mao announced that China would overtake the industrial production of the United Kingdom in 15 years. This sounded the death knell for conventional Soviet-style planning and gradual development and was the prelude to the dramatic social and economic mobilisation of the Great Leap Forward in 1958.

Land Reform

In twentieth century China, the expression Land Reform, or alternatively Agrarian Reform [*tudi gaige*], is usually reserved for the policy of confiscating land from the landowning classes and redistributing it to the poorest peasants. Occasionally the meaning is extended to include the process of collectivisation that followed the redistribution of land and led eventually to the formation of the People's Communes in 1958. It should be noted that land reform is not purely a policy of Communist parties. Japan underwent a similar process during the period of American occupation after the Second World War, the Guomindang government on Taiwan has carried out its own land reform programme and so have right-wing military regimes in Latin America.

The earliest experience that the CCP had of rural policies was in 1922–3 when Peng Pai (1896–1929) organised peasant associations in Guangdong province. He was later ignored in official Communist Party histories principally so that Mao Zedong would appear to have been the first senior party figure to have taken an interest in the peasantry. Serious attempts at Land Reform under the auspices of the Communist Party began in the Jiangxi Soviet period (1929–35) when the beleaguered CCP, surrounded by Guomindang armies, carried out a ruthless land redistribution campaign which cost the lives of many landlords. This period can be seen as the laboratory in which many policies were first tested. In their land policies, the CCP tried at first to copy procedures that at the time were believed to have succeeded in the USSR, and, to paraphrase Mao, they relied on the poor peasants and landless labourers as the core of their support while trying to rally the middle peasants to the cause. During the United Front period of 1937–45, attempts at an alliance with the Guomindang to resist the Japanese invasion led the Communist Party to moderate its land policies, and the large-scale redistribution of land was replaced by an emphasis on demands for the reduction of land rent and of interest on loans, the dual financial burden on poor peasant farmers. Patriotic sentiment predominated during the occupation and this meant that, in this phase of the CCP's revolutionary endeavour, even landlords were brought into the struggle if they were prepared to resist the Japanese, although the peasants remained the prime interest of the Party. Increased production to support the war effort became a key part of their agrarian policies.

When the Japanese were defeated in 1945 and China was dragged into yet another civil war, far harsher land reform policies were set in motion by the CCP, many landlords were killed, excess land was compulsorily purchased and redistributed and a conscious attempt was made to eliminate the rich peasant farmers as a class. The chief motives of the CCP at this time were to increase farm production in the ever expanding rural areas under their control and to increase the already substantial support that they enjoyed among the poorer farmers. By the time the Communist Party came to power as the government of the People's Republic in October 1949, the land reform process was already well advanced and the party and its cadres had amassed considerable experience in implementing it. The main task of the new government was to consolidate and codify the procedures for implementing the confiscation and redistribution of land and, in many cases, to restrain overzealous activists who were redistributing land and killing people who they alleged were landowners with little regard to their actual status or individual track records. The legislation designed to resolve this was the Agrarian Reform Law which was promulgated in 1950. The general principles were expressed in Article 1 of the law:

> The land ownership system of feudal exploitation by the landlord class shall be abolished and the system of peasant landownership shall be introduced in order to set free the rural productive forces, develop agricultural production and thus pave the way for New China's industrialisation.[11]

It bears repeating that the CCP had far more experience and better trained personnel available to carry out land reform than it had for its urban campaigns. Different approaches were tried, based on the understanding that the CCP had acquired in the 'liberated areas' of Manchuria and North China and the methods of ensuring compliance were gradually refined. In 1950, Mao Zedong's view was that the 'agrarian reform in the north was carried out in wartime, with the atmosphere of war prevailing over that of agrarian reform, but now, with the fighting practically over, the agrarian reform stands out in sharp relief and the shock to society will be particularly great'.[12] A major difference was that land reform was now carried out over a much wider geographical area. Actual seizures of land still involved only a relatively small proportion of the rural population. Although the land owned by families classified as landlords was confiscated and redistributed to the poorest farmers, in many cases land owned by farmers classified as rich peasants was not expropriated. This was because the food produced by the farms belonging to rich peasants was vital for the reconstruction of the country and the CCP did not want to alienate them. The criteria for classifying individuals and families as landlords or rich, middle and poor peasants were complex and convoluted. They afforded ample opportunities for settling old scores and doing down rivals or enemies and the Agrarian Reform Law was designed partly to encourage a more rational and fairer system of classification. The results of this process were of vital importance as not only did the class label determine how much land a family might gain or lose, but it remained with the family for decades and could determine work and even marriage prospects.

Land reform could not begin until an area was firmly under the control of the new regime and the military played a crucial role in the agrarian revolution. PLA units spread across China, first taking the major cities and then fanning out to the rural market towns and the villages. 'Bandit Suppression Campaigns' were launched, in the course of which potentially hostile groups and individuals were disarmed and new village militia units were organised. The land reform campaign was coordinated at county town level, where work teams of from 3 to 30 people were established. These included local people considered by the CCP to be reliable, particularly if they were veteran party and army officials or members of the PLA, but there were also many students and other urban intellectuals who had been politicised in the resistance to Japanese occupation.

The first task of the work teams was to organise a system for collecting taxes and this was not an easy undertaking because of the reluctance of peasants to pay taxes to a regime that, for all they knew, might not survive for very long in power. The tax campaign cost the lives of more than 3,000 cadres during the first year of land reform, although the resistance lessened once the tax burden was switched from the poorest farmers to the better off. Peasant associations were then set up on the model that had been established by Peng Pai, rent and interest reductions were secured and mass meetings were held to attack those who were identified as the cruellest and most oppressive members of the former village elites.[13] The objective of these meetings was to break down traditional patterns of social control, deference to the clan and landowning elites and mutual dependence that had characterised rural China for centuries. Work teams identified landlords and sought to isolate them from the poorer members of their extended families. Landlord families would often find ways to reduce their apparent standard of living dramatically so that they seemed to be no wealthier than middle-ranking peasants: they might kill and eat their livestock, rather than have cattle and sheep calculated as part of their wealth; they might even ignore traditional, social or charitable activities that would have marked them out as landlords. Peasants, unsure of how long the new order was likely to survive, sometimes secretly gave back the amount by which their rent had been reduced to their landlords with whom they may have had family or other ties. Peasant associations were not always dependable and in some areas as few as 40 per cent of peasants were members. The traditional power and influence of the gentry and landlords were difficult to overcome in a rural culture where traditional bonds of family, clan and local association were extremely powerful. The problems that work teams encountered were increased by the fact that many of them were cadres from outside the area in which they were working: they often had little knowledge of local conditions and might not even understand the local rural dialect.

There has been much debate over whether the land reform policy of the early 1950s were ever intended to be an end in itself, with every peasant family owning its own plot of land, or whether it was from the outset conceived as a halfway house on the road to full collectivisation. In a report by Liu Shaoqi on the Agrarian Reform Law of June 1950, he outlined the economic rationale as 'freeing the rural productive forces and paving the way for industrialisation', echoing the principles enshrined in the preamble to the legislation. There was a genuine economic motive but land reform was also a formidable political tool.[14]

In November and December 1950 while the Korean War raged on China's borders, more radical policies of land reform were again implemented, and there was greater emphasis on class struggle and mass mobilisation. Class identification was carried out more rigorously, landlords' holdings were ruthlessly confiscated and work teams from their headquarters in the county towns were sent down to the villages to clean up and reform any of the Peasant Associations that were considered to be weak or unreliable. A new leadership of poorer peasants emerged in the associations, and 'speak bitterness' meetings, at which landlords were publicly criticised, accused and humiliated, were frequently followed by executions. It is possible that as many as 2 million landlords were killed during this period.

The outcome of these land reform policies in terms of crude statistics was that, after the campaign, roughly 60 per cent of the rural population now owned 43 per cent of cultivable land, a substantial redistribution. Although the poorest farmers benefited, it was probably the middle-ranking peasants who gained most. There may also have been an overall national improvement in agricultural productivity but it is difficult to determine how much this was due to redistribution and how much was simply the benefit of an extended period without war or foreign occupation. The main achievement, at least as far as the Chinese Communist Party was concerned, was a political one. 'The old village institutions of clan, temple and secret society had been replaced by the new, which assumed their education, mediatory and economic functions.' A new elite of village cadres from a poor and middle-ranking peasant background had emerged and the members of this new elite owed their positions entirely to the CCP.[15]

Collectivisation and Cooperatives

Land reform had begun in the liberated areas as early as 1948 and it spread across the country with the victories of the PLA and the enactment of the Agrarian Reform Law. The process of collectivisation or cooperation in agriculture began in 1952 and was promoted in some areas even before land reform had been completed in others. It drew not only on the experiences, negative as well as positive, of the Soviet Union's programme of collectivisation in the 1930s but also on experiments in China which had taken place at the same time. The leadership of the CCP were conscious of the disastrous consequences of the attempt by Stalin to eliminate the *kulaks* (rich peasants) as a class in the USSR and were determined to avoid this by introducing collective farming gradually in China.

The first stage, which took place roughly between 1952 and 1955, was the introduction of Mutual Aid Teams [*huzhu zu*]. Labour and tools were pooled but remained the property of individual families. These teams were not entirely an innovation as in certain areas there was a tradition of peasants cooperating, often at busy times such as the harvest or spring planting. The difference was that the system was now formalised and managed by the peasant associations and the new local government. The CCP favoured these teams because they encouraged a collective spirit and took the peasants out of their traditional small family units.

Agricultural Producers' Cooperatives or APCs [*nongye shengchan hezuoshe* or *nongye she*] followed in 1955. These were created by combining a number of successful Mutual Aid Teams and comprising 30 or 40 peasant families. Membership was voluntary, the land was still considered to be privately owned and the cooperative paid rent to the members for the land that they contributed to the enterprise. Families were able to retain some land for their own use. Farming families derived about half of their income from renting out their land to the cooperative and the other half from work points. This was an incentive for families with larger landholdings to participate. By March 1955, approximately 14 per cent of rural households were members of APCs. This was far too slow for Mao Zedong and his supporters and in July 1955, Mao insisted on a 'high tide of socialism' [*shehuizhuyi gaochao*] in the Chinese countryside which would increase the speed at which families were incorporated into cooperatives. The argument put forward at the time was that the party was in danger of lagging behind an overwhelming surge of popular support for collectivisation. The reality was that there was an excess of zeal among local party officials reporting on the success of cooperation in their own areas. Between July and November 1955, the proportion of households enrolled in cooperatives increased to 60 per cent with very little outright opposition. A compilation of articles on agricultural cooperation that reflected this enthusiasm was presented to the Seventh Central Committee of the CCP which met in Beijing from 4 to 11 October 1955. A collection of 176 of these articles was then edited into a three-volume book which was published in January 1956, adorned with a glowing preface by Mao Zedong and circulated widely.[16] The adoption of the 'high tide' was an abandonment of the gradual approach to the collectivsation of Chinese agriculture and an indication of the shape of things to come.

An even greater degree of collectivisation was planned and a new level of organisation came into force between the spring of 1956 and August 1958 with the creation of the Higher Agricultural Producers' Cooperatives, HPCs [*gaoji nongye shengchan hezuoshe*, often abbreviated to *gaojishe*]. The HPCs were intended to be 'fully socialist' in that all the land they farmed would be collectively owned and the rights of individual families to ownership were thereby rescinded. The income of the farming families would now depend entirely on the work points that they earned through their labour in the cooperative. The HPCs were also much larger than the APCs and may have contained between 100 and 300 families. They were subdivided into production brigades [*shengchan dadui*] of 30–40 families, corresponding approximately to the old APCs, and production teams [*shengchan dui*] which were effectively the same as the old Mutual Aid Teams.

But what precisely did this collectivisation mean for the families involved? In most cases there was probably very little physical movement if any: they lived where they had always lived and they farmed the same fields. The changes were essentially in the management of agriculture and in the impact that this had on the local government in the rural areas. The main differences were organisational changes to ensure that the control of agriculture was firmly in the hands of local supporters of the CCP. With the move to larger collective units, decision making moved up to a higher administrative level, out of the hands of the farming families, so that planning could be carried out over a wider area. The names attached to the sub-divisions of the cooperatives – brigades and divisions – are interesting as an indication of the changes in the style of management. They are essentially military terms and would have been familiar to many peasants who had served in the PLA or even the old GMD army. They certainly reflected the type of organisation with which the PLA work teams that had spearheaded land reform would have been comfortable. The rhetoric that frequently accompanied the push towards collectivisation was also militaristic. Super-ficially this could be seen as the militarisation of the Chinese countryside, but it would probably be more accurate to consider it as a military-style movement towards the centralisation of decision making and control by the Communist Party and its local government. After problems had been en-countered in the management of cooperatives, there was a move to decen-tralise and to return a degree of control to the lower levels of management. The tension between centralisation and decentralisation remained a con-stant feature of cooperatives and of the even larger People's Communes that were to follow in 1958.

Marriage Reform

Reforming the traditional system of marriage was one of the highest social priorities of the CCP. Arranged and forced marriages, which were the norm in the rural areas, were regarded as serious problems for a modernising country and the CCP wished to attract the support of women. Once again, there was the powerful model of the USSR where the emancipation of women had played a key role in the initial successes of the Russian revolu-tion, but there was also an influential group of women revolutionaries with-in the CCP who drove forward these policies.

The Central People's Government adopted the Marriage Law of the People's Republic of China on 13 April 1950 and it was formally put into effect on 1 May. The general principles set out in the beginning of the document proclaimed the abolition of 'feudal' marriage which had 'held sway for centuries, based on arbitrary and compulsory arrangements' and declared that a new form of marriage had now taken effect, based on the free choice of partners, monogamy, equal rights for men and women and 'the protection of the lawful interests of women and children'. Bigamy, the taking of concubines and the betrothal of very young children were all specifically outlawed. It became illegal to prevent widows from remarrying if they wished to do so and the demanding of dowries and bride prices was also prohibited. The details of the law covered the nature of the marriage contract, the rights and duties of husbands and wives, the relationship be-tween parents and children and divorce.[17]

Simply publishing a law does not solve a problem and this legislation was no exception. Nevertheless, the Marriage Law did give cadres the authority that they needed to act on some of the worst cases of abuse that were uncovered. The trend towards freely contracted marriages in the decades that followed the enactment of the Marriage Law was, not surprisingly, far stronger in the towns and cities than in the rural areas. Arranged marriages persisted (and continue to do so into the twenty-first century) but in many of these cases the element of coercion has at least been replaced by negotiation and family pressure. The implications of the new law posed a serious challenge to the authority of the immediate and extended family: this was the intention of the CCP.[18]

Intellectuals: Feng Xuefeng and Hu Feng

During the 1950s and 1960s, the CCP struggled to build a working relationship with the Chinese intelligentsia, many of whom had been positive if not entirely enthusiastic about the Party's role in the resistance to the Japanese and the construction of a New China. Within the CCP, which had spent decades in the countryside and was more used to dealing with peasant farmers and waging war against the Guomindang than with the educated urban professional and business classes, there was considerable suspicion and distrust of 'intellectuals'. No one was more suspicious or distrusting than the former student and assistant librarian, Mao Zedong. The intelligentsia themselves were attempting to establish a role for themselves, often in the tradition of the loyal but critical court intellectuals of the imperial period. Nevertheless it is surprising how much of the political discourse of the period was really, or apparently, related to the role of the intelligentsia. The term for intelligentsia or intellectuals in China, *zhishi fenzi* (literally the 'knowledgeable elements') covers a somewhat wider range than its counterpart in most European languages; it is frequently used to refer to teachers and at times to anyone with even a secondary-level education, although this usage may be accounted for partly by political expediency and the sycophancy of the Communist Party leadership towards workers, peasants and soldiers in the more radical periods.

The first sign that a confrontation between the Party and the intelligentsia was inevitable came as early as 1950 during the tense period of the Korean War when university lecturers, writers, artists and other professional and cultural workers were required to undergo a period of 'thought reform': this applied particularly to anyone who had studied in Europe or the US. There was also a drive to rid libraries and bookshops of any literature that was deemed to be counter-revolutionary and the main targets of this campaign were the translations of works by foreign writers, novels and certain categories of other books from the classical Chinese tradition. The energy and resources that were required to carry out the Three-Anti and Five-Anti Campaigns and the social transformation of the commercial and industrial sector provided a brief respite for the intellectuals and the number of 'struggle and criticism' meetings in universities and other cultural institutions diminished, but only temporarily.

It was in the autumn and winter of 1954, after the leadership had resolved the Gao Gang and Rao Shushi issue, that the Party turned again to the cultural and artistic world and in particular to the cases of Feng Xuefeng and Hu Feng. Feng Xuefeng was the managing editor of the leading literary publication *Literature and Art* [*Wenyi bao*] and was one of the first targets of a campaign against 'bourgeois idealism' which the Party's cultural police believed they had detected in his journal. The campaign was designed to expose and root out those intellectuals who clung stubbornly to liberal ideas of an independent role for art and literature in society as opposed to the CCP's understanding that the only function of art was to serve the revolution, a concept which had been developed in Yan'an in the 1940s under the close supervision of Mao Zedong. The principal cultural target as far as the CCP were concerned was Hu Shi, one of China's leading writers in the 1930s and 1940s and a committed anti-Communist, so anyone who could be associated with his cultural views was automatically classified as an enemy of the Party and of New China.

The new cultural inquisition launched attacks on the literary historian Yu Pingbo who had written extensively about the classic Qing dynasty novel of manners and society *Dream of the Red Chamber*. Yu was denounced for having adopted an uncritical, individualistic and romantic approach to the social mores depicted in the novel which were now judged to have been 'feudal'.[19] Feng Xuefeng and his editor Chen Qixia were then dismissed from their posts, having been accused of supporting Yu's analysis by allowing it to be published. At this point, Hu Feng, a writer who had supported the CCP almost since its foundation, turned against the Party's cultural policy. Hu could not be dismissed easily as a reactionary or a closet supporter of the Guomindang. He had joined the Communist Youth League as early as 1923 and had been a member of the League of Left Wing Writers and an admirer of the iconic left-wing writer and satirist Lu Xun. Unfortunately for him, he had also made an enemy of the doctrinaire Stalinist cultural bureaucrat and propaganda chief, Zhou Yang, who had been in charge of both education and the party line on literature in the CCP's Yan'an base. Zhou Yang took the opportunity of the new cultural inquisition to make an example of him.

Hu had complained that the CCP's policies were thrusting five daggers into the backs of writers and other intellectuals. These 'daggers' were the demands that intellectuals should study Marxism; live among the workers, peasants and soldiers; counter bourgeois ideology; conserve and support selective national traditions and serve politics enthusiastically. Hu Feng's robust counterattack enraged the conservative cultural authorities within the CCP establishment and after a campaign organised by the Chinese Writers' Union, the organisation to which he belonged, he was required to compose a formal self-criticism in May 1955. Even this proved not to be sufficient for his critics and he was denounced not only as a counter-revolutionary but as a leading member of a counter-revolutionary organisation. He was personally vilified by Mao Zedong who provided a preface and a note to a collection of documents denouncing him. Hu Feng was deprived of all of his posts on state-run cultural bodies and effectively lost his livelihood as a writer. During the Cultural Revolution, Red Guard newspapers reported that he had died in prison in 1958, after having suffered serious mental illness as a result of his treatment.[20] In fact he survived this ordeal even though the original sentence of 14 years imprisonment, which he served first in Beijing's Qincheng prison and subsequently in the city of Chengdu, was increased during the Cultural Revolution to life imprisonment without the possibility of parole. Hu was eventually released in 1980, and resumed his writing until his death in 1985. The attacks on Hu Feng were broadened out into a campaign against hidden counter-revolutionaries, the *Sufan* campaign, *sufan* here being an abbreviation for *Suqing ancang fangeming*, 'Clear out hidden counter-revolutionaries', the implication being that Hu Feng was merely one example of a kind. This was the shape of things to come for creative writers and artists. They were to continue to face bizarre attacks on their readings of obscure aspects of classical literature, mass campaigns, self-criticism, disgrace and imprisonment for at least the next 20 years.

1956 – Khrushchev's 'Secret Speech', Hungary and Poland

For many Westerners, the year 1956 was the year of the Suez crisis, the British and French intervention in partnership with Israel to prevent the nationalisation of the Suez Canal by the Egyptian President Nasser. China's concerns, however, were more with dramatic events in Eastern Europe and the Soviet Union, her allies in the Communist bloc and economic partners in Comecon, the trading community of the Communist world.

The first act of the drama was not made public immediately. During the Twentieth Congress of the Communist Party of the Soviet Union in late February, the first secretary of the Party, Nikita Khrushchev, made what is usually referred to as a 'secret speech', which would be either a contradiction in terms or a pointless exercise. It was, in fact, a speech to a closed session that was not announced in advance on the agenda, and it was made after journalists and foreign communists had been ordered to leave the meeting (although not all did leave and the news leaked out). The title of Khrushchev's speech was 'On the Personality Cult and Its Consequences' and in it he launched an unprecedented attack on the tyrannical rule of his predecessor, Stalin, who had died in 1953. The detailed denunciations of Stalin's crimes and personality shocked the delegates, or at least the public acknowledgement shocked them. Much of what Khrushchev said had been discussed in private and in whispered tones for many years.

When the existence of the speech was first made public within the USSR a few months after the Congress came to an end, it was at first reported in a bowdlerised form and only referred to serious mistakes that had been had made during the last few years of Stalin's life. However in the de-Stalinisation process that followed the speech, many thousands of political prisoners were released, and Khrushchev announced his intention of following a policy of 'peaceful coexistence' with the West. The revelations of the speech cast doubt not only on the policies and the character of Stalin but also on the viability of the Soviet model of a Communist state.

In Beijing, it set alarm bells ringing. Mao Zedong had consciously fashioned his political style on Stalin and the attack on the cult of Stalin's personality that had developed in the USSR looked uncomfortably close to an attack on the cult of Mao that was already beginning to develop in China. Mao had been thinking seriously about an alternative way forward to Communism that did not slavishly follow the Soviet model and after Khrushchev's revelations he began to consider how he could distance himself even further from the USSR. Beijing had habitually seen the countries of eastern Europe as a barometer for the kind of change that might happen in China. During 1956, the atmospheric pressure was high. Czech students demonstrated in favour of freedom of the press and the right to travel abroad. Demonstrations and strikes flared up in Poland with workers at the Stalin Locomotive Works in Poznan in the vanguard. They demanded better working conditions and wages and also called for freedom from control by Moscow, but their protests were suppressed by the police and the military, and many demonstrators were killed. Unrest continued into the autumn. In Hungary, dissident intellectuals and writers had formed themselves into a Petöfi Club which took its name from the romantic nationalist poet, Sandor Petöfi, who had been martyred at the age of 26 in Hungary's 1848 revolution. The club met in the summer of 1956 and formulated demands for an end to the rule of the Moscow-controlled Hungarian Workers' Party. In October, demonstrators in Budapest and other cities called for free elections and the immediate withdrawal of Soviet troops as well as the return to power of the pluralist and reform-minded prime minister, Imre Nagy, who had been dismissed in 1955 after pressure from Moscow. The Hungarian government called for Soviet troops to help them to put down the insurrection. Nagy went ahead and formed an independent government but on 4 November the Hungarian rising was crushed by tanks and troops from the Soviet Union.

For the Chinese Communist Party, the risings of 1956 in Poland and Hungary were seen as an advance warning of what could go wrong for them. Although both revolts were characterised by the Communist parties as the results of conspiracies by reactionaries and fascists, it was patently obvious that the vast majority of the demonstrators and strikers were ordinary workers whose main ideological motivations were an anti-Russian nationalism and in some cases their religion: the role of Roman Catholicism in Poland was particularly significant. In both countries, but above all in Hungary, a group of dissident intellectuals had played a key role in focusing the demands of the demonstrators. If China were to avoid a similar confrontation there would have to be policy changes to try to keep the intellectuals on the side of the CCP.

Hundred Flowers and Anti-Rightist Campaign

After the attacks on Feng Xuefeng and Hu Feng, many educated and professional Chinese were angry, frustrated and frightened. It became clear to some senior members of the Party leadership, notably Zhou Enlai, that something had to be done urgently to mollify them if the state and the Party were to retain their loyalty while allowing them to maintain their initiative and independence. The CCP's Cultural Committee met between 14 and 20 January 1956 to discuss the question of what should be done about the educated classes. Zhou Enlai, in a 'Report on the Question of Intellectuals', argued that the majority of educated and professional men and women were loyal to the working class (for which one should read the CCP) and the new order. The meeting was asked to endorse the development of 'science and technology in socialist construction' and by implication the training and education of scientists and engineers. A new approach and new policies were needed. This was not intended as a liberalisation but it was supposed to be a relaxation of the ideological pressures on the intelligentsia.

The new policies for dealing with intellectuals were framed around a slogan that was first suggested by Lu Dingyi, the director of the Propaganda Department of the CCP's Central Committee, at a meeting of members of the Chinese Academy of Sciences and the All-China Federation of Literary and Art Circles on 26 May 1956. This was the celebrated call to 'let a hundred flowers bloom and a hundred schools of thought contend' [*baihua qifang, baijia zhengming*], a phrase that had echoes of the glorious days of ancient Chinese philosophy at the end of the Zhou dynasty (c.1045–221 BC) when ideas and religious and philosophical schools proliferated as thinkers searched for a new political order. The slogan was vague enough to allow for a range of interpretations but the message it was intended to convey was that there was room for a plurality of views. The fact that it was conveyed with a classical slogan was intended to reassure traditional scholars and the older professionals and to bolster the idea that this was a specifically Chinese way of resolving the problems that had arisen and not a foreign, Russian, approach. The implication was that there would now be greater intellectual freedom and also that it would be possible for the educated classes to criticise the bureaucracy. It was hinted that this criticism would assist government by ironing out problems and reducing inefficiency – once again the loyal intelligentsia could be enlisted in the service of the Chinese state.

Such was the concern and apprehension of the educated Chinese public that it was only when this slogan was endorsed personally by Mao Zedong that the campaign could get underway. Mao's support for the policy of letting a hundred flowers bloom in the fields of art, literature and academic research was aired publicly in a speech that he made to a Supreme State Conference on 2 May 1956 and the Hundred Flowers Movement is conventionally dated from this speech. After the object lesson of the way Hu Feng had been treated, it was hardly surprising that the intelligentsia were slow to respond to the request for honest criticism. On 27 February 1957, Mao spoke again on this subject in an address to 1,800 delegates attending the Supreme State Conference and his speech was later published as 'On the Correct Handling of Contradictions among the People'.[21] He insisted that what he referred to as 'non-antagonistic contradictions' should be aired publicly so that they could be resolved. 'Antagonistic' contradictions or conflicts were deemed to be those between 'ourselves' and 'the enemy' and could not be resolved easily, while 'non-antagonistic' contradictions were those which could be found among 'the people' and could be resolved. The awkward, obfuscatory phrasing and the oblique quasi-philosophical style of the speech does not make it easy to read (either in Chinese or in the English translation) but the implications are not as complex as they appear. Essentially Mao was allowing the authorities to define certain conflicts as 'non-antagonistic', in which case the parties to the conflicts would not face the risk of being demonised as 'enemies of the people' but could put forward their views freely and without fear. Following Mao's speech, a series of articles began to appear in the press promoting the idea of the Hundred Flowers and soliciting criticisms in the spirit of 'non-antagonistic contradictions'.

As Mao acknowledged directly in his 'Contradictions' speech in May 1957, there had been a tense atmosphere throughout China in the previous year. In addition to the trouble over the intellectuals, there had been a series of strikes by industrial workers in the cities, peasant demonstrations and (particularly relevant to the issue of intellectuals) student boycotts and demonstrations in at least 29 different colleges and universities.[22] It was not until the spring of 1957 that articles finally began to appear in the press criticising bureaucracy, maladministration and corruption. Articles critical of government policies appeared in the leading literary journal *People's Literature* [*Renmin wenxue*] and in *Guangming ribao*, the daily newspaper that fulfilled in China a similar role to that of *Izvestia* in the Soviet Union and had a wide readership among teachers, writers and the scientific and technical community. Once the criticism had begun, the movement acquired a momentum of its own. Student protest intensified, wall newspapers that were highly unsympathetic to the CCP were posted on the campus of the prestigious Beijing University and unofficial journals began to appear. In addition to general complaints, students also objected to the second-rate jobs to which they were being allocated without any choice after graduation. Historians and social scientists openly questioned the necessity for studying Mao Zedong's works which had been made a compulsory part of the curriculum of universities and colleges. Members of the designated democratic parties, the small group of eight parties that were allowed to function alongside the CCP although they had no power and little authority, demanded more consultation and participation. Journalists complained of the regime of censorship and control under which they were obliged to work. Many individual cases of corruption, nepotism and maladministration were also raised. Taken together they amounted to a general atmosphere of dissent and discontent.[23]

The degree of criticism stunned the authorities and Mao was taken aback by the acrimony of the attacks and, by all accounts, personally affronted. The leadership had allowed for and expected technical evaluations of the impact of their policies, conceivably negative ones, but within the framework that the Party had established. What they experienced was root and branch criticism of the entire structure of the PRC, particularly the role of the CCP, and stinging attacks on the lifestyle and attitudes of senior cadres, sometimes by name. The reaction of Mao and the Party was draconian and what had been a debate about the future role of the intelligentsia in a Communist society rapidly turned into a witch hunt. The ferocious backlash against those who had dared to criticise the Party was dignified by the name Anti-Rightist Campaign [*fan youpai yundong*]. This new campaign, which was essentially just another old-style mass campaign, followed the publication of a revised version of Mao's 'Contradictions' speech in June

1957. The tone of the new text was defiant and imposed firm guidelines on the type of dissent that would be tolerated. Those who had overstepped the mark were attacked as 'rightists' (*youpai*). The Central Committee issued a directive on 'mustering forces to repulse the Rightists' attacks' on 8 June and *People's Daily* published an editorial on the same day calling for a mass national campaign against 'rightists'. Those identified as 'rightists' were subjected to public vilification in meetings at their own work units [*danwei*], whether they were schools, colleges, newspaper offices or publishing houses, as well as in the national press and they were obliged to undergo a process of 'thought reform' [*sixiang gaizao*] or 'reform through labour' [*laogai*] which usually meant that they were sent to farms far away from the cities or to factories where contact with peasants and workers was intended to cure them of their bourgeois and elitist attitudes. It has been estimated that between 400,000 and 700,000 educated and professional men and women lost their jobs and were sent down to the countryside or to industrial plants in this campaign. Not only did this destroy careers, it created havoc for families: many of those who were rusticated suffered severe health problems and not a few died during the process. The mastermind behind this illiberal and repressive campaign was none other than Deng Xiaoping, secretary-general of the CCP, who ensured that it was carried out throughout the length and breadth of China.

The repression of the Anti-Rightist Campaign was not restricted to prominent intellectuals. It gave the CCP the opportunity to control, punish and silence all forms of opposition. Three student leaders at colleges in Wuhan were executed in August 1957 after a perfunctory trial and across the country as many as 1,000 people may have been sentenced to death in this period. Thousands of people from all walks of life were rounded up as criminals or vagrants and sentenced to imprisonment or reform through labour and the boundaries between dissent and criminality were deliberately blurred by the authorities. Members of the democratic parties, the non-Communist parties that had been allowed to operate openly in keeping with the spirit of the United Front were also targeted. The democratic parties had provided much of the trenchant criticism of CCP practices that had been published during the Hundred Flowers period and it was now time for them to be brought under control. Those members of the democratic parties who were recognized as most sympathetic to the CCP, or who even had dual membership, were given the task of identifying and denouncing 'rightists' in their ranks and those branded as 'rightists' in this way were handed over to the Public Security Bureau during August and September 1957. As many as 12,000 members of the democratic parties were dismissed from their jobs as 'rightist' and sent for labour re-education. Any vestige of influence that these parties had previously exercised was destroyed in this campaign. They were unable to attract new members and they became completely irrelevant to the political process in China.[24]

13

GREAT LEAP FORWARD
(1958–1965)

The radical policy initiative and mass mobilisation of 1958 that is popularly known as the Great Leap Forward marked a major shift in the CCP's approach to governing China. It also changed China's relations with the USSR and the rest of the Communist bloc as China veered away from the rather staid and plodding bureaucratic path set by Moscow and searched for its own radical style of Communism. To be strictly accurate, the Great Leap Forward was only one part of the new CCP policy which was known at the time by the general term of the Three Red Banners [*sanmian hongqi*]. The Three Red Banners were the General Line for Building Socialism [*shehuizhuyi jianshe zong luxian*] under which industry and agriculture were to develop concurrently, relying on traditional and modern technologies; the Great Leap Forward [*Dayuejin*] itself, which represented the labour mobilisation necessary for this development and the creation of the People's Communes [*Renmin gongshe*] which were initially presented as a model for the collectivisation of the whole of Chinese society.

These policies emerged out of bitter factional disputes within the CCP. Intent on pushing forward his radical agenda in the face of the strong opposition of some of the most senior figures in the Party's central organisations, Mao had sought support from powerful regional Party leaders and used a working meeting of provincial party secretaries, convened by the Central Committee and held in the Sichuan provincial capital of Chengdu to steamroller the opposition. He persuaded some of the key provincial leaders to demonstrate their support for him by their actions and even before the conference, Agricultural Producer's Cooperatives had been merged into larger bodies in Henan and the backyard furnaces for producing steel, later to become notorious as a symbol of the folly of the entire Great Leap Forward, first saw the light of day in the small towns and villages around Shanghai.[1]

Eighth Party Congress

The Second Plenary session of the Eight Party Congress that launched the new political direction was held in Beijing from 5 to 23 May 1958. It formally approved the introduction of Mao's General Line and the radical new policy for dragging China out of its economic and cultural backwardness. The meeting called on the people of China to catch up with, or even overtake, the economic achievements of Britain within 15 years. It also accepted Mao's theories about the persistence of class conflict in socialist society and his contention that the main conflict in Chinese society at that time was still between the bourgeoisie and the proletariat and therefore between the 'socialist road' and the 'capitalist road'. The Great Leap Forward policies were designed to ensure that it adhered firmly to the 'socialist road'.

From this meeting onwards, a Great Leap Forward fever swept the land. Lin Biao was brought into the Central Committee as an additional vice-chairman and he became a member of the Standing Committee of the Politburo. The Central Committee decided that it should publish its own theoretical journal *Hongqi*, always known in English as *Red Flag* (although, in the context of the Three Red Banners movement, *Red Banner* might have been more appropriate). The first issue of *Red Flag* was published on 1 June 1958, and it included an article by Mao Zedong entitled 'Introducing a Cooperative' in which he argued that China's industry and agriculture could catch up with, and indeed overtake, that of the capitalist West much more quickly than had been predicted. He went on to say that one of the most remarkable characteristics of the 600 million people of China was that they were 'poor and blank' (*yiqiong er bai*). Although that might appear to be a bad thing on one level, on another level, he argued, it was a good thing. 'Poverty produces thought of change, the desire to act and the desire for revolution' [*Qiong ze si bian, yao gan, yao geming*]. He declared that the beauty of a blank sheet of paper was that on it could be created the freshest and most beautiful written characters or paintings.[2] This assessment by Mao seems quite extraordinary in its lack of understanding of the power of traditional rural cultures of China from which the CCP had drawn almost its entire support during the 1930s and 1940s and his dismissive attitude towards the peasantry.

One of Mao's most implacable opponents by this time was the minister of defence and Marshal of the People's Liberation Army, Peng Dehuai, whose history as a revolutionary of long standing and as a successful military leader during the civil war period carried a great deal of weight. Peng accused Mao of spouting empty rhetoric and putting forward theories of development that bore no relation to reality. The roles played by Liu Shaoqi and Deng Xiaoping are less clear. Both were later accused by Mao's supporters of having sided with Peng, but by the time of the conference, Liu had apparently been won over and the Work Report that he presented to the conference explicitly supported Mao's radical central concept of the necessity for an uninterrupted revolution [*buduan geming*] even under a socialist or communist government. He was in turn backed by the power brokers of the Party machine and by a sufficient number of other senior figures for Mao to win the day.[3]

Great Leap Forward

In the late 1950s and early 1960s, the Great Leap Forward dominated the press and newsreel film in China as well as the nascent television industry. There were constant images of the mass mobilisation of people from all walks of life, leaving their routine jobs and delighting in voluntary labour in the service of the state to complete some essential public works project. The drab and uniform clothing that men and women wore at the time, approximating to military battledress in blue or sometimes green or grey denim, gave rise to the notion that China was a nation of an 'army of blue ants' on the move. The images of labour mobilisation were accompanied by dramatic and naive political slogans and, with increasing frequency, by portraits of Mao Zedong, an illustration of the growing 'cult of the personality' that Mao and his supporters had borrowed from Stalin.

On 22 June, the Report on the Steel Output Plan was distributed. It included an unprecedented projected increase in steel production for 1959 to more than 30 million tons and a target of 50–90 million tons by 1962. These targets were completely unattainable but, in the spirit of *duo, kuai, hao, sheng*, this report established a pattern in which region after region and sector after sector competed to outbid each other in setting the highest targets. This approach was ratified by the Politburo which met in enlarged session at the Party's seaside conference venue in Beidaihe on the coast of Bohai Bay from 17 to 30 August. The main item on the agenda was a discussion of the annual economic plan for 1959 which should have formed part of the Second Five-Year Plan: by this time, orthodox Communist planning had been discarded completely and had given way to the creation of wildly overoptimistic targets for industrial and agricultural production. The meeting also adopted a Resolution on the Establishment of People's Communes in the Rural Areas, and the impression was given to the people of China that the achievement of full Communism was but a step away and that commodity production and the operation of a market would be outlawed. The rhetoric of rapid economic development was accompanied by an upsurge of patriotic or nationalist sentiment which reached its peak on 23 August while the Politburo was still in session. Artillery units of the People's Liberation Army on the coast of Fujian shelled the outlying island of Mazu (Matsu), which, in spite of its closeness to the mainland, was and is still occupied by Guomindang troops together with the neighbouring island of Jinmen (Quemoy). Jinmen and Mazu remain under the control of Taiwan to this day.

People's Communes

Inspection tours in outlying regions of China, after the fashion of some of the Qing emperors, were an important part of Mao's style of leadership. They enabled him to claim that he was acting on the basis of first-hand knowledge of local conditions and also gave him the opportunity to broaden his support by winning round local Party leaders to his own radical policies. At the beginning of August 1958, Mao was undertaking one of these tours in Hebei, Henan and Shandong, three provinces in north central China. While in rural Shandong he discussed the creation of agricultural cooperatives with local party leaders and uttered his celebrated quotation, 'People's Communes are good. Their advantage is that they can combine industry, agriculture, commerce, education and military affairs, making it easier to exercise leadership'. This was the cue for an enormous upsurge in the merger of cooperatives with local township administrations to create People's Communes. The term People's Commune [*Renmin gongshe*] may not have been Mao's creation. It had first appeared in *Red Flag* on 1 July 1958 in an article written by his political secretary and adviser, Chen Boda, about the merging of cooperatives that was already being undertaken by some counties in Henan. When Mao spoke approvingly of the Commune idea, he was telling the Shandong leadership that they should adopt the model that was being tried just over the provincial border in Henan.[4] Most communes were relatively small and rural and were often identical geographically to the previous township [*xiang*] administrations, but there were also larger communes which were closer in size to a whole county. Urban communes were also created, mostly based on either a large factory or a residential district, but they never achieved the political support or the status which rural communes enjoyed and they died out very quickly.[5] The rural People's Communes have been in turn mythologised and reviled. For the majority of China's farming families over a period of 20 years, they were the only way of life that they knew. Two examples of how communes were created and how they operated will have to represent thousands across China, all with their own local variations and idiosyncrasies.

A People's Commune 1: Qiliying

Qiliying (Seven League Camp) People's Commune in Xinxiang county, Henan province was the experiment that had impressed Mao Zedong:

On 6 August, 1958, a light blue sedan drew up before the office building of the Qiliying People's Commune in Henan Province. A strongly-built senior comrade alighted, a warm smile on his face. 'Look, it's Chairman Mao!' some onlookers shouted in glad surprise… Chairman Mao looked over the commune's flour mill, ball-bearing workshop and experimental cotton plot. Everywhere he went he chatted warmly with the men and women members. He was photographed in a white open-necked shirt and a broad brimmed peasant hat standing in a field full of shoulder high maize. That same day Chairman Mao left Qiliying to continue his rural inspection tour. On 9 August, he came to Shandong Province. When told by comrades of the Shandong Provincial Committee of the Chinese Communist Party that some townships there were going to organise big farm collectives, Chairman Mao said, 'It is good to set up people's communes'.[6]

The rest is history.

In the spring of 1958, the township government of Qiliying claimed that it was under pressure from its advanced agricultural cooperatives that wanted to merge so that they would have the capital and labour necessary to carry out large-scale projects including the construction of vital roads, the installation of electricity power lines and the mechanisation of agriculture. Mergers were approved and these larger units also took responsibility for marketing, the provision of education and the local militia. Sensing that they were now operating a different kind of local organisation they looked for a new name and the name that they chose was inspired by the Paris Commune of 1871.[7] The Paris Commune was the radical, elected organisation set up in Paris largely by the working people who had been involved in the citizen's militia when France was defeated in the Franco-Prussian War and it was celebrated by Karl Marx in *The Civil War in France*.[8] The Chinese term used to translate 'commune' [*gongshe*] means roughly 'public society', but the *gong* also has connotations of fairness and equality and *she* is an old term for a village or hamlet and also the altar to the local gods of the earth around which such a village would have been organised.

The population of Qiliying Commune in 1958 was 53,200 and it had at its disposal 93,000 *mu* (1,394,303 hectares) of agricultural land and had been formed by the merger of 56 advanced cooperatives. It was subdivided into 38 production brigades [*shengchan dadui*] each of which was effectively one existing village. Each brigade was further subdivided into production teams [*shengchan dui*] and Qiliying had a total of 298 of these teams. There were therefore three levels of management and also three levels of ownership: as the commune struggled to establish itself, the responsibilities of the different levels would change. Teams were usually too small to own much equipment: the larger brigades owned several tractors and the commune itself ran a tractor station which provided tractors for those brigades that could not afford their own and maintenance work was carried out centrally. The larger brigades and the commune itself also had the resources to run factories and other enterprises and these included a flour mill, brick and tile works, a repair shop for agricultural tools and a pig-breeding farm.

The commune was, however, more than just a collective farm. It replaced the existing local government at the township level and took responsibility for finance, commerce, education, public health, policing and the local militia. The township governments ceased to function and the new local authority was the Qiliying People's Commune Revolutionary Committee which reported to the Revolutionary Committee of Xinxiang County.[9]

How much real change had taken place? To some extent the move to the commune system was an exercise in rebranding. The villages remained where they had always been, the peasants spent a lot of their time working with the same family and village groups that they had always worked with, but there was now an extra sense of communal identity and the commune was able to mobilise its workforce for large-scale projects in a way that had not been possible before. The merging of the management of agriculture with local government was supposed to give greater priority to the needs of farming and it ensured that supporters of Mao's radical policies, mostly drawn from officials of poorer backgrounds who had come to prominence in the land reform movement, were moved into key positions in local government. The terminology of the communes is also important. The lower level bodies were organised as brigade [*dadui*] and team [*dui*] and, as has already been observed, these are terms which have a military connotation and which chimed in well with the patriotic ethos of the times and the experience of those running China at local level, most of whom had emerged from the People's Liberation Army during the civil war and the Korean War.

A Peoples' Commune 2: Yangyi

The commune of Yangyi is one of the most thoroughly documented in English as it included the village of Ten Mile Inn. The process of land reform in Ten Mile Inn was described in detail by Isabel and David Crook and they returned to the village in 1959 and 1960 to follow its progress into the commune. Yangyi is some 275 miles to the south west of Beijing in the 'dry and rugged' Taihang Mountains which dominate the southwestern corner of Hebei province.

The impetus for merging existing cooperatives in Yangyi came from a need to develop water conservancy and irrigation projects but it did not meet with the wholehearted support of local farmers. Some activists had seen films about collective farms in the Soviet Union at mobile cinemas that had visited the village and were enthusiastic about trying the same kind of experiment by merging their own cooperatives. Others had heard reports about collectives elsewhere in China when they had travelled as delegates to conferences in the provincial capital Shijiazhuang or in Beijing.

The Central Committee resolution of 29 August spurred on the activists, meetings were held in the villages and 'the ferment of discussion even bubbled over into the day's work in the fields'. A group of 430 households in Ten Mile Inn supported the application for the establishment of a commune and there was similar support in other villages. Yangyi People's Commune was formally constituted in September 1958 with the merger of 33 existing cooperatives. This brought together a grand total of 10,000 households with 37,000 people who had access to 16,000 acres of farming land. A new Commune Party Committee was established to take overall control of the merger and the 'Yangyi Commune Council reorganised existing township committees into Commune Departments of Industry and Trade, Culture and Education, Security and Defence. Meanwhile the constituent co-operatives went on farming as before – but under the new name of "production brigades"'. There was a transfer of power and resources from the villages to the new Commune Council which functioned as the local government.[10]

Backlash against the Great Leap Forward

Mao was never able to have his own way entirely and as early as November 1958, the more rational members of the CCP leadership were beginning to find ways of voicing their serious reservations about the direction that China was taking. At a working conference of senior party figures convened at the chairman's request on 2 November in Zhengzhou, the great railway hub and capital of Henan province that is just to the south of Mao's favoured commune at Qiliying, Mao began to revise his public pronouncements on what he now described as erroneous ideas about the possibility of abolishing the market economy in the countryside. Blaming these ideas on his amanuensis Chen Boda, he used this First Zhengzhou Meeting to affirm the need to develop a commodity economy in the rural areas and reassured the peasants that the new policies had not been put in place simply to expropriate their property and their produce.

The Sixth Plenary Session of the Eighth Central Committee of the CCP met in Wuchang between 28 November and 10 December 1958. It adopted a policy document, entitled Resolution on Some Problems Concerning the People's Communes, which built on Mao's partial repudiation of the excesses of the commune movement at the First Zhengzhou Meeting and reaffirmed the need to retain and develop a commodity economy in the countryside. The meeting also began work on reducing the unrealistic targets for industrial production that had been set at the Beidaihe meeting the previous August. Mao proposed that he should not serve a further term as chairman of the People's Republic of China, the post of head of state and the equivalent of president. This proposal was accepted but Mao remained chairman of the Chinese Communist Party although his power and authority were seriously diminished by the negative reaction to the policies of the Great Leap Forward.

When the Politburo met in Zhengzhou between 27 February and 5 March 1959 (the Second Zhengzhou Meeting) the only item on the agenda was the issue of People's Communes and Mao continued to try to dissociate himself from the excesses. In early April 1959, the Central Committee met again in full session, the Seventh Plenary Session, and in its document, Eighteen Questions Concerning the Peoples' Communes, it supported a process which would lead to the decentralisation of power in the Communes and the restoration of ownership and management to the production teams, in other words to the smaller local units rather than the central Commune leadership. When China's quasi-parliamentary body, the National People's Congress met in Beijing from 18 to 28 April 1959, Mao was replaced as chairman of the People's Republic of China by Liu Shaoqi and the central leadership of the CCP was beginning to appear polarised and unstable.[11]

The background to this division of opinion was a growing concern that the communes had been established without proper preparation. The new administrative bodies often did not have adequate office accommodation, and services such as canteens, care homes for the elderly and nursery schools were promised before suitable premises could be found. Some nurseries were trying to operate in the cold winter of 1958 without heating. There were insufficient numbers of trained personnel and this was a particular problem in the case of commune accountants. The new communes in many cases attempted to operate independently of the other state organisations, the supply of grain was interrupted and there was a lack of adequate winter clothing. It became clear that an economic crisis was looming in China's countryside. There was also a growing resistance by peasants, who by convention and tradition are independent, if not bloody-minded, to the military-style regime which involved marching to the fields and eating only in communal dining halls. This resistance spread throughout the southern and western provinces in November and December 1958 and was so serious in some areas that it amounted to a local insurrection: the PLA was called in to suppress the disorder.[12]

Insurgency in Tibet

In March 1959 the attention of the leadership in Beijing was diverted from its factional disputes and the debates over the Great Leap and the Communes by grim news from China's far western frontiers. An armed revolt had broken out in Tibet directed against the administration that the CCP had established in Lhasa in 1951. This was seen by Beijing as a serious assault on the territorial integrity of the People's Republic of China and it was decided that an immediate and determined response was required.

The status of Tibet has been a matter of international controversy since the mid-twentieth century. To many Tibetans, the position is simple: Tibet is and has always been an independent state that was occupied illegally by the Chinese in 1951. For the present government of the PRC, the position is equally simple: Tibet has always been and will be part of China. The legal justification for this claim is extremely dubious but that is the premise on which Beijing's actions in Tibet were based in 1959 and are still based. What is incontestable is that from the fall of the Qing dynasty in 1911 until the People's Liberation Army marched into Tibet in 1951, Tibet functioned *de facto* as a fully independent state, ruled by a combination of secular and Lamaist bureaucracies.[13] The situation is complicated further by the fact that the Tibetan Autonomous Region as it is constituted today is only the core region of what was the old Tibet before 1951: substantial portions of the former Tibetan lands have been transferred to the Chinese provinces of Gansu, Qinghai and Sichuan.

When the CCP was victorious in the civil war that ended in 1949, Tibet, like Xinjiang, became part of the PRC. The intention was that this would happen by means of a process that was known as 'peaceful liberation' [*heping jiefang*]. This took place in Xinjiang where there had been a long-standing Chinese official presence, but Mao and the CCP acknowledged that the position of Tibet was different because of its isolation and the absence of a significant Han Chinese community there. In December 1949, judging that Tibet could only be 'liberated' by military action, Beijing began to make preparations for an invasion of the eastern provinces of Tibet, particularly Chamdo, while opening negotiations with the existing Tibetan government. The Tibetans failed to send a delegation to Beijing and on 7 October 1950, the Eighteenth Army of the PLA crossed the frontier into Chamdo with the intention of rendering inoperative the Tibetan Army units based there and cutting off Lhasa. The poorly led and somewhat amateurish Tibetan forces were no match for their battle-hardened opposite numbers in the PLA and the entire Tibetan army was defeated within two weeks. The PLA could have moved directly to Lhasa as there were no significant military obstacles, but Mao's strategy was to hold Chamdo and to try for a negotiated settlement that would have the approval of the Dalai Lama and, it was therefore assumed, the majority of the population of Tibet.

The Tibetans launched an appeal to the United Nations asking that the independent status of their country be recognised but this was rejected after Britain and India vetoed any discussion. Britain believed that any demand for China's withdrawal from Tibet would be unenforceable and India was reluctant to compromise its developing diplomatic relations with China. Reluctantly, the Tibetan government decided to send a delegation to negotiate with its new masters in Beijing and the result was the Seventeen Point Agreement, signed in Beijing on 23 May 1951, which gave the Tibetans limited autonomy within the PRC in return for agreeing to assist the PLA in its occupation of Tibet and ceding to Beijing its right to conduct diplomatic relations with foreign countries. PLA troops moved to garrison Lhasa under the terms of this agreement on 16 October. The circumstances under which the agreement was concluded remain controversial as it was clearly signed under duress. The Dalai Lama did not take part in the negotiations. He had moved from the Potala Palace in Lhasa to the small town of Yadong, a Tibetan community close to the border with India and Sikkim in preparation for a swift withdrawal should the PLA march on Lhasa. He returned to Lhasa in August 1951 and, in a telegram to Mao Zedong on 24 October, he agreed to lend his support to the Seventeen-Point Agreement. The agreement preserved most of the traditional government and politico-religious structures of Tibet, including the unique role of the Dalai Lama, in exchange for the acknowledgement of Chinese suzerainty over the country. Beijing was eager to demonstrate that its policy was moderate and *laissez-faire* and therefore the traditional and monastic economy remained intact – there was no confiscation of land from the feudal landlords or the monasteries at this stage.

The agreement only applied to central Tibet (which later became the Tibetan Autonomous Region) that is the area around the capital Lhasa and the city of Shigatse and westwards into the high plains and the mountains. It did not apply to the Tibetan-speaking communities in Sichuan and Qinghai, and when the land reform and collectivisation policies were carried out in these areas it provoked great hostility among the Tibetan population (who were a minority in those regions) and there were large-scale migrations westwards towards central Tibet. In the mid-1950s, the radical collectivisation programmes reached central Tibet and resistance to Chinese rule, largely organised by refugees from Sichuan and Qinghai, was growing apace. Mao tried to reassure the Dalai Lama that Tibet would be protected from the radical reforms that were tearing apart the old rural society across China, but the resistance movement proved too powerful and the Dalai Lama found himself on the sidelines. The Tibetan revolt broke out on 10 March

1959 and the headquarters of the PLA and the Chinese government in Lhasa were surrounded by demonstrators. Forces loyal to the Tibetan government turned on the PLA garrison in the Tibetan capital on 19 March. The rising had little chance of succeeding and assistance from the CIA that had been promised did not materialise in time. Over the next four days, the PLA suppressed the revolt, both in Lhasa and elsewhere in Tibet. The Dalai Lama had once again left Lhasa two days previously and he crossed the border into India on 31 March, where he formally renounced the Seventeen-Point Agreement. The Tibetan government that had been in power since 1951 was dissolved on the instructions of Beijing and a preparatory committee was set up to establish a new Tibetan Autonomous Region government. The Chinese also decided that the Seventeen-Point Agreement no longer applied and moved against the theocratic and landed elites, confiscating the largest landholdings and closing down some monasteries. The Dalai Lama established a government in exile in the town of Dharamsala which sits on the slopes of the Himalayas in the state of Himachal Pradesh in northwestern India: the Panchen Lama, traditionally viewed as the link between China and the Tibetans, became the highest ranking spiritual leader within Tibet. The Panchen Lama was appointed chairman of the preparatory committee for the Tibetan Autonomous Region on 28 March 1959 on the specious grounds that the Dalai Lama was being held by rebels against his will. In 1965 Tibet became an Autonomous Region of the PRC.

Confrontation at Lushan

The mounting conflict within the CCP leadership became even more intense over the course of two meetings – of the Politburo and the Central Committee – that were held in the summer of 1959 at the hill-station on Mount Lushan, which is near the Poyang Lake in the northeastern part of Jiangxi province. The first of these meetings, the Lushan Conference, which was technically an enlarged meeting of the Political Bureau of the Chinese Communist Party, lasted from 2 July to 1 August.[14] By the end of the meeting, Mao Zedong had launched a ferocious attack against Peng Dehuai, China's defence minister and one of the ten Marshals of the People's Liberation Army, and had set in motion the procedures necessary to replace Peng with Marshal Lin Biao. The Chinese military subjugation of the pro-independence forces in Tibet was fresh in the minds of the participants in the conference as were the problems that had become apparent with the communes and the growing rumours of serious food shortages in some of the more remote rural areas which were becoming more and more difficult to ignore.

Peng Dehuai's sympathies and closest political relationships were with the older PLA marshals, with his officers and rank and file soldiers in the PLA and with the peasants, from whose ranks almost the entire soldiery was recruited. As a result of these connections, Peng was in constant contact with developments in the countryside through the military postal service and other formal and informal sources within the armed forces. He was a strong supporter of the professionalisation of the Chinese armed forces and disapproved of the increased emphasis on politicisation and on the popular militia which Mao favoured. Peng had also recently made an extended visit to the Warsaw Pact countries on an official military mission: he had left Beijing on 24 April 1959 and returned on 13 June. He is known to have met Khrushchev in Tirana, the capital of Albania, and to have had a long discussion with him which almost certainly included conversations about the communes, Sino-Soviet relations and the Chinese army. In June Khrushchev cancelled the Soviet nuclear aid agreement with China and publicly attacked the communes. Mao interpreted this as evidence of collusion between Khrushchev and Peng. It was certainly an early sign that Sino-Soviet relations were not as amicable as public pronouncements had consistently suggested.

There have been suggestions that Zhang Wentian, the deputy minister of foreign affairs and an old rival of Mao, worked closely with Peng at Lushan, and may have prompted him to launch his attack on the communes and the other policies of the Great Leap Forward. Zhang Wentian, who was hardly ever mentioned in China between 1959 and Mao's death was the general secretary of the CCP during the Long March but was forced out by Mao and had been marginalised since 1949.[15] Peng may also have been involved with Gao Gang and Rao Shushi before they were purged in 1954–5. Gao and Rao had mounted the only serious challenge to Mao's position in the early years of the People's Republic and Mao saw Peng Dehuai's Lushan intervention as a repeat of this and an attempt to put himself in a position to take over the leadership. Before the Lushan meetings, Liu Shaoqi had taken over as chairman of the PRC, the post which Mao had relinquished. He was looked on as Mao's likely successor and his picture was given equal status to Mao's in public. Liu's strong position in 1959 may also have been one of the factors that pushed Peng into making his challenge.

Peng Dehuai's attack on Mao and on the whole approach of the Great Leap Forward was a *tour de force*. It was in turns emotional, sarcastic and mordant. He attacked the fanaticism of the collectivisation frenzy and the unreality of Mao's ambitions, but in particular he condemned the sycophancy and craven performance of party leaders who had encouraged the exaggeration of both targets and achievements in industrial production. The majority of those present at the conference may have sympathised with Peng's strictures but his condemnation of the Great Leap was not just an argument about policy: it was a direct assault on Mao and the nature and quality of his leadership. This was more than Mao could bear and his counter-attack was furious, vicious and personal. He linked Peng with the 'revisionist' factions that he had defeated in the past and, in an extra-ordinary proclamation, he made it clear that if Peng's ideas were formally endorsed he, Mao Zedong, would be prepared to break up the CCP:

> If we have done ten things, nine of which have been bad, and are reported in the papers, we must perish. And if we deserve to perish then I shall go. I shall then go to the countryside to lead the peasants to overthrow the government. If you from the PLA do not follow me, I shall find myself a Red Army. But I believe that the PLA will follow me.[16]

No one was prepared to call Mao's bluff and the conference backed him. Peng Dehuai's political fate had been sealed.

The second of the two high level meetings, the Eighth Plenum of the Eighth Central Committee, which took place from 2 to 16 August, con-tinued the battle at Lushan. The attack on Peng at the Eighth Plenum began indirectly and it was Zhang Wentian who was criticised in the initial stages of the meeting. Peng said very little but was finally compelled to make a self-criticism in which he implicated Zhang Wentian and Huang Kecheng in a factional plot against Mao. When the documents of the plenum were published by the Xinhua news agency on 26 August, it became clear that the opponents of the Great Leap Forward had achieved some degree of success at the meeting as the economic targets for 1959 had been reduced significantly, but the price for this was a purge of the leadership and those who lost their posts were criticised for their 'right opportunist' ideas. There were two key resolutions at the close of the Eighth Plenum. The first was the condemnation of the 'anti-Party clique headed by Peng Dehuai' and the decision to remove him from his post as minister of defence and first vice-chairman of the powerful Central Military Commission, although he was allowed to retain his membership of the Central Committee and the Polit-buro. The second resolution was in support of the decentralisation of power in the People's Communes with a substantial degree of authority being de-volved to the production brigades. Peng was formally removed from his post as minister of defence at the September meeting and Zhang Wentian, Huang Kecheng and Zhou Xiaozhou were also purged as members of an oppos-itional military clique at an enlarged meeting of the Military Affairs Commit-tee which was convened in September. The conflict reverberated throughout the entire national organisation of the Chinese Communist Party as a drive against 'right-opportunist' supporters of Peng Dehuai was launched.[17]

Great Famine

Between 1959 and 1962 China suffered a devastating famine that cost the lives of 30 to 40 million people. It was one of the worst episodes of mass starvation that China has suffered in its recent history, not excluding the severe north China famines of the 1920s. China has always been subject to famine and other natural disasters: it is primarily an agricultural society and its climate periodically produces extremes of drought and flood. However the food shortages and deaths of 1959–62 followed immediately on the heels of the Great Leap Forward, so the question has to be asked: was the famine simply the result of the economic and social policies implemented by the CCP under Mao Zedong, or was it an unavoidable natural disaster similar to those of previous decades? The disputes in Lushan did not end Mao's dreams of a Great Leap Forward. A new political drive that was organised early in 1960 by his most committed followers included renewed support for communes and even for urban communes: there was also a campaign to send cadres down to the countryside for ideological education. It has been argued that it was this second 'leap' rather than the original 1958 policy that caused the disastrous failure in agricultural and industrial production and rural famine.

Information on the extent of the problems in China's countryside emerged slowly, even within the country. As late as the spring of 1959 there were glowing reports of a huge increase in agricultural production but already there were rumours of severe but localised natural disasters appearing in the local press.[18] In March there was news of serious flooding in Hunan and a significant percentage of the harvest in southwest China was lost when a severe drought developed. The year 1960 was the first of what became known as the 'three bitter years'. Hebei, Henan, Shandong and Shaanxi provinces were all badly affected by drought: in some areas there had been virtually no rain and therefore no harvest at all. The year 1961 brought only a slight improvement but food shortages were already at famine levels. Rationing was introduced but it provided less than the minimum requirements for survival. News began to seep out from the rural areas of a serious crisis: whole families were dying of hunger and desolate villages showed no sign of life. The press began to acknowledge that the problems in the countryside were the worst for almost a century but the word 'famine' was not used until it appeared in a report in the Guangdong provincial newspaper, *Southern Daily* [*Nanfang Ribao*], on 5 July 1963. China was obliged to import wheat from Canada and Australia and it became apparent that the human cost of the famine had reached levels that were almost incomprehensible. Analysts in the 1970s began to suggest that as many as 10 million people died either as a direct result of malnutrition or from the epidemic diseases that had accompanied the famine. It only gradually became clear that this was a considerable underestimate.[19]

The difference in the way that the 1958 Great Leap Forward and its consequences were treated by commentators during Mao Zedong's lifetime and by historians today highlights many of the problems that plague the student of contemporary Chinese history. As late as 1970, it was possible for commentators sympathetic to the revolution in China to write as follows:

> In agriculture, 1958 was certainly a good year, though not as good as had been thought. The three succeeding years were extremely bad. In 1959, almost half the cultivated area was affected by heavy floods or serious drought. In 1960, drought, typhoons, floods and pests struck 800 million *mou*, more than half of the cultivated area, and seriously affected another 30 to 360 million *mou*, some of which bore no crop at all. The Yellow River practically dried up for a month in Shandong, an almost unheard-of event. A serious food shortage developed, but famine was avoided by rationing and collective effort. The commune system, by its ability to mobilise large numbers of people, undoubtedly helped in avoiding famine in these difficult years.[20]

It was being argued within the Chinese leadership that serious problems, caused by unusually difficult weather conditions and also by the withdrawal of Soviet aid and technicians, had been alleviated by the new commune system that emerged during the Great Leap. Historians today, both Western and Chinese, now concede that the 1958 policies were a complete disaster and that there were at least 20 million (and some analysts go as far as 40 million) excess deaths attributable to starvation and diseases that can be linked to the famine.[21] Policy errors, including the insistence that peasants should leave large areas of land fallow because they would otherwise have insufficient storage facilities to cope with the expected surplus, and the transfer of labour from the land to impressive construction projects of dubious practical value, led to a serious shortfall in the supply of foodstuffs. High quotas of grain taxation bled the countryside of much needed food supplies as late as 1961, by which time the problems on the ground should have been obvious to all. Bad weather and the withdrawal of Soviet technicians were without doubt contributory factors but they alone could not account for more than 20 million excess deaths that were recorded between 1959 and 1961.

The scale of the disaster was such that the government had no option but to retreat from its programme of creating communes. In the teeth of a second Anti-Rightist Campaign during 1959–61, which targeted among others the respected economist Chen Yun, the Politburo at a meeting in 1960 and the Ninth Plenum of the Eighth Central Committee that met in Beijing from 14 to 18 January 1961 agreed to a radical decentralisation in the management and ownership of communes. Land, cattle, tools and seed were all put back under the control of the production team, the lowest level of the commune, which corresponded in most cases to the pre-commune villages. The production brigade would in future have authority over schools, nurseries and industry and the commune's powers would be restricted to public works and security matters.[22]

In the final analysis, who was to blame for the famine and the catastrophic loss of life? Jasper Becker's investigation of the Great Leap Forward, *Hungry Ghosts: China's Secret Famine* is a powerful account, which uses eyewitness reports from the Chinese countryside and some Chinese primary documents but it relies heavily on information from Western analysts. He comes down firmly in favour of blaming the CCP for the famine although he does give due consideration to the judgement of many contemporary Chinese thinkers that the weight of China's past and the traditional mindset of Chinese society, which is particularly strong in the rural areas, must take some of the responsibility. Dali Yang has argued that the famine was caused in part by the unforeseen consequences of well-intentioned policies. He even includes in this the intervention of Peng Dehuai at the Lushan Plenum, arguing that Peng's confrontation with Mao made it impossible for those who favoured retrenchment to have any influence as they would have appeared to be taking a stand against Mao. This is an uncomfortable thought for those who have taken the view that Peng's stand could have been the saving of the peasants. Dali Yang was brought up in rural Shandong where memories of the famine years were raw and where the legacy of the years of scarcity affected life in the countryside for decades afterwards: his approach reflects both an informed view from the grassroots and an academic analysis.[23]

Lin Biao, Liu Shaoqi and Deng Xiaoping

The political consensus of the Yan'an period leadership was by now disintegrating and the conflict at Lushan was a dress rehearsal for the final rift which would occur in the Cultural Revolution. There were two distinct political responses to the failure of the Great Leap Forward and these were the basis for the complete polarisation of the Chinese political elite.

The writings of Mao Zedong had been published widely throughout China and his speeches and essays had been collected in *Selected Works* of which the fourth volume, containing some of Mao's key texts from the period between the surrender of Japan and the foundation of the PRC, was published on 30 September 1960.[24] At an enlarged meeting of the Central Military Commission which met in Beijing in September 1960, Marshal Lin Biao, the new minister of defence who had replaced Peng Dehuai, called for the 'concentrated study of Mao's works' in the People's Liberation Army. Lin argued that political work of this nature would counter the low morale among peasant soldiers that had been become apparent since the famine. Because this concentrated study was intended primarily for recruits from the rural areas who were some of the least educated people in China, it inevitably involved a considerable simplification of Mao's ideas. From this process emerged *Quotations from Chairman Mao Zedong*, the legendary, 'little red book'. Many CCP members in the cities hoped that this over-simplification would never be useful outside the military but when the Central Committee of the CCP supported the drive to increase ideological work in the army it was agreed that the basic principles would also be helpful for Party organisations, for government departments and also for schools and some businesses. The stage was set for the widespread use of *Quotations* as a basic educational resource throughout Chinese society. This joint initiative of Mao Zedong and Lin Biao found its expression in the Socialist Education Movement and the promotion of the People's Liberation Army as the model to be emulated by all, especially the young.

Liu Shaoqi and Deng Xiaoping adopted a completely different approach. In 1961–2, they were responsible for drafting a series of weighty policy documents with the most uninspiring titles imaginable. These included, Sixty Articles on Peoples Communes, Seventy Articles on Industry, Fourteen Articles on Science, Thirty-five Articles on Handicraft Trades, Six articles on Finance, Eight Articles on Literature and Art, Sixty Articles on Higher Education and Forty Articles on Commercial Work. This administrative and highly bureaucratic approach, dull but highly practical, was in great contrast to the drama and the politicisation advocated by Lin Biao and Mao. Party leaders were in charge of the drafting, but non-party specialists were also consulted. The thrust of most of the documents went completely against the spirit of Great Leap Forward policies and emphasised quality, professionalism, modernity and large-scale developments. Experts and expertise were accentuated. Mao did not openly oppose these but was completely opposed to the direction that policy was taking.[25]

Socialist Education Movement

Although Chinese politics during 1962–5 appeared to be relatively stable in the hands of the compromise coalition that had emerged from the Lushan conflict, below the surface the polarisation was every bit as acute as it had been before Lushan. The radicals around Mao Zedong decided to launch another campaign, the Socialist Education Movement, to advance their agenda and to counter the bureaucratic style of Liu Shaoqi and Deng Xiaoping. As with many of China's political campaigns, the name is misleading and unhelpful: it had nothing to do with education in the conventional sense. The initial aim of the Socialist Education Movement was to restore the impetus of the drive for collectivisation in the rural areas and to reverse the decision to decentralise commune management that had followed the famines, but it rapidly became refocused on what was seen as a growing problem, grassroots corruption in the countryside.

At the 10th Plenum of the Central Committee of the Chinese Communist Party which took place in September 1962, there was a call for the party to focus on the shortcomings of cadres and the need for class struggle. Essentially this was a response to growing discontent in the countryside and a distinct lack of enthusiasm for the collectivisation programme. In addition, the old rural elite which had lost much of its power during the land reform movement was attempting to stage a comeback in some areas and became the core of conservative opposition to the collectivisation. In December 1962 the Four Cleanups [*Siqing*] campaign was launched on an experimental basis in Hebei and Hunan provinces, but it was soon extended throughout the whole of the country.

In February 1963 a Draft Resolution of the Central Committee, entitled 'Some Problems in Current Rural Work', made it clear that the Socialist Education Movement would focus on 'the administration of collective accounts, communal granaries, public property and work points' (the four issues that needed 'cleaning-up'). The campaign concentrated on reforming the leadership in the rural areas and using the administrative technique of *xiafang*, the sending down of experienced urban cadres to the countryside, to replace or reinforce existing senior cadres because of what was perceived as a problem with the quality of leadership at the lowest levels. As part of this reform, the role of poor and lower-middle peasants in the management of agriculture was to be enhanced and poor peasants' representative groups were established. Cadres were also encouraged to spend more time in manual labour so that they would identify more closely with the poorest section of the rural community. A follow-up work conference on 20 May 1963 established the guidelines for the campaign and authorised the dispatch of work teams into the countryside to monitor the movement. These work teams rapidly realised that they faced considerable resistance from the peasant population, far more than they had been led to believe. A Politburo resolution of September 1963 was approved in an attempt to moderate Mao's policies by arguing in favour of greater toleration for private plots and the preservation of a market economy in the rural collectives.[26]

People's Liberation Army as Model

The re-politicisation of the PLA had begun in 1960 after the appointment of Lin Biao as minister of defence: the decision to use *Quotations from Chairman Mao Zedong* as a basic text during military training was the first clear evidence of the new policy, which was accompanied by the increasing militarisation of Chinese society. During the early 1960s, the PLA and its values were increasingly taken as the model to which the whole of Chinese society should aspire. There were many campaigns within the PLA in which individuals or units competed to show that they embodied all the military and political virtues, but of all these it was the Lei Feng campaign that was the greatest success and the cult of Lei Feng took root among the civilian population as well as in the military. In March 1963, Mao put forward the slogan 'Learn from Comrade Lei Feng' [*Xiang Lei Feng tongzhi xuexi*]. Lei Feng was a soldier who had been killed at the age of 22 while on duty, some say when a lorry reversed into a telegraph pole which fell on him, hardly a glamorous demise. However, he was of unimpeachable character, reliable and unquestioningly loyal to the Party and happened to have been born and brought up in Changsha in Hunan, Mao's home area. He had received several commendations for being a model worker and after his death, his journals *Diary of Lei Feng* [*Lei Feng riji*] were published and revealed him to have lived his life by basing it on his studies of the works of Mao Zedong. It is widely assumed that Lei Feng's diaries were invented by propaganda units in the PLA and that, even if he had actually existed, his life had been rather different from the way it was portrayed in the media at the time. Nevertheless, there was something about the myth of Lei Feng, his peasant simplicity, devotion to duty and self-abnegation and his banal and far from heroic death that struck a chord with many young Chinese at the time and made him an effective, if unlikely, hero. He remained popular with younger members of the CCP long after the original campaign had come to an end. A collection of songs and dialogues about him in the form of a traditional *xiangsheng* or 'cross-talk' dialogue was published in 1978 and a successful film of his life was released as late as 1996. [27]

As the tempo of the Socialist Education Movement increased during 1964, the role of the PLA as a model became increasingly important. In July 1965 the press mounted a formal campaign to encourage the study of Mao Zedong's works. Initially this was a distinct movement and was kept quite separate from the Cultural Revolution which broke out in the summer of 1966, but the two were subsequently linked closely together.[28]

Sino-Soviet Dispute

The increasing radicalism of Mao's policies exacerbated the differences between Beijing and Moscow that had been simmering since Khrushchev's attack on Stalin's legacy in February 1956. The USSR had not supported the Great Leap Forward or the PLA's shelling of the island of Jinmen that was still under Guomindang control, and in 1960 a series of events revealed the extent of the split for the first time. The first of these was the conference of Communist and Workers' Parties held in Bucharest, the capital of Romania, from 24 to 26 June: during the meeting the Soviet delegation began a concerted campaign against the policies of the CCP. This was followed on 16 July by the decision of the Soviet Union and its Eastern European allies to withdraw all of their technical and economic experts from China and to renege on many existing agreements, including contracts for the supply of equipment that the Chinese leadership considered vital to their economic plans. The decision was communicated to the Chinese government on 16 June 1960 but was not made public for another two years.

Another significant international meeting of the Communist bloc, the Moscow Conference of Communist and Workers' Parties began on 5 November 1960 and the Chinese delegation to this conference was led by Liu Shaoqi and Deng Xiaoping. The dispute between China and the USSR became even more acrimonious than in Bucharest and the focus of the disagreement was the USSR's wish to move towards a policy of 'peaceful coexistence' with the Western capitalist world. Khrushchev wished to turn his back on the policy of confrontation to which Moscow had returned after the anti-Fascist alliance during the Second World War and which it had maintained until the death of Stalin in 1953. This was not a policy with which Beijing felt comfortable and it was also another attack on the legacy of Stalin and therefore, in the eyes of the Chinese, an implicit attack on Mao Zedong, who saw himself as Stalin's successor. The conference agreed on a communiqué which was issued on 1 December: this Moscow Statement appeared to show unanimous support by the delegates for Khrushchev's policy of 'peaceful coexistence' but among insiders there was no doubt about the depth of antagonism between the two Communist Parties. There was an attempt to preserve the show of unity after the conference, and the Chinese and Soviet press refrained from attacking each other directly. Instead, there were bizarre attacks by the Chinese media on Yugoslavia, and by the press and broadcasters of the Soviet Union on Albania. Yugoslavia, the most liberal of all of the communist bloc countries was taken by the Chinese to be a representative of the 'revisionism' that endangered the world Communist movement and Albania, soon to become China's only ally in Europe, was singled out by Moscow as a proxy for China's ultra-radicalism.

Third Front

The existence of the Third Front was a closely guarded secret for decades: it involved the strategic redistribution of resources between 1964 and 1971 to create a self-reliant economy in the interior of China and away from potential military threats on China's borders. It raises many questions about the military impetus behind the radicalism of the 1960s and the Cultural Revolution: in particular, to what extent the Cultural Revolution was a facade to conceal the work being done to create a military–industrial complex in the seclusion of the Chinese interior. Between 1964 and 1971 the government of the People's Republic carried out a gigantic programme of investment in some of the more inaccessible parts of western China. This was designed to establish an industrial foundation which could be virtually self-sufficient in the event of war between China and its neighbours.

The term Third Front had been first used publicly in China during a speech that Lin Biao made at the Seven Thousand Cadre Conference, an enlarged working conference of the CCP Central Committee that took place in Beijing between 11 January and 7 February 1962. The conference had been called primarily to deal with the political and economic fallout of the failure of the Great Leap Forward. Lin raised the spectre of an attack on the PRC by Guomindang forces while the mainland was in crisis, possibly with the backing of American naval power. He speculated that Shanghai might be a target and that the appropriate response would be withdrawal from the coast and resistance at a Second Front in the region of Suzhou. If the attack persisted, the forces of the PLA could then retreat to a Third Front further inland where they could begin a long-drawn-out campaign of resistance. Lin argued that it was necessary to prepare the groundwork in the areas to which the CCP would withdraw. This was more than just a possible military strategy: it also represented a bunker mentality which reflected the mood in an increasingly isolated and encircled country.

Economic problems associated with the failure of the Great Leap Forward prevented the immediate implementation of the plan. The USA became more deeply involved in the Vietnam War during 1964 which meant that its air force, including long-range bombers, was operating within easy striking distance of China. Mao called for greater investment in the Third Front including the building of a large-scale steel plant in Sichuan province. On 4 August 1964, American bombers attacked North Vietnam in a reprisal raid for torpedo attacks on American ships. On 17 August, Mao, speaking to a special party conference demanded a dramatic stepping up of the development of the interior, on the assumption that war might be imminent. He was not exclusively contemplating a possible war with the USA because the estrangement between China and the Soviet Union had by then become a major cause for concern in Beijing and China could no longer regard its inner Asian borders as secure. Although an imminent attack by the USSR seemed unlikely in 1964, hostilities were eventually to break out on the borders in 1969. The Third Front had serious consequences for China's subsequent programme of economic modernisation. It was a costly programme carried out on the basis of strategic and military reasoning and gave little thought to civilian economic development. From the point of view of the post-1979 reform programme, it left many enterprises unviable and uneconomic and extremely difficult to convert into private businesses.[29]

14

CULTURAL REVOLUTION
(1966–1980)

In 1966 China entered a period of turmoil which was to last for 14 years. The Communist Party appeared to be at war with itself and it was a war that had been instigated primarily by its own leader, Mao Zedong. Social conflict, often violent, affected all of the major urban centres and much of the countryside. The most dramatic clashes were in the great cities of Beijing, Shanghai and Wuhan but in the rural areas, even in the most remote villages, it was still possible 20 years later to see traces of Cultural Revolution slogans on the walls of granaries, schools and houses. After months of unrest, the military was deployed and by 1968 stability was beginning to return. The Cultural Revolution is one of the most difficult periods to interpret in the whole of modern Chinese history. Much of the documentation that has been available since the 1960s is no more than rhetoric; the language of the political documents was arcane and mystifying and much of what happened appeared to have been at worst senseless and at best incomprehensible, although the rationale of the various actors did gradually become apparent.[1] Ten years after the beginning of the Cultural Revolution, the nation lost its most charismatic leader: Mao Zedong died in September 1976, and his death was followed by a bitter struggle for power in which Mao's widow and her supporters (the Gang of Four) were defeated. Deng Xiaoping came to power and set China on a new course that took it towards a market economy and ended its commercial and diplomatic isolation.

The Cultural Revolution began in 1966 but there is no general agreement on when it came to an end. Many Chinese commentators have argued that it lasted for ten years and it has been called the 'decade of disaster' [shinian haojie], the 'decade of turmoil' [shinian dongluan] or the 'decade of internal chaos' [shinian neiluan], the implication being that it continued unabated until the death of Mao in September 1976 and the arrest of his closest supporters, the Gang of Four, the following month and then came to an end. In fact, the most turbulent phase of the Cultural Revolution was over by 1969 and by 1972, after the fall from power and death of Lin Biao, most central government organs were functioning normally enough to accommodate the unprecedented visit by the president of the USA, Richard M. Nixon. The revolutionary rhetoric persisted into the late 1970s, and even later in some parts of the country, but the trial of the Gang of Four which began in November 1980 was the final nail in the coffin of the Cultural Revolution.

The full and formal name for the Cultural Revolution was the Great Revolution in Proletarian Culture [*Wuchanjieji wenhua da geming*, which is usually abbreviated to *wenge*]. Its name derives from its ostensible origins in a move to replace the remnants of bourgeois culture with genuine proletarian art, a policy which not only reflected Mao Zedong's contention that class struggle remained an important factor in Chinese society but also owed a great deal to the involvement of Mao's wife, the former actress Jiang Qing, with the radical cultural and artistic circles of Shanghai. As the Cultural Revolution unfolded, it became clear that it was not in fact a struggle about culture but was a battle for the leadership of the Chinese Communist Party and a continuation of the power struggles of the 1950s. Where it differed from these earlier conflicts was the strategic and widespread exploitation of social groups by members of the political elite in support of their factions, most famously the creation of the Red Guards.

Beijing and Shanghai

In the time-honoured fashion, the factional politics of the Cultural Revolution acquired geographical bases. Beijing was initially the centre of the cautious and conservative faction led by Liu Shaoqi and Deng Xiaoping. As the seat of government and of the central organisations of the CCP, it represented an impregnable political and bureaucratic fortress which the radicals were unable to penetrate. Mao Zedong's standing had been reduced significantly when he ceded the State Chairmanship (the post equivalent to president and thus the head of state) to Liu Shaoqi in April 1959. From that time onwards, Liu was often referred to as Chairman Liu, [Liu *zhuxi*] and although this was technically correct it was seen as a slight by Mao and his supporters since the title of Chairman had previously been reserved for Mao alone. Liu's portrait began to appear more frequently in the media and at rallies from the spring of 1965: on 1 October of that year, National Day, the images of Liu and Mao were carried by participants in the rally 'in roughly equal numbers'. Some of Mao's conservative opponents who had lost their positions in 1959 were beginning to re-emerge, albeit in relatively minor appointments. Peng Dehuai was given a low-level bureaucratic post in Sichuan and Huang Kecheng became deputy governor of Shanxi province. Mao felt that he no longer had the support of the majority of senior Party members in Beijing and decided that the time had come to make a strategic retreat to the south of the country. In October 1965 he left Beijing and was to spend the following nine months either in Shanghai or in the nearby city of Hangzhou.[2]

Mao Zedong thus transferred his attention and his allegiance to Shanghai and the region around it. Shanghai had a radical tradition; it was the birthplace of the Chinese Communist Party but, of more immediate and practical significance, it was the power base of his wife Jiang Qing, who had established a reputation for herself in the literary and art world there and, as the wife of the chairman, had also accumulated a considerable and loyal political following. The nucleus of the group that was to lead the Cultural Revolution came together in Shanghai. The key actors in this intrigue were Chen Boda, who was Mao's political secretary, Jiang Qing herself and Zhang Chunqiao who had only recently taken over the post of First Secretary of the powerful East China Bureau of the Communist Party. Their new political grouping operated entirely independently of the Party authorities in Beijing and used the Shanghai media to attack what they identified as the resurgence of a new right-wing political current in the capital.[3]

Opening Salvoes 1965–6

The early skirmishes of what was to become the Cultural Revolution were conducted entirely through the press and were directed in such an oblique manner that, although readers sensitised to the use of the media by political factions knew that a major conflict was underway, the targets and the implications of the conflict were far from clear.[4] The Cultural Revolution began in the media in the most obscure and confusing way imaginable with articles attacking Wu Han for his play *Hai Rui Dismissed from Office* [*Hai Rui baguan*]. Wu Han was the deputy mayor of Beijing and a senior member of the Democratic League, one of the legal but ineffectual minority parties. He was also a writer of some distinction and a historian specialising in the Ming period and his acclaimed biography of the first emperor of the Ming dynasty, Ming Taizu, had been published in 1948. Between 1961 and 1964 he had collaborated with two other writers, Deng Tuo and Liao Mosha, on a regular satirical column in the local newspaper *Beijing Daily*. The column, entitled 'Evening Talks at Yanshan' had, among other targets, attacked many of the more extravagant and overoptimistic policies of the Great Leap Forward period in a bitter and witty style. This had not endeared the authors to Mao and his supporters.

Hai Rui Dismissed from Office was a historical drama based on the real life story of Hai Rui (1513–87), an official of the Ming dynasty who had dared to criticise the Jiajing emperor for neglecting affairs of state while spending all his time on the quest for longevity by practising Daoist rituals. Hai Rui was imprisoned and tortured, but he was released after the death of the emperor and appointed to a senior position on the board of the Censorate of the Ming Imperial Court. He became the symbol of the incorruptible official who suffered for daring to speak the truth. The play was first published in the magazine *Beijing Literature and Art* [*Beijing wenyi*] on 9 January 1961 and appeared in book form in November of the same year. The parallel with the career of Peng Dehuai and his suffering at the hands of Mao at the Lushan meetings of 1959 was not lost on Wu Han's readership. Mao and his supporters, particularly his wife Jiang Qing, were incensed by the play but because of Wu Han's stature as a leading intellectual and also because he was protected by the mayor of Beijing, Peng Zhen, they could not find any way to attack it effectively in the Beijing media. Jiang Qing apparently tried to persuade Mao to take action against Wu Han but he would not agree to this for several years, partly because he himself had invoked the name of Hai Rui during the Lushan confrontation.

An article by a previously unknown Shanghai journalist, Yao Wenyuan, attacking the play as a 'poisonous weed' was eventually published on 29 November 1965 in the Shanghai daily newspaper *Wenhui bao* after its publication had been blocked in Beijing by Peng Zhen. On Mao's instructions it was then reprinted and published throughout the country. The article took months to prepare and had been revised several times by Jiang Qing and Zhang Chunqiao as well as by Yao. Mao does not seem to have been involved in the writing or editing of the article as he is said to have criticised it for not making the parallel with Peng Dehuai clear enough, but he was prepared to put his name to the authorisation of publication.[5]

Cultural Revolution Groups and Big Character Posters

On 7 February 1966, Peng Zhen, the mayor of Beijing, issued a document, graced with the bland title of Outline Report on Current Academic Discussions. This was a report from the Cultural Revolution Group, a small working party that Peng had convened at the request of the Central Committee to consider the implications of the Wu Han affair. The report was an attempt by Peng to keep the mounting political conflict within the confines of historical and literary debates and this in turn was his way of protecting Wu Han and other moderates in the Beijing Communist Party. Peng showed the report to Liu Shaoqi in the hope of obtaining his authorization to publish it, but Liu advised him to get personal clearance from Mao. Mao queried a few points in the report and did not raise any objection to its publication at the time. He later convened a meeting of the Standing Committee of the Politburo, reinforced by his own supporters who did not normally sit on that committee, at his Hangzhou retreat and it met on 4 May

1966. The main item on the agenda was the ousting of Peng Zhen, and the method that he adopted for achieving this was the creation of a rival Cultural Revolution Group in direct opposition to the one that Peng had organised. This new Cultural Revolution Group would naturally be sympathetic to Mao's radical views, and it was supported by Lin Biao and Jiang Qing and had its political base in Shanghai rather than in Beijing. During an enlarged meeting of the full Politburo this new group was incorporated into the Party machine as the Central Committee's Cultural Revolution Group and the activities of Peng's original group were terminated. The document that announced this coup was the May Sixteenth Circular, a document issued by the Central Committee of the CCP, which had met in Beijing from 14 to 19 May 1966 and was chaired by Liu Shaoqi: Mao did not attend the meeting himself and remained in the south. The May Sixteenth Circular condemned Peng Zhen's original document, attacked 'representatives of the bourgeoisie who have sneaked into the Party', in crude class-conflict terms and announced the dissolution of Peng's Group of Five. Peng was dismissed from all of his posts before the end of May. The newly created Cultural Revolution Group reported directly to the Standing Committee of the Political Bureau, which was now firmly under Mao's control. The May Sixteenth Circular was written in a rhetorical style that had all the hallmarks of Lin Biao who, towards the end of the meeting of the Politburo, had made a lengthy and histrionic speech, warning of an anti-Party coup and heaping praises on Mao, declaring that as a historical figure he was head and shoulders above Marx, Lenin and Engels, none of whom had led a proletarian revolution in person.[6]

On 25 May 1966, within ten days of the appearance of the May Sixteenth Circular, Nie Yuanzi and other members of the Department of Philosophy at Beijing University put up a wall poster [*dazibao*, literally 'big character poster') criticising the Vice-Chancellor of the university, Lu Ping, for undermining the Cultural Revolution in the university.[7] Nie Yuanzi was a junior lecturer at the time but, more important, she was also a niece of Marshal Nie Rongzhen, who was an old comrade in arms of Lin Biao and her action was a forerunner of the way that warring political families were to use the younger generation to fight their battles in the universities. The poster, which had been produced at the instigation of Kang Sheng, the *eminence grise* of the covert security apparatus under Mao, was initially suppressed by the conservative authorities in Beijing who were the target of the poster. On 28 May the Maoist version of the Cultural Revolution Group reconstituted itself as the Central Cultural Revolution Group. The head of the Group was to be Chen Boda, Mao's political secretary, and Kang Sheng was its senior adviser: Jiang Qing and Zhang Chunqiao of the radical Shanghai faction were deputy heads and the membership included Yao

Wenyuan, the author of the attack on Wu Han. This Central Cultural Revolution Group took control of the campaign for a Cultural Revolution and it gradually supplanted the Politburo and the Central Committee as the most powerful political body in China.[8]

Chen Boda took over the running of the Communist Party newspaper *People's Daily* on 31 May by arriving at the offices with a work team and the personal authorisation of Mao Zedong. He was also able to determine the content of press releases issued by the *Xinhua* (New China) news agency and radio news bulletins and was therefore in control of all the most powerful sections of the Chinese media. On 1 June *People's Daily* carried an editorial urging the populace to 'sweep away all monsters and demons'. On 2 June it published a reproduction of Nie Yuanzi's poster, which had been suppressed by Peng Zhen's supporters in Beijing, praising it as the 'first Marxist–Leninist big character poster'. This was taken as evidence that Mao personally supported the actions of the radicals in the universities. The CCP Central Committee approved a reorganisation of the Beijing Municipal Party Committee, Peng Zhen's former power base, and this was announced on 4 June. The new Beijing Party Committee decided to send work teams into Beijing University to promote the Cultural Revolution there: there were widespread demonstrations by students in Beijing and in towns and cities around the country and it became clear that the focus of the Cultural Revolution had now moved to the universities.[9]

In early June, work teams under the overall direction of Liu Shaoqi and Deng Xiaoping were sent into other universities and secondary schools (middle schools) in Beijing, and Party committees in the rest of China began to follow suit when they saw which way the wind was blowing. Work teams had been used successfully during the Socialist Education Movement and this was taken as the model for the Cultural Revolution. By sending in their own teams, Liu and Deng were attempting to wrest the initiative away from Mao's group and to retain control of the movement themselves. Initially the work teams were welcomed by large groups of students but this changed when it became clear that their remit was to bring the radicals under control rather than to support them. Groups of students who were opposed to the work teams created their own organisations which they designated as 'revolutionary'. Students who were sympathetic to the aims of the work teams also formed organised groups. The composition of the two parallel groups of student organisations was to a large extent determined by the family backgrounds of their members. The more radical groups often comprised children from educated families whose members had been discriminated against by the CCP, whereas in the organisations supporting Liu and Deng's work teams there was a preponderance of the children of senior Party and government officials. The division between the social backgrounds of the two groups was not always as clear cut as this but the polarisation was bitter and prolonged. The student movement was thus divided from the start and the dispatch of the work teams was the cause of this polarisation. Political battles between pro-Mao and anti-Mao groups (which also claimed to be pro-Mao) brought the universities to a standstill. The first battles were in Beijing University, the most prominent institution of higher education in the country and Tsinghua (Qinghua) University, the leading scientific and technological institution, and also the most political of China's universities by virtue of its strong connections with the CCP hierarchy. The conflict spread nationwide; by June colleges in Guangzhou were in turmoil and the Vice-Chancellors of Nanjing and Wuhan Universities had been physically attacked by radicals.

In July 1966 Mao finally emerged from his retreat in Hangzhou. He travelled to Wuhan on 16 July and took a prolonged and very public swim in the Yangzi River, apparently to demonstrate his fitness and to indicate that he was on his way back to power. This attracted enormous publicity and swimming suddenly became a symbol of patriotism and an indication of political support for the chairman. On 18 July he returned to Beijing, which was by this time surrounded by troops and firmly under the control of the PLA and the minister of defence, Lin Biao. The military had been on a state of high alert since January when Lin Biao had effectively put the PLA on a war footing, although it was never made clear precisely against which enemy this war was going to be fought.[10] Mao ordered that Nie Yuanzi's poster be immediately published across the whole country and on 25 July an enlarged meeting of the Cultural Revolution Group, which was now the highest decision-making body in the country, met in Beijing to discuss the role of the work teams in the universities. Mao forced through a motion for their withdrawal against the explicit wishes of Liu Shaoqi. Mao was beginning to make his long-planned comeback and at last felt able to function again in Beijing.[11]

The Eleventh Plenum of the Eighth Central Committee of the CCP convened in Beijing from 1 to 12 August. It was inquorate according to its own constitution but it was packed with radical supporters of Mao. Mao published his own big character poster, which was modelled on the poster put up by Nie Yuanzi and entitled 'Bombard the Headquarters', on 5 August: it attacked the work teams for 'adopting the reactionary stand of the bourgeoisie' and enforcing a 'bourgeois dictatorship' and declared that the Central Committee was full of 'monsters and demons'.[12] This was an attack on Liu Shaoqi and although this was obvious to everyone involved, he did not mention Liu's name directly. On 8 August the document known colloquially as the Sixteen Points, or more formally as the Decision concerning the Great Proletarian Cultural Revolution, was adopted as official Party policy. This portrayed the Cultural Revolution as a completely new stage in the socialist revolution rather than a political campaign about art and culture which is how it had started. It called for activists to arouse the masses and let them educate themselves in the movement. Good cadres would be sorted out from the bad in the heat of the struggle and the PLA would continue to act under instructions from the Military Commission of the Central Committee. The Party centre was completely reorganised and a new Standing Committee of the Politburo, comprising entirely of Mao's radical supporters was chosen. Lin Biao was appointed as vice-chairman of the CCP which made him, to all intents and purposes, Mao's heir apparent.

Students at universities and in secondary schools were by this time forming themselves into rebel bands both for and against the work teams, and these groupings gave themselves a variety of exotic and romantic names. Even those opposed to Mao's policies had to present themselves as Maoists so the names of the student groups were extremely confusing. Of all these names, the one that became most widely used was Red Guard [*Hongweibing*]. The original Red Guards were the members of a student organisation that was created at the secondary school attached to Qinghua University on 29 May, and they in turn took their name from the Red Guard (*krasnaya gvardia*) of the Russian Revolution. The Russian Red Guards were a workers' militia set up in the summer of 1917 in Petrograd to defend the new Soviets and were the forerunner of the Red Army. Mao Zedong liked the name and wrote to the Qinghua schoolchildren on 1 August (the anniversary of the foundation of the Chinese Workers' and Peasants' Red Army in 1927) saying that they were right to 'rebel against the reactionaries'. He also encouraged them to link up with like-minded groups, and this was the signal for the Red Guard movement to spread like wildfire throughout China. On 18 August in Tian'anmen Square in the centre of Beijing there was a mass rally of Red Guards, who had travelled to the capital from all over the country. On the rostrum of the Gate of Heavenly Peace, over-looking the square, stood Mao Zedong, flanked by Lin Biao, Zhou Enlai, Tao Zhu, Chen Boda and Deng Xiaoping, the inner core of the leadership of China during the Cultural Revolution period. Possibly as many as one million young people participated in the rally. Mao publicly donned a Red Guard armband signifying his support for the movement which was to express its aspirations through personal loyalty to Mao. This theatrical gesture was an echo of an earlier occasion on 26 June 1959 when a photograph of Mao wearing the red neckerchief of the Young Pioneers had been widely circulated. After the 18 August gathering, similar Red Guard rallies took place on almost a monthly basis for the remainder of 1966.[13]

The Red Guards were given permission to 'liaise' with similar groups around the country in pursuit of their struggle against the 'capitalist-roaders' and many seized this opportunity to travel to parts of China that they had never seen before. The more adventurous also used the opportunity to seek out new personal experiences and to break away from the constraints of a highly disciplined society. Under the slogan of attacking the 'four olds' (old ideas, culture, customs and habits), groups of Red Guards attacked and destroyed many cultural relics including works of art, books and buildings. Religious institutions such as Buddhist and Daoist temples, mosques and churches were a favourite target for young radicals desperate to demonstrate their revolutionary credentials in what often became a battle between the generations. Although the Red Guard movement is associated with student radicals, it is important to note that many of them were young teenagers, of secondary school rather than university age. They teamed up with young workers who had never progressed beyond a secondary education and what had started as limited student demonstrations in support of Mao Zedong was turning into a nationwide youth movement with rival groups battling for supremacy in the name of factions within the CCP hierarchy.

Power Seizure in Shanghai

The most spectacular phase of the Cultural Revolution developed over the autumn and winter of 1966–7 when there was a dramatic shift from rhetoric and student demonstration to political action. From September 1966, the attack on the moderates in the CCP had begun to evolve into a mass movement that was ostensibly anti-bureaucratic in its orientation and therefore highly attractive to students and young workers. It struck at the structures of power that the Party had established in the major cities in China, beginning with Shanghai where verbal and written attacks on alleged 'rightists' gave way to a genuine coup d'état as the radical supporters of Mao seized control of their local Party organisation from his conservative opponents.

On 9 September a group of Red Guards from Beijing who were liaising in Shanghai attempted to occupy the Shanghai CCP headquarters. The group included the originator of the first Cultural Revolution wall poster, Nie Yuanzi, and Kuai Dafu a radical student leader who was at the centre of the Maoist activists at Qinghua University. Local students and young workers were outraged by this arrogant interference by outsiders (and, what was worse, outsiders from Beijing) in the affairs of Shanghai and fought them off, and this intervention polarised the student movement in Shanghai as it had in Beijing. The conflict in Shanghai took a different direction because it spread outside the universities so rapidly and soon involved young factory and dock workers in increasingly large numbers.

On 1 November journalists from Shanghai's local daily newspaper *Wenhui bao* demanded the right to take part in the Cultural Revolution and put up their own *dazibao* wall newspapers. On 9 November the creation of a new type of organisation, the Shanghai Workers' Revolutionary Rebel Headquarters, was announced. This was unprecedented as it was described as a non-party mass organisation which was acting on its own initiative, and the CCP had gone to great lengths to ensure that organisations of this nature that could rival the authority of the Party were never allowed to emerge. To justify setting up such an extraordinary entity, the organisers were able to refer to the fourth of the Sixteen Points of the Cultural Revolution which had been adopted as CCP policy on 8 August and which encouraged measures that 'let the masses educate themselves in the movement'. Workers' Headquarters, as it became known, was the political vehicle of the pro-Mao radicals, created by supporters of Jiang Qing and Zhang Chunqiao and established in direct opposition to the existing Communist Party organisation in Shanghai. It only remained for the radicals to overthrow the old party organisation and replace it: this they accomplished during the January Storm of 1967.

The power seizure by the Maoist radicals in Shanghai, the January Storm [*yiyue fengbao*], began with the occupation of the *Wenhui bao* offices by Red Guard supporters of Workers' Headquarters on 4 January 1967. On 5 January they also took control of the Communist Party's Shanghai newspaper *Liberation Daily* [*Jiefang ribao*] and arrested the mayor of Shanghai Cao Diqiu and the city's Communist Party Secretary Chen Bixian. The main opponents of Workers' Headquarters were the Scarlet Guards [*chiweidui*] who had been mobilised in support of the existing Party organisation. Scarlet could be seen as redder than mere red and in any case the name Scarlet Guards had a sound revolutionary pedigree as the originals after whom they were named had been armed workers' militias during the 1930s. To counter the growing influence of Workers' Headquarters, the Scarlet Guards organised a general strike and this was highly effective among the dockers and the railway workers. By 10 January local radio in Shanghai was reporting on the seriousness of the strike. The city was paralysed and the political activists were polarised between the Municipal Committee with their Scarlet Guards and the Red Guard supporters of Workers' Headquarters.

The radicals issued a series of proclamations to reinforce their coup d'etat. The first of these was the Message to the People of Shanghai which was released on 5 January in the name of the Shanghai Workers' Revolutionary Rebel Headquarters and 'ten other revolutionary mass organisations'. It declared that 1967 would be the year in which the bourgeois reactionary line would finally be vanquished in the wake of a mass movement supporting the Cultural Revolution in the factories of Shanghai but then warned against 'a handful of reactionary elements [who] were even plotting to cut off water and electricity supplies and bring public transport to a standstill'. The message also complained that 'in many factories and plants, it has occurred that some or even the majority of the members of the Workers' Red Militia Detachments have suspended production and deserted their posts...' If the Maoist radicals had assumed that the massed ranks of the industrial workers of Shanghai would be solidly behind them they were soon to be disappointed as the strikes and boycotts were almost entirely in support of the existing Shanghai Party and local government bodies.

By 9 January 1967, when the radicals issued their second proclamation, the Urgent Notice, they were clearly alarmed at the impact of the industrial action and blamed a 'handful of Party persons in authority who are taking the capitalist road', inciting 'one group of people against another, causing breakdowns in factory production and railway and road traffic. They have even incited dockers to stop work, causing difficulties in running the port and damaging the international prestige of China'. This state of affairs was attributed to the underhand actions of the Shanghai Municipal Committee. The Urgent Notice called on people to remain at their posts; demanded that radicals from Shanghai who were 'exchanging revolutionary experiences' in other parts of China return to Shanghai; cancelled documents authorising radical students and others to travel to 'exchange revolutionary experiences' and froze the funds of government departments apart from wages and necessary day-to-day running expenses. The Urgent Notice also gave authority to the Public Security Bureau, the police, to prevent the unlawful seizure of property and suppress disorder and illegal acts: it had previously been prevented from carrying out what would have been its normal duties by the atmosphere of justifiable rebellion that Mao's supporters had created.

The Central Committee of the CCP in Beijing, by now completely under the control of the radicals, sent a Message of Greeting to Revolutionary Rebel Organisations in Shanghai on 11 January, supporting the Urgent Notice and reminding those who supported Workers' Headquarters of Mao Zedong's exhortation that they should 'take firm hold of the revolution and promote production'. The Message of Greeting was also endorsed by the State Council, the Military Commission of the Central Committee and the Cultural Revolution group of the Central Committee, in other words by all the big guns of the political and military authorities. It was radical in tone but also indicated firmly that things had gone too far and that the wave of strikes that was paralysing Shanghai was unacceptable.[14]

Shanghai Commune

During the January Storm in Shanghai, hundreds of different political mass organisations (one estimate suggests the number was as high as 700) were described as revolutionary, but it is difficult to determine with any certainty which were 'Maoist' and which were primarily loyal to the old Municipal Committee since most of them carried out their activities in the name of Mao. This led to considerable confusion and conflict between organisations that were trying to outdo each other in their revolutionary zeal. The radical leaders urgently needed to find a way of unifying the disparate groups and Zhang Chunqiao and Yao Wenyuan established a Preparatory Committee for the Shanghai People's Commune to try to create some kind of united body. After three weeks of bitter wrangling, the Preparatory Committee met at one o'clock in the morning on 5 February 1967 with representatives from 38 of the radical mass organisations in attendance. The name Commune drew on the idea of the urban communes, which had been proposed during the Great Leap Forward, but which had never really attracted much support, and also on the historic Paris Commune of 1871. The Commune Committee issued a manifesto in which it claimed that it was 'a new type of local organisation born on the Yangzi Delta' and urged all regions to follow its example. It issued an order dissolving the Shanghai Municipal Committee, the old Communist Party committee that had been running the city since 1949 and revoking any decisions that the committee had made since 16 May 1966.

The Maoist radicals led by Zhang Chunqiao and Jiang Qing appeared to have routed the conservatives in Shanghai but, although they could count on the support of the mass organisations, the idea of a Shanghai Commune had very little credibility among the working population in the factories and the docks. The Commune did not appear to be an organisation capable of managing a metropolitan area the size of Shanghai and the internal wrangling between the different constituent organisations weakened it fatally. Its demise was never formally announced but the term Commune simply disappeared and Shanghai gradually came under the control of a new, and ultimately more enduring, form of organisation, the Revolutionary Committee.[15]

Revolutionary Committees

The Central Committee of the CCP, the State Council, the Central Military Affairs Committee and the Cultural Revolution Group issued a joint decree on 23 January 1967 which ordered the PLA to 'support the left' and to intervene on the side of the revolutionary left in the Cultural Revolution. This was not what the decree really meant. The purpose of this order from the most powerful central bodies of the Cultural Revolution period was to ensure the establishment of Revolutionary Committees across the whole of China rather than the ultra-radical Commune model of local government that had been proposed in Shanghai.

The idea of a Revolutionary Committee [*geming weiyuan hui*], commonly abbreviated to *geweihui*] had been pioneered in the northeast of China in common with many other policy experiments that had been introduced since 1949. The origin of the Revolutionary Committee concept was in Heilongjiang province and the committees were designed to channel the energies of political activists along moderate or even conservative lines. The first Revolutionary Committee had been established in Heilongjiang on 31 January 1967 at the same time that the January Storm had been raging in Shanghai: it was intended to be a temporary structure and other provinces followed suit and set up their own committees. The composition and the remit of these bodies was far from uniform and it was the Shanxi Revolutionary Committee, which took shape in March 1967, rather than the Heilongjiang version, that was eventually presented as the model to be copied on a nationwide basis. Approximately half of the members of the Shanxi committee had been associated with Cultural Revolution mass organisations, one-quarter of them were pre-Cultural Revolution Party cadres and one-quarter were serving soldiers of the PLA. However the Standing Committee of the Shanxi Revolutionary Committee, which wielded the greatest power, was more heavily weighted towards the old cadres and the military, giving little opportunity for the Maoist radicals to exercise any real influence. It took many months for some provinces to create Revolutionary Committees because of internal wrangling and factional disputes and the final two, in Tibet and Xinjiang, were not established until September 1968.

These 'support the left' policies were applied across the whole of the country and the composition of the committees gave the military extraordinary powers which they had not had since 1949: some regions in which the old political structures had broken down completely were for all practical purposes under martial law. As more and more Revolutionary Committees were created, the proportion of mass organisation representatives decreased even further and the influence of the PLA increased. There was a brief revival of the spirit of the Cultural Revolution in 1968 when the influence of the Maoist radicals was temporarily revived but this was countered by the dispersal of thousands of Red Guards under the policy of *xiafang* or 'sending down', usually despatching them to rural areas, which removed them from their places of work or study and had the desired effect of extinguishing their political organisations.[16]

Wuhan Incident

As spring turned into summer, conflict between rival mass organisations had become increasingly violent, especially in the major cities of the southwest and the Communist Party central organisations in Beijing sent a delegation to Chengdu, Chongqing and Kunming in an attempt to resolve the problems that this was creating. Two members of the delegation then continued to the great city of Wuhan on the Yangzi River where more than 500,000 workers were reported to be striking and demonstrating. The Wuhan incident of July 1967 was the high point of revolutionary turbulence and was a critical stage in the course of the Cultural Revolution. After the call for the PLA to intervene in the conflict, the military authorities under the command of the head of the Military District, Chen Zaidao, did intercede, but they openly took the side of the more conservative former Party committee against the explicit wishes of the Central Committee.

Serious violence had broken out in Wuhan as early as February 1967, and there were reports of hundreds of deaths in the conflict between radical and conservative factions. Strikes had spread through the factories of the city, and in June and July the railways were regularly disrupted and the impressive new bridge across the Yangzi River had been closed on more than one occasion. Two representatives of the Central Committee, Xie Fuzhi and Wang Li travelled to Wuhan on 14 July to try to restore order and enforce the policies of the radical CCP centre. Zhou Enlai and the acting Chief of the General Staff had also travelled there. Between them, they decided that one of the most active militant factions, the One Million Warriors [*Baiwan xiongshi*], which had been backed by Chen Zaidao and the local Military District, was in fact a conservative group which should not be supported and clearly favoured the radical General Workers' Council Headquarters. At the time Wuhan was firmly under the control of the One Million Warriors and Unit 8201, a regular detachment of the PLA which supported them. Unit 8201 patrolled the streets and had set up machine gun posts on the roofs of key buildings. Xie and Wang were kidnapped on 20 July and held prisoner by members of the PLA and workers' organisations loyal to the conservatives. Wang Li was injured during the altercation and sported a black eye in subsequent photographs and film shots. Their incarceration lasted less than two days as they managed to negotiate their way to the airport, with the help of units of the PLA Air Force: from the airport they flew to Beijing. Far from the situation having been resolved by their intervention, the crisis had deepened. PLA units from other parts of China were deployed by the Central Military Affairs Committee in Beijing to bring Unit 8201, which was now deemed to be a renegade unit, under control. The 8191 Airborne Division which was in the Wuhan area and the Fifteenth Army from Hubei were mobilised against Chen Zaidao and Unit

8201, and at least five gunboats of the East Sea Fleet were dispatched west-wards up the Yangzi River and were positioned to shell Wuhan. Lin Biao arrived to take charge personally, sent a telegram on 21 July dismissing Chen Zaidao and increased his own political standing by doing so. The political conflict had now also become a conflict between the central mili-tary authorities in Beijing loyal to Mao and the local military in Wuhan, who favoured the existing conservative Party organisations. A combination of overwhelming force and tough negotiations finally resolved the situation by early August. Chen Zaidao was arrested and taken to Beijing. He was replaced by Zeng Siyu and most senior local party officials were forced to retire. Wuhan was once again under control and more or less orderly. The Wuhan incident [*Wuhan shibian*] was confusing as it involved belated sup-port by the central Cultural Revolution bodies for a local radical organisa-tion, in contrast to Shanghai and in most of the revolutionary committees where the military and the conservatives were by this time generally coming out on top. It had also cast doubt on the reliability of the PLA and its loyalty to Mao and his supporters which had seemed unshakeable after Lin Biao had taken command. The incident was treated as if it had been an attempt at a military coup and in all probability civil war was only narrowly averted.[17]

Attack on Liu Shaoqi

Between April and September 1967, criticisms of Mao's main rival Liu Shaoqi had appeared regularly in the Chinese media. However, such was his status that for many months he was never mentioned by name: there were simply denunciations of 'China's Khrushchev' or the 'Top Party Person taking the Capitalist Road'. On 14 August a joint editorial in the CCP organs *People's Daily* and *Red Flag* accused him of having tried to undermine the socialist system for decades. Specifically he was charged with having put forward the idea of converting the Chinese People's Consultative Confer-ence and the National People's Congress into a bicameral parliamentary system, a notion condemned as bourgeois. He was also castigated for his failure to support Mao in the battle with Peng Dehuai at the meetings in Lushan in 1959.[18] He was not named in the article but it was made clear, through the parallel informal systems of communication that the Party had always operated, that Liu was the target. There were growing demands from the more radical Maoists that he be put on trial publicly for his counter-revolutionary crimes.

Red Guards had taken up positions near the Communist Party com-pound of Zhongnanhai, which is just to the west of the Forbidden City in central Beijing, and on 1 August when *People's Daily* reprinted Lin Biao's influential article, 'Long Live the Victory of People's War' (his clarion call for a third world revolution led by China) they set up stalls, printed leaflets and cartoons attacking Liu and demanded that he be handed over to the Party Centre as a criminal. There were even demands that he be put to death. Peasants from the suburbs and workers from the capital's factories came into the centre in lorries festooned with red flags, shouting 'down with Liu Shaoqi'. Under this pressure the Party leadership agreed that Liu would be kept in the Party compound in Zhongnanhai and would come under severe criticism. No doubt they recognised that if Liu Shaoqi were thrown to the wolves any one of them could be next.[19] The struggle against Liu continued but he remained in post as State Chairman until he was finally dismissed in October 1968. Deng Xiaoping, Zhu De, Zhou Yang and many others who took a similar pragmatic line and preferred to rely on government rather than mass politics were also purged at the same time.

Demobilising the Red Guards

The Red Guards, that is the revolutionary mass organisations of young students and workers who were loyal to Mao and his romantic ideas of a revolution, had played a vital role in the overthrow of the old Party committees. These committees had been the political base of Liu Shaoqi and the moderates or conservatives within the CCP both nationally and throughout the country. Once that task had been completed the Red Guards had outlived their usefulness: indeed they now represented a threat as they had been operating entirely outside the Party machine and this went against all the practices that the CCP had adopted since coming to power. Even the radicals in the Party centre realised that it was now time to reign in their student supporters, but it was left to Zhou Enlai, whose position throughout the attacks on the conservatives had appeared unassailable but inscrutable, to order them back to their schools and colleges. In a speech to the Beijing Municipal Committee on 1 September Zhou announced that he was ordering the Red Guards to cease their revolutionary liaison activities forthwith, to abandon violence and attacks on foreigners and to return to their homes. Speaking directly to an audience of Red Guards on 17 September, Zhou passed on a message from Mao Zedong. The 'little revolutionary generals' of the Red Guard movement had begun to make serious mistakes, Mao had said, and it was time for them to resume their studies.[20]

This was far easier said than done so the task of ensuring compliance was given to the PLA. Army units moved into primary and secondary schools, and they were reopened with new syllabuses which were heavily weighted towards political education and quasi-military training. It took much longer for the universities and other tertiary colleges to resume their teaching and the first did not reopen until the autumn term of 1970. The army was able to restrict the free travel, the 'revolutionary exchanges of experience' which had kept the Red Guards of different cities in touch with each other and was given authority to scrutinize any leaflets or posters that the Red Guards wanted to publish.

Even this did not bring to an end the radical current among the youth of China. Many students and young workers had acquired a taste for dissent and the notion of an anti-bureaucratic and egalitarian continuous revolution struck a chord with many of those who knew only the dull and stifling officialdom of China in the 1950s. In spite of the repression carried out by the military, independent Red Guard units continued to exist and radicals in Inner Mongolia, Guangdong and other provinces declared themselves to be part of a new trend or new wave [*xin sichao*] of the Cultural Revolution. In Hunan a group claiming to be the Hunan Proletarian Revolutionary Alliance Committee [*Hunan sheng wuchanjieji geming da lianhe weiyuanhui*, usually abbreviated to *Shengwulian*] published documents in December 1967 and January 1968 supporting the revival of the idea of a Shanghai Commune and attacking what they saw as the return of the bureaucrats whom they had so successfully overthrown in the spring of 1967. The military response to this new leftist current was swift and ruthless. Universities across China were occupied by the PLA and there were many injuries among the radical students and significant loss of life. The Party Centre which during the previous year had lauded their 'bombardment of the headquarters' now turned a deaf ear and by the autumn of 1968 the Red Guard movement had to all intents and purposes been eradicated. Former Red Guards, particularly those who had played a leading role in the organisations, were sent down [*xiafang*] to the villages where it was intended that they would learn from the poor and lower middle peasants. Some of the most recalcitrant were tried and executed as anarchists or hooligans.[21]

Rebuilding the Communist Party

The Twelfth Plenary Session of the Eleventh CCP Central Committee was held in Beijing from 13 to 31 October 1968. This was an enlarged, in other words a carefully packed, meeting of the Central Committee and was the first that had been held since August 1966. In addition to the regular and alternate members of the Central Committee, members of the Cultural Revolution Group, leading Party figures from the provinces and senior PLA officers were also present. This October Plenum sought to legitimise the changes at the top of the CCP that had resulted from the mass action and the purges of Liu Shaoqi and his supporters. A communiqué was issued on 1 November and published in *People's Daily* the following day. In this communiqué, Liu Shaoqi was mentioned by name for the first time as China's Khrushchev, 'a renegade, traitor and scab hiding in the Party', who was also 'a lackey of imperialism, modern revisionism and the Guomindang reactionaries who had committed innumerable crimes'.[22] The Plenum approved the Report on the Crimes of the Traitor, Enemy Agent and Scab Liu Shaoqi, which had been produced by Jiang Qing and Kang Sheng. It also adopted a draft constitution for a radically reconstructed CCP which was put before the Ninth Party Congress when it finally took place in April 1969.

The Ninth Congress was long overdue according to the Party's own constitution as the Eighth had been held more than ten years previously in 1958 and the normal term was five years. It was convened in Beijing on 1 April 1969 and was attended by some 1,500 delegates, many of them in PLA uniform. Security was tight and the conference was stage-managed even more carefully than normal. At the congress, Lin Biao was formally designated Mao's successor, and Jiang Qing and her supporters became members of the Political Bureau. Lin's report was notable for its attack on the legacy of Liu Shaoqi while calling for the unity of the Party. The new CCP constitution that was adopted at the conference enshrined Marxism–Leninism Mao Zedong Thought as the theoretical basis of the Party. Liu Shaoqi was permanently expelled from the CCP and lost all of his state and government positions. He died in prison in Kaifeng on 12 November 1969 at the age of 71 after prolonged ill-treatment. The Ninth Party Congress gave the Cultural Revolution Group the authority that they had sought to force through Mao's policies but it also left the PLA in an immensely powerful position. Fifty per cent of the members of the Central Committee that was elected by the Ninth Congress had been senior officers of the PLA.[23] In many ways the end of the Ninth Congress was also the end of the Cultural Revolution. The conservatives who were close to Liu Shaoqi had been defeated and most had been expelled from the Party; the mass organisations that had been used to achieve this had been brought under control or dissolved and a new political coalition of radicals and PLA officers with whom Mao could identify had been put in place.[24]

China and the USSR on the Brink of War

The Sino-Soviet dispute had been almost completely eclipsed by the Cultural Revolution but it had by no means disappeared. Although the principal targets of the Red Guards were the conservative leadership of the CCP, they did keep back some of their vitriol and spleen for foreign adversaries. The USA and its allies, notably the United Kingdom, were condemned: there were demonstrations outside their diplomatic compounds in China and the office of the British *chargé d'affaires* was occupied and seriously damaged by fire in August 1967. However the greatest venom was reserved for China's erstwhile ally, the Soviet Union, whose government was now reviled as revisionist and social-imperialist and its leaders excoriated as the New Tsars. The street in which the Soviet embassy was situated was re-named Anti-Revisionism Street [*Fanxiu lu*] and was the scene of many anti-Soviet demonstrations.

Acrimonious diplomatic exchanges and mutual criticism continued in the Chinese and Soviet press but the focus of the conflict between China and the USSR shifted to questions relating to their common border. Border problems between the two states were far from new: they were the legacy of the expansion of the Chinese and Russian empires in the seventeenth and eighteenth centuries. Although treaties such as those signed at Nerchinsk in 1689 and Kiakhta in 1727 had produced agreements on border demarcation, there were still long-standing disagreements about who should control certain sectors of the territory in the border areas. As the Cultural Revolution escalated, tension on the borders mounted, more troops were deployed on both sides and the rhetoric that appeared in the rival media made it clear that China and the USSR were no longer allies with ideological differences but potential enemies. The total length of the Sino-Soviet border is more than 2,500 miles and by 1969 there were more than one million Soviet troops deployed along its length.

The government in Moscow had made it clear that it possessed the means to destroy China's nuclear capacity which was still in its infancy. A Chinese nuclear test at the Lop Nur site in Xinjiang on 27 December 1968 did nothing to reduce tensions and on 2 March 1969, there was an armed clash between Chinese and Soviet troops and naval personnel on a disputed island in the Ussuri River in northeastern China, an island that is known in Chinese as Zhenbao and in Russian as Damanskiy. A second exchange of fire followed on 14 March, and there was loss of life in both of these incidents and during a further clash on 8 July which took place on an island in the Amur River, which forms the border between the states, close to the Russian city of Khabarovsk. On the northwestern border of China where Xinjiang borders on what is now the independent state of Kazakhstan, there had been a number of skirmishes between Chinese and Soviet troops. On 10 June there was a serious battle at the border in Yumin County, which is to the north of the city of Yining (Ghulja in the local Uyghur language). A further skirmish occurred in the same area on 13 August.

While both sides continued to stake their claims to the border areas that they wished to control, talks between the Chinese foreign minister, Zhou Enlai, and the prime minister of the Soviet Union, Alexei Kosygin, began in Beijing on 11 September and were followed by working sessions which opened on 20 October. China had issued a statement on 8 October demanding that the existing 'unequal treaties' on the Sino-Soviet border be replaced by a new agreement. The tension on the border lessened after the convening of these negotiations but normal relations between the two governments were not restored and would not be during the remainder of the life of the Soviet Union.[25]

Fall of Lin Biao

At the conclusion of the Ninth Party Congress on 24 April 1969, Lin Biao had emerged as the heir apparent. He was the anointed crown prince, Mao Zedong's 'close comrade in arms' who appeared on official photographs standing next to the chairman and wearing a military green *zhongshan zhuang* (the Sun Yat-sen jacket that is often referred to in the West as the Mao jacket) in contrast to Mao's grey jacket and frequently brandishing *Quotations from Chairman Mao* which he had turned into the political training Bible for his PLA troops. By September 1971 it was all over: Lin was dead after a mysterious air crash, amid allegations of a coup d'etat against his mentor. What went wrong? The answer is to be found partly in the convoluted and deadly feuding of factions in the CCP and PLA and partly in the changing international situation, in particular China's dramatically changing relationship with its one time ally the USSR and its erstwhile bitter enemy the USA.

The bond between Mao Zedong and Lin Biao had never been as solid as the propaganda photographs suggested. Lin was deeply implicated in the ultra-leftism of the Cultural Revolution from which Mao was now trying to distance himself and many senior members of the CCP had serious concerns about the growing power of the PLA in internal affairs. The conflict between the two men became more apparent at the second plenary session of the Ninth Central Committee which was held in the old gladiatorial arena of CCP political infighting, Lushan, from 23 August to 6 September 1970. The key issue on the agenda was Mao's proposal, made in March 1970, that the new Constitution that was being prepared during that time should omit the role of chairman of the People's Republic of China (State chairman or president) the position held most recently by Liu Shaoqi. Lin saw this as a political ploy to deny him a senior position – his inference was almost certainly correct – and he persuaded his supporters in the PLA and the Party to restore it to the agenda. Their proposal was that Mao should once again assume the role of State Chairman while serving concurrently as Party Chairman, returning to the position that he had occupied before the decision of the Eighth Central Committee in Wuchang on 10 December 1958. However Lin Biao's allies were also engaged in forward planning and were actively considering what Lin's role would be after the death of Mao

Zedong who was known to be ailing. Mao perceived Lin's move as a conspiracy and went to some lengths to ensure that the Beijing Military Region, which was responsible for the security of the capital and consequently of Mao, was not under the control of generals loyal to Lin.

Both Mao and Zhou Enlai had become concerned at developments in the foreign policy of the Soviet Union. As well as the direct threat of troops on China's borders which had already led to armed conflict during the early years of the Cultural Revolution, the invasion of Czechoslovakia in 1968 had demonstrated beyond a shadow of a doubt that the USSR was prepared to act outside its own borders in defence of its own interests and regardless of international opinion. Realising that this posed a grave threat to China's security, Mao Zedong commissioned four of the most senior marshals of the People's Liberation Army to write a report on China's foreign policy priorities. Their proposals were that China should abandon any idea of either continuing its alliance with the USSR based on shared ideology or of assuming the leadership of a world revolution. Instead it should move towards a pragmatic stance that would place the country's interests and national security at the top of the agenda and deal with the major powers accordingly. Lin Biao could not countenance the thought of any rapprochement with the USA, and although his position has often been represented as pro-Soviet his track record, and in particular his polemical essay, 'Long Live the Victory of People's War', suggest that he wished a plague on the houses of both the superpowers and resisted an alliance with either.[26]

What finally persuaded Mao appears to have been not political logic or modern international relations theory but a parallel that he perceived between the political situation that China faced in 1969 and the period of the Three Kingdoms (AD 220–65), a tumultuous historical period after the fall of the Han Dynasty with which Mao felt a particular affinity. The legendary strategist of the Three Kingdoms period, Zhuge Liang, was prime minister of the kingdom of Shu. Shu was under threat from the kingdom of Wei, which was located to its north. Zhuge Liang's strategy was to form an alliance with the kingdom of Wu to the east to counter the power of Wei. The implications were obvious: the threat from the Soviet Union was so great that China would be obliged to ally itself with the USA. Mao accepted this proposal and so began a dramatic and bewildering diplomatic *volte face* that took the world, and the population of China, completely by surprise.[27]

The decision has been attributed to Mao but the strategy and the planning were the work of Zhou Enlai who had become aware of a change in the attitude of the USA. There was a new willingness in Washington to move closer to China to isolate the Soviet Union. The Foreign Ministry was one of Zhou's highest priorities as prime minister: he controlled it through his protégé, the Foreign Minister Chen Yi, and he had been personally affronted when it was occupied by radicals of the May Sixteenth Group during the Cultural Revolution. He had fought ferociously to regain control of the Foreign Ministry so that China could maintain some degree of normality and credibility in diplomacy and foreign relations during this period of turbulence, but he was unable to prevent Chen Yi from becoming the subject of Red Guard criticism. The ministry had been taken over by radicals for a period of 16 days from 7 August 1967 and it was during this period that the office of the British Chargé d'affaires was sacked. Zhou Enlai is credited with having ordered in the police and PLA units to protect the British diplomats.[28]

The People's Republic of China, since its establishment in 1949, had been excluded from the United Nations, where the Chinese seat was occupied by the administration of the Republic of China based in Taiwan, the heirs of the pre-1949 Nationalist government of the mainland. Debates and votes on the legitimacy of Taiwan's retention of the seat and the counter claims of the PRC had taken place regularly in the United Nations but on 20 November 1970 there was, for the first time, a simple majority in favour of the PRC taking the Chinese seat. This vote lacked the two-thirds majority needed to effect the change but it was an important step forward for Beijing's case. On 15 March 1971, the US State Department lifted restrictions on US citizens who wished to travel to the PRC, restrictions that had been in force since the Korean War. One month later, on 14 April, Zhou Enlai formally welcomed a team of table tennis players from the USA to China. President Richard Nixon announced a relaxation in the embargo on Sino-US trade and the use of American dollars by the PRC. This ping-pong diplomacy, as it became known, was followed by the shuttle diplomacy of Henry Kissinger, Richard Nixon's National Security Adviser, who made an unannounced visit to Beijing in early July. Kissinger held talks with Zhou Enlai on the possibility of a rapprochement between the two countries. As a token of his good faith he offered the Chinese government access to top secret intelligence on the disposition of Soviet military forces that had been acquired by the USA using its satellite monitoring systems. Initially this included the deployment of Soviet troops at the time of the war between India and Pakistan that had led to the emergence of an independent Bangladesh and an assessment of the nuclear weapons available to the Soviet Union in any future attack on China.[29]

On 13 September 1971 Lin Biao fled China in a British-made Trident aircraft which was on its way towards the Soviet Union when it crashed over Mongolia, killing Lin and several members of his family. According to one official account:

Lin Biao and his die-hard followers had devised a plan for a coup d'etat in March to be launched on 8 September. When their plot was discovered, Lin Biao, his wife Ye Qun and his son Lin Liguo tried to flee the country in the early morning on 13 September. They were all killed when their plane crashed near Ondorhaan in Mongolia. After the 13 September incident, a nationwide rectification movement to criticise and denounce Lin Biao was unfolded and the crimes of the Lin Biao counter-revolutionary clique were investigated.[30]

The precise details of the night flight, what preceded it and why it crashed, have been the subject of intense speculation ever since that day in September 1971. Rumours abounded that Lin had not been on the aircraft but had been killed in Beijing; there were claims that the plane had been shot down and there was intense speculation about the nature of the plot that Lin was said to have been hatching. Mao had certainly been extremely suspicious about the genuineness of Lin's support and presumed that his creation of the cult of personality and his sycophantic elevation of Mao's works was part of a strategy to promote himself rather than any genuine admiration for Mao. He was also deeply distrustful of Lin's wife Ye Qun who had complete control over her husband's office and of Lin's son, Lin Liguo, a PLA Air Force officer and a relatively minor functionary in the defence department who had been organising an independent intelligence network to support his father. It appears that Lin Liguo had arranged for contingency plans that could be put into operation in the event of Lin Biao being purged. These vague and ill-thought-out notes became dramatised as Project 571 and Mao appears in them as B-52, the tyrannical leader whose erratic deployment of political power had cost the careers of many senior Party figures.[31]

It may well be that Mao was actively planning to exclude Lin from power and that Lin had got wind of this. It is not impossible that Lin Biao was actively plotting to overthrow Mao, although it is more than likely that he realised that Mao was a sick man and was trying to ensure that after the chairman's death it would be Lin, and not Jiang Qing, who succeeded to the highest office of the state and the party. Lin Liguo appears to have been considering a military coup based on the Air Force. Whatever the case, the facts, and then the exact circumstances, of Lin's death remain confusing and ambiguous.[32]

Nixon Visits China

On 25 October 1971 after fierce lobbying, and this time with the sponsorship of the USA and Japan, the UN General Assembly voted to admit the

PRC to membership of the United Nations and to exclude the Republic of China administration on Taiwan. The first delegation from Beijing to the UN arrived at UN headquarters in New York on 11 November. The People's Republic of China was finally able to participate in international diplomacy and the psychological impact on the Communist government of defeating and humiliating its Guomindang rivals should not be under-estimated. The Nationalist government in Taipei expressed its anger at what they perceived as a great betrayal and the bitterness at this treachery was to persist for decades.

The most public manifestation of the change in China's international position was the official visit made by the president of the US, Richard M. Nixon, to the PRC, the first visit made by a US president to the country that had been the bitter enemy of America during the Korean War. The presidential aircraft *Air Force One*, a Boeing 707, carrying Nixon, his wife, his entourage and attendant journalists and photographers, arrived at Hongqiao airport just outside Shanghai at 8.55 in the morning of 21 February 1972. Nixon met Chairman Mao Zedong and Premier Zhou Enlai, was enter-tained at a performance of the Cultural Revolution ballet, *The Red Detach-ment of Women*, visited cultural, industrial and agricultural sites, toured the cities of Hangzhou and Shanghai and climbed up to the Great Wall, where he stopped and is reputed to have commented, 'This is a great wall!'

Nixon spent some 15 hours in closed working sessions with the Chinese leadership, mostly with Zhou Enlai, in addition to informal discussions and social occasions. Much of the detailed business, however, was carried out by his secretary of state for foreign affairs, Henry Kissinger, whose explora-tory trip the previous year had made possible Nixon's visit and by the dep-uty foreign minister of China, Qiao Guanhua. These two seasoned negoti-ators hammered out the official communiqué that was issued jointly at the end of the visit on 28 February. While recognising the differences between China and the USA, the communiqué expressed the wish for continued ties; mutual cooperation in science, technology, culture and sport; the development of bilateral trade and progress towards the normalisation of diplomatic relations.[33] The US and China did not in fact establish normal diplomatic relations and exchange ambassadors until 1 March 1979. The Taiwan issue, above all, was the cause of the delay. Following the example of Richard Nixon, the Japanese Prime Minister Kakuei Tanaka visited China from 25 to 30 September 1972 and appended his signature to a Joint Statement on 29 September. This was the beginning of the normalisation of Sino-Japanese relations, after a long gap following Japan's invasion of China and its defeat in the Second World War: the process or normalisation was concluded in 1978 and was vitally important to the Chinese economic reforms of the 1980s.[34]

Deng Xiaoping and the Gang of Four

Deng Xiaoping's name appeared in press reports of a banquet in honour of Prince (later King) Sihanouk of Cambodia, which Deng had attended on 12 April 1973 in his capacity as vice-premier. This was the first time that his name had been mentioned in the press since he had been purged during the Cultural Revolution and with hindsight it can be seen to have marked the beginning of his rise to power. It was far from being the end of the struggle with the radical Maoists. In January 1974 a new campaign had been launched, the Movement to Criticise Lin Biao and Confucius (*pi Lin pi Kong*). This was originally mounted by the Cultural Revolution group around Jiang Qing as an attack on Confucianism and thus as a not very subtle attack on Zhou Enlai, 'the greatest Confucian mandarin of them all who is negating the Cultural Revolution'. Zhou skilfully managed to take control of this campaign, converted it into a campaign against Lin Biao, and by implication against the radicals with whom Lin had been allied before his flight, and confused everyone as to whom the real target had been. The key documents of the campaign which were published as *Selected Documents Criticizing Lin Piao [Lin Biao] and Confucius [Pi Lin pi Kong wenxuan]* were a collection of apparently academic articles on a range of recondite topics connected with the history and philosophy of the period before the unification of China in 221 BC. Confucius was condemned as 'an outwardly stubborn and ferocious but inwardly extremely weak and empty man; he was sinister and cunning and rotten to the core. This was the nature of the declining slave-owning class he represented – it is a feature common to representatives of all reactionary classes on the verge of extinction'.[35] It did not take a great leap of the imagination to realise that the target was not Confucius, but Zhou Enlai, who was really being damned as a representative of the bourgeoisie.

Two significant events that took place outside the People's Republic had an impact on its internal politics in 1975. On 5 April, Chiang Kai-shek, the arch rival of the Beijing government died at the age of 87. Chiang had been the personification of the enemy Guomindang regime and with his passing a powerful symbol of anti-Communism was removed. On 30 April, the Vietnam War finally came to an end with the liberation of Saigon and the ignominious withdrawal of American forces. The war had been a major bone of contention between China and the USA, with China supporting the North Vietnamese and, in the south, the National Liberation Front coalition. The conclusion of the war made the move towards full diplomatic relations with the USA more realistic.

Zhou Enlai had been seriously ill for some time and his health worsened during the spring of 1974. He had two heart attacks in June and July and was confined to bed for long periods. Deng Xiaoping was effectively in control of the day-to-day running of the government although Zhou continued to meet visiting dignitaries. Zhou Enlai recovered sufficiently to complete a report on a new draft constitution that was to be placed before the session of National People's Congress scheduled for January 1975 and which would be the first to be held for ten years. His report had to compete with one from the Shanghai radical, Zhang Chunqiao, but the NPC did agree with his insistence on the priority of progress towards the Four Modernisations [sige xiandaihua] in agriculture, industry, science and technology and defence, which can be seen as Zhou Enlai's most important legacy as it was the prelude to the agreement on Deng Xiaoping's reform and opening policies. Deng Xiaoping was elected as first deputy prime minister and chief of the general staff at the congress but Jiang Qing and her ultra-leftist allies from Shanghai had still not given up the idea of taking control of the Party.

Zhou Enlai's condition deteriorated during the winter of 1975 and he died on 8 January 1976. He was 78 years old, was genuinely mourned by many who had never met him and was credited, probably far more than he deserved, with having curbed many of the excesses of the Cultural Revolution and having protected many individuals from attacks by the ultra-radicals. Zhou's passing was the first in what was to be a year of politically significant deaths.[36]

Tian'anmen 1976

Qingming [clear and bright] is the traditional Chinese festival for honouring departed members of the family. It takes place at the beginning of the third lunar month, close to Easter in the Christian calendar. The most important activity of the festival is visiting, sweeping and repairing the graves of the ancestors [*saomu*]. Family members of all generations visit the tombs of their closest relatives and take paper money and offerings of food which are set out either on the ground in front of the grave or on a stone table. If the inscription on the headstone is worn, it is repainted. Since 1949, the festival has also been the occasion on which to remember martyrs who fell during the years of revolution. In 1976, the *Qingming* festival fell on 4 April but, long before the day of the festival, wreaths commemorating Zhou Enlai had been placed on the Revolutionary Martyrs' Memorial that stands at the southern end of Tian'anmen Square. The first floral tributes were placed on the memorial on 19 March, and these tributes were all the more poignant because the inscription on the monument is in Zhou Enlai's own handwriting. On 30 March poems and eulogies to Zhou began to appear and a steady stream of people, determined to commemorate the premier, brought wreaths, bouquets and verses, which covered the base of the monument. On 4 April, the eve of *Qingming*, the police arrived in force without warning and took away all the tokens of grief and respect. Tian'anmen Square was cordoned off by police barricades and the crowds of people who were still attempting to leave their tributes were held back. In the face of these clumsy and boorish tactics, the commemoration of Zhou rapidly turned into a political demonstration. The demonstrators moved to surround the Great Hall of the People and a police station in the corner of the square was attacked and badly damaged. Several police and government vehicles were overturned and set on fire. The crowd rejected appeals by the mayor of Beijing, Wu De, to disperse and the police and military were deployed to put down the demonstration. Hundreds were arrested on the day and many more in the days that followed and there were many executions of those accused of being the ringleaders. The events of 5 April 1976 became known as the Tian'anmen Incident [*Tian'anmen shijian*] but also as the April Fifth [*Siwu*] Movement: in Chinese this is the reverse of *Wusi*, the name for the May Fourth Movement of 1919. The Tian'anmen Incident of 1976 should not be confused with the democracy movement demonstrations in Tian'anmen Square which were suppressed on 4 June 1989 and which overshadowed the earlier protests.

As the demonstrations grew in number and intensity, the nature of the poems and eulogies changed radically from simple praise of Zhou Enlai to political diatribes against Jiang Qing. They revealed a deep revulsion towards the policies of the ultra-Maoists and they marked the beginning of a new period of dissent that was to erupt again in the democracy movement of the late 1980s. Deng Xiaoping was blamed personally by Jiang Qing and her radical supporters for encouraging the demonstrations and was once again stripped of all of his Party and government positions. On 7 April it was announced that Hua Guofeng, who was virtually unknown, would replace Deng as first vice-chairman of the Central Committee of the CCP, second only to Chairman Mao.[37] Demonstrations had also taken place in other large cities and indeed the protests in Nanjing had started even before those in Beijing.

Zhu De, who was once Mao's military opposite number and his alter ego in the revolutionary civil wars, but had been purged during the Cultural Revolution, died on 6 July 1976. On 28 July the northern industrial city of Tangshan, which lies to the east of Beijing, and the rural area nearby experienced one of the most serious earthquakes to hit China during the twentieth century. It registered 7.8 on the Richter scale and struck early in the morning: it cost the lives of at least 242,000 people and left a further 164,000 injured. Although there were many offers of assistance from abroad, China preferred to deal with the crisis alone and units of the PLA and many civilians were deployed in the rescue and reconstruction efforts.[38]

Death of an Emperor?

Everyone in China who had any appreciation of the mythology of earth-quakes in the country's history and culture was aware that a quake on this scale must presage a political event of momentous proportions. Mao Ze-dong died on 9 September 1976: it was the end of an era. Mao had been incapacitated for months and had not been in control of state affairs for some considerable time. Many of his pronouncements in the final years were mediated through the office of his wife, Jiang Qing, and after his death her radical supporters moved swiftly to try to inherit his mantle on the basis of what they claimed were clear deathbed instructions from Mao. Wang Hongwen, who was the youngest of the Shanghai radical leaders, installed himself in an office in the Zhongnanhai party and government complex and had staff working for him round the clock, contacting local Party organisations throughout China and instructing them to report direct-ly to him. On 4 October, an article appeared in *Guangming Daily* under the name Liang Xiao, a pseudonym that had been used previously by the Shanghai radicals. It was entitled 'Always act in accordance with the policies laid down by Chairman Mao' and appeared to transfer authority to Jiang Qing's group, claiming that Hua Guofeng was a 'revisionist'. The radical faction led by Jiang Qing also attempted to mobilise military units in sup-port of their claim to the succession, once again creating the very real possibility that China could slide into a civil war.

Gang of Four

Two days later on 6 October, a group of senior members of the Politburo, principally Hua Guofeng, Ye Jianying and Li Xiannian, ordered the arrest of the four leading Shanghai radicals, Jiang Qing, Zhang Chunqiao, Yao Wenyuan and Wang Hongwen – the Gang of Four [*Siren bang*] as they would now be branded. This manoeuvre was carried out by Unit 8341 of the PLA under the command of Wang Dongxing after the four had been summoned to what they were told was an emergency meeting of the Polit-buro. Wang Dongxing, who had been loyal to Chairman Mao, had switched his allegiance to Chairman Hua. On 7 October Hua Guofeng was appoint-ed as chairman of the Central Committee of the CCP and of the Central Military Committee, the key posts that Mao had held until his death. Mao's alleged last words to Chairman Hua, 'With you in charge I can set my mind at rest' [*ni banshi, wo fangxin*], were relayed across the entire Chinese media. The following July, Deng Xiaoping was reinstated as the vice-chairman of the Chinese Communist Party, but Hua was confirmed in his position as chairman and there was an uneasy alliance between the two. A victory parade, celebrating the downfall of the Gang of Four, brought a million soldiers and civilians to Tian'anmen Square on 24 October 1976.[39]

The Gang of Four and their supporters were accused almost immediately of having attempted to seize power by taking over the Chinese Communist Party illegally; contaminating the political instructions handed down by Mao Zedong and acting against Hua Guofeng both before and after Mao's death. It would take more than four years before they were brought to trial: this was an indication of the political, rather than the legal, complexities involved in the process. First, they were tried alongside supposed supporters of Lin Biao although they had clearly parted company with Lin well before their attempt to succeed Mao. Second, and far more problematic, was their association with Mao. None of them could have achieved the level of influence that they had attained without the support of the chairman and they could with considerable justification claim that in many ways they were merely continuing the policies that Mao would have followed had he lived. China was not yet ready to divest itself of the legacy of Mao so an intricate balancing act was called for.

The trial began on 20 November 1980 and was presided over by the chief justice of the Supreme Court, Jiang Hua. The panel of 34 judges included many who had no legal training or experience, but this was the norm for China at that time as it had only the most rudimentary legal structures and little in the way of a trained legal profession. The central charges against the defendants were that they were responsible for the following:

1. Framed and persecuted party and state leaders and plotted to overthrow the dictatorship of the proletariat.

2. Persecuted, killed and tortured more than 34,000 officials and ordinary people.

3. Planned an armed coup in Shanghai after the death of Mao (this was alleged to have been a coup organised by Wang Hongwen who had distributed weapons and ammunition to the militia).

4. Planned to assassinate Mao and organised an armed counter-revolutionary coup.

In addition to the Gang of Four, Chen Boda who was Mao's former political secretary and speech writer until he was purged in 1970 was on trial as were a group of generals who had been close to Lin Biao. A further six names were given to the court, the names of people who had died but who would otherwise also have been on trial. These included Lin Biao and his wife and son, the former security chief Kang Sheng and Xie Fuxhi who had succeeded Kang. The trial was notable for the histrionics of Jiang Qing who attempted to portray herself as a revolutionary martyr and for the way that the co-defendants readily implicated each other while attempting to defend themselves.[40] After intense political wrangling that involved the judges and the new CCP leadership, a verdict was finally reached on 25 January 1981. Jiang Qing and Zhang Chunqiao were sentenced to death with a two-year reprieve (the equivalent of a sentence of life imprisonment) and deprived of political rights for life. As many in the CCP hierarchy, and almost certainly the public, favoured the death penalty this could be regarded as quite a lenient sentence. The two more junior Shanghai radicals, Wang Hongwen and Yao Wenyuan, and several of their other political allies including Chen Boda received long prison sentences.[41] Jiang Qing refused to acknowledge the authority of the court and was defiant until the end. While incarcerated in Qincheng prison she developed cancer of the throat and was allowed to serve the remainder of her sentence under house arrest. She died on 14 May 1991, in all probability by her own hand.[42]

15

MODERNISING AND OPENING CHINA

The trial and conviction of the Gang of Four was a clear indication to the people of China that the Maoist era had finally come to an end, although the rhetoric of the Cultural Revolution was to persist for some years. Behind the scenes the new age of reform and modernisation had already been quietly underway for some time, although without any formal announcement. Hua Guofeng's position as chairman of the Chinese Communist Party, never a strong one, had been seriously undermined by the trial and by his closeness to the Shanghai radicals. Although he had not himself been charged with any political offences, he had clearly been implicated in their policies during the last years of Mao's life. People began to speak of a Gang of Five rather than a Gang of Four: at first this normally referred to the Four plus Hua but as time went by, when people referred to the Gang of Five they meant the Four plus Mao as Mao's role in the ultra-leftism of the 1960s and 1970s was revealed and reassessed. Hua had been a proxy for Mao but it gradually became possible to criticise Mao directly.

Return of Deng Xiaoping

With hindsight, the re-emergence of Deng Xiaoping should not have been a surprise but it was by no means a foregone conclusion: during the attacks on the Gang of Four, Deng had also been severely criticised in the press as Hua Guofeng fought to maintain his position. Hua had given his approval to the publication of an editorial that was printed simultaneously in the authoritative newspapers *People's Daily* and *Liberation Army Daily* and the Party's theoretical journal *Red Flag* on 7 February 1977 and called on the Party to defend 'whatever policy decisions Chairman Mao made' and follow 'whatever instructions Chairman Mao gave'. These slogans became known as the 'two whatevers' (as with so many political catchphrases this sounds less inelegant and ridiculous in Chinese than it does in the English translation) and were used to justify Hua Guofeng's takeover of Chairman Mao's mantle.

At a working conference of the Central Committee that occupied the Party leadership between 10 March and 22 March 1977, respected elder statesmen of the CCP, including Chen Yun and Wang Zhen, called for the reinstatement of Deng Xiaoping but Hua insisted that they should carry on condemning him. One popular story that was much repeated at the time told of Deng being recognised while eating out in a Beijing restaurant at the time of the Central Committee meeting and being applauded by some of his fellow diners. He is reported to have clapped them in return, in the traditional Chinese response, but to have told them: 'Carry on criticising Deng' [*jixu ping Deng*]. Deng wrote to the Central Committee on 10 April criticising the 'two whatevers': his argument was accepted by the Central Committee and his letter copied to all branches of the Party. This marked the beginning of Deng's second political resurrection and a change of tone, and eventually of policy, within the CCP. However it was not until the third plenary session of the Tenth Central Committee which met in Beijing from 16 to 21 July 1977 that Deng's reinstatement was publicly acknowledged: even then Hua Guofeng was once gain confirmed as chairman of the CCP and Deng had to argue his case on the basis of the need for a deeper study of Mao Zedong Thought. This position was reiterated at the conclusion of the Eleventh National Congress of the CCP on 19 August when Deng was nominated as a vice-chairman of the Party.

Third Plenum and Reform

Hua Guofeng continued to act as chairman of the Party and made several official visits abroad but it gradually became clear that his position was almost entirely ceremonial and that he was being retained purely as a concession to the ultra-leftists in the Party and the memory of Chairman Mao. At the third plenary session of the Eleventh Central Committee which occupied the most powerful people in China from 18 to 22 December 1978, although the rhetoric remained firmly Maoist, the real agenda was the introduction of a reformist programme. The main topic of discussion was the urgent need for China to embark on the path of modernisation, or socialist modernisation as it was put to the meeting. Many in the Party argued that this was not a radical departure but a return to the correct policies from which China had strayed in 1958 under Mao's leadership. The key issues discussed by the Central Committee were how to correct imbalances in the economy and reform the over-centralised economic management of the country; the development of economic cooperation with the advanced economies of the world; improvement in science and education to support modernisation and, last but not least, the reform of the agricultural economy. This was the beginning of the policy shift that was initially simplified into the slogans of 'four modernisations' [*sige xiandaihua*] and later 'reform and opening' [*gaige kaifang*]. This historic meeting is often referred to simply as the Third Plenum and it was a political triumph for Deng Xiaoping and for his key ally, the veteran economic planner Chen Yun. Some information has emerged about the horse trading and battles that took place during the Third Plenum, but the full story of how Deng and Chen succeeded in driving through their dream of a modern China has not yet been told.[1]

The Third Plenum also sought to redress serious past injustices against senior party leaders including Peng Dehuai and it elected new members whose track record of pragmatism and economic rationality contrasted markedly with the radicals of the Mao era. Hu Yaobang, who was later to become a prominent reformer, was nominated secretary-general of the Party at the 25 December meeting of the Politburo. His appointment was confirmed by the fifth plenary session of the Eleventh Central Committee in February 1980 and he and Zhao Ziyang were elected to the powerful Standing Committee of the Politburo. The Central Committee also decided to adopt a resolution on the injustice done to the former State Chairman Liu Shaoqi: this was rather too late for Liu who had been hounded to death ten years previously but it was nevertheless another nail in the coffin of the Mao era.

The most radical change, and almost certainly the most difficult for the older generation of CCP leaders to accept, was the reform of agriculture. Although it had been flagged up in the December meeting of the Central Committee, the details were not revealed until 11 January 1979 when two draft policy documents were released. These were the Decision on Some Questions Concerning Acceleration of Agricultural Development and the Regulations on the Work of Rural People's Communes. The bland and obfuscatory titles of these two documents concealed a decision to launch a revolution (or depending on one's point of view, a counter-revolution) in China's countryside. Hidden among 25 policy measures to speed up agricultural production and modernise agriculture was the proposal to introduce the 'responsibility system' [*zeren zhi*]. Behind this previously little-known policy lay the complete dismantling of the system of People's Communes and the return of collectivised land to farming families. The 'responsibility system' was not entirely new and a version of the policy had existed during the period when cooperatives were decentralised in the early 1960s, but in 1979 it became the key policy for bringing the commune system to an end. It was not spelled out as bluntly as this but that was the effect. On the same day that these documents were issued, the Central Committee decided that the categories of landlord and rich peasant should be formally abolished.

The lives of people in the countryside who had carried these labels had been blighted for decades.

The dominant theme of the late 1970s and early 1980s was the restructuring and modernisation of the Chinese economy, both agricultural and industrial. However the Party also realised that it could not simply abandon the legacy of the Mao years without a great deal of political groundwork and there was much discussion of the role of Mao and his mistakes. In the short term, the CCP resolved the dilemmas involved in dealing with the legacy of Mao by accepting that the great man had made mistakes, some of them extraordinarily serious, and mainly since 1958. As with so much in Chinese political life, this was to become simplified into the slogan that Mao had been 70 per cent good and 30 per cent bad. Even this was too much for some cynics who would hold up three fingers when saying 70 per cent and seven when saying 30 per cent. The Party, however, continued to emphasise the importance of Mao Zedong Thought as the guiding principle of the Chinese state. Perhaps the most damning indictment of the Mao years was that Deng Xiaoping, the man who succeeded him as the internationally acknowledged leader of China, refused to take the title of Chairman.[2]

When the Politburo of the CCP met in November and December of 1980, after the arrest of the Gang of Four and at the beginning of their trial, the spotlight fell on Hua Guofeng. The link between Hua and the Gang of Four during the Cultural Revolution was now made explicit and he was accused of having attempted to create a new personality cult. Unlike the Four, Hua was not charged with any offences against the state and was allowed to resign. Hu Yaobang became chairman of the Central Committee and Deng Xiaoping took the powerful post of chairman of the Central Military Commission, which ensured that he was in overall political control of the People's Liberation Army.

During 1981 and 1982, the reformers consolidated their dominance over the Party throughout the provinces. New cadres were recruited, Communist Party members who had been involved in the worst factional disputes during the Cultural Revolution were excluded and many older cadres were persuaded to retire. By 1986 as many as 1.8 million older cadres had retired and 150,000 had been expelled from the Party for various infractions. The Party was being rejuvenated and the new younger cadres were on the whole far better educated than their predecessors.[3] In spite of this commitment to change and renewal, there was no question of the Chinese Communist Party relinquishing its hold on power or of the introduction of any political reforms which might allow that possibility. Deng's policies were intended to strengthen the Party and to make it more capable of retaining its leading position in Chinese society.

On 12 September 1981, *People's Daily* carried a report on an experiment to hold direct elections to people's congresses at the county level that had begun in the second half of 1979. This was hailed as a breakthrough in grassroots democracy. It was indeed a new departure and it extended the pool of suitable candidates but it was not the beginning of an open Western-style electoral system because the nomination process was entirely under the control of the CCP. These new style elections were further encouraged by the Organic Law on Village Committees which was passed by a meeting of the Standing Committee of the National People's Congress held in Beijing from 12 to 24 November 1987 and came into force during 1988.

International Relations in the Reform Period

In 1978, the developments that had begun with the visit of Richard Nixon in 1972 began to come to fruition. China's foreign policies were transformed as it prioritised its domestic economic development and looked to ways in which its international relations could support the much needed expansion of the economy. The Sino-Japanese Treaty of Peace and Friendship, which was signed in Beijing on 12 August 1978 and ratified later that year during Deng Xiaoping's visit to Tokyo from 22 to 29 October, was the most important example of this because technology transfer and capital investment from Japan were to play a critical role in the economic modernisation of China. Since Japan was China's near neighbour and shared many cultural assumptions, its contribution was more valuable, at least in the early stages, than that of the more distant Western nations. The treaty, which ended a period of 33 years in which there had been no officially acknowledged contact between China and Japan, went some way to repairing the damage to Sino-Japanese diplomatic relations that had been caused by Japan's wartime occupation of China. It was the essential precursor to the establishment of economic relations.

China and the USA also agreed to establish normal diplomatic relations from 1 January 1979. A joint communiqué issued on 16 December 1978 by the governments of the two countries announced that ambassadors would be exchanged with effect from 1 March 1979. One of the main reasons for the delay in establishing relations after the Nixon visit had been the intractable problem of Taiwan. The USA had been compelled to accept that Beijing was now the de facto government of China, whether it liked it or not, but it still had loyalties and existing ties to Taiwan that had to be taken into consideration (not to mention the powerful Taiwan lobby in the USA). In the negotiations that led to the joint communiqué, China accepted, but could not acknowledge, that informal relations between Taiwan and the USA would have to continue.

Not all of China's international initiatives were so peaceful. On 17 February 1979, China went to war with Vietnam, its small neighbour and erstwhile Communist ally. China and Vietnam had been at odds for some years over Vietnam's presence in Cambodia. Prince Norodom (later King) Sihanouk, the Cambodian head of state who was close to Beijing, was deposed in 1970 while he was on holiday in Paris and his Prime Minister Lon Nol was compelled to support what was essentially a Vietnam-backed coup d'etat at gunpoint. Sihanouk attempted to lead a coalition of Cambodian and Vietnamese communists but an autonomous and uncompromising Cambodian guerrilla organisation had been developing in the isolated rural areas. These guerrillas, the Khmer Rouge, were not only vehement opponents of what they considered to be Sihanouk's corrupt regime, they were also bitterly opposed to Vietnam's attempt to control their liberation struggle. On 17 April 1975, two weeks before the end of the Vietnam War, young guerrillas of the Khmer Rouge had marched into the Cambodian capital, Phnom Penh, and established a brutal and secretive regime, Democratic Kampuchea, which resulted in the deaths of 2 million of its citizens, the flight into exile of hundreds of thousands of Cambodians and the depopulation of the major cities.[4] This nightmare came to an end only when, on 16 December 1978, Vietnam took control of Cambodia by establishing a National United Front which it controlled. Vietnamese forces moved into Cambodia from 25 December 1978 and took control of Phnom Penh on 7 January 1979. On that day, China denounced Vietnam's 'war of aggression' against Cambodia. Ten days later, on 17 January, Chinese troops moved into Vietnam claiming that China's security had been threatened at Vietnam's borders with Guangxi and Yunnan provinces. PLA troops remained in Vietnam until 16 March and negotiations to avoid further conflict between the two sides dragged on for several months in Beijing.

The Vietnam War had been the greatest symbol of American imperialism in Asia, and in the 1960s and 1970s China had issued many statements of support for the national liberation struggle of the Vietnamese people. These professions of assistance and cooperation were complicated by the fact that Vietnam had been politically far closer to the Soviet Union than China in the dispute that had split the Communist bloc and also by China's historic claims over at least the northern part of Vietnam. In the dispute between Vietnam and Cambodia, the Soviet Union supported Vietnam's invasion of Cambodia; China sided with the Cambodians at the urging of Prince Sihanouk who was in exile in Beijing even though the Khmer Rouge were not supporters of his government. Pragmatic regional power politics and concern for border security had completely replaced ideological considerations in China's international relations.[5]

Open Door and Democracy Movement

Among the educated population of China, there was considerable dissatis-
faction at the fact that economic reform was being promoted but not political reform. In November 1978 wall posters after the fashion of those put
up by Red Guards during the Cultural Revolution and the 1976 Tian'anmen
incident began to appear on Xidan Street, a major thoroughfare in central
Beijing. The wall on which they were pasted became known as Democracy
Wall; it was after a similar wall that had been a focus for dissent during the
Hundred Flowers period of 1956. The posters that were displayed included
attacks on the memory of Mao Zedong, including critiques that accused
him, with some justification, of having been part of the Gang of Four;
political poems; and the writings of diverse dissidents, including Wei Jingsheng whose celebrated demand that the four modernisations needed a
fifth – democracy – earned him a 15-year prison sentence.

During the 1980s and 1990s, China experienced a process of rapid economic development. New industries developed, towns and cities expanded
and there was a great migration from the rural areas to the cities and particularly to the cities of the south and southeast which were the initial focus
of the government's economic development plans.[6] This economic miracle
was accompanied by social and political confusion. Old certainties and old
value systems began to seem irrelevant and there was uncertainty at all
levels of society as to how China should deal with what were seen as
strange and alien values that were coming from the West and from Japan.

Once again it was the actions of Japan rather than the West that provoked a response from the Chinese population. Japan, by virtue of its
geographical proximity and its economic success, had led the way in international investment in China's economic reform programme. Although the
investment was welcomed by the government, there was considerable
popular resentment at the Japanese presence in China: some claimed that
the nation that had attempted to control China by military means in the
1930s and 1940s was now trying to do that same in the 1980s by deploying
its economic power. In September 1985 students began a series of protests
against what they argued was Japan's new economic aggression. The demonstrators were also highly critical of the Chinese government's craven attitude to the former aggressors, mirroring complaints made by their predecessors in the response to Japan's Twenty-One Demands of 1915. The
1985 demonstrations were timed to coincide with the fifty-fourth anniversary
of the Japanese invasion of Manchuria on 18 September 1931. Although
Japanese investment was the catalyst for the campaign, the protestors also
complained vociferously about a number of purely domestic issues that had
been causing concern for some years, including inflation which China had
not experienced since the currency stabilisation of the 1950s and, in par-

ticular, price rises in basic foodstuffs and other goods. The protestors also publicised longstanding and deeply felt concerns about corruption within the Party and the government. These criticisms had been circulating informally for many years but this was the first time that they had been aired openly. The issue that caused greatest anger was the rise of nepotism as jobs in the growing and lucrative modern economic sector were given to the sons and daughters of senior officials [*gaogan zidi*]. Major demonstrations were planned by students at the prestigious Beijing and Tsinghua (Qinghua) Universities in December 1985 but the government intervened to prevent them. Although the demonstrations were suppressed, the anger at official corruption did not die down. Further protests were planned in 15 major Chinese cities for December 1986 and by this time the demands of the demonstrators had gone beyond the immediate issue of corruption and had become more general political protests, with calls for free speech, freedom of assembly and of the press and genuine democratic elections.

The first demonstration of 1986 took place at the Chinese University of Science and Technology in Hefei, the capital city of Anhui province. The university had been optimistically planned as a Chinese rival to the Massachusetts Institute of Technology and was attracting some of China's leading academics, including the astrophysicist, Fang Lizhi. Fang called for the government to take decisive action on political democracy to match China's progress on economic modernisation and the demonstrators demanded genuine consultation over the nomination of delegates to the National People's Congress, China's quasi-parliamentary body. A wave of demonstrations spread throughout the country. In Shanghai more than 30,000 students and at least 100,000 workers marched on the offices of the municipal government on 19 December 1986. In Beijing, 4,000 students marched to Tian'anmen Square and burned copies of *Beijing Daily*, not the national publication *People's Daily*, but the local newspaper controlled by the Beijing CCP Committee, which had criticised the demonstrations. The protests reflected not only the immediate concerns of the participants but also the long-term unease among the general population about the growth of corruption and the lack of democracy. The leadership of the CCP was deeply divided on how to deal with these demonstrations. The conservative hardliners used the only tactic of which they had any experience, or in which they genuinely believed, the mass campaign: they launched a sustained media campaign against 'bourgeois liberalisation' [*zichanjieji ziyouhua*] the code name for the more open attitudes that were spreading at the same time alongside the economic reforms. The CCP Secretary-General Hu Yaobang and his supporters were broadly sympathetic to the demonstrators and favoured a policy of leniency, but the conservative old guard, who still wielded enormous influence in the Party, won out. Under pressure from conservative hardliners, Hu Yaobang was relieved of his duties by Deng Xiaoping in January 1987, although Deng had been extremely reluctant to dismiss him.

Thirteenth Party Congress

Deng's response to this crisis came at the Thirteenth National Congress of the CCP, which met in Beijing from 25 October to 1 November 1987. It was a milestone as it was the occasion for the retirement of the older generation of political leaders who had won their spurs on the Long March and in the war and civil war of the 1940s. A total of 1,936 delegates, representing 46 million party members, attended the conference. The main item on the agenda was 'speeding up and deepening reform' The delegates reaffirmed their support for the Reform and Opening policies that Deng Xiaoping had initiated and gave a clear indication to the conservatives, who looked back with nostalgia to the Maoist days of an all-powerful centrally planned economy, that they were yesterday's men and women. To underline this change a group of Long March veterans and well-known senior party leaders agreed to take voluntary retirement and they were replaced by promising cadres of the younger generation. Those who retired included Peng Zhen, the former mayor of Beijing, who had served as chairman of the Standing Committee of the National People's Congress; the respected economist Chen Yun; Hu Qiaomu, a former editor of *People's Daily* and the official historian of the CCP; Deng Liqun who had led the campaign against bourgeois liberalisation and the president, Li Xiannian. Deng Xiaoping himself retired from all his posts to set an example but was persuaded (or persuaded himself) that he should retain the chairmanship of the Central Military Commission, the Party body that is the final political authority behind the People's Liberation Army. Li Peng, a technocrat with a background in hydraulic engineering became prime minister, replacing Zhao Ziyang who took over as CCP general secretary from Hu Yaobang.

In spite of the atmosphere of reform and the radical personnel changes that were taking place, it was still considered essential to cast set political changes within a Marxist theoretical framework and to justify the need for market reforms in terms of China's eventual progress towards communism. This had been the subject of Zhao Ziyang's report, 'Advance along the Road of Socialism with Chinese Characteristics'. Zhao, the former prime minister who had become secretary-general of the CCP on 16 January after the resignation of Hu Yaobang, presented an outline of the changes that had taken place in China during the reform period. He argued that China was already a socialist society but that it was still in the primary stage of socialism and that a programme of reform was required for China to be able to move on to the next stage. Zhao also proposed reforming the political structure as a prerequisite for improving the efficiency of economic reform. The key element of this scheme for political reform was to be the separation of the functions of the Communist Party and the government, so that the organisations of the CCP would no longer have any day to day involvement in the operation of either the administration or economic enterprises. This was the most far-reaching reform proposal in the history of the CCP since it had come to power in 1949.

Eastern Europe and the Road to 4 June

Even before the new year of 1989 had dawned, it was clear that it was going to be a year of great political significance in China. It was after all the fortieth anniversary of the founding of the People's Republic of China and the seventieth anniversary of the May Fourth Movement of 1919, out of which the Chinese Communist Party (and indeed the nationalist Guomindang) had emerged. For historians, and particularly for Marxist historians, it was also notable as the two-hundredth anniversary of French Revolution.

Of more immediate and direct concern was the rise of dissenting and anti-communist movements in Poland, Hungary and the Baltic States and the impact of Mikhail Gorbachev's policies of *perestroika* [reconstruction] and *glasnost* [openness] on the Communist Party of the Soviet Union and its hold on power. In spite of China's acrimonious disengagement with the USSR and its allies in the 1960s, a breach which had never been repaired, China constantly looked to the USSR and particularly to Eastern Europe as a barometer for what might happen in its own society. They had of course been the model for the political structures that China had created in the 1950s and they shared a common political rhetoric. The collapse of Soviet power began in 1989. On 6 January, Moscow made it known that tens, or possibly hundreds, of thousands of Soviet citizens who had been the victims of Stalin's purges were to be rehabilitated, in many cases posthumously. On 14 February, the USSR withdrew its armies from Afghanistan where they had been fighting, and losing, a brutal war against the *mujahidin* resistance since 1979. When the first national elections in which candidates from non-Communist parties were allowed to stand were held in the Soviet Union on 26 March, the CCP suffered serious losses, particularly in the non-Russian republics. There were demonstrations in the Republic of Georgia, Stalin's home state in the Caucasus, on 9 April demanding independence and strikes by thousands of miners in the coalfields of the USSR began in early July.

In Hungary, legislation permitting the establishment of new independent political parties was approved by parliament on 11 January and a report 'reversed the verdict', to use the popular Chinese phrase, on the rising of 1956. When elections were held on 28 March, there was a widespread vote against the Hungarian Workers' (Communist) Party and in favour of a pro-European reform bloc. After strikes and protests in Poland, the mass organisation Solidarity, with its base in the trades unions and the Roman Catholic laity, was legalised on 21 April and in Czechoslovakia the government agreed to multiparty elections. When changes of this magnitude had been proposed in the 1950s and 1960s, the Soviet Union had reacted by suppressing dissent with overwhelming military force but in 1989 Gorbachev signed an agreement with the West German Chancellor Helmut Kohl under which the USSR agreed not to act against changes in Eastern European countries. Hungary abolished border controls with Austria, which permitted and even encouraged many to leave the country for the first time, but the Berlin Wall, a symbolic as well as a concrete barrier, remained so that East Germans who wished to leave the country had to flee to the West via Hungary en route to Austria. There was political turmoil in the Baltic states and in Moldavia and in August Ukrainians demonstrated in favour of independence. Yugoslavia began to collapse, eventually with tragic consequences, especially for Bosnia. East Germany had been the most obdurate in holding out against reform but after demonstrations in Dresden on 6 October and Berlin on 4 November, the anti-government movement spread across the nation with perhaps 750,000 people marching. The East German government resigned on 7 November and on 9 November the Socialist Unity Party (the East German Communist Party) announced that its borders would be opened. The following day large sections of the Berlin Wall were dismantled by East Berliners who clambered over the rubble to join their fellow Germans in the West. Gorbachev had been unable to keep Eastern Europe within the Soviet fold and now his attention turned to keeping what remained of the USSR together.[7]

The collapse of Soviet power was viewed with mounting alarm by the authorities in Beijing, who were determined not to make the same type of mistake for which they considered Gorbachev responsible. If the unthinkable could happen and the Soviet Union could collapse, the continued existence of the People's Republic of China could certainly not be taken for granted. On the contrary, the demands for democracy that were being raised in the former Soviet bloc were welcomed by many in China, in particular by students and young intellectuals.

Democracy Movement

The nationwide upsurge of student demonstrations that had galvanised many young Chinese in 1986 had abated after the dismissal of Hu Yaobang but the mood for reform remained buoyant, and political discussion groups and salons continued to debate the thorny question of how to add political reform to the agenda of the CCP which was almost completely preoccupied with economic modernisation. On 6 January 1989, the distinguished astrophysicist and political activist Fang Lizhi sent an open letter to Deng Xiaoping asking for an amnesty for all China's political prisoners and in particular raising the case of Wei Jingsheng who had been sentenced to 15 years in prison in 1979 at the end of the Democracy Wall period, ostensibly for communicating state secrets to a foreigner: it was Wei's demand that Deng add a fifth modernisation – democracy – to the four that he was promoting that really infuriated the leadership. As a result of his letter and the threat that the CCP believed he posed, Fang Lizhi was prevented from attending a reception organised by President George Bush in Beijing to which he had been invited. The open letter generated a movement to petition the government in support of Fang's demands and this found a ready audience in the nation's student body. Fang subsequently went into exile in the USA.

Hu Yaobang, the dismissed secretary-general, died on 15 April 1989. He died from natural causes but there were persistent rumours that the heart attack that was the cause of his death had occurred while he was arguing the case for reform with members of the Politburo. The following day, more than 300 students from Beijing University marched to Tian'anmen Square to pay tribute to him and by 20 April thousands of students had gathered outside the CCP headquarters in Zhongnanhai which lies to the west of the square, demanding an audience with the prime minister, Li Peng. Police were deployed to disperse the demonstrators and several students were injured. The fact that there were now martyrs, albeit still alive, gave the movement added impetus. An independent organisation of Beijing University students had been established on 18 April and two days later the first all-Beijing autonomous student federation was created. The demonstrators were fragmented and many disparate groups emerged, all with their own leaders and their own agendas. When one group began a hunger strike this became the focus of attention and the hunger strikers acquired great moral authority. Groups of Beijing residents began to join what had been at first almost exclusively a student demonstration. These included employees of a range of diverse organisations, including journalists and academics, especially those who were connected with think tanks sympathetic to the reformers within the CCP. Towards the middle of May, the movement became more specific and focused on demands for the dismissal of Li Peng and Deng Xiaoping who were by now identified as the main obstacles to political reform. To the elderly CCP leadership, almost under siege in Zhongnanhai, it must have looked as if a mass organisation similar to the Polish Solidarity union were building up to overthrow them. The scale of

the demonstrations escalated and by mid-May as many as a million participants, students and Beijing residents were involved.

During the reform period an unusual newspaper, the *World Economic
Herald* [*Shijie jingji daobao*], had made its appearance in Shanghai. It was independent, a solid supporter of reform and close to Zhao Ziyang. The dramatic and disturbing collapse of Soviet power had been covered in great
detail in its pages. The *World Economic Herald* had been responsible, together
with other bodies, for organising a meeting to commemorate the life and
career of Hu Yaobang and was planning to print the speeches made on that
occasion in its issue of 24 April. However, Jiang Zemin, who was at that
time the secretary of the Communist Party in Shanghai but was later to
become the national leader, took the view that this would be too inflam-
matory and ordered the paper to be closed down. Zhao Ziyang, the General secretary of the CCP, had been out of the country on a visit to North
Korea and when he returned on 10 May the situation was spiralling out
of control.[8]

The crisis came to a head with the visit on 15 May of the president of
the USSR, Mikhail Gorbachev, himself a vigorous advocate of the reform
of the communist system. His visit had been planned long before the
political turbulence and was the first visit of a Soviet head of state to China
since 1959. His mission was intended to heal the longstanding breach between the two Communist states but it turned into an embarrassing fiasco
when his motorcade was unable to reach the Great Hall of the People,
which is on the west side of Tian'anmen Square, and the official reception
had to be held at the Capital Airport a long way outside Beijing. Gorbachev
met Deng Xiaoping, Li Peng and other senior Chinese leaders and the two
governments issued a communiqué proclaiming the resumption of normal
diplomatic relations, but what should have been the announcement of a
triumphant diplomatic breakthrough was completely overshadowed by the
turmoil on the streets of Beijing.

Bitter arguments on how to resolve the crisis divided the Politburo with
Zhao Ziyang arguing strongly for the need to achieve a peaceful resolution.
He lost the argument on 19 May and, like Hu Yaobang before him, was dismissed from his post of general secretary of the CCP. On 20 May, Li Peng,
the premier of the State Council (prime minister) issued an Order of the
State Council declaring martial law in Beijing with effect from ten o'clock
that morning. The mayor of Beijing, Chen Xitong, then signed Orders 1, 2
and 3 of the Beijing Municipal People's Government specifying the districts
of the capital in which martial law applied. Units of the PLA moved into
Beijing, declaring that they were there to restore and maintain public order
but that they had not been deployed to suppress the student demonstrations. The Communist Party had been divided into two factions with Zhao

Ziyang and Li Peng on opposite sides. With Zhao's removal from office, the rift was resolved and the CCP could act with one voice, that of Li Peng. This only strengthened the resolve of the demonstrators who intensified their demands for the resignation of the hardliners. When the demonstrators erected a statue, which they called the Goddess of Democracy, in Tian'anmen Square on 30 May, it was like a red rag to a bull. The sculpture was unmistakably an imaginative if unsophisticated blend of the American Statue of Liberty and the traditional Chinese Buddhist deity, Guan Yin, the goddess of mercy.

During the night of 3–4 June, the PLA moved in to clear Tian'anmen Square of all demonstrators. A Radio Beijing announcer reporting the onslaught in the English language service exhorted his listeners to remember 3 June but it was in the early hours of the morning of 4 June that the military assault began. At about four o'clock, the troops advanced from west to east down Chang'an Boulevard towards the square, dispersing demonstrators at Muxidi, which lies a little to the west of the CCP headquarters, with great loss of life and moving through the Tian'anmen Square southwards to the great gate of Qianmen. The tents of the demonstrators were crushed by tanks and many were killed and injured in the offensive. Official figures put out later by the Chinese government claimed that 200 civilians had been killed, including 36 students, and that more than 3,000 had been injured. Independent sources have estimated the numbers to be far higher than this. It is probably true that there were relatively few deaths in Tian'anmen Square itself and that the greatest number of casualties were outside the centre of the protests, at Muxidi and Qianmen. Similar demonstrations took place across China, with major protests erupting in the cities of Shanghai, Guangzhou, Wuhan, Chengdu, Guiyang, Harbin and Lanzhou. Relatives of the dead and injured continue to campaign for justice for the victims of the military suppression of what has become known as the 4 June Democracy Movement.[9]

The formal removal of Zhao Ziyang from his post of general secretary and from the Politburo and its Standing Committee was announced at the Fourth Plenary Meeting of the Thirteenth Central Committee which convened in Beijing from 23 to 24 June. Li Peng introduced a Report on Comrade Zhao Ziyang's mistakes in the Anti-Party, Anti-Socialism Turmoil which severely criticised the former secretary-general for taking the side of the demonstrators and splitting the CCP. Zhao was not allowed to defend himself and this was the end of his political career. He spent the next 15 years under house arrest, in increasingly poor health and was hospitalised on 11 January 2005 after having suffered heart and respiratory problems. He died on 17 January at the age of 85 and his funeral took place on 29 January at the Babaoshan cemetery, the last resting place for China's revolutionary martyrs and other major political figures. It had been delayed because of disagreements between his family and political supporters who thought that a state funeral was the only proper farewell for a man who had held such senior political office. In the end it was a low-key affair heavily guarded by police and security officials who feared that it might become a focus for demonstrations by dissidents. Zhao Ziyang's successor as secretary-general of the CCP was Jiang Zemin who had been the head of the Party in Shanghai and who had suppressed the liberal newspaper the *World Economic Herald*. Jiang was appointed president in 1993.

16

TIBET AND XINJIANG

Tibet and Xinjiang are today both administered by the People's Republic of China and are part of the vast and underdeveloped western region of the country. Both also have long-standing and controversial claims to independence which are vehemently and consistently disputed by Beijing. Although they are neighbours, geographical boundaries and religious and cultural differences have restricted the contact between them and their histories are very separate. Tibet experienced an uprising against the PRC in 1959. Parts of Xinjiang had independent governments on two separate occasions before 1949 but the movement for independence remained dormant until the 1990s.[1]

Tibet

After the collapse of Tibetan resistance to the armies of the CCP in 1959, the Dalai Lama retreated to Dharamsala, a hill station in the northern Indian state of Himachal Pradesh. The Dalai Lama and his senior religious and political officials remained in exile in Dharamsala, depriving Tibet of its traditional religious and secular leadership.[2] The prime minister of India, Jawaharlal Nehru, formally invited the Dalai Lama to establish his government in exile in Dharamsala, an area that although predominantly Hindu also had a tradition of Tibetan Buddhism that can be traced back to the eighth century. Dharamsala, and especially the part of Upper Dharamsala that is known as McLeod Ganj, is home to a large community of Tibetans in exile. Its name hints at its history as a nineteenth century hill station of the British Raj, popular as a summer escape for expatriate members of the civil service working in Delhi.

Tibet was designated an autonomous region of the PRC on 9 September 1965. This status which was also accorded to Xinjiang, Inner Mongolia and Ningxia was a concession to the non-Han population of the region but it did not confer genuine autonomy: Beijing attempted to include ethnic Tibetans in the local government but overall control was always vested in the Chinese Communist Party backed by the People's Liberation Army. During the Cultural Revolution, which began in 1966, there were determined attacks on Tibetan Buddhism and its material culture that built on a repression that had begun during the suppression of the 1959 rising. Red Guards, many of them ethnic Tibetans, participated in assaults on monasteries to demonstrate their loyalty to Chairman Mao. As well as physical damage to monasteries, shrines and other manifestations of Buddhist culture, there were organised campaigns against religious practices, and monks and nuns were condemned and ridiculed by Red Guards. The authority for this movement was Mao's instruction to the Red Guards to destroy the Four Olds: 'old customs, old habits, old culture and old thinking'. In Tibet, 'old' was considered to be synonymous with Tibetan, whereas Chinese styles and methods were identified as new, modern and progressive. Even at this early stage the transformation of Tibet under the CCP looked uncomfortably like a campaign directed by predominantly Han Chinese politicians against Tibetan culture.[3]

Hu Yaobang and 1987–9 Demonstrations

The death of Mao Zedong in September 1976 led to a period of relative liberalisation throughout the PRC and in the mid-1980s, influenced by CCP secretary-general Hu Yaobang (whose premature death in 1989 had precipitated the Democracy movement and the demonstrations in Tian'anmen Square), there had been an increase in the number of Tibetans participating in local government in Tibet: the repression of Tibetan Buddhism was relaxed and the status of the Tibetan language and local culture was also enhanced in government and education.[4] Hu Yaobang visited Tibet in 1980 on the twenty-ninth anniversary of the Seventeen-Point Agreement that had been signed under duress in 1951 and was openly critical of the condescending and, in many cases, frankly racist policies and attitudes of Han Chinese cadres towards Tibetan officials and the populace in general.[5]

Partly because of the more relaxed atmosphere in Tibet and partly in response to a major international diplomatic initiative by Dharamsala to try to procure a definitive settlement to the Tibet question, a wave of demonstrations began in October 1987. The demonstrations were led by monks and nuns who supported the idea of a return to an independent state of Tibet under the Dalai Lama. The first protests were by monks of Drepung monastery, which is to the west of Lhasa and is the senior monastery in the Gelugpa or Yellow Hat tradition. They carried out religious circumambulations of Lhasa and were arrested when they marched on government offices. The protests became violent after demonstrators were arrested and assaulted and police fired on the crowds killing some demonstrators. Demonstrations continued in response to this new wave of repression and were once again led by monks and nuns, whose courage and fortitude in the face of brutality by the armed police was recognised internationally. A further serious disturbance broke out in March 1988 after the Panchen Lama had visited Tibet in an attempt to ensure the success of the Great Prayer Festival that is traditionally held during celebrations of the Tibetan New Year. Many monks felt that their festival had been hijacked by the CCP and what had started as a minor contretemps exploded into riots that were followed by mass arrests and a political and religious clampdown.

Protests continued in the spring of 1989 but later that year, after the fourth major disturbance in Lhasa, the Chinese authorities appeared to lose patience and decided to declare martial law. Units of the People's Armed Police were deployed in Lhasa and elsewhere in Tibet and used their expertise in riot control to considerable effect. The policies of the Hu Yaobang period were reversed in a decision that was taken by the Politburo in the winter of 1989 and a new tough and repressive regime was imposed on Tibet. The regional secretary-general of the CCP in Tibet at this time was Hu Jintao, later to become China's president. In the teeth of this repression, a nationalist Tibetan Buddhist movement had coalesced: it had been stimulated by support for the leadership of the Dalai Lama in Dharamsala, but was isolated from it and acted independently.[6]

Panchen Lama

The unexpected death of the Tenth Panchen Lama in January 1989 and the search for his reincarnation, who would become the Eleventh, precipitated another crisis. The Panchen Lama is second only to the Dalai Lama in the Tibetan spiritual hierarchy and some Buddhists in Tibet even place his spiritual authority ahead of that of the Dalai Lama: in the twentieth century, successive Panchen Lamas have generally been closer to governments in Beijing than any other high lamas, and this has resulted in divisions and disagreements over spiritual and political precedence. Beijing tried to take control of the selection process but the choice of a new Panchen incarnation also required the confirmation of the Dalai Lama. The Dalai Lama announced the name of his candidate, Gedhun Choeki Nyima, on 14 May 1995 but in November Beijing endorsed a different contender, Gyaltsen Norbu, and the whole process ended in complete disarray.[7] Conflict between the Tibetan religious leadership and Beijing over the succession to the Panchen Lama was highlighted when the Abbot of Kumbun monastery in the province of Qinghai, part of old Tibet, was formally expelled from the Chinese People's Consultative Conference in June 2000 after he had left China for the USA in 1998. Agyo Lobsangtubdain Gyurma had been a member of the committee established by the Chinese that was entrusted with locating the reincarnation of the Panchen Lama but he spoke out in support of the Dalai Lama and rejected the Chinese choice of Gyaltsen Norbu.[8] The Dalai Lama gave an interview to the journal *Asiaweek* in October 2000, in which he reflected on the effect that his eventual demise would have on the Tibetan people. He said, 'If I passed away, the re-incarnation would logically come outside Tibet, in a free country. But China will choose a boy as the next Dalai Lama, though in reality he is not.' He added that Tibetans would reject the Panchen Lama nominated by Beijing.[9] Reports of ill-treatment and brutality continued to come out of Tibet, and monks and nuns, the standard-bearers of Tibetan national and religious identity, were frequently the primary targets. Five nuns, arrested after dem-onstrations in May 1998, were interrogated in Drapchi prison and beaten with belts and electric batons after calling out Tibetan nationalist slogans when ordered to sing Chinese patriotic songs. They committed suicide.[10]

A young lama, virtually unknown outside the Tibetan community, left Tibet in December 1999 to join the Dalai Lama in Dharamsala. The Seventeenth Karmapa Lama, who was 14 years old at the time, left the Tsurphu monas-tery which is located to the northeast of Lhasa having declared that he was going to travel outside Tibet so that he could buy musical instruments and the black hats that had traditionally been worn by previous incarnations of the Karmapa. Unusually the Karmapa Lama, Ugyen Trinley Dorge, the son of nomads, had been recognised by both Beijing and the Dalai Lama as a reincarnation of the previous head of the Kagyu sect in 1992.[11] The flight of the Karmapa Lama embarrassed the authorities and was followed by a crackdown on monasteries in Tibet. Thirty monks were expelled from the Jokhang temple in Lhasa in June 2000, and the government threatened reprisals against anyone who took part in pilgrimages to monasteries during the festival of Sagadawa, the festival of the illumination of Buddha, which takes place on the fifteenth day of the fourth month in the Tibetan calen-dar. Children were told they would be expelled from school, officials that they would be dismissed from their posts and pensioners that their pen-sions would be stopped. There were also reports of houses being raided and the seizure of religious objects and photographs of the Dalai Lama. Members of the CCP and teachers who had photographs of the Dalai Lama in their possession were fined.[12]

In September 2000, the Tibetan government in exile published a report on China's policy in Tibet in which it claimed that Beijing was aiming at the 'total destruction' of Tibetan culture. The report also argued that the Dalai Lama had moderated the more extreme elements of Tibetan nationalism and that China's refusal to have any contact with him could lead to further violent expressions of dissent.[13]

Qinghai–Tibet Railway

Tibet's isolation has been a decisive factor in the development of its distinctive culture, in both earlier and modern times. The construction of a new railway link between China Proper and Tibet, the Qing–Zang railway, was a major project by Beijing to bring Tibet closer to China. The line which links Xining, the capital city of Qinghai province, with the Tibetan capital Lhasa was regarded as an indispensable infrastructural project, without which the economic development of Tibet and its integration into China could not be guaranteed. Construction of the key final stage from Golmud to Lhasa began in 2001 and was complete by the autumn of 2005. The formal opening ceremony took place on 1 July 2006 after months of testing of both track and rolling stock in the difficult mountainous conditions. Services using this line include long distance trains which run to Lhasa from Beijing, Chengdu, Chongqing, Xining and Lanzhou.[14]

Critics of the railway have argued that, far from improving the lives of Tibetans, the new rail link would simply serve to strengthen China's control over Tibet. There were also concerns that it would encourage the migration of young Tibetans away from their homeland in search of employment and the migration to Tibet of Han Chinese from the east who would obtain preferential treatment in employment opportunities. Nevertheless, the opening ceremony was turned into a high-profile event by the Chinese government, and the railway became a symbol for the entire economic and political relationship between Beijing and Tibet.

Xinjiang – Eastern Turkestan

The history of Tibet's neighbours to the north, the Muslims of Xinjiang, and their own nationalist struggle against Chinese control are less well known. The network of mosques across Xinjiang provides the framework for a complex system of worship, education and law that dominated the region before it came under the control of the Chinese Communist Party but has been considerably depleted since 1949. It is difficult to obtain credible statistics on the total number of mosques but one estimate has suggested that in 1949 there were 29,545 mosques in the whole of Xinjiang. By the start of the Cultural Revolution in 1966 this had been reduced to 14,119: many had fallen into disrepair, some had been requisitioned by the government and others had been demolished or closed down during anti-religious and land reform campaigns. During the chaos of the Cultural Revolution in the 1960s there were said to be only 1,400 active mosques, but by 1990 the number had risen again to more than 17,000 and there were more than 43,000 other 'places of religious activity', which must have included Sufi shrines and *madrasas* (religious schools).[15]

Although mosques in Xinjiang are found in villages, towns and cities, the *mazar* tombs of the Sufi sheikhs and the religious complexes that have grown up around them are usually in isolated settings.[16] These tombs are the bases of the Sufi orders, predominantly the Jahriyya and Khufiyya branches of the Naqshbandiyya. Members of the orders make pilgrimages to the tombs on the anniversary of the death of the founding *sheikh* and on major religious festivals. These pilgrimages have on occasion attracted crowds of such a size that the authorities have banned or restricted them. The *mazar* culture is viewed by the Chinese state as a serious threat to its authority and has been the subject of frequent repression by the authorities: it has also been attacked by conservative Muslims and by Islamic reformers influenced directly or indirectly by austere teachings that originated in Saudi Arabia and are usually characterised as Wahhabism.

As with the extent of the mosques, it is impossible to estimate with any confidence how many active *mazars* there are in Xinjiang, but a serious and authoritative study by an Uyghur scholar lists 73 major sites.[17] Because of the unpopularity of government regulation of mosques, this parallel Islam is becoming more popular. The fact that these Sufi orders are part of a transnational Islamic movement (in particular the highly political Naqshbandiyya) is also attractive to the isolated Turkic-speaking Muslim Uyghurs of Xinjiang but troubles the Chinese authorities.[18]

Turkic-Islamic Republic of Eastern Turkestan

Yang Zengxin became governor of Xinjiang in 1911 and ruled until his assassination in 1928. In many ways he maintained the status quo in the region, retaining for all practical purposes the framework of civil administration that had been employed by the Qing Imperial Court to govern its most distant subjects. He kept the region tightly under control, partly by isolating it from the political factionalism of the republican politicians in China Proper but also kept open a weather eye for Russian and later Soviet interference and influence. In Owen Lattimore's words, he was 'an experienced official of the civil service, who flew the flag of the Republic but ruled the province for himself until his assassination in 1928'.[19] His successor Jin Shuren had none of the power or authority that Yang had wielded: under his administration there was a marked increase in tensions between the Chinese administration and the native Uyghur leaders with whom Chinese officials had to negotiate.

In the 1930s, Uyghurs and other Turkic peoples throughout Xinjiang, influenced to some degree by pan-Islamic and pan-Turkic sentiments, rose against Chinese control and the Turkic-Islamic Republic of Eastern Turkestan was proclaimed in Khotan on 12 November 1933. Its policies were based on an Islamic identity but with the addition of modern educational, economic and social reforms. It also strove to remain outside the control of the Soviet Union which was eager to influence the politics of its neighbour Xinjiang. The republic lasted only until 6 February 1934 when the major city of southern Xinjiang, Kashghar, was taken by the forces of the Hui or Dungan warlord Ma Zhongying as part of his own strategic campaigns against the new Governor Sheng Shicai. The republic had been in many ways the direct descendant of the regime of Yakub Beg that had controlled the Kashghar region between 1867 and 1877 and this continuity of an Islamic political tradition is important to Uyghur nationalists today. In its short life, the republic had created the framework of an independent state with a cabinet, a national assembly and a constitution. It issued its own currency and had its own flag, which consisted of a white star and crescent on a light blue, or turquoise, background. The flag and banknotes, together with those of the later East Turkestan Republic of 1944–9, are revered by contemporary supporters of Xinjiang independence as symbols of a once and future state.

Sheng Shicai and the Three Districts Revolution

Jin Shuren was ousted in a *coup d'état* and replaced as governor by Sheng Shicai, a native of northeastern China who had fought alongside Chiang Kai-shek during the Northern Expedition. Sheng had arrived at an accommodation with the Soviet authorities with whom he was to cooperate until 1942, and they decided to intervene on his side against the Hui forces of Ma Zhongying. Ma was forced to retreat to southern Xinjiang, and eventually fled. Sheng then had effective control over the whole of Xinjiang apart from the Yarkand and Khotan area which was still held by Hui or Dungan forces loyal to Ma Zhongying.

Opposition to Chinese control continued and an independent Kazakh and Uyghur East Turkestan Republic emerged to take control of the northwestern Ili or Ghulja region of Xinjiang from 1944 to 1949.[20] This was only a brief period of independence but it has had a profound impact on the culture and psyche of the Uyghurs and the other non-Han Chinese people of the region. The Eastern Turkestan Republic (ETR), which lasted from 1944 to 1949 is known in the official Chinese histories as the 'Three Districts Revolution' [*sanqu geming*] and is regarded by the Chinese Communist Party as having been a necessary precursor of the 'peaceful liberation of Xinjiang' in 1949 during which the CCP took control of the region. However, it is the independent, non-Chinese, and indeed anti-Chinese, nature of the East Turkestan Republic of this period that is remembered by many Uyghurs and others in Xinjiang today and the flag of the East Turkestan Republic remains a symbol of Turkic and Muslim nationalism and is anathema to the Chinese authorities as a symbol of separatism.

In August 1945, as the Second World War came to an end, the leaders of the Eastern Turkestan Republic began negotiations with Guomindang representatives in Dihua (now called Urumqi). Chiang Kai-shek sent the head of the political department of the GMD Military Committee, Zhang Zhidong, to negotiate with the rebels in September 1945. Zhang became chairman of the Xinjiang Provisional Government Council and thus effectively governor of Xinjiang, but his authority did not extend to the Three Districts of the Ili region. A new provisional government was formed in October 1945, but the negotiations with the GMD were superseded by the outbreak of the civil war between the GMD and CCP.

Peaceful Liberation

Xinjiang came under the control of the CCP in what the official accounts refer to as the 'peaceful liberation' [*heping jiefang*] of the region and which Burhan Shahidi, one of the most significant political leaders of early twentieth century Xinjiang calls, in an outbreak of humour rare in the political history of modern Xinjiang, the 'telegram uprising' [*tongdian qiyi*], referring to the exchange of telegrams between himself, Zhang Zhidong, Tao Zhiyue and CCP Chairman Mao Zedong in September 1949 in which Xinjiang was surrendered to the PLA and during which Burhan pledged his allegiance to the CCP.[21] In this way, the independent Eastern Turkestan government was absorbed into the revolutionary administration of the CCP. Eight of the leaders of the Eastern Turkestan Republic were invited to Beijing to negotiate the precise details of the relationship between Xinjiang and the PRC with the Communist Party leadership early in 1950. They were reported to have been killed when the aircraft they were travelling in crashed and their deaths are still seen by many Uyghurs as the deliberate elimination by the Chinese authorities of that section of the ETR leadership who were in favour of genuine autonomy or independence. Indeed some of those closely connected with the East Turkestan Republic maintain to this day that the leaders never made it to the aircraft but were killed in the Kazakhstan town of Panfilov on the orders of Stalin.[22] The official Chinese account is simply that it was an accident.

A programme to encourage the immigration of Han Chinese from the east was announced in 1950. Two major political campaigns which were launched by the CCP in the early years of its rule, the movement against counter-revolutionaries and the Land Reform programme, which included the confiscation and redistribution of mosque-owned *waqf* land (land owned by mosques or other religious and charitable foundations), were used to break down the traditional social structure and political and religious authority of

Xinjiang.[23] Although these campaigns also took place throughout the rest of China, they were modified in Xinjiang (as in Tibet) to take account of the special social and religious conditions of the region. Campaigns against Pan-Islam and Pan-Turkism were added to campaigns against landowners and in a retrospective article written in 1994, *Urumqi Evening News* estimated that millions of *yuan* were confiscated and over half a million people killed or sent to labour camps as part of these campaigns.[24]

On 1 October 1955 the Xinjiang Uyghur Autonomous Region was created, with a number of autonomous Mongol, Kyrgyz, Kazakh and Hui counties. Burhan Shahidi, an ethnic Tatar born in the village of Aksu in Tetesh county in the Kazan region which was the centre of the Tatar community of Russia, and Seypidin Aziz (Saifudin), an Uyghur, headed the regional government, although real power rested with Wang Zhen, commander of the PLA units which had taken control in 1949, and the regional Communist party secretary, Wang Enmao, both of whom were ethnic Hans. After the 1958 Great Leap Forward, radical policies, even less sensitive to local feelings replaced what in comparison appears to have been a relatively cautious approach to ethnic relations in the early 1950s. 'Local nationalism' and Han and Muslim leaders who were thought to be too sympathetic to the USSR were systematically criticised, and bazaars and Islamic organisations were closed down. Wang Enmao introduced more moderate policies in 1962 after the exodus of 60,000 Kazakhs to Kazakhstan,[25] but the 1966 Cultural Revolution, during which he was dismissed, caused chaos which was only brought to an end by the imposition of direct military control in 1971.

Uyghur Resistance in Xinjiang

The Uyghurs did not simply accept the regime that the PRC imposed on them. The first major incident of resistance to CCP control over Xinjiang is generally acknowledged to have been the Khotan rising of December 1954 by a Pan-Turkic organisation, known to the Chinese authorities as the Emin group, which was led by Abdimit (Abudu Yimiti). Declaring its intention of establishing a Muslim state, the Emin group published a document entitled 'Guidelines for an Islamic Republic', issued many posters and pamphlets and elected a government of which Abdimit was to be president. On 31 December, Abdimit led more than 300 supporters from the Karakash, Hotan and Lop areas, all of them followers of one of the Sufi orders collectively known in Xinjiang as *ishan*, in an attack on a prison camp [the Chinese term for this is *laogai nongchang* labour reform farm] in Karakash during which an officer, an NCO and seven soldiers were killed.[26]

Disturbances in the Ili region in 1962, including the insurrection of 29 May and the mass exodus westwards from Xinjiang of Kazakhs and Uyghurs, arose out of objections to the grain rationing system, Han Chinese immigration and competition between the military land reclamation units of the quasi-military Xinjiang Production and Construction Corps which farmed large areas of the region and local residents for scarce agricultural land, water and pastures. Among those who fled to the USSR were senior political and military officials who had been appointed by the CCP, almost all of them Kazakhs or Uyghurs. Many of these became involved in the establishment of a Turkestan People's Liberation Committee, which acted as a focus for emigré political activity in Kazakhstan and neighbouring parts of the USSR and became the basis for a number of organisations run by political exiles.[27]

Of all dissenting organisations in Xinjiang, the Eastern Turkestan People's Revolutionary Party (ETPRP) is considered by some Chinese researchers to have been the single largest resistance organisation in Xinjiang since 1949. It was founded in 1967 or 1968, during the most chaotic phase of China's contemporary history, the Cultural Revolution, and was naturally a clandestine group. The party had originally been called the Uyghurstan Peoples' Party but changed its name to echo that of the Eastern Turkestan Republic which ruled parts of Xinjiang between 1944 and 1949. In addition, the name Uyghurstan was, not surprisingly, less attractive to the Kazakh and Kyrgyz population of the region. Chinese writers have alleged that the ETPRP was formed by Soviet spies. This may simply mean that it was formed by individuals on both sides of the Sino-Soviet border or by Uyghurs who were based in the Soviet Union, but it is perfectly possible that Soviet intelligence was involved in its creation and organisation, given the difficult relations between China and the USSR at the time.

Antagonism between Uyghur Muslims and the Chinese authorities had persisted since the suppression of the insurrections of the 1950s, but the conflict became more acute and more visible in the 1980s and 1990s. It was most intense in two areas of Xinjiang: the southwest which is dominated by the great Uyghur cultural and Islamic centre of Kashghar and the Yining/Ghulja region in the northwest which is close to the border between China and Kazakhstan. Major disturbances began in April 1980 with riots in the town of Aksu, which lies almost midway between Urumqi and Kashghar, following clashes between local people, members of the Xinjiang Production and Construction Corps (XPCC) and demobilised the Red Guards. This led to similar disturbances in Kashghar, student protests in Urumqi and demonstrations by Uyghurs studying in the Central Nationalities Institute in Beijing protesting against racial and religious insults. Generalised disaffection at Chinese rule was gradually evolving into a broad opposition movement.

On 5 April 1990 in the town of Baren, close to Kashghar, the regular prayers at a mosque in the town turned into demonstrations against the

CCP's policies towards ethnic minorities. Some protesters called for a *jihad* against the unbelievers and there were demands for the establishment of an East Turkestan state. The demonstrators were able to ward off the police, and it took the intervention of units of the People's Armed Police and regular troops from the Kashghar garrison to subdue them. The Baren rising was not simply a spontaneous act of defiance: it was the result of a carefully planned and organised operation by a group which identified itself as the Eastern Turkestan Islamic Party and explicitly linked politicised Islam with the call for the independence of Xinjiang. The rebels attacked military vehicles and the town hall which was the local symbol of Chinese administration. Police, troops and the militia of the XPCC put down the rising after an early morning counter-attack on 6 April. The incident revealed the depth of anti-Chinese feeling, the degree of organisation of the rebels and the Islamicisation of the independence struggle, which had previously been dominated by Uyghur nationalism. There were bomb attacks by separatist units on a bus in Urumqi in 1992 and on government buildings in the city of Kashghar in 1993.

The focus of opposition moved to the town in the Ili region which is known as Yining to the Chinese and Ghulja to the Uyghurs. Unrest in the spring of 1995 began with demonstrations calling for an end to Chinese rule in the region, and police stations and local government offices were attacked and looted. There were also attacks on imams who were considered to have been compromised by their cooperation with the Chinese authorities. The government mobilised 20,000 troops under the command of the Lanzhou Military Region to put down the insurrection. Its political response was to launch a nationwide Strike Hard campaign: this was ostensibly a campaign against organised crime and hooliganism but, in the ethnic minority areas including Xinjiang, it was also designed to strike at the roots of opposition to Beijing's rule.

The Strike Hard campaign in Xinjiang led to harsh and sustained repression during 1996, and there were public trials of Uyghurs who were accused of serious criminal offences but were also alleged to be linked to the separatist movement and many were executed. There were also reports of secret executions of separatists. In this atmosphere of repression and anger young Uyghurs took to the streets of Yining [Ghulja] on 5 April 1997, attacking Han Chinese residents of the city. Police action to stop the violence led to an escalation of the protests and the following day there were further attacks on Han people and property. The Yining rising has become notorious for the violence with which it was suppressed. Official figures claim that there were fewer than 200 people killed by the police and military, but eyewitness reports suggest that the death toll was much higher and may have run into the thousands. The violence continued sporadically until 9 April and there were also bomb attacks by separatist groups in Urumqi on 25 February and in Beijing on 7 March. Public security organisations were placed on the highest alert nationwide and launched a major crackdown in Xinjiang, arresting thousands of people in what was essentially an intensification of the Strike Hard campaign. The authorities also embarked on campaigns of political education around the theme of national unity.[28]

Religious Affairs Bureaux and Control of Islam

The Chinese Communist Party has sought to regulate all religions throughout the whole of China, including Islam, by using the authority of the Religious Affairs Bureau, which was established by the State Council in 1954. It created the Chinese Islamic Association with which all mosques, *madrasas* and other Muslim organisations are legally obliged to register. Many groups, including some of the Sufi orders, have refused to register on the grounds that the atheist state should have no authority over their doctrines and forms of worship. This has created a conflict, not only between unregistered Muslim organisations and the government but also between registered and unregistered Muslim groups. The Chinese Islamic Association fell into abeyance during the Cultural Revolution but was resurrected after Deng Xiaoping came to power in 1978. New mosques were built and older ones that had been damaged during the Cultural Revolution were restored or even extended and worship became more open and relaxed.

When the rise of political and ethnic dissent began to alarm the authorities in the 1990s, the situation changed abruptly. A confidential internal *Document No. 7*, issued by the Chinese Communist Party in 1996 identified separatism in Xinjiang as a major threat to the region and to the nation as a whole. Inter alia the document ordered a crackdown on illegal *madrasas*, a restriction on the construction of new mosques and the independent teaching of martial arts and Qur'an study sessions. It called for the purge of party cadres who were also devout Muslims and who had refused to give up their beliefs in spite of years of CCP ideological indoctrination.[29] State control over Muslims in Xinjiang was reinforced after the publication of *Document No 7* and further intensified after the uprising in Yining/Ghulja in February 1997. The attacks by Al Qaeda on New York and Washington in September 2001 reinforced China's fears of the links between separatism and political Islam, but by that time the repression in Xinjiang had already been in place for five years. Under the new restrictions, children under the age of 18 were prohibited from entering mosques and the wearing of the *hijab* (veil) and other forms of Islamic dress was strictly forbidden in schools. Members of the CCP and the Communist Youth League and employees of government organisations, including retired members of staff, were forbidden to enter mosques and notices outlining these restrictions appeared in Uyghur at the entrance to mosques. Mosques were also barred from any involvement in disputes over marriage and family planning, and there was a specific prohibition on reading out the *nikah*, the Islamic marriage contract, in the mosque before the couple had been issued with a valid civil marriage certificate. The aim of these restrictions was to assert the primacy of civil laws over Islamic law and to restrict the authority of the local Islamic judge [*qadi*]. Printed or taped materials, which related to anything deemed to be religious extremism or separatism, were also explicitly banned and the teaching of religion anywhere other than in a registered mosque was also outlawed. The restrictions limited the sale of religious literature in general and a list of banned books was issued to booksellers.

Training 'Patriotic Religious Personnel'

It has been estimated that there were 54,575 imams or more senior religious leaders in Xinjiang in 1949 but that, as a result of the campaigns of the 1950s, this had been reduced to 27,000 by the start of the Cultural Revolution in 1966. It was assumed that there were few active religious leaders during the Cultural Revolution but in reality, imams simply operated without the knowledge of the Chinese authorities. The only organisation for training imams from the whole of China, including Xinjiang, in the 1950s and 1960s was the Chinese Islamic Academy in Beijing. In 1987 an Islamic Academy was established in Urumqi specifically to cater for imams from Xinjiang and the first graduates left the academy in 1992 to staff the mosques of the region. The Qur'an was also published in an Uyghur translation to cater for those whose grasp of Arabic was poor. The Religious Affairs Bureau exercised considerable control over the training and curriculum of Islamic education.[30] During 2001, as many as 8,000 imams from the mosques of Xinjiang were compelled to take part in a 'patriotic education campaign'. This was organised by a special work team under the control of the central government in Beijing and ran from 15 March to 23 December 2001. Imams were required to attend seminars during which they were instructed in the CCP's thinking on legal, political and religious topics, and they were ordered to avoid any involvement with mosques or other groups that were judged to be involved in separatist activities. This campaign was designed to strengthen government control over the registered mosques and increase the divide between them and those Muslims who refused to register their organisation. There were no serious outbreaks of violence associated with separatists or with political Islam between 1997 and 2006, but Xinjiang remained tense and Uyghur Muslims continued to be subjected to severe and ongoing surveillance and repression. There have been sporadic outbreaks of violence since, notably a grenade attack on a police post in Kashghar in August 2008 during the prelude to the Olympic Games, but the most dramatic were the Urumqi riots of July 2009. At least 200 people were injured in disturbances that followed a demonstration to protest at the murder of an Uyghur worker in Guangzhou and six Uyghurs were sentenced to death for their part in the violence.

17

HONG KONG AND TAIWAN

The only similarity between the histories of Hong Kong and Taiwan is that they are both Chinese communities outside the mainland of China that avoided the military conquest by the CCP in 1949 and the subsequent political and economic campaigns and policies that shaped the People's Republic. Hong Kong was a British colony until it was returned to China by agreement in 1997. The island of Taiwan, a colony of Japan since 1895, regained its independence in 1945 at the end of the Second World War but then became the base for the Guomindang, the Nationalist party, which had been defeated in the civil war on the mainland. It has continued an uneasy and anomalous existence as the Republic of China, independent to all intents and purposes but not recognised by Beijing and, since 1971, with no official representation in most international bodies. In spite of the different trajectories that they have taken, the histories of Hong Kong and Taiwan have been inextricably linked to the dramatic transformation that the mainland has undergone in modern times.

Hong Kong under Japanese Occupation

The Japanese occupation of Hong Kong lasted from the surrender of the British garrison by the Governor Sir Mark Young on 25 December 1941 until the capitulation of Japan in August 1945. This period is known to many Hong Kong residents simply as the 'three years and eight months'. The colony was governed by the Japanese under martial law, thousands of British servicemen and women and civilians were imprisoned in internment camps and there were widespread food shortages which led to malnutrition and the spread of disease and the consequent loss of life. Conditions were much harsher for the majority of the population of the colony, the Chinese, than for the Europeans. Japanese troops behaved towards them with at best callousness and at worst brutality. Although some sections of the population, particularly certain elements of the business class of Indian origin, were initially seduced by the Japanese claim that they would liberate fellow Asians from the racist rule of European colonialists, this illusion did not last for long and reality soon set in. Japan established its own colonial administration and Japanese specialists were brought in to occupy the most senior government and administrative posts with Chinese employees being retained in subordinate positions. Some members of the local business community of all ethnic backgrounds felt that they had no alternative but to cooperate with the Japanese occupiers as had happened in other parts of China. There was also resistance but it was in vain.[1]

Return of the British

In August 1945, after the dropping of atomic bombs on Hiroshima and Nagasaki and the unconditional surrender of the Japanese empire, plans were put into effect almost immediately for the reoccupation of the colony and a British naval task force entered Hong Kong harbour on 30 August 1945. Rear Admiral C.H.J. Harcourt, the commander of the task force, sailed into Hong Kong on board the cruiser *HMS Swiftsure* to re-establish control over the colony. A British military administrative office was set up in Victoria on Hong Kong Island on 1 September and the new administration accepted the formal surrender of the Japanese on 16 September at Government House.[2] The reoccupation was effected with a certain amount of diplomatic sleight of hand because it did not entirely meet with the approval of Chiang Kai-shek. Chiang assumed that his Guomindang government was going to resume its control over China that had been so rudely interrupted by the Japanese attack on Nanjing in 1937. As nationalists the Guomindang were adamantly opposed to the occupation of Hong Kong by the British and wished it to be returned to China. Chiang had made it clear that he wished the surrender of the Japanese forces in Hong Kong to be taken by his own Nationalist forces but circumstances obliged him to compromise and the surrender was in fact taken by the British but under Chiang's nominal authority as a courtesy. Sir Mark Young returned as governor for a year but he was replaced by Sir Alexander Grantham in July 1947.

Even by this stage the shadow of the eventual handover had fallen over Hong Kong, and there was a division between those who thought they could somehow avoid the inevitability by economic and political reform and those who accepted it and tried to work towards the best possible outcome. In both cases there was an agreement that the priority for Hong Kong should be economic development. The assumption was that prosperity would reduce demands from the Chinese population of Hong Kong for a return of the colony to China. It was also hoped that Hong Kong would be so valuable to China as an intermediary during a time of China's isolation, and subsequently as a financial services centre, that Beijing would not wish to exert overwhelming pressure on the colony. Many in the administration and the populace in general simply avoided the issue and went about their normal business.

The British presented the new post-war administration as simply a case of carrying on where they had left off after a brief, ill-mannered, interruption by the Japanese occupation. In reality the character of Hong Kong society was never to be the same again: it changed subtly but it changed profoundly. Some of the changes were as a result of legislation: restrictive regulations on the Chinese language press were rescinded and non-Europeans were no longer prevented by law from living in the exclusive residen- areas of the Peak. More significantly for social change in the colony, there was a drive to recruit additional Chinese employees into government ser- vice at all levels. The colonial apparatus remained but it was being opened up to the local majority population.

As the civil war in China came to an end in 1948–9 and it became clear that the Chinese Communist Party was going to form the next government on the mainland, what had been a gradual flow of refugees moving south turned into a mass migration and thousands of Chinese citizens headed towards the colony. Most of the migrants were farmers who settled in the New Territories, the largest land area of the colony that is attached to the mainland. They were able to rent small parcels of land – market gardens – and grow vegetables for which there was an increasing demand in the urban areas of Hong Kong. This new market-oriented economy disrupted the older rice-growing economy of the New Territories which faced collapse. Emigration to the United Kingdom from Hong Kong began in this period as village families chose to migrate rather than change to a different way of earning a living in Hong Kong.[3]

Negotiating with Beijing

The political and personnel changes that occurred in the People's Republic of China in the 1970s made it easier for progress to be made in its in rela- tions with Hong Kong .After the death of Lin Biao in 1971, Zhou Enlai's moderate foreign policy and more cosmopolitan approach made high level contacts with the USA and other Western governments possible. Mao Zedong died in 1976 and the 'reform and opening' policy agenda of Deng Xiaoping indicated an awareness of the need for China to engage with the wider world. At the same time, the new governor of the colony, Sir Murray Maclehose, who had been appointed in 1971, took a practical and positive approach to contacts with Beijing. He broke precedent by developing a cordial working relationship with the Xinhua (New China) News Agency office in Hong Kong. Xinhua is the official news agency of the PRC and its office in Hong Kong was the only form of representation that Beijing had established in the colony: it acted both as an unofficial embassy and as an important conduit for information and unacknowledged negotiations in addition to its news agency role.

Sir Murray made an official visit to China in 1979 to discuss an improvement in trade between Hong Kong and China and in particular to discuss with Beijing how the colony could assist in China's ambitious programme of economic modernisation. Although this was not the beginning of official negotiations about the terms and timetable for the formal handover of Hong Kong to China, it was a useful reconnaissance mission and enabled the governor and his closest colleagues to form an opinion of the attitudes of the new reform-minded leadership in Beijing on the Hong Kong issue.[4] One of Governor Maclehose's significant policy initiatives was the establishment in 1974 of the Independent Commission against Corruption (ICAC) which attempted to stamp out what was perceived to be an unacceptable level of corruption in the civil service and the police. He became Lord Maclehose in 1982.

The task of initiating the formal negotiations fell to Lord Maclehose's successor as governor, Sir Edward Youde, who took office in 1982: these negotiations took place that same year, before and during the visit to China of the British prime minister, Margaret Thatcher. Mrs Thatcher was taking an uncompromising stance on the continuation of a British presence after what she regarded as her success in the Falklands War. However, the Chinese under Deng Xiaoping were equally, if not more, intransigent and were insisting on the return of Hong Kong to Chinese control. In theory there was an important difference between the legal status of Hong Kong island, which had been ceded to Britain in perpetuity in 1842, and the New Territories which were British by virtue of a 99-year lease that was due to expire in 1997. In practice there was common consent that the two parts of the colony were not viable separately and would have to be treated as a whole and that some accommodation between Britain and China was essential for Hong Kong's continued economic success and social stability.[5]

Joint Declaration and Basic Law

Negotiations between Britain and China continued until September 1984, by which time it was clear to the British negotiators that Beijing was not going to retreat on its determination that Hong Kong would return to China. Britain had hoped to be able to continue administering Hong Kong, after the transfer of sovereignty but this was unacceptable to the Chinese side. The Sino-British Joint Declaration on Hong Kong was agreed and initialled in Beijing on 29 September 1984 by Sir Richard Evans, Britain's ambassador to the PRC and Zhou Nan, the Chinese deputy minister of foreign affairs. The formal signing ceremony by Mrs Thatcher and the Chinese prime minister, Zhou Enlai, took place in Beijing on 19 September and the agreement became effective from May 1985.

Under the terms of the Joint Declaration, or Joint Agreement, it was established that the sovereignty of the entire territory of Hong Kong would be transferred to China on 1 July 1997. Britain would continue its responsibilities for administering the territory in the interim and the PRC would cooperate in this. China agreed that it would create a Special Administrative Region (SAR) to govern Hong Kong (there were already Special Economic Regions such as Hong Kong's close neighbour Shenzhen within the PRC but the concept of an SAR was an interesting innovation) and allowed that the SAR would enjoy a considerable degree of autonomy in all questions with the exception of foreign policy and matters connected with defence. The agreement provided for a chief executive to be nominated by China in place of the governor, but it was accepted that existing personnel, including foreign nationals would be able to remain in post. Social and economic practices that were in place at the time, the legal system and the rights and freedoms that the colony had enjoyed would be respected. It was also announced that a Basic Law would be drawn up and that this would be enacted and ratified by the National People's Congress in Beijing. This law would guarantee the status quo in Hong Kong for 50 years under a formula that went by the name of 'one country two systems' [yiguo liangzhi]. In other words, although Hong Kong would be deemed to have become a constituent part of the PRC, it would be governed according to the long-established capitalist system and the distinctive way of life that prevailed in the former colony rather than the state-dominated economic system of the mainland. There had been great apprehension in Hong Kong about the outcome of these negotiations and although there was still concern and lack of confidence in the willingness and ability of China to comply with the terms of the Joint Agreement, the feeling overall was one of relief and there was a general acknowledgement that things could have been much worse.

The Basic Law was drafted by a joint committee which included members from both Hong Kong and the PRC. There was considerable public consultation in Hong Kong and rather less on the mainland. The law was adopted by the Seventh National People's Congress of the PRC on 4 April 1990 and it became effective on the day of the handover, 1 July 1997. The text of the Basic Law concerned the autonomy of the Special Administrative Region; the maintenance of the status quo for 50 years and the preservation of the existing system of legislation, including protection from arbitrary detention or imprisonment, and freedom of speech, the press and assembly. A number of issues remained contentious, notably the question of the right to abode of mainland residents who might wish to settle in Hong Kong; the possibility of a move towards complete universal suffrage and the term of office of Chief Executives who would follow the first holder of the post. When the Joint Agreement became effective in May 1985, Hong Kong entered a period of uncharted waters. An issue that had concerned both residents and foreign observers for decades but had been largely avoided by the administration, Hong Kong's lack of democracy, suddenly acquired greater importance in this transitional period. It had been argued by many in the business and administrative elite in Hong Kong that the absence of democracy in the colony in the post-war period had been owing to the lack of grass roots demand and a popular perception that it was unnecessary because the government was delivering the goods. There had, however, been a long established core of activists who argued for re-dressing the democratic deficit. The spilling over of the Cultural Revolution into Hong Kong in 1967 certainly did not help the cause of democracy and the demonstrations provoked more alarm than sympathy. The colonial government did use the opportunity this presented to increase the degree of public participation in the processes of government and the positive response that this generated suggested that democratisation was long overdue.[6]

Governance of Hong Kong

Hong Kong did not have a democratically elected parliament. The legislative body of Hong Kong, the Legislative Council (known almost universally as Legco) was created in 1843 by the British colonial administration under the terms of the Charter of Hong Kong, Letters Patent of Queen Victoria. Its members were not democratically elected but were appointed to advise the governor, who alone had the authority to enact legislation. When the 1843 Charter was replaced in 1917, the wording of the new Letters Patent was altered to clarify the relationship between the governor and the Legislative Council by stressing that the council was not merely an advisory body but that its consent was required for legislation. Membership of the Legislative Council was increased from time to time until by 1976 it had 23 official and 23 unofficial members (the unofficial members were members who did not have government posts and were in large part drawn from the business community). The first elections to the Legislative Council took place in 1985 and the number of unofficial members was increased so that it exceeded the number of official members. In 1995, the final Legislative Council before the handover saw 20 of the members returned by direct elections. The Legislative Council had evolved very slowly from an advisory to a legislative body but resistance to the idea of elections by full universal suffrage continued to the very end. The last governor, Chris Patten, was a British conservative politician who had lost his seat in the House of Commons for the constituency of Bath in the 1992 elections. His governorship was controversial because of his abrasive approach to officials in Beijing and the changes he made to the functional constituencies from which the unofficial members were elected: these alterations had extended the franchise in the last elections before the handover against the understanding that had been reached in the negotiations. The formal transfer of Hong Kong's sovereignty from the United Kingdom to the People's Republic of China took place at midnight on 1 July 1997, at a ceremony held at the Convention and Exhibition Centre which overlooks Victoria Harbour. Chris Pattern stood down as governor and was replaced by Tung Chee Hwa who became the first Chief Executive of the new Hong Kong Special Administrative Region. The Portuguese colony of Macao, Hong Kong's near neighbour agreed to revert to Chinese rule under a similar agreement in 1999.[7]

Taiwan after the Second World War

Between 1945 and 1988 the economy of Taiwan grew at an impressive and unprecedented rate. Supporters of the Free China concept choose to attribute this to the superiority of Guomindang [usually spelled Kuomintang in Taiwan] policies over their Communist rivals on the mainland or to the greater capacity of the island's population for hard work and creativity. However the level of economic development and prosperity that Taiwan achieved in the 1950s could not have been achieved without the financial support of successive US administrations, initially by aid packages and, when these were withdrawn in 1965, by Taiwan's role in supplying the US forces during the Vietnam War.

The government in Taipei implemented a programme of Land Reform at the same time that the CCP was carrying out its own policies of confiscation and redistribution of agricultural land on the mainland. For the Guomindang, this programme of rural reconstruction was not a socialist policy as such but a practical realisation of Sun Yat-sen's policy of 'land to the tiller'. It was a three-stage programme which began with an overall reduction in the rent paid by tenant farmers; continued with the sale to farmers of publicly owned land originally retained by the Japanese colonial administration to encourage immigration from Japan; and was completed with a compulsory purchase programme under which the government acquired land from large land holdings and resold it to farmers at cost plus interest. Agricultural productivity and the rural standard of living increased as a result of these policies. Taiwan's industrialisation was even more successful than its agricultural transformation. A post-war reconstruction phase was followed by a four-year economic plan which invested in small and medium-sized enterprises. By 1956, the number of factories and factory workers and their per capita income had risen dramatically. During the 1960s, Taiwan gradually moved towards a policy of encouraging the production of consumer durables for the export trade and established itself as a major player in the international export markets.[8]

Taiwanese and Mainlanders

Since 1949, Taiwan (or Formosa as it continued to be known in the West for many years) has been presented in contrasting political guises. To many Westerners, and to the Guomindang government of Chiang Kai-shek during what it believed was its temporary exile on the island, it was Free China [*Ziyou Zhongguo*].[9] The government, and its allies overseas, continued to regard Chiang's administration as the legitimate government of the whole of China and accepted the assertion of the Guomindang that it would one day resume its rightful position and govern the mainland once more from its capital in Nanjing. To the newly established government of the People's Republic of China in Beijing, Taiwan was a bastion of the defeated Guomindang where they had been able to find short-term refuge, but, once they were finally crushed, it would return to control by China as a province and submit to the authority of the Communist Party's government.

The Cold War in Asia, exacerbated by the Korean War caused these two positions to become firmly entrenched. For the people who lived in Taiwan it was never as simple as this. The group of military officers and civilian administrators, who had crossed to the island in advance of and accompanying the retreating Nationalist government during the civil war of the late 1940s, gradually established themselves, not as members of a transitory administration but as a new ruling elite. They displaced the colonial administration that had been controlled by Japan and replaced it with a Chinese government, but this Chinese government was not a government of Taiwanese but a government of mainlanders who spoke Mandarin and brought with them the culture and political networks of the mainland. The indigenous Taiwanese, the descendants of the much earlier generation of migrants from Fujian, who spoke the language of that southeastern province of China in a modified Taiwanese form, were effectively excluded from power. The ethnic and political conflict between these two groups was to affect every aspect of the development of Taiwan's history from the 1940s until the present day but it is a conflict that for most of that time has been obscured, rarely referred to and little understood by outsiders. If the confrontation with the Chinese Communist Party was the Guomindang's major international challenge in the years after the Second World War, its confrontation with the movement for Taiwanese self-government was its greatest domestic challenge. Taiwan gradually evolved into a one-party state, ironically a mirror image of its Communist adversary on the mainland: the Guomindang was the only political party legally permitted to exist until 1986 and martial law, which had been proclaimed in 1947, remained in force until 1987.

Movement for Democracy in Taiwan

The beginnings of a movement for a democratic Taiwan can be traced to the periodical *Free China* [*Ziyou Zhongguo*]. In its inaugural edition in November 1949, the liberal intellectual, Hu Shi, set out the journal's twin objectives of supporting the idea of a free and independent China and opposition to Communism. Initially the outlook of *Free China* chimed with the views of the Guomindang, which was on the point of taking power. However, when the Korean War broke out Taiwan began to receive aid from the USA which strengthened its political position. The Guomindang no longer felt able to tolerate the discordant voices of the liberal intelligentsia: it began a rectification campaign and arrested dissidents. *Free China* responded by attacking the economic and social policies of the Guomindang administration in articles and editorials, including pieces published in a special edition of the magazine which criticised Chiang Kai-shek on the occasion of his seventieth birthday. It grew more and more unsympathetic to the government and opposed a third term in office for Chiang Kai-shek in 1960. The constitution of the Republic of China specified that a president should be elected for a term of six years and that this could be extended for a second term but not for a third. The National Assembly voted to suspend this constitutional requirement in February 1960 in the light of the tension between Taiwan and the mainland and on 21 March Chiang was elected for a third term in office as president: he was subsequently returned for fourth and fifth terms. *Free China* also called on the government to abandon the idea of a counterattack on the mainland and proposed the establishment of a separate Democratic Republic of Chinese Taiwan to oppose the PRC. A group associated with *Free China* formed a political party, the China Democratic Party, to contest elections but on the eve of the party's launch in September 1960, its leaders were arrested by troops of the Taiwan garrison headquarters on suspicion of involvement in an armed rebellion and the party was strangled at birth. *Free China* was outlawed and ceased publication in 1960.

The repression was so severe that an open and organised opposition did not reappear until the 1970s by which time Taiwanese society was undergoing great changes as a result of the industrialisation of the island and the emergence of a new middle class. In the early 1970s, the periodical *University Review* [*Daxue zazhi*] took on the role of the government's main critic although it did not actively engage in politics. It was joined by *Taiwan Political Commentary* [*Taiwan zhenglun*] in 1975. The Extra-Party [*Dangwai*] movement which developed in the 1970s became the major focus for dissidents. The term *Dangwai* (literally outside the party) had originally meant anyone who was not a member of the Guomindang but it became used more widely for members of the opposition movement who did not belong to any political party. This group was beginning to coalesce into an influential movement. When the fifth issue of *Taiwan Political Commentary* was banned in 1977, a number of opposition members associated with it stood in elections for the Taiwan Provincial Assembly. Some were elected and the movement benefited from a higher profile and a more organised presence throughout the island.[10]

Taiwan after Chiang Kai-shek

Chiang Kai-shek died in 1975, having been effectively president of Taiwan for life, although he had never been acknowledged as such. On 6 April, he was succeeded by C.K. Yen (Yen Chia-kang) who had been his vice-president, this succession being in accordance with the provisions of the constitution. However, this was a presidential appointment in name only. Chiang Ching-kuo, Chiang Kai-shek's son, became chairman of the Guomindang in 1975 and it was he who exercised real power. In 1978 Chiang Ching-kuo formally succeeded Yen as president and he was elected to serve for a second term as president in 1984. His vice-president in this second term was Lee Teng-hui, who was not a member of the mainlander elite but a Taiwan-born politician who had been mayor of Taipei and governor of Taiwan and who had been educated at Cornell University in the USA where he had completed a PhD in agricultural economics. Lee Teng-hui was the most significant of a group of native-born Taiwanese who were protégés of Chiang Ching-kuo who had been strongly in favour of advancing non-mainlanders who showed promise.

Now that there was no longer the powerful guiding hand of Chiang Kai-shek to rein in dissent, divisions began to emerge within the Kuomintang between factions that can be characterised broadly as the old guard and the modernisers. The Kuomintang had been transformed from a revolutionary party with a strong link to the military to a more mainstream political party concerned with policy and with the minutiae of the day-to-day running of an administration: this reduced the requirement for unquestioning loyalty and the existence of a range of political views became more acceptable.

'Formosa' Incident

In August 1979, a group of political dissidents opposed to the Guomindang's monopoly of power, many of them lawyers, and others who had been part of the *Dangwai* movement, launched a new journal. The Chinese name of the journal was *Meili dao*, a literal translation of the Portuguese name *Ilha Formosa* (Beautiful Island) by which Taiwan had been known until the mid-twentieth century and it is generally known in English as *Formosa*. During the autumn of 1979, it established 15 branch offices throughout Taiwan, offices that were effectively the branches of an embryonic political party, albeit a party without a party name [*meiyou dangming de dang*] or an openly acknowledged existence in view of the fact that parties remained illegal under martial law. The magazine experienced continual harassment from supporters of the Guomindang, the police and military intelligence which culminated in simultaneous attacks on the home of the publisher in Taipei and the offices of the magazine in Kaohsiung and Pingtung on 29 November 1979.

On 10 December 1979 opposition politicians organised a demonstration in the great port city of Kaohsiung (Gaoxiong) in southwestern Taiwan in association with *Formosa* magazine to mark International Human Rights Day. The demonstration resulted in serious disturbances after the intervention of police and undercover agents of the security services and a number of the organisers were arrested, including Annette Lü who was later to become vice president and others who were later to become senior figures in the Democratic Progressive Party.[11]

Reforms of 1986

In March 1986 a commission appointed by President Chiang Ching-kuo, and consisting of 12 members of the Central Committee of the Guomindang, was convened to make recommendations on six major reform proposals. These were the revoking of the Emergency Decree on Martial Law which by then had been in force for thirty-eight years; the lawful formation of new political parties, some of which had already been operating illegally; the reinforcement of local sovereignty; the creation of a parliamentary system; the internal reform of the Guomindang and confronting crime and corruption. On 28 September 1986 six organisations applied to be registered formally as political parties. The largest of these, the Democratic Progressive Party (DPP), went on to capture 11 seats in the National Assembly and 12 seats in the Legislative Yuan in the elections that were held in December 1986. This was a turning point in the political history of Taiwan because, for the first time, it introduced to the legislature politicians who were openly in favour of a genuinely independent Taiwan and did not claim the right to rule the mainland. Martial law was finally lifted on 15 July 1987. In November of the same year, residents of Taiwan were permitted to visit relatives across the Taiwan Straits for the first time since 1949.

Lee Teng-hui Era

Chiang Ching-kuo had been in poor health for some time and died on 13 January 1988. Lee Teng-hui was sworn in as president and at the Thirteenth Congress of the Kuomintang in July 1988 he was also confirmed as party chairman, a notable achievement for a native Taiwanese. At the same meeting, many Taiwan-born politicians were elected into key posts in the new leadership. Of the 31 members of the Standing Committee of the Party, 16 were Taiwanese in origin and Lee Teng-hui's first cabinet brought eight Taiwanese politicians into government. The Thirteenth Congress had also agreed on a number of measures to relax relations with the mainland and to enable personal, family, cultural and business exchanges between Taiwan and the People's Republic. The only proviso was that none of these exchanges should imply recognition of the PRC or endanger Taiwan's security. There was no question of dealings between the two sides of the Taiwan Strait being carried out on the basis of equal relations between two independent states. The government in Taipei, in common with the government in Beijing, remained committed to the idea of a reunified China at some point in the future and was not prepared to compromise.[12]

In July 1999, President Lee Teng-hui issued a statement in which he argued that future contacts between China and Taiwan should be on the basis of 'special state-to-state relations'. This was a step closer to asserting formal independence and was viewed as dangerous brinkmanship which was bound to provoke the wrath of the government in Beijing. By this time Lee was becoming detached from mainstream Guomindang politics and was already planning his retirement. Both of these factors were used to limit the damage his remarks caused and to reduce cross-straits tension. He was subsequently expelled from the Guomindang in September 2001 when he broke party discipline by publicly endorsing election candidates from another political party, the Taiwan Solidarity Union (TSU), which was formed in August 2001 by defectors from the Guomindang, many of whom were supporters of Lee. The TSU was the first political party to use the name Taiwan in its official title and this was a deliberate move to emphasise its pro-independence credentials at a time when the DPP was seen to be too willing to reach an agreement with Beijing.

Chen Shui-bian's Presidency

Chen Shui-bian, the leader of the Democratic Progressive Party (DPP) was elected president in a historic election that brought to an end 50 years of unbroken rule by the Kuomintang. Chen Shui-bian was born into a poor farming family in the south of Taiwan, the heartland of the independence movement. He practised law and was drawn into pro-independence politics when he represented several of the defendants in the Formosa incident in 1979. He became active in the Extra-Party [*Dangwai*] movement and served on the Taipei City council where he became mayor in 1994. His style was populist and he was often referred to by the familiar soubriquet of A-bian which can be either affectionate or slightly disdainful depending on the context. Although he had been a vociferous supporter of the idea of an independent Taiwan, he moderated his calls for immediate formal independence in order not to provoke Beijing. The Democratic Progressive Party was one of the new parties that first registered in 1986 and has been the most successful of the pro-independence groups. President Chen defeated the Guomindang candidate Lien Chan, a protégé of former President Lee Teng-hui and an independent James Soong, but his government did not have a majority after this election. In the December 2001 Parliamentary Elections, the Kuomintang lost its parliamentary majority for the first time since 1949. The DPP secured 87 seats in the legislature, the Kuomintang 68 and other parties had 70.

China-Taiwan Relations

On 24 January 2001, Vice Premier Qian Qichen of the PRC, who had been a widely respected former foreign minister, called on the Taiwan authorities to accept what had become known as the 1992 consensus on the principle of One China. The consensus was the result of a meeting between the two organisations established in China and Taiwan to manage cross-straits relations. The Association for Relations Across the Taiwan Straits, ARATS (PRC), and the Straits Exchanges Foundation, SEF (Taiwan), met in Hong Kong in 1992. The consensus, which was that both sides should abide by the One-China Principle, may not have been a consensus at all as the Taiwan side rejected it, but as the rejection came after the election of the pro-independence DPP, the status of the agreement was not at all clear.[13]

Political relations between China and Taiwan remained strained for some years but economic relations continued to develop in a way that belied the reports of cross-straits tension. Taiwanese firms invested heavily in the mainland economy and by 2002 there were at least 50,000 businesses based in the island that were operating in the PRC.[14] In Shanghai alone, there is a resident Taiwanese community numbering at least 300,000 which

runs its own schools and a newspaper. Direct trade, transport and communications were banned for decades but, after lengthy negotiations to
relax these restrictions, direct flights became a reality in December 2008.
The economies of China on both sides of the Taiwan Strait are linked
closely together and, after the financial crisis of 2008, there was pressure for
even closer economic integration and greater mainland investment in Taiwan although the lack of political accommodation is still a barrier.

Changes in the Guomindang

The role of the Guomindang has changed significantly since it went into
opposition in 2001. In spite of the historical antipathy between the GMD
and the Communist Party, the Guomindang was prepared to enter into
discussions with Beijing and continued to insist on a policy of reunification
in the long term in the face of the growing wave of pro-independence
sentiment. At a GMD congress that was held in the city of Taoyuan in June
2007, major changes were made to the constitution of the Party, enabling it
to concentrate on the island of Taiwan and the 'people's welfare' (the old
reformist term used by Sun Yat-sen) rather than having reunification as its
main objective. The party leader, Ma Ying-jeou, who was the GMD's
candidate in the 2008 presidential elections, indicated that he would be
willing to conclude a peace agreement with the PRC. These moves reflect
the party's willingness to bow to the contemporary political reality of Taiwan's de facto independence rather than the historical commitment to one
China which has both united and divided the GMD and the CCP since the
1920s.[15]

In the elections of March 2008 the GMD candidate for president, Ma
Ying-jeou, was elected and the former DPP leader Chen Shui-bian was
charged with corruption and imprisoned while awaiting trial. This return to
GMD control was welcomed by the authorities on the mainland who greatly preferred to deal with their old adversaries on the basis that both parties
were broadly committed to the idea of one China. Several high-profile cross-
straits visits took place, culminating in the visit of the GMD Chairman Wu
Po-hsiung to Beijing in May 2009. DPP members and other supporters of a
formally independent Taiwan argued that the de facto independence of the
island was under threat because of the massive investment that the PRC
was beginning to direct towards Taiwan. Many pro-independence commentators argued for a reduction in negotiations between the two sides but
even the DPP mayor of Kaohsiung, Chen Chu, was to be found in Beijing
during the same month as Wu Po-hsiung, negotiating for support for the
World Games that the city was due to host later that year.

18

CHINA AFTER DENG XIAOPING

The transformation of the Chinese economy after the launch of Deng Xiaoping's reform programme in the late 1970s has astonished and impressed the world. The physical manifestation of the transformation was dramatic, particularly in the prestigious construction projects of Shanghai and Beijing: the contrast between the new palaces of glass and concrete and the drab neo-Stalinist edifices that typified China of the 1950s and 1960s was emblematic of a profound change in attitude and a new national purpose. However this brand new face of China was only part of the story and diverted the attention of many observers from serious problems that remained unresolved. Vast swathes of the countryside are still awaiting development and, especially in the western regions, economic and cultural backwardness and dire poverty continue to present serious challenges to the political leadership and pose a serious threat to social stability and therefore to the government's stated aspiration of a China that is rising peacefully and evolving into a harmonious society.

Jiang Zemin and the Third-Generation Leadership

After the death of Deng Xiaoping in February 1997 political circles in China began to use a new expression to classify the successive leadership groups of the Party: political generations. The concept of generations of leadership in the Communist Party and the PRC had begun to enter the public discourse in the 1990s during the final years of Deng Xiaoping's life. The issues of succession and the balance of change and continuity were always in the minds of the Party hierarchy and its collective memory in the Secretariat. The concept of a fourth generation was the first to be used widely, to refer to Hu Jintao and Wen Jiabao, and it became necessary to be more precise in reclassifying the earlier leadership into three predecessor generations. Chinese commentators projected backwards to the period under Mao's control as the first generation and Deng's incumbency as the second. Jiang Zemin was therefore the third-generation leader. The key figures of the first generation, although that term was never used while they were in power, were Mao Zedong, Liu Shaoqi, Peng Dehuai, Lin Biao and Zhou Enlai. They were the first generation of the CCP to achieve power, and they had brought with them the legacy of the Long March, the revolutionary struggle in the countryside, the guerrilla resistance to the Japanese occupation and the victories on the battlefields of the civil war where they had defeated the armies of the nationalists. They also carried with them the considerable political baggage of factional, ideological and personal differences which were to bedevil China's domestic politics during the 1950s and came to a head in the Cultural Revolution.

The second generation were Deng Xiaoping and the group of veteran party leaders (often designated as moderate or conservative) who had come to power following the death of Mao Zedong in 1976 and after the elimination of his political supporters including the Gang of Four. Their major contribution to the political development of the country was a willingness to tackle the thorny problem of economic reform as China emerged from the chaos of the Cultural Revolution, including the dismantling of the commune system and the attraction of foreign capital to fuel the new programme of industrialisation. Among the key members of this group were Chen Yun, highly respected as the Party's economics supremo, and Hu Yaobang and Zhao Ziyang, who were premiers in succession and who were both on the liberal wing of the Party, although that is not a term that the CCP would officially recognise. This political combination, which appeared to promise so much in terms of reform, came to grief after the military suppression of the Democracy Movement in Beijing on 4 June 1989.

The demise of the USSR and the Communist states of Eastern Europe were constantly in the minds of Deng and his colleagues of the second-generation leadership: the lessons that they drew from what they inevitably perceived as a political debacle included the necessity of creating sound economic growth as the only way of ensuring the stability of the state and the legitimacy of the CCP. Part of this strategy was the decision to develop close links between the growing business sector and the CCP, at the same time consolidating the Party's authority over the military apparatus. The second-generation leadership was far from being the liberal administration that some Western observers had hoped for, but the pragmatism that was demonstrated by Deng and his supporters did ensure the stability and continuation of the regime. Stability was, above all else, the main aim of the CCP. According to their own lights they were extremely successful.

The final collapse of the Soviet Union in 1991 concentrated the minds of Deng Xiaoping, Jiang Zemin and the CCP leadership. Even though criticising Mikhail Gorbachev for destabilising socialism in the USSR, Deng and Jiang were obliged to concede that control of China by the CCP could also be in danger if the reforms did not succeed in providing the population with substantial material gains. Deng Xiaoping took the lead by embarking on a tour of southern China in January and February 1992, an extended visit that was distinctly reminiscent of the grand excursions made by the Qing emperors and their entourages to the farthest corners of their domains. Deng's purpose was to rally support for a further acceleration of his reform programme in the face of opposition from 'leftists' who felt that the scheme had already gone too far. In the following September, the prime minister, Li Peng, toured the northwest of China, including Xinjiang, to encourage the expansion of trade across the borders with the newly independent republics of former Soviet Central Asia. Among the 'leftist' intransigents who were attempting to slow down the reforms against the wishes of Deng Xiaoping was the very same Li Peng, but when the fourteenth congress of the CCP met in March 1992, Deng's call for the speeding up of the reform enterprise carried the day. When Deng Xiaoping died on 19 February 1997, his legacy seemed secure: China was characterised by rapid economic reform but tight political control.

Jiang Zemin, who succeeded Deng to take the helm of the third-generation leadership, was widely regarded by foreign analysts as a nondescript caretaker leader. He was held to be dull and uninspiring and treated as something of a joke. However he had entered the highest echelons of Chinese politics on the basis of considerable local and regional success in Shanghai, where he had been the head of the municipal CCP organisation. Jiang had succeeded Zhao Ziyang as secretary-general of the CCP in 1989 after Zhao had been ousted for failing to resolve the issue of the democracy demonstrators in Beijing which led to the military assault on 4 June. In addition to Jiang's decisive action in closing down the reformist *World Economic Herald*, one of the most interesting and controversial newspapers to be published since 1949, but which was presenting ideas that the CCP leadership considered to be dangerous, Jiang's major achievement before moving to Beijing was that he had also managed to control the pro-democracy demonstrations that had taken place in Shanghai without any loss of life. The chief task that faced him on his appointment as secretary-general of the CCP was to revive confidence in the reform programme which had been badly shaken by the social dislocation that had occurred during and after the demonstrations. Many foreign companies had withdrawn their employees and embassies had removed non-essential staff. Foreign direct investment, which was vital to China's reforms, also appeared to be under threat although, in the event, business returned swiftly with Japanese companies in the lead. The government made a gesture towards the grievances of the demonstrators by launching a campaign against corruption in national politics which had been one of the main targets of the protestors: government ministries, the Supreme People's Court and the Supreme People's

Procurate (the prosecuting authority) attempted to persuade corrupt officials that they should confess to their crimes and offered to show them leniency if they did so.

Jiang had been appointed State Chairman (president) of the People's Republic of China in 1993 in addition to his position as secretary-general of the CCP: since 1989 he had also held the post of chairman of the Central Military Commission which exercises ultimate political authority over the military. By the time that Deng Xiaoping died in February 1997 Jiang had become the head of the state, the party and the military and theoretically had a status equivalent to that of Deng Xiaoping, although he possessed neither Deng's authority nor his personal and political power base within the CCP. Jiang's administration followed Deng's prescription for stability and growth but he will be remembered above all for the confusing, inelegant and much derided slogan of the 'Three Represents' [*sange daibiao*] which was intended to provide a theoretical justification for his policy of admitting senior people from the business community to membership of the Party: membership had previously been restricted to workers, peasants and the military during the Cultural Revolution and other social groups were only gradually being encouraged to join.

Many Chinese political slogans seem inelegant or ludicrous in English but are more pleasing to the ear and to the eye in the original language. The theory of the 'Three Represents' is a notable exception. It became something of an embarrassment and was quietly dropped when Jiang Zemin completed his period in office. There are various interpretations of what it might have meant. According to an interpretative note by the International Department of the Central Committee of the CCP:

> An important conclusion can be reached from reviewing our Party's history over the past 70-odd years; that is, the reason our Party enjoys the people's support is that throughout the historical periods of revolution, construction and reform, it has always represented the development trend of China's advanced productive forces, the orientation of China's advanced culture, and the fundamental interests of the overwhelming majority of the Chinese people. With the formulation of the correct line, principles and policies, the Party has untiringly worked for the fundamental interests of the country and the people. Under the new conditions of historic significance, how our Party can better translate the Three Represents into action constitutes a major issue that all Party members, especially senior officials, must ponder deeply.

At the end of his term in office, Jiang seemed decidedly reluctant to relinquish the authority and influence of his position, which was unusual even for a CCP leader. This was assuaged somewhat by the possibility that his ideas would be preserved for posterity, partly as a result of a strange biography written by an American investment banker, Robert Kuhn, but approved by the Chinese authorities, which tried to present Jiang, in the eponymous but tendentious title, as *The Man Who Changed China*. This was followed in 2006 by a multi-volume compilation of his speeches and writings in a *Selected Works* that ran to 654 pages.[1] Jiang Zemin finally stepped down in November 2003 after the Sixteenth CCP congress which chose Hu Jintao as the new general secretary. Hu was later nominated as State Chairman (president) and, after some delay, as chairman of the CCP's Central Military Commission, the political body that directs the army. The delay was apparently caused by Jiang Zemin's unwillingness to relinquish this powerful position: it was also the last Communist Party post that Deng Xiaoping had held before he finally retired. More significant in the long term than Jiang as a man who changed China was his premier, Zhu Rongji who, like Jiang, was a former mayor of Shanghai. Zhu was renowned for bluntness and the shortness of his temper, but he was also highly respected for his competent management of the transition to a semi-market economy and he is credited as having been largely responsible for the technical aspects of China's successful application to join the World Trade Organisation.

The pattern of economic progress and political reaction continued. At the Fifteenth National Congress of the CCP in September 1997, and the Ninth National People's Congress in March 1998, new reform policies were announced. At the same time, the CCP continued to suppress any organised dissent as soon as it surfaced: the embryonic China Democracy Party was crushed and its leaders were arrested in November 1998. In April 1999 the new religion of Falungong was ruthlessly suppressed. It offered its adherents a synthesis of traditional Buddhist and Daoist teaching with some new age accretions and advocated the combination of an apparently admirable exercise programme with bizarre and possibly dangerous medical remedies. The government had tolerated its activities while it remained a loose amalgam of groups practicing *qigong* exercises but when it grew into a national organisation and recruited widely, including from families with military and police connections, and mounted high profile demonstrations, the decision was made to proscribe it. The government's strategy was to encourage economic reform while firmly suppressing any demands for political reform and any political, religious or social dissidence that posed a threat to the status quo and in particular to the status of the CCP. Falungong was clearly deemed to fall into that category.

China's Accession to the WTO

China joined the World Trade Organisation in December 2001 on terms that had finally been agreed in November 1999 after complex and long drawn out negotiations. China's application to join the World Trade Organisation was deemed, both within the PRC and by the international community, to be the most important indication of the success of China's economic modernisation; or at least of the acceptance by worldwide opinion that it was an economy that other advanced industrial economies could deal with. By its accession it moved closer to the government's aim of being accepted as a world-class market economy. This new status was endorsed by the visit of the president of the USA, George W. Bush, to Beijing in February 2002 and by Jiang Zemin's return state visit to the USA in October 2002 when he was accorded the rare honour of being entertained at the Bush family's Prairie Chapel ranch near Crawford, Texas.

The origins of the World Trade Organisation were in the peace settlement that followed the Second World War. A conference was held in Bretton Woods, New Hampshire in the USA in July 1944 to set out the parameters for the post-war economic and financial order. It was attended by representatives of the victorious allied powers. The conference failed to agree on the creation of an International Trade Organisation, which had been one of the key objectives, but instead set up the General Agreement on Tariffs and Trade (GATT): the International Monetary Fund and the International Bank for Reconstruction and Development were also established as part of this agreement. GATT's role was to regulate international trade and particularly to encourage the growth of free trade by reducing tariff and other barriers. Technically, it always remained an agreement rather than a fully-fledged international organisation, although it exercised much greater authority than this status might suggest: it was replaced on 1 January 1995 by the World Trade Organisation (WTO).

Membership of the WTO confers many benefits but there are also responsibilities and China's accession to the organisation was delayed because of concerns by both sides about the implications of these conditions and whether China, as a 'socialist market economy', was in a position to fulfil them. Above all, the requirement that the PRC should open its doors to international financial markets created many difficulties in the negotiations. The thorny question of the status of Taiwan vis-a-vis the WTO was also a major stumbling block. Nevertheless, China's accession was essential for the Chinese government. The PRC had been excluded from the United Nations for 22 years until 1971 and securing membership of this powerful international economic club was as much a matter of self-respect as of economic necessity. It was also vital for the international community because it was the only effective mechanism that could be used to oblige China to open its commercial and financial sectors to overseas businesses and banks. The PRC finally joined the WTO on 11 December 2001 after protracted negotiations which had throughout been fraught with technical and diplomatic obstacles. The complete application process had taken a total of 15 years which was the longest on record in the history of either GATT or the WTO. Bringing such a Herculean task to a successful conclusion was regarded as a great success both for China and for the WTO. Taiwan also became a member of the WTO but not until 1 January 2002. It did not join as the Republic of China, which would have been completely unacceptable to Beijing, but as the Customs Territory of Taiwan, Penghu, Kinmen and Matsu.

Hu Jintao and the Fourth-Generation Leadership

When the Central Committee of the Chinese Communist Party was due to meet in full session from 9 to 11 October 2000, the published agenda indicated that it would be concentrating on the Tenth Five-Year Plan for the development of the national economy and, in particular, the Western Development programme, the grand plan for developing the impoverished western regions of the country. In reality the meeting was at least as concerned to establish the basis for a smooth transition from the generation of leaders led by Jiang Zemin to what would become known as the fourth-generation [di sidai] leadership of the People's Republic. The planned retirement within two years of President Jiang Zemin, Premier Zhu Rongji and the chairman of the National People's Congress, Li Peng, was confirmed and the names of the men who were to lead the new generation were given new prominence: they were Hu Jintao as vice-president, Wen Jiabao who became vice-premier and Zeng Qinghong, promoted to be the head of the CCP's influential Organisation Department. The new generation of leaders formally emerged after the Sixteenth Congress of the Communist Party of China that was held in November 2002. They took over at a time when the CCP was in flux, throwing off some of its old ideological baggage, committed to economic modernisation to be sure, but also unswervingly dedicated to maintaining its own central and unchallengeable role in preserving the stability of the state.

The two most prominent fourth-generation figures in the Politburo Standing Committee that emerged from the Sixteenth Congress were the president, Hu Jintao, and the premier, Wen Jiabao. The vice-president, Zeng Qinghong, who was part of the powerful Shanghai faction associated with former President Jiang Zemin, had a much lower profile, but he was known to have considerable influence and had the reputation of being a shrewd political operator. He was also widely assumed to see himself as

Hu's successor as president. There was much speculation about the emergence of a Hu-Zeng axis which would eventually eliminate Premier Wen Jiabao. Wen, however successfully consolidated his own position, in part by embracing populist causes such as the reduction of poverty, opposition to political corruption and environmental protection. Zeng Qinghong unexpectedly lost his posts after the Seventeenth Congress of the CCP in 2007, largely it can be assumed as a result of the retirement of his patron, Jiang Zemin.

Hu Jintao was born in Anhui province in southern China in 1942. He studied hydroelectric engineering at Tsinghua (Qinghua) University in Beijing and joined the Communist Party while he was a student in 1964. He is a classic product of the 'double burden' system under which China's future potential leaders were simultaneously educated in technology and trained as politicians. His early career was in the Ministry of Water Conservancy and Power, an unexciting post but one in which he learned to deal with some of the fundamental issues in the development of China's economy. Hu Jintao's political history is often described as obscure but this is mainly because his formative years were spent in important but low-profile positions in the west of China. He is best known for the authoritarian style with which he ruled Gansu, the poor and remote province in the northwest in the 1970s and 1980s and for his role as CCP secretary in Tibet in the 1980s and 1990s, when he imposed martial law. He also served as head of the Central Party School which provides political and ideological education for senior party members. One of his power bases is a group of former members of the Communist Youth League (CYL), of which he was First Secretary during 1984–5. He was recalled to Beijing in 1992 as a member of the all-powerful Standing Committee of the Politburo under Deng Xiaoping. When he became president of China in 2003, he brought in a number of officials from the CYL and promoted them to key positions.

Like previous leaders of the CCP he realised that he needed to ensure that the military remained firmly under the control of the Party and that it was necessary for him to guarantee the support of the army for him personally to consolidate his power. When Jiang Zemin retired, somewhat reluctantly, from the post of chairman of the Central Military Commission [CMC] on 19 September 2004, Hu Jintao rapidly moved to strengthen his personal relationship with senior military officers. He was responsible for promoting several key officers, including members of the CMC, to the rank of general and appeared publicly at PLA functions and exercises. He has also made a point when being photographed with senior officers of wearing the *zhongshan zhuang* (often called the Mao jacket) in military green rather than his usual trademark Western-style suit, collar and tie.[2] Hu Jintao has also strengthened the CCP's links to the increasingly important business class, continuing the process that was begun by Jiang Zemin. His 2006 New Year broadcast address focused on his commitment to 'peaceful development', the consensus term for China's non-aggressive rise to power and multilateralism. However, he also made a point of stressing his continuing support for the 'one-China principle' and the active promotion of the peaceful reunification of Taiwan with the mainland and opposition to Taiwanese secessionists (that is the DPP of Chen Shui-bian), probably the political cause dearest to the heart of the military. His priority is to maintain the legitimacy and longevity of the CCP and all other matters are subordinate to that. He is seen as a cautious but determined politician, a steady hand on the tiller and someone who is not easily rattled. He is prepared to tolerate administrative reforms but is unlikely to be willing to countenance any fundamental political change.

When he took office, Prime Minister Wen Jiabao's image was of a meticulous, perhaps even dull, functionary who is more concerned about results than political slogans. He was trained as a geologist and also worked in Gansu province, and during China's long drawn out period of applying to join the WTO he was given the crucial task of developing policies on agriculture, finance and the environment. He had previously worked with Hu Yaobang, Zhao Ziyang and Jiang Zemin when they were in turn chairmen of the CCP, and in June 1989 he had accompanied Zhao Ziyang when he made his celebrated visit to the students who were on hunger strike in Tiananmen Square. Unlike Zhao, who was dismissed and placed under house arrest, Wen survived politically. He has identified himself publicly with popular causes especially the environment, openness, decreasing the wealth gap and attacks on corruption. Wen visited Harbin on 26 November 2005 to observe the recovery work after the pollution of the Songhua River. He admonished local officials for not having acted quickly enough and warned them against any attempt at a cover-up. He has stressed the need for putting the protection of the environment ahead of the push for economic growth at any cost. On New Year's Eve 2006, he visited the cities of Jiujiang and Ruichang in the northeast of Jiangxi province which had been devastated by an earthquake on 26 November. The quake cost the lives of 13 people and left more than 100,000 homeless and Wen emphasised the need for reconstruction, not only of housing but also schools which had also been damaged or destroyed. He is himself from a humble family background and has acquired the reputation of having genuine concern for the lot of the common people, although as with all CCP leaders, it is difficult to know to what extent these are his genuine views.[3]

The third member of the ruling triumvirate at the beginning of the twenty-first century, and the man who was for some time believed to be the heir apparent to Hu Jintao, was Zeng Qinghong. He is the son of Zeng

Shan, a civil war veteran who became deputy mayor of Shanghai after the victory of the CCP in 1949 and later served as minister of internal affairs. Zeng Qinghong was educated as an engineer and joined the CCP in 1960. Chinese analysts point to the fact that he is both the scion of a revolutionary family and a member of the powerful Shanghai faction in the Chinese Communist Party. His position in the faction was consolidated in the 1980s when he worked for the then CCP secretary in Shanghai, Jiang Zemin. When Jiang took over from Zhao Ziyang as secretary-general of the CCP after 4 June 1989, Zeng Qinghong moved to Beijing with him. Respected for his political acumen but not popular, Zeng is regarded as having been Jiang's hatchet man and thus responsible for removing Jiang's political opponents. After the retirement of Jiang from front-line politics, Zeng was his master's voice in the Politburo Standing Committee and the effective head of the Shanghai faction. In 1999, he became head of the CCP's powerful Organisation Department which has administrative responsibility for appointments and promotions within the Party. Although, like any successful Chinese machine politician, Zeng Qinghong plays his cards close to his chest, some insiders believed that he was be the most liberal or at least the most open-minded of the ruling triumvirate. However, when Jiang stepped down, Zeng's career came to a speedy and unexpected end.

China and the USA

After the normalisation of diplomatic contacts between the USA in China in the 1970s, the main emphasis in bilateral dealings was on economic relations, primarily trade but also the technical but increasingly acrimonious debates on the relative value of the Chinese currency, the *renminbi*, and the US dollar. However, a series of political crises revealed that critical differences remained between China and the USA. The three most serious were the NATO bombing of the Chinese embassy in Belgrade in May 1999; the collision between a US reconnaissance aircraft and a Chinese fighter over Hainan Island in April 2001 and allegations in 1999 that a Chinese-born American scientist had been passing nuclear secrets to Beijing.

On 7 May 1999, during NATO operations in Yugoslavia, which was in a state of civil war, the Chinese embassy in the capital Belgrade was hit by bombs. The building was badly damaged and three Chinese citizens, all journalists, were killed. The CIA took responsibility for the attack, and maintained that it was at fault because it had been using a map that was out of date. However rumours spread that the bombing was a deliberate act by the USA because the Americans believed that the embassy was being used to assist the Yugoslav army in its radio communications. In China students demonstrated outside foreign embassies and on some university campuses foreign students were threatened. The atmosphere was tense. Relations between the USA and China improved towards the end of the year and the two parties came to an understanding on ex gratia payments to the families of the victims and compensation for the damage to the embassy. This did not entirely resolve the matter, especially in the eyes of many Chinese who persisted in the belief that the attack had been deliberate: rumours and counter-rumours circulated, and continue to circulate, about possible reasons for the bombing although the US government continues to insist that it had merely been a dreadful error.

On 1 April 2001, a Lockheed EP-3E Aries II signals reconnaissance aircraft, operated by the US Navy, was patrolling close to the island of Hainan which is off the southern coast of China. US sources claimed that the EP-3E had been operating legitimately in international air space but Shenyang J-8 fighters of the PLA Air Force intercepted it on the grounds that it was within Chinese air space and was on an espionage mission. The reconnaissance aircraft and the wing of one of the fighters collided. The fighter crashed and the pilot was presumed killed, although his body was never found: the US aircraft was damaged but was able to make an emergency landing on Hainan. US diplomats were hurriedly dispatched to the island to negotiate for the release of their crew, all of whom had survived and the men were released ten days later. However the Chinese authorities did not release the EP-3E for several weeks and it was assumed that they availed themselves of the opportunity to assess and possibly even remove any advanced technology with which the aircraft was equipped. The fact that the aircraft was intercepted was an indication of the tension between the Chinese and American military on the borders with Chinese airspace but the speed with which a negotiated settlement was reached was a mark of the importance attached by the two governments to maintaining diplomatic relations.

Political Anniversaries

The manner in which the Chinese Communist Party has treated the anniversaries of the deaths of its former leaders is very revealing and can furnish useful evidence about the internal balance of power. The commemorations of the deaths of both Hu Yaobang and Zhao Ziyang pointed to interesting tensions within the ruling triumvirate in the Politburo Standing Committee. In the final months of 2005 there was considerable debate behind the scenes in Beijing on the appropriate ceremonials to mark what would have been the ninetieth birthday of Hu Yaobang, who had died in 1989, and the first anniversary of the death of Zhao Ziyang. In terms of the range of political views within the CCP, Hu, whose death provided the impetus for the Democracy Movement which was crushed on 4 June 1989, and Zhao were both considered to have been liberal reformers who were considerably ahead of their time: attitudes to their legacy offered pointers to the state of internal party politics in 2005 and 2006. A commemoration of the ninetieth anniversary of Hu Yaobang's birth was held in the Great Hall of the People on Friday 18 November 2005. It was a low key affair, described as a symposium by *People's Daily*, and attended by three members of the Politburo Standing Committee, including Wen Jiabao and Zeng Qinghong. Hu Jintao did not attend, although he had supported the original decision to hold the memorial meeting. This was perhaps surprising as Hu Jintao had been appointed head of the Communist Youth League by Hu Yaobang in the 1980s and continues to associate himself with the liberal and tolerant ethos that his mentor encouraged.[4] Hu Yaobang was secretary-general of the CCP in the mid-1980s and not only was he seen as liberal minded, he was personally responsible for the rehabilitation of a number of political figures who had lost their posts during the Cultural Revolution. He was dismissed as premier in 1987 after a series of demonstrations by students which began as protests against the increasing involvement of Japanese business in the Chinese economy but expanded into a movement to condemn corruption and to demand greater democracy.

Zhao Ziyang died on 17 January 2005 but there were no public ceremonies to mark the first anniversary of his death in 2006 as would have been customary in the Chinese tradition of mourning public figures. Instead it was commemorated by a small gathering of family and friends: campaigners for democracy were firmly discouraged from attending. The former premier was honoured for his role in extending the market reforms that he had developed in Sichuan province to the whole of China in the 1980s. However his role in the 1989 crackdown, when he appeared to side with the demonstrating students, led to his house arrest for 15 years and made him a powerful symbol for reformers within the CCP. For years there had been persistent rumours that Zhao had left behind a manuscript of his testament giving his own version of the bitter political battles behind the scenes that led to the unleashing of units of the PLA on unarmed demonstrators on 4 June 1989 and a book, *Prisoner of the State: The Secret Journal of Premier Zhao Ziyang*, based on testimony recorded during his house arrest was eventually published in May 2009. It was available in Hong Kong but not initially in China.[5]

The thirtieth anniversary of the death of Zhou Enlai on 8 January 2006 was commemorated by the publication of a substantial *Pictorial Biography of Zhou Enlai* [*Zhou Enlai hua zhuan*]. The book was launched at a symposium, held in the Zhou Enlai Memorial Chamber in the Mao Zedong Memorial Hall and presided over by Gu Xiulian the deputy chairwoman of the Standing Committee of the National People's Congress. The former premier is still venerated as a great revolutionary and many Chinese believe, rightly or wrongly, that he ameliorated some of the harshest policies of the Cultural Revolution and saved the lives of many individuals.

In different ways, Hu Jintao and Wen Jiabao both followed the Hu Yaobang and Zhao Ziyang style of government. Zeng Qinghong, as the protégé of Jiang Zemin who succeeded Zhao, did not have the same devotion to their memory. The subdued commemoration of the two former leaders suggests that there was a determination to keep alive their legacy without seriously disturbing the delicate factional balance within the Party. The legacy of Zhou Enlai is less divisive but tends to benefit the reformers. Hu and Wen have functioned as part of a team as well as being rivals. It is tempting to see them as respectively a hardliner and a liberal but that would be simplistic. Wen succeeded in enhancing his authority by his championship of popular causes. Zeng's influence was understated but he was in a strong position because of his leadership of the Shanghai faction and was considered to be a serious candidate for the presidency after Hu Jintao until his rapid fall from power.

CONCLUSION

CHINA RISING
AND A 'HARMONIOUS SOCIETY'

The fundamental question that effects all long-term developments in China is the future of the uneasy alliance of the CCP-run state with the market economy as it continues to expand nationwide beyond the major urban areas of the south and southeast. It is a question that could be posed to the leadership of the Chinese Communist Party in terms of the classic Marxist analysis of conflict between the economic base and the social and cultural superstructure, but it rarely is.

The argument that was put forward by senior Chinese political figures in the early days of the reform programme was that they were creating a specifically Chinese type of socialism, 'socialism with Chinese characteristics' in the official jargon, although on closer inspection the concept is little more than ethnocentric rhetoric. Marxist or Communist political ideology is no longer a significant factor in twenty-first-century China and even the half-hearted attempts to invoke the spirit of Yan'an, the self-sacrificing soldier Lei Feng, or the model official Jiao Yulu that were revived during the 1990s disappeared rapidly below the horizon. Economics was the only thing that mattered and it was quite common when discussing problems of democracy with people in China to hear them say that they were not concerned whether China achieved political democracy as long as there was economic democracy. What mattered to them was whether they could earn a living, preferably in the way that they chose.

Part of the reason for these changes in attitude was the emergence of new social groupings in China. Over the last few decades, an elite group of managers and technocrats has emerged as the most important political force. Many of its members have been educated abroad and they are deeply committed to modernisation as the primary goal for China. These men and women are often, although by no means exclusively, the children of senior party, military and government officials. They are highly sceptical of political theories, especially anything to do with socialism, and are more interested in Western management techniques and economic principles although that has not prevented many of them from joining the CCP.

During the 1980s another group also came into view, the nouveau riche individual entrepreneurs [*getihu*] who were prevented from operating in Mao's lifetime. Most started with small businesses, but many are now extremely wealthy, even by Western standards and by the beginning of the twenty-first century some were functioning in ways that are indistinguishable from their counterparts in the West. They own their own businesses and all seek the same trappings of success – prestigious houses and cars and private, possibly foreign, education for their children. The relationship between the new business class and the party elite is still evolving, but it has been an important factor in the emergence of one of China's major problems – corruption.

Corruption

Criticism of corruption by party and government officials, which was largely absent from political life during the radical Maoist period, has been one of the features of the reform period. Corruption exists on a vast scale and at all levels, and political demonstrations in 1986 and in the run up to the 1989 democracy movement included campaigns against nepotism and corrupt practices. It is difficult to quantify the level of corruption, but it remains a matter of serious concern to the Chinese authorities. There have been many public criticisms of corrupt officials, including some in highest ranks of the party and the government, and exemplary punishments have been imposed by the courts.

One of the most dramatic denunciations was in a speech by president and secretary-general of the CCP, Jiang Zemin that was published on 1 July 1993. The speech coincided with a suspended death sentence that had been handed down to a senior Chinese banker for his involvement in the illegal sale of bonds in return for bribes, a case in which a deputy minister was also implicated. The overheating economy and frozen official salaries have encouraged this behaviour and although some of the most spectacular cases involved central government and party officials, corruption was also rife among local officials in rural areas. County town officials were accused of the worst excesses and were blamed by Jiang Zemin for not following central government guidelines. What marked out Jiang's speech on 1 July was his warning, unprecedented for a Chinese leader, that unless corruption was brought under control, the party could lose power. The formal attack on corruption continued under President Hu Jintao and there have been many more high profile convictions including that of Chen Xitong, the mayor of Beijing, who was sentenced to 16 years imprisonment in 1998, and the execution of some corrupt senior officials. Zheng Xiaoyu, who had served as the director of the State Food and Drug Administration, was accused of taking bribes from manufacturers of food products in exchange for issuing licences and was executed in July 2007 during a period of international concern about the safety of food and other products that were being exported.

Order and Disorder

In the tradition of the Confucian emperors of old, what the cautious and conservative leadership in China fears most is disorder [*luan*]. There is a consensus among Chinese official spokesmen and Western observers, particularly those who have a business background, that since the death of Mao Zedong China has completely abandoned its radical past and is on a stable path towards a capitalist, or at least a mixed, economy and that this will automatically and inevitably result in continued stability. There have however been many outbreaks of violence and disorder, some on a large scale, particularly in the rural areas. Some Chinese commentators have suggested that a period of serious social disorder leading to nationwide unrest is a distinct possibility. This could be ignited by popular revulsion against official corruption or by bankruptcies, strikes and demonstrations against mass redundancies that could result from an overheating economy.

However if there is unrest on a significant scale, it is in the peasant heartland of China that it could spread most rapidly. Wan Li, the chairman of China's quasi-parliamentary body, the National People's Congress, in a report in 2004 complained of peasants being exploited. They were being given IOUs, known as 'white slips', for government payments due to them and 'green slips' were issued in lieu of post office payments of remittances sent by peasants working on construction sites in south China to their families at home. These were handed over by the authorities instead of money payments, and the recipients were not being allowed to cash them. Given the problems of high taxation that they also faced, a rural unemployment rate that may be as much as 50 per cent in some areas and endemic corruption, it is clear that conditions in many rural areas are becoming intolerable. Peasant farmers have been reported as saying that they need a new Cheng Sheng and Wu Guang, referring to the leaders of the peasant revolt that helped to overthrow the Qin dynasty in 206 BC. In the 1990s there were persistent reports of farmers attacking officials and refusing to pay levies and taxes, and influential independent local leaders have emerged in some rural areas. Demonstrations and riots involving thousands of people have been reported in the provinces of Sichuan, Henan and other rural areas and official sources accepted that there had been tens of thousands of major disturbances across China.[1]

The Ministry of Public Security issued statistics to show that the number of protests during 2006 had declined in comparison with the unusually high number recorded in 2005. According to the official announcement, in the first nine months of 2005, there had been 17,900 'mass incidents', but the number of 'public order disturbances', a term which is normally used to refer to smaller-scale and less serious incidents increased by 6 per cent to 87,000. It is not clear whether the reduction in serious disorder was a genuine figure or a result of under-reporting or redefinition by local officials, but the number of serious incidents and the fact that they were being reported publicly, in a society where the tendency had been to keep silent about embarrassing issue such as these, indicates the level of concern felt by the authorities.[2]

There were also well-documented accounts in legal journals and newspapers of the resurrection of rural secret societies which were said to have been wiped out in 1949. Detailed knowledge of what really happens in the whole of the Chinese countryside is elusive. The sheer size of the rural areas, poor communications and the censorship of the official media make it difficult to arrive at a realistic assessment of the problem. From the 1990s into the twenty-first century, the number of disturbances over tax gradually diminished as the government adjusted its policies and eventually abandoned the unpopular land tax in 2006, but this conflict was replaced by disputes over the sale of farming land to builders and developers in deals which also involved official corruption.

The last resort for the government in dealing with rural revolts or other serious disturbances is the People's Liberation Army. It could once have been regarded as unswervingly loyal and enjoying great national prestige, but doubts were cast on its efficiency and reliability in the reform period. During the 1980s there was a move to reduce the size of the PLA by one-quarter, and many men and women in the services were moved to non-military duties which include manufacturing and other money-making activities. Recruitment suffered as fit young peasants, the backbone of the army for 40 years, preferred more attractive and profitable occupations such as private farming or business. Some sections of the PLA were discontented at the image of the military after the suppression of the Tian'anmen demonstrations in 1989 and there were suggestions that senior officers might be unwilling to act in a similar way in the future. The Hong Kong news magazine *Zheng Ming*, which has highly placed sources in Beijing, reported that army garrisons have been reshuffled to avoid the threat of factional disputes at a senior level within the PLA and CCP about the nature of 'reform' within the military.

The approach to social crises that was adopted by conservatives in the party's leadership in the past was to fall back on military training accompanied by political education and ideological pressure, using tired revolutionary models such as the soldier hero Lei Feng and the exemplary official Jiao Yulu. The response of young Chinese to this kind of exhortation has been even more unenthusiastic than in the past, and military training for university students, which was briefly introduced after the suppression of the 4 June demonstrations, has also lapsed. Although these moralistic campaigns failed and it was widely agreed that China's problems could no longer be resolved by returning to the old leftist thinking of control, ideological education and military training, no viable alternative was put forward by the central political leadership apart from an emphasis on patriotism.

Patriotism, Nationalism and National Humiliation

As the economic reform programme progressed, even though the authority of the Communist Party was maintained, the ideology and political tradition from which it had emerged was in crisis. This crisis was exacerbated when the Soviet Union collapsed in 1991: for many in China as in the former USSR, this was a confirmation that Marxism–Leninism of the Stalinist variety had been completely discredited or at the very least was irrelevant to the needs of a society in the process of such dramatic change. Whether this amounted to a political vacuum is debatable but during the late 1990s, any remaining Marxist rhetoric was gradually being supplanted by appeals to patriotism or nationalism. This was particularly noticeable during the periods when there was increased tension between China and the USA, notably after the bombing of the Chinese embassy in Belgrade by NATO forces in May 1999.

There were also appeals to redress China's 'national humiliation' (*guochi*). National humiliation is sometimes used to refer to the entire process of Western encroachment and the semi-colonialism of the treaty ports in the nineteenth and early twentieth centuries. It is, however, often reserved more specifically to refer to the humiliation suffered at the hands of the Japanese from the Twenty-One Demands of 1915. On 18 September 2006, the seventy-fifth anniversary of the invasion of Manchuria by the Japanese Imperial Army commemorations and rallies took place across the whole of China. In the northeastern (Manchurian) city of Shenyang, close to where the Japanese invasion had begun, sirens had been sounded on the anniversary since 1995 at the suggestion of an elderly resident, but this practice spread and in 2006 it was emulated in at least 100 other cities across the nation, and cars and buses sounded their horns in response to the sirens. Shenyang has a museum, the 9.18 Historical Museum which is one of 150 in China that commemorate the 18 September invasion of 1931 and the subsequent war against Japan.[3] There have been persistent pleas for 18

September to be formally declared a 'national humiliation day', including a proposal from a Shandong delegate to the National People's Congress in March 2007. This was resisted, as were plans to declare 7 September, the anniversary of the signing of the Boxer Protocol in 1901 as a day of national defence. In the end 18 September became National Defence Day, a more positive designation than a day of national humiliation, although the name is not widely used.[4]

Unity and Division

One notable feature of the reform decade was a discernible growth in the regionalisation of the economy, initially in the southeast but also in the border areas of the northwest, the northeast, Tibet and the southwest, where liberalisation of cross-border trade with the former Soviet Union, India and Pakistan had brought local economic growth that is unprecedented in post-war China. Although there had been other periods of decentralisation, including the Cultural Revolution years, it became possible to detect stronger feelings of regional political and economic consciousness, even in the northwest border area that had long been regarded as one of the most backward in China. Where there was a conflict of interest between local financial needs and national requirements, as in the case of a celebrated dispute between Guangdong province and Beijing over the payment of taxes, it could no longer be assumed that Beijing would automatically get its way.

Could this decentralisation lead to division and disorder with echoes of the warlord period of the 1920s? Economic logic seems to have been pushing China towards decentralisation and the growth of regional power centres, with a weakened political centre. The precise regional powers which might emerge are far from certain, but those most likely to succeed economically are the south of Guangdong province including the Shenzhen special economic zone in cooperation with Hong Kong; Fujian, increasingly in cooperation with Taiwan; Shanghai, which has a local government determined to take over from Hong Kong as China's financial powerhouse, and its hinterland; and the Beijing–Tianjin nexus. Other possibilities include the Northeast in trading partnership with Korea and the Russian Far East; Xinjiang and the other regions of northwestern China; and Tibet, although progress in these areas depends to a large extent on the satisfactory solution of long-standing and intransigent ethnic conflicts. The rapid development of the coastal regions has already raised a number of serious questions about the future of the poor interior, which is far less likely to attract capital; the possibility of inter-regional conflict for scarce resources; the effect of migration towards provinces with greater job opportunities and the consequent danger of additional social unrest. These regional issues are exacerbated by the question of inter-ethnic conflict in some of the border areas. Although, as has been suggested, the movement for Tibetan autonomy is the best known outside China it is not the only one, and the Beijing leadership is certain to face further demands for autonomy from the Uyghurs of Xinjiang and the Mongolians of Inner Mongolia – demands which seem less unrealistic since the dissolution of the USSR, the creation of new Central Asian states based partly on ethnic divisions, and the opening of China's borders which have encouraged contacts with related ethnic groups outside China.

It has long been an article of faith of both the Communist Party and the Guomindang that China must remain as a single unified state within the boundaries set by the Manchu Qing emperors in the eighteenth and nineteenth centuries. The centrifugal forces of regionalism are a threat to central power, but to what extent they pose a genuine threat to the unity of China is still unclear. Further decentralisation, if not actual political division, is likely to accompany and sustain the economic and social modernisation of China, but it also poses a grave threat to the future of the Communist Party.

Peaceful Development and a 'Harmonious Society'

On 22 December 2005 the Information Office of the State Council, China's cabinet, issued a white paper on the future development of the nation. The watchwords were peaceful development, harmony and prosperity and the document systematised a debate that had been under way within the political elite of the PRC for some years. Although it had echoes of both Nikita Khrushchev's peaceful co-existence policies of the 1950s and Zhou Enlai's proposals for the Five Principles of Peaceful Co-existence in China's relations with Third World countries, it was presented as a new and modern approach to China's development and its relationship with the outside world.[5] Central to this position is successful economic development and the creation of a society that is described as *xiaokang*. *Xiaokang* is a new term in contemporary political discourse but it has a substantial historical pedigree in Confucian writings where it was often used as a description of the society that would immediately precede the Confucian utopia of Datong (Great or Universal Harmony) It was resurrected by Hu Jintao and Wen Jiabao in the early years of the twenty-first century and can be translated approximately as 'comfortably off', that is not necessarily very wealthy but certainly not poor. The Chinese leadership may have in mind the generally affluent and middle class population (by their own assessment) of their economically successful neighbour Japan, or possibly even Taiwan. It is certainly the antithesis of the class conflict approach to social change that the Communist Party pursued under Mao Zedong's leadership.

President Hu Jintao in a speech to leading members of the Communist Party at his old stamping ground, the Central Party School, on Monday 25 June 2007, reaffirmed his commitment to the policy of spreading wealth more widely and tackling corruption as the main tasks for the CCP if it is to achieve its goal of a 'comfortably off' society by 2020. The extension of social services, particularly health and education to the 800 million residents of rural China, many of them desperately poor, was identified as an important part of this strategy. Hu accepted that the struggle against corruption was going to be a long haul and an extremely complex and difficult process.

In addition to senior figures from the Party centre, that meeting was also attended by senior officers of the military and security services and by delegates from regional and provincial party and government organisations, the key figures in the ruling elite. In keeping with his track record of caution on political reform, Hu warned that any reform of the political system would have to keep pace with economic and social development which he identified as the main priority. While he conceded that participation in the decision-making process could be improved by opening up new channels for consultation and that the rule of law was essential, he insisted that maintaining the leading role of the CCP was non-negotiable. The conference was not open to foreign journalists but it was reported in *People's Daily* the following day. Hu Jintao's speech was clearly intended to set the tone for political discussions about the future direction of the reform programme in the run-up to the CCP's Seventeenth quinquennial conference which took place in October 2007 and at which the next generation of the Chinese leadership made their appearance. The most significant of these were Xi Jinping, who was elected as vice-chairman of the CCP and is almost certain to succeed Hu Jintao as chairman of the Party and president in 2012, and Li Keqiang, who became senior deputy premier.

Olympic China

The decision in 2001 to award China the Olympic Games for the summer of 2008 was considered by Beijing to be both a colossal achievement and a just recognition of the nation's new status in the world. The creation of a successful games became a matter of national pride, and China invested heavily in the renovation of old sporting venues and the creation of new ones, including iconic constructions, notably the Beijing National Stadium that is known universally as the Bird's Nest, and the Watercube which was built for swimming and other aquatic activities. Even after the end of the games, these have remained major tourist attractions, particularly for Chinese tourists visiting Beijing, and symbols of China's national self-esteem. In addition to the sporting facilities, tens of millions of *renminbi* were spent on renovating hotels and improving the transport infrastructure, in particular the expansion of the underground rail network and the creation of the spacious new international Terminal 3 at Beijing Capital Airport. The total cost of the games to China is not known precisely but some estimates have put the figure as high as $40 billion.

The games were held from 8 to 24 August and brought to the city hundreds of thousands of foreign athletes and spectators who might otherwise never have visited China. Across the globe, millions more watched some or part of the games on television by virtue of the massive presence of the world's media and for many viewers this was their first impression of contemporary China. As a whole the games were an organisational and presentational triumph for the government of the PRC. They demonstrated that Beijing had the ability to commit resources and finish a complex project on time and that, in spite of all the problems that China faces in the twenty-first century, it was possible to mobilise a large proportion of the population around the patriotic obligation to show China at its best. Many Chinese, even those who were not necessarily committed supporters of the CCP, found it difficult to understand the political protests and criticisms of China's human rights record that took place during the torch relays outside China and in Beijing while the games were under way.

The games were not without controversy and even during the construction process conflict arose over the acquisition of land and properties. There was criticism of the lack of open media access and the suppression of protests by Chinese citizens: questions were also raised about the ages of some of the participating athletes from China. The major ceremonies were orchestrated with style and commitment but at times the patriotism and national pride with which they were imbued spilled over into jingoism.

The way the Olympic Games were organised and presented is a pointer to how China will conduct itself in the future. Patriotic pride and a rejection of what the leadership considers to have been a century and a half of 'national humiliation' will continue to be a major factor in the way that China interacts with the rest of the world. The ability to accumulate and deploy vast resources centrally will remain a high priority and this will restrict the degree of privatisation in the economy. Although China is more inclined than previously to recognise the importance of human rights, it will not recognise the right of other countries or outside bodies to instruct it how to run its own society. This was amply demonstrated on 4 June 2009, the twentieth anniversary of the suppression of the democracy movement in Tian'anmen Square, when a spokesman for the Chinese Ministry of Foreign Affairs, Qin Gang, angrily rejected a statement by the US secretary of state, Hillary Clinton that China should 'provide a public accounting of those killed, detained or missing, both to learn and to heal'.[6] This exchange symbolises a prickly relationship between the USA and China which is a pointer to potential conflict in the long term. China and the USA are already commercial competitors and are political rivals: they may be the only two superpowers of the late twenty-first century. Managing this problematic relationship and ensuring that economic and political rivalry does not develop into military confrontation will preoccupy the leaderships of China and the USA and observers of the Chinese scene for many years to come.

NOTES

Introduction
1 Herbert A. Giles *The Civilisation of China* (London: Williams and Norgate, 1911).

1 Rise and Fall of the Chinese Empire
1 The Han people take their name from the Han dynasty and ultimately from the Han River valley that was home to the family that founded the dynasty. Many southern Chinese, however, prefer to think of themselves as people of Tang (*Tangren*, a name which is used for many Western Chinatowns) rather than Han, and they, in turn, attribute their name to the Tang dynasty. This distinction is further evidence of the great differences between the people classified as Han in contemporary China.
2 The name Manchuria went out of favour in China because of its associations with the Japanese puppet state of Manzhouguo (Manchukuo) in the 1930s, and the region is now generally referred to on the mainland as the Northeast [*Dongbei*] or the Three Provinces of the Northeast [*Dongbei sansheng*].
3 Pamela Kyle Crossley *The Manchus* (Oxford: Blackwell, 1997); Mark C. Elliott *The Manchu Way: The Eight Banners and Ethnic Identity in Late Imperial China* (Stanford: Stanford University Press, 2001).
4 The most comprehensive account of the Manchu conquest is Frederic Wakeman Jr. *The Great Enterprise: The Manchu Reconstruction of Imperial Order in Seventeenth Century China* (Berkeley: University of California Press, 1985). The banner organisations, based on clans, were the foundation of the Manchu military achievements.
5 Peter C. Perdue *China Marches West: The Qing Conquest of Central Asia* (Cambridge: Belknap Press of Harvard University Press, 2005), pp. 161–73.
6 Dawa Norbu *China's Tibet Policy* (Richmond: Curzon, 2001).
7 Joseph Fletcher 'Ch'ing Inner Asia c. 1800' in John K. Fairbank (Editor) *Cambridge History of China* (Cambridge: Cambridge University Press, 1978), Volume 10, pp. 90–106.
8 Perdue *China Marches West: The Qing Conquest of Central Asia*, pp. 289–92.
9 Owen Lattimore *Nationalism and Revolution in Mongolia* (Leiden: E.J. Brill, 1955), pp. 6–7.
10 Lattimore *Nationalism and Revolution in Mongolia*, p. 7.

11 Lloyd E. Eastman *Family Fields and Ancestors: Constancy and Change in China's Social and Economic History, 1550–1949* (New York: Oxford University Press, 1988), pp. 3–6. It is necessary to treat population figures for this period with great caution: until 1953 there was no national census of China that was even remotely reliable.

12 Susan Naquin and Evelyn S. Rawski *Chinese Society in the Eighteenth Century* (New Haven: Yale University Press, 1987).

13 Peng Zeyi (Editor) *Zhongguo jindai shougongye shi ziliao 1840–1949* [*Materials on the History of Modern Chinese Handicraft Industries, 1840–1949*], 4 volumes (Beijing: Sanlian shudian, 1957).

14 Eastman *Family Fields and Ancestors: Constancy and Change in China's Social and Economic History, 1550–1949*; Harriet Zurndorfer *Change and Continuity in Chinese Local History: The Development of Hui-chou Prefecture, 800–1800* (Leiden: E.J. Brill, 1989); Michael Dillon 'Commerce and Confucianism: The Merchants of Huizhou' *History Today*, February 1989.

15 Richard J. Smith *China's Cultural Heritage: The Qing Dynasty 1644–1912*, second edition (Boulder: Westview, 1994), p. 71.

16 Chang Chung-li *The Chinese Gentry: Studies on Their Role in Nineteenth-Century Chinese Society* (Seattle: University of Washington Press, 1955).

17 Mark C. Elliott *The Manchu Way: The Eight Banners and Ethnic Identity in Late Imperial China* (Stanford: Stanford University Press, 2001). Pamela Kyle Crossley *Orphan Warriors: Three Manchu Generations and the End of the Qing World* (New Jersey: Princeton University Press, 1990), pp. 28–9.

18 Smith *China's Cultural Heritage*; Jean Chesneaux *Secret Societies in China* (Hong Kong and London: Heinemann, 1971).

19 Crossley *The Manchus*, pp. 67–8.

20 Naquin and Rawski *Chinese Society in the Eighteenth Century*, pp. 38–9, 108–9.

21 Crossley *The Manchus*, pp. 87–90.

22 Crossley *The Manchus*; Crossley *Orphan Warriors*.

2 China and the West: the Road to the Opium War

1   Edward H. Schafer *The Golden Peaches of Samarkand: A Study of T'ang Exotics* (Berkeley: University of California Press, 1963). Strictly speaking, the remains of Tang dynasty Chang'an lie outside the modern city of Xi'an.

2   J.D. Legge *Indonesia* (Sydney: Prentice Hall, 1980), pp. 50–1. For the development of Malacca as the major port of the spice trade see D.G.E. Hall *A History of South-East Asia* (London: Macmillan, 1961), pp. 179–85. Benzoin is a gum resin used in ointments and perfumes.

3   Chen Dasheng *Quanzhou yisilanjiao shike* [*Islamic Stone Carvings of Quanzhou*] (Fuzhou: Ningxia and Fujian People's Press, 1984).

4   Hall *A History of South-East Asia*, p. 198, Legge *Indonesia*, p. 75; J.H. Parry *The Spanish Seaborne Empire* (London: Hutchinson, 1971).

5   Hall *A History of South-East Asia*, pp. 257–8.

6   H.B. (Hosea Balou) Morse *The Chronicles of the East India Company Trading to China 1635–1834*, 5 volumes (Oxford: Clarendon Press, 1926), Volume I, p. 5.

7   Louis Dermigny *La Chine et l'Occident: Le Commerce à Canton au XVIIIe siècle 1719–1833* (Paris: S.E.V.P.E.N., 1964).

8   Hall *A History of South-East Asia*, pp. 224–35; Morse *Chronicles*, Volume I, p. 4. Hall points out that those beheaded by the Dutch in the 'massacre' included ten Japanese nationals and one Portuguese. The British and Dutch navies later came into conflict much closer to home and fought major battles in the North Sea during the three Dutch Wars of the seventeenth century. The Treaty of Westminster, which was concluded after the first of the three conflicts, included an agreement that the Dutch would pay compensation for the Amboina massacre, pp. 249–50.

9   Morse *Chronicles*, Volume I, p. 6.

10   Morse *Chronicles*, Volume I, p. 7.

11   Morse *Chronicles*, Volume I, pp. 9–11.

12   Morse *Chronicles*, Volume I, pp. 14–30.

13   Morse *Chronicles*, Volume I, pp. 50–65.

14   Morse *Chronicles*, Volume I, pp. 85–98.

15   Morse *Chronicles*, Volume I, p. 99.

16   Morse *Chronicles*, Volume I, pp. 181, 301.

17   Morse *Chronicles*, Volume I, p. 113.

18   Morse *Chronicles*, Volume I, pp. 154–60.

19   Morse *Chronicles*, Volume I, pp. 161–70

20   Cheng Hao *Guangzhou gang shi, jindai bufen* [*History of the Port of Guangzhou, the Modern Period*] (Beijing: Haiyang Press, 1985), pp. 10–12.

21   Xiao Yishan *Qingdai tongshi* [*Comprehensive History of the Qing Dynasty*] (Taipei: Shangwu Yinshuguan, 1952), p. 91.

22   Li Jiannong *Zhongguo jin bainian zhengzhi shi* [*Political History of China in the Last 100 years*], 2 volumes (Shanghai: Shangwu Yinshuguan [Commercial Press], 1947), pp. 17–19.

23   Bao Zhenggu *Yapian zhanzheng* [*The Opium War*] (Shanghai: Xin zhishi chubanshe, 1954). This book was produced, according to the publisher, so that people would understand the history of foreign imperialism in China and be on their guard against future threats.

24   J.L. Cranmer-Byng (Editor) *An Embassy to China: Being the Journal Kept by Lord Macartney during His Embassy to the Emperor Ch'ien-lung 1793–1794* (London: Longmans, 1962), p. 353.

25   Cranmer-Byng *An Embassy to China*, p. 61. The Spithead, which lies of the south coast of England between Portsmouth and the Isle of Wight, is a sheltered natural harbour and has been the main home anchorage for the British navy for centuries. The geographical parallels with Guangzhou or Hong Kong are quite striking. An 'Indiaman' or 'East Indiaman' was the contemporary term for a large merchant ship trading with India and designed to take both passengers and freight, while a brig was a square-rigged sailing ship with two masts.

26   Cranmer-Byng *An Embassy to China*, p. 63.

27   Cranmer-Byng *An Embassy to China*, p. 64.

28   Cranmer-Byng *An Embassy to China*, pp. 71–2.

29   Cranmer-Byng *An Embassy to China*, pp. 74–6.

30   Cranmer-Byng *An Embassy to China*, pp. 78–93.

31   Cranmer-Byng *An Embassy to China*, pp. 78–93.

32   Morse *Chronicles*, Volume II, p. 214.

33   Morse *Chronicles*, Volume II, pp. 224–5; Cranmer-Byng *An Embassy to China*, pp. 106–17, 122–4, 131–6.

34   Li *Zhongguo jin bainian zhengzhi shi*, p. 22.

35   Harley Farnsworth MacNair *Modern Chinese History Selected Readings: A Collection of Extracts from Various Sources* (Shanghai: Commercial Press, 1927), pp. 3–4.

36   Alain Peyrefitte *The Collision of Two Civilisations: The British Expedition to China, 1792–4* (London: Harvill, 1993) and Aubrey Singer *The Lion and the Dragon: The Story of the First British Embassy to the Court of the Emperor Qianlong in Beijing 1792–4* (London: Barrie and Jenkins, 1992) were the most significant books published at or near the time of the anniversary.

37   Zhang Shunhong, 'Historical Anachronism: The Qing Court's Perception of and Reaction to the Macartney Embassy' in Robert A. Bickers *Ritual and Diplomacy: The Macartney Mission to China 1792–1974* (London: British Association for Chinese Studies and Wellsweep Press, 1993), pp. 31–42.

38   Hsin-pao Chang *Commissioner Lin and the Opium War* (Cambridge: Harvard University Press, 1964), pp. 16–17; Li *Zhongguo jin bainian zhengzhi shi*, pp. 31–2.

39   Chang *Commissioner Lin and the Opium War*, p. 18; Fan Wenlan *Zhongguo jindai shi [Modern Chinese History]* (Beijing: Renmin chubanshe, 1962), pp. 5–6; Li *Zhongguo jin bainian zhengzhi shi*, pp. 31–3; Xiao *Qingdai tongshi*, Volume 2, pp. 906–27.

40   A chest was the usual measure for opium as it was for tea. In practice, tea chests were of different sizes, depending on the port of origin. Quarter chests as used in Whampoa held ten catties and were popular as they were the easiest to store. The port of Fuzhou favoured half chests and full chests. Tea from Shanghai normally came in full chests. Opium (Malwa) weighed 100 catties – 1 picul or 133 1/3 pounds, per chest. Patna or Benares opium weighed 12 catties to the chest. Basil Lubbock *The China Clippers* (London: Century, 1914), p. 122; Basil Lubbock *The Opium Clippers* (Glasgow: Brown, Son and Ferguson, 1933), pp. 28–9.

41   Chang *Commissioner Lin and the Opium War*, pp. 19–21; Arthur W. Hummel *Eminent Chinese of the Ch'ing Period* (Washington, D.C.: Government Printing Office, 1943–4), pp. 399–402.

42   Chang *Commissioner Lin and the Opium War*, pp. 21–2. During the early nineteenth century, the trade in Malwa opium played an important role in the development of the economy of western Madhya Pradesh. Bombay, in the neighbouring state of Maharashtra, was emerging as the main commercial and financial centre and the sale of Malwa opium to China played an important part in this development. Malwa opium poppy growers challenged the monopoly of the East India Company which attempted to restrict the production of the poppy and trade in its product.

43   Chang *Commissioner Lin and the Opium War*, pp. 22–32, 223.

44   Fernand Braudel *Civilisation and Capitalism 15th–18th Century*, Volume 3, *The Perspective of the World* (London: Collins, 1984), pp. 420–5.

45 Li *Zhongguo jin bainian zhengzhi shi*, pp. 33–4.

46 Beijing Normal University, Modern Chinese History Group *Zhongguo jindai shi ziliao xuanbian* [*Selected Documents in Modern Chinese History*], 2 volumes (Beijing: Zhonghua Shuju, 1977), Volume 1, pp. 1–5.

47 Chang *Commissioner Lin and the Opium War*, pp. 85–119; MacNair *Modern Chinese History Selected Readings*, pp. 85–103; Xiao *Qingdai tongshi*, pp. 911–15; Fan Wenlan *Zhongguo jindai shi* [*Modern Chinese History*] (Beijing: Renmin chubanshe, 1962), pp. 14–17.

48 Hummel *Eminent Chinese of the Ch'ing Period*, pp. 574–6; MacNair *Modern Chinese History Selected Readings*, pp. 112–13.

49 Hummel *Eminent Chinese of the Ch'ing Period*, p. 511.

50 Chang *Commissioner Lin and the Opium War*, p. 111; Hummel *Eminent Chinese of the Ch'ing Period*, pp. 716–17.

51 www.jardines.com/profile/history.html.

52 *Chinese Repository*, Volume VI, 1838 in MacNair *Modern Chinese History Selected Readings*, pp. 91–2.

53 Chang *Commissioner Lin and the Opium War*, pp. 120–6.

54 Li *Zhongguo jin bainian zhengzhi shi*, pp. 35–6.

55 Li *Zhongguo jin bainian zhengzhi shi*, p. 36; MacNair *Modern Chinese History Selected Readings*, pp. 106–8; *Zhongguo jindai shi ziliao xuanbian* [*Selected Documents in Modern Chinese History*], pp. 13–15.

56 Chang *Commissioner Lin and the Opium War*, pp. 141–60.

57 MacNair *Modern Chinese History Selected Readings*, pp. 108–10.

58 MacNair *Modern Chinese History Selected Readings*, pp. 111–13; Chang *Commissioner Lin and the Opium War*, pp. 161–72.

59 Chang *Commissioner Lin and the Opium War*, pp. 122–4.

60 Li *Zhongguo jin bainian zhengzhi shi*, p. 39.

61 MacNair, *Modern Chinese History Selected Readings*, p. 128.

62 *Chinese Repository*, Volume VIII, pp. 264–5 in MacNair *Modern Chinese History Selected Readings*, pp. 128–9.

63 Chang *Commissioner Lin and the Opium War*, pp. 189–208; Li *Zhongguo jin bainian zhengzhi shi*, p. 40; MacNair *Modern Chinese History Selected Readings*, pp. 128–34.

64 Chang *Commissioner Lin and the Opium War*, pp. 208–10; Li *Zhongguo jin bainian zhengzhi shi*, pp. 40–51.

65 MacNair *Modern Chinese History Selected Readings*, p. 138.

66 Hummel *Eminent Chinese of the Ch'ing Period*, pp. 126–7, 512–13.

67 Li *Zhongguo jin bainian zhengzhi shi*, pp. 44–6.

68 Li *Zhongguo jin bainian zhengzhi shi*, pp. 46–7.

69 John Ouchterlony (Lieutenant) *The Chinese War* (London 1844), pp. 125–7 in MacNair *Modern Chinese History Selected Readings*, p. 160.

70 Li *Zhongguo jin bainian zhengzhi shi*, pp. 47–8.

71 Ouchterlony in MacNair *Modern Chinese History Selected Readings*, pp. 161–3.

72 Li *Zhongguo jin bainian zhengzhi shi*, pp. 48–9.

73 Hummel *Eminent Chinese of the Ch'ing Period*, pp. 582–3.

74 Captain Granville G. Loch *Closing Events of the Campaign in China* (London, 1843), in MacNair *Modern Chinese History Selected Readings*, p. 171.

75	S. Lane-Poole *Sir Harry Parkes in China* (London 1901) in MacNair *Modern Chinese History Selected Readings*, p. 172. Sir Harry Parkes became a distinguished British diplomat in China and Japan. John Robert Morrison (1814–1843) was the son of the missionary and pioneering sinologist Robert Morrison (1782–1834). He succeeded his father as interpreter to the East India Company and later became secretary to the government of Hong Kong. The colour yellow is associated with the emperor. 'Tiffin' was the term for a light lunch in India during the Raj (and among the British in many other parts of Asia), as Henry Yule and A.C. Burnell *Hobson Jobson* the dictionary or Anglo-Indian usage, published in 1886 attests and as every English man and woman of a certain age knows. Main and Mizen (normally spelled mizzen) were masts on sailing ships.

76	MacNair *Modern Chinese History Selected Readings*, pp. 174–8; Godfrey Hertslet *Hertslet's China Treaties* (London: HMSO, 1908); Chinese text in *Zhongguo jindai shi ziliao xuanbian* [*Selected Documents in Modern Chinese History*], pp. 33–6.

77	MacNair *Modern Chinese History Selected Readings*, pp. 182–8.

78	Sir John Francis Davis *China during the War and since the Peace* (London 1852), Volume 1, pp. 6, 7, in MacNair *Modern Chinese History Selected Readings*, pp. 172–3.

79	Lin Fuxiang 'Sanyuanli dazhang riji' [*Diary of the Fighting in Sanyuanli*] from *Pinghai xinchou* [*New Plans for Pacifying the Oceans*] in *Zhongguo jindaishi ziliao xuanbian* [*Selected Documents in Modern Chinese History*], pp. 23–4.

80	Lin 'Sanyuanli dazhang riji'; Frederic Wakeman Jr. *Strangers at the Gate: Social Disorder in South China, 1839–1861* (Berkeley and Los Angeles: University of California Press, 1966), pp. 11–21, 39–40.

3 Taiping, Nian and Muslim Uprisings

1	Jean Chesneaux *Secret Societies in China* (Hong Kong and London: Heinemann, 1971).

2	Li *Zhongguo jin bainian zhengzhi shi*, pp. 53–81; Sir John Francis Davis *China during the War and since the Peace* in MacNair *Modern Chinese History Selected Readings*, pp. 328–33; S.Y. Teng *The Taiping Rebellion and the Western Powers*; Franz Michael *The Taiping Rebellion: History and Documents* (Seattle and London: University of Washington Press, 1966). The three-volume collection, edited by Franz Michael, which consists of one volume of historical narrative and analysis and two volumes of translated primary documents, provides detailed primary source material in English translation for the Taiping period that is unrivalled in Western studies of modern Chinese history.

3	*Bendi*, also found in a transcription of its Cantonese pronunciation as *punti*, simply means 'local' or 'belonging to this land'. Unlike the Bendi, the Hakka or *Kejia*, whose name translates as 'guest families', were looked upon as outsiders or interlopers even after they had been settled in the region for centuries.

4	Michael *Taiping Rebellion*, Volume 2, p. 3. Hong Rengan played a role that is perhaps analogous to that of John the Baptist in his relationship with Jesus of Nazareth, a comparison that is appropriate in the light of the adoption by the Taiping of many of the trappings of Christianity.

5 Michael *Taiping Rebellion*, Volume 1, pp. 21–3; Jonathan D. Spence *God's Chinese Son: The Taiping Heavenly Kingdom of Hong Xiuquan* (New York and London: Norton, 1996), pp. 46–50.

6 Taiping Heavenly Chronicle [*Taiping tianri*] in Michael *Taiping Rebellion*, Volume 2, pp. 51–76.

7 Gospel jointly witnessed and heard by the Imperial Eldest and Second Eldest Brothers. Michael *Taiping Rebellion*, Volume 2, pp. 7–10.

8 Michael *Taiping Rebellion*, Volume 2, pp. 3–4.

9 Michael *Taiping Rebellion*, Volume 1, pp. 24–6; the missionary career of the Reverend I.J. Roberts in Guangzhou from May 1844 can be followed in the *China Mission Reports* of the Southern Baptist Convention (www.sbc.net) but his encounter with Hong Xiuquan is not mentioned; Jonathan Spence *God's Chinese Son: The Taiping Heavenly Kingdom of Hong Xiuquan* (New York: Norton, 1996).

10 Joseph-Marie Callery and Melchior Yvan *History of the Insurrection in China* (London, 1853) in MacNair *Modern Chinese History Selected Readings*, p. 334.

11 Michael *Taiping Rebellion*, Volume 1, pp. 37–50.

12 Michael *Taiping Rebellion*, Volume 2, p. 103.

13 Michael *Taiping Rebellion*, Volume 1, p. 43. Proper names have been rewritten in *pinyin* spellings. The Zhou military model of farmer-soldiers has had powerful resonances throughout subsequent Chinese history right up to the present day: it influenced the creation of the Ming dynasty's border guard system, the relationship between the CCP and the Red Army before 1949 and the Xinjiang Production and Construction Corps in present-day China.

14 Michael *Taiping Rebellion*, Volume 1, pp. 45–6.

15 Michael *Taiping Rebellion*, Volume 1, pp. 51–71; Volume 2, pp. 107–8, 124–31.

16 Wuchang is now part of the city of Wuhan and was to be the scene of the first actions in the outbreak of the 1911 Revolution.

17 Michael *Taiping Rebellion*, Volume 1, pp. 64–71.

18 William James Hail *Tseng Kuo-fan and the Taiping Rebellion* (New Haven and London: Yale University Press, 1927).

19 Michael *Taiping Rebellion*, Volume 1, pp. 75–8.

20 Michael *Taiping Rebellion*, Volume 1, pp. 78–88, Volume 2, pp. 364–408.

21 Michael *Taiping Rebellion*, Volume 1, pp. 92–5.

22 Michael *Taiping Rebellion*, Volume 1, pp. 109–15, 118.

23 Michael *Taiping Rebellion*, Volume 1, pp. 66–7.

24 Michael *Taiping Rebellion*, Volume 1, pp. 96–109. *Xiang* is an archaic name for Hunan province: it is also commonly used as an abbreviation for the province in modern China. Wuchang and Hanyang are both within the modern city of Wuhan.

25 Michael *Taiping Rebellion*, Volume 1, pp. 164–75; Hummel *Eminent Chinese of the Ch'ing Period*, p. 753.

26 Frank Houghton *China Calling* (London: China Inland Mission, 1936), pp. 36–7, 111.

27 Li *Zhongguo jin bainian zhengzhi shi*, pp. 95–6; Prescott Clarke and J.S. Gregory *Western Reports on the Taiping* (London: Croom Helm, 1982).

28   Chiang, Siang-tseh *The Nien Rebellion* (Seattle: University of Washington Press, 1954); Elizabeth J. Perry (Editor) *Chinese Perspectives on the Nien Rebellion* (New York: M.E. Sharpe, 1981).

29   Sorghum is a cereal grain which can be grown successfully in hot and dry conditions because of its ability to resist drought and heat. It is often grown for animal feed but is also suitable for human consumption. It usually forms part of the diet of rural people only when rice and other better quality grains are not available.

30   Chiang, *The Nien Rebellion*, pp. 2–3; Perry (Editor) *Chinese Perspectives on the Nien Rebellion*, pp. 38–42.

31   Dictionary definitions are only useful to a limited extent in such a context as there is not necessarily a one-to-one correspondence between a character and a dialect word like *nian*. One secret society among many in the border region of Huaibei was known as the *Niezi hui*, a group of outlaws who 'pinched' (*nice*) themselves together into bands and there may be a connection between local pronunciations of these two words for which quite separate written characters are used.

32   The activities and organisation of the Nian are remarkably similar to those of the Border Reivers, family based raiding bands that operated in the disputed Borders – the territory between England and Scotland – until they were suppressed in the sixteenth century.

33   Chiang, Siang-tseh *The Nien Rebellion*, pp. 20–31.

34   Chiang, Siang-tseh *The Nien Rebellion*, pp. 32–44.

35   Sechin Jagchid and Paul Hyer *Mongolia's Culture and Society* (Boulder: Westview Press, 1979), p. 145. His name in modern romanised Chinese is Senggelinqin.

36   Chiang *The Nien Rebellion*, pp. 100–30.

37   Chiang *The Nien Rebellion*.

38   Michael Dillon *China's Muslims* (Hong Kong: Oxford University Press, 1996); *China's Muslim Hui Community: Migrations, Settlements and Sects* (London: Curzon, 1999).

39   Lin Gan *Qingdai huimin qiyi* [*Muslim Risings of the Qing Dynasty*] (Shanghai: New Knowledge Press, 1957); David G. Atwill 'Blinkered Visions: Islamic Identity, Hui Ethnicity and the Panthay Rebellion in Southwest China 1856–1873' *Journal of Asian Studies*, Volume 62, Number 1, November 2003, pp. 1079–1108; Wang Jianping *Concord and Conflict: The Hui Communities of Yunnan Society in a Historical Perspective* (Lund: Lund Studies in African and Asian Religions, 1996) gives much valuable information on the historical background and religious and social position of the Hui in Yunnan.

40   *Huizu jianshi bianxie zu* [*Editorial Group for Brief History of the Hui*] (Yinchuan: Ningxia People's Press, 1978).

41   Chu Wen-djang *The Moslem Rebellion in North-West China 1862–1878* (The Hague: Mouton, 1966), pp. 23–4.

42   Chu, *The Moslem Rebellion in North-West China 1862–1878*, pp. 23–4.

43   Jonathan Lipman *The Border World of Gansu, 1895–1935* unpublished PhD (Stanford University, 1981) p. 24; Jonathan Lipman *Familiar Strangers: A History*

of Muslims in Northwest China (Seattle and London: University of Washington Press, 1997).

44 Chu *The Moslem Rebellion in North-West China 1862–1878*, p. 25; Lipman *Familiar Strangers*, pp. 24–5.

45 *Huizu jianshi* [*Brief History of the Hui*], pp. 42–3; Chu *The Moslem Rebellion in North-West China 1862–1878*, pp. 27–45. Guyuan and Pingliang are both in the present-day Ningxia Hui Autonomous Region.

46 *Huizu jianshi* [*Brief History of the Hui*], pp. 43–4; Chu *The Moslem Rebellion in North-West China 1862–1878*, pp. 45–50.

47 Chu *The Moslem Rebellion in North-West China 1862–1878*, p. 44. *Ahong*, derived from the Persian *akhond* is the usual title for imams in the Hui communities.

48 Chu *The Moslem Rebellion in North-West China 1862–1878*, p. 51.

49 Ma is by far the most common surname among Hui Muslims and it is generally assumed that it is derived from the name Mohammed: these insurgent leaders were therefore not necessarily related.

50 Personal observation 1991.

51 The Salars and Dongxiang are also Muslim ethnic groups with their own distinctive languages and cultures.

52 *Huizu jianshi* [*Brief History of the Hui*], pp. 45–7; Lipman *Familiar Strangers*, pp. 27–9.

53 Commandant Henri d'Ollone *Recherches sur les Musulmans Chinois* (Paris: Leroux, 1911), p. 236.

54 *Huizu jianshi* [*Brief History of the Hui*], pp. 47–8.

55 Chu *The Moslem Rebellion in North-West China 1862–1878*, pp. 151–5.

56 Marshall Broomhall *Islam in China*, p. 155. Broomhall's evidence comes partly from two articles published by Colonel Mark Bell VC, CBE in *The Asiatic Quarterly Review* of January and July 1896 which drew on his first-hand experience of Gansu.

57 *Pingding Shaan-Gan Xinjiang Huifei fanglue* [*On the Pacification of the Muslim Bandits in Shaanxi, Gansu and Xinjiang*] in Chu *The Moslem Rebellion in North-West China 1862–1878*, p. vii. The refugees who fled with Bai Yanhu eventually settled in Central Asia and were the founding fathers of the Chinese Muslim community who are known as Dungans in that region.

58 For further information on the history of the Hui in this period, see Dillon *China's Muslim Hui Community: Migrations, Settlements and Sects*.

59 James Millward *Beyond the Pass: Economy, Ethnicity and Empire in Qing Central Asia* (Stanford: Stanford University Press, 1998).

60 Joseph Fletcher 'The Heyday of the Ch'ing Order in Mongolia, Sinkiang and Tibet' in Denis Twitchett and John K. Fairbank (General Editors) *The Cambridge History of China, Volume 10: Late Ch'ing, 1800–1911, Part 1*, p. 374 (Cambridge: Cambridge University Press).

61 Chu *The Moslem Rebellion in North-West China 1862–1878*, pp. 163–96. Aspects of the 'Great Game' of Russo-British rivalry in southwestern Xinjiang are described in C.P. Skrine and Pamela Nightingale *Macartney at Kashgar* (Hong Kong and Oxford: Oxford University Press, 1987).

4 Restoration and Western Colonisation

1   James M. Polachek *The Inner Opium War* (Cambridge, MA: Harvard University Press, 1992).

2   J.Y. Wong *Deadly Dreams: Opium, Imperialism and the Arrow War (1856–1860) in China* (Cambridge: Cambridge University Press, 1998), pp. 43–4 and *passim*.

3   This is not the Summer Palace in the northwestern suburbs of Beijing which features the marble boat and is a popular weekend destination for excursions by foreign tourists and local people alike. That is the Yiheyuan which was restored in 1888 on the instructions of the Empress Dowager Cixi. The ruins of the other Summer Palace, the Yuanmingyuan (Garden of Perfect Brightness) that was begun by the Kangxi emperor in 1709 and substantially reconstructed by the Qianlong emperor, are located further north and slightly to the east of the Yiheyuan. British visitors, especially historians, are likely to be taken there as a reminder of the damage that British troops did in 1860. Carrol Brown Malone *History of the Peking Summer Palaces under the Ch'ing Dynasty* (Urbana: University of Illinois Press, 1934, reprint 1966 New York); Susan Naquin *Peking: Temples and City Life 1400–1900* (Berkeley: University of California Press, 2000), pp. 311–18.

4   *Tsungli Yamen* in the Wade-Giles system of romanisation.

5   A more literal translation of *Tongwen guan* would be Joint Languages Academy.

6   Li *Zhongguo jin bainian zhengzhi shi*, pp. 133–4.

7   Mary Clabaugh Wright *The Last Stand of Chinese Conservatism: The T'ung-chih Restoration, 1862–1874* (Stanford: Stanford University Press, 1957), pp. 43–50. This remains the classic account of the Tongzhi period.

8   Li *Zhongguo jin bainian zhengzhi shi*, p. 126.

9   Beiyang was the term used in the Qing dynasty to denote the northern coastal provinces that are today known as Liaoning, Hebei and Shandong. The prime task of the Beiyang Fleet was the defence of this coastline which in turn controlled access to the capital, Beijing.

10   Wright *The Last Stand of Chinese Conservatism*, pp. 241–8.

11   *Hobson Jobson*. It is also rather a double-edged name as the original compradors in Bengal and at first in China were house-servants or butlers, whereas the commercial intermediaries in the Chinese Treaty Ports were often from powerful and high status families.

12   Frances Wood *No Dogs and Not Many Chinese: Treaty Port Life in China 1843–1943* (London: John Murray, 1998); Brian Power *The Ford of Heaven* (London: Peter Owen, 1984).

13   Cornelius Osgood *The Koreans and their Culture* (New York: Ronald Press, 1951), pp. 204–10; James Hoare and Susan Pares *Korea: An Introduction* (London: Kegan Paul International, 1988).

14   MacNair *Modern Chinese History: Selected Readings*, pp. 515–48. The name Formosa means 'beautiful' in Portuguese and early Portuguese traders knew it as Ilha Formosa, 'beautiful island'. The name Formosa was regularly used in the West until the 1960s, but Taiwan is now used almost exclusively.

15   Chen Hongtu (Editor) *Taiwan shi* [*History of Taiwan*] (Taipei: Sanmin, 2004).

16 Luke S.K. Kwong *Mosaic of the Hundred Days: Personalities, Politics and Ideas of 1898* (Cambridge, MA: Harvard University Press, 1984); Li *Zhongguo jin bainian zhengzhi shi*, pp. 176–87.

17 MacNair *Modern Chinese History Selected Readings*, p. 578.

18 Hummel *Eminent Chinese of the Ch'ing Period*, p. 733.

19 MacNair *Modern Chinese History Selected Readings*, pp. 572–87.

20 Li *Zhongguo jin bainian zhengzhi shi*, pp. 179–82.

5 Boxer Rising and Imperial Decline

1   Victor Purcell *The Boxer Uprising: A Background Study* (Cambridge: Cambridge University Press, 1963) is the classic English language account.

2   Joseph W. Esherick *The Origins of the Boxer Uprising* (Berkeley: University of California Press, 1987).

3   Shandong University History Department *Shandong yihetuan diaocha ziliao xuanbian* [*Selected Material from an Investigation into the Boxer Movement in Shandong*] (Jilin: Shandong People's Press, 1980); Chesneaux *Peasant Revolts in China 1840–1949*.

4   The best known and by far the most gripping of the accounts of the relief of the legations in English is Peter Fleming *The Siege at Peking* (London: Hart-Davis, 1959).

5   Albert Feuerwerker *The Chinese Economy, ca. 1870–1911* (Ann Arbor: Michigan Papers in Chinese Studies No. 5 1969), pp. 17, 29. This was subsequently included as a chapter in the *Cambridge History of China*.

6   Li *Zhongguo jin bainian zhengzhi shi*, p. 197.

7   The eight trigrams or eight diagrams are an arrangement of complete and divided lines in groups of three lines. They are said to have originated with the mythical emperor Fu Xi and represent the creative forces of the universe. Two trigrams combine to form a hexagram and hexagrams are the basis for the classical book of divination the *Yijing* (more commonly written *I Ching* in the West).

8   Bao Shijie *Quanshi shanyu* [*Imperial Edicts from the Time of the Boxers*] in *Zhongguo jindaishi ziliao xuanbian* (Beijing: Zhonghua Shuju, 1977), p. 95.

9   Jean Chesneaux *Secret Societies in China in the 19th and 20th Centuries* (Hong Kong: Heinemann, 1971), p. 120 and *passim*.

10 The character for *tan* is the same as that found in Tiantan, the Temple of Heaven, and in the names of the other imperial altars in Beijing.

11 Chesneaux *Secret Societies in China in the 19th and 20th Centuries*, pp. 120–2.

12 Li *Zhongguo jin bainian zhengzhi shi*, pp. 202–3.

13 *Zhongguo jindaishi ziliao xuanbian*, pp. 104–5.

14 Li *Zhongguo jin bainian zhengzhi shi*, p. 186.

15 B.L. Putnam Weale *Indiscreet Letters from Peking* (London: Hurst and Blackett Ltd, 1900), p. 5. Putnam Weale was the pseudonym of B.L. Simpson who had worked for the Chinese Customs Service. He distinguished himself during the relief of the Legations to the extent that the British Minister put him forward for a commendation but, according to Fleming in *The Siege at Peking*, he was later accused of having been involved in looting. Fleming considered Weale's

book to be odious and advised that it should be used with caution. It is certainly waspish and irreverent but it is also a convincing first-hand account of the siege from within.

16   Weale *Indiscreet Letters from Peking*, p. 22.

17   Weale *Indiscreet Letters from Peking*, pp. 34–42.

18   Weale *Indiscreet Letters from Peking*, pp. 52–3. The name Tartar City refers to the northern part of Beijing, the home of the Manchus (who, together with the Mongols, are commonly referred to as Tartars). It enclosed the Imperial City, which in turn surrounded the Imperial Palace or Forbidden City. The Chinese City was to the south. The Legation Quarter was in the south of the Tartar City, adjacent to the Chinese City.

19   Weale *Indiscreet Letters from Peking*, pp. 59–60.

20   Weale *Indiscreet Letters from Peking*, p. 68.

21   Li *Zhongguo jin bainian zhengzhi shi*, pp. 202–6; Weale *Indiscreet Letters from Peking*, pp. 65–72; MacNair *Modern Chinese History Selected Readings*, pp. 589, 606.

22   'In Peking' in *The Boxer Rising: A History of the Boxer Trouble in China* reprinted from the *Shanghai Mercury*, October 1900 (New York: Paragon Books, 1967), pp. 69–71.

23   MacNair *Modern Chinese History Selected Readings*, p. 606.

24   Rev. Gilbert Reid D.D. 'The Siege of Peking' in *The Boxer Rising: A History of the Boxer Trouble in China*, pp. 89–105.

25   Captain J. Boyce-Kup 'The Taking and Occupation of Peking' in *The Boxer Rising: A History of the Boxer Trouble in China*, pp. 106–9.

26   A. Henry Savage Landor *China and the Allies* (London: William Heinemann, 1901). Henry Savage Landor, grandson of the more famous Walter, the poet, details looting by individuals of all nationalities in Beijing and Tianjin and points out that there were also Chinese looters.

27   French text with annexes in Godfrey Hertslet *Hertslet's China Treaties* (London: HMSO, 1908), pp. 123–47; English version in MacNair *Modern Chinese History Selected Readings*, pp. 618–24.

28   MacNair *Modern Chinese History Selected Readings*, pp. 639–53.

29   F.R. Sedgwick *The Russo-Japanese War on Land* (London, 1906) in MacNair *Modern Chinese History Selected Readings*, pp. 658–61. Roosevelt was awarded the Nobel Prize for Peace in 1906 for his role in mediating in the Russo-Japanese War.

30   MacNair *Modern Chinese History Selected Readings*, pp. 661–2.

31   MacNair *Modern Chinese History Selected Readings*, p. 663.

32   W.F. Tyler 'Memorandum on China's neutrality in the Russo-Japanese War' (The Hague: International Congress, 1907), in MacNair *Modern Chinese History Selected Readings*, pp. 663–70. The Hague Conventions (the first had been convened in 1899) were instituted to establish internationally acceptable regulations for the conduct of war and the peaceful settlement of international disputes. The best known long-term outcome of these negotiations was the Geneva Protocol on the limitation of chemical and biological warfare which was based on the Hague discussions and was signed in 1925.

33   Li *Zhongguo jin bainian zhengzhi shi*, p. 276.

34 William L. Tung *The Political Institutions of Modern China* (The Hague: Martinus Nijhoff, 1968). This thorough but neglected study analyses the evolution of political organisations and constitutions from the late Qing period to the 1950s with translations of key documents.

35 Feuerwerker *The Chinese Economy, ca. 1870–1911*, pp. 58–9.

36 H.B. Morse *The International Relations of the Chinese Empire* (Shanghai: Kelly and Walsh, 1918), Volume 3, pp. 99–100.

37 Li *Zhongguo jin bainian zhengzhi shi*, pp. 295–8.

38 Chinese text (part) of *Geming jun* in *Zhongguo jindaishi ziliao*, pp. 189–212. English translation in John Lust *The Revolutionary Army, A Chinese Nationalist Tract of 1903* (The Hague: Mouton and Company, 1968).

39 Mary C. Wright (Editor) *China in Revolution: The First Phase 1900–1913* (New Haven: Yale University Press, 1968); Li *Zhongguo jin bainian zhengzhi shi*, pp. 224–6; Leonard Shilien Hsü *Sun Yat-sen: His Political and Social Ideals, A Source Book* (Los Angeles: University of Southern California Press, 1933), pp. 53–74. *Geming* [revolution] can be translated literally as 'casting off the mandate [of heaven]', a radical concept for anyone still wedded to the idea of a traditional Confucian empire.

40 Li *Zhongguo jin bainian zhengzhi shi*, pp. 286–7.

41 Wu Yu-chang (Wu Yuzhang) *The Revolution of 1911* (Beijing: Foreign Languages Press, 1962), p. 118.

42 Wu *The Revolution of 1911*, pp. 117–23.

43 Li *Zhongguo jin bainian zhengzhi shi*, pp. 304–5; Sir John Jordan *Blue Book, China No 1* (1912) in MacNair *Modern Chinese History Selected Readings*, pp. 699–702; Hsü *Sun Yat-sen: His Political and Social Ideals, A Source Book*, p. 77.

44 Li *Zhongguo jin bainian zhengzhi shi*, pp. 305–7.

6 Struggle for the Republic of China

1 The 1911 revolution was also known as the 'war of 1911' (*Xinhai zhi yi*). The period 1926–7 is considered to have been a revolutionary civil war but 1949 is always known as the 'liberation' of China. Since the two characters that are read *xin* and *hai* can, in certain contexts, be read as 'bitter' and 'north', it is possible read an allegorical meaning into the date but it is really only a way of naming the year.

2 Hsü *Sun Yat-sen: His Political and Social Ideals, A Source Book*, p. 82.

3 *Sun Zhongshan xuanji* [*Selected Works of Sun Yat-sen*] (Hong Kong: Zhonghua shuju, 1956), pp. 82–3; *China Mission Yearbook* (Shanghai 1912) in MacNair *Modern Chinese History Selected Readings*, pp. 719–21.

4 For this and other abdication edicts, see MacNair *Modern Chinese History Selected Readings*, pp. 721–9.

5 MacNair *Modern Chinese History Selected Readings*, pp. 722–7.

6 Li *Zhongguo jin bainian zhengzhi shi*, pp. 272–3; Chinese text of the *Provisional Constitution* in *Jindaishi ziliao*, pp. 246–51; translation in MacNair *Modern Chinese History Selected Readings*, pp. 729–34.

7 Li *Zhongguo jin bainian zhengzhi shi*, pp. 361–72.

8   Li *Zhongguo jin bainian zhengzhi shi*, pp. 382–90; Jerome Ch'en *Yuan Shih-k'ai* (Stanford: Stanford University Press, 1972), pp. 128–31.

9   Li *Zhongguo jin bainian zhengzhi shi*, pp. 391–5.

10 Li *Zhongguo jin bainian zhengzhi shi*, pp. 304–9; Ch'en *Yuan Shih-k'ai*, p. 163.

11 Li *Zhongguo jin bainian zhengzhi shi*, p. 419; MacNair *Modern Chinese History Selected Readings*, p. 758.

12 MacNair *Modern Chinese History Selected Readings*, p. 758.

13 *Shantung Treaties and Agreements* (Washington: Carnegie Endowment for International Peace, 1921), pp. 65–7, 81–2. Qingdao is also well known as Tsingtao, the origin of the high quality Tsingtao beer, brewed in the manner of German lager. Jiaozhou was often spelled Kiaochou or, by the Germans, Kiaotschou.

14 *Shantung Treaties and Agreements*, pp. 72–3, citing *Manchuria Daily News* 7 December 1914.

15 MacNair *Modern Chinese History Selected Readings*, p. 766.

16 MacNair *Modern Chinese History Selected Readings*, pp. 766–7; Li *Zhongguo jin bainian zhengzhi shi*, pp. 419–21.

17 The Chinese text of the original demands can be found in *Zhongguo jindaishi ziliao*, pp. 281–4; English translation in MacNair *Modern Chinese History Selected Readings*, pp. 768–71. There were several different versions of the demands in circulation at the time including the edited and watered down version published by the Japanese, counterproposals by China and a revised version produced by the Japanese government. Details of these and related diplomatic correspondence can be found in MacNair *Modern Chinese History Selected Readings*, pp. 758–801.

18 Li *Zhongguo jin bainian zhengzhi shi*, pp. 310–12.

19 MacNair *Modern Chinese History Selected Readings*, pp. 742–6. According to MacNair, Dr Goodnow was not prepared to make the English original of his report available to scholars at the time.

20 H.A. Van Oort *Porcelain of Hung-hsien: A Study of the Socio-Cultural Background and Some Characteristics of the Porcelain Produced at Ching-te-chen during the Imperial Reign of Yuan Shih-k'ai* (1916) (Brill: Leiden, 1970), pp. 31–2, 144; Ch'en *Yuan Shih-k'ai*, pp. 174–5.

21 *North-China Daily News* 3 July 1916.

22 Ch'i Hsi-sheng *Warlord Politics in China 1916–1928* (Stanford: Stanford University Press, 1976), pp. 41–7.

23 Li *Zhongguo jin bainian zhengzhi shi*, pp. 384–5.

24 Hindustani is the immediate ancestor of modern Hindi and Urdu and *mantri* was originally derived from the even more venerable Sanskrit. See Henry Yule and A.C. Burnell *Hobson-Jobson: The Anglo-Indian Dictionary* (1986), new edition edited by William Crooke (London: John Murray, 1903). The word *mantri* survives in the modern Malay *mìntìri*, the title of a hereditary chief and of the prime ministers of the pre-federation Malay states, and, by association, any official; R.O. Winstedt *An Unabridged Malay-English Dictionary* (Singapore: Kelly and Walsh, n.d.). This serves as a reminder of the linguistic connections between what appear to have been quite disparate cultures in Asia.

25 Nguyen-Ton Nu Hoang-Mai *Parlons Vietnamien* (Paris: L'Harmattan, 2005), pp. 128–9.

26 De Francis, John, *Nationalism and Language Reform in China* (Princeton: Princeton University Press 1950), pp. 55–65.

27 Lattimore *Nationalism and Revolution in Mongolia*, p. 22.

28 Lattimore *Nationalism and Revolution in Mongolia*, p. 22.

29 Lattimore *Nationalism and Revolution in Mongolia*, pp. 31–2, 34.

30 C.R. Bawden *The Modern History of Mongolia* (London and New York: Kegan Paul, 1989), p. 189; Peter S.H. Tang *Russian and Soviet Policy in Manchuria and Outer Mongolia 1911–1931* (Durham: Duke University Press, 1959), pp. 299–310.

31 Lattimore *Nationalism and Revolution in Mongolia*, p. 117.

32 According to the western calendar, the revolution took place in November.

33 Bawden *The Modern History of Mongolia*, pp. 238–60. Sukhebatur and Choibalsan are often referred to rather lazily as the Lenin and Stalin of Mongolia and Mongolia's complicated political and economic relationship with the Soviet Union has habitually been reduced to one word – 'satellite'.

34 Melvyn C. Goldstein *A History of Modern Tibet, 1913–1951: The Demise of the Lamaist State* (Berkeley: University of California Press, 1989), pp. 44–88; See also Patrick French *Younghusband: The Last Great Imperial Adventurer* (London: HarperCollins, 1994).

35 Dawa Norbu *China's Tibet Policy* (Richmond: Curzon Press, 2001), p. 97.

36 Owen Lattimore *Inner Asian Frontiers of China*, p. 187 (Boston: Beacon Press, 1967).

37 Michael Dillon *Xinjiang: China's Muslim Far Northwest* (London: Routledge Curzon, 2004), pp. 17–20.

7 May Fourth Movement: Communists and Nationalists

1 Martin Bernal 'The Triumph of Anarchism over Marxism 1906–7' in Wright *China in Revolution: The First Phase 1900–1913*.

2 Edward Hallett Carr *The Bolshevik Revolution 1917–1923* (London: Pelican, 1969), Volume 1, p. 81.

3 Carr *The Bolshevik Revolution 1917–1923*, Volume 1, pp. 81–2.

4 Carr *The Bolshevik Revolution 1917–1923*, Volume 1, pp. 100–11; John Reed *Ten Days That Shook the World* (London: Penguin, 1970), pp. 115–16; Geoffrey Hosking *A History of the Soviet Union 1917–1991* (London: Fontana, 1992), pp. 50–1.

5 Carr *The Bolshevik Revolution 1917–1923*, Volume 3, pp. 484–5, 235; Gavan McCormack *Chang Tso-lin in Northeast China 1911–1928: China, Japan and the Manchurian Idea* (Folkestone: Dawson, 1977), pp. 35, 40, 112.

6 Hu Shih (Hu Shi) *The Chinese Renaissance* (New York: Paragon, 1963), pp. 44–62.

7 Hu *The Chinese Renaissance*, pp. 44–62; Lucien Bianco *Origins of the Chinese Revolution 1915–1949* (Stanford: Stanford University Press, 1971), pp. 28–35.

8 MacNair *Modern Chinese History Selected Readings*, pp. 839, 842–5.

9 Chow Tse-tsung *The May Fourth Movement: Intellectual Revolution in Modern China* (Cambridge: Harvard University Press, 1960), pp. 99–109. Some sources have

suggested that the number of demonstrators was as high as 5,000 but Chow Tse-tsung's figure of over 3,000, which is based on an analysis of a number of contemporary sources, is credible. *Tian'anmen*, the Gate of Heavenly Peace, is the southern gate of the Forbidden City. Tian'anmen Square, the square that now spreads out in front of the gate to the south, did not exist at that time: it was constructed during the 1950s.

10 Joshua A. Fogel *Nakae Ushikichi in China: The Mourning of Spirit* (Cambridge: Harvard University Press, 1989).

11 Chow *The May Fourth Movement: Intellectual Revolution in Modern China*, pp. 109–16.

12 Chow *The May Fourth Movement: Intellectual Revolution in Modern China*, pp. 194–5.

13 Tony Saich (Editor) *The Rise to Power of the Chinese Communist Party: Documents and Analysis* (New York: M.E. Sharpe, 1996); Arif Dirlik *The Origins of Chinese Communism* (New York: Oxford University Press, 1989); Hans J. Van de Ven *From Friend to Comrade: The Founding of the Chinese Communist Party 1920–1927* (Berkeley: University of California Press, 1991).

14 Saich *The Rise to Power of the Chinese Communist Party*, pp. 11–13. Earlier sources have suggested that it was founded in May 1920 but the later date is now thought to be more probable.

15 Stuart Schram *Mao Tse-tung* (London: Penguin, 1966), p. 65; Saich *The Rise to Power of the Chinese Communist Party*, p. 15.

16 Dirlik *The Origins of Chinese Communism*, pp. 156–7; Philip Short *Mao: A Life* (London: Hodder & Stoughton, 1989), pp. 119–20.

17 Saich *The Rise to Power of the Chinese Communist Party*, pp. 13–19.

18 Saich *The Rise to Power of the Chinese Communist Party*, pp. 40–3.

19 Hsü *Sun Yat-sen; His Political and Social Ideals, A Source Book*, pp. 44–82.

20 Li *Zhongguo jin bainian zhengzhi shi*, pp. 425–8.

21 Li *Zhongguo jin bainian zhengzhi shi*, pp. 440–4.

22 Li *Zhongguo jin bainian zhengzhi shi*, pp. 624–35; Hsü *Sun Yat-sen; His Political and Social Ideals, A Source Book*, pp. 119–41. The Chinese word *xuanyan* is used in the title of both documents. Hsü translates the title of the 1923 version as 'Manifesto' and the 1924 equivalent as 'Declaration'.

23 J.O.P. Bland *China: The Pity of It* (London: William Heinemann, 1932), p. 8.

24 MacNair *Modern Chinese History Selected Readings*, pp. 848–51. Warren Gamaliel Harding (1865–1923), the 29th President of the United States, held office in 1921–3 and died in office on 2 August 1923. The Department of State is the equivalent of a Ministry of Foreign Affairs. The Memorial Continental Hall, designed in 1905, is the oldest building in the headquarters complex of the elitist, conservative and patriotic organization, the Daughters of the American Revolution.

25 MacNair *Modern Chinese History Selected Readings*, p. 855.

26 *Pacific and Far Eastern Questions, Being the Second Part of the Report of the American Delegation Submitted to the President, February 9, 1922 by the American Delegates, the Honorable Messrs Charles E. Hughes, Henry Cabot Lodge, Oscar W. Underwood, Elihu Root* in MacNair *Modern Chinese History Selected Readings*, pp. 854–8. Charles Evans Hughes was Secretary of State, Henry Cabot Lodge (1850–1924) was the leader of the conservative wing of the Republican Party (and the grandfather of

the twentieth century American senator and diplomat Henry Cabot Lodge Jr.): the other delegates were leading United States senators.

27 *Pacific and Far Eastern Questions* in MacNair *Modern Chinese History Selected Readings*, pp. 858–62.

28 Gregoriy Evseyevich Zinoviev was a close collaborator of Lenin who later sided with Stalin in his battle with Trotsky. He is assumed to have been the author of the infamous forged Zinoviev Letter of 1924.

29 *The First Congress of the Toilers of the Far East 1922*, Hammersmith Reprints of Scarce Documents – originally published in Petrograd 1922 (London: Hammersmith Books), pp. 24, 235, 239; Saich *The Rise to Power of the Chinese Communist Party*, pp. 11, 61, 95.

8 Northern Expedition and United Front

1 Sun Yat-sen's original order, *Da yuanshi ling* (order from the Generalissimo) appointing Chiang as Principal of the Military Academy (*Lujun junguan xuexiao xiaozhang*), signed Sun Wen and dated 2 May in the 13th year of the Republic, is reproduced in S.I. Hsiung *The Life of Chiang Kai-shek* (London: Peter Davies, 1948), opposite p. 174.

2 Chiang Kai-shek, pp. 19–25 *A Summing Up at Seventy: Soviet Russia in China* (London: Harrap, 1957).

3 Chiang *A Summing Up at Seventy.*

4 Li *Zhongguo jin bainian zhengzhi shi*, pp. 639–41; Carr *The Bolshevik Revolution 1917–1923*, Volume 3, p. 540. Huangpu, which is better known as Whampoa, a form reflecting more closely the Cantonese pronunciation, is in Guangdong province, ten miles east of Guangzhou on an island in the Pearl River Delta. It should not be confused with the Huangpu River in Shanghai.

5 Harold R. Isaacs *The Tragedy of the Chinese Revolution* (Stanford: Stanford University Press, 1961), p. 64.

6 F.F. Liu *A Military History of Modern China: 1924–1949* (Princeton: Princeton University Press, 1956), pp. 14–15.

7 Hollington K. Tong *Chiang Kai-shek: Soldier and Statesman* (authorized biography) (Shanghai: China Publishing Company, 1937), pp. 77–8; Richard B. Landis, Training and Indoctrination at the Whampoa Academy, in F. Gilbert Chand and Thomas H. Etzold *China in the 1920s: Nationalism and Revolution* (New York; New Viewpoints, 1976); Jane L. Price *Cadres, Commanders and Commissars: The Training of the Chinese Communist Leadership, 1920–1945* (Folkestone: Dawson, 1976), pp. 53–72; Jiang Weiguo (Editor) *Beifa tongyi* (Taipei: Liming wenhua shiye gongsi, 1981), Volume 1, pp. 133–9.

8 Dick Wilson *Chou: The Story of Chou Enlai 1898–1976* (London: Hutchinson, 1984), pp. 73–6.

9 Li *Zhongguo jin bainian zhengzhi shi*, pp. 462–4.

10 Edward L. Dreyer *China at War 1901–1949* (New York: Longman, 1995), pp. 112–16; Ch'i His-sheng *Warlord Politics in China 1916–1928* (Stanford: Stanford University Press 1976); James Sheridan *Chinese Warlord: The Career of Feng Yuxiang* (Stanford: Stanford University Press, 1966), pp. 133–7.

11 Donald A. Jordan *The Northern Expedition: China's National Revolution of 1926–8* (Honolulu: University Press of Hawaii, 1976), pp. 63–4, quoting a photograph of the document in the National Military Museum in Taibei. The *Guominjun* National Army, as has been noted, was the name given by the warlord Feng Yuxiang to his forces after he had occupied Beijing on 23 October 1924.

12 Jordan *The Northern Expedition*, pp. 67–82, 83–92; F.F. Liu *Military History of Modern China*, pp. 22–35.

13 Marie-Claire Bergère, Lucien Bianco and Jürgen Domes *La Chine au XXe siècle: D'une révolution a l'autre 1895–1949* (Paris: Fayard, 1989), pp. 153–5.

14 Much of this sounds remarkably and uncomfortably similar to China's later industrial development in the years after Mao Zedong's death in 1976.

15 Beijing University *Zhongguo jindaishi ziliao*, Volume 2, pp. 323–35.

16 Ho Kan-chih *A History of the Modern Chinese Revolution* (Beijing: Foreign Languages Press, 1959), pp. 51–7. The most comprehensive treatment of the trade union movement in China before 1927 is Jean Chesneaux, *The Chinese Labour Movement, 1919–1927* (Stanford: Stanford University Press, 1968).

17 David Strand *Rickshaw Beijing: City People and Politics in the 1920s* (Berkeley: University of California Press, 1989), pp. 182–91.

18 Gail Hershatter *The Workers of Tianjin: 1900–1949* (Stanford: Stanford University Press, 1986), pp. 212–20.

19 Jean Chesneaux *The Chinese Labour Movement, 1919–1927*, p. 322.

20 Peng Zeyi *Zhongguo jindai shougongye shi ziliao*, Volume 2, p. 604.

21 Chesneaux *The Chinese Labour Movement*, pp. 322–28.

22 Michael Dillon 'Fang Zhimin, Jingdezhen and the Northeast Jiangxi Soviet' *Modern Asian Studies* Volume 26, Number 3, 1992, pp. 569–89.

23 Isaacs *The Tragedy of the Chinese Revolution*, pp. 156–74; 175–185.

24 Marie-Claire Bergère 'The Other China: Shanghai from 1919 to 1949' in Christopher Howe (Editor) *Shanghai: Revolution and Development in an Asian Metropolis* (Cambridge: Cambridge University Press, 1981), p. 3.

25 Richard Gaulton 'Political Mobilization in Shanghai, 1949–1951' in Howe (Editor) *Shanghai: Revolution and Development in an Asian Metropolis*, pp. 46–7. Although these proposals to dismantle the economic structure of Shanghai seem ludicrous, very similar anti-urban policies of dispersing the population of the capital city to the countryside were carried out by the leadership of the Khmer Rouge when they took control of the Cambodian capital Phnom Penh in 1975.

26 R.H. Tawney *Land and Labour in China* (London: Allen and Unwin, 1932), pp. 23–6. Population statistics are notoriously unreliable for China before the government of the People's Republic carried out its first census on 30 June 1953 and even after that date they leave much to be desired. The figure of 450 million for the total population of China in the first half of the twentieth century was used by the League of Nations and widely quoted, but demographic specialists acknowledge that this can only be considered an estimate because of the lack of uniform procedures in previous censuses. There is, however, a general consensus on the proportion of the population engaged in agriculture. Leo

A. Orleans *Every Fifth Child: The Population of China* (London: Eyre Methuen, 1972), pp. 14–28.

27 Chesneaux *Secret Societies in China*, pp. 43, 170, 173–5; Li Dazhao *Li Dazhao xuanji* [*Selected Works of Li Dazhao*] (Beijing: Renmin chubanshe, 1959), pp. 564–70; A. Ivine *Krasnye piki* [*Red Spears*]Moscow, 1926; Ralph A. Thaxton Jr. *China Turned Rightside Up: Revolutionary Legitimacy in the Peasant World* (New Haven: Yale University Press, 1983), pp. 70–6; Ralph A. Thaxton Jr. *Salt of the Earth: The Political Origins of Peasant Protest and Communist Revolution in China* (Berkeley: University of California Press, 1997), pp. 145–6. The Yiguandao society remains active, although illegal, in the People's Republic of China and has a strong following in Taiwan, surpassed only by mainstream Buddhism and Daoism.

28 Tawney *Land and Labour in China*, p. 26.

29 Peking United International Famine Relief Committee *The North China Famine of 1920–22 with Special Reference to the West Chihli Area* (Peking: Commercial Press, 1922), pp. 11–15.

30 *Hongqi piaopiao* [*Red Flags Flutter*] (Beijing: Zhongguo qingnian chubanshe, 1957–66), Volume 5, pp. 32–45; Roy Hofheinz Jr. *The Broken Wave: The Chinese Communist Peasant Movement, 1922–1928* (Cambridge: Harvard, 1977); Stuart Schram *Mao Tse-tung* (Harmondsworth: Penguin, 1966), pp. 79, 92; Yong-Pil Pang '*Peng Pai: From Landlord to Revolutionary*' *Modern China*, Volume 1, Number 3, July 1975; Chen Ye 'Nongmin yundong de da wang: jieshao Peng Pai lieshi de guanghui shiji he wenwu' (King of the Peasant Movement: The Glorious Deeds and Legacy of the Martyr Peng Pai) *Geming Wenwu* [*Revolutionary Legacy*] 1978, Volume 5, pp. 40–47. This article was probably the first in China to rehabilitate Peng Pai in the popular imagination after the death of Mao Zedong.

31 Saich *The Rise to Power of the Chinese Communist Party*, pp. 182–194, 198–210.

32 Lu Hsun (Lu Xun) *A Brief History of Chinese Fiction* (Beijing: Foreign Languages Press, 1964) is a study of the Chinese traditional novel by the leading exponent of vernacular fiction in the 1920s.

33 Perry Link *Mandarin Ducks and Butterflies: Popular Fiction in Early Twentieth Century Chinese Cities* (Berkeley: University of California Press, 1981).

34 Zhou Liangpei (Editor) *Zhongguo xin shi ku: Xu Zhimo juan* [*Treasury of China's New Poetry: Xu Zhimo*] (Wuhan: Changjiang wenyi chubanshe, 1988).

35 Zhou (Editor) *Zhongguo xin shi ku: Wen Yiduo juan*; Tao Tao Sanders *Red Candle: Selected Poems by Wen I-to* (London: Jonathan Cape, 1972)

36 Colin Mackerras *The Chinese Theatre in Modern Times from 1840 to the Present Day* (London: Thames and Hudson, 1975).

9 Nanjing Decade and the Long March

1 H. Owen Chapman *The Chinese Revolution 1926–27: A Record of the Period under Communist Control as Seen from the Nationalist Capital Hankow* (London: Constable, 1928), pp. 104–5.

2 Isaacs *The Tragedy of the Chinese Revolution*, pp. 270–1.

3 Chiang Kai-shek had already been married twice. His first wife was a young peasant woman whom he had married in 1901 and they had a son, Jiang

Jingguo (Chiang Ching-kuo) who was later to succeed his father as President of the Republic of China in Taiwan. Chiang Kai-shek married Chen Jieru (Jenny Chen) in December 1921 in the Great Eastern Hotel in Shanghai. Her account of their marriage can be read in Ch'en Chieh-ju (edited and with an introduction by Lloyd Eastman) *Chiang Kai-shek's Secret Past* (Boulder: Westview Press, 1993).

4   Guandong (or Kwantung) should not be confused with the name of the province Guangdong (Kwangtung). It refers to the region 'east of the passes' in Manchuria where this Japanese army, to a great extent independent of the Japanese government in Tokyo, was originally stationed to guard the South Manchurian Railway and Japanese interests in the leased territory of the Liaodong peninsula.

5   The Institute of Politics was an annual convention on international affairs held under the auspices of Williams College: its first session was in 1921.

6   Chao-Chu Wu *The Nationalist Programme for China* (New Haven: Yale University Press, 1929), pp. 1–31.

7   Wu *The Nationalist Programme for China*, pp. 33–57, 59–78, 98–101.

8   The English text of the Organic Law can be found in Wu *The Nationalist Programme for China*, Appendix II, pp. 81–9.

9   Patrick Lescot *Before Mao: The Untold Story of Li Lisan and the Creation of Communist China* (London: HarperCollins), 2004.

10 Dillon 'Fang Zhimin, Jingdezhen and the Northeast Jiangxi Soviet,' pp. 569–89; Kamal Sheel *Peasant Society and Marxist Intellectuals in China: Fang Zhimin and the Origin of a Revolutionary Movement in the Xinjiang Region* (Princeton: Princeton University Press, 1989). The Chinese name for the Xin river region is written as Xinjiang in the *Hanyu pinyin* romanisation and this has led to some confusion with the Xinjiang of northwestern China.

11 Trygve Lötveit *Chinese Communism 1931–1934: Experience in Civil Government* (Lund: Scandinavian Institute of Asian Studies, 1973); William Wei *Counterrevolution: The Nationalists in Jiangxi during the Soviet Period* (Ann Arbor: University of Michigan Press, 1985).

12 Saich *The Rise to Power of the Chinese Communist Party*, pp. 509–17; Party History Research Committee of the CCP *History of the Chinese Communist Party: A Chronology of Events (1919–1990)* (Beijing: Foreign Language Press, 1991), pp. 78–9. It can be surprisingly difficult to obtain a trustworthy factual version of an event or of a subject which appears to be straightforward such as the membership of CCP committees and the holders of party posts. These appointments have often been revised subsequently in the light of the rise and fall of individual leaders and their supporters.

13 Chi-hsi Hu 'The Sexual Revolution in the Kiangsi Soviet' *China Quarterly*, Volume 59, July/September 1974, pp. 477–90.

14 Lötveit *Chinese Communism 1931–1934*.

15 Donald A. Jordan *Chinese Boycotts versus Japanese Bombs; the failure of China's 'Revolutionary Diplomacy' 1931–2* (Ann Arbor: University of Michigan Press, 1991).

16 Mei Jian *Guo Gong mishi* [*Secrets of the Guomindang and Communists*] (Beijing: Zhonguo wenshi chubanshe, 2001), pp. 298–301.

17 Mao Zedong *Mao Zhuxi shici sanshiqi shou* [*Thirty Seven Poems of Chairman Mao*] (Beijing: Wenwu chubanshe, 1974), p. 4. For an alternative translation see Wong Man *Poems of Mao Tse-tung* (Hong Kong: Eastern Horizon Press, 1966), p. 20.

18 Mei *Guo Gong mishi*, pp. 298–301.

19 Saich *The Rise to Power of the Chinese Communist Party*, pp. 517–18.

20 *Xinghuo liaoyuan* [*A single spark can start a prairie fire*] (Hong Kong: Sanlian Press, 1960), p. 1.

21 One example will have to represent many. Chen Chi-tung's *The Long March* (Beijing: Foreign Languages Press, 1956) is a drama in six acts with an epilogue, written by a man who took part in one section of the Long March and the English translation includes an appendix in which the author explains how he wrote the play.

22 The two most reliable and accessible sources in English are Dick Wilson *The Long March 1935: The Epic of Chinese Communism's Survival* (London: Hamish Hamilton, 1971) and Harrison E. Salisbury *The Long March: The Untold Story* (London: Macmillan, 1985).

23 Party History Research Committee of the CCP *History of the Chinese Communist Party: A Chronology of Events (1919–1990)*, pp. 105–6.

24 Thomas Kampen *Mao Zedong, Zhou Enlai and the Evolution of the Chinese Communist Leadership* (Copenhagen: Nordic Institute of Asian Studies, 2000); Mei *Guo Gong mishi*, pp. 313–15.

25 Huaqing Hot Springs is still a popular resort for Chinese, and foreign tourists and local people take great delight in pointing out precisely where Chiang Kaishek was captured. Its history as a resort dates back at least to the Tang dynasty and legend has it that Yang Guifei, the celebrated concubine of the Tang Emperor Xuanzong, bathed in its waters. The springs are not far from the tomb of the first emperor of China, Qin Shihuangdi, and the site of the terracotta army.

26 Saich *The Rise to Power of the Chinese Communist Party*, pp. 663–5; Mei *Guo Gong mishi*, pp. 393–421; Frederic Wakeman Jr. *Spymaster: Dai Li and the Chinese Secret Service* (Berkeley: University of California Press), pp. 233–6; Luo Ruiqing, Lü Zheng'ao and Wang Bingnan *Zhou Enlai and the Xi'an Incident* (Beijing: Foreign Languages Press, 1983); Zhang Xueliang's own account of this incident and also the rest of his life and political career is given in Zhang Xueliang *Zhang Xueliang koushu zizhuan* [*Zhang Xueliang's Autobiography: An Oral Account*] edited by Wang Shujun (Hong Kong: Xianggang shidai chubanshe, 2004).

27 Luo, Lü and Wang *Zhou Enlai and the Xi'an Incident*.

28 Saich *The Rise to Power of the Chinese Communist Party*, pp. 770–1, 769.

10 Japanese Invasion, Second United Front and Civil War

1 J. Gunnar Andersson *China Fights for the World* (London: Kegan Paul, Trench, Trubner & Co, 1939), pp. 138–40. There is now a Chinese People's Memorial Museum of the War of Resistance against Japan in Wanping.

2 Richard Storry *A History of Modern Japan* (Harmondsworth: Penguin, 1960), pp. 202–7.

3   Owen Lattimore *Reminiscences of China*, tape recordings, University of Leeds, 1976.

4   Bergère 'The Other China: Shanghai from 1919 to 1949.'

5   Charles S. Maier 'Foreword' in Joshua A. Fogel (Editor) *The Nanjing Massacre in History and Historiography* (Berkeley: University of California Press, 2000), pp. vii–viii. The comparison made by some Chinese writers with the Holocaust of European Jewry has been one of the more controversial aspects of the debate on the Nanjing massacre.

6   Perhaps the most influential of these eyewitness reports were the diaries of the German businessman John Rabe, which are published in *The Good German of Nanking* (London: Abacus, 1998).

7   Takashi Yoshida 'A Battle over History: the Nanjing Massacre in Japan' in Fogel (Editor) *The Nanjing Massacre*, pp. 70–132; Iris Chang *The Rape of Nanjing: The Forgotten Holocaust of World War II* (London: Penguin Books, 1998). Iris Chang was found dead, apparently by her own hand, in California in 2004.

8   Dreyer *China at War 1901–1949*, pp. 206–64.

9   With the exception of the disputed archipelagos of the Xisha, Nansha and Zhongsha islands in the South China Sea.

10 Balujun Xi'an banshichu jinianguan (Editor) *Zhou Enlai yu Qixianzhuang* (Balujun Xi'an banshichu jinianguan: Xi'an, 1988); Balujun Xi'an banshichu jinianguan (Editor) *Balujun zhu Shaan banshichu [Eighth Route Army Office in Shaanxi]* (Balujun Xi'an banshichu jinianguan: Xi'an, 1979); Luo, Lü and Wang *Zhou Enlai and the Xi'an Incident*.

11 CCP Central Committee Party History Research Centre *History of the Chinese Communist Party: A Chronology of Events (1919–1990)*, p. 139; Dreyer *China at War 1901–1949*, pp. 252–3.

12 Gregor Benton *Mountain Fires: The Red Army's Three Year War in South China 1934–1938* (Berkeley: University of California Press, 1992); Gregor Benton *New Fourth Army: Communist Resistance Along the Yangze and the Huai 1938–1941* (Richmond: Curzon Press, 1999).

13 The Southern Anhui Incident is also known as the Wannan Incident. *Wannan* is a term for southern Anhui, combining the traditional single character name *Wan* for the name of the province and the word *nan* for south.

14 Dreyer *China at War 1901–1949*, pp. 254–5; Gregor Benton *New Fourth Army: Communist Resistance Along the Yangze and the Huai 1938–1941* (Richmond: Curzon Press, 1999).

15 Blake Clark *Pearl Harbour: An Eye-Witness Account* (London: John Lane The Bodley Head, 1942).

16 Boyd Compton *Mao's China: Party Reform Documents, 1942–44* (Seattle: University of Washington Press, 1952).

17 David Smurthwaite *The Pacific War Atlas 1941–1945* (London: HMSO, 1995).

18 Often translated simply as the Anti-Japanese War.

19 Stuart Gelder *The Chinese Communists* (London: Gollancz, 1946), p. xiii. All place names, and the party name Guomindang, have been converted into *pinyin* romanisation in this and the following quotation. The *News Chronicle* was a

popular British newspaper that was published from June 1930 until 1960, when it merged with the *Daily Mail.*

20 Gelder *The Chinese Communists*, pp. xiv–xv.

21 Dreyer *China at War 1901–1949*, pp. 265–311.

22 Dreyer *China at War 1901–1949*, p. 266.

23 Theodore White and Annalee Jacoby *Thunder Out of China* (New York: William Sloane, 1946), pp. 5–8.

24 White and Jacoby *Thunder Out of China*, pp. 11–19.

25 White and Jacoby *Thunder Out of China*, p. 129.

26 Lattimore *Reminiscences of China.*

27 White and Jacoby *Thunder Out of China*, pp. 129–31.

28 Dreyer *China at War 1901–1949*, pp. 266–71, 284–9; Chiang *A Summing Up at Seventy*, pp. 117–19.

29 David D. Barrett *Dixie Mission: The United States Army Observer Group in Yenan, 1944* (Berkeley: Centre for Chinese Studies China Research Monographs, No 6, 1979). The reason for the nickname 'Dixie' is not entirely clear but it was probably a name used informally by the U.S. forces in China for the mysterious rebel areas, with echoes of the name for the southern Confederate states in the American Civil War and the popular song 'Is it true what they say about Dixie?'.

30 John Israel 'Southwest Associated University: Preservation as an Ultimate Value' in Paul K.T. Sih (Editor) *Nationalist China during the Sino-Japanese War, 1937–1945* (Hicksville, NY: Exposition Press, 1977), pp. 131–54.

31 Delia Davin *Woman-Work: Women and the Party in Revolutionary China* (Oxford: Oxford University Press, 1976).

32 John Dower *Embracing Defeat: Japan in the Aftermath of World War II* (London: Penguin, 1999), pp. 74–81.

33 Dreyer *China at War 1901–1949*, pp. 305–6

34 Saich *The Rise to Power of the Chinese Communist Party*, pp. 1244–53.

35 Details of the Liao-Shen and Huai-Hai battles in their political and social context can be found in Liu Tong *Zhongguo de 1948 nian liang zhong mingyun de juezhan* [*China in 1948: Two Fateful and Decisive Battles*] (Beijing: Sanlian, 2006).

36 Chalmers A. Johnson *Peasant Nationalism and Communist Power: The Emergence of Revolutionary China 1937–1945* (Stanford: Stanford University Press, 1962).

37 Mark Selden *The Yenan Way in Revolutionary China* (Cambridge: Harvard University Press, 1971).

38 Ralph Thaxton *China Turned Right Side Up* (New Haven: Yale University Press, 1983) is an example of this kind of rural history based on detailed fieldwork and local studies.

39 H. Maclear Bate *Report from Formosa* (London: Eyre and Spottiswoode, 1952), p. 20.

40 Bate *Report from Formosa*, pp. 20–1; *Twenty-Sixth Anniversary of the 'February 28' Uprising of the People of Taiwan Province* (Beijing: Foreign Languages Press, 1973).

41 Tang Tsou *America's Failure in China, 1941–1950* (Chicago: University of Chicago Press, 1963), p. 497.

11 Liberation and the Birth of the People's Republic of China

1 Derk Bodde *Peking Diary* (New York: Henry Schuman, 1950), pp. 98–101. His translation of Feng Youlan's *History of Chinese Philosophy* was finally published in 1952.

2 Colin Mackerras *Modern China: A Chronology from 1842 to the present* (London: Thames and Hudson, 1982), p. 436.

3 Peter Townsend *China Phoenix: The Revolution in China* (London: Jonathan Cape, 1955), pp. 217–27.

4 Zhou Enlai 'Renmin zhengxie gongtong gangling caoan de tedian' [Distinguishing Features of the CPPCC's Draft Common Programme] in Zhonggong Zhongyang wenxian yanjiu shibian *Jianguo yilai zhongyao wenxian xuanbian* [*Selections of Important Documents since the Establishment of the People's Republic*] (Beijing: CCP Documentary Press, 1993), Volume 1, pp. 14–18. Hereafter *Jianguo yilai*.

5 *Jianguo yilai*, Volume 1, pp. 1–13.

6 Zhou Enlai 'Renmin zhengxie gongtong gangling caoan de tedian' *Jianguo yilai*, Volume 1, pp. 14–19; Townsend *China Phoenix*, pp. 224–7.

7 Mao Zedong *Selected Works* (Beijing: Foreign Language Press, 1967), Volume 4.

8 Zhu De 'Zhongguo renmin jiefangjun zongbu mingling' [Instruction from the Headquarters of the Chinese People's Liberation Army] *Jianguo yilai*, Volume 1, pp. 22–3.

9 *Jianguo yilai*, Volume 1, p. 509.

10 *Jianguo yilai*, Volume 1, pp. 44–7; Laszlo Ladany *The Chinese Communist Party and Marxism 1921–1985* (Stanford: Stanford University Press, 1988), pp. 178–9.

11 Ladany *The Chinese Communist Party and Marxism 1921–1985*, p. 179.

12 *Xinhua yuekan* quoted in Ladany *The Chinese Communist Party and Marxism 1921–1985*, p. 181. For a discussion of the nature of the suspended death penalty, see Andrew Scobell 'The Death Penalty in Post-Mao China' *China Quarterly* 123, September 1990, pp. 503–20. For Peng Zhen on suppressing counter revolutionaries, see *Jianguo yilai*, Volume 2, pp. 48–53.

13 Ladany *The Chinese Communist Party and Marxism 1921–1985* citing *People's Daily* 12 July 1951. The campaign in Tianjin in 1999 against the neo-Buddhist group, Falungong, had close parallels with the 1951 campaign against the Yiguandao.

14 Townsend *China Phoenix*, pp. 373–86.

15 Ladany *The Chinese Communist Party and Marxism 1921–1985* citing *People's Daily* 19 May 1957.

16 The Government Affairs Council was the supreme body of the Chinese state until it was superseded by the State Council after the adoption of the Constitution of September 1954.

17 *Jianguo yilai*, Volume 2, pp. 471–85, 500–1 and 552–3.

18 Ralph Lapwood and Nancy Lapwood *Through the Chinese Revolution* (Letchworth: People's Books Cooperative Society, 1954), pp. 162–74.

19 *Jianguo yilai*, Volume 3, pp. 53–4.

20 *Jianguo yilai*, Volume 1, pp. 95–7. The text of the treaty, ancillary agreements and the official communiqué can be found in *Jianguo yilai*, Volume 1, pp. 117–25; Isaac Deutscher *Stalin* (London: Penguin, 1966), pp. 575–83; Sergei N.

Goncharov, John W. Lewis and Xue Litai *Uncertain Partners: Stalin, Mao and the Korean War* (Stanford: Stanford University Press, 1993); Robert Service *Stalin: A Biography* (London: Macmillan, 2004), pp. 509–10. CCP Central Committee Party History Research Centre *History of the Chinese Communist Party: A Chronology of Events (1919–1990)*, p. 219.

21 Mao Zedong 'Bu yao simian chuji' [Don't Strike Out in All Directions] *Jianguo yilai*, Volume 1, pp. 257–60.

22 *BBC Summary of World Broadcasts*, 3 September 1992.

23 Chen Jian *China's Road to the Korean War* (New York: Columbia University Press, 1994), pp. 111–13; Goncharov, Lewis and Xue *Uncertain Partners: Stalin, Mao and the Korean War*.

24 Chen *China's Road to the Korean War*, p. 110.

25 Jürgen Domes *Peng Te-huai: The Man and the Image* (London: Hurst, 1985), pp. 605.

26 Kuang Chen and Pan Liang *Women de 1950 niandai* [*Our 1950s*] (Beijing: Zhongguo youyi chuban gongsi, 2006), p. 17.

27 Domes *Peng Te-huai: The Man and the Image*, pp. 605.

28 *Constitution of the People's Republic of China* (Beijing: Foreign Languages Press, 1954); Chinese text in *Jianguo yilai*, Volume 5, pp. 520–42.

29 *Handbook on People's China* (Beijing: Foreign Languages Press, 1957), pp. 47–51, 52–80.

30 Gregor Benton (Editor) *Wild Lilies and Poisonous Weeds: Dissident Voices from People's China* (London: Pluto Press, 1982).

31 CCP Central Committee Party History Research Centre *History of the Chinese Communist Party: A Chronology of Events (1919–1990)*, pp. 244–5; Jürgen Domes *The Internal Politics of China 1949–1972*, pp. 52–3 (London: Hurst, 1973).

32 Gao Gang had committed the serious political error (as far as his Chinese colleagues were concerned) of sycophancy towards Stalin in the meetings that preceded the signing of the Sino-Soviet Treaty of 1949. Goncharov, Lewis and Xue *Uncertain Partners: Stalin, Mao and the Korean War*.

12 Economic and Social Policies

1 Rudolf Hommel *China at Work an Illustrated Record of the Primitive Industries of China's Masses, Whose Life Is Toil, and Thus an Account of Chinese Civilization* (Cambridge, MA: MIT Press, 1969 [1937]).

2 *Chronology of the Peoples Republic of China 1949–1984* (Beijing: Foreign Languages Press, 1986), pp. 2–3. The GAC functioned as the cabinet in the early 1950s.

3 Although some senior CCP figures had experience of working in Europe they did not necessarily return to China with a positive view of the way that modern capitalist economies had operated in the 1930s and 1940s.

4 Li Fuchun 'Bianzhi diyi ge wunian jihua ying zhuyi de wenti' [Problems to be Considered in Drawing Up the First Five Year Plan] in *Jianguo yilai*, Volume 1, pp. 402–6.

5 Audrey Donnithorne *China's Economic System* (London: Allen and Unwin, 1967), pp. 457–95.

6 Donnithorne *China's Economic System*, pp. 457–8.

7　Domes *Internal Politics of China 1949–1972*, p. 42.

8　'The total value of Soviet assistance amounted to only 3 per cent of the overall sum assigned for the fulfilment of the Five Year Plan...' Rodzinski *The People's Republic of China: A Concise Political History* (New York: Free Press, 1988), p. 32.

9　Nicholas R. Lardy 'Economic Recovery and the 1st Five Year Plan' in Denis Twitchett and John K. Fairbank (General Editors) *Cambridge History of China Volume 14 The People's Republic, Part 1: The Emergence of Revolutionary China 1949–1965* (Cambridge: Cambridge University Press, 1987), pp. 155–6.

10　Donnithorne *China's Economic System*, p. 460.

11　*Agrarian Reform Law of the Peoples Republic of China* promulgated by the Central People's Government, 30 June 1950, Chinese text in *Jianguo yilai*, Volume 1, pp. 336–45.

12　Mao Tse-tung *Selected Works* (Beijing: Foreign Languages Press, 1977), Volume V, p. 24.

13　Frederick C. Teiwes 'Establishment and Consolidation of the New Regime' in Twitchett and Fairbank (General Editors) *Cambridge History of China Volume 14 The People's Republic, Part 1: The Emergence of Revolutionary China 1949–1965*, pp. 83–8.

14　*Jianguo yilai*, Volume 1.

15　Teiwes 'Establishment and Consolidation of the New Regime', pp. 83–8. For detailed information on the evolution of land policies, see Chao Kuo-chun *The Agrarian Policy of the Chinese Communist Party 1921–1959* (London: Asia Publishing House, 19600. Contemporary first-hand accounts of the movement in specific villages can be found in the classic *Fanshen* by William Hinton (Harmondsworth: Penguin Books, 1972) and two books by Isabel and David Crook *Revolution in a Chinese Village: Ten Mile Inn* (London: Routledge and Kegan Paul, 1959) and *Mass Movement in a Chinese Village: Ten Mile Inn* (London: Routledge and Kegan Paul, 1979). A recent critical account of long-term change in rural China is Zhang Yongdong *1949 nian hou Zhongguo nongcun zhidu biange shi* [*History of the Transformation of China's Rural System*] (Taipei: Ziyou wenhua chubanshe, 2008).

16　General Office of the Central Committee of the Communist Party of China *Socialist Upsurge in China's Countryside* (Beijing: Foreign Languages Press, 1957).

17　Central People's Government Council *The Marriage Law of the People's Republic of China* (Beijing: Foreign Languages Press, 1950) 1973; Kuang Chen and Pan Liang, pp. 9–10.

18　Elisabeth Croll *The Politics of Marriage in Contemporary China* (Cambridge: Cambridge University Press, 1981).

19　The original Chinese title of *Dream of the Red Chamber* by Cao Xueqin is *Honglou meng*, and it has also been translated into English as *The Story of the Stone*.

20　Mao Zedong *Mao Zedong xuanji* [*Selected Works of Mao Zedong*] (Beijing: People's Publishing House, 1977), pp. 157–67; Domes *Internal Politics of China 1949–1972*, pp. 53–5.

21　The Supreme State Conference [*Zuigao guowu huiyi*] is not the National People's Conference but a body that could only be convened on the direct authority of the Chairman of the People's Republic of China (President), at the time, Mao Zedong. 'The Chairman of the Republic may, whenever necessary, convene a Supreme State Conference, and put the views of the Conference on important matters of state before the National People's Conference, its Standing Committee, the State Council or other bodies concerned, for consideration and decision.' *Constitution of the People's Republic of China* (Beijing: Foreign Languages Press, 1954), Article 43; *Handbook on People's China*, p. 58.

22 Roderick MacFarquhar, Timothy Cheek and Eugene Wu (Editors) *The Secret Speeches of Chairman Mao: From the Hundred Flowers to the Great Leap Forward* (Cambridge, MA: Harvard University Press, 1989), pp. 174–7.

23 Roderick MacFarquhar *The Hundred Flowers Campaign and the Chinese Intellectuals* (New York: Octagon Books, 1974).

24 Domes *Internal Politics of China 1949–1972*, pp. 83–93.

13 Great Leap Forward

1 CCP Central Committee Party History Research Centre *History of the Chinese Communist Party: A Chronology of Events (1919–1990)*, p. 269.

2 Mao Zedong 'Jieshao yige hezuoshe' (Introducing a commune) *Jianguo yilai*, Volume 11, pp. 274–6. Writing from Guangzhou, Mao was recommending that other regions follow the example of a cooperative in Fengqiu county in Henan province, which he had visited during his inspection tour; CCP Central Committee Party History Research Centre *History of the Chinese Communist Party: A Chronology of Events (1919–1990)*, pp. 271–2.

3 Domes *Internal Politics of China 1949–1972*, pp. 88–93; Liu Shaoqi 'Zhongguo gongchandang zhongyang weiyuanhui xiang diba jie quanguo daibiao dahui dier ci huiyi de gongzuobao' [Work Report of the Eight Central Committee of the Chinese Communist Party to the Second Meeting of the National People's Congress] *Jianguo yilai*, Volume 11, pp. 285–325.

4 Domes *Internal Politics of China 1949–1972*, pp. 97–9; CCP Central Committee Party History Research Centre *History of the Chinese Communist Party: A Chronology of Events (1919–1990)*, p. 273.

5 Domes *Internal Politics of China 1949–1972*, pp. 97–8.

6 Chi Li and Tien Chieh-yun *Inside a People's Commune* (Beijing: Foreign Languages Press, 1975), pp. 5–6. The spelling of place names has been transcribed into *pinyin*.

7 Chi and Tien *Inside a People's Commune*, pp. 9–10.

8 The image of the Chinese communes abroad has probably been affected negatively by the name, especially in the English-speaking world. In France, the name *commune* is nothing special: although the concept does have radical origins in the French Revolution of 1789 and the Paris Commune of 1871, it is now simply the term for a level of local government, run by a municipal council and led by the mayor. It has none of the connotations of alternative lifestyles in hippy communes such as those that flourished in the Haight-Ashbury area of San Francisco in the 1960s or Christiania in Copenhagen.

9 Chi and Tien *Inside a People's Commune*, pp. 10–16.

10 Crook and Crook *The First Years of Yangyi Commune*, pp. 32–8.

11 CCP Central Committee Party History Research Centre *History of the Chinese Communist Party: A Chronology of Events (1919–1990)*, pp. 275–7.

12 Domes *Internal Politics of China 1949–1972*, pp. 101–3.

13 Goldstein *A History of Modern Tibet 1913–1951*; Melvyn C. Goldstein *The Snow Lion and the Dragon: China, Tibet and the Dalai Lama* (Berkeley: University of California Press, 1997).

14 CCP Central Committee Party History Research Centre *History of the Chinese Communist Party: A Chronology of Events (1919–1990)*, p. 280. Enlarging, or packing, a meeting was a technique employed by the leadership to ensure that policies which might not be acceptable to the regular membership would be endorsed.

15 In the year 2000, the CCP organised a series of activities to mark the commemoration of the birth of Zhang Wentian (1900–1976). The published text of an article by then President Yang Shangkun includes the sentence 'After the Zunyi Conference, he took total control of the CCP Central Committee (everybody liked to call him "general secretary". Zhang had a senior position during the Long March, but by 1943 had "stepped down from the leading posts of the Party Central Committee"'. *BBC Summary of World Broadcasts*, 31 August 2000.

16 Domes *Internal Politics of China 1949–1972*, pp. 101–3.

17 CCP Central Committee Party History Research Centre *History of the Chinese Communist Party: A Chronology of Events (1919–1990)*, pp. 280–1; Domes *Peng Tehuai: The Man and the Image*, pp. 81–106.

18 Local newspapers were considered to be *neibu*, classified internal documents and were authorised for circulation only within China.

19 Domes *Internal Politics of China 1949–1972*, p. 113.

20 E.L. Wheelwright and Bruce McFarlane *The Chinese Road to Socialism* (London, Penguin Books 1973), p. 55. A *mou*, *mu* in *pinyin* romanisation, corresponds to ·0667 hectares of land. This view was common at the time and Wheelwright and McFarlane's analysis is only one example, albeit a widely circulated one.

21 Excess deaths in this context indicates deaths over and above the statistically projected normal death rate for the years in question.

22 Domes *Internal Politics of China 1949–1972*, p. 117; Jasper Becker *Hungry Ghosts: China's Secret Famine* (London: John Murray, 1996).

23 Dali L. Yang *Calamity and Reform in China: State, Rural Society and Institutional change since the Great Leap Famine* (Stanford: Stanford University Press, 1996).

24 Mao's key writings, *Mao Zedong xuanji*, were published in an English translation as *Selected Works of Mao Tse-tung*, Volumes 1–4 (Beijing: Foreign Languages Press, 1967). Volume 5 appeared in 1977. These authorised versions of Mao's speeches and writings are heavily edited and incomplete and Western and Japanese scholars have worked to compile complete editions.

25 Richard Baum and Frederic C. Teiwes *Ssu-ch'ing: The Socialist Education Movement of 1962–66* (Berkeley: University of California Press, 1968).

26 Baum and Teiwes *Ssu-ch'ing: The Socialist Education Movement of 1962–66*; Domes *Internal Politics of China 1949–1972*, pp. 137–9.

27 *Yidai xinren xue Lei Feng* [*A New Generation Learns from Lei Feng*] (Shenyang: Liaoning People's Publishing House, 1978).

28 Baum and Teiwes *Ssu-ch'ing: The Socialist Education Movement of 1962–66*.

29 Barry Naughton 'The Third Front: Defence Industrialisation in the Chinese Interior' *China Quarterly* 115, September 1988, pp. 351–86, and 'Industrial Policy during the Cultural Revolution: Military Preparation, Decentralisation and

Leaps Forward' in William A. Joseph, Christine P.W. Wong and David Zweig (Editors) *New Perspectives on the Cultural Revolution* (Cambridge: Harvard, 1991).

14 Cultural Revolution

1   Roderick MacFarquhar and Michael Schoenhals *Mao's Last Revolution* (Cambridge: Belknap Press of Harvard University Press, 2006) is highly recommended as a balanced and detailed attempt to make sense of this critical and problematic period, using the most up-to-date Chinese sources.
2   Domes *The Internal Politics of China 1949–1972*, p. 141.
3   Domes *The Internal Politics of China 1949–1972*, pp. 151–2.
4   MacFarquhar and Schoenhals *Mao's Last Revolution*, pp. 14–31
5   CCP Central Committee Party History Research Centre *History of the Chinese Communist Party: A Chronology of Events (1919–1990)*, pp. 318–19; MacFarquhar and Schoenhals *Mao's Last Revolution*, pp. 32–51, 52–65.
6   Jean Esmein *The Chinese Cultural Revolution* (London: Andre Deutsch, 1975), pp. 61–4; *Important Documents on the Great Proletarian Revolution in China* (Beijing: Foreign Languages Press, 1970), pp. 107–28. CCP Central Committee Party History Research Centre *History of the Chinese Communist Party: A Chronology of Events (1919–1990)*, pp. 323–4.
7   Some sources have suggested that this poster was not put up until 1 June.
8   CCP Central Committee Party History Research Centre *History of the Chinese Communist Party: A Chronology of Events (1919–1990)*, pp. 324–5.
9   *Beijing daxue wuchanjieji wenhua da geming yundong jieshao* [Introduction to the Cultural Revolution Movement at Beijing University] (Beijing: Beijing University Cultural Revolution Committee Propaganda Group, 1966).
10 Jean Esmein *The Chinese Cultural Revolution* (London: Andre Deutsch, 1975), p. 62.
11 Domes, pp. 156–8; CCP Central Committee Party History Research Centre *History of the Chinese Communist Party: A Chronology of Events*, pp. 327–8.
12 CCP Central Committee Party History Research Centre *History of the Chinese Communist Party: A Chronology of Events (1919–1990)*, p. 328.
13 CCP Central Committee Party History Research Centre *History of the Chinese Communist Party: A Chronology of Events (1919–1990)*, pp. 328–30; MacFarquhar and Schoenhals *Mao's Last Revolution*, pp. 155–69.
14 English translations of these documents can be found in *Important Documents on the Great Proletarian Revolution in China* (Beijing: Foreign Languages Press, 1970) and also in Joan Robinson *The Cultural Revolution in China* (Harmondsworth: Penguin, 1969); MacFarquhar and Schoenhals *Mao's Last Revolution*, pp. 166–9.
15 Jean Esmein *The Chinese Cultural Revolution*, pp. 159–62; MacFarquhar and Schoenhals *Mao's Last Revolution*, pp. 169, 170–83.
16 Jürgen Domes 'The Role of the Military in the Formation of Revolutionary Committees, 1967–68' *China Quarterly* 44, October–December 1970; Domes *The Internal Politics of China 1949–1972*, pp. 201–5.
17 Domes *The Internal Politics of China 1949–1972*, pp. 183–4; Jean Esmein *The Chinese Cultural Revolution*, pp. 224–8; Thomas W. Robinson 'The Wuhan Incident: Local Strife and Provincial Rebellion during the Cultural Revolution'

China Quarterly 47, July–September 1971, pp. 413–38; MacFarquhar and Schoen-hals *Mao's Last Revolution*, pp. 199–220.

18 *China Quarterly* 32, October–December 1967, pp. 201–2; MacFarquhar and Schoenhals *Mao's Last Revolution*, pp. 273–84.

19 Esmein *The Chinese Cultural Revolution*, pp. 228–32; MacFarquhar and Schoen-hals *Mao's Last Revolution*, pp. 239–52.

20 Domes *The Internal Politics of China 1949–1972*, pp. 194–5.

21 Domes *The Internal Politics of China 1949–1972*, pp. 194–6.

22 *China Quarterly* 37, January–March 1969, pp. 15–18.

23 Domes *The Internal Politics of China 1949–1972*, pp. 205–7, 210.

24 MacFarquhar and Schoenhals *Mao's Last Revolution*, pp. 285–307.

25 MacFarquhar and Schoenhals *Mao's Last Revolution*, pp. 308–23.

26 John Gardner *Chinese Politics and the Succession to Mao* (London: Macmillan, 1982), pp. 40–7.

27 Xiong Xianghui 'Dakai Zhong Mei guanxi de qianzou: 1969 nian siwei laoshuai dui guoji xingshi de yanjiu yu jianyi' [The Prelude to the Opening of Sino-US Relations: 1969 Study of the International Situation by Four Veteran Com-manders] *Xin Zhongguo waijiao fengyun* [*New China's Changing Diplomacy*] (Beijing: Shijie zhishe chubanshe, 1996) Volume 4, pp. 7–34.

28 Wilson *Chou: The Story of Zhou Enlai 1898–1976*, pp. 258–69; Han Suyin *Eldest Son: Zhou Enlai and the Making of Modern China 1898–1976* (London: Pimlico, 1994), pp. 345–8.

29 Documents released by the National Security Archive, George Washington University, 10 January 1999.

30 Cheng Jin *Chronology of the Peoples Republic of China 1949–1984* (Beijing: Foreign Languages Press, 1986).

31 The numbers 571 are individually pronounced *wu, qi* and *yi* and together they bear a close resemblance to a Chinese phrase that means 'armed uprising' *wuzhuang qiyi*. It could also stand for May 1971, a possible date for the plot which may have been hatched as early as March 1971. To give Mao the code name of the American bomber that had devastated so much of Vietnam during the war is ironic indeed. MacFarquhar and Schoenhals *Mao's Last Revolution*, pp. 324–86.

32 Gardner *Chinese Politics and the Succession to Mao*, pp. 47–61; Li Zhisui *The Private Life of Chairman Mao the Inside Story of the Man Who Made Modern China* (London: Chatto and Windus, 1994), pp. 533–41.

33 Richard Wilson (Editor) *The President's Trip to China: A Pictorial Record of the His-toric Journey to the People's Republic of China with Text by Members of the American Press Corps* (New York: Bantam, 1972).

34 MacFarquhar and Schoenhals *Mao's Last Revolution*, pp. 320–3.

35 Wilson *Chou: The Story of Zhou Enlai, 1898–1976*, p. 286; *Selected Articles Criticizing Lin Piao and Confucius* (Beijing: Foreign Languages Press, 1974).

36 MacFarquhar and Schoenhals *Mao's Last Revolution*, pp. 379–95, 396–412.

37 David S.G. Goodman *Beijing Street Voices: The Poetry and Politics of China's Democ-racy Movement* (London: Marion Boyars, 1981); additional information from par-ticipants in the demonstrations in private communications.

38 CCP Central Committee Party History Research Centre *History of the Chinese Communist Party: A Chronology of Events (1919–1990)*, p. 376; MacFarquhar and Schoenhals *Mao's Last Revolution*, pp. 413–30.

39 Immanuel C.Y. Hsü *China without Mao: The Search for a New Order* (Oxford: Oxford University Press, 1982), pp. 12–28; CCP Central Committee Party History Research Centre *History of the Chinese Communist Party: A Chronology of Events (1919–1990)*, pp. 377–83.

40 Hsü *China without Mao: The Search for a New Order*, pp. 21–2; 126–42.

41 CCP Central Committee Party History Research Centre *History of the Chinese Communist Party: A Chronology of Events (1919–1990)*, p. 413.

42 MacFarquhar and Schoenhals *Mao's Last Revolution*, pp. 440–43, 447–49.

15 Modernising and Opening China

1 Zhu Jiamu *Wo suo zhidao de shiyi jie sanzhong quanhui [The Third Plenum of the Eleventh Central Committee That I knew]* (Beijing: Dangdai Zhongguo chubanshe, 2008) is a personal account of the Third Plenum by a participant who had served as Hu Qiaomu's private secretary. James M. Ethridge *Changing China: The New Revolution's First Decade*, 1979–1988 (Beijing: New World Press, 1988) is a useful account of the first decade of the reform period based on official documents.

2 In the West there was great confusion about Deng's title. He was regularly called the 'paramount leader', a term that was never used in China and does not have a Chinese equivalent. In China he was simply referred to as Comrade Deng Xiaoping and later as Secretary-General Deng Xiaoping.

3 Roderick MacFarquhar *The Politics of China: The Eras of Mao and Deng* (Cambridge: Cambridge University Press, 1997).

4 David Chandler *A History of Cambodia* (Boulder: Westview Press, 1996).

5 Michael Yahuda *The International Politics of the Asia-Pacific* (London: Routledge-Curzon, 2004), pp. 79–80.

6 Delia Davin *Internal Migration in Contemporary China* (London: Macmillan, 2004).

7 Martin Gilbert *A History of the Twentieth Century: Volume Three 1952–1999*, pp. 671–93.

8 Li Cheng and L.T. Whyte 'China's Technocratic Movement and the World Economic Herald' *Modern China* July 1991; *World Economic Herald [Shijie jingji daobao]* Numbers 407–41 (September 1988 to May 1989).

9 Tony Saich *The Chinese People's Movement Perspectives on Spring 1989* (New York: M.E. Sharpe, 1990); Michel Oksenberg (et. al.) *Beijing Spring 1989: Confrontation and Conflict, the Basic Documents* (New York: M.E. Sharpe, 1990); Radio Beijing International, 3 June 1989.

16 Tibet and Xinjiang

1 Inner Mongolia has a similar contested history but it has never been fully independent: it was part of a greater Mongolian entity until it was separated from Outer Mongolia in 1924. There is a clandestine movement for independence from China and reunification with the independent republic of Mongolia

but it is very low key and to date it has not been as prominent as the movements in Tibet and Xinjiang.

2   Tsering Shakya *The Dragon in the Land of the Snows: A History of Modern Tibet since 1947* (London: Pimlico, 1999), pp. 163–211.

3   Shakya *The Dragon in the Land of the Snows*, pp. 314–47.

4   Goldstein *The Snow Lion and the Dragon*, pp. 61–75.

5   Shakya *The Dragon in the Land of the Snows*, pp. 381–2.

6   Goldstein *The Snow Lion and the Dragon*, pp. 79–83.

7   Goldstein *The Snow Lion and the Dragon*, pp. 100–11.

8   *South China Morning Post 29* June 2000; Isabel Hilton *The Search for the Panchen Lama* (London: W.W. Norton, 2001).

9   Press Trust of India, New Delhi, 11 October 2000.

10 *BBC News* 6 October 2000; personal communication from Tibetan nun.

11 *Financial Times* 9 January 2000; *BBC News* 8 January 2000.

12 Agence France Press, 27 August 2000.

13 *South China Morning Post* 30 September 2000.

14 Qing-Zang combines the customary abbreviations for Qinghai and Tibet (Xizang).

15 Wang Wenheng *Xinjiang zongjiao wenti yanjiu* [*Studies on Religion in Xinjiang*] (Urumqi: Xinjiang People's Press, 1993), pp. 93–5. These figures appear to reflect only the registered and officially sanctioned mosques and other bodies.

16 The Uyghurs use the Arabic and Turkic term *mazar* (tomb or shrine, which is *mezar* in the Turkish of Turkey) for the tombs of their founding sheikhs but it should be noted that there is also a Sufi tomb culture among the Chinese-speaking Hui Muslims (both within and outside Xinjiang) who use the term *gongbei* a Chinese transliteration of the Arabic *qubba* (dome or cupola, after the dominant architectural feature of these tombs).

17 Reyila Dawuti (Rayila Dawud) *Weiwuerzu mazha wenhua yanjiu* [*Studies of Uyghur Mazar Culture*] (Urumqi: Xinjiang University Press, 2001).

18 Thierry Zarcone 'Le Culte des saints au Xinjiang (de 1949 à nos jours)' *Journal of the History of Sufism* 3 (2001), pp. 133–72.

19 Owen Lattimore *Inner Asian Frontiers of China* (New York: American Geographical Society, 1951), p. 87.

20 For detailed accounts of this period of Xinjiang's history, see Andrew D.W. Forbes *Warlords and Muslims in Chinese Central Asia: A Political History of Republican Sinkiang 1911–1949* (Cambridge University Press, 1986) and Linda Benson *The Ili Rebellion: The Moslem Challenge to Chinese Authority in Xinjiang 1944–1949* (New York and London: M.E. Sharpe, 1990).

21 Burhan (Shahidi) *Xinjiang Wushinian* [*Fifty Years of Xinjiang*], pp. 355–61.

22 Personal communication, Almaty, September 1998.

23 For Chinese policies in the strongly Islamic south of Xinjiang, see Wang Jianping 'Islam in Kashghar in the 1950s (unpublished paper).

24 BBC *Summary of World Broadcasts* 21 October 1997.

25 McMillen (1984); Yan Ruiding 'Historical Storm on the Pamirs' *Minzhu Zhongguo*, Number 8, February 1992.

26 Zhang Yuxi 'Xinjiang jiefang yilai fandui minzu fenliezhuyi de douzheng ji qi lishi jingyan' [The Struggle against Ethnic Separatism since the Liberation of Xinjiang) in Yang Faren, Li Ze and Dong Sheng, *Fan yisilanzhuyi fan tujuezhuyi yanjiu [Research on Pan-Islam and Pan-Turkism]* (Urumqi: Xinjiang shehui kexueyuan, 1994), pp. 333–4. *Ishan* is simply the third person plural personal pronoun, 'they', in the Persian language, but in Xinjiang it has come to acquire the special meaning of a Sufi devotee.

27 Zhang Yuxi 'Xinjiang jiefang yilai fandui minzu fenliezhuyi de douzheng ji qi lishi jingyan', pp. 334–36.

28 The Chinese authorities initially suppressed information about these disturbances although details leaked out through émigré publications and the monitoring of local broadcast and print media by the BBC and FBIS. In-depth accounts, heavily slanted towards the Chinese government's perspective, were later published in Xu Yuqi and Chen Yishan (Editor) *Xinjiang fandui minzu fenliezhuyi douzheng shihua [Narrative History of the Struggle against Separatism in Xinjiang]* (Urumqi: Xinjiang People's Press, 1999) and the authoritative Ma Dazheng *Guojia liyi gaoyu yiqie: Xinjiang wending wenti de guancha yu sikao [The Interests of the Nation above All: Observations and Reflections on the Stability of Xinjiang]* (Urumqi: Xinjiang People's Press, 2003). See also Michael Dillon *Xinjiang: China's Muslim Far Northwest* and 'Uyghur Separatism and Nationalism in Xinjiang' in Benjamin Cole (Editor) *Conflict, Terrorism and the Media in Asia* (London: Routledge, 2006), pp. 98–116.

29 Chinese Communist Party Central Committee *Central Committee Document No. 7: Record of the Meeting of the Standing Committee of the Politburo of the Chinese Communist Party concerning the Maintenance of Stability in Xinjiang* (in Uyghur), 19 March 1996.

30 Wang Wenheng *Xinjiang zongjiao wenti yanjiu*, pp. 91–2. A separate academy was also established in Yinchuan, the capital of the Ningxia Hui Autonomous Region, where it trains Chinese-speaking Hui imams.

17 Hong Kong and Taiwan

1 Steve Tsang *A Modern History of Hong Kong* (London: I.B.Tauris, 2007), pp. 119–32

2 Steve Tsang *Hong Kong: An Appointment with China* (London: I.B.Tauris, 1997), pp. 51–3; Philip Snow *The Fall of Hong Kong: Britain China and the Japanese Occupation* (Harvard: Yale University Press, 2003).

3 James L. Watson *Emigration and the Chinese Lineage: The Mans in Hong Kong and London* (Berkeley: University of California Press, 1975); Tsang *A Modern History of Hong Kong*, pp. 145–60, 160–79.

4 Tsang *Hong Kong: An Appointment with China*, pp. 83–94.

5 Tsang *A Modern History of Hong Kong*, pp. 211–27.

6 Tsang *Hong Kong: An Appointment with China*, p. 119; Tsang *A Modern History of Hong Kong*, pp. 228–44.

7 The official history of the Legislative Council and an account of its current operation can be found on its website http://www.legco.gov.hk; Steven Tsang *A Modern History of Hong Kong*, pp. 245–67.

8   Chen Hongtu (Editor) *Taiwan shi [History of Taiwan]* (Taibei: Sanmin, 2004), pp. 159–70; Huang Xiuzheng, Zhang Shengyuan, and Wu Wenxing *Taiwan shi [History of Taiwan]* (Taibei: Wunan tushu, 2004), pp. 281–5, 286–95; John F. Copper *Taiwan: Nation-State or Province?* (Boulder: Westview, 1996).

9   The spelling of Kuomintang and its abbreviation KMT is often used for the Nationalist Party on Taiwan to distinguish it from the pinyin spelling of Guomindang for the party when it ruled China from 1927–45. These two romanised variants represent exactly the same Chinese characters so Guomindang is used for both in this text.

10   Chen Hongtu *Taiwan shi*, pp. 145–50; Huang, Shengyuan, and Wu *Taiwan shi*, pp. 202–67.

11   Chen Hongtu *Taiwan shi*, pp. 147–9; Huang, Shengyuan, and Wu *Taiwan shi*, pp. 264–7.

12   Chen Hongtu *Taiwan shi*, pp. 173–85.

13   Press release, Chinese Embassy in the United Kingdom, 25 January 2002.

14   *Economist* 3 January 2002.

15   *Financial Times* 27 June 2007.

18   China after Deng Xiaoping

1   *Financial Times* 9 August 2006.

2   *People's Daily* (Overseas edition) 27 September 2006.

3   *People's Daily* 1 January 2006.

4   *People's Daily* 18 November 2005.

5   *South China Morning Post* 6 May 2006; Zhao Ziyang *Prisoner of the State: The Secret Journal of Premier Zhao Ziyang* (New York: Simon & Schuster, 2009).

Conclusion: China Rising and a 'Harmonious Society'

1   Chen Guidi and Wu Chuntao *Will the Boat Sink the Water: The Life of China's Peasants* (London: Public Affairs, 2006); Ian Johnson *Wild Grass: China's Revolution from Below* (London: Penguin, 2004).

2   *Financial Times* 8 November 2006.

3   *Northeast Network* www.liaoning-gateway.com; www.china.org.cn.

4   *People's Daily* 19 September 2004.

5   'China's Peaceful Development Road' *People's Daily* 22 December 2005.

6   BBC News 4 June, 2009.

BIOGRAPHICAL NOTES

These are brief notes to assist in identifying individuals who played major roles in the history of modern China and putting them in context. More information is available in the main text.

Aisin Gioro

The family name of the leading Manchu lineage which provided the emperors of the Qing dynasty. The last in the line was Aisin Gioro Pu Yi.

Borodin, Mikhail Markovitch (Michael) 1884–1951

Comintern agent of Russian Lithuanian origin who as a young man lived in the USA. He was responsible for Stalin's policy on cooperation between the GMD and CCP in the 1920s and was expelled from China in 1927 during the purge of Communists. He returned to the USSR to work in propaganda and journalism and was Head of the Soviet Information Bureau from 1941 to 1949.

Bai Chongxi 1893–1986

Guomindang military officer from a Muslim background in Guangxi. He commanded units of the Northern Expedition and as garrison commander in Shanghai ordered the attack on communists and trade unionists on 12 April 1927. He became Minister of War from 1946 to 1949 and escaped to Taiwan at the end of the Civil War.

Bo Gu 1907–46

Pseudonym of Qin Bangxian, one of the Twenty-Eight Bolsheviks who dominated the CCP in the 1930s and General Secretary of the Party from 1931 to 1935. He was killed in an aircraft crash during the war against Japan.

Bo Yibo 1908–2007

Leading CCP member, wartime guerrilla leader in Shanxi province and aide to the warlord Yan Xishan. He joined the Central Committee in 1945, became deputy premier and held important posts in the State Planning Commission and the State Financial and Economic Commission under the PRC.

Braun, Otto 1900–74

Also known by his Chinese name of Li De, Braun was the Comintern military adviser assigned to China in 1932. He was a fierce opponent of guerrilla warfare, favouring traditional positional warfare. He was responsible for the evacuation from Jiangxi that led to the Long March and left China in 1935 after his military policies had been discredited.

Cai Yuanpei 1868–1940

Leading educational reformer and Principal of Beijing University during the May Fourth movement. He had studied in Europe and was the founder of the research institute Academia Sinica in 1928; however resigned when the Guomindang began to repress dissidents.

Chen Boda 1904–89

Mao Zedong's chief political adviser, speech writer and editor from the Yan'an period. He became a member of the CCP Politburo in 1956 and editor of the theoretical journal *Red Flag* in 1958. He was the leader of the Cultural Revolution group with Jiang Qing as his deputy and became an ally of Lin Biao. He was charged with ultra-leftist crimes along with the Gang of Four and sentenced to 18 years in prison but was released early because of ill health. He died in 1989.

Chen Cheng 1897–1965

The Nationalist General who led operations against the communists in the encirclement campaigns during the 1930s, he was commander of the Wuhan Defence Area during the Japanese occupation and was second in command to Chiang Kai-shek during the civil war of 1946–9. He was appointed governor of Taiwan in 1948 after the massacres of 27 February and became Deputy President of the Republic of China on Taiwan in 1954.

Chen Duxiu 1879–1942

Founder member of the CCP and leading light of the May Fourth and New Culture movements. He had initially been influenced by Western ideas of democracy but moved gradually towards Marxism. He established the influential journal *Xin Qingnian* [New Youth] and, with Li Dazhao the political review *Meizhou pinglun* [Weekly Review]. He remained a member of the

CCP and served as its General Secretary until 1927, when he was accused of supporting Trotskyist groups and expelled.

Chen Shui-bian 1950–

Taiwanese politician and leading member of the Democratic Progressive Party. He was President of the Republic of China on Taiwan from 2000 to 2008, the first from a party other than the GMD, but following his defeat in the 2008 elections was charged with corruption and detained pending trial.

Chen Yi (1) 1883–1950

Guomindang officer and former military commander in the army of the warlord Sun Quanfang. He was appointed governor of Taiwan in 1945 but his repressive policies led to demonstrations, and he was responsible for the massacre of 27 February 1947. He was expelled from the GMD and executed as a traitor in 1950 after having made contact with members of the CCP.

Chen Yi (2) 1901–72

Officer in the CCP's Red Army and New Fourth Army. He became Mayor of Shanghai in 1947 and Foreign Minister in 1958. The given names of the two Chens are written with different characters.

Chen Yonggui 1913–86

Model peasant and Party secretary of the Dazhai production brigade in Shanxi which Mao Zedong eulogised as his model of a frugal, self-reliant agricultural unit. He became a member of the National People's Congress in 1964 and a member of the CCP Central Committee. He was Deputy Premier until 1980.

Chen Yun 1905–95

CCP economic supremo and influential figure in the economic modernisation of China in the post-Mao period. He was both a veteran of the Long March and an economic planner trained in the Soviet Union and was an intransigent opponent of China's move away from the planned economy. He gave up his government functions in 1987 with the group of veterans who stood down when Deng Xiaoping retired.

Chiang Kai-shek (Jiang Jieshi) 1887–1975

Leader of the Guomindang and President of the Republic of China on the mainland until 1949 and on Taiwan until his death. He had a military background and was a protégé of Sun Yat-sen who had him appointed commandant of the Huangpu (Whampoa) Military Academy in 1924. He took control over the Guomindang in a coup after the death of Sun Yat-sen in 1925 and consolidated his political power after the successful completion of the Northern Expedition to reunite warlord-torn China. He led the Guomindang government during the Nanjing decade (1928–37) and in internal exile in Chongqing during the Japanese occupation. After being defeated in the civil war of 1946–9, he presided over the beginnings of the Taiwanese economic miracle with financial support from the USA but ruled the island under conditions of martial law, never losing sight of his main political goal – the reconquest of the mainland.

Cixi 1835–1908
Empress Dowager and de facto ruler of China for most of the period from 1861 until her death in 1908. She is blamed for the failure of the Qing dynasty to reform in the face of the threat from the West and in particular for obstructing the Hundred Days Reform of 1898.

Deng Tuo 1912–66
Editor in Chief of *People's Daily* from 1950 to 1957 and its managing director from 1957 until he was denounced in the Cultural Revolution. He was responsible for a series of sharp satirical articles in *Beijing Evening News* in 1961–2, many of which were obliquely but unmistakably critical of Mao Zedong and his Great Leap Forward policies.

Deng Xiaoping 1904–97
Military commander and political commissar of the Second Field Army of the CCP immediately before 1949. After the foundation of the PRC he was secretary of the CCP's southwestern bureau but became deputy premier under Zhou Enlai in 1952 and General Secretary of the CCP in 1956. He was associated with the pragmatic and managerial policies of Liu Shaoqi rather than the revolutionary romantic approach of Mao and was purged during the Cultural Revolution. He returned as Deputy Premier after the Cultural Revolution but was forced to step down after the 1976 Tian'anmen Incident. After the fall of the Gang of Four he was able to return to power and spearhead the drive for economic reform, and it is this for which he will be remembered although his reputation was tarnished by his suppression of the Democracy movement in Beijing in June 1989.

Deng Yingchao 1904–92
Political activist and wife of Zhou Enlai. Her major political interests were in women's issues but she was also responsible for the creation of an

important publication of oral historical documents in the *Wenshi ziliao* (*Historical and Cultural Materials*) series.

Duan Qirui 1865–1936
Aide to Yuan Shikai and head of military planning for the late Qing modernisation programme. He served as commander of a division of Yuan's Beiyang army and as commandant of the Beijing Military Academy from 1886 to 1889. In 1912 he was Yuan Shikai's Minister of War in the new Republic and was head of the government of the Beijing region between 1924 and 1926.

Elgin, Lord (James Bruce) 1811–63
British envoy and negotiator in the period following the Arrow War. He led the military mission to enforce the Convention of Beijing on China in 1860. During this mission he ordered his troops to destroy the Yuanmingyuan, the old Summer Palace.

Elliot, Captain Charles
British Superintendent of Trade in Guangzhou who was responsible for handing over opium to Lin Zexu to be destroyed. He was second in command and later the commander of the British Expeditionary Force in the Opium War when the original commander, his cousin Admiral George Elliot, became ill.

Empress Dowager *see* Cixi

Fan Wenlan 1893–1969
Historian, writer and member of the Chinese People's Consultative Conference. The first volume of his *Modern History of China* was published in Yan'an in 1947.

Fang Zhimin 1900–35
Communist martyr who was executed by the Guomindang in 1935. He was the head of the independent Xin River Soviet in Northeast Jiangxi province and left behind a collection of essays and letters.

Fei Xiaotong 1910–2005
Pioneer of social anthropology in China after training under Bronislaw Malinowski at the London School of Economics. His books *Peasant Life in China* and *Earthbound China* are classic accounts of rural life in China before the Second World War. He was also active in the Democratic League and

a delegate to the Chinese People's Consultative Conference and held senior posts in the Chinese Academies of Sciences and Social Sciences.

Feng Guifen 1809–74

Leading advocate of Western-style economic reforms in the middle of the nineteenth century. His major contributions were as an adviser to Li Hong-zhang and his development of ideas to fuse Western technological methods with traditional Chinese values. He was instrumental in setting up factories and arsenals, and translation and interpreting colleges. His ideas permeated the reform movement through to the end of the nineteenth century and provided much of its theoretical foundation.

Feng Xuefeng 1903–76

Poet, translator and literary theorist who was the target of severe criticism in the 1950s. He had been a friend and literary follower of Lu Xun and wrote lyrical poetry. He was editor of the official journal *Wenyibao* [Literary Gazette] but was declared a rightist and lost his position.

Fu Zuoyi 1895–1974

Guomindang general who negotiated the surrender of Beijing to the Communist PLA in 1949. A native of Shanxi province he had served in the army of the provincial warlord Yan Xishan and fought against the Japanese army in Inner Mongolia in 1936. After 1949 he was active in the Chinese People's Political Consultative Conference.

Gao Gang 1905–55

Served as Red Army soldier and senior CCP official in Yan'an and Chairman of the North East People's Government in 1947 and was appointed Chairman of the State Planning Commission in 1952. Together with Rao Shushi he was expelled from the CCP in 1954 on the grounds that he was trying to split the Party and establish an independent kingdom. He was close to Soviet political leaders, which was a contributory factor in his downfall.

Gong, Prince 1833–98

Younger brother of the Qing Xianfeng emperor who played a prominent role in negotiations with the British at the end of the Arrow War and during the talks over the Convention of Beijing. He was a firm supporter of the Self-Strengthening Movement and largely responsible for the creation of the Zongli Yamen. Conservative elements at court marginalised him and he lost all authority and influence.

Guangxu Emperor 1871–1908

Zairian was the nephew of the Empress Dowager Cixi who adopted him when the Tongzhi emperor died and had him installed as emperor at the age of four. He attempted to reign in his own right when he became a major but Cixi and the court conservatives were frightened by his involvement with the Hundred Days reformers. He died at the age of 37 just one day before his aged aunt.

Guo Moruo 1892–1978

Writer and literary bureaucrat who held important cultural posts in the PRC and was President of the Academy of Sciences. He was criticised for not having supported writers who were attacked in the 1950s and preserved his position by making a comprehensive self-criticism.

Hart, Sir Robert 1835–1911

Inspector General of the Chinese Imperial Maritime Customs Service from 1863 and also head of the Imperial Postal Service from 1896 to1908. He promoted the opening of China to Western trade and technology and was instrumental in the development of railways, mining and the telegraph to China.

He Long 1896–1969

General of the Workers' and Peasants' Red Army who commanded the Twentieth Army during the Long March and fought in the war against the Japanese occupation. He served in the CCP's Military Affairs Commission after 1949.

He Yingqin 1890–1987

Nationalist commander of troops in the second Encirclement Campaign against the CCP and signatory with the Japanese commander Umetsu of the agreement under which GMD forces withdrew from northern China in 1935. He served the GMD in various military and political capacities in Taiwan.

Hong Xiuquan 1814–64

Charismatic leader of Taiping Rebellion. Hong failed the imperial examinations three times and had a psychological crisis following which he claimed that he had ascended to heaven and had been instructed by God to drive out demons on the earth. On re-reading Christian tracts that he had obtained earlier, he came to believe that he was the younger brother of Jesus. He gathered a group of mainly Hakka supporters in the God Worshippers Society and after the establishment of the Taiping Heavenly Kingdom he was proclaimed Heavenly King. He died as the kingdom was about to fall to the forces of the Qing empire.

Hu Feng 1902–85

Literary critic and target of a major CCP propaganda campaign in 1955. He was a well-established left wing writer and supporter of the CCP but he fell foul of the Party's cultural commissar Zhou Yang and was criticised for refusing to subordinate literature to the interests of the Party. He was imprisoned for over 20 years and not released until 1979.

Hu Qiaomu 1911–92

CCP historian and ideologue. Hu became editor of *People's Daily* in 1949 and his official history of the CCP, *Thirty Years of the Communist Party of China*, was published in 1951. He was the editor of Mao Zedong's *Selected Works* and also one of Mao's speechwriters.

Hu Shi 1891–1962

Distinguished scholar of Chinese literature and philosophy. Hu Shi was a pioneer of the May Fourth Movement and a supporter of writing in the vernacular; however rejected Marxism in favour of a pragmatic liberal approach. He gravitated towards the GMD and was the ambassador in Washington for their government from 1938 to 1942. He settled in Taiwan and became head of Academia Sinica in 1958.

Hu Yaobang 1915–89

CCP veteran of the Long March and Secretary General of the Party from 1982 to 1987. He was dismissed after having been blamed for a series of student demonstrations and replaced by Zhao Ziyang. His death on 15 April 1989 led to a period of mourning and demonstrations by students who considered him to have been a champion of democracy. These were the prelude to the Democracy Movement which ended in tragedy on 4 June 1989.

Hua Guofeng 1920–2008

Caretaker Chairman of the CCP after the death of Mao Zedong. He was closely associated with the ultra leftists and, even though he ordered the arrest of the Gang of Four, he soon lost power to Deng Xiaoping.

Huang Xing 1874–1916

Founder of the radical China Revival Society. He met Sun Yat-sen in Japan in 1905 and agreed to merge his organisation with others to form the Tongmenghui and became Minister of War in Sun's short-lived administration.

Jiang Qing 1914–91

Wife of Mao Zedong and leading member of the Gang of Four. With a background in acting in the Shanghai film industry, Jiang Qing's main interests were in the cultural sphere, and she launched a movement to reform traditional Beijing opera and ballet, making it more radical and ostensibly proletarian. She used her power base in Shanghai to support Mao's leftist position during the Cultural Revolution and became a leading member of the Cultural Revolution Group and the Politburo that was dominated by the radicals. Arrested in 1976 she was tried with the other members of the Gang of Four and sentenced in 1981 to death with a two-year stay of execution. She committed suicide in 1991.

Joffe, Adolph 1883–1927

Comintern agent sent to China in 1922 to negotiate cooperation between Sun Yat-sen and the Chinese Communist Party. The Sun-Joffe agreement announced in 1923 was the basis for the united front work of Mikhail Borodin in China.

Kang Sheng 1899–1975

CCP internal security supremo for much of his career and closely associated with the Cultural Revolution Group. He was posthumously stripped of all his Party posts and implicated in the deaths and persecution of hundreds of senior CCP members during the Cultural Revolution.

Kang Youwei 1858–1927

Radical reformer, leading light of the Hundred Days Reform Movement and forced into exile when it failed in spite of the support of the Guangxu Emperor. Kang remained loyal to Confucianism and drew his inspiration from the New Text School. He proposed that China should become a constitutional monarchy but even this modest reform was too extreme for the Empress Dowager and the idea lost credibility after the collapse of the reform movement.

Kung, H.H. 1881–1967

Financier and politician who married Song Ailing, the elder sister of Song Meiling and Song Qingling. Kung supported Sun Yat-sen during the 1911 Revolution and served Chiang Kai-shek's Guomindang government as Minister of Industry and then Finance.

Lee Teng-hui 1923–

President of Taiwan who had previously served as Mayor of Taibei and Governor of Taiwan. He was the first native Taiwan-born politician to achieve this office under the Guomindang regime. He became an out-spoken supporter of the recognition of the independence of Taiwan and this attracted criticism from Beijing. He retired from office and joined the new pro-independence grouping, the Taiwan Solidarity Union.

Lei Feng 1939–62

Soldier and model communist who died on duty when he was hit by a fall-ing telegraph pole. His diaries which were published posthumously showed that he had been a dedicated follower of Mao and had tried to live his life according to Mao's works. His transparent honesty and the banality of his death struck a chord with young Chinese during the Cultural Revolution but it is widely assumed that his diaries were invented, or at least improved, by the PLA's propaganda department.

Li Dazhao 1888–1927

One of the founding fathers of Chinese Marxism who studied in Japan and worked as a journalist before becoming a librarian and then an academic historian. He worked with Chen Duxiu and was associated with several key journals of the May Fourth era. He pointed out the implications of the Russian Revolution for China at an early stage and was killed by Zhang Zuolin's police in the Soviet embassy in Beijing during the anti-Communist purge of April 1927.

Li Fuchun 1899–1975

Senior CCP economic official, Chairman of the State Planning Commission and Deputy Premier. He remained in office during the early stages of the Cultural Revolution but was left out of the reconstructed Politburo in 1969.

Li Hongzhang 1823–1901

Moderniser and key figure in the Self-Strengthening Movement who was a protégé of Zeng Guofan. He played a significant part in the suppression of the Taiping and Nian rebellions and supported the development of modern technology and communications in northern China as Governor-General of Zhili and was also responsible for the creation of the Nanjing Arsenal and the China Merchants' Steam Navigation Company. His Huai army and Beiyang fleet were defeated by the Japanese in 1895 and he signed the Boxer Protocol on behalf of the Qing court.

Li Lisan 1899–1967

CCP activist who advocated disastrous military offensives in the cities after the break with the GMD in 1927. His policies were contrasted with the suc-cess of Mao's guerrilla warfare and he lost authority in the Party. He became a senior official and a Minister in the PRC but was attacked by Red Guards in the Cultural Revolution and committed suicide.

Li Zongren 1890–1969
Guangxi warlord who joined the Guomindang resistance to Japan in the 1930s. He was elected the vice-president of the Republic of China in 1948 and took over the government in 1949 when Chiang Kai-shek stepped down temporarily but handed the post back to Chiang in 1950.

Liang Qichao 1873–1921
Supporter of Kang Youwei and leading proponent of reform through newspaper and journal articles. He advocated the establishment of provincial assemblies and a constitutional monarchy and was opposed to the revolutionary movement. He held the post of Finance Minister in the warlord government of Duan Qirui in Beijing but became completely disillusioned with politics after seeing the devastation of Europe after the First World War.

Lin Biao 1901–71
Successful CCP commander during the civil war who became Marshal of the PLA and Minster of Defence in 1959 after Peng Dehuai was forced out. In the internal CCP conflict of the 1950s and 1960s he backed Mao and threw the weight of the armed forces behind the leftist faction. He was designated Mao's successor after the Ninth Party Congress in 1969 but died mysteriously in an air crash in 1971 amid allegations that he had tried to stage a military coup to overthrow Mao.

Lin Zexu 1785–1850
Career official and national hero when he burned foreign-owned opium on the orders of the Daoguang emperor in 1839. He was exiled after the war when the British complained about the way he had treated them during the early stages of the Opium War.

Liu Shaoqi 1898–1969
Chairman of the People's Republic of China from 1959 to 1969 and 'top party-person taking the capitalist road' during the Cultural Revolution. His machine politics and pragmatism contrasted with Mao's revolutionary romanticism and he died after prolonged ill-treatment by Party inquisitors.

Lu Xun 1881–1936
Literary icon of the radical left and the CCP. Zhou Shuren who took the pen name of Lu Xun, was a writer of fiction and essays who was one of the

first significant figures to attempt to writing in the vernacular in the May Fourth period. He studied medicine in China and Japan but devoted himself to writing as a cure for China's national sickness. His best-known works are *Diary of a Madman* and the *True Story of Ah Q*. He claimed to be a Marxist but never joined the CCP, thus avoiding accusations of factional mistakes.

Luo Ruiqing 1906–78

Marshall of the PLA and Public Security Minister in the PRC who was purged after being attacked by Red Guards during the Cultural Revolution. He was accused of downplaying the importance of Mao Zedong Thought and insisting on professional expertise in the military.

Macartney, Lord 1737–1806

Governor of Madras who led the first British diplomatic mission to China in 1793. He secured an audience with the Qianlong Emperor, but disputes over the kowtow contributed to the failure of the mission.

Mao Zedong 1893–1976

Most prominent leader of the CCP, Chairman from 1943 and the instigator of the Great Leap Forward and the Cultural Revolution. Mao was famed for his advocacy of guerrilla warfare and for his recognition of the importance of the peasantry for China's revolution. In office he was impatient with pragmatism and gradual change, and he has been held responsible for millions of deaths that have been attributed directly or indirectly to his policies.

Nie Yuanzi 1921–2006

Author of the first big character poster of the Cultural Revolution, produced while she was CCP secretary in the Philosophy Department at Beijing University and an influential Red Guard.

Panchen Lama

Senior Tibetan Lama considered by some to possess higher spiritual authority than the Dalai Lama, by others to be the second-highest ranking lama. Panchen Lamas have often been under the influence of the Chinese court. The tenth Panchen Lama lived in Beijing from 1959 until his death in 1989 and was accused by some Tibetans of having betrayed their cause. There is a dispute over the eleventh reincarnation with one candidate named by the Dalai Lama and one by the religious authorities of the PRC.

Peng Dehuai 1898–1974

Minister of Defence from 1954 to 1959. Peng had spoken out courageously against the Great Leap Forward because of the threat to China's economic development and the future of the armed forces. Conflict with Mao Zedong came to a head at the Lushan Plenum of 1959 and he was purged. He was arrested during the Cultural Revolution and died in prison.

Peng Pai 1896–1929

Pioneer CCP peasant activist in Guangdong province in the early 1920s whose interest in rural issues preceded that of Mao Zedong. He was killed by the GMD in 1929.

Peng Zhen 1902–97

Mayor of Beijing under the PRC from 1951 who was purged in 1967 at the beginning of the Cultural Revolution as an opponent of Mao. Imprisoned but returned to the Politburo after the death of Mao.

Pu Yi, Henry Aisin Gioro 1905–67

Last emperor of the Qing dynasty as a child, restored unsuccessfully by the warlord regime in Beijing in 1917 and by the Japanese occupation forces as emperor of Manzhouguo in 1934.

Qiu Jin 1875–1907

Revolutionary activist and women's rights campaigner executed by the Qing authorities. She was a highly educated woman, which was unusual at that time, and wrote articles and established a paper to advocate equal rights for women.

Song Meiling 1897–2003

Wife of Chiang Kai-shek and sister of Song Qingling. Educated in the USA, she was a professed Christian, a fluent speaker of English and the international face of Chiang Kai-shek's presidency, especially during the Second World War. She died in New York at the age of 105.

Song Qingling 1892–1981

Wife of Sun Yat-sen and a leading member of the left wing of the Guomindang. She remained in China after 1949 and played a role in united front organisations. She became vice-president of the National People's Congress. She founded the English-language magazine *China Reconstructs* which has since renamed *China Today*.

Soong, T.V. 1894–1971

Brother of Song Meiling and Song Qingling and thus brother-in-law of Chiang Kai-shek in whose administration he served as Minister of Finance and later Minister of Foreign Affairs. He was the governor of the Chinese central bank and also involved in private finance which had enabled him to underwrite the nationalist political enterprise.

Stilwell, Joseph 1883–1949

US Army General and wartime adviser to Chiang Kai-shek for whom he had little respect. As an old China hand who spoke the Chinese language he was opposed to Chiang's preference for fighting the communists rather than the Japanese. He was relieved of his duties in 1944 at Chiang's request. He was known as 'Vinegar Joe'.

Sun Yat-sen 1866–1925

The leading advocate of the Chinese Republic who served briefly as its first president before being ousted by Yuan Shikai in a deal that Sun hoped would keep China unified. He had a history of revolutionary activity but was forced to spend much of his life outside China. He ended his career as a local military leader in Guangdong province dreaming of reuniting China. His book of edited speeches *Three People's Principles* [*Sanmin zhuyi*] remains influential among Chinese nationalists and he is still acknowledged as the founding father of the Republic by the CCP.

Tongzhi Emperor – reigned 1862–75

Emperor after whom the Tongzhi restoration is named. He played no part in this as he was a minor and then under the control of the Empress Dowager.

Wang Hongwen 1935–92

Former Shanghai cotton mill security guard and founder of the Shanghai Workers' Revolutionary General Headquarters in 1967. He became vice-chairman of the CCP in 1975 but fell from grace with the other members of the Gang of Four and was sentenced to life imprisonment.

Wang Jingwei 1883–1944

Member of the GMD from 1924 but sympathetic to the CCP and therefore on the left wing of his own party. After the split between the CCP and GMD in 1927 he tried to maintain a left Guomindang government in Wuhan but was expelled from Chiang Kai-shek's GMD which he had re-joined and eventually decided to cooperate with the Japanese occupation forces in a puppet government based in Nanjing. He is regarded by many Chinese as a traitor.

Wang Ming 1904–75
One of the Soviet-trained Twenty-Eight Bolsheviks and leader of the Jiangxi Soviet in the 1930s until he was ousted to make way for Mao Zedong's takeover.

Wen Yiduo 1899–1946
Modernist poet who was also involved in politics as a leading member of the China Democratic League which was trying to develop a third way between the CCP and the GMD. He was assassinated by GMD agents in Kunming in 1946.

Wu Han 1909–69
Respected historian, writer and deputy mayor of Beijing whose play *Hai Rui Dismissed from Office* was the first target of the radicals in the Cultural Revolution. He died after severe ill-treatment in prison.

Yan Xishan 1883–1960
Independent Shanxi warlord who collaborated with the central Nationalist government. He was an enlightened military dictator who implemented a number of economic and social reforms in his province and served briefly as premier of the Republic of China after fleeing to Taiwan in 1949.

Yao Wenyuan 1931–2005
Shanghai radical and literary critic whose article on Wu Han's play initiated the debate that launched the Cultural Revolution. He was sentenced to 20 years imprisonment as one of the Gang of Four.

Yuan Shikai 1859–1916
Qing dynasty military official who advised the Korean army in the 1880s and dabbled in the reform movement. He supported the Empress Dowager in 1898 but when the Qing were on the point of collapse became a republican and manipulated himself into the post of President by ousting Sun Yat-sen. He then discovered that he was a monarchist after all and tried to have himself declared emperor.

Zeng Guofan 1811–72
Qing dynasty official who created the Hunan army to suppress the Taiping Rebellion. This military experiment was repeated with other armies and

these became the backbone of the Self-Strengthening Movement of which he was a dedicated supporter.

Zhang Chunqiao 1917–2005

Shanghai journalist and director of propaganda for the city's Party Committee in the 1960s. He was as supporter of Jiang Qing's drive to revolutionise opera and film and was the initiator of the Shanghai Commune idea. He became Chairman of the Shanghai Revolutionary Committee in 1967 and as one of the Gang of Four was sentenced to death with a two-year stay of execution.

Zhang Guotao 1897–1979

Founding member of the CCP and one of its leaders in the 1930s. He was at the head of one of the columns on the Long March and arrived at Yan'an separately from Mao's forces. His differences with Mao led to his expulsion from the CCP. He defected to the GMD and later settled in Hong Kong where he wrote his memoirs and Canada where he died.

Zhang Xueliang 1898–2001

Warlord of Manchuria in succession to his father Zhang Zuolin until he was expelled by the Japanese occupation forces in 1931. He continually pressed Chiang Kai-shek to ally with the CCP against Japan and engineered Chiang's capture in the Xi'an Incident to try to force his hand. He released Chiang after negotiations that led to the Second United Front but was imprisoned by the Nationalists and remained in prison until 1962 and under house arrest until 1990.

Zhang Zuolin 1873–1928

Warlord of Manchuria whose sphere of influence also included northern China and at times Beijing. He was responsible for the execution of Li Dazhao in 1927 and was killed when a bomb planted by members of the Japanese Guandong army exploded under his train in 1928. He was succeeded by his son, Zhang Xueliang.

Zhou Enlai 1898–1976

First Premier of the PRC. Urbane but ruthless, he maintained his position in the hierarchy throughout the Cultural Revolution. Widely regarded as a pragmatist and a statesman, he acquired a reputation for having saved the lives and careers of many senior Party figures in the turmoil of the 1960s but it has been suggested that he was also implicated in the persecutions.

Zuo Zongtang 1812–85

Assistant to Zeng Guofan and responsible in part for the defeat of the Taiping and Nian rebellions and the recovery of Xinjiang. He recommended that Xinjiang be incorporated into China as a regular province in 1884. He was also a prominent supporter of the Self-Strengthening Movement and created the Fuzhou dockyard.

FURTHER READING

Much of modern Western thinking on the history of China (and also Japan and Korea) in the nineteenth and twentieth centuries was shaped by John K. Fairbank and his colleagues Edwin O. Reischauer and Albert Craig in the famous 'rice paddies' course (Soc. Sci. 101) at Harvard University in the 1960s, and their joint textbooks *East Asia: the Great Tradition* and *East Asia: the Modern Transformation*, subsequently combined in *East Asia: Tradition and Transformation* (with the Chinese history chapters also published separately as *China: Tradition and Transformation*) are still a valuable source of factual information although they are inevitably somewhat dated. Some of the assumptions behind the Fairbank approach, particularly the importance of the Western impact on China and the usefulness of the terms traditional and modern were challenged by the subsequent generation of American scholars, notably Paul A. Cohen in *Discovering History in China*.

Volumes 10 and 11 of the *Cambridge History of China* provide a comprehensive and authoritative summary of historical writing on the late Qing. These two volumes were edited by John K. Fairbank (Volume 11 with Kwang-ching Liu), whose *Great Chinese Revolution 1800–1985* draws on the research done for the Cambridge History as well as on Fairbank's own encyclopaedic knowledge of Chinese history. This one-volume treatment of the period does not replace the *Cambridge History* but has been available in paperback. Volumes 12 and 13, Parts 1 and 2, *Republican China: 1912–1949* of the *Cambridge History of China* are similarly a standard source for the period leading up to the formation of the People's Republic of China in 1949. *Volume 14, The Peoples Republic, Part I: The Emergence of Revolutionary China 1949–1965* and *Volume 15, The Peoples Republic, Part 2: Revolution within the Revolution* bring the story up to the Cultural Revolution.

Alternative approaches can be found in Jean Chesneaux *China from the Opium Wars to the 1911 Revolution* and *China from the 1911 Revolution to Liberation* which broadly speaking belong to the tradition of French academic Marxism, Wolfgang Franke's *A Century of Chinese Revolution 1851–1949*, and

China Readings 1: Imperial China and *China Readings 2: Republican China*, both edited by Franz Schurmann and Orville Schell. Joseph R. Levenson's *Modern China: an Interpretative Anthology* is a series of readings which explores cultural and nationalist responses to the West, and this theme is also central to Jerome Ch'en's *China and the West: Society and Culture 1815–1937*.

Modern China: a Chronology 1842 to the Present Day, edited by Colin Mackerras is an important reference tool which gives precise dates for major events. The journals *Late Imperial China* (formerly *Ch'ing-shih wen-t'i* – but published in English in spite of its name), *Republican China* and *Modern China* are useful for the period up to 1949. *China Quarterly* and *China Journal* focus primarily on post-1949 China.

Qing Dynasty (General)

By far the best single volume account of the Qing dynasty is *China's Cultural Heritage: the Ch'ing Dynasty, 1644–1912* by Richard J. Smith (Boulder: Westview Press, 1983, re-printed 1994). It is a thoughtful and authoritative work that provides a reliable introduction to the last dynasty of imperial China. It includes material on the historical background to the rise of the Qing, the political, social and economic institutions created to govern China, the languages of the period (Chinese and Manchu), philosophy, religion, art, literature and China's transformation under the impact of the West.

Qing Conquest

Franz Michael's *Origin of Manchu Rule in China* (Baltimore: The Johns Hopkins Press), 1942, was the first major English language account of the Manchu rise to power. It is based on close readings of Chinese historical texts and was influenced by Owen Lattimore's pioneering work on China's Inner Asian frontiers which considered China's history in terms of its relationship with its Central or inner Asian neighbours. *From Ming to Ch'ing: Conquest, Region and Continuity in Seventeenth Century China* edited by Jonathan D. Spence and John E. Wills, Jr. (New Haven and London: Yale University Press, 1979) is a collection of nine essays on the 'dynamic transition' from Ming to Qing. The essays examine the chronology of the transition, the effects that the Qing conquest had in the various regions of China and the consequences of the dynastic change for the economy and the literate elite. Frederic Wakeman's magisterial account of the Manchu conquest of China *The Great Enterprise: the Manchu Reconstruction of Order in Seventeenth Century China* (Berkeley and Los Angeles: University of California Press, 1985) runs to more than 1,300 pages in two volumes and is based on a detailed examination of an impressive range of sources in Chinese and Japanese.

Two books by Lynn Struve give an account of different aspects of the crisis of the seventeenth century as it affected China and help us to understand the consequences of the establishment of the Manchu state for the *ancien régime* of the Ming and its citizens. *The Southern Ming* (New Haven and London: Yale University Press, 1984) is an account of the Ming dynasty's desperate attempts to cling to power between the Manchu occupation of Beijing in 1644 and the final defeat of its forces and the death of its last representative, the Prince of Lu in 1662. *Voices from the Ming-Qing Cataclysm* (New Haven and London: Yale University Press, 1993) is an anthology of translations of first-hand accounts of the trials and tribulations of the transition from Ming to Qing designed to give a variety of views of the period from a range of individuals in different parts of China.

Borders

For an English language account of the Qing government's attempts to integrate Xinjiang (one of the most important of the border regions) into their empire, both politically and economically, there is *Beyond the Pass: Economy, Ethnicity and Empire in Qing Central Asia 1759–1864* by James A. Millward (Stanford: Stanford University Press, 1998). This covers the military conquest of Xinjiang and official trade with the region but its main focus is on Chinese merchants who flocked to Xinjiang in search of commercial opportunities in this untapped market. Peter Perdue *China Marches West: The Qing Conquest of Central Eurasia* (Cambridge: Bellknap Press of Harvard University Press, 2005) chronicles in detail the military and political aspects of the late Qing conquest in Central Asia.

Chinese Society and Government under the Qing

Richard J Smith *China's Cultural Heritage: The Ch'ing Dynasty, 1644–1912* is the best starting place for reading on the social and political history of the Qing as it is for other aspects of the dynasty. Susan Naquin and Evelyn S. Rawski *Chinese Society in the Eighteenth Centre* (New Haven and London: Yale University Press, 1987) is an important study. The first part of the book examines Qing society in a general way, concentrating on the policies of the government and the institutions it created to enforce them; kinship, social and economic organisations; and the culture of the educated literati (or gentry) class and festivals and rituals which affected elite and non-elite alike. The second part is particularly interesting as it explores both the social and cultural diversity of Qing China (it is hardly surprising that there was such diversity in an empire the size of Europe but this has not always been acknowledged) and the profound social changes that accompanied an increase in the population and greater social mobility. Although it covers a broader period and includes much material on the Ming dynasty *Popular*

Culture in Late Imperial China edited by David Johnson, Andrew J. Nathan and Evelyn S. Rawski (Berkeley: University of California Press, 1985) is valuable for its coverage of both secular and religious popular culture, operas, drama and literature, all in their social context. Lloyd Eastman *Family, Field and Ancestor: Constancy and Change in China's Social and Economic History, 1550–1949* (New York: Oxford University Press, 1988) provides an excellent overview of social and economic change, in imperial and modern China.

Although it was first published as long ago as 1955, Chang Chung-li *The Chinese Gentry: Studies on their Role in Nineteenth Century Chinese Society* (Seattle: University of Washington Press, 1974) remains an essential source: it has been republished regularly and has established itself as a classic. The gentry or *shenshi* (literati in Max Weber's accounts of Qing China) were essentially the rural elite, but their status and economic power did not solely depend on the ownership of land, rent and the sale of products. Success in the gruelling state examination system was a prerequisite for entry into this privileged stratum, and this could only be achieved by many years of commitment to studying the classical Confucian texts. Chang's study examines the different layers of gentry society and the mechanisms for mobility within this society as well as the informal social functions that the gentry performed. He also analyses the size and growth of the gentry in the nineteenth century and the nature of the examination system and applies techniques of quantitative analysis to 5,473 biographies of members of the local gentry taken from the local histories or gazetteers [*fangzhi*] that were produced for every town, county, prefecture and province during the Qing dynasty.

Kung-chuan Hsiao *Rural China: Imperial Control in the Nineteenth Century* (Seattle: University of Washington Press, 1961) was a product of the remarkable Modern Chinese History Project at the University of Washington, as was Chang Chung-li's book on the gentry and like Chang's book it has stood the test of time. It is a monumental study of the mechanisms developed by the Qing to control the Chinese countryside, including the police and tax collection systems and the use of the leadership of lineages to control their members. Ch'ü Tung-tsu also looks at control and government in his *Local Government in China under the Ch'ing* (Stanford: Stanford University Press, 1962) but focuses on the formal structures of prefectural and county government, the magistrates, clerks, personal secretaries and other staff of the *yamen*. The final chapter complements Chang Chung-li's study, examining as it does the formal and informal roles of the gentry in local administration.

Huang Liu-hung *A Complete Book Concerning Happiness and Benevolence: A Manual for Local Magistrates in Seventeenth Century China* (Tucson: University of Arizona Press, 1984) is a magistrate's view of his role and was written for other magistrates, an excellent insider's view of the most important administrative position in the Chinese empire. A magistrate in Qing dynasty China was not primarily a judge as the conventional but rather imprecise translation of his title might suggest: he was the local representative of the emperor and enjoyed considerable power and authority. Pao Chao Hsieh *The Government of China 1644–1911* (London: Frank Cass, 1966) was originally published in 1925 and is a detailed account of the formal organisation of the central government in the latter part of the Qing dynasty, reflecting the attitudes of the late Qing and of the Republic that followed it.

Manchus and Chinese

Although it is usually regarded in China as a Manchu, and therefore foreign, conquest dynasty, in contrast to its predecessor, the 'Chinese' Ming, there is considerable scope for debate about the ethnic, cultural and linguistic nature of the Qing. Pamela Kyle Crossley has examined the Manchus in Qing China in two important studies. *Orphan Warriors: Three Manchu Generations and the End of the Qing World* (Princeton: Princeton University Press, 1990) was an early attempt at the demolition of the myth that China always absorbs and sinicises its foreign conquerors. It does so by examining the fate of the descendants of Manchu troops sent throughout China to establish garrisons to defend the empire of their aristocratic lords. It demonstrates that Manchu (as distinct from Chinese) identities persisted through to the end of the Qing dynasty, and this is attested to by the movements for the revival of the Manchu identity in China and Taiwan that developed in the late twentieth century. *The Manchus* (Oxford: Blackwell, 1997) is a more general examination of the people we now know as the Manchus, their Urchin ancestors, and their language, society and history. It concludes with a chapter on the twentieth century, in which the role of the central character Aisin Gioro (Henry) Puyi, the last Qing emperor and puppet of the Japanese invaders in Manzhouguo (Manchukuo) can be seen as a symbol of the bankruptcy of Manchu identity at the end of the Qing dynasty. Mark C. Elliot *The Manchu Way: The Eight Banners and Ethnic Identity in Late Imperial China* (Stanford: University of California Press, 2001) is the most recent history of the Manchus in the Qing dynasty and makes extensive use of documentation in the Manchu language.

Arrival of the West

J.K. Fairbank (ed.) *The Chinese World Order: Traditional China's Foreign Relations* (Cambridge: Harvard University Press, 1968) remains an essential source for the way China related with the outside world before its contacts with the West in the eighteenth and nineteenth centuries. *La Chine et l'Occident: le Commerce à Canton au XVIIIe siècle (1719–1833)* by Louis Dermigny is the best starting point for an understanding of trade between the West and

China before the Opium War. The two-hundreth anniversary of the Macartney embassy to China was marked by a number of publications about the ill-fated diplomatic mission. By far the best was Alain Peyrefitte *The Collision of Two Civilisations: The British Expedition to China in 1792–4* (London: Harvill, 1993). *Un Choc de Culture: La vision des Chinois* (Paris: Fayard, 1998) by the same author is a collection of primary sources, mainly letters and court memorials translated into French. Taken together, the two volumes show the complete lack of understanding and clash of cultures that was eventually to lead to the Opium Wars and the British invasion of China in 1842. J.K. Fairbank *Trade and Diplomacy on the China Coast: The Opening of the Treaty Ports 1852–1854* (Cambridge: Harvard University Press, 1953) is still the classic account of the development of the Treaty Ports.

The Opium War through Chinese Eyes by Arthur Waley (London: Allen and Unwin 1988) and Maurice Collis' *Foreign Mud* (London: Faber and Faber, 1946) give contrasting pictures of the naval battles between Britain and China from 1831 to 1842. Peter Ward Fay's *The Opium War 1840–1842* (Chapel Hill: University of North Carolina Press, 1975) is more recent but focuses on the Westerners involved and uses no Chinese sources.

Rebellion and Its Suppression in Late Qing China

Susan Naquin has investigated two of the popular insurrections of the late Qing period. *Shantung Rebellion: The Wang Lun Uprising of 1774* (New Haven and London: Yale University Press, 1981) demonstrates the power of the White Lotus sect and its ability to mobilise thousands of peasants in an attack, ultimately unsuccessful, on the representatives of the Qing state in Shandong province. *Millenarian Rebellion in China: The Eight Trigram Uprising of 1813* (New Haven and London: Yale University Press, 1976) is an even more detailed account of the attempt by one White Lotus sect to attack the Qing capital, Beijing.

The major rebellion of the ninteenth century, and the one that almost succeeded in bringing about the collapse of the dynasty, was the rising of the quasi-Christian Taiping movement whose formal name was the Heavenly Kingdom of Great Peace [*Taiping tianguo*]. The standard work is Franz Michael (with Chang Chung-li) *The Taiping Rebellion* (Seattle: Washington University Press, 1966) in three volumes. Volume 1 is a chronological history of the uprising; whereas Volumes 2 and 3 have an invaluable collection of original Taiping documents in translation. C.A. Curwen *Taiping Rebel: The Deposition of Li Hsiu-cheng* (Cambridge: Cambridge University Press, 1977) views the rebellion through the trial documents of one of its leaders.

For the lesser known but not necessarily less important Nian rebellions of the same period, there is Chiang Siang-tseh *The Nien Rebellion* (Seattle: University of Washington Press, 1954) an account of the social banditry of the Yellow River area and Teng Ssu-yu's *The Nien Army and Their Guerrilla Warfare, 1851–1868* (La Haye: Mouton, 1961). Chu Wendjang *The Moslem Rebellion in Northwest China 1862–1878* (Paris: Mouton, 1966) chronicles the brutal conflict between Hui Muslim and Han in Gansu in northwest China which threatened Qing control over the region. Philip A. Kuhn *Rebellion and Its Enemies in Late Imperial China* Cambridge, Mass: Harvard University Press, 1970 and Mary C. Wright *The Last Stand of Chinese Conservatism: The Tung-chih Restoration 1862–1874* (Stanford: Stanford University Press, 1957) demonstrate how the Qing re-established its authority after the rebellions were suppressed.

End of the Qing Dynasty and the 1911 Revolution

The declining years of the Qing were defined by the failure of a reform movement led by Kang Youwei and Liang Qichao, which is chronicled in *A Mosaic of the Hundred Days: Personalities, Politics and Ideas of 1898* by Luke S. Kwong (Cambridge, Mass: Harvard 1984) the regency of the enigmatic Empress Dowager Cixi, and the final rebellion of the dynasty, the Boxers. Victor Purcell *The Boxer Rising* (Cambridge: Cambridge University Press, 1963) is the classic account and Joseph Esherick *The Origins of the Boxer Rising* (Berkeley: University of California Press, 1987) is the most recent study.

For the mutiny and revolution that finally brought down the Qing, Wu Wuchang *The Revolution of 1911* (Beijing: Foreign Languages Press, 1962) is a contemporary narrative by a participant translated from the Chinese, whereas Mary C. Wright *China in Revolution: The First Phase 1900–1913* (New Haven: Yale University Press, 1968) is a more analytical study of the transition from empire to republic.

Harold C. Schiffrin *Sun Yat-sen and the Origins of the Chinese Revolution* (Berkeley: University of California Press, 1968), *Sun Yat-sen Reluctant Revolutionary* (Boston: Little Brown, 1980) and Marie Claire Bergere *Sun Yat-sen* (Stanford: Stanford University Press, 1998) are the most authoritative biographies of the major political figure of the revolutionary period.

May Fourth Movement and the Guomindang State

The May Fourth Movement of 1919 is credited with the birth of the major political movements that were to shape the rest of Chinese history. Chow Tse-tsung *The May Fourth Movement: Intellectual Revolution in Modern China* (Cambridge: Harvard University Press, 1960) was the first detailed study of this phenomenon. The question of whether the Chinese Communist Party at its inception in 1921 was primarily an indigenous Chinese organization or mainly a creation of Moscow-based advisers has been examined in, among other works, Arif Dirlik *The Origins of Chinese Communism* (New York: Oxford

University Press, 1989) and Maurice Meisner *Li Ta-chao and the Origins of Chinese Marxism* (Cambridge: Harvard University Press, 1967).

For the history of the Guomindang, its Northern Expedition and the attempt to build a national government, see Donald Jordan *The Northern Expedition: China's national revolution of 1926–8* (Honolulu: University of Hawai'i Press, 1976); Lloyd Eastman *The Abortive Revolution: China under Nationalist Rule 1927–1937* (Cambridge: Harvard University Press, 1990) and John Fitzgerald *Awakening China: Politics, Culture and Class in the Nationalist Revolution* (Stanford: Stanford University Press, 1996). Frederic Wakeman Jr. *Policing Shanghai 1927–1937* (Berkeley: University of California Press, 1995) suggests greater continuity between nationalist China and the PRC than is often appreciated.

Chinese Communist Party Before 1949
For the period in which the CCP was in the countryside, Edgar Snow *Red Star over China* (London: Gollancz, 1937) stands out as a rare first hand account by a Westerner of life in Yan'an under the CCP. Dick Wilson's *The Long March 1935: The Epic of Chinese Communism's Survival* (London: Hamilton, 1971) is a readable and reliable account of the retreat that became a myth and Harrison Salisbury *The Long March: The Untold Story* (London: Harper Collins 1985) is a more recent version with the benefit of interviews with many of the survivors. Mark Selden *The Yenan Way in Revolutionary China* (Cambridge: Harvard University Press, 1971) and Chalmers Johnson *Peasant Nationalism and Communist Power: The Emergence of Revolutionary China 1937–1945* (Stanford: Stanford University Press, 1962) initiated an important debate on the reasons for the success of the CCP in 1949.

People's Republic of China 1949–89 (General)
John Gittings *China Changes Face: The Road from Revolution 1949–1989* (Oxford: Oxford University Press, 1989) and *The Changing Face of China: From Mao to Market* (Oxford : Oxford University Press, 2005) reflect the rapid changes taking place in China as seen by one of the best informed and most reliable journalists of his generation. Roderick MacFarquhar *The Origins of the Cultural Revolution*, 2 volumes (Oxford: Oxford University Press, 1974) does far more than the title suggests and is a detailed political history of the first decade of the PRC. Witold Rodzinski *The People's Republic of China: Reflections on Chinese Political History Since 1949* (London: Collins, 1988) is an interesting and concise account by a Polish diplomat who was accredited to Beijing in that period.

Chinese Communist Party and 'Liberation' 1949
Derk Bodde *Peking Diary: A Year of Revolution* London: Cape, 1951, is a unique eyewitness account of the CCP's takeover of Beijing. Boyd Compton *Mao's*

China: Party Reform Documents 1942–44 (Seattle: University of Washington Press, 1952) presents documentary evidence and analysis of the rectification campaign within the CCP preparatory to the takeover of China. Tony Saich *Governance and Politics of China* (Basingstoke: Palgrave, 2004) is a useful account of the political structures of the PRC.

Korean War and China

The most useful works on the Korean War and on China's decision to enter the conflict are Bruce Cumings *The Origins of the Korean War*, 2 Volumes (Princeton: Princeton University Press, 1981 and 1990), John Gittings *The Rôle of the Chinese Army* (London: Oxford University Press, 1967) and Allen S. Whiting *China Crosses the Yalu: The Decision to Enter the Korean War* (Stanford: Stanford University Press, 1960). The most recent which takes advantage of material from the Soviet archives is Sergei N. Goncharov, John W. Lewis and Xue Litai *Uncertain Partners: Stalin, Mao and the Korean War* (Stanford: Stanford University Press, 1993).

China's Economy

Most material written on China's economy is difficult for non-specialists to use but Christopher Howe *China's Economy: A Basic Guide* (London: Elek, 1978) is useful for understanding the Mao era and the same author's *China's Economic Reform: A Study with Documents* with Y.Y. Kueh and Robert Ash (London: RoutledgeCurzon, 2003) is equally valuable for the reform period. Stephen Green *Reforming China's Economy: A Rough Guide* (London: Chatham House, RIIA, 2003) is a basic introduction to the changes in the economy of China in the 1990s and Peter Nolan *China at the Crossroads* (Cambridge: Polity, 2004) is a thoughtful study which recognises what China has lost as well as gained during the reform period. He Kang (editor-in-chief) *China's Township and Village Enterprises* (Beijing: Foreign Languages Press, 2005) is a positive account of changes in one of the most important sectors of the new economy.

Social Control

Bao Ruowang *Prisoner of Mao* (Harmondsworth: Penguin, 1976) was one of the earliest first-hand accounts on the prison system in the PRC to become widely available. Jean Luc Domenach *Chine: l'archipel oublié* (Paris: Fayard, 1992) is the most serious account of the prison camp system and its role in the Chinese economy, while Harry Hongda Wu *Laogai: The Chinese Gulag* (Boulder: Westview, 1992) is an account by a former inmate.

Hundred Flowers Period

For this period which requires an understanding of literary and cultural politics as well as China's national politics, the most useful sources are Merle Goldman *China's Intellectuals: Advise and Dissent* (Cambridge: Harvard University Press, 1981); Merle Goldman *Literary Dissent in Communist China* (Cambridge: Harvard University Press, 1967) and Roderick MacFarquhar *The Hundred Flowers Campaign and the Chinese Intellectuals* (New York: Octagon Books, 1974)

Great Leap Forward

Two contrasting studies of 1958 and its aftermath are Roderick MacFarquhar *The Origins of the Cultural Revolution, Volume 2, The Great Leap Forward* (Oxford: Oxford University Press, 1974) and Jasper Becker *Hungry Ghosts: China's Secret Famine* (London: John Murray, 1996).

Sino-Soviet Split

Two thorough studies that were carried out during the period of the Sino-Soviet dispute indicate how serious an issue this was believed to be at the time. John Gittings *Survey of the Sino-Soviet Dispute: A Commentary and Extracts from the Recent Polemics 1963–1967* (London: Oxford University Press, 1969) and Donald S. Zagoria *The Sino-Soviet Conflict 1956–1961* (Princeton: Princeton University Press, 1962).

Cultural Revolution

Much of the literature published during the Cultural Revolution, was polemical and ephemeral. Among the more serious studies is Simon Leys *The Chairman's New Clothes* (London: Allison and Busby, 1981) which is an acerbic and iconoclastic account of the period. Liang Heng and Judith Shapiro *Son of the Revolution* (New York: Alfred A. Knopf, 1983) is the best of the accounts by former Red Guards of life for the young activists during the Cultural Revolution. Livio Maitan *Party, Army and Masses in China* (London: NLB, 1976)was a contemporary attempt to apply a sophisticated and non-Stalinist Marxist analysis to the seemingly incomprehensible events taking place in China. The most recent study, Roderick MacFarquhar and Michael Schoenhals *Mao's Last Revolution* (Cambridge: Belknap Press of Harvard University Press, 2006) is a detailed balanced and scholarly analysis of the period and likely to become the standard text on the Cultural Revolution.

Mao Zedong

Stuart Schram, *Mao Tse-tung* (London: Allen Lane the Penguin Press, 1967) was the standard biography for many years and although it is dated it still repays reading. Philip Short *Mao: A Life* (London: Hodder and Stoughton, 1999) is by far the most detailed and the most reliable of recent accounts. Jung Chang and Jon Halliday *Mao the Unknown Story* (London: Random House, 2005) offers an account that is not particularly unknown and is better on character assassination than balanced assessment: it is simplistic and has been criticised severely by most specialists on the Mao period. Lin Chun, Gregor Benton *Was Mao Really A Monster?: The Academic Response to Chang and Halliday's 'Mao, The Unknown Story'* (London: Routledge, 2009) brings together the most valuable criticism.

Taiwan and Hong Kong

Simon Long *Taiwan: China's Last Frontier* (New York: St Martin's, 1990) is an accessible general history which challenges the claim that Taiwan has always been part of China; John F. Copper *Taiwan Nation-State or Province* (Boulder, Colorado: Westview Press, 1996) is a useful and comprehensive introduction to society politics and economics of Taiwan. Christopher Hughes *Taiwan and Chinese Nationalism: National Identity and Status in International Society* (London: Routledge, 1997) examines the thorny question of Taiwan's current status. Of the many books on Hong Kong, Steve Tsang *A Modern History of Hong Kong* (London and New York: I.B.Tauris, 2004) is both authoritative and readable.

Contemporary China

Stephanie Hemelryk Donald and Robert Benewick *The State of China Atlas* (Berkeley: University of California Press, 2005) is useful for putting the changes in China into geographical context. Michael Dillon *Contemporary China: An Introduction* (London: Routledge, 2009) is a broad introduction to the main issues in the contemporary period. For critical views of contemporary development from the bottom up see Chen Guidi and Wu Chuntao *Will the Boat Sink the Water? The Life of China's Peasants* (London: Public Affairs, 2006) and Ian Johnson *Wild Grass: China's Revolution from Below* (London, Penguin 2004). There are many books written by journalists on the basis of their tours of duty in China. The following can be recommended: Philip Pan *Out of Mao's Shadow: The Struggle for the Soul of a New China* (London: Picador, 2008); Rob Gifford *China Road: A Journey into the Future of a Rising Power* (London: Bloomsbury, 2007); John Gittings *The Changing Face of China: From Mao to Market* (Oxford: Oxford University Press, 2005); Duncan Hewitt *Getting Rich First: Life in a Changing China* (London: Vintage, 2007) and James Kynge *China Shakes the World: The Rise of a Hungry Nation* (London: Phoenix, 2007)

Other useful studies include Susan L. Shirk *China: Fragile Superpower* (Oxford: Oxford University Press, 2007); Pierre Haski *Le Sang de la Chine: quand le silence tue* (Paris: Bernard Grasset, 2005) which is by far the most detailed study of the Hunan blood transfusion disaster; Colin Mackerras *China's Ethnic Minorities and Globalisation* (London: RoutledgeCurzon, 2003); Norman Stockman *Understanding Chinese Society* (Cambridge: Polity, 2000) and Elizabeth J. Perry and Mark Selden (eds.) *Chinese Society: Change, Conflict and Resistance* (London: Routledge, 2003).

For political developments in the modern period, see Joseph Fewsmith *China since Tiananmen: The Politics of Transition* (Cambridge: Cambridge University Press, 2001); Willy Wo-Lap Lam *Chinese Politics in the Hu Jintao Era: New Leaders, New Challenges* (New York: M.E. Sharpe 2006); Tony Saich *Governance and Politics of China* (Basingstoke: Palgrave 2004) and Michael Yahuda *The International Politics of the Asia-Pacific 1945–1995* (London: RoutledgeCurzon, 1997).

Tibet and Xinjiang

Books on Tibet tend to produce more heat than light but the following are balanced and based on knowledge on the ground as well as serious research: Melvyn C. Goldstein *The Snow Lion and the Dragon: China, Tibet and the Dalai Lama* (Berkeley: University of California Press, 1997); Melvyn C. Goldstein *A History of Modern Tibet, 1913–1951: The Demise of the Lamaist State* (Berkeley: University of California Press, 1989); Dawa Norbu *China's Tibet Policy* (Richmond: Curzon Press, 2001); Tsering Shakya *The Dragon in the Land of Snows: A History of Modern Tibet since 1947* (London: Pimlico, 1999). Patrick French *Tibet, Tibet: A Personal History of a Lost Land* (London: HarperCollins, 2003) is a revealing study of the pro-Tibet campaign from the inside.

For Xinjiang, which still receives far less coverage than Tibet, see Michael Dillon *Xinjiang: China's Muslim Far Northwest* (London: RoutledgeCurzon, 2004); S. Frederick Starr (ed.) *Xinjiang: China's Muslim Borderland* (New York: M.E. Sharpe, 2004); Christian Tyler *Wild West China: the Taming of Xinjiang* (London: John Murray, 2003) and James Millward *Eurasian Crossroads: A History of Xinjiang* (London: Hurst, 2007).

INDEX